THE
NON-WESTERN WORLD

Environment, Development, and Human Rights

Pradyumna P. Karan

ROUTLEDGE
New York • London

Published in 2004 by
Routledge
270 Madison Avenue
New York, NY 10016
www.routledge-ny.com

Published in Great Britain by
Routledge
2 Park Square
Oxon, OX1 4RN
www.routledge.co.uk

10 9 8 7 6 5 4 3 2 1

Library of Congress Cataloging-in-Publication Data
    Karan, Pradyumna P. (Pradyumna Prasad)
    The non western world : development, environment, and human rights / Pradyumna P. Karan ;
Cartography by Richard Gilbreath.
        p. cm.
    This book was developed for Routledge by the Center for American Places."
    Includes bibliographical references and index.
        ISBN 0-415-94713-8 (hb : alk. paper) – ISBN 0-415-94714-6 (pb : alk. paper) 1. Economic development–Social aspects–Asia. 2. Economic development–Social aspects–Middle East. 3. Economic development–Social aspects–Africa, Sub-Saharan. 4. Asia–Social conditions. 5. Middle East–Social conditions. 6. Africa, Sub-Saharan–Social conditions. I. Center for American Places. II. Title.
    HC412.K318 2004
    338.9–dc22
                            2004002286

Preface

The focus of this book is on critical issues of development, environment, and cultural conflicts facing the non-Western world. The first chapter provides an introduction to the non-Western world and emphasizes important contemporary cultural, socioeconomic, environment, and development issues. Each of the major cultural areas of the non-Western world—China, Japan and Korea, Southeast Asia, the Indian subcontinent, the Middle East, and sub-Saharan Africa—is covered in subsequent chapters. In each regional chapter significant geographic, socioeconomic, political, cultural, environmental and sustainable development, human rights, and gender-related issues as they pertain to the specific area are discussed. Discussion topics are adapted to each country's specific political, economic, social, and environmental circumstances. Wherever desirable, national and regional comparisons have been included on topics such as population, environment, and development in India and China, and Asia and Africa.

The last chapter on challenges facing the non-Western world pulls together some of the ideas described in the regional chapters and discusses three challenges: adoption of an ecodevelopment model to achieve sustainable development and environmental management; integration of poverty alleviation programs, development, and environmental protection strategies with population policy; and resolution of ethnic and religious conflicts. To help readers interested in further exploration of some of the themes discussed in the book, a reading list of recent publications is given at the end of each chapter. Unless indicated otherwise, all data in this book are from the United Nations and the World Bank.

The origins of this book lie in my experiences and early education in the colonial setting. As a student in British India, I learned from textbooks printed in England about the most powerful Western world powers—their symbols of prosperity, economy, and culture. During the same period I witnessed how a scantily clothed man—Mohandas Gandhi—brought the downfall of the mighty British Empire through a nonviolent movement, which eventually began the process of decolonization of the non-Western world. As I graduated

v

from college, the massive decolonization of the non-Western world was in full swing. Nothing expressed the downfall of the Western colonial powers so starkly as the independence of India, the earth's largest colony, parts of which Britain had held since 1757. A major political and economic transformation of the world had commenced.

Rarely—and usually, only grudgingly—have scholars scrutinized the Western domination of non-Western lands from the perspective of the people of the non-Western world. Viewed through the eyes of the colonized, the development of this part of the world during the last two hundred years becomes rather sobering and more meaningful. As the changes resulting from decolonization unfolded, I was not satisfied with the lists of answers or explanations given in the textbooks on the changing global economic, political, and cultural patterns. When I went to graduate school, I began to direct my studies toward understanding patterns of development and modernization of the non-Western societies of India, China, Southeast Asia, West Asia, and Africa as these areas were beginning to emerge from Western domination, and Japan as it began to develop after the destruction of the Second World War. My goal was to understand how this non-Western world I knew had come to be, its virtues and faults, its economy, its environment, and its culture. This book is the result of studies and observations, travel across the reaches of the non-Western world, and ideas gleaned from interviews with scholars and ordinary folks. For whatever limitations the book has, I alone am responsible.

Acknowledgments

A work of this scope would not have been accomplished without the generous help of many people. First, I am indebted to Cotton Mather, a geographer, colleague, and friend for many years. From Cotton Mather I gained a sense of the cultural world, and the world of ideas and intellect, that has shaped the contemporary Western and non-Western worlds. He offered insightful evaluations of the Western and non-Western cultures based on his many years of experience in both the West and the East.

I am grateful to several colleagues:—Professor Stan Brunn, University of Kentucky; Professor Shigeru Iijima, Tokyo; Professor M. P. Thakore, Delhi University; Professor Todd Stradford, University of Wisconsin-Platteville; Dr. Unryu Suganuma, Hokuriku University, Kanazawa, Japan; Professor Kohei Okamoto, Nagoya University; Noritaka Yagasaki, Tokyo Gakugei University; Kenichi Nonaka, Research Institute for Humanity and Nature, Kyoto; Kazuaki Imoto, Yatsushiro; and Professor T. Chao—who provided suggestions and ideas. I am particularly grateful to Professor Chao for providing comments on the China section, to Professor Iijima for comments on Japan, to Professor Thakore for a critique of the chapter on the Indian subcontinent, to Professor Ulack for suggestions to improve the Southeast Asia chapter, to Dr. Mohammad Carami for suggestions on the Middle East, and to Professor Ruth Besha, University of Dar es Salaam, for comments on sub-Saharan Africa. The comments and expertise of these scholars from various areas of the non-Western world contributed significantly to this book.

My students, graduate and undergraduate, read extended sections of the book. Seminar classes on development and environmental management offered uplifting discussion of parts of the manuscript. In particular, students Masae Miyasaka, Chris Jasparro, Jon Taylor, Gregg Goldstein, Gary O'Dell, David Mast, Soedono Adji, Christopher Riegert, Bob Beatty, Tae Kim, Xin Jin, Manish Patel, Abdalla Misalati, Chad Cottle, Julien Mercille, and hundreds of undergraduates who used this as a text in my course on the non-Western world offered many insights and comments. The arduous task of transforming my rough map drafts into finished drawings for publication required the painstaking efforts of Richard Gilreath, Director of the University of Kentucky Cartographic Lab, and Brian Mayfield, GIS technician/cartographer. Shin-ichi Asabe, Todd Stradford, UNICEF, Robert Beatty, Cotton Mather, the International Fund for Agricultural Development, and others provided a number of photographs used in this book. Their contribution is acknowledged in the photographs' captions.

Contents

Chapter 1

Introduction to the Non-Western World

THE NON-WESTERN WORLD

What is the non-Western world, and why it is important to learn about its peoples and cultures? When we speak of the non-Western world we are referring to the areas in which cultures developed essentially apart from the Greco-Judaic-Christian tradition of the Western culture. Thus, it includes East Asia (China, Japan, and Korea), Southeast Asia, the Indian subcontinent, the Middle East and Sub-Saharan Africa. Latin America, Russian Asia, and Oceania are excluded. The indigenous cultures of Latin America and Oceania are not Western, but they are also not non-Western in the same sense as the ancient civilizations of China and India. Moreover, the culture of the pre-Columbian settled communities in Yucatan and Andes (600 B.C.), the empire of the Mayas in Central America, the Inca civilization (1200–1535 A.D.), and the Aztec empire (1325–1521 A.D.) in the valley of Mexico were conquered.

Colonization by the West played a role in the decay of indigenous peoples and their culture. The migration of swarms of Europeans and the transplanting into the new lands of languages, religion, arts, and institutions of Europe represented a great outward growth of Western culture on the other side of the Atlantic. Where the natives were not numerous in North America, the English drove them back into wilderness beyond the pale of the European settlements. In other regions, however, where the Spaniards and Portuguese penetrated, the new Western culture was merely overlaid like a veneer upon the older, indigenous culture of the natives. Throughout the hemisphere and also later on in Australia, New Zealand, and Oceania, power—economic, social, and political—was in the hands of the settlers of European stock, and this power assured the dominance of the Western culture. Therefore, the contemporary cultural pattern in Latin America and Oceania, unlike the

1

non-Western cultures of Asia and Africa, is based dominantly on Western traditions and values.

Culture in this book refers to the distinctive ways of life such as language and writings; value and belief systems; and forms of social, political, and economic organization that characterize human groups. It is the sum total of ways of living built by a group of human beings and transmitted from one generation to another. Often, regional cultures fused into one, creating larger cultural zones. Civilization resulted from this process of fusion into larger units such as India or China. Civilizations systematized ideas into organized stories, philosophies, and formal religions. Civilizations spread common belief patterns over wide areas as a means of linking diverse peoples. Civilization persists when these common belief patterns are maintained by a large population over a considerable period of time. Generally speaking, tribal societies or cultures are without them. In addition, tribal cultures are usually smaller and local. There are some exceptions such as the Yoruba of West Africa, whose tribe numbered hundreds of thousands, who maintained large cities and specialists, but lacked writing and large public works, which usually accompany civilizations.

The use of writing is a major clue for identifying cultures because the introduction of writing into a society improves transmission of social and cultural traits and enhances the availability of knowledge to affect and change all else in society. Likewise, the maintenance of cities and the specialization of occupation (such as blacksmiths, priests, traders, and rulers, and the technology and economic organization to support them) cannot exist without a rural hinterland to feed the city dwellers and without transport for food supplies. Once this economic basis is available, there is more effective energy and wealth for the development of culture.

There is a core of solidarity among non-Western societies of Asia and Africa that derives from non-European cultural roots, shared memories of the past, domination by Western powers, a resolve to remove the remaining traces of Western colonialism, and a feeling that they are a distinct part of humanity, long victimized and now sharing a common aspiration to protect their independence and development. Except for Japan, Singapore, South Korea, and Taiwan, the non-Western lands range from the least developed nations to some that are close to crossing the threshold that Japan and Western nations crossed during the twentieth century.

Our focus in this book is on six major non-Western culture areas: China, India, Japan, Southeast Asia, the Islamic Middle East, and Sub-Saharan Africa (Figure 1.1). Civilizations in China, India, and the Nile and Tigris-Euphrates valleys of the Middle East were already old when the Europeans rose out of barbarism. Sumeria, Tigris-Euphrates valleys around 4,000 B.C., Egypt (Nile Valley) five hundred years later, China (Yellow River Valley) around 3,500 B.C., and India (Indus Valley) about 2,500 B.C. all reached cultural maturity centuries before the Greeks appeared as the first

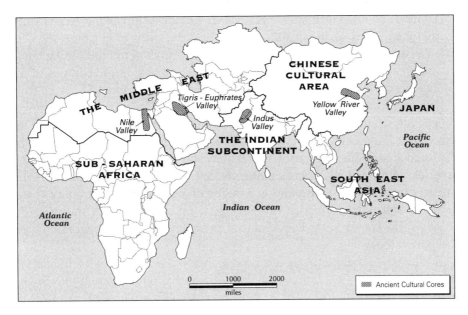

Figure 1-1. The non-Western world.

civilized culture in the West (about 800 B.C.). Except for China and India, all of these ancient civilizations had lost their power by the time of Christ, and with few exceptions had been assimilated into later peoples. Distinctive cultural areas discussed in this book are delimited from one another partly by geography; partly by history; partly by cultural traits such as language, religion, political and economic organization; and most of all by value systems, behavior, and attitude.

The non-Western cultures of China (based on Confucianism) and India (based on Hinduism) survived to our day with national cultural ideals that were substantially unchanged for twenty-five centuries. Both are now engaged in a struggle for development in a modern age. China and India are patriarchs among the world's civilizations, but they are also relatively new in the contemporary political family of nations. The experiences of the Chinese and Indians have marked similarities. China and India have each known an almost changeless civilization during two thousand years, securely based on a national belief system and an ethical code that reflects a national soul at peace with itself. Even the challenge of foreign religions—Buddhism in China and Islam in India—has not upset the basic pattern. Both nations have lived self-contained lives with relatively little curiosity about the lands beyond their borders, except in commerce. But both have been exploited for four centuries by more aggressive peoples from the West. Both countries hold immense lands and resources which still may be inadequate to support sustainable development of their large populations. As a result, both face bewildering problems of development, resource use, and environmental management.

Chinese cultural influence has been dominant in Japan and Korea since early times. Political and institutional forms were taken from China; the Chinese system of writing was adopted in Japan, which permitted the Japanese to gain ready access to the Confucian classics and to Chinese editions of the Buddhist scriptures. Buddhism was introduced in Japan about 552 A.D. from China and Korea, and has thrived alongside the indigenous Shinto religion. For several centuries Japan lived in splendid isolation under the rule of the Shoguns (1336–1868). Perry's visit in 1854 led to the opening of Japan, and initiated a period of rapid growth. Japanese borrowed first from the Chinese and later from the West those elements that fitted their needs and environment. The resulting combination has been unique, and Japan today represents a distinctive culture of great interest and of much importance. Post–World War II Japan has advanced as one of the major economic superpowers in the world.

Culturally, Southeast Asia has been a zone of convergence for Indian and Chinese cultures. People from southern areas of China migrated into Southeast Asia. About 100 A.D. Hindu states were established in the East Indies by the Dravidian Kings of South India. By the second century A.D. several Indian colonies had developed in Cambodia. Hinduism expanded with the Hindu colonization of Java and there was expansion of Buddhism between 700 and 800 A.D. Islam was introduced about 1000 A.D. The Hindu states of Southeast Asia fell shortly before the discovery of the Philippines by the Portuguese navigator Ferdinand Magellan in 1521. As a crossroad between Europe and East Asia (China and Japan), Southeast Asia attracted Europeans. Batavia (formerly named Jakarta) was founded by the Dutch in 1619; two centuries later Raffles (1781–1826), an English governor in Sumatra founded Singapore in 1819. Most of Southeast Asia became colonies of Britain, France, and the Netherlands. Today, Southeast Asia is a dynamic region ruled mostly by authoritarian governments. Some nations such as Cambodia and Thailand are making slow progress toward democracy. The region's most populous country, Indonesia, is engaged in a struggle between democratization and Islamic fundamentalism.

Torn between ancient traditions and the modern world, the Islamic countries of the Middle East search for a balance. It has become, as in ancient times, a nexus of bitter conflict. Some disputes are battles within nations, as a surging younger generation challenges autocratic regimes for opportunity and political reform. Others pit nation against nation, over issues ranging from weapons proliferation to the proper interpretation of Islam. The clash of Israelis and Palestinians over tiny parcels of land continues to make headlines around the world. In this land of crisis, oil-rich nations, and the birthplace of three great faiths—Judaism, Christianity and Islam—the United States is currently involved in establishing a foothold for democracy in Iraq. If this attempt is successful, it may change the political landscape of the region.

The political and economic development of Sub-Saharan Africa presents a major challenge in the twenty-first century. Most of its nations are among the non-Western world's youngest and poorest. Colonial inroads beginning in the sixteenth century led to the exploitation of the region's human and natural resources. By the mid-nineteenth century, European, American, and Arab slave traders had robbed the continent of perhaps as many as 25 million human beings. At the 1884 Berlin Conference, the competing European powers gerrymandered Africa with their own political boundaries. In the aftermath of the wind of decolonization which began to sweep across Africa in the mid-1950s, Sub-Saharan nations became independent. Arbitrary political boundaries, which often divide language and tribal groups, have resulted in ethnic fragmentation. It has helped touch off civil wars and numerous coups led by military dictators during the post-independence period. Warring factions and regimes sell off diamonds, oil, timber, and ore to build armies and buy weapons, deepening conflicts and poverty. Meanwhile, about two thirds of Africans depend on agriculture for their livelihoods. The fate of agricultural production, therefore, directly affects economic growth, social improvement, and political stability. As the region's population continues to grow, rapidly outpacing the growth rate in other regions of the non-Western world, its agricultural land is becoming increasingly degraded. Unless African governments, supported by the international community, take the lead in confronting the problems of land degradation, deteriorating agricultural productivity will undermine the foundations of sustainable development in Sub-Saharan Africa.

SOURCES OF IDEAS SHAPING THE ROOTS OF NON-WESTERN CULTURE

All of the six non-Western cultural areas are distinct from the West. Western culture is the product of Greco-Judaic-Christian tradition, Roman law, Greek philosophy (ideas of democracy and civil liberty), and the ideas and value systems derived from the Renaissance (1400–1650) in Europe. Writing as a part of technology has been an intellectual tool used by various cultures, and the great literary works have been a source of ideas that have shaped cultures. Writing led to achievements in astronomy, arithmetic, and geometry, and also in the accumulation of social surplus and the distinctive quality of the cultures that were established in Western and non-Western worlds. The great literature of the Western culture such as the Bible, the writings of Plato (427-347 B.C., the Greek philosopher), Homer (the eighth-century Greek epic poet), Thomas Moore (1478–1536, English humanist and statesman), Machiavelli (1469–1527, Italian philosopher and author), Martin Luther (1438–1546, German theologian and author, leader of the Protestant Reformation), Galileo (1564–1642, Italian physicist and astronomer), Voltaire (1694–1778, French philosopher and historian), Karl Marx (1818–1883, German economist, philosopher, and socialist), Charles Darwin (1809–1882, English naturalist), and Sigmund Freud (1856–1939, Austrian neurologist and founder of psychoanalysis) provide sources of ideas that helped to shape the Western culture. Literature in both Western and non-Western worlds represents reflection and refinement of thought that relates the community to the wider society and culture and often exemplifies the behavior of the people in that culture.

The ideas and values enunciated in these great books and by the authors noted in the preceding paragraph are clearly distinct from the literature of the non-Western world. Among the great literature of the non-Western world are the works by Confucius (551–470 B.C.), Li Po (701–762 B.C.), and Tu Fu (713–770 B.C.), the Vedic Hymns (2000–800 B.C.), the Upanishad (eighth to sixth century B.C.), the *Mahabharat* (about 1000 B.C.), works of Kalidasa (fifth or sixth century A.D.), the Koran (between 610 and 632 A.D.), *The Arabian Nights* (786–809 A.D.), and the poems of Omar Khayyam (eleventh century A.D.) and Hafiz (1300–1383 A.D.). These classical works tell us about sources of ideas that shaped the cultures of the non-Western world. Through the poems and essays one can capture the distinctive cultural values of the people.

Chinese literature had ethical content and its specialists influenced the people by precept and example. Li Po and Tu Fu in their poetry open a new world—a delicate, fragile world of bamboo and jade, yet inhabited by intensely human characters—revealing the distinctive aspects of the Chinese culture amd life. Confucius pointed out a sensible way of life. No others could possibly represent the great Chinese culture to the world so well as these three master spirits. Despite periodic civil wars and invasions, the cultural unity of China has reasserted itself time and again and absorbed many would-be conquerors in its long history. The Chinese have assimilated foreign ideas and political systems without losing their essential point of view.

The persistent cultural stability of China has been due to four elements: rapport with earth and nature, the family, veneration of ancestors, and the Confucian code. The identification of the Chinese peasant with the land (to a greater extent than elsewhere) strengthened stability. The Chinese learned in the family from the beginning that individual preferences must be subordinated to the welfare of the group; Chinese family members deferred to the head of the family, who was the oldest male member. The old not only retained their authority during life but also after death through the veneration of ancestors. Veneration of the past did restrain hasty changes and the disruptions that invasions brought to most other peoples. Confucius concentrated on human relationships, and his teachings codified how to get along in this life.

In India there has been more reciprocal influence between literati and common people, between sacred literature and popular tradition. The ancient hymns of the Vedas, composed anonymously between 2000 and 800 B.C., are the foundations of the Indian culture and are the oldest writings in any

Indo-European language. They are the ultimate source of Hindu religion and culture. Of the four great collections, the *Rig-Veda* (verse-knowledge) is the oldest and is the source of the other three. Compiled in stages over a long period, it contains hymns to the folk gods of nature such as sky (Varuna) and fire (Agni), and later hymns to abstract concepts such as the "Origin of All Things," which lead into the philosophical discussion of the Upanishads. These lyrics project an exalted sympathy with nature through noble imagery, vivid descriptions, simple, concrete diction, and a fine reverent tone. India's greatest folk epic, the *Mahabharat,* dating back to perhaps 1000 B.C. and the longest poem in the world with 100,000 couplets, abounds in loosely connected stories and essays. The central plot of the epic concerns a great struggle between two families of royal cousins for succession to the throne. Like the Trojan War of the Greeks, the struggle has foundation in a protracted war between rival kingdoms. The most famous section of the Mahabharat is the Gita, a philosophical dialogue between the god Krishna and Arjun, hero of the epic. The subject of the Gita is the Hindu reconciliation of work and necessary activity in this world with the idea that the world is a mere illusion to be ignored. Krishna explains that disinterested performance of duty in this world involves no desire and hence no sin. This subtle interpretation of actions in terms of attitude and intention is a central feature of Indian culture.

Kalidasa, as a great playwright of India, has often been called "the Shakespeare of India," and the parallel goes far. Like Shakespeare, he was equally at home in narrative, lyric, and dramatic poetry. In the plan of his dramas, too, Kalidasa reminds us of Shakespeare, in his combination of serious and comic elements within the same play, especially in the use of clowns, and in his frequent interpolation of lyric verse in the midst of dramatic scenes. Kalidasa did not write tragedies. To the Hindu, defeat and death in this world have no tragic meaning.

The fantastic love theme of Kalidasa's *Shakuntala* attracted the German poet Goethe (1749–1832), who borrowed from the play for his *Faust,* and Goldmark's overture to Shakuntala has long been a standard concert selection. Kalidasa's work shows that all the pessimism and asceticism in the Hindu view of life do not stifle the longing for worldly beauty and love for nature, seasons, and landscape.

In contemporary times Mohandas Karamchand Gandhi's life and work provided a source of ideas that influenced Indian society and has had effects beyond the non-Western world in Martin Luther King, Jr.'s struggles for racial and political equality in America. Born in 1869, M. K. Gandhi spent twenty-one tumultuous years in South Africa resisting racism using his weapon of nonviolent *satyagarha* (pursuit of truth). He was 45 years old when he returned to India and transformed both the tactics and the purpose of India's struggle against the British. This "half naked *fakir*," as the British called him, converted an elite struggle into a mass movement, a violent uprising into a nonviolent but nonetheless insistent struggle, and political demands into a testament of faith (Figure 1.2). Gandhi's ideas and life carry a remarkable message for many oppressed people who daily wrestle with the challenges of social and political reform. Gandhi's nonviolent resistance served well both Aung San Suu Kyi of Myanmar (Burma) and Nelson Mandela of South Africa during their years of arrest for demanding political and social justice.

The Koran, the first important body of Arabic prose, is the great book of authority for the morals, laws, theological doctrines, and social ethics for the Muslims everywhere from North Africa to Southeast Asia. Its 114 chapters, or suras, of varying length are accepted as the word of Allah, revealed to his only prophet, Mohammed. From the first to the last it preaches the unity and soleness of the Most High, the Most Merciful, and Most Compassionate God, Allah; to serve him and to die for him are the greatest of privileges, to neglect him and to disregard his commandments are the unforgivable sins. The imagery of the Koran is the imagery of the desert, of the lonely places of body and soul, of the unsophisticated pastoral and rural scene rather than the crowded bazaar and teeming city streets. It entertains the promise of idyllic sensual existence for the faithful after the Day of Judgment. Millions of people today live by its words in the non-Western world.

African cultures have powerful persistence through deeply rooted religious beliefs connecting Africans with their environment through worship of ancestors and gods of nature, including a creator god, combined with strong community and family ties. Transmission by story and memory, in a largely oral tradition, add to the mix and maintain the vitality of the traditional cultures.

Some of the great works of the non-Western world noted above are in part a record of the ideas and customs, the special visions and feelings of the non-Western peoples. Through these works students of the non-Western world can understand the nations and cultures that created the great books. They

Figure 1-2. Mohandas Gandhi addressing a public meeting in 1946. A nonviolent movement led by Gandhi led to the independence of India, marking the beginning of decolonization of the non-Western world. The teachings of Gandhi inspired Martin Luther King, Jr. to nonviolent resistance in the civil rights movement. (Photo: G. R. Jani.)

tell us about their past and they help us understand the context of their present society. Knowing and understanding the great books of the non-Western cultures leads us into contact with ideas that may be new to many readers in the West, but such contact frees us from provincialism in the realm of ideas and gives us respect for other points of view.

We can summarize some of the major differences between non-Western and Western cultures (Table 1.1). These differences center around three related issues: the relation between society and nature, the role of religion in society, and the structure and nature of cultural values and the role of individuals and groups in the society. The common elements underlie all non-Western cultural areas, but there are other elements that distinguish each culture within a major cultural cluster and each major cluster from other clusters. The non-Western world should be viewed as a mosaic of cultures rather than as a big homogenous, undifferentiated area.

Many non-Western values involve blending some of the world's intellectual traditions such as Confucianism, Buddhism, Hinduism, and Islam. As in the West, some of the non-Western values have gone wrong in parts of Asia. The attachment to the family has fostered nepotism in countries such as Indonesia and China. The importance of personal relationships rather than formal legality has become cronyism. Consensus has become wheel-greasing and corrupt politics. Conservatism and respect for authority has become rigidity

TABLE 1-1

MAJOR DIFFERENCES BETWEEN WESTERN AND NON-WESTERN CULTURES

Western	*Non-Western*
1. Superiority over nature	1. Adaptation to nature
2. Christianity concerned with absolute moral values, differences between good and evil, and redemption of the soul.	2. Non-Western religions focus on virtue. Confucianism provides an ethical code of behavior.
3. Society is built on legalistic contractual relationships.	3. Society is built on direct personal relationships.
4. Individualistic orientation.	4. Group orientation: clan, caste, tribe.
5. Behavior controlled by rules, punishments and rewards	5. Behavior controlled by group adaptation. Departures from the group norm are accompanied by feelings of shame.
6. Attribution groups are important (family, class, occupation).	6. Frame groups are important (village, neighborhood, company, region, and nation).
7. Weak hierarchical structure	7. Strong hierarchical structure.
8. Important values are freedom and personal conscience.	8. Important values are security and obedience.
9. Need for self-assertion.	9. Need for coordination.
10. Contractual relationships based on rights and duties.	10. Personal relationships based on mutual obligations and mutual dependence.

and inability to innovate. Much-vaunted educational achievements have
become rote learning and a refusal to question those in authority.

INTERACTION BETWEEN WESTERN AND
NON-WESTERN PEOPLES

More than 2,000 years ago, commercial interaction between the non-Western
world and Europe was via the Silk Road, perhaps history's most famous highway (Figure 1.3). The route wound for 5,000 miles from China across vast
steppes, through the mountains of Central Asia and Northern India to the open
ports of the Mediterranean. Precious bales of silk from China, exotic spices,
muslin, gems, and ivory from India were ferried on the backs of camels on the
Silk Road to markets in Europe. Large-scale Western interaction with Asia
and Africa began chiefly as a capitalist search for markets and commodities,
but it soon grew into a movement of much greater scope. It intensified after
1500 A.D. following the discovery of the sea route to India by Vasco da Gama
in 1498, six years after the discovery of the New World by Columbus.

Five hundred years ago, on the eve of Europe's intrusion into Asia and
Africa, non-Western societies were stagnant. Many African societies were
subsistence oriented and weak. Asian societies were more feudal and science
and technology were "frozen." Between the feudal class and an oppressed
peasantry, only a rudimentary class of merchants had arisen, except in China,
among the Arabs, and perhaps in India and Japan.

Western Europe, on the other hand, rose on the strength of a dynamic
economic system. An agricultural revolution in the twelfth century was
followed by the growth of trade and industry, and the "rebirth of Europe"
in the fifteenth century. A merchant-led middle class gradually rose to
power, committed to the application of science and industry. Denied access
to Eastern silk and spices, Europeans embarked on the Age of Exploration
(see box on spices). Science and technology led to naval superiority and
Western dominance of the non-Western world. A period of some five
hundred years followed in which the Western trade and economy
overwhelmed Asia and Africa.

In the Age of Colonialism (1500–1800), Europeans founded colonies all
over the non-Western world and, with arrogance and inhumanity, imposed
slavery on Africa, although most of Africa was colonized after 1800. Only
Japan and Thailand escaped colonial rule. It was followed by the Age of
Imperialism (1800–1947), which marked a period of intensified colonialism.
With the evolution of West European capitalism, there was an intensified need
for colonies to provide investment opportunities abroad, secure sources of raw
materials, and guaranteed markets. The colonies brought profit and wealth to a
substantial section of the European population. The desire for profitable trade,
plunder, and enrichment were forces that led to the establishment of the

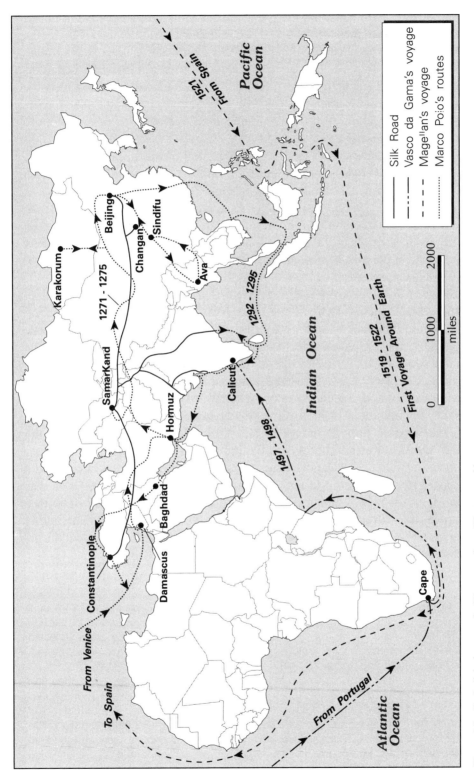

Figure 1-3. Early links between the Western and non-Western worlds.

imperial structure. For example, India was the main provider of employment for substantial numbers of the upper and middle classes in Britain. The Indian Empire also helped Britain to maintain its military power because the Indian Army could be shipped all over the world to fight wars on Britain's behalf, as in 1914 and 1939. Indian troops raised in the subcontinent and paid for by the people of India helped maintain Britain's global military status. The importance of economic factors varied; sometimes political factors were more important in colonial activities.

The cultural interactions between Africa and the West began following the European discovery of the New World during the fifteenth and early sixteenth centuries. Labor needs on plantations prompted Europeans to turn to Africa as a source of slave labor. Slave collection centers were established along the west coast of Africa, and during three centuries of slave trade, ships carried millions of Africans to the Americas. After the scramble for Africa was over by the end of the nineteenth century, European powers had partitioned most of the Sub-Saharan Africa.

There was widespread contact between Arabs and the West from ancient times. Translations of Greek and other texts led to an Islamic intellectual awakening in the ninth century. All of Spain except Granada—including the great libraries of Cordoba and Toledo—was lost to Islamic rule by 1250. The rise of Islam created fear in Christian Europe. European Crusaders sought to win back the Holy Land from the Muslims. Muslims often scorned European backwardness and crudeness, and when Europe became powerful, they often evaded opportunities for imitation and interaction.

The Western impact on non-Western societies varied according to the intensity of European interest and the internal strength of the Asian society concerned. Where European interest was marginal, even weakly organized societies were left more or less undisturbed. Where European interest was intense, the impact varied according to the internal strength of the victimized society. Even in the post-independence period (since 1947), the interaction between the Western and the non-Western worlds is taking place within the constraints of a strongly entrenched global capitalist system.

GEOGRAPHY OF SPICES

In 1992 America, Spain, and Italy celebrated the 500th anniversary of Columbus's voyage; they also should have paid tribute to spices. After all, when Columbus bumped into America, he was on a mission for the King and Queen of Spain to locate a new and speedier route to a place called the Spice Islands, now part of Indonesia.

In the fifteenth century, any country that dominated the market in spices from Asia–the equivalent of controlling massive oil reserves today–was rich. Today, the effect of spices on the balance of trade is inconsequential, at least in the United States, and competition in the spice market is between companies, not countries. But the fortunes in spices are still substantial. Their use has more than doubled in the last 20 years, to over 762 billion pounds in 2000, when Americans spent an estimated $2 billion on dried herbs and spices for cooking, according to the American Spice Trade Association in New York.

Elite Europeans 500 years ago needed spices to mask the taste and aroma of food that was often putrid; Americans are now using spices to add zest to dishes that are underseasoned, having little or no salt. The increased interest in highly seasoned ethnic cuisines such as Cajun, Mexican, Indian, and Chinese has also boosted demand. To further pump up usage, manufacturers are coming out with new varieties of blended spices such as special concoctions for microwave cooking. Some manufacturers also are trying to tap the fastest-growing segment of the market, the food processing industry.

In the trade, spices include all the plant material used as seasonings in dried or shelf-stable form. That includes the spices derived from tropical trees and plants such as black pepper, cinnamon, cloves, turmeric, ginger, nutmeg, cardamom, and allspice, in addition to dehydrated onion and garlic, and capsicums such as dried chilies and paprika.

Historically, the quest for rare tropical spices led to the quest for the most efficient trade routes. Cutting a few months from a two-year voyage or reducing the likelihood of shipwreck could give the spice merchant an advantage, and at various times, Venice, Portugal, and the Netherlands all reaped fortunes from trading in spices.

In early times, black pepper was the most valued spice; at one point, it accounted for 25 percent of the world's trade. When Alaric, the king of the Visigoths, first arrived at the walls of Rome in 408 A.D., he demanded not only gold and silver as a tribute, but also 3,000 pounds of precious pepper. In Antwerp, Belgium, by the mid-1500s, the price of pepper had become theDowJones of the day.

With few exceptions such as the Mediterranean spices, virtually all aromatic spices used in the United States are still imported from the tropics in the non-Western lands, some directly by companies, others through brokers. America's biggest spice companies are also the oldest. McCormick, Schilling, and the Durkee brand date back to the late nineteenth century. McCormick & Company, the nation's biggest spice maker, bought Schilling in 1947 and has since marketed the McCormick brand east of the Mississippi and Schilling to the west. The R.T. French Company bought Durkee Famous Foods of Cleveland in 1985; today, its Durkee-French division is the number two producer. Besides McCormick and Durkee-French, the other major spice marketers include Spice Islands, Lawry's, and such supermarket chains as Kroger, Safeway, and Winn-Dixie, which are believed to control 17 percent of the market.

The memory of colonial rule by Western countries—Britain, France, Belgium, the Netherlands, Germany, Italy, Portugal, and, briefly, the United States—is still vivid in the non-Western world; so are the consequences of colonial rule's end. It is hard to imagine so comprehensive a change as decolonization in so little time. Suddenly, in Asia and Africa the colonial rule was a thing of the past by the end of 1950s. The very word *imperialism* acquired a strong overtone of condemnation, as did *colonialism*. This was true not only in the former colonies, but also in the former imperial or colonial powers in the West.

Why did imperialism and colonialism come so suddenly, so dramatically, to an end? Of course, the people of the former colonial territories actively sought independence. Some non-Western countries ceased to be governed because they had become ungovernable by outside authority. Self-assertion and self-determination was too strong. This was undoubtedly true in India, where dissent had sophistication and a resulting force far in excess of what could be mobilized in opposition by the Western colonial power. Here, *Satyagraha* (which literally means "the force for truth") was shaped into a powerful political philosophy by M. K. Gandhi to assert and advance civil and political rights. Drawing on the ancient Indian tradition that evil could best be countered by nonresistence, *Satyagraha* became associated with noncooperation and nonviolent civil disobedience. The protestors used techniques such as nonpayment of taxes and refusal to cooperate with authority. It became a potent weapon in Gandhi's hands, a nonviolent means of confronting the big battalions of imperial supremacy. This step may be viewed as an important watershed in the history of resistance to imperialism and in the development of peaceful techniques to assert nationalism. There was organized military resistance to the colonial power in Indo-China against the French, in Indonesia against the Dutch, and in Malaya against the British. The rise of nationalism emerged as the most effective Asian and African response to Western colonialism.

Nationalism arrived late in Africa, in part because European conquest came late, and in part because most of the colonial units were arbitrary, with no relationship to political tradition. John Sarbah (1865–1910) from the British Gold Coast colony (now Ghana) argued for customary laws and virtues. In the 1920s and 1930s a larger number of Africans trained in the West led a more sweeping nationalistic agitation. The first meeting of the Pan-African Congress was held in 1919.

The British encouraged Arab and Jewish nationalism in the Middle East in the early twentieth century, hoping to undermine the Ottoman Empire. A steady increase of nationalistic agitation and identification has persisted in Asia and Africa.

Often nationalism was fueled by mounting repression and aided by a common language (the colonial ruler's), the mass media, and the new network of roads and railroads. In much of the colonial world, the Western powers were allowed to go in peace. In the United States there was no thought of keeping the Philippines by force.

There was also another important reason for sudden decolonization. After World War II colonialism no longer served any important economic interest. Economic factors joined hands with idealism and became a vital force for rapid decolonization. Once, the acquisition of colonial territory brought revenues and exploitable resources that benefited the merchant and industrial interests within the governments of colonial powers. With colonial possessions went a national monopoly of trade centered on import of raw materials from colonial lands and export of industrial factory products. After World War II economic development became centered internally rather than externally; it was from domestic economic growth that nations prospered. Trade between the industrial countries became dominant; economic relations with the colonial world became marginalized. The colonies could depart without major economic cost to the Western colonial powers. Few in the United States suffered financial loss from the liberation of the Philippines.

In the years following decolonization, the extension of superpower influence of the United States and the Soviet Union over the newly independent and poorer nations of the non-Western world was seen as the new form of imperialism during the decades of the Cold War. The superpower rivalry had disastrous military aspects in Afghanistan, Vietnam, and other places in the non-Western world. The end of the Cold War, the downfall of communism, and the break-up of the Soviet Union in 1991 brought this to an end.

As we enter the twenty-first century there are great economic powers (the United States, Japan, and Germany) and lesser ones (such as China and India) with varying military strengths, but imperialism and colonialism belong to the past. The non-Western nations must now deal with the imperial legacy of grave, indeed intolerable, human suffering left in its wake. When the former colonial possesions achieved independence, they were forced to take on the most demanding of human tasks—the provision of honest, reliable, and responsible government. Many non-Western countries have failed in this regard. From this, in turn has come economic failure, for economic success depends on the support and supervision of a stable, efficient, and effective governmental structure. Instability, incompetence, corruption, and the dictatorship of the favored few have been all too frequent in the non-Western world during the last fifty years. In extreme, but not exceptional instances, there is civil disorder and conflict. Cambodia, Afghanistan, Nigeria, Congo, and Burma are recent examples. Even where things are better, the routine tasks of the state—the collection of taxes, the rendering of essential services, and the provision of a firm legal basis for economic progress—are poorly performed or not performed at all (Figure 1.4).

Without stable and efficient government, the essential requirement for social and economic development is unrealized. In most of the non-Western nations, stark poverty is still endemic. The West cannot set itself apart from this poverty and feel comfortable and content in its affluence while its former colonies are poor; it must be on the conscience of the former colonial powers. Since decolonization, the poor non-Western countries have received attention from the West. During the Cold War period (1950–1989) most of this attention was the result of the hope or fear of Communism. An influential constituency in the Western countries, and recently in Japan, has consistently expressed sympathy and supported aid for the poor lands, as have the World Bank and other international agencies. In recent years, the United States has spent $12 to $15 billion for bilateral and multilateral international development and security assistance. As the leader in an increasingly integrated global order, the United States has a vital stake in promoting sustainable development, political stability, and democracy in the non-Western world.

Figure 1-4. "Down with pro-imperialist new economic policies" written on the wall of a government build-ing in Patna, India. Many people in the non-Western world are still concerned with neocolonial economic policies that have led to the economic domination of the non-Western world by the West. (Photo: P. P. Karan.)

In the early days of development, assistance agriculture was frequently neglected. Emphasis was on the cities and their inhabitants, and that was where development occurred. Food prices were often fixed to favor the urban population, and this had a depressive effect on agricultural production. There are exceptions, the leading example, as is so often the case, being in India.Since independence, the Indian population has more than doubled, but, supported by grain hybrids, fertilizer, irrigation, other soil and water manage-ment, and assured prices for farmers, so has food production. In more recent times, the role of agricultural and rural development has become evident and accepted, and the importance of good education—particularly the education of women—environment, and infrastructure for effective development has been appreciated.

Most of the non-Western nations have followed the West's frontier economics model of development, in which the environment has been treated as an infinite supply of physical resources (raw materials, energy, water, soil, and air) for use. At the same time, the environment has been viewed as an infinite sink for the by-products of development in the form of various types of pollution (waste) and ecological degradation. Some countries such as Japan have moved to the environmental protection model of development, in which the focus is on clean-up and repair of ecological damage resulting from development activities. A sustainable development program will involve three dimensions: economic, environmental, and sociocultural. These three dimensions must be addressed by the non-Western countries with equal emphasis to ensure sustainability. The economic dimension involves achieving the maximum flow of income while maintaining the stock of assets (or capital—environmental, human, and industrial) that yields these benefits. The focus of the environmental dimension is on the maintenance of the stability of biological and physical ecosystems. The sociocultural dimension involves maintenance of the stability of social and cultural systems, particularly reduction of destructive social conflicts and preservation of cultural diversity. These three dimensions of sustainable development form a closely integrated triangle with interactions among them (Figure 1.5).

RESPONSE OF THE TWO MAJOR NON-WESTERN CIVILIZATIONS TO THE WEST

The non-Western world is dominated by two great systems of civilization, the Indian and the Chinese (from which the Japanese society is in some measure derivative). The two systems have represented two opposite methods of organizing the energies and purposes of humans in society. India—decentralized, fragmented in thousands of village councils, yet held together by great pilgrimages and the common celebration of great feasts—has remained in many ways a singularly uncoercive society. Princes fought, dynasties rose and fell, but at the base of the social order authority remained with the village. China, on the other hand, early demonstrated some of the characteristics of an organized, centralized, bureaucratic, and authoritarian society. The number of issues that the emperor could directly decide may have remained limited, but he had instruments of coercion. His bureaucracy—the mandarinate—was empirewide, and succeeding dynasties were able to experiment with large-scale planning and control. Drastic land reforms and forced procurement of

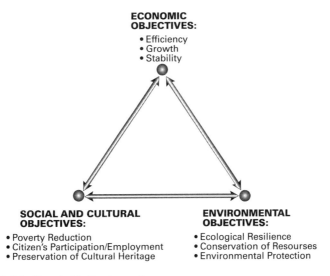

Figure 1-5. Model of Sustainable Development.

grain were all attempted 700 years before Marx proposed the end of all private enterprise.

These fundamental differences between India and China did not prevent both of these great societies from suffering the same vicissitudes of external conquest and internal dissension. In both countries the dynasties rose and fell: Mauryas, Guptas, Rajputs, and Moguls in India; Han, T'ang, Sung, Ming, and Ch'ing in China. Yet behind these common upheavals one can discern a deeper pattern. India's conquerors attempted to impose unity on its diverse people, whereas in China an organized centralized instinct in the community imposed unity on the conquerors.

In the past two and half centuries, Asia lived through a wholly new type of invasion by the West. Hitherto Asia's conquerors had been either people at the same level of culture, such as the Moguls, or of a much lower but fiercer kind of culture, such as the Manchus. The West introduced the first elements of a completely unprecedented civilization based on science, technology, a rational administration, and the rights—both national and personal—of humans. Once again, the underlying ethos of the two great civilizations dictated different responses.

After a century and more of Western impact, both societies found themselves, after World War II, with developed export sectors dispatching raw materials to industrialized markets abroad and served by vast coastal cities that were linked with some development of modern transport and power, some small beginnings of industry and, in the social sphere, with a growing number of men and women educated in the modern manner. But these changes had barely touched the vast countryside where most of the people lived and where age-old farming methods, landlordism, and the growing pressure of population were all producing a condition of stagnation at best, and, at worst, of growing despair.

After 1945, both countries faced comparable tasks of rapid modernization to ensure that modern education, modern industry, and modernized agriculture could help the people in the race against a rapidly rising birthrate: 8 million more Indians every year, and 12 million more Chinese. Both set out to achieve the objective through a series of national economic plans. There, the resemblance ends.

In the modern period, as in the old, India and China proceed by different routes and different philosophies. The difference is partly a matter of history. Between 1800 and 1945, India underwent a generally stable period of British control and administration. Universities where Edmund Burke and Jeremy Bentham could be studied were opened as early as 1855. The process of drawing Indians into an elective, representative system began in the 1880s. Administration as a creative tool of change and law as the impartial custodian of the citizen's rights and interests were inherent in British concepts of government—even authoritarian, imperial government.

To their own traditions of tolerance within a plural society, educated Indians added a profound grasp of what was best in the Western constitutional tradition. They showed a unique capacity to fuse the new ideals with a living legacy from their own past. From Ram Mohan Roy in the early nineteenth century to M. K. Gandhi in the twentieth, India produced a line of leaders in whom new and old could coexist, producing not a superficial copying of Western ideas but a true Asian form of the liberal ideal.

The Chinese had no such opportunity. As the nineteenth century advanced, the Manchus, unlike the Moguls in India a century earlier, did not collapse. They ossified. The state structure remained nominally in being. Outside forces could not, as in India, usurp central authority and hence inherit responsibility. They could only nibble away at the edges, exacting treaty ports and concessions. China's official reaction was a deepening rigidity. Modern ideas were fended off in the name of tradition. As modernizing pressures grew on the edge of the system, a deepening anti-modern reaction paralyzed the core. No fruitful fusion took place, only collision. Moreover, after the collapse of the Manchus in 1911, China could not settle down to a period of peaceful adjustment to modernity since, save for brief intervals, the country was continuously exposed to external Japanese attack and internal civil war. By 1949 the divisions and incoherences in China called for drastic solutions and Communism, with its strict orthodoxy, its centralized planning, its all-powerful mandarinate of commissars, appealed to deep authoritarian trends in Chinese life and at the same time offered a shortcut to modernization.

The Communist seizure of power carried the old historical trend into the new age. Modern China, like ancient China, would be practical, forceful, centralized, and authoritarian. India would remain, or attempt to remain, plural, decentralized, tolerant, and permissive. During the last half-century, India has demonstrated that the Western ideal of constitutional government, personal freedom, and the open society has validity outside the Atlantic culture that gave it birth. In only one non-Western culture so far has the liberal order put down real roots, drawing on the temperament and philosophy of the people and on decades of practical experience. That place is India.

Emergence of the Non-Western World

The emergence of the non-Western World from largely dependent status under the tutelage of colonial powers of the West was one of the major events of the post–World War II period. The Second World War was in this context a watershed, separating the two great periods of human history: the European or Atlantic period and the Asian period.

In the Asian section of the non-Western world the rapid growth of Japan, Taiwan, South Korea, Hong Kong, Singapore, and, more recently, Thailand,

Malaysia, Indonesia, China, and India has poised the region to become potentially a vibrant leader in the global economy of the twenty-first century (Figure 1.6). The success of the region has been attributed to export-oriented economic policy of East Asian countries; a well-educated, disciplined, hard-working labor force; a favorable global economy; an innovative, dynamic business sector; industrial policies that supported development of key sectors; and high rates of saving and investment.The average growth rates in the last two decades have been 6 to 8 percent for China, 7 percent for Southeast Asia, and 9 to 12 percent for Taiwan, South Korea, and Singapore.

The financial trauma and recession of late 1990s in South Korea, Thailand, Indonesia, Malaysia, and Singapore was a setback. But pressure from international agencies and overseas investors is whittling away at the financial and banking problems and encouraging more open and efficient markets. China and India did not share the financial turmoil that faced South Korea, Thailand, Malaysia, and Indonesia.

The non-Western countries are in the grip of a complex series of agricultural, industrial, and post-industrial revolutions which are occurring in three waves, the nature and intensity of which vary according to the time, the country, and the country's historical and political traditions. The revolutions

Figure 1-6. Hong Kong, with a per capita income of about $23,000, ranks among the most-developed areas of East Asia. Hong Kong became a British colony in 1843. By an agreement reached in 1984, China recovered sovereignty over Hong Kong in July 1997. It is now a Special Administrative Region of China. In 2003 Hong Kong's economy was on the verge of recession with unemployment at a record 8.3 percent. A bill to limit civil rights in 2003 drew half a million protestors into the streets and threw Hong Kong government into its biggest crisis since the territory returned to China. (Photo: P. P. Karan.)

have broad similarities to the European Renaissance, Reformation, and the Industrial Revolution. Because of the compression in time, these three distinct revolutions intermingle in Asia.

The first wave crested across Japan, South Korea, Taiwan, Hong Kong, and Singapore (with a combined population of 210 million). These countries have served the role of internal dynamo in the evolving Asia-Pacific economies. Japanese, Korean, and Taiwanese investment strategies have fueled progress in other Asia-Pacific countries. Singapore and Taiwan are following in the footsteps of Japan and have emerged as leading investors in Southeast Asia and Hong Kong. The first wave is far from ebbing.

The second wave reached the Southeast Asian countries (population 320 million) in the 1970s. Since independence, Southeast Asian economies have been relying on the world trading system for the export of their oil and commodities. Active trading in farm exports, plantation products, and mineral resources has left many Southeast Asian countries with a basic infrastructure of ports, airports, roads, railways, and telecommunications. Forty years of experience in self-government has established the public administration and private sector organizations and mechanics. By tapping the international market for tourism (Thailand) and investments (Singapore and Malaysia), the countries have achieved high growth rates.

The planned or regimented economies of China, India, Myanmar (Burma), and Vietnam (population over 2 billion) make up the vanguard of the third wave in the Asian region. These countries suffer from more bureacratic government control. But the Chinese economy has been growing very rapidly since the 1980s, and India's economic growth has moved rapidly under the impetus of market reforms since 1991. Vietnam is also beginning to attract foreign investment.

Despite their different political systems, China and India, the world's two most populous countries, followed similar development strategies from the early 1950s through the early 1980s, both focusing on an industrial-oriented strategy under heavy state control. Both are now engaged in attempts to liberalize and revitalize their economies. China began its reforms in 1978. India began in a piecemeal fashion in the 1980s and comprehensively in 1991. In agriculture, in 1978 China replaced the communal farm system that had led to the starvation deaths of 30 million people with the household responsibility system. India, soon after independence, passed reforms to reduce over-concentrations of land ownership. Although agrarian institutions evolved differently in the two countries, their overall agricultural performance has remained roughly identical. In the area of trade, China moved away from monopolies by national corporations to the development of export-oriented trade zones in coastal areas. Although the large industrial state enterprise system has yet to be reformed significantly, exports of all goods and services, particularly manufactures, rose rapidly and significantly. In India, attempts to reform trade were unsuccessful until 1991, and a diversified and dynamic export sector has not emerged. Both nations are discovering that international trade holds great promise for economic growth.

Because of China's continental size (two to three times larger than Europe in its geographical area and population), the revolutions are uneven and are focused on the coastal or capital cities in China. Both in India and Vietnam, signs of rapid change have emerged, but the main tidal waves will probably not start until the turn of the century. The primary force for the revolutions in the Asian Pacific has been the rapid advance of powerful technologies. Whereas iron, steel, coal and steam powered the spread of European influence, microchips, telecommunications, and jet transport are powering the spread of a vast array of technological and commercial empires.

A significant problem facing development in non-Western countries is corruption. Indeed, according to a report on Asian corruption by a Hong Kong firm, Political and Economic Risk Consultancy (PERC), the biggest risk that business firms face in the non-Western world is corruption. China is among the three most corrupt countries in Asia, according to a survey of expatriate managers carried out by PERC. The managers were asked to grade corruption in each country on a scale from zero to ten. Rather than corruption itself, what bothers foreign companies most in Asia are the shortcomings within a country that allow corruption to flourish, such as the lack of a reliable legal system (a big problem in China) or poor pay for civil servants in most countries. In China, a purge against corruption has seen some officials executed and resignations in the highest places.

Despite Asia's teeming millions, shortage of both labor and skills are among additional constraints on the region's economic growth. From dusty construction sites in Malaysia to gleaming microchip plants in Taiwan and boardrooms in Shanghai and Mumbai (Bombay), companies are struggling to find skilled workers and managers. Finding, training, and hanging on to qualified local employees is a problem. In Penang, Malaysia, and Bangalore, India, high-tech firms try to retain staff by offering perks such as overseas travel and share options. In many places, economic development has simply outpaced the skills of the workforce. Across the region, a boom in infrastructure projects has created a massive demand for construction workers. In 1994 Thailand sent some 400,000 workers to building sites in Singapore, Hong Kong, Malaysia, and Taiwan. Laborers from Myanmar work illegally on many Thai building sites. Immigrants from Bangladesh work on many building sites in major Indian cities. Both Hong Kong and Singapore have migrant workers, mostly Filipino maids, for cheap labor they can no longer provide for themselves.

Skilled managers and technicians are even more in demand. There is a shortage not just of engineers or specialists such as tax accountants, but also of staff who know how to deal face-to-face with customers in service businesses such as hotels. Many companies are investing in training facilities. Even so, the armies of migrant workers are likely to be a feature of the Asian labor market. The Philippines alone has some 4.5 million workers overseas who send home an estimated $6 billion a year. The skills overseas workers acquire can be useful when they return home. Many of Taiwan's new high-tech firms are led by Taiwanese engineers and scientists who have returned from working overseas, especially in the United States. Something similar is now happening in Bangalore, India. Bangalore used to be a recruiting ground for Western companies seeking to hire cheap computer programmers. Now many of those who went abroad are returning to start up their own software firms.

The Twenty-First Century in the Non-Western World

Despite the problems of corruption, financial turmoil, and the resulting economic slow down in Japan, South Korea, and Southeast Asia; conflict in the Middle East; and ethnic/tribal hostilities in Africa, the non-Western world is standing on the verge of the most enormous changes that have ever occurred in world society. With its vast population and ancient traditions, it is joining the modern industrialized world. During the first decade of the twenty-first century, one billion Asians and Africans, roughly the population of the United States and Europe today, will have reached the threshold of middle-class income. Their entry into the world marketplace will transform nearly every business on earth, creating unprecedented demand for goods and services of all kinds.

Visit any Asian city from Beijing to Cape Town and you will witness an economic miracle: fast-growing industries, rising incomes, bustling trade, and twenty-first century skylines built on ground that, twenty to forty years ago, could barely support subsistence farming. Some of the most dynamic economies on earth—China, India, Hong Kong, Singapore, South Korea, Taiwan, Malaysia, Indonesia, Thailand, and the Philippines—were third-world countries ravaged by war and famine four decades ago. Notwithstanding the current financial crisis, since the 1970s Asia has produced more economic growth for more people than any other region in the history of humankind.

And the long-term future looks to be more astonishing and exciting than the past forty years were. By 2020, experts anticipate that some 2 billion will have climbed from poverty, creating the world's largest industrial consumer society. And the rise of a modern non-Western world won't just change life in the Asia and Africa; the development will affect every aspect of Western culture also, including business, investment, language, education, and entertainment.

The forces that will carry these age-old non-Western cultures into the future are already under way. Consider the impact of the Industrial Revolution, first in England, then in Europe, then in America in the twentieth century. Now imagine the effect of an even more sudden economic revolution currently sweeping through the non-Western world. Economies are moving into the machine age and beyond into the information and technology age, all within a few decades. Over half the world's population, including China and India, is on the brink of the modern era.

Historically, the fuel for Asia's success can be summed up in one word: exports. Over the past four decades rising exports have pushed one Asian country after another to increasing levels of affluence. First Japan, then the four tiger territories of Hong Kong, Korea, Taiwan, and Singapore, and now China and the less-developed Asian nations have staked their futures on manufacturing. And that effort has succeeded. Today, Asia makes 40 percent of the world's goods, up from 25 percent in the early 1970s. Europe and North America, by comparison, each contribute about 25 percent of the total.

Non-Western countries have followed a pattern in economic development:

- Countries start with relatively simple, labor-intensive industries that pay low wages.

- As modernization takes hold, wages and education levels rise. Countries then graduate to more complex, capital-intensive industries, often moving their labor-intensive businesses to less-developed neighbors.

- In the final stage, countries enter technology and service-based industries such as computer and telecomunications equipment, software, banking, consulting, and finance.

Some Southeast Asian countries and South Korea kept a tight political control on financial institutions and the economy. In 1997 they faced financial turmoil resulting from this strategy which often ignored sound financial practices and lent money to good friends instead of lending money to good borrowers.

Right now countries such as China, India, Vietnam, Thailand, and Indonesia are at various points in the first stage, South Korea and Malaysia are in the second stage, and Hong Kong, Taiwan, and Singapore are at the final stage. The future clearly lies with value-added, technological industries. Taiwan has already made this shift, drawing an increasing flow of Taiwan-born managers and engineers educated abroad back home to establish a high-tech industry. South Korea now has a thriving semiconductor industry, trailing only the United States and Japan in world production. Singapore, too, has begun to emphasize high-tech manufacturing, particularly biotechnology, pharmaceuticals, microelectronics, computer software, and imaging. And Bangalore, India, is now one of the world's largest exporters of computer software.

As rising incomes push millions into a thriving middle class, non-Western lands have become an important consumer market (Figure 1.7). Already the newfound wealth is shifting the patterns of trade within the region. In 1985, the countries of South Korea, Taiwan, Singapore, and Hong Kong split their trade almost evenly between the United States and the rest of Asia and Africa. By 2000, these countries' trade with Asia and Africa was double their trade

Figure 1-7. The Ginza shopping area in Tokyo. Japan's export-based economy grew rapidly after World War II, partly as a result of close government–business cooperation that fostered poor lending practices leading to the burst of the "bubble" economy in 1989 and economic slowdown. Japan's economic recovery has been very slow. (Photo: P. P. Karan.)

with the United States. Regional trade should intensify further as consumers see their buying power increase. If current growth trends continue, by 2010 nearly 1 billion people in Asia will command as much as $10 trillion in spending power. That's half again as big as the U.S. economy. And that's why, in industry after industry, Asian consumers provide the greatest potential for future growth. For example, Boeing predicts that Asians will account for two thirds of the growth in air travel between 1995 and 2005. As phone usage increases, China and India represent stunning opportunities for the world's telecommunication industries.

Although the changes will reach the countryside someday, their most immediate impact is on fast-growing cities. And as life in the metropolis grows more modern, the process of urbanization will accelerate. In 2000, fewer than a third of the non-Western world's people lived in cities. The United Nations estimates that by the year 2020, some 60 percent will live in cities— an influx of about 1.5 billion people.

Three Large Nations of the Non-Western World: China, India, and Japan

Of the non-Western World's three giant nations, two (China and India) are the world's most populous, and the other (Japan) is the second largest economically. These three countries rank among the top five in the primary global structures—economic, military, and knowledge power. They are strong states with the ability to mobilize the country's human and natural resources in the service of its worldview and policy objectives. By conventional measurements of great powers (in terms of international military and economic power balances), China and India are rising powers. Japan, a great power before World War II, possesses all the requisites of a great power, but the Japanese appear to have little desire to pursue that status. For the time being, Japan is content to remain under the American nuclear and military protection. Yet in a rapidly changing world where transnational nonmilitary challenges to sources of power are becoming increasingly important, the future of China, India, and Japan as complete great powers remains indeterminate. At best, both China and India are emerging and assertive regional military powers, and Japan's role is constrained by its military record in East Asia during the Second World War.

The growth of China's economic power during the last twenty years has been impressive (Figure 1.8). The downside is that this remarkable economic growth has been made possible by China's growing involvement and dependence on the capitalist world economic system. The greater involvement in the global political economy—external trade dependency and external

Figure 1-8. Towering new high-rise buildings replacing old structures symbolize the growing economy of China based on export of goods dependent on low-cost labor. Shanghai is an economic bright spot, as China girds itself to defend its huge yet fragile economy from an invasion by foreign companies following its membership in the World Trade Organization. Some of the manufacturing industries such as the domestic car makers may not be able to compete with cheaper, higher-quality imports as import quotas that limit competition are abolished by 2005 under the new trading rules. The service industry, which has replaced manufacturing as Shanghai's engine of growth, is bringing an economic transformation of the city. (Photo: P. P. Karan.)

debt—more easily translates into greater economic vulnerability and sensitivity than into a great power. A growing mismatch between China's population and resources, and a possible eruption of ethno-national conflict accompanied by domestic, social, political, demographic, and environmental problems, could make the nation's continuing success far from assured. The Chinese communist legitimacy is threatened by growing middle-class expectations created by the free market economy but frustrated by government repression.

Despite its growing economic vulnerability and dependence, authoritarian China seems poised to mobilize significant resources for the exercise of power outside its borders. China is a member of the exclusive nuclear club, possessing the world's third-largest nuclear arsenal. It also maintains the world's largest army with 3 million soldiers. China at 2000 is what Germany was in 1900: a large nondemocratic, have-not power of rising ambition and growing military might. Indeed, while every other Great Power has drastically reduced military expenditures, China's have significantly increased.

India, the world's largest democracy with its near-billion population, growing but largely self-reliant economy, efficient army and nuclear arsenal, and strong sense of cultural and national identity, is a growing and assertive power that is striding confidently on to the world stage as a contender for great power. In 1998, after a remarkably smooth electoral process, a new Indian government was sworn in, a government free from the ideological baggage that, coming from the left, had slowed economic performance. In contrast to authoritarian China, India is constrained by a democratic framework in the transformation of its socioeconomic structure. India's concern with both democracy and development poses a good counterexample within the non-Western world to the Chinese model of development in which the state presides over the introduction of a capitalist sector. An authoritarian Chinese government is better capable of running a vigorous economic and military policy than democratic governments, because it does not need its people's consent. When Deng Xioaping ordered troops to crackdown on pro-democracy demonstrators in Tianamen Square in 1989, he was not worrying about what it would mean and how he would do in the next election. But a totalitarian government can make a serious mistake if dictatorial over-confidence leads it to ignore hard facts. On the other hand, a democracy can be vigorous because decisions are arrived after discussion, debate, and consent of the masses.

India has now begun remedying its weaknesses. The economy has reached a size at which it can support a burden of military spending that is significant by global standards. Located between East Asia and West Asia, at the head of the Indian Ocean, India has clear interest in a favorable geopolitical balance in both areas of Asia as well as in eastern and southern Africa.

Japan has much of what it takes to be a great power. Its military technology and defense spending are well ahead of all other non-Western countries. Japan knows what role it wants to play in the world. Japan faces China, across the

East China Sea, where feelings about Japan's wartime occupation are still raw. Japan faces problems arising from its location. East Asian countries do not want a strong Japan. China would like to keep Japan militarily weak. With dependence on the U.S. nuclear arsenal and defense, Japan has a problem making itself an independent great power.

How will power redistribute itself in the non-Western World in the opening decades of the twenty-first century? It appears that China, India, and Japan will emerge along with the United States, Russia, and the European Union as centers of political, economic, and military power. However, what happens in the next generation will depend largely on the behavior of three Asian powers—China, India, and Japan—and the United States' strategic interests in the region. Despite the presence of American military forces in Japan and South Korea, the United States does not enjoy much political leverage to influence the policies of India and China, as recent events have indicated. The ability of America and Europe to exercise control over balance of power in Asia will continue to decline.

DEMOCRACY, DEVELOPMENT, AND ENVIRONMENT

Population and Food Supply

Rapid population growth presents a problem in the non-Western world's development. The faster the population grows, the harder it is to achieve rapid rates of economic growth per head (Figure 1.9). Within the non-Western world, population growth has been fastest in the Islamic Middle East. Since 1975 the number of people in this region has increased by an average of 3.1 percent a year. Next is Sub-Saharan Africa, with an average annual population growth rate of 2.9 percent. In the Indian subcontinent the growth rate is 2.2 percent per year. In East Asia, where the economies have been more success-ful, the figure is a modest 1.6 percent per year.

As a result of broad social and economic development and effective national family planning programs, Asian fertility rates declined by 39 percent, or 62 percent of the way toward the population-replacement level of 2.1 children per woman, between the late 1960s and the late 1980s. Although every region of Asia participated in the decline, the amount varied greatly, ranging from 20 percent in the Islamic West Asia (Figure 1.10) to 57 percent in East Asia. Qualified observers did not expect that in Asia's populous countries fertility would fall substantially or contraceptive prevalence rise rapidly in just two decades. Six Asian countries with strong national family planning programs—Bangladesh, China, India, Indonesia, Sri Lanka, and Vietnam—collectively have a contraceptive use rate of 64 percent and total fertility rates ranging from 4.5 to 2.1 children per woman. Together, they account for 76 percent of Asia's population.

Figure 1-9. Young children at a school in Gangtok, Sikkim, India. Populations in the non-Western world will continue to grow for many decades to come, increasing pressure on the natural resources. Between 2000 and 2050, national populations are expected to grow in every country except Japan. Much of the growth will occur in countries that are least capable of coping with additional stress on land, water, and other natural resources. Countries where population is projected to grow fastest have some of the lowest income levels in the world. These countries already rank high in terms of environmental stress. (Photo: P. P. Karan.)

China, Indonesia, Sri Lanka, and Vietnam, the four countries with the largest fertility declines, have, in addition to strong national family planning programs, two important development indicators: low mortality and high adult female literacy. China has mobilized its peasant population. India's moderately strong program is not always well implemented in the field, and national mortality and illiteracy rates remain high. In Bangladesh, which, despite high mortality and low female literacy, has had a substantial fertility decline, with 40 percent of the population of childbearing age now using contraceptives. Two countries, Pakistan and Nepal, still have high mortality and low female literacy. Their family planning programs are ineffective, and fertility remains high.

Six countries in East and Southeast Asia already have below-replacement fertility. For Hong Kong (a special territory of China) and Japan, the explanation is social and economic development combined with private family planning services. For South Korea, Singapore, Taiwan, and Thailand, it is broadly based development combined with strong family planning programs. Ideas about family planning and new lifestyles, carried by modern communication networks, play a role; but in some of these countries traditional familial values persist despite low fertility rates. The movement from replacement to below-replacement fertility

Figure 1-10. Health clinic in Jordan. Fertility continues to be high in most countries of the Middle East. Increasing population has major implications for political, social, and economic development. The status of women and tension between Islam and modernity affect population growth patterns. The growing number of people in Muslim countries ruled by kings, emirs, sheiks, sultans, religious leaders, and strongmen face major development challenges. How will the Muslim countries in which Islam offers a code for many aspects of life that is often enforced in a legal system meet the challenge of demographic transition and modernization? (Photo: UNRWA by Munir Nasr.)

has resulted from delayed marriage and increased singlehood, linked to women's improved status.

Slower rates of population growth in East Asian countries have accelerated economic development. Experience over the past thirty years demonstrates that a rapid decline in fertility in conjunction with effective economic policies and other favorable conditions can have a strong positive impact on economic development. Women in East Asia have reduced their childbearing at a remarakable speed, from an average of six children or more to two children or fewer in a single generation. Singapore completed this fertility transition in only 22 years, Japan and South Korea in 24, Taiwan in 26, and Thailand in 28 years. The developed countries of Europe and North America completed a similar transition more slowly. Countries such as India and the Philippines are projected to take as long as 60 years.

Enhancing the educational, political, and economic opportunities for women is perhaps the surest way to curb further population growth in the non-Western world. It is intuitively right to assume that women, as bearers of children, are in the best position to slow birth rates and that, if given greater opportunities, they will forgo continuous childbearing (Figure 1.11). Beyond intuition, there is empirical evidence. The state of Kerala in populous India, though poor, has reduced its fertility rate to replacement levels, thanks in large part to high levels of female literacy and education and growing economic opportunities for women.

For centuries, many writers have been predicting food shortages and famine in non-Western countries such as China and India. Thomas R. Malthus (1766–1834) argued two centuries ago that the growth of population must outstrip that of food supplies. In 1968 Gunnar Myrdal, a Swedish Nobel laureate, declared that India would have trouble feeding more than 500 million people. Some have argued that China's growing demand for food imports could trigger food price shocks, in turn causing starvation for hundreds of millions.

Although population doubled in many countries between 1950 and 1990, food supply kept pace with demand. Pessimists had failed to anticipate the "green revolution," in which use of fertilizers, irrigation, and new crop varieties spread and allowed food production to keep pace with population growth. In Asia, wheat yields rose fivefold between 1961 and 1991. Output was boosted further by better farming methods, more irrigation, and more chemical fertilizers. Apart from some blips in the 1970s, food prices continued their long-term decline. Asia, which grows almost half of the world's

Figure 1-11. Young women feeding a child in Zhi village, Shaanxi Province, China. Fertility decline and better nutrition has boosted both family well-being and national economic growth in China. Over the 50-year period between 1950 and 2000, life expectancy in China increased from 41 to 71 years. Because fertility is much lower in China, Japan, and Korea, the population will grow more slowly in this region than the other areas of the non-Western world. (Photo: UNICEF by Roger Lemoyne.)

cereals, produced 20 million tons more in 1995 than the 900 million tons of 1994. The green revolution has transformed Asian farming since the 1970s, making India and several other countries self-sufficient in food.

Certainly, the challenge of food supply is daunting, particularly in Sub-Saharan Africa (Figure 1.12). Every year the population of the non-Western countries expands by almost 90 million. The United Nations estimates suggest that by 2020 world population will exceed 8 billion, up 45 percent from 1995. Food demand will rise faster still as people are lifted out of poverty. There are some worrying signs, too, on the supply side. Yields of rice and wheat in Asia are still rising, but much more slowly than they did in the 1960s and 1970s. Growth in the use of fertilizers has slowed worldwide.

The green revolution has brought problems too. In Asia many irrigated areas have become saline or waterlogged. Pests have developed resistance to chemicals. In many countries, fertile areas still uncultivated are often precious habitats for wildlife. In some areas, such as northern China, irrigation has led

Figure 1-12. Two women winnow rice from the local harvest, near the town of Nyagatare, Rwanda. Humans and nature have conspired to create an unparalled food crisis in Sub-Saharan Africa. Back-to-back droughts, compounded by disease, corruption, foolhardy economic policies, misguided nationalism, and government mismanagement have crippled agricultural production. Many African governments invest little in improving farming techniques, soil conservation, or scientific research that can boost crop yields. Among the continent's strongman regimes and feeble democracies, leaders have seldom been ousted by food crises, making feeding the population a low priority. In addition, powerful homegrown forces have magnified Africa's agricultural problems. In Zimbabwe, with the onset of land reform, whites lost farms, blacks lost jobs, and the country that once fed much of southern Africa lost the means to feed itself. In contrast, until the mid-1970s, many Asian countries, as underdeveloped as African ones, were suffering from droughts and famines. Today, better seeds, fertilizers, and pesticides, as well as investments in science and technology, have produced silos overflowing with surplus grain. For example, India is now the world's second-largest exporter of rice and the sixth-largest exporter of wheat. (Photo: UNICEF by Maggie Murray-Lee.)

to water shortages. The environmental problems brought by modern farming methods are real enough, but it is unlikely that the world will let them seriously restrain food production.

Along with fertility decline, growing agricultural productivity, and robust economic growth rates, advances in Asia will continue in the twenty-first century, and the forces of change will have an effect on more than 3 billion people. In Asia, the Western world's Calvinist work ethic has met, fused with, and been reinforced by Chinese and Indian business principles. The result is an area where the wave of future development will rise and crest. It's a concept that's often hard to grasp in the United States—a nation that has spent 200 years looking across the Atlantic Ocean toward Europe, drawn by ethnic and cultural heritages, political goals, and economic needs. But that doesn't change what's happening in the Asian region of the non-Western world.

Modernization and Development

Modernization may be defined as the application of science and technology to the problems of life and society. The resulting patterns of change offer prospects for the betterment of human conditions, but also may threaten mankind in some cases with environmental destruction. Colonial rule in the non-Western world stressed westernization—the adoption of Western customs—without modernization. In general, colonialism and modernization were contradictory. Independence is a necessary condition for modernization involving upgrading of the application of science and technology to society.

Development is a process of directed social and economic change. Drawing on the experience of several decades of development efforts, the concept of sustainable development emerged in the 1980s. Historically, the development of the Western world and Japan focused on production. Not surprisingly, therefore, the model followed by the developing nations of the non-Western world in the 1950s and 1960s was output and growth dominated, based mainly on the concept of economic efficiency. By the early 1970s the large and growing numbers of poor in the developing countries, and lack of "trickle down" benefits to them, led to greater efforts to directly improve income distribution. The development paradigm shifted toward equitable growth, in which social (distributional) objectives, especially poverty alleviation, were recognized as distinct from, and as important as, economic efficiency.

Protection of the environment has now become the third major objective of development with the economic and social objectives noted in the preceding paragraph (Figure 1.13). By the early 1980s, a large body of evidence had accumulated that environmental degradation was a major barrier to development. The concept of sustainable development has therefore evolved to encompass three major points of view: economic, social, and environmental. The economic approach to sustainability places emphasis on growth,

Figure 1-13. Bhopal, India. In 1984 a poisonous gas escaped from a Union Carbide plant in this city, killing and injuring thousands of people. Chemical factories, producing toxic or radioactive materials, often located in densely populated areas, present potential high risk to the local population in many non-Western world countries. (Photo: P. P. Karan.)

efficiency, and stability. The social-cultural concept of sustainability is people oriented, and seeks to maintain the stability of social and cultural systems. Elimination of poverty, equity, and the rights of future generations are important aspects of this approach. Preservation of cultural diversity and the better use of knowledge concerning sustainable practices embedded in indigenous cultures are emphasized. For socially sustainable development a society must encourage and harness pluralism and grassroots participation into a more effective decision-making framework. The environmental view of sustainable development focuses on the stability of biological and physical systems. The emphasis is on preserving the resilience and dynamic ability of natural systems and habitats, including human-made environments such as cities. Natural resource degradation, pollution, and loss of biodiversity reduce the resilience of the system.

To achieve sustainable development, the economic, social-cultural, and environmental concepts must be integrated. Integrating and operationalizing them to achieve sustainable development is a formidable task. Most development decisions in the non-Western world continue to be based on economic efficiency criteria; often attempts are made to incorporate social-cultural approaches, but these have not been very successful. There is a need to develop a broader conceptual framework that integrates the economic, social-cultural, and environmental approaches. The major goals of development in the non-Western world must be growth with equity, and cultural and environmental preservation.

The United Nation includes Nepal, Bhutan, Bangladesh, Myanmar (Burma), and Laos among the least-developed countries in the Asian Pacific region. The obstacles to development are measurably greater in Africa than in Asia, where growth-oriented nations have quickened the pace of innovation, investment, and social and economic change. Among the criteria used for measuring development are income per capita, structure of the economy (employment in primary, secondary, and tertiary sectors), and social indices such as literacy, health, and infant mortality. A recent report by the International Monetary Fund (IMF) suggests that some non-Western countries are less poor than official figures indicate. Rather than convert local-currency GDPs (gross domestic product) into dollars at market exchange rates, the IMF now has decided to use purchasing power parities (PPP), which take into account international differences in prices. The result is a sharp jump in the developing countries' share of the world's output, to 34 percent with the new method from 18 percent with the old method. By contrast, the share of industrially advanced countries has dropped from 73 percent to 54 percent.

The central issues in development in non-Western lands involve continued emphasis on improving agricultural production through higher yields, the reform of land tenure, development of modern industry, and protection of the environment through better management of growth. The speed of development has been determined by the amount of funds available through investment by multinational corporations.

Significant development will continue in the future, if the governments of less-developed countries in the non-Western world put people, rather than ideology, at the center of their national development goals. This would involve emphasizing education, primary health care, family planning, safe water, and feasible growth and resource development strategy. In addition, long-term development in any country will not be possible without the establishment of human freedom indicated by multiparty elections, freedom of the press, rule of law, right to travel and assembly, and opportunities for gender and ethnic equality.

In 1990 the United Nations Development Program (UNDP), an independent agency which in 1990 channeled $1.4 billion in aid, introduced a human development index (HDI) ranking 130 countries on a composite index. The *1991 Human Development Report* refined that index and expanded it to cover 160 countries, while introducing a new "human freedom index" to show the relationship between freedom and development. It shows that the world's poorest nations are generally also the least free, and concludes that "overall there seems to be a high correlation between human development and human freedom." Among the non-Western countries, Japan ranks at the top with 32 of a possible 40 points and Iraq as the least free, with a score of zero. Most of the non-Western world's poor countries including China, Pakistan, Indonesia, and Bangladesh score 10 points or less.

Five Sins of Development in the Non-Western World

Development efforts in the non-Western countries have been bedevilled by a lack of appropriate emphasis in five major areas. An emphasis on these items is necessary to make the development efforts a success.

1. **Development without infrastructure**. Development efforts of recent years have yielded a range of techniques and strategies that could accelerate real development even in the difficult decades that lie ahead. Most of the cost-effective techniques now available, from immunization to oral rehydration therapy, and from new seed varieties to new hand-pumps, are of little value without a reliable delivery mechanism for informing and supporting people in their use. The backbone of infrastructure is made up of a properly trained staff and informed people.

2. **Development without participation**. Sustained development ultimately depends on enhancing people's own capacities to improve their lives and to take more control over their own destinies. External assistance, whether from a capital city or a foreign country, cannot long be the star of the show, and must learn the skills of the supporting role. Whether in agriculture or industry, water supply or housing schemes, development experience to date has shown that there is an absolutely crucial distinction between the kind of assistance that enables and involves and the kind that alienates and disenfranchises. The success or failure of any development effort will usually depend on which side of that sometimes subtle line such assistance falls.

3. **Development without environment**. Twenty-five years ago it was widely thought that environmental degradation was a problem of the industrialized world, a function of affluence, and of little relevance to the less-developed nations. Today the deforestation of lands, erosion of soils, silting of lakes and rivers, the new propensity to drought and flood, and industrial disasters such as the Bhopal tragedy have shown that the environment is also a problem in Asia and Africa. At the same time, rising concern over the depletion of the ozone layer, global warming, and the unknown consequences of the destruction of the world's forests should have made it clear to all that the environment is *everyone's* problem. In every development initiative the environment ought to be a part of the forethought and not an afterthought.

4. **Development without the poor**. Development has for too long been confined to showcase examples and pilot projects. Such projects have shown what can be done: the emphasis must now shift toward doing it for the poorest third of the families in non-Western lands. The problems

of malnutrition, poor growth, frequent ill-health, child deaths, maternal mortality, illiteracy, and low productivity are concentrated among the poorest third of the population.

The challenge of reaching the very poorest is the greatest challenge of social development. Over the last fifteen years, almost every initiative, large or small, has come up against the same problem of reaching the unreached. Even the most serious and politically difficult attempts at shifting priorities in favor of the poor—via primary schools or adult literacy campaigns, rural clinics, or supplementary feeding programs—have often failed to reach substantial numbers among the very poorest groups.

There is no one answer to this problem. Just as the impact on the environment must now be borne in mind at every stage of every development initiative, so pressure must be maintained at every stage to keep the focus on the poorest communities. In particular, the pressure must be kept up for the increasing representation of the poor in decision making and for the inversion of spending pyramids so that the majority of resources available for development are devoted to actions that benefit the poorest.

5. **Development without women**. The women of the non-Western World are responsible for producing and marketing most of its crops; they also carry the main responsibility for food preparation and homemaking, for water and fuel, for nutrition and health care, for hygiene, and for the education of the young (Figure 1.14). Not least, they are almost entirely responsible for the physical and mental development of the next generation. Yet the bulk of the development assistance efforts to date, most of the education and training, the technology and the inputs, the investments and the loans, have gone to men.

The gender-based imbalance in development is difficult to correct because it is part of a landscape of fundamental social inequities in all countries. But the inefficiency involved in this bias, not to mention its injustice, costs the development effort dearly. The effects of female education on family size, child health, and the use of available government services are already known. But the possibilities for increased productivity and incomes through credit, training, and technology for women have hardly begun to be explored. Similarly, investments in safe motherhood and in labor-saving devices of particular relevance to women are among the most productive but the most ignored of all investments in social and economic development.

It is no exaggeration to say that the avoidance of these "five sins" could more than double the cost-effectiveness of the development effort.

Figure 1-14. A woman of the Ouro village, near Ouahigouya on the central plateau of Burkina Faso, weeding millet planted along a stone diguette. Women play an important role in agricultural economies, compared with their status and access to resources. Development efforts in Africa are beginning to focus on better integration of women in the development processes through emphasis on all spheres of women's lives, including social realities that shape views of sex and assign specific roles, responsibilities, and expectations to women and men. It is critically important for policy makers to listen to and work with women to improve their positions and thereby accelerate Africa's development. (Photo: International Fund for Agricultural Development by J. Hartley.)

Women in the Non-Western World: A Neglected Resource

The vast majority of the people who live in the non-Western world's poorest countries lead lives of grinding poverty, unrelenting toil, and ignorance. And those who are the poorest, who toil the hardest, and are the most uneducated are women.

It was once assumed that development efforts aimed at people in general would automatically benefit everyone, male and female. Not so. For a variety of reasons—women's inferior status, their relative invisibility in national economic reckonings, their traditionally small voice in decision making—women were virtually left out of the development process in many countries. In fact, the lot of most of the women has worsened as populations have grown, as technology and training have been awarded to men, as farmland has been increasingly taken over for cash crops, and as natural resources have been depleted.

Women account for two-thirds of the work hours. They produce 60 to 80 percent of the food in the Asian Pacific. Yet they officially constitute only one-third of the labor force in the non-Western world, receive only 10 percent of its income, and own less than 1 percent of its property. The work women do in the home and on the farm is never calculated into the gross national product of any country. Women's unpaid contributions to their national economies are largely overlooked.

The gap between women's work and their rewards is largest in Asia and Africa. As populations have exploded (mainly because of a decline in infant mortality) women's burdens have increased and their health has deteriorated. Most women spend all their childbearing years either pregnant or nursing children. Largely because of the male urban migration, women end up heading at least 17 percent of the households—30 percent or more in some rural areas of the non-Western lands.

Depletion of the land has meant that millions of women are fleeing to the cities and crowding into often primitive slums. Conditions there are even harder than in the countryside. Back on the land, deforestation, poor land management, and emphasis on cash crops have shrunk the arable acreage available to food producers, most of whom are women. At the same time, environmental decay has forced women to spend more time each day walking greater and greater distances to find water and firewood for their families.

By keeping food prices low, government policies in many countries have sacrificed the welfare of rural peasants—most of whom are women—to appease the growing, more politically focused demands of the city dwellers. These policies have encouraged cash crops in a desperate attempt to generate hard currency and pay off national debts. In many areas, local wars or drought and floods, have relegated large numbers of women and children to the crowded and dehumanizing conditions of refugee camps.

As if all of this were not enough, a breakdown in the pattern of traditional marriage has left many women with children to fend for themselves. Alcoholism, mainly among men, and the domestic violence that results from it have become major problems in several countries. And while the world economic crunch has meant that few families are able to survive on only one income, women often have neither the training nor the freedom from family responsibilities to enable them to find gainful employment.

A major effort is underway throughout the non-Western world to widen women's horizons beyond childbearing and the collecting and preparing of food. Jobs and education are essential if more and more women are to be given a chance. Literacy and education are also vital in freeing women from the drudgery of village and slum life.

To increase equality of opportunity for women, it will be important to remove the long-standing laws and social practices that have either explicitly or effectively discriminated against women in the non-Western world. In many countries, laws and practices restrict women's right to own property, secure credit, enter certain occupations, and access education. It is often difficult to change traditional social practices without strong and widespread involvement of women in national and local social movements. National laws to ban dowries in India and prohibitions on prostitution in Thailand are significant steps, but they had limited effects in removing long-standing practices. Public policy such as subsidies for girls' education, employment preference for qualified women, and assistance such as flexible working hours, on-site child care, maternity leave, and child care tax credits to women who are combining the role of worker and household manager can play an important role in alleviating gender inequality.

Inequity and Rural Poverty

Rural poverty, a dominant feature of life in all regions of the world, affects the lives of close to 900 million people in the non-Western world. The proportion of rural population whose incomes and consumption fall below nationally defined poverty lines is estimated at 31 percent (633 million) in Asia (46 percent or 262 millions if China and India are excluded), 60 percent (204 million) in Sub-Saharan Africa, and 26 percent (27 million) in the Middle East.

These rural poor are largely untouched by the recent progress in the non-Western world. The goal of lifting this impoverished majority out of its hopelessness and misery through development has largely failed. The development quest continues, but problems such as poverty, ignorance, unemployment, hunger, and disease (which the developers set out to solve) still afflict vast millions. Development is not reaching the rural poor in any decisive degree. Countries such as China and India are growing in gross economic terms, but the individual lives of the bulk of their people living in rural areas are stagnating (Figure 1.15). Even though many nations in Asia and Africa are dotted with showcase factories, modern urban areas, new universities, high-yielding fields of rice and wheat, and shops filled with consumer goods, there is widespread evidence in the rural landscape that the development efforts have failed.

Not only has development failed to give significant help to the poor, it has also contributed to widening the gap between rich and poor in many non-Western countries. The failure is rooted in two major factors: the inability to curb the relentless growth of population in most countries and the inability and, in many cases, unwillingness of officials in governments plagued by inefficiency and corruption and preoccupied with other concerns to push social development with enough vigor to transfer some of the fruits of economic growth to the rural poor.

Throughout the non-Western world the advantaged minority in the rural areas—those with power, influence, money, or education—has pushed quickly ahead since the 1970s, but the rest of the rural poor have remained behind. Although the average per capita income has increased, the per capita income of the majority of the people remained below the poverty line. The social tensions caused in large part by the population burden and economic inequities have often produced political turmoil. For example, in Pakistan, the East Pakistanis revolted, charging neglect, deprivation, and exploitation, and

Figure 1-15. Yangtze valley, near Wuhan, China. Rural poverty in China has declined substantially during the last two decades. Yet, even as China's economy continues to grow and it enters into the World Trade Organization, it is becoming harder to reduce poverty and inequality further. China's beleaguered farmers are among those most threatened by the changes resulting from the country's membership in the World Trade Organization, which calls for relaxation in duties and quotas on imported agricultural products. This will increase the competition farmers face from imports. Already, Chinese farm incomes are falling, and poverty is spreading in some areas where rural households depend on money sent home by relatives working on construction sites in cities. Labor is plentiful and cheap in the countryside, but total production costs on China's small farm plots are actually higher than in the West, where large mechanized farms provide economies of scale. For example, American wheat can be bought in China for about $36 less a ton than domestic wheat, putting downward pressure on local prices. That pressure will intensify after China raises its ceiling on wheat imports from the current 2 million tons annually to 9.3 million tons by 2004. Competition from efficient foreign agriculture is expected to hasten the already huge migration of people from the countryside into China's cities. The influx will strain urban social services and worsen urban unemployment. (Photo: P. P. Karan.)

with the help of India won a two-week war for independence in December 1971, as the new nation of Bangladesh. Nonetheless, the Pakistanis, though relieved of what was seen as a burdensome Bengali majority, continue to have an impoverished and anxious rural population of 23 million living below the poverty line. With large populations of poor people estimated in 1997 at 251 million in India, 119 million in China, 82 million in Bangladesh, 34 million in Indonesia, 22 million in the Philippines, and 14 million in Thailand, the major battle in some non-Western countries is just to keep the numbers of poor from increasing further.

There is no doubt that, individually and collectively, the obstacles facing the rural poor are formidable. They are not, however, insuperable. Most of the forces creating poverty are essentially social. They reflect systems of resource allocation that are made by societies, and as such they can be reversed. Basic elements in the effort to render the rural poor in non-Western countries more productive are the provisions of economic services and assets that the rural poor have tended not to receive in the past. The prosperity of the rural poor depends on the improvement in the means of production directly available to them. Health and education are very important, but they offer more if they are combined with the material means of making a living. To pull people out of poverty, it is also important to first empower them with self-esteem and with the hope that change is always possible (Figure 1.16). When confronting major challenges such as traditional poverty, small steps are more effective than monumental antipoverty programs.

Massive Urbanization

˙The cities of the non-Western world are growing at an extremely rapid pace and many are becoming unmanageable. Millions of people in Africa and Asia pour each year from the impoverished countryside, swelling the ranks of the unemployed and straining the already limited supply of urban services. Of

Figure 1-16. Human needs of mothers and children are reflected in the naïve smile of a child and a mother's expression of despair in this photo of a shanty town near Dhaka, Bangladesh. Nowhere is the problem of development more urgent than in the slums and shanty towns that ring the major cities of the non-Western world. Large numbers of people are drawn to the cities from the rural hinterland by dreams of better economic opportunities. But megacities of the non-Western world are choking with pollution, congestion, and appalling squalor engulfed by poverty. The poor in-migrants who contribute vitally to a city's economy have little access to urban resources and amenities. The growth of megacities exemplifies how the urban boom signals expanding economic opportunities, but the poor who contribute to this economic growth continue to live outside the mainstream of these cities in terms of access to housing, sanitation, basic healthcare, safe drinking water, and secure employment. (Photo: UNICEF by Bernard P. Wolff.)

the world's urban population of 2.6 billion, nearly 1.2 billion are in the non-Western world. By 2025, the urban population is projected to increase to 2.7 billion in Asia and 804 million in Africa. An estimated 600 million people in urban areas of the non-Western world today cannot meet their basic needs for shelter, water, and health. The population living in urban slums in megacities of the non-Western world varies between 12 percent in Seoul to 84 percent in Cairo. The slum population of other cities, according to estimates made by the International Labor Organization, is 20 percent in Shanghai, 57 percent in Mumbai, and 58 percent in Lagos. National studies in Asia show large percentages of the urban population in slum and squatter settlements: Bangladesh at 47 percent, Sri Lanka at 21 percent, Malaysia at 15 percent, Thailand at 15 percent, and Indonesia at 54 percent.

The rapid growth of cities and the development of slums and squatter settlements in much of the non-Western world is an outgrowth of a failed strategy of development that emphasized industrial and urban growth at the expense of agriculture and rural development. The urban-based development strategy fueled substantial rural-to-urban migration and the concentration of economic activity in urban areas. Housing, urban infrastructure, and water supplies failed to keep pace with urban growth. In many non-Western cities, modern districts are set apart from the traditional city centers and expanding slums settlements are frequently on the periphery. One can see these slums on the outskirts of Delhi, India, and on the periphery of many other cities. Less than a half-hour drive from New Delhi's dazzling architectural wonders, comfortable neighborhoods, and splendid gardens, there are abject slum settlements along the Jamuna river on government-owned land. From the levee above the river one can look down on a staggering clutter of rusted and crumbling corrugated iron roofs secured only by stones. Here, over 20,000 marginalized people are crammed into makeshift homes. Dirt, disease, and squalor cast a spell of hopelessness in such slums in the major cities.

Most cities do not have the resources to provide adequate sanitation and public health. Poor living conditions lead to increased risks from pollution to environmental health, the quicker spread of infectious diseases, and the interactions of viral and bacterial infections. Crowding and poor-quality water are major elements in disease transmission.

Historic areas are threatened by expanding urban development, and preservation efforts often conflict with economic restructuring priorities. The feminization of poverty in the cities is a cause for increasing concern. Women in the larger cities are either unemployed or work in the lower ranks of clerical, sales, and menial occupations rather than in production and manufacturing. In some Asian cities such as Karachi, civil disturbances, violent social movements, and periodic unrest have displaced growing numbers of women and their children. Such women become heads of their households with few resources to provide for their families' basic needs and limited opportunities to improve their situation.

Most non-Western countries have lately become concerned about the degree of urbanization and the resulting social, economic, and environmental problems. The 1996 U.N. Conference on Urbanization held in Istanbul highlighted the problems of the rapid growth of cities. Overurbanization did not occur in the development of the Western countries because, broadly speaking, migrants were absorbed by industry in the cities, or they moved to new territories overseas. But non-Western countries today are in a different situation from that of the Western countries on the eve of their industrialization. The major difference is that there are many more people today attempting to enter industries that require much less labor.

Two policy approaches, undertaken simultaneously, are necessary to retard the current urban growth rate in major cities by redirecting the flow of migrants to smaller cities in rural areas and by increasing the attractiveness of rural areas. The first, rural development is now widely accepted—in theory at least, if not always in practice. Its aim is to increase employment and incomes in the countryside so that fewer people feel compelled to migrate to cities in search of a livelihood. The second, urban bias in development policy such as special tax breaks, subsidized interest rates, excessive tariff protection and other privileges enjoyed exclusively by urban large-scale industry, must be eliminated. The governments must expand urban public services in rural towns and small city service centers. This is not an argument that non-Western countries should remain rural and disregard industrialization. Rather, it asserts that in the absence of participatory rural development, few countries will be able to achieve their industrialization goals without severe and chronic urban problems. If the countryside does not prosper, the cities will continue to deteriorate. National leaders in the non-Western world will need courage, political skill, administrative ability, and self-confidence—not the most common combination of leadership attributes in the non-Western countries—to enact development policies to reverse current urbanization trends. These policies are generally opposed by the urban wealthy classes.

Environmental Degradation

Environmental degradation is a rapidly growing problem for most of the non-Western World, but the least-developed countries, especially their poorest citizens, are facing the most immediate and extreme consequences. Perhaps the most dramatic are the chronic droughts and desertification that are swallowing up large parts of the countries of Sub-Saharan Africa, turning millions of farmers and shepherds into permanent refugees. Erosion and deforestation on the slopes of the Himalayas (Figure 1.17) may partially contribute to the flooding of millions of acres of arable land in the Indo-Ganges plain.

The steady deterioration of their environment and dwindling resources have made it clear that the environment must become a top priority for the least-developed nations of the non-Western world. Otherwise, in some cases, their populations will simply no longer have any life support system left. It is

Figure 1-17. Environmental degradation threatens the productivity of agricultural and forest resources on which many non-Western countries depend for their economic growth. The problem is most pervasive in the least-developed countries such as Nepal, where poverty and population pressure compel people to deplete the natural resources to meet their immediate needs for survival. Although deforestation, seen here in the Himalaya, has yielded considerable short-term benefits through timber exports and agricultural production on previously forested land, it has entailed huge (and largely unmeasured) long-term costs to the people of the areas directly affected. Among the more direct and visible of these costs are the losses of forest products such as timber, fuel wood, fibers, canes, resins, oils, pharmaceuticals, fruits, spices, and animal hides. More indirect, but equally important, long-term costs include soil erosion, flooding, and the siltation of reservoirs and hydroelectric facilities; destruction of wildlife habitats; climate changes; and the irreversible loss of biological diversity. (Photo: P. P. Karan.)

no exaggeration to say that halting environmental degradation is one of the most formidable, difficult, yet inescapable challenges facing the non-Western lands in the 1990s.

In the past, most of the inhabitants of the non-Western world devised ways of adapting their lifestyles to the environment, establishing a harmonious relationship with the natural habitat surrounding them. Simple techniques were developed to cope with drought, to exploit water resources, to contain erosion, and to protect forests and rivers. When the colonial powers introduced modern methods of cultivation and fishing, and large commercial companies began to exploit the natural resources, the fragile ecological balance in the non-Western world was disturbed. The unabated expansion of commercial operations has meant the shrinking of the physical resource base of the poor. In many cases this has led to the destruction of the environment and its productive capacity. Tree loss and deforestation are also partly the result of a heavy dependence on fuelwood, but as the area of woodland diminishes, it can no longer sustain the cutting rate. The seas along the coastlines formerly fished only by small unmechanized boats, have been pillaged by modern fleets, resulting in depleted stocks and less food for the coastal state.

Well-meaning development projects have wreaked unintentional havoc in many areas. In particular, ecologically sound traditional practices have been spurned in favor of ill-adapted Western technologies. For example, the introduction of modern irrigation systems has caused widespread losses of once-productive land through salinity and water logging.

Many of the poor non-Western countries have become cheap garbage depositories for the industrialized nations. Millions of tons of toxic waste, some of it radioactive, are deposited in the poor countries of the non-Western world in exchange for much-needed dollars. The state of Washington sends about two-thirds of the plastic it collects from individual recyclers to Asia. In Hong Kong, China, Indonesia, the Philippines and elsewhere, these U.S.-made plastic soda bottles and milk jugs are sorted by low-wage laborers, melted down, reused, burned or buried, often without strict environmental or labor law enforcement. Greenpeace, an environmental watchdog, has reported the unloading of wastes from Europe in non-Western countries. The waste business has flourished not only because of the poor countries' desperate need for foreign exchange but also because of the corruption of government officials, weak national legislation, and unclear international law. But will improved international laws stop the illegal trade in toxic wastes?

Hazardous smelting dust, sludge, rubble, bloody hospital syringes, amputated limbs, expired chemicals and paints, shredded clothing, broken furniture, rusted refrigerators, scrap tires consigned to burning—what the West cannot use, Asia and Africa receive, despite laws on both sides that sharply restrict such trade. The pressure is mainly financial. Under U.S. and European environmental laws, the cost of disposing of hazardous industrial and mining waste can reach as high as several thousand dollars per ton, depending on content. Shipping such material abroad often is much cheaper.

In the rapidly growing economies of the Asian Pacific, the environment has become the victim of their success. Rapid economic development in countries such as South Korea, Thailand, Taiwan, China, Malaysia, India, and Indonesia has created spectacular development and a consumer boom. Much of Asia has adopted a growth-first strategy that puts investment above environment. Governments have given priority to infrastructure projects to promote economic activity such as power plants and ports, rather than sewage and water treatment plants. Now, across the Asian Pacific region, rapidly industrializing economies are attracting millions of migrants from the poorer rural areas to the urban centers. With few exceptions, the governments in Asia are failing to provide even the most basic services such as sanitation and piped water for much of their burgeoning populations.

China, Indonesia, Bangladesh, India, and Pakistan face urban environmental problems on such a vast scale that the viability of their major cities is at stake, as is the sustainability of the capitals of medium-size nations such as Thailand and the Philippines. The reality in many of the large cities in the non-Western world is foul air and waterways and a severe shortage of basic facilities such as water, sewage systems, garbage disposal services, and transportation.

The Indonesian government has long considered the growth of the capital, Jakarta, a major problem, and in 1971 the city was closed to new rural migrants. Despite efforts to stem the arrival of these migrants, the population of the greater Jakarta region grew from 5.8 million to 17 million between 1960 and 1990. Reams of statistics reveal the consequences: shrimp in Jakarta Bay are contaminated by mercury from some 30,000 small factories that dump untreated effluent upstream. On the international air pollution index, particle pollution has exceeded the standard on a maximum of 268 days a year and an average 173 days a year since 1975.

World Health Organization data point to the special risks for residents of the most densely populated cities (except those in Japan, which have benefited from two decades of investment in pollution-control technology). The large cities of China and India, both of which have recently liberalized their economies to promote foreign investment and rapid development, top the list. Mukden, China, has exceeded international safety standards for particle-pollution levels on 347 days of the year and for sulfur-dioxide levels on 326 days. In all Chinese cities, lung cancer mortality rates are four to seven times the national average. In Delhi, India, 30 percent of the population suffers from respiratory diseases, 12 times the national average, and particle-pollution levels exceed the safety limit on an average of 294 days of the year. In Manila, the failure of infrastructure is particularly obvious. No new power stations have been built since the mid-1980s, and blackouts are now scheduled daily. The result is that businesses and households that can afford to generate their own electricity use diesel generators, which create noise and air pollution.

In 1992 the United Nations Environmental Program and the World Health Organization concluded that all of the non-Western megacities—places with more than 10 million inhabitants in 2000—already exceeded the level the WHO deems healthy in at least one major pollutant. Several exceeded the guidelines for two pollutants. In Beijing, Seoul, Delhi, Calcutta, Cairo, Mumbai, and Shanghai the major pollutants are gases comprising small particles of unburnt carbon, forming various oxides of sulphur, which dissolve in water to produce acid. Their presence in the air turns rain into acid. Along with gases is gunge, small particulate matter less than ten-millionths of a meter across. The smaller the particles, the deeper into the lungs they seem to penetrate.

The cities in the non-Western world will continue to grow, despite their deteriorating environments. One factor is simply the weight of numbers.

Rural populations have continued to grow at such a rate that migration to the cities has not reduced total numbers, and the opportunity to find a job in the city is forcing more and more people off the land (Figure 1.18). At the same time, new middle classes are emerging in the cities with the same energy consumption expectations as their Western counterparts: cars, air travel, labor-saving household goods, power, running water, air conditioning, heating, and high-quality housing.

Japan offers a contrast to the rest of the non-Western world in environmental preservation. In forty years, Japan has left behind its reputation as one of the dirtiest industrial powers and gone on to set world standards with its technology to control pollution and use energy efficiently. Japanese politicians and civil servants are now asking whether their achievements have provided them with a long-awaited opportunity to exercise global political leadership. Could Japan really set the pace in the battle to clean up the planet?

Compared with other industrial nations, Japan uses less energy per head of population, produces less carbon dioxide, has stricter standards for airborne pollutants, and provides its citizens with cleaner water. Japanese industries are

Figure 1-18. Rural migrants arriving in Dhaka, bustling capital of Bangladesh. Each year cities in Asia and Africa receive thousands of migrants from the countryside. Some of these migrants find jobs in factories producing clothing for the Gap, Disney, the Kathie Lee Gifford line, and others. Other migrants remain unemployed or find part-time work. Working conditions in the factories producing goods for foreign companies are often unsatisfactory. Women are forced to quit if they become pregnant; they receive no vacation, holiday, or sick days and earn about 15 cents an hour, which means that they earn about 5 cents for a shirt that sells for $17.99 in the United States. (Photo: UNICEF by Jason Laure.)

already working on dozens of projects to develop new technologies that use energy and materials even more sparingly. Business is, of course, looking for profits from its activities.

In the 1950s and 1960s, Japan's fledgling industries belched millions of tons of noxious pollutants into the country's waterways, atmosphere, and homes. The results were horrific. In Minimata, on the southern island of Kyushu, mercury from a factory left thousands crippled. Cadmium pollution in the industrial city of Yokkaichi, some 185 miles south of Tokyo, caused another horrific disease, simply named *tai, tai* ("it hurts, it hurts") for the endless cries of its victims. The eventual outcome was uniquely Japanese—industry and government cooperated to set new standards for clean emissions and devised new technologies to meet them.

One priority in the 1960s was to develop the technology for filtering heavy metals out of industrial effluent. Alongside the purge of waterborne effluent came the speedy introduction of scrubbers to filter out sulfur dioxide and oxides of nitrogen from smokestacks. By 1989, Japan's 2,189 desulfurization and denitrification units represented three-quarters of all those installed around the world. With the oil crises of the 1970s, Japan redoubled its efforts to use materials efficiently and developed the world's most sophisticated industrial technology for saving energy. While the country's gross domestic product grew by more than 65 percent between 1973 and 1986, energy consumption rose by a mere 10 percent.

It is this history that helps make Japan believe that it has something to offer to other nations. The Japanese experience should be invaluable to the nations of Asia and Africa (Figure 1.19). But there is a worm in Japan's rosy plans to lead the world in solving global environmental problems. Plenty of people outside Japan see the damage its timber industry has wrought in the tropical forests of Southeast Asia, and its heartless pursuit of whales, as making it unfit to speak about the environment.

Differences in the way Japan perceives its successes, and in the way the outside world sees its failures, may be partly cultural. Japan has earned the most international condemnation for its continued insistence on the right to kill whales. Yet many Japanese cannot see why. To them, a whale is just another fish, like a tuna or a sardine.

The non-Western world must focus on improving quality of life through environmental preservation. To this end, support from Japan and other industrialized countries, and international agencies, can be valuable in implementing policies to protect and preserve the environment.

DEMOCRACY AND HUMAN RIGHTS

For most of the past four decades South Korea, Taiwan, Singapore, Thailand, Malaysia, and Hong Kong, and recently China, have been known

Figure 1-19. Lake Toya, Japan, where environmental preservation and development interests have clashed. The area is part of the Shikotsu-Toya National Park in southern Hokkaido, which contains a number of volcanoes, caldera lakes, and hot springs. Its pristine beauty has rendered Lake Toya a site for one of the countless disputes in Hokkaido pitting preservationists against developers of hotels and related tourist facilities. Environmentalists are opposed to the building of hotels, souvenir shops, and spas in the mountainous forests around Lake Toya. In recent years, local groups have begun fighting the developers. Some groups have also sprung up to battle the construction of hydroelectric dams and nuclear power plants in Hokkaido. Among the most active groups are those representing the aboriginal people of Hokkaido, the Ainu. (Photo: P. P. Karan.)

largely as countries with rapid economic growth but stilted political development, with most countries led by military regimes, autocratic strong men, or all-powerful ruling parties that kept power through money, patronage, and a measured amount of repression. Yet recent events are converging to challenge some of the old certainties, upending some long-held political orthodoxy, despite the fact that leaders in countries such as Singapore, Malaysia, and China still advocate the idea of "Asian values," a system that prizes stability and consensus while eschewing Western-style democracy with its emphasis on individual freedoms.

In the early twenty-first century there are stirrings of democracy in East Asia that are testing the much-repeated axiom that Asians, by and large, care little about democracy and human rights and favor authoritarian governments. South Korea, the Philippines, Thailand, and Indonesia—where general elections were derisively called "election of generals"—have embraced democracy. Some Asian countries have a tradition of democracy, including Japan, which became a Western-style liberal democracy after World War II;

the Philippines, where democracy was aborted by the Marcos dictatorship; and India, the world's most populous democratic nation. But Asia's autocrats have brushed aside these countries as unsuitable models for the rest of the region because of their unique circumstances: Japan's war-time defeat and occupation, for instance, and the Philippines' history as a U.S. colony. And India, with its endemic poverty, often still is viewed as a negative example showing that democracy does not generate economic development and stability. Asian countries compare the limits India encounters in speedy or radical economic reforms to the relatively free hand of governments in authoritariam societies such as China.

Nonetheless, democracy is becoming more entrenched, most remarkably in South Korea, Thailand, Taiwan, and the Philippines—countries where armed forces once exercised control. There are few exceptions and holdouts to the democratizing trend. Burma (Myanmar) is still run by a military junta that refuses to recognize the National League of Democracy as the party that won national elections in 1990. Communist-run Vietnam is also lagging behind in the democratization trend. Cambodia had ushered in a new democratic government after the UN-brokered elections, but in July 1997 a bloody coup destroyed the fragile democracy.

The region from North Africa to the Persian Gulf is full of authoritarian regimes whose claims to power come from God (Iran), genealogy (Saudi Arabia), or the barrel of a gun (Libya). Yet some Middle Eastern nations have started to embrace democratic reforms. Turkey is the only Muslim democracy in the Middle East. In recent years it has made great strides in addressing human rights. One of the United States' more ambitious goals for Iraq is a democratic government that would be an example for the region.

The Sub-Saharan Africa region is also dominated by authoritarian regimes. In new South Africa widespread unemployment, crippled schools, and rampant corruption have produced a violent, hopeless young population that threatens the stability of the elected government. Ethnic disputes resulting from lack of representation of local people in the government have disrupted oil production in Nigeria. Values such as individual freedom and democracy have been a disappointment in Sub-Saharan Africa, often producing sham elections, continued misrule, and poverty.

In the long term, development operating within a democratic framework is more enduring because growth and development take place through the participation of the electorate rather than by the command or dictates of a single person or a small group of people. In Asia, China and India offer contrasting examples in this regard. Many Asian countries overlook the fact that democratic politics in India, over time, have provided an enduring foundation for economic and social development. The consensus-building process required by democracy has helped to ensure that developments are broadly based and will survive changes of government leadership. The results of development and economic reforms in turn have helped strengthen democracy in India.

The development challenges facing many countries of the non-Western world are monumental. Unlike Western countries, they do not have the luxury of executing the process of nation building, economic growth, and democracy in a sequential fashion, spread over centuries. Instead, these three processes must be carried out simultaneously, even though they are not always mutually reinforcing.

Compounding their problems, these developing countries must deal with these challenges in an open, and increasingly networked, global economy. To be successful in such an environment, they must become further integrated into the world economy. Yet, by being more open, these countries run the risk that international players, with agendas of their own, could undermine their efforts at nation building by competing for economic resources as well as political and cultural loyalties. The resources of the non-Western world countries to meet these challenges are severely limited, especially in the least-developed states.

Civil Strife and Human Rights

What makes one group of people ready to kill another group? The answer is usually a conflict of interests, or a clash of life-shaping ideas, or one group's belief that it is in blood and bone superior to the rest. Have those causes of conflict disappeared from the face of the earth? Of course they have not. In the non-Western world the major civil strifes are the result of all these factors: ideology, conflict of interest, and blood-and-bone animosity. In Asia, several areas of conflict are located in the overlapping sections of Islamic and non-Islamic cultures: Kashmir, Sinkiang, Chakmas in Bangladesh, Malay Muslims in Thailand, Christians in East Timor, and Muslims in Mindanao

In China, the Tibetans seek independence, while the Kurds want to carve a state out of Turkey (Figure 1.20). Muslim Indonesia fights a separatist movement in mostly Christian North Sumatra, as deaths in Kashmir's Muslim insurgency against India pass the 8,000 mark. Indigenous Uighurs in Xinjiang, China, want independence for the land they call East Turkestan. The 6 million Han Chinese immigrants have reduced the Muslim Uighurs to 54 percent of the population. The Uighurs fears that, if the influx continues, they will become the minority. As it is, the Chinese get the best paid jobs, while about 25 percent of adult Uighurs are unemployed. Hundreds of mosques have been closed. Uighur schools are neglected. Thousands of angry Uighurs have taken to the streets to protest Chinese rule. Likewise, Buddhist Chakmas in Bangladesh, Pathans in Pakistan, and Tamils in Sri Lanka all seek varying degrees of self-rule or statehood.

Figure 1-20. A Tibetan refugee in Sikkim, India. The era of Chinese influence in Tibet ended with the uprising against China in Lhasa in 1911. Between 1912 and 1950 Tibet enjoyed full independence. In 1950 the new communist government in China decided to "liberate" what China called oppressed and exploited Tibetans and reunite them with the "great motherland." The Peoples Liberation Army invaded Tibet and easily took control of the country. China's attempt to dismantle Tibetan's traditional society, Buddhist spiritual values, and customs led to the uprising in 1959 and the flight of the ruler Dalai Lama to exile in India. Several thousand Tibetans have fled the country as refugees. The Dalai Lama, who is reviled as a "separatist" by the Chinese government, opposes violence in the quest for Tibetan autonomy. Hu Jintao, who became China's president in 2003, took responsibility for Tibet in 1989. The three years he oversaw Tibet are described by human rights groups as brutal oppression. The crackdown appeared to earn him some credit and he joined the Politburo standing committee in 1992. Tibetans, who have a distinct language and culture, demand autonomy. (Photo: P. P. Karan.)

The non-Western world's dizzying array of ethnic hot spots starkly illustrate how, of all the features of the twenty-first-century world, the most consistently troubling are turning out to be the hatreds that divide humankind by race, faith, and nationality. The explosion of ethnic and religious violence is the paramount issue facing the human rights movement today. Indeed, xenophobia, religious rivalry, and the general intolerance of anything different are often now more anguishing and cruel than the ideological differences that until recently divided the world.

Why are ethnic, religious, and tribal conflicts so widespread? The end of totalitarian regimes (colonial or communist) that repressed old political and cultural rivalries has been linked to the proliferation of clashes. In Indonesia, one of Asia's large states, the war pitting Christians and Muslims in Timor has long roots. To a large extent, history provides only the context. Most ethnic conflicts have a background of domination, injustice, or the oppression of one group by another. These historic elements have been shaped and given form by a growing number of regimes that have recently tried to build followings by exploiting ethnic, religious, and other differences. Contemporary leaders in many non-Western countries use accumulated historical animosity for their own political and economic gains. In Bangladesh, the Muslim-dominated government uses that animosity to promote the Islamic agenda, which the Buddhist Chakmas of southern Chittagong consider a threat to their way of life and a violation of their human rights. The hatred is built around traditional differences that, but for appeals of opportunistic leaders, might not have been transformed into hostility or warfare.

Transitions to democracy can also create an uncertainty that fuels ethnic and religious passions, and eventually rivalries. The problem is not democracy per se, but the turbulent transition to democracy. Along the way, secular democratic governments such as in India have faced increasing unemployment, inflation, public disillusionment, and even resistance. The tremendous psychological pressure on human populations from political change creates a sense of anxiety that frequently makes people seek refuge in belief systems that involve definitions of membership and the value of belonging to a specific ethnic or religious group. So people fall back on their primordial identities such as religion and ethnicity. The most visible case is the explosion of political Islam in places such as Afghanistan, Indonesia, and Pakistan. But as Islamists redefine identities and agendas ethnic minorities have sensed new threats.

Limited resources and the struggle to survive can also spawn or deepen ethnic or religious conflicts. The more limited the resources, the greater the danger of ethnic strife. In Sudan, the multilayered hostility between northerners and southerners, Arabs and Africans, Muslims and Christians has been exacerbated by a hostile desert environment and the chronic recent cycle of drought and famine. In India, the Sikhs' separatist movement is in part related to the water resources, which are of vital importance to the 80 percent of Punjabi Sikhs who are farmers. The green revolution was successful in Punjab because of the excellent system of irrigation and the steady flow of water from the Sutlej, Ravi, and Beas rivers. In 1976, however, a substantial amount of water from these rivers was diverted to the neighboring Indian states of Rajasthan and Haryana. The water problem enlarged the potential base of support of the militant Sikhs seeking an independent Khalistan in the 1970s.

In Sri Lanka an estimated 20,000 persons have been killed and more than 1.5 million displaced since 1990 in a contemporary conflict sparked by the age-old discrimination by the predominantly Buddhist Sinhalese against the minority Hindu Tamils. In dealing with the ethnic separatist or independence movements, many governments have responded with actions such as torture, abductions, and murder that violate human rights. National security, or the need to combat insurgency, is not a justification for political killings, arbitrary arrests, or the stifling of free expression.

What Are Human Rights?

Definitions can be controversial. The U.N. Universal Declaration of Human Rights, adopted in 1948, includes both civil rights and economic rights. Some examples follow.

- Life, liberty, and the security of person
- Entitlement to equal protection under the law
- Freedom of movement and residence within the borders of each state and freedom to leave and return to any country
- Freedom of thought, religion, and expression, including the freedom to seek, receive, and impart information and ideas through any media
- Freedom to own property
- Free choice of employment, just and favorable conditions of work and protection against unemployment, and equal pay for equal work
- A standard of living adequate for health and well-being, including food, clothing, housing, medical care, and the necessary social services
- Protection of the moral and material interests that result from an individual's scientific, literary, or artistic productions
- Participation in government, directly or through freely chosen representatives
- Freedom from subjection to torture or to cruel, inhuman, or degrading treatment or punishment
- Freedom from being held in slavery or servitude
- Freedom from arbitrary arrest, detention, or exile

At the 1993 World Conference on Human Rights there was a debate between countries such as Japan, India, and Western democracies that defended the universal human rights enshrined in the 1948 Declaration, and countries such as China, Syria, Iran, Malaysia, and Indonesia (countries not exactly renowned for their love of democracy); that wanted to water down the concept of universal rights with economic, cultural, and religious arguments. They have been promoting an "Asian" concept of human rights in which political and civil liberties are subordinated to economic development.

The nongovernmental organizations attending the 1993 conference, such as the human rights lawyers from Pakistan and Sri Lanka; representatives of indigenous peoples from Bangladesh; women's rights activists from India and the Philippines; Japanese, Thai, Indian, and Korean civil liberties groups; environmentalists from Malaysia; Buddhists and Baha'is; a group working on behalf of refugees from Bhutan; and another for human rights in China, refuted or contested every major premise of the "Asian" concept of human rights. They effectively exposed the governments' line for what it is: a pretext of largely authoritarian governments to justify their unchecked power in the name of meeting economic and social needs. The nongovernmental organizations stressed the universality of human rights and stated that neither a lack of resources nor cultural differences could justify abuse by the governments. It is not surprising that the countries most adamant about the primacy of economic development are those in which alternative voices are silenced or harassed. Citizens of non-Western countries such as China, Indonesia, Malaysia, and Singapore do not want their political and civil rights traded in the name of development.

The French embrace 1789. Americans pledge allegiance to 1776. Britons, when not romanticizing the Magna Carta, snap a salute to the Glorious Revolution of 1688. All were landmarks in the emergence of a political system that is now widely hailed as the best guarantor of human rights, life, and liberty. The increasingly self-confident and prospering Confucian societies of the Asian Pacific region are challenging democratic liberalism with their own Asian model of democracy—a system sometimes called "soft authoritarianism"—that exists in Singapore and other of the region's economically vibrant states. These countries have no scruples about using their reserve powers of arbitrary arrest and detention or about using the tame news media to blacken the credentials of opponents. Along with harsher restraints on civil liberties, Malaysia bans satellite-television dishes, while Singapore censors music and the movies and belabors its citizens with all manner of preachments. China carries out tortures and summary executions.

The major problem with the Asian model of democracy in Southeast Asia and China is that it has not developed the art of the adversarial relationship. How does one disagree with the government without being disagreeable? In China anyone who criticizes the government is "unpatriotic." Unconventional figures are considered misfits and egotists—nails that stick out and must be hammered down. The leadership protects itself and prevents any opposition from emerging. The only systemic change that the Confucian tradition sanctions is revolutionary: toppling a hierarchy that is bad at its job.

Western models of democracy in non-Western nations such as India and Japan strive to protect the freedom of expression of their citizens and guard them against abuses by the state. Here the concept is that people, who created the government, granted it the minimal rights of interference, not the other way around. Democracy's ultimate strength in these countries is the capacity for political change, which most of the other Asian and African countries have yet to demonstrate. China and Southeast Asian countries have grown rich in large part due to Confucian ethics, not Confucian government, and due to the more tangible benefits of U.S.-supplied strategic defense, Western investments, and Western markets. The Asia Pacific is more self-reliant now, but without the freest nation in its midst—Japan,—those startling economic statistics would make a much poorer show. With the exception of Japan and India, human rights remain severely circumscribed in most non-Western countries.

GEOPOLITICAL LANDSCAPE

World political geography has entered a new phase in the twenty-first century in which the fundamental source of conflict is not ideological or economic but cultural. The principal conflicts are occurring between groups of different cultures. The clash of cultures will dominate global political geography. During the Cold War (1946–1989), the world was often divided into the first (the United States, Canada, Western Europe, Australia, and New Zealand), second (the Soviet Union and Eastern Europe), and third worlds (Asia, Africa, and Latin America). Those divisions are no longer relevant. It is far more meaningful to group countries in terms of their cultures than in terms of their political or economic systems or their level of economic development. A culture is the important grouping of people. Western culture has two major variants, European and North American; non-Western cultures have four major variants: Chinese, Indian, Islamic, and African. Islam has its Arab, Turkic, and Malay subdivisions.

Cultural identity has become increasingly important, and the world is being shaped in large measure by interactions among half a dozen major cultures, including the Western, Confucian, Japanese, Islamic, Hindu, and African. Conflicts often occur along the borders separating these cultures because of the differences among them: their history, language, tradition, and, most important, religion. Different cultures have different views on the relations between nature and society, citizens and the state, parents and children, liberty and authority, equality and hierarchy. These differences are centuries old.

As the world becomes smaller, interactions between people of different cultures are increasing, intensifying the awareness of differences and sameness within cultures. For example, Americans react far more negatively to investments from Japan and China, non-Western countries, than to larger investments from Western nations such as Canada and Britain or the Netherlands. In much of the world, religion has become a dominant fact of life, often in the form of movements such as that of the fundamentalists. Such movements are found in Western Christianity, Judaism, Buddhism, Hinduism, and Islam.

Conflict along the border line between the Western and Islamic cultures has been ongoing for 1,300 years. The centuries-old conflict is unlikely to decline. On the northern border of the Islamic world, conflict has increasingly erupted between the Orthodox and Muslim peoples, including the 1990s conflict in Bosnia and the tense relations between the Russians and Muslims in Central Asia. On the southern border area of the Islamic world the antagonistic interaction of the Arab Islamic culture has been with the pagan, animist, and increasingly with the black Christian people of Africa. On the eastern margins of the Islamic world, the historic clash between Muslims and Hindus in the Indian subcontinent and Muslims and other groups in Southeast Asia are manifest in religious strife.

Non-Western cultures have attempted to become modern without becoming Western. Only Japan has fully succeeded in this quest. Non-Western cultures will continue to acquire the wealth, technology, skills, machines, and weapons that are part of being modern. They will continue to reconcile this modernity with their traditional culture and values. Their economic and military strength relative to the West is increasing. Hence, the West must accommodate these non-Western cultures such as Japan, China, and India, whose power will, in the twenty-first century, approach that of the West but whose values and interests differ significantly. This will require the West to develop a much more profound understanding of the basic religious and philosophical assumptions underlying other cultures and the ways in which people in those cultures perceive their interests.

Non-Western nations are of great importance to the industrialized nations of Europe, the United States, and Japan. These countries occupy nearly half of the world's surface and contain two-thirds of its population. They contain vast material and human resources and are of great consequence to the North American, European, and Japanese economies as suppliers of both raw materials and manufactured goods, and markets for farm products and high-technology products. The 1997–1998 bank failures, plunging currencies, and stock market turmoil in South Korea, Thailand, Indonesia, and Malaysia, after two decades of rapid growth, had negative effects on the economies of the United States, Japan, and Europe. Until the economic rebound began in 2000, Asian fallout reduced or slowed the economic growth in the Western industrialized nations and Japan, which are dependent on Asian export markets.

A large share of American manufactured goods are exported to the non-Western world, which also receives over 50 percent of American agricultural products. A substantial percentage of the Western world's and Japan's crude oil imports come from the non-Western world, as does the bulk of industrial raw materials. Increasingly, non-Western countries, including many without impressive natural resource endowments, exert a powerful force on investment flows and world trade in manufactured products through their entrepreneural prowess, their capacity for innovation, and their marketing skills.

The strategic location of many non-Western countries also gives them a special military and geopolitical importance to the United States. Some, such as South Korea, Japan, and Israel are close allies; others such as Kuwait, Qatar, and Bahrain provide America access to important facilities.

Spending on Weapons

Although the world became a safer place with the end of the Cold War, the spending on weapons in the non-Western countries is awesome. While the global arms spending is on the wane, two regions—the Middle East and East Asia—are running counter to the trend. The Middle East is perpetually among the world's most unstable areas, but China and Southeast Asian countries are arming even as the area enjoys a period of relative peace and prosperity.

Countries such as Iran, Iraq, Israel, Libya, and Algeria in the Middle East, India, Pakistan, China, North Korea, South Korea, Taiwan, Indonesia, Thailand, and Malaysia have substantially increased military spending. Nearly 50 percent of the world's conventional weapons are sold to the Middle East by the United States and other industrialized nations, and at a time of shrinking defense markets in Europe and America, the arms bazaar in the non-Western countries will be all the more important in the future. According to Stockholm International Peace Research Institute's *Yearbook 2003*, military spending in Southeast Asia, Taiwan, and South Korea increased between 1993 and 2002. China boosted its military spending by 18 percent in 2002. Viewed on a global basis, arms spending in Asia in 1981 accounted for only 15 percent of the world's total. By 2002, the figure had reached 23 percent of the global total. Japan ($46.7 billion), China ($31.1 billion), Saudi Arabia ($21.6 billion), Iran ($17.5 billion), South Korea ($13.5 billion), India ($12.9 billion), Turkey ($10.1 billion), and Israel ($9.8 billion) were major spenders in terms of market exchange rate. However, on the basis of purchasing power parity (PPP) rates, in which dollar figures are converted to purchasing power of the local currency (calculated by the World Bank PPP project), the leading spender countries were China, India, Japan, Saudi Arabia, South Korea, Turkey, Iran, and Pakistan. China's increased spending reflects in part pursuit of military reform and in part the effort to strengthen its position as a regional and global power. India's increase is the result of both heightened tension with Pakistan and regional power ambition, where it is in competition with China. In Sub-Saharan Africa military spending increased by a modest 4 percent during 1993–2002.

China, India, and Pakistan have nuclear weapons; Israel has nuclear weapons, although it has not declared itself a nuclear state. North Korea and Iran have or could be within range of obtaining nuclear weapons. Most of these countries already have a significant number of ballistic missiles and many are looking to acquire more. In the Asian Pacific, China's soaring military spending could destablize the entire region as wary neighbors watch the arms buildup. Ominously, China also has reasserted its claim to the entire South China Sea. Taiwan, Vietnam, the Philippines, Malaysia, and Brunei have also made conflicting claims in the South China Sea, particularly to the Spratly Islands. Rich undersea oil fields are believed to be in the area, and the major shipping lanes for oil from the Middle East to Japan and South Korea pass through the Spratlys.

The military intentions of China worry Taiwan, Thailand, Vietnam, Indonesia, and South Korea. Which is the real China? The one that professes peaceful intentions or a China with a historical view of itself as "the center of the Earth" surrounded by dutiful tributaries? The evidence is mixed. Vietnam accuses China of speaking peace and practicing hegemony by bullying its smaller neighbors. Indeed, Vietnam's effort to establish diplomatic relations with the United States is linked to fears of China's growing military punch. India also views China as a bigger threat in terms of firepower, including the nuclear kind, which prompted India to carry out nuclear tests in 1998 to develop its own nuclear arsenal.

There are a number of areas that have the potential to produce international conflict in Asia. Three major points of tension in Asia—the Korean peninsula, relations between China and Taiwan, and the dispute over the Northern Territories involving Japan and Russia—although difficult to resolve, have stabilized. Regional conflicts in Kashmir, in the Persian Gulf, or over the Spratly Islands in the South China Sea remain a distinct possibility, and there are a number of other domestic and international trouble spots. But their potential to involve competing major powers and affect regionwide security is limited.

The international political system that is still taking shape as a result of the end of the Cold War, the implosion of the Soviet Union, and Asia's growing economic dynamism has the potential to produce conflicts in the non-Western world. But despite the fact that many countries are using their economic wealth to purchase arms and strengthen their military capabilities, the stabilizing forces in the region outweigh the destabilizing ones. Many Asian countries have pursued economic modernization through outward, export-oriented policies that place a high premium on a stable and healthy international environment. They have a vested interest in preventing the outbreak of violent conflict. Deepening economic integration in the region will also increase the cost of and raise the threshold for using force. By and large, the non-Western world will be a zone of peace, especially at the level of the major powers of Japan, China, Russia, India, and the United States. Of course, there will still be periods of tension among these powers, but these will be periods of tension leading to accommodation, not conflicts.

There is greater potential for continuing conflict in the non-Western world at the domestic level in Tibet, Burma, Sri Lanka, Rwanda, Sudan, Turkey, Egypt, Kashmir, Palestinians in Israel, and many more. But again, although these disputes incite armed violence, their potential to involve competing major powers (except in Israel) and affect regionwide peace and stability is limited.

Rise of Terrorism

The last two decades have seen a rapid increase in terrorist activity in the non-Western world with major negative effects on economic development and political stability. Individual countries in the non-Western world have suffered terrorist attacks and endured continued terrorist group activities in 2003. Terrorism is generally defined as premeditated, politically motivated violence perpetrated against noncombatant targets by subnational groups or clandestine agents, usually intended to rattle and influence a wide audience. The aim is to use the psychological impact of violence or of the threat of violence to effect political change.

Among the terrorist organizations, al-Qaeda has emerged as an international terrorist network that seeks to rid Muslim countries of the profane influence of the West and replace their governments with fundamentalist Islamic regimes. Al-Qaeda has also targeted American and other Western interests, Jewish targets, and the Indian territory in Kashmir. From 1991 to 1996, al-Qaeda worked out of Sudan. From 1996 until the collapse of the Taliban in 2001, al-Qaeda operated out of Afghanistan and maintained training camps there. After al-Qaeda's September 11, 2001, attacks on the United States, the United States launched a war in Afghanistan to destroy al-Qaeda bases there and overthrow the Taliban, the country's Muslim fundamentalist rulers. Now, al-Qaeda's senior leadership has regrouped in lawless tribal regions just inside Pakistan, near the Afghan border. Al-Qaeda has underground cells in some 100 countries, including the United States. Al-Qaeda–linked attacks include the May 2003 car bomb attacks in Riyadh, Saudi Arabia; a November 2002 car bomb attack in Mombasa, Kenya; an October 2002 attack on a French tanker off the coast of Yemen; and the September 11, 2001, hijacking attacks on the World Trade Center and the Pentagon. It is reported that senior officials of Saudi Arabia may have funneled hundreds of millions of dollars to charitable groups and other organizations that may have helped finance al-Qaeda activities.

In Japan, the Aum Shinrikyo religious cult attacked the Tokyo subway system with sirin gas in 1995. The Philippines continues to experience violent attacks in the southern province of Mindanao from rebels in the Moro Islamic Liberation Army and the Abu Sayyaf Group. In Thailand, a strong military offensive against Muslim separatists of the New Pattani United Liberation Organization helped restore calm in the south, which has experienced a wave of bombings. In addition to the sectarian ethnic and religious violence that affects lives and property in Karachi and elsewhere in Sind and

Punjab, there were credible reports of official Pakistani support for Kashmiri militant groups that engage in terrorism. In 1998 the militant terrorist group Harakat-μl-Ansar kidnapped four Western visitors, including a U.S. citizen in India's Kashmir.

Ongoing civil wars and ethnic violence in some regions of Africa overshadow individual incidents of terrorism. Major areas of violence were in Angola, Congo, Ethiopia, Liberia, Nigeria, Rwanda, Somalia, and Uganda.

Many scholars argue that a well-focused, sustained development program that encourages employment, institution building, public security, and education could help some of the poor countries in the non-Western world and thereby reduce their risk of becoming havens for terrorism. It may also reduce the anti-Americanism in the Arab and Muslim world that al-Qaeda and other terrorist groups often exploit. Indonesia, the Philippines, and Yemen have received funding to combat terrorism.

ORGANIZATION OF THE NON-WESTERN WORLD

The following discussion of the non-Western World is organized under six major cultural regions: the Chinese cultural area, Japan and Korea, Southeast Asia, the Indian subcontinent, the Islamic Middle East, and Sub-Saharan Africa.

Each major cultural area is characterized by well-marked distinguishing features and occupies a distinctive geographic environment. Countries in each cultural area have grown out of a shared body of religious or philosophical beliefs and a shared experience of history. The various regional chapters of the book are devoted to the discussion of distinctive features of each area. In regional chapters themes of physical and cultural diversity, population and food supply, environment and sustainable development, human rights, and economic restructuring are discussed to present a contemporary picture of the region blending history, geography, politics, economy, and culture of the area.

The Chinese Culture Area

The cradle of the Chinese or Sinic culture lies in the irrigable middle reaches of the Huang He (Yellow River). Like the cultures of the Indus, Nile, and Tigris-Euphrates, civilized life began through the gifts of a river that permitted food to be raised in such quantity that some inhabitants were released for other pursuits. Chinese civilization subsequently spread south toward the tropics, displacing or absorbing the indigenous Thai and related groups. The need to defend China against the incursions of nomadic tribes led to a progressive assertion of political control over the grasslands of Mongolia and the desert basins of Turkestan. Western economic development in

Southeast Asia acted as a magnet, drawing millions of Chinese south into Malaya and the adjoining areas in the nineteenth century. In recent years these overseas Chinese (estimated at 60 million), particularly those in Taiwan, Hong Kong, and Singapore, have been important sources for almost half the foreign direct investment in China.

Since reforms began in 1979, China has become one of Asia's fastest-growing economies. The country's population of 1.2 billion offers incredible purchasing potential as incomes rise. Foreign investments have poured into China at an accelerating rate, from $3 to $4 billion in the late 1980s and early 1990s to some $34 billion in 1994. Though China's inefficient state-owned companies still monopolize much of the country's technology and assets, a burgeoning private sector should drive continued growth.

Hong Kong, which became part of China in July 1997, employs three quarters of its population in services. Banking and finance are particularly important, and this tiny area provides much of the capital for developing mainland China. Hong Kong's port is the main outlet for Chinese goods on their way to the United States, with $168 billion in exports passing through it each year. China's commitment to Hong Kong's development appears firm, but Hong Kong's economy contracted in 1998, the first negative growth in thirteen years.

Despite tensions with China, Taiwan continues its global economic expansion as the sixteenth-largest economy in the world. Taiwan has a per capita income of $11,640, rivaling some developed countries in the West. Recent free elections highlight the country's drive and determination. Taiwan has led the charge in investing in Asia's less-developed countries, pouring capital, equipment, and manufacturing know-how into China, Vietnam, Malaysia, and Indonesia.

Japan and Korea

Japan and Korea, whose early civilizations and subsequent development were strongly influenced by China, are related to the Chinese culture area. In Japan and Korea, the Chinese written language, or a derivative of it, has been or is still used. The Chinese classics played the same molding role that the Greek and Latin classics played in Europe, and Confucianism, a secular philosophy of the state and of man's role in society, deeply influenced political thinking in these countries. A major contribution of the Confucian ethos for Japan's modernization was its openness to Western learning.

Japan's unusual combination of localism and globalism makes it not only one of the most enigmatic modern postindustrial states but also a most intriguing case in comparative cross-cultural studies. Japan arose as a new power in a part of the Western Pacific Rim that was ravaged after World War II. By the late 1960s Japan had become the world's third-largest economic power. In the postwar period the annual growth of Japan's gross national product approached 10 percent, nearly three times that of the United States, and it climbed to 11.1 percent between 1960 and 1969. The Japanese worked hard at jobs six days a week. They lived simply. Their frugality enabled the Japanese to save for the future and promoted Japanese success. In the 1980s Japan became a major financial power, and its economic might is second only to that of the United States. Close cooperation between government and industry enabled Japan's rapid growth. Despite its major economic strength, its economy is vulnerable. It experienced a severe recession that started in 1992 and lingered into 1998. Commercial land prices plunged to less than half of what they were earlier, and office vacancies soared.

Japan is the most densely populated nation in the non-Western world; its land area is about the size of California, but its population is 124 million, compared to 30 million in California. Most of its land is mountainous and nonarable. Lacking mineral resources, it imports about 80 percent of its coal, 90 percent of its minerals, and 98 percent of its oil and gas. It had to import rice in 1994. It desperately needs a continued flow of surplus trade and dollars to import raw materials and food.

The Japanese economy in the late 1990s became more like that of an older industrial economy. It is importing more, paying more for labor, suffering from financial downturns and recessions, and carrying a postwar baby-boom population that is becoming an aging and unproductive population. The tight Japanese political fabric is becoming frayed. The Liberal Democratic Party lost its majority in parliament in 1993, after twenty-eight years of governance without challenge. Japan faces major economic, political, and environmental challenges in the twenty-first century.

Led by the country's *chaebols* (or conglomerates), South Korea's economy has tripled every decade since the 1960s. Its economy now is the eleventh-largest in the world. South Korea made a comprehensive use of public instruments to achieve rapid development. Government began a coordinated campaign in 1971 to build up firms in six designated industries: steel, shipbuilding, machinery, electronics, petrochemicals, and metals. The most important measure was heavily subsidized credit and tight controls on the financial system. The policy was successful in the development of South Korea, but there were long-term costs borne by the banks resulting from the shackles of directed credits. In 1997 South Korea's fifty largest firms, and the banks that lent to them, found themselves overburdened with debt. Banks raised billions in foreign currency to finance over-expansion and passed them on in Korean currency (the won) to the firms. As the won fell in value, South Korea required ever more won to repay loans denominated in foreign currency. The financial crisis has put South Korea's erstwhile development miracle in serious trouble.

Southeast Asia

Southeast Asia is a composite region, lying in the contact zone of Indian and Chinese civilizations. It is from these major civilizations that the "high cultures" of the region are derived. These high cultures are essentially lowland cultures based on the cultivation of rice. They include the Indianized cultures of the Burmese; the Thai and Khmers, which developed in the river valleys of the Irrawaddy, the Menam, and lower Mekong; and the Sinicized culture of the Vietnamese, which developed in the Red River lowland. The upland areas were little touched by these high cultures; they remain to this day occupied by more backward tribal groups only partially integrated into the states within whose frontiers they live.

To the south, the peninsulas and islands of Southeast Asia have, from early times, been the center of the Malaya peoples. In the west the maritime fringes of the region were Indianized, then strongly influenced by Islam, which became the dominant religion of Malaysia and Indonesia, and which spread as far east as the southern Philippines. Subsequently, the Catholic Spanish influence thrusting westwards from the Spanish parts of Latin America came to dominate the northern Philippines, introducing a new element of cultural diversity which has only partly been effaced by half a century of American control.

Within the island world of Southeast Asia there is, as in the mainland, the same ethnic contrast between the lowlands and the forested uplands of the interior and, in the east, the tribal peoples of New Guinea link the Southeast Asian world with the Melanesian section of the Pacific.

This region of spectacular beauty has done a remarkable job of encouraging economic growth and reducing poverty. The number of abjectly poor in Indonesia has fallen from 68 million to 18 million over a twenty-year period. Malaysia, once an economy entirely based on commodity production, has turned itself into a manufacturing powerhouse. The Philippines, long among Asia's least-developed countries, has launched an ambitious program of infrastructure development. As the United States reduced its military presence there, this island nation converted the former Subic Bay naval base into a hotbed of entrepreneurship. In 1993, Subic Bay attracted foreign direct investment. Thailand, Indonesia, and Malaysia were fast making the transition from economic backwater to modern industrial states until the financial crisis of 1997.

One of Asia's newest emerging economies, Vietnam has proved adept at putting capitalist ways into practice. Today Ho Chi Minh City has become a capital of commerce, and private entrepreneurs in Vietnam have created some 4.7 million new jobs in just four years. Vietnam's future is bright, too, because of its educated population and the government's commitment to economic reforms. The problem in Vietnam is that a rigid communist regime talks about economic reforms on the one hand, but obstructs liberalization on the other.

Mixing authoritarian government with free-market capitalism has made Singapore a center for high-tech manufacturing, finance, and services. It is among the world's most competitive economies, ranked second behind the United States in 1995 for manufacturing efficiency. Along with Hong Kong, Singapore has successfully made the transition to a modern consumer-oriented society, with average per capita incomes topping $19,000.

But not all of Southeast Asia has developed rapidly. Laos, Cambodia, and Myanmar lag behind in development.

Malaysia, Thailand, and Indonesia pursued a development policy model employed by South Korea and Japan. They coined the term "Look East Policy" in 1981. Malaysia brought in Korean advisors to help pick and produce industrial winners. Indonesia encouraged foreign investment and liberalized trade. In Thailand Japanese investment was heavy. Like in South Korea, banks in all these countries face unbearable levels of bad debt—the result of cozy relationships between businesses, banks, and governments. The poor investments will slow down the economies of these leading Southeast Asian countries as they enter the twenty-first century.

The Indian Cultural Area

The cradle of the Indian culture lies in the alluvial river valleys of the north, those of the Indus and the Ganges. The Indian civilization subsequently became subcontinental in extent, integrating the peoples of the Deccan and the coasts of peninsular India. The extension of Islam brought the Indus valley and much of Bengal into the Muslim world, and the partition in 1947 followed religious lines, leading to the emergence of the Islamic state of Pakistan and the dominantly Hindu, but secular, Indian Union. At an early stage of history Indian influences penetrated deep into Southeast Asia, shaping the civilization of Burma, Thailand, and Cambodia, and leaving a strong Indian imprint on the cultural and political life of Indonesia. This imprint survives, in a slightly modified form, on the island of Bali. The extension of British control over Burma and the Malayan peninsula made possible a new diffusion of Indian settlers, which has left a major legacy in the plural societies of Southeast Asia.

In the Indian subcontinent past political philosophies do not appear to have created the same barriers to the growth of Western-style democracy as has the Confucian legacy of China. The Indian subcontinent—or its elite group—has been much more effectively Westernized; the leaders of India, Pakistan, Bangladesh, and Sri Lanka have tended to think in at least the forms of Western-style institutions and to work through a Western-style bureaucracy, the latter inherited in part from the colonial period.

Recently, India pledged to put forty years of experimentation with socialism and central planning behind it and convert its bureaucracy-ridden economy into a market economy. As a result, foreign direct investment is rising. Like China, India commands an enormous population whose sheer numbers promise a tempting market. A long entrepreneurial tradition, a commitmment to growth, and an expatriate business class much like the ethnic Chinese all point toward accelerating growth in India.

The Islamic World of the Middle East

The term *Middle East* applies to the region that stretches from Morocco in the west to Iran in the east, and from the Caspian Sea in the north to Sudan in the south. The region contains one of the major culture hearths in the world, a source area or innovation center from which cultural traditions were transmitted. The culture hearths lie in the Tigris-Euphrates Plain (in ancient Mesopotamia) and in the Nile Valley of Egypt. Two other culture hearths are located in the Huang He Valley of North China and in the Indus Valley of the Indian Subcontinent. In the Middle Eastern culture hearth people first learned to domesticate plants such as wheat and barley and to gather harvests. They made implements out of bronze and learned to use draft animals. They employed the wheel, a revolutionary invention, and built some of the world's oldest cities 6,000 years ago.

The Middle East has a crossroads location at the junction of Europe, Asia, and Africa. The central location favored dissemination of culture and the receipt of culture brought by invaders. Its location has given the area strategic importance in global air and sea routes. It is a dry land, a vast belt of deserts and dry grasslands with an average annual precipitation of less than 10 inches. Two of the world's large deserts, the Empty Quarter in Arabia and the Sahara in North Africa, lie within this region. In the valley of the Nile in Egypt and the Tigris and Euphrates in Iraq, the soil is rich and fertile. Here several crops can be grown during the year with irrigation, and the population concentration is heavy.

The Middle East is the birthplace of three great monotheistic religions—Judaism, Christianity, and Islam—but it is a world of Islam, with Muslims (practitioners of Islam) dominant in all countries except Israel (Judaism), Lebanon, and Ethiopia (ancient form of Christianity). The region lacks most of the natural resources, but it contains over 50 percent of the world's petroleum resources.

Sub-Saharan Africa

Sub-Saharan Africa covers over 9 million square miles—more than three times the size of the continental United States. Most of its nations are among the world's youngest and poorest. In the Great Rift system, where manlike beings were walking upright 3.6 million years ago, Ethiopians today subsist on an annual income of $100. In Upper Volta, only 6 percent of the population can read, and a newborn child is not expected to live to celebrate a fortieth birthday. Many of Africa's 450 million people, who speak more than a thousand languages, till drought-prone farmland. Their governments struggle with numerous economic, social, and environmental challenges.

Missionaries, traders, and adventurers penetrated the continent in the nineteenth century. They were followed by government officials engaged in extending colonial domains. Most of the area was controlled by France, Britain, Portugal, and Belgium. Europeans settled in various areas of the continent, traded, extracted minerals, and established governments reflecting the different policies and institutions of the colonial powers.

The wave of African independence began in 1957, and now all countries are free. But the political evolution of these African countries during the last four decades has been tumultuous, with most of the countries undergoing nonconstitutional changes in their governments. More than half of the nations are led by military leaders, and conflicts between tribal or ethnic groups are rampant. The vast majority of Africans suffer from a variety of diseases and from malnutrition. In recent years the AIDS epidemic has continued through Africa, outracing the preventive campaigns.

As these six culture areas of the non-Western world continue their transformation from poverty to prosperity—from dominoes to dynamos—the reader should look at a combination of change and continuity to understand the evolving social and economic patterns. One of the consequences of prosperity has been the emergence of a rising middle class in all countries from Korea to South Africa, which exemplifies change and continuity. In Singapore, Shanghai, Bangalore, and Bangkok, educated, highly skilled young men and women are much like their American counterparts, while retaining elements of the traditional Asian ethic that includes discipline, sacrifice, and frugality.

FURTHER READINGS

Asian Development Bank. 1997. *Emerging Asia: Changes and Challenges*. Manila: Asian Development Bank.

Asian Development Bank. 2001. *Asian Environment Outlook 2001*. Manila: Asian Development Bank.

Asian Development Bank. 2001. *Growth and Change in Asia and the Pacific: Key Indicators*. New York: Oxford University Press.

Basu, Amrita, ed. 1995. *The Challenge of Local Feminisms: Women's Movements in Global Perspectives*. Boulder, CO: Westview Press.

Blomstrom, Magnus and Mats Lundahl, eds. 1993. *Economic Crisis in Africa*. New York: Routledge.

Borthwick, Mark. 1992. *Pacific Century: The Emergence of Modern Pacific Asia.* Boulder, CO: Westview Press.

Davison, Jean, ed. 1988. *Agriculture, Women and Land: The African Experience*. Boulder, CO: Westview Press.

Dean, Vera Micheles and Harry D. Harootunian, eds. 1963. *West and Non-West: New Perspectives.* New York: Holt, Rinehart and Winston.

Dixon, Chris and Michael Heffernan. 1994. *Colonialism and Development in the Contemporary World.* London: Mansell

East-West Center. 2002. *The Future of Population in Asia.* Honolulu, HI: East-West Center.

Fischer, Louis, ed. 2002. *The Essential Gandhi: An Anthology of His Writings on His Life, Work, and Ideas,* 2nd ed. New York: Vintage Books, Random House.

Fuchs, Roland, Ellen Brennan, Joseph Chumie, Fu-Chen Lo, and Juha I. Uitto, eds. 1994. *Mega-City Growth and the Future.* Tokyo: United Nations University Press.

Global Environment Facility. 2002. *The Challenge of Sustainability.* Washington, D.C.: Global Environment Facility.

Huntington, Samuel P. 1996. *The Clash of Civilizations and the Remaking of the World Order.* London: Touchstone Books.

Islam, Nurul, ed. 1995. *Population and Food Supply in the Early Twenty-First Century: Meeting Future Food Demand of an Increasing Population.* Washington, D.C.: International Food Policy Research Institute.

Karan, P. P. 1994. "The Distribution of City Sizes in Asian Countries." In *The Asian City: Processes of Development, Characteristics and Planning.* Edited by Ashok K. Dutt, Frank J. Costa, Surinder Agarwal and Allen G. Noble Dordrecht, the Netherlands: Kluwer Academic Publishers.

Krishnan, R., ed. 1994. *Growing Numbers and Dwindling Resources.* New Delhi: Tata Energy Research Institute.

Mason, Karen. 1995. *Is the Situation of Women in Asia Improving or Deteriorating?* Asia-Pacific Population Research Reports, No. 6. Honolulu, HI: East-West Center.

Panikkar, K. M. 1959 edition. *Asia and the Western Dominance.* London: George Allen and Unwin.

Prescott-Allen, Robert. 2001. *The Well-Being of Nations: A Country-by-Country Index of Quality of Life and the Environment.* Washington, D.C.: Island Press.

Rush, James. 1991. *The Last Tree: Reclaiming the Environment in Tropical Asia.* Boulder, CO: Westview Press.

United Nations. 2001. *World Population Prospects: The 2000 Revision.* New York: Population Division, Department of Economic and Social Affairs.

United Nations. 2001. *World Urbanization Prospects: The 1999 Revision.* New York: Population Division, Department of Economic and Social Affairs.

United Nations. 2001. *State of the Environment in Asia and the Pacific 2000.* New York: United Nations Economic and Social Commission for Asia and the Pacific and Asian Development Bank.

United Nations Environmental Program and World Health Organization. 1992. *Urban Air Pollution in Megacities of the World.* Oxford: Blackwell.

United Nations Population Fund. 2001. *Population, Environment and Poverty Linkages: Operational Challenges.* Population and Development Strategies Series, No.1. New York: United Nations.

Chapter 2

The Chinese Cultural Area

PEOPLE'S REPUBLIC OF CHINA

For nearly 1400 years after the fall of the Roman Empire, there was one preeminent power in the world: China. No other nation came close to matching the colossus of Asia in terms of size, population, wealth, and inventiveness. Even after they conquered China, the Mongols and Manchus quickly succumbed to, and were absorbed by, the splendors of Chinese civilization. But decline set in during the nineteenth century, when aggressive European powers ushered in a century of humiliation with their victories in the Opium Wars. As foreigners plundered, China convulsed in a nightmarish sleep of famine, revolution, and anarchy. Mao Zedong's communist triumph brought respite and new hope. But it was soon dashed by fresh upheavals. As Deng Xiaoping's reforms took root in the 1980s, China finally woke up. "There lies a sleeping giant," Napoleon once said of this ancient land. "Let her sleep, for when she wakes she will shake the world." For better or worse, China has awakened.

Throughout Asia and beyond, China is receiving growing attention. What will China be like as a great political, economic, and military power? Will it be expansionist or inward-looking? Will the country become more democratic, or will its leaders maintain their millenia-long tradition of authoritarian rule? What opportunities does its economic expansion hold? How will China address its serious environmental problems resulting from a combination of a booming economy and a teeming population? And how should other nations respond to a resurgent China?

Underpinning the nation's revival is its thriving economy. The figures tell the story. Since China embarked on its economic reforms in 1978, the GNP has averaged a 9 percent yearly growth rate—more than three times the

United States' rate. The Guangdong province, which adjoins Hong Kong, recorded a 13 percent growth. Throughout the 1980s China's manufacturing output rose by 14.4 percent annually, fastest by far among the fifty biggest economies. Already the country has the third-largest economy in the world.

China faces some basic choices. It can either use its newfound wealth to fuel more growth, particularly the growth of interior lagging areas, or it can use part of those riches to buy weapons and technology and beef up its armed forces to assert itself globally. For the moment it seems to be doing both. China's rise is being keenly watched in the United States and by its Asian neighbors.

A MAJESTIC COUNTRY

The ancestors of today's Chinese people invented printing with movable type, gunpowder, astronomy, paper money, and spaghetti. They also were pioneers in metallurgy, ceramics, and the weaving of silk and cotton cloth. Thinkers and teachers such as Confucius and Lao-tzu expressed philosophic ideas and ideals that have survived to the present and continue to influence human relationships throughout the world. As painters and sculptors, the Chinese created matchless arts and crafts.

The demand for Chinese silk among wealthy Romans led to the establishment in about 200 B.C. of the first commercial trade route linking the East and the West. This network of trails, which ultimately became known as the Silk Road, helped to shape the spiritual and material history of the world. On its route, the Silk Road passed around the Tarim Basin. Camel caravans moved silks and spices from ancient Cathay to Constantinople, returning with gold, jewels, furs, cosmetics, and perfumes. History's most famous traveling salesman, Marco Polo, took the Silk Road to Cathay in the thirteenth century and returned to Venice years later with treasures and tales that astonished all of Europe.

China, the third-largest country in the world, covers an area of 3.7 million square miles, stretching 3,100 miles from east to west and 3,400 miles from north to south. Its 12,400-mile land frontier is shared with Hong Kong, Vietnam, Laos, Myanmar, India, Bhutan, Nepal, Pakistan, Afghanistan, Tajikistan, Kyrgyzstan, Russia, Mongolia, and North Korea. Its 8,700-mile coastline fronts on the Yellow Sea, the East China Sea, the Taiwan Strait, and the South China Sea (Figure 2.1).

With 1.2 billion people, China is the most populous nation on earth. It is home to scores of different ethnic groups that speak more than 400 languages and dialects. The official language is Mandarin Chinese, the dialect spoken in Beijing. China's ethnic minorities (over 100 million) straddle its central Asian borders. Currently exempt from population policies, minorities have a growth rate triple that of the Chinese majority. Muslims are most numerous in the

Figure 2-1. China's administrative units and physical regions.

northwest and Buddhists in Tibet. Tibetans rebelled in 1959 against China's tightening grip. China has quashed separatist demands among Tibetans and Uighurs of Xinjiang and set out to eliminate their ancient cultures through massive settlements of Han Chinese in these areas.

Topographically, China is divided into three major regions. The east contains virtually all of the country's low-lying areas—lands mostly below 1,500 feet in elevation. Surprisingly, arable land constitutes just 15 percent of

China's total land area, and most of the fertile lands are in the east. The south-western region features the Tibetan Plateau (Figure 2.2), with an average elevation of 13,000 feet, and the northwestern region is marked with broad desert basins ringed by mountain ranges. China shares with Nepal the highest peak in the world, Mount Everest.

The Shandong Peninsula and North China Plain form a rough triangle smaller than Texas yet more populous than the United States. The Sichuan Basin, the size of Michigan, is home to over 70 million people. Some 150 million live by the Chang Jiang (Yangzte River). A long growing season and a mild, humid climate make the Sichuan Basin one of China's most productive farming regions. Abundant rice crops are supplemented by wheat, corn, sugarcane, and soybeans.

EVOLUTION OF THE CHINESE STATE

A key to understanding China lies in its long history. The civilization that first appeared in the second millennium B.C. in the Huang He (Yellow River) Valley of North China Plain is the direct ancestor of the culture of modern China. Their written language is an early form of the present script, and the connection between the spoken Chinese of today and that of a remote age can

Figure 2-2. Most of Western China is mountainous and semi-arid. The Tsangpo River, seen in this photo, rises at above 16,000 feet in western Tibet near the sources of the Indus and the Sutlej. It flows east across Tibet and bends around a series of gorges as it enters India as the Brahmaputra. A ferry crosses the Tsangpo near Samye in central Tibet. (Photo: P. P. Karan.)

be traced. The present-day Chinese, especially in north China, are the descendents of the people of Shang, the first certainly known kingdom of the area. In the north China kingdom of Shang, confined to the valley of Huang, the priest kings presided over ancestor cults in the villages and artisans made elaborate bronze vessels.

By 1100 B.C. Shang rulers had succumbed to the state of Zhou. After three centuries of tranquillity the fuedal states began vying for dominance. The country was divided by warring feudal lords. The western state of Qin—bolstered by surplus grain from fields irrigated from the Min River and Zheng Guo Canal—had mastered all others by 221 B.C. Its king, Qin Shi Huangdi, declared himself first emperor, and initiated tremendous public works, notably the consolidation of fortifications into the Great Wall of China.

After the death of the first emperor the country was engulfed in a civil war from which emerged the Han Dynasty, which restored the central unified empire. Before the Qin-Han empire there had been no political unity in China. The Han Empire expanded the frontiers of the country, and also extended its conquests far into central Asia. Ruling all China for over four hundred years (206 B.C.–221 A.D.), it was contemporary with the great age of the Roman Republic and the first centuries of the Roman Empire. During this period the Chinese extended their sway toward the west across the Central Asian oases, toward the north over Manchuria and Korea, and toward the south over the non-Chinese Tai people beyond the alluvial plains of Yangtze and into the hill country of south China. The Chinese expansion was achieved through conquest and colonization. Floods and drought in the north and the lure of new lands in the south spread the colonists to the south. The southward advance of Chinese colonization spread a network of walled cities called *hsien* or country capitals throughout the valleys of China. *Hsien* served as the administrative and economic centers for the surrounding regions.

The imperial state as constructed by the Han remained the model for subsequent regimes, right down to modern times. The emperor was the supreme and absolute monarch, and in 2 A.D. China counted 57,671,400 people in its first recorded census. The ideological cement the Han rulers used was Confucianism, which formed the basis of Chinese society.

Confucius (551–449 B.C.) indicated that the emperor was given a mandate from heaven to be the universal monarch. The emperor had to conform to the will of heaven through good government and moral conduct. The evidence of good government and moral conduct was found in human conditions in the realm. Floods, drought, and famine were signs that the emperor was failing to conform to heaven's will, which justified his replacement by a new dynasty. Confucian principles emphasized excellence as the result of education and conduct rather than inheritance; the value of submission to authority; respect for tradition; the reverence of the past; an emphasis on traditional learning in the classics and fine arts; decorum in social relationships; prudence, caution, and a preference for moderation; and living in harmony to fit into the rhythmic pattern of the universe.

In the early third century A.D. the Han Empire collapsed due to a variety of internal tensions, and civil wars divided the country into three kingdoms. Tartar tribes seized the northern provinces. Chinese dynasties, which ruled from Nanking, held the south. This period of division lasted for more than 250 years (316–589). During these centuries Buddhism was introduced from India, establishing a major place in the Chinese civilization, from whence it spread to Japan.

The reunion of the empire was accomplished by the short-lived Sui Dynasty (589–618) and then consolidated by the great Tang Dynasty (618–907). This period of three hundred years marked the apogee of the old Chinese civilization (contemporary with the European Dark Ages). Tang China was a cultural watershed. Buddhism had already permeated the nation and reinvigorated the arts; Buddhist texts were spread by the invention of block printing, as were dictionaries and calendars. The second half of the Tang dynasty was disturbed by a major rebellion, which weakened the central government's control in the provinces. Turkic strength checked Chinese advances in the northwest and menaced China. Arab invaders reached the Amu Darya River by 651 and slowly converted their subjects. A Tang defeat at Talas (751) opened Central Asia to Islam. When the Tang fell in 907 an interval of fifty years of confused struggle and separation divided it from the rise of the next great unifying dynasty, the Sung (960–1280). During the Sung Dynasty the economy made great advances; shipping and overseas commerce were for the first time more important sources of revenue than the land tax. In 1086 a census was conducted which revealed that China had 108 million citizens. This vast population was governed by an elite bureaucracy, chosen through competitive examinations in classic Confucian texts. For centuries the Chinese civil service examinees indoctrinated themselves in a state orthodoxy by memorizing the official commentaries on the Confucian classics. A successful candidate spent ten or fifteen years of hard work at this task. Not surprisingly, he seldom thereafter produced a novel or rebellious idea. Yet he had put himself through this intellectual wringer by his own choice and at his own expense.

Equally neat and useful was the legal system of mutual or collective responsibility, in which all family members were responsible for one another and all neighbors were responsible for neighboring households. If your brother did wrong and absconded, you would pay. So you kept an eye on him. As a result, everybody watched everybody—again at no cost to the state. This ancient invention lies behind the networks of informers that operate in China today.

Innumerable other devices and self-balancing institutions helped to keep society in order. All were the handiwork of the scholar-official ruling class—the mandarins—who were the inheritors of the statecraft and supervised the activities of the peasants, merchants, and artisans. Indissolubly wedded to Confucian principles and dependent on imperial patronage, they became the world's most formidable establishment, highly conservative in outlook and highly skilled in manipulating people.

Beyond the northern frontiers of Sung China, powerful and violent nomadic people emerged and broke into the empire, first in 1127 when they conquered north China, and later, from 1212 to 1280, when the Mongol ruler Genghiz Khan and his successors maintained continuous attacks on China until they conquered the whole country and extinguished the Sung Dynasty. In 1215 Genghiz Khan took Beijing (Yanjing). By 1280 his grandson Kublai Khan ruled all of China and established the Yuan (Mongol) Dynasty. Kublai's Empire of the Great Khan was one of the four Mongol khanates. Europe learned of the glory of Kublai Khan, the first Mongol to rule all China, from Marco Polo's accounts of his travels during 1271 to 1295. The successors of Kublai were weak; in 1368, after less than a century of full control, the Mongols were driven out by a large-scale Chinese rebellion, which was led and organized by the founder of the following Ming Dynasty.

The Ming Dynasty expanded the limits of the empire, but from the middle of the fifteenth century China was menaced by the growth of a new power in Manchuria. The Manchu tribes threw off their allegiance to the Ming and began to encroach on Ming territory. By the middle of the seventeenth century they were raiding the Great Wall frontier of China proper. In 1644 an internal rebellion overthrew the Ming government; the Manchu occupied north China and later extended their rule over much of south China.

The Qing or Manchu Dynasty (1644–1912) was the last age of imperial China. The Qing Dynasty expanded briskly into the west, doubling the population and providing a buffer for the heartland. In 1762 China had some 200 million people; by 1830 the population had nearly doubled (to 395 million) in less than 70 years. With the doubling of the population, land became hard to find and prices rose; tenants were rack-rented and free peasants were bought or squeezed out. Industry had not yet developed to meet the demands of the rising population and provide new employment.

As the nineteenth century got underway, the scale and grandeur of China's ancient culture seemed proof against any radical change. The Manchus and those who served them had sunk into lethargy and corruption. Mechanically they continued the rituals of rule while Western guns were aimed at the gates, and civil unrest—a sure sign of dynastic decline—flared across the lovely land.

Wars for Opium and Privilege

The Qing authority was fatally challenged by Europe. Western resentment of the restrictive trading permitted them at Guangzhou (formerly Canton) grew into the Opium Wars of 1839 and 1856, which China lost. China distrusted the foreign traders who were coming to the country in increasing numbers. China confined them to the single port of Canton, forced them to deal only with a selected group of Chinese merchants, and hedged them with numerous vexatious restrictions. Tensions built up at Canton, and the discovery that opium, which was produced by the British in India, could be sold in China turned the favorable trade balance from China to Britain. Opium was an illegal import; the British traders and their officials connived at an extensive opium smuggling trade. Early in the nineteenth century the opium trade was an open scandal that was doing great harm to China's economy and to social life. When the Manchu court totally suppressed the opium trade, the Opium War resulted.

China was defeated; her navy was wholly inadequate to face the British fleet, and her old-style army could not overcome the more modern arms of the small British landing forces. China was compelled to sue for peace; this was consummated by the Treaty of Nanking, which established the system of Treaty Ports, concession areas, and the right of extraterritorial jurisdiction. Treaty Ports were cities, not always on the coast, that were designated as places where foreign traders could reside and trade (Figure 2.3). At such cities foreigners were granted concessions (usually outside the walls) that were beyond Chinese control. In 1842 China ceded the island of Hong Kong to Britain. Soon China was divided into spheres of Western colonial influence (Figure 2.4).

The Treaty of Nanking represented a severe encroachment on Chinese sovereign rights. Each time China involuntarily opened new treaty ports, Qing rulers acquiesced as European powers carved out spheres of influence and posted troops. The Qing was weak within. When the empress dowager died in 1908, no strong character remained to carry on the regency in the name of her grandson, Pu-Yi, who ruled for four years until the Revolution of 1911. In 1912 a series of rebellions led to a republic and the abdication of Emperor Pu Yi. The overthrow of the Manchu Dynasty in 1911 also threw out the Son of Heaven as an institution. A government that for more than two thousand years had centered on the monarchy now had no monarch. As Mongolia and Tibet broke away from the Chinese Republic, the empire disintegrated.

Revolution of 1911

For the majority of Chinese, the Revolution of 1911 in favor of democratic abstractions meant little. Famine had always stalked the towns and villages, and the end of the Manchus made no difference. Between 1900 and 1925 there were at least eight severe famines, with death tolls up to 500,000. In the Kansu Province, famine, typhus, bandits, and war killed one-third of the population between 1926 and 1930.

Figure 2-3. The former International Settlement on the Huangpu waterfront in Shanghai. Formed in 1863 from the original British (1843), American (1862), and French (1849) concessions, it was an autonomous and extraterritorial unit until 1943. The former International Settlement contains fine boulevards and the famed Bund, or waterfront. It was the site of the great business houses, banks, shipping companies, and wharves. Though the municipal government here was foreign (English and French) the people were mainly Chinese. The Shanghai metropolitan area today has a population of over 17 million. (Photo: P. P. Karan.)

As the Manchu dynasty declined, it progressively yielded up more and more power to local strongmen or warlords. Essentially, a warlord was a strongman who could put together a military force, arm it, and feed it. During 1917–1927 warlords numbered in the hundreds, and their wars, alliances, treacheries, and fallings-out defy description. By the early 1920s the principal warlords were an ex-bandit who was a protege of the Japanese (who ultimately killed him) with a base in Manchuria, a classical scholar who became the boss of North China, and a "Christian General" (he was baptized by a Methodist minister in 1914).

The absence of a clear central authority made China an easy prey for Japan, which set up a puppet state in Manchuria in 1932 and held it through World War II. The period from 1917 to 1927—"the warlord era"—was marked by a series of short civil wars fought entirely between rival militarists to gain control of the weak government and its revenues in Beijing. Within the country there was an increasing breakdown of law and order, with rampant banditry and rural distress. In a real sense the seeds of revolution were rapidly maturing.

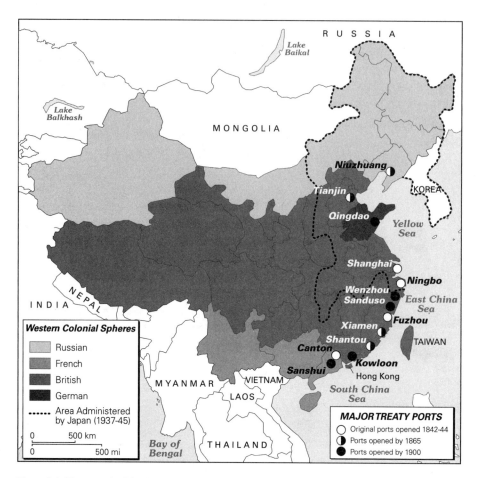

Figure 2-4. Western colonial spheres and Treaty Ports.

In 1921 the Chinese Communist Party was formally set up at a meeting in Shanghai; eleven members, one of whom was Mao Zedong, attended. At almost the same time a Chinese Communist Party was also formed in France by Chinese students living in Paris. One of the founders was Chou En-lai.

The Nationalist (Kuomintang) government in Canton prepared for war against the southern warlords in 1926 under the command of Chiang Kaishek. In much of south China, particularly the Hunan Province, a social revolution, inspired by Mao Zedong, was sweeping the country. From 1929 to 1935 Chiang launched successive extermination campaigns against the Communists, who had now, under the leadership of Mao, established an area of control in the hill country on the Hunan-Jiangxi border. The Communists were not defeated; they set out on the Long March in 1935 with about 100,000 men and many of their dependents. A year later they reached Yanan, in Shaanxi, after marching and counter-marching for more than 6,000 miles, with 30,000 fighting men.

In 1936 the Nationalists and Communists formed a united front to face the Japanese during the Second World War. In 1937 Japan struck near Beijing, and the fighting soon escalated into a large-scale, but still undeclared war.

Like all of East Asia, Japan for centuries had deferred to Chinese cultural superiority and had coveted its natural wealth. In the 1890s Japan, along with other foreign powers, extorted concessions from China's decaying Manchu Dynasty. This continued during the Boxer Uprising in 1900 (when more than 50 percent of the invading troops were Japanese) and the Russo-Japanese War, and culminated in the 1930s when Japan's modern armies clanked across the nearly helpless Chinese mainland. The Chinese forces were pushed back from the coast to the mountainous interior of western China, losing nearly two thirds of the provinces to the Japanese. In those conquered territories, particularly north China, the Communists were organizing the guerrilla resistance, which challenged Japanese authority.

For the Chinese people, the coming of the Japanese meant suffering and death on a scale difficult to comprehend. After seizing the Beijing-Tianjin area and north China, Japan occupied Shanghai. During ten days in 1937 the Japanese onslaught reduced the population of the city of Nanking (Nanjing) from 1.1 million to 250,000. Forced to trade terrain for time, Chiang Kaishek moved his capital up the Chang Jiang (Yangtze River) from Nanking (Nanjing) to Hankow (Wuhan) in 1937, only to fall back to Chungking (Chongqing) a year later.

The Chinese Communists steadily expanded their guerrilla war until large areas were liberated, and in these they set up their own administration. Japanese retaliation was brutal and ruthless. "Three All" campaigns were launched against guerrilla areas (Kill All, Burn All, Loot All). This policy had the effect of forcing the Chinese peasantry to rely on the communist guerrillas for their sole protection. It roused the national consciousness of an indifferent apolitical peasantry and was the main factor in building the power of the Communist Party of China to a national level.

After the capitulation of Japan during the Second World War, China was left deeply divided. The Nationalists took over from the Japanese in the south and eastern provinces. The Communists controlled the rural north. The civil war widened in 1945, and by the end of 1948 near Hsuchow (Suzhou) the Communists decimated the Nationalists. Within months the Nationalists fled to the island of Taiwan and established the Republic of China on the island on December 8, 1949. On October 1, 1949, the People's Republic of China was proclaimed. In October 1971 China was admitted to the United Nations, displacing Nationalist China (Taiwan).

A citizens' group in China—the Committee for Japanese War Reparations—is asking Japan to compensate them for its World War II aggression. The group, which claims 300,000 members across China, demands that Japan pay victims of the war 180 billion yuan ($30 billion). There are still 10 million

Chinese war victims living. China renounced government demands for war compensation in an agreement that established diplomatic relations with Japan in 1972. But now the government openly encourages citizens to seek payment, despite the fact that the emperor of Japan during a historic visit to China in October 1992 expressed remorse over the atrocities of the Imperial Army. The Imperial Japanese Army forced Asian women to serve as "military comfort women."

After the 1931 conquest of Manchuria, a bacteriological laboratory was established by Japan in northeastern China in the vicinity of Pingfang Station, about 12 miles from the city of Harbin. About 600 prisoners of war from the undeclared Sino-Japanese war of the 1930s and 1940s are estimated to have been killed annually in experiments at this laboratory. Between 1940 and the day of Japan's surrender in August 1945, no less than 3,000 prisoners of war and civilians were put to death. These victims included Chinese and Korean resistance fighters and Russian and Mongolian citizens arrested by military police on suspicion of engaging in anti-Japanese actvities.

Fifty-Five Years of the People's Republic, 1949–2004

The People's Republic of China was born after a long period of struggle into an uncertain world. It inherited many economic and social developments and has tackled some of these problems. Its development over the last fifty-five years has been very impressive in many areas. These improvements have not been painless or smooth. Between 1949 and 1965 China concentrated on land reforms from the simple redistribution of land to the formation of cooperative farms, and finally communes in 1958–1959. Droughts, floods, and misman-agement brought starvation and the largest famine in this century in 1959–1961, which killed millions of people. A period of centrally planned and discontinuous economic development continued until 1960, followed by several years of turmoil preceeding, during, and after the Cultural Revolution (1966–1976).

Chinese today acknowledge Mao Zedong's "mistakes"—the politically correct term for the famines and massive violence he caused—but they prefer to remember the "good things"; Mao inspired them, spoke for them, and tapped their immense power. In 1966, Mao ignited his most violent campaign of all, the Great Proletarian Cultural Revolution. The Cultural Revolution began with a power struggle. Mao's leadership had been challenged by the Communist Party Congress; in May 1966 he struck back. Mao attacked the moderates for lacking revolutionary zeal, then targeted his rivals in the leader-ship. Mao called on millions of patriotic youths to form the Red Guards, "bombard the headquarters" of government, and dislodge his opponents. What followed was a reign of terror. Marauding Red Guards hunted down "class enemies," smashed Buddhist temples and other so-called symbols of feudalism, and effectively paralyzed China's government. The Cultural Revolution wreaked havoc with the economy, injecting ideology into economic planning, disrupting foreign trade, and practically shutting down educational and training facilities. The Cultural Revolution ended with the death of Mao Zedong in 1976.

With the death of Mao and Deng Xiaoping's ascension to power, China's official passions reverted from revolution to modernization. The goal of "four modernizations" (agriculture, industry, science and technology, and national defense) was first proposed by Chou En-lai, but the means with which Deng pursued it went so far beyond what Zhou envisioned that some refer to Deng's policies as China's "second revolution." Agricultural communes were dismantled, the scope of central planning shrank, and foreign investment was actively courted. The results have been outstanding.

Deng's transformation from Communist to pragmatist began with the disastrous Mao-inspired Great Leap Forward, which precipitated the largest famine in humankind's history, leaving between 27 million and 43 million Chinese dead. In July 1962 Deng made the pronouncement that has guided him ever since: "Whether white or black, a cat is a good cat so long as it catches the rat." Any means, socialist or not, was good so long as production increased. Deng's assertive pragmatism increased agricultural production and led to his two purges—once in 1966 at the outset of the Cultural Revolution and again in 1976 during the radical reaction that followed Zhou's death.

Deng's pursuit of economic reform within tightly circumscribed political limits was single-minded, and he did not hesitate to purge those who would undermine his delicate balance between economic liberalism and political control. Three Communist party chiefs were purged after Deng's return. Deng's hard edge was most apparent to China and the rest of the world on the night of June 3, 1989, when he ordered the army into Beijing to suppress the demonstration that had been going on for more than six weeks (Figure 2.5). Students occupied Tiananmen Square, but they had massive overt support from the city's citizens. Democracy was the slogan under which everyone demonstrated, but few really wanted to overthrow the Communist Party rule or had more than a rudimentary conception of Western-style democracy. Inflation, corruption, and the special privileges of the sons and daughters of the Party elite were the dominant concerns.

Tiananmen Square marked a major landmark in China's recent history. It was the first time since the revolution of 1949 that Chinese troops shot at citizens in Beijing's streets. Hundreds of young people died. Many thousands more were jailed, and for every one person put in prison, a hundred more were harassed, and a thousand scared into silence. The army's attack brought one of those sudden, violent changes in direction that have punctuated communist China's fifty years of history. For several weeks before the massacre, students in more than eighty cities and towns, backed by millions of their countrymen, had captured the world's attention by calling for democracy in

Figure 2-5. Beijing. Tiananmen Square and The Gate of Heavenly Peace from which Mao Zedong proclaimed the People's Republic in 1949. In June 1989 Chinese tanks crushed pro-democracy demonstrations
at Tiananmen Square. An unleashed military committed a massacre against its own people. In the thousands
of years spanned by Chinese history, unspeakable atrocities have occurred. Millions have suffered from the
machinations of cloistered emperors, empresses, and eunuchs; whole cities were slaughtered by marauding
invaders and warlords. Until June 1989 that all seemed safely in the past. (Photo: P. P.Karan.)

China. With the massacre, Deng Xiaoping, who initiated bold economic
reforms, dashed the hopes of the young for political reform and freedom of
the mind. Of the 1.2 billion Chinese, nearly two-thirds, some 759 million, are
under 35 years old; their hope for a free future was killed by the government
gunfire at Tiananmen Square. A loosened economy and a richer flow of information allowed the youth of China a mobility and political awareness unheard
of before the 1980s. Deng could not stop the social consequences of his
opening of China, but in the year after the Tiananmen Square the government,
out of fear of losing control over an awakened youth, reverted to nationalistic
authoritarianism.

The gradual establishment of the government under Deng Xiaoping
reduced the role of ideology in China. Since 1978, the fundamental premise of
China's development policy has been that consumer welfare, economic
productivity, and political stability are indivisible. The emphasis has been on
raising personal income and consumption and introducing new productivity
incentives and management systems.

Looking over China's history since 1949, it can be said that Mao Zedong
united China and Deng Xioaping took China from a period of struggle
to one of economic reform. Jiang Zemin tried to keep China stable and

growing smoothly. For Hu Jintao, the current leader, simply steering China through intensifying economic and social dislocation will be a major achievement. State-enterprise reform could throw as many as 40 million people out of work, and Asia's financial crisis is slowing China's growth, hampering efforts to get those people reemployed. The potential for unrest is real, and is growing.

TRANSFORMATION OF ONE-FIFTH OF MANKIND

China's economic transformation began with an eclectic mix of capitalism and socialism in 1978. The first step was the liberalization of agriculture, replacing communes with long-term land leases. That permitted peasants to keep the proceeds from their extra production, nearly duplicating the incentives of private enterprise while maintaining state ownership of land. And it paid off. While the farm output grew by 5 percent annually from 1978 to 1995, the portion of the workforce on farms fell to 53 percent from 72 percent. In the second wave of near-capitalist reforms, small community-owned industrial enterprises were permitted to blossom, absorbing much of the labor freed by productivity gains in agriculture. "Special economic zones"—free markets, by another name—were created in southern coastal cities. And their success induced some ninety other cities to demand partial exemption from labor, taxes, and foreign investment regulations. Strikingly, the growth of free enterprises did not come at the expense of the socialist sector.

The economic reforms introduced by Deng Xiaoping have produced great successes. China's economic performance in the years between 1978 and 2003 has brought about one of the biggest improvements in human welfare anywhere at any time. The real GNP has grown by an average of almost 9 percent per year. China's economy in 2000 was about eight times larger than it was in 1978.

The overall figures mask a startling rise in the standard of living. About 75 percent of the Chinese population—around 800 million people today—still live on the land. Deng's first reforms concentrated on freeing the farmers from the suffocation of the commune system. This increased farm production enormously. Tens of millions of peasants left the land for factory and construction jobs, powering a transformation of China's coastal provinces and major urban centers. Linked with foreign capital and skills, their low-wage labor makes China a major force in world trade.

The rapidly modernizing parts of China are home to at least 400 million of the country's nearly 1.2 billion people. China is on its way to becoming two nations, politically united but economically divided, with roughly one third of its people in the prosperous coastal and urban areas and two thirds in the isolated villages and towns of the interior. Life may continue to gradually improve even in the poorer areas, but only the modern coastal areas have real economic weight in the world. Hundreds of millions of Chinese in the booming coastal provinces are now able to change jobs, take vacations, and complain on talk radio. But about 3,000 are in prison for their political views—more than in any other nation.

A new openness in China allows powerful outside influences—including many from America—to come flooding in, undermining the old ways. Everything from blue jeans and running shoes to the Goddess of Democracy statue erected on Tiananmen Square in 1989 reflects the allure of American culture and ideas. But advocates of political reform and American ideas of democracy have been silenced.

Two millenia separate China's imperialist despot (the first emperor Qin Shi Huangdi) from the contemporary communist revolutionary rulers (Mao Zedong, Deng Xiaoping, Jiang Zemin, and Hu Jintao), yet they are cut from the same silk. They achieved power by force. They suppressed dissent without scruple. And they made China whole. No theme recurs more frequently in Chinese history than the drive to preserve, or reassemble, a country threatened by splintering and invasion. China's perennial answer to chaos has been severe, central authority. China's regime has introduced far-reaching economic reforms during the last twenty-five years, but the communist government grips the nation's time-tested formula for cohesion.

The Communist Party and Capitalist Society in China: Conflicts

China's reaction to the collapse of communism in the former Soviet Union was to speed up economic reform. The logic was that if the party delivered economic goods it would keep its power. This means that the Communist Party at every level is intent on doing whatever is needed to ensure that the economy keeps on growing.

Even so, the paradox of communism and the free capitalist market economy has to be resolved. At some point the Chinese Communist Party has to stop being communist if the economic growth is to continue. China will have to choose between political communism and economic growth. This need not mean the disintegration of the party. The party has already considerably relaxed the totalitarian controls. Decision making of all kinds has been decentralized, both geographically and to firms and lower-level governments. As long as they steer clear of politics, the Chinese people have freedoms that were undreamed of ten years ago. A modern economy, with a rule of law in which people are free to move from one place to another, from one job to another, and from one house to another is flatly inconsistent with the principles behind the system of communist political control.

The economic changes have locked China on a course that seems destined to sharpen some fundamental contradictions in Chinese society—conflicts between central control and individual incentive, between collectivist doctrines and free-market dictates. The economic reforms have widened the gap between the haves and have-nots, and have already created a new entrepreneurial class—an economic elite—that is changing China from the bottom up. The new economic elite use money to do virtually whatever they want in the economic sphere. The self-made capitalists represent the fastest-growing class among China's 51 millon party members.

At the same time, China's age-old problem of the central government's difficulties in dealing with rebellious provinces has increased. The central government's control has been eroding for several years—an erosion that is most easily measured in money. This is most evident in Beijing's inability to collect revenue. Government authorities have been engaged in bitter fights with provincial leaders over how much money they can keep and how much money they must give to Beijing. The central government has backed down, causing its worst budget deficit ever.

Encouraged by Deng Xiaoping's remark—"Never miss a chance for economic development"—provincial governments have enthusiastically drawn up plans to create economic and technological development zones in their territories. In fact, plans for economic development have gathered such momentum in the provinces that the central government will not find it easy to apply the brakes. The provinces in the coastal area that are experiencing high rates of growth are poised to continue aggressive development policies.

The old control system on the economy was the Communist Party and its control over administrators, but the old system cannot be used to control a market economy which is not run by state administrators. The normal control mechanisms that exist in the market economies—taxes, regulations, and monetary policies—are not adequately developed in China. The result is a rapidly growing but very unstable economy.

Another problem facing the capitalist development in a communist state is that foreign investment is flooding the country, but China's paranoia about the management of information remains as strong as ever. China does not like to broadcast things that go wrong. The management of news remains very centralized. In 2003 China was slow to report the outbreak of the SARS epidemic, prompting suspicions that officials are eager to suppress news that might be considered unfavorable to the Communist Party leadership.

After June 1989, China was synonymous in the world with a bloody, repressive government, and scant attention was paid to how economic reforms were largely left in place. Over the last several years, in contrast, the paradigm has shifted to one in which China is most often assessed in the light of its economic growth and its modernization plans and lucrative opportunities for foreign business. Far less emphasis is given to the shortcomings and contradictions that persist. A common mistake that outsiders, particularly foreign investors, make is to believe that communist ideology and the old communist way of doing things have disappeared. Even though few people in China still believe in Marxism-Leninism as an economic system, fifty-five years of Communist Party rule has left a heavy legacy of dilapidated factories, millions of poorly trained workers, and heavy-handed bureaucrats. At present China's leaders are attempting what no other communist country has managed: modernizing a vast economy and integrating it into the free world while maintaining absolute control within a monolithic single-party system.

Centrifugal Forces Grow Stronger in China

A proud accomplishment of the Chinese Communist Party is that it reunited a nation torn apart by warlords and recreated a central government that could successfully lead the country. This achievement is being undermined by the provinces that are practicing local protectionism to keep their factories running. Provincial authorities quietly order retailers in their domain to sell only local goods. In one of the most flagrant violations of national policy, in 1990 the Xinjiang region in far-western China quietly banned the importation from other provinces of 48 kinds of products, ranging from color televisions to soap and bicycles. Some department stores in the Hubei, Jilin, and Liaoning provinces were told not to sell products made outside the province. The provinces back their demands not with any law but with the knowledge that they can make life extremely difficult for anyone who disobeys their rules. The bans are often instituted only informally in conversations with industrial concerns and retailers, which are difficult to control.

Rivalries among the provinces grew steadily during the 1980s, but until 1990 they were generally concerned with the competition for scarce raw materials. Some provinces even stationed guards at their borders to prevent silk cocoons, hogs, cotton, and other materials from going to other regions. Now the battle for scarce supplies has slackened, and the interprovincial combat is focused on the local markets and excluding competitors.

If retailing were mostly in private hands, the shops might protest and the shop owners might well try to evade the protectionist rules. But in China, with the partial exception of Guangdong Province in the south, most retail shops are still relatively large and are state owned. As a result, there is less incentive for them to find the cheapest merchandise available.

Some experts believe that the problem reflects deeper flaws in the economic system and is a by-product of the decentralization strategy that has been the centerpiece of China's reform efforts. Errant provinces are difficult to bring back to heel. The provinces going their own way arouse a traditional Chinese apprehension of *luan*, or chaos. It underscores the strength of the centrifugal forces that some fear could lead to the same fragmentation of the country that has happened periodically in China for thousands of years.

As decentralization gains momentum, local leaders are getting increasingly bold about defying national policies. Separatist movements exist in Tibet, Xinjiang, and Inner Mongolia. It seems less likely that China's other provinces would want to leave, but in places such as Guangdong, which is growing very fast, the possibility of eventual secession cannot be ruled out. Other analysts discount such fears as alarmist and point out that powerful regions like Guangdong Province depend on the interior provinces for their markets, raw materials, and fuel. For the moment, China's rulers are banking on a combination of forces to hold the country together: the weight of the Communist Party bureaucracy, coercion, and a fundamental desire for social order that is ingrained in the unifying tradition of a country with a 5,000-year-old history.

Many empires disintegrated in the twentieth century, as the British, the French, and the Russians discovered. Today the Chinese empire—stretching from Buddhist Tibet to Korean enclaves in Manchuria, from Muslim Xinjiang near Pakistan to Cantonese-speaking Guangdong next to Hong Kong—is arguably the last great multiethnic transcontinental empire left in the world. And although its grasp is enormous, its reach is even greater; Chinese claims stretch across the seas to encompass Taiwan and the Spratly Islands near the Philippines and Malaysia. The ideology and the fear that Mao used to keep the provinces in the orbit of Beijing are no longer sufficient. Chinese leaders are searching for a new unifying force to keep the empire together. They have in mind two possible unifying forces. One is a sustained economic boom to raise living standards and thus give the government a new legitimacy and the people a sense of purpose. The second is nationalism.

There are problems with both. China's economic boom has tended to worsen regional disparities and tensions rather than alleviate them. One basis for fragmentation may be economic disparities, with rich coastal regions going their own way, led by Guangdong and Shanghai. Economically, the non-Han minorities such as the Tibetans, Muslims, and Mongolians feel left out, while prosperous Guangdong Province and the coastal regions are growing so quickly that they feel dragged down by the rest of the country. Tibet and parts of Xinjiang, culturally distinct from the rest of China, might seize the chance to break away altogether. As income disparity deepens in China's cities, divisive forces increase. The number of city dwellers living in poverty is growing rapidly. A decade ago, this group was virtually nonexistent. Now, Chinese researchers estimate that anywhere from 12 million to more than 22 million urban residents of an urban population of 200 million live in "absolute poverty," meaning that they cannot afford basic food, clothing, and shelter. These urban poor are distinct from the large number of poor migrants from the countryside, who come to cities in search of work but are not counted as residents. The urban poor are mostly unskilled workers, the losers in China's rapid transformation to a market economy; the income gap between rich and poor in China is probably growing faster than anywhere else in the world.

Under the old planned economy, nearly all Chinese who lived in the cities were assigned to governmental "work units," which guaranteed them a place to live and subsidized food staples, medical care, pensions, and often schooling for their children. Under this system, living standards of urban residents rose steadily, en masse, throughout the 1980s. But in the 1990s that system started to crumble; many state companies shut down or downsized, laying off vast numbers of workers. Government figures put the unemployment rate at 3 percent in 2000, but World Bank estimates it at closer to 8 percent in the urban areas. With a higher unemployment rate has come more social and economic unrest.

Chinese nationalism could threaten Asian stability. China's neighbors are naturally concerned that rising nationalism could encourage China to become more aggressive, particularly since it is engaged in a far-reaching military build-up. Nationalism is clearly on the rise also among ethnic minorities, and in their case it is directed against China.

ENVIRONMENTAL DIVERSITY

China shows a unique diversity of geographic and environmental conditions. It extends over a vast area that varies from 500 feet below sea level in the Turpan (Turfan) depression in Xinjiang (Sinkiang) to over 29,000 feet in Qomolangma Feng (Mount Everest) on the southern edge of the Xizang (Tibet) Plateau. It includes continental and insular environments. Its climates range from the perpetual frost climate of some areas of Xizang to the rain forest climate of Hainan and the extreme south. The concept of duality permeates Chinese thought; it can be extended to the physical and environmental aspects of China, providing us with a means of organizing and describing the diversity of the country.

The key areas of China are the lowlands, where some four-fifths of the population is concentrated. These areas include the lowlands of Manchuria, the Great Plain, the Chang Jiang (Yangtze), and the valley of the Zhu (Pearl River). The loess-derived alluvium area of the Great Plain is highly productive, but it is dependent on flood control and irrigation. The mastery of China's rivers has been of decisive importance to agricultural development.

The upland areas are thinly populated. The warmer upland areas of China originally carried a forest cover varying from the coniferous forest of the cooler north to the luxuriant broad-leaf forest of the tropical south. For countless centuries, however, the forest has been ravaged by man; clearing for farming destroyed much of the forest country of central and south China from the seventeenth century onward, and millennia of felling and cutting for fuel, construction timber, and fodder left a scrubby and degraded second-growth vegetation. Almost half of the total forest area is in the northeastern and southwestern regions. Extensive northwest and north China have little or no forest. There are only small areas of forest cover in Gansu, Ningxia, Qinghai, Xinjiang, western Tibet, and central-western Inner Mongolia, and these areas make up 50 percent of the total land area of China. Only recently has affforestation begun to change the landscape, though these areas, even where climate is favorable, still remain largely marginal in terms of agriculture.

Two types of upland environment are found in the interior of China: the high deserts of the Tibetan Plateau, which is bitter cold throughout the year; and the true sand and gravel deserts of the interior basins of northwest China, with their cold winters and hot summers. Settled agriculture on the Tibetan Plateau is confined to limited areas where summer temperatures rise sufficiently high for crop growth, as in the climatically more favored areas of the Yarlung (Tsangpo) Valley. In the interior basins agriculture is confined to the girdle of oases on the fringes of the desert basins. These oases are nourished by streams rising in the snows and by the glaciers of mountain ranges such as the Tian Shan, Kun Lun, and Altai. The Altai Mountains have an average height of 6,000 feet, some peaks reaching an altitude of 10,000 feet. The mountains are separated by a series of valleys and basins that provide the basis for agricultural and pastoral economies combined with lumbering and mining in the surrounding mountains. To the south, Tian Shan rises to more than 12,000 feet above the Dzungarian and Tarim basins, which are situated in northern and southern Xinjiang, respectively. The Tian Shan does not form a continuous chain; the rift found between the cities of Turpan and Urumqi provides a natural route across the Tian Shan, between Tarim and Dzungaria from southern to northern Sinkiang. The Kun Lun Mountains separate the Tarim Basin from the high plateau of Tibet. To the east, Kun Lun branches off into three separate chains: the Altun Shan range in the north divides the inland drainage of the northwest from the Huang (Yellow River); the Tsinling range in the center forms the major watershed between the Huang and the Chang Jiang (Yangtze); and the Tanggula range in the south meets the eastern end of the Himalayan system in western Sichuan and northwestern Yunnan.

The aridity of the Dzungarian Basin (Junggar Pendi), the Tarim Basin, and the Turpan Depression are closely linked to location and relief. These desert basins comprise sandy dune areas (Shamo) and stony areas of weathered rock surfaces called *Gobi*. Although the mountains surrounding the desert basins cause their aridity, the mountains also provide the deserts with the largest part of their water. For example, 52.4 percent of the entire surface run-off of Xinjiang comes from the Tian Shan. The main oases such as Hotan, Yutian, and Minfeng on the southern edge, and Aksu, Kuqa, Luntai and Korla on the northern edge of the Tarim Basin are located on the alluvial fans or cones of the rivers that originate in the Kun Lun and Tian Shan. They follow the southern and northern branches of the old Silk Road. Wheat, cotton, fruit, and vegetables are grown where water is available. Over wide areas of western China, however, the dominant economy is that of pastoral nomadism. During the last decade new resources have been developed in these formerly marginal areas: oil in the basins of northwest China, a wide range of metallic minerals, and energy sources in the shape of coal and water power on the outer margins of the uplands. These resources are providing the basis for new patterns of industry and settlement.

After 1958, and subsequently during the Cultural Revolution, the land was developed at a rapid rate in Xinjiang, mainly by destroying the natural vegetation cover, under the slogan "Every soldier a farmer—every farmer a fighter." Large numbers of Han Chinese were settled in the area under "colonization" schemes. The Han Chinese now make up 96 percent of the population of most of the desert basins. Xinjiang had a population of 5.6 million in 1960; it increased to 13.1 million in 1982. As a result of settlements and land development, the sand dunes have become mobile and now threaten the farms in the Dzungarian Basin. In many places shifting sand dunes are moving at rates of 7 to 30 meters a year, and protective measures are required to fix the sand in the colonized regions. Efforts are being made now to establish strips of woodland or trees to protect the cultivated land. Salinization of the soil is another major problem; nearly 1 million hectares of all cultivated land in Xinjiang is affected by salt.

Environmental conditions certainly pose problems throughout China. The area of arable land is limited; the vagaries of climate and of river regimes are unpredictable. With 22 percent of the world's population and only 7 percent of the world's farmland, China faces a critical situation. These problems are related to the present development of China.

ENERGY RESOURCES

From the time Marco Polo reported the Chinese way of burning black stones and forging metals to recent reports, the accounts of China's natural resources have varied from glowing optimism to cautious underestimates. In general, China has adequate resources to support industrialization. Chinese policies encourage investments in the exploration of vast and largely untapped energy resources. Until the mid-1990s China was largely energy independent, but it is quickly challenging Japan and the United States as the world's largest importers of oil, prompting efforts to secure new supplies domestically and building pipelines into Russia and Central Asia. China has put more emphasis on exploiting its own supplies of natural gas in places such as southwestern Sichuan, where the wells are as deep as 4,000 meters, or over 13,000 feet. An accident in this natural gas field in December 2003 killed nearly 200 persons and spread poisonous fumes into the surrounding communities.

Coal is by far the most important source of primary energy (Figure 2.6). With 750 billion metric tons of identified and recoverable reserves, China's total coal resources are exceeded only by those of the United States and the Commonwealth of Independent States. In July 1985 Occidental Petroleum signed a thirty-year joint venture agreement with the Chinese to develop the world's largest open-pit coal mine at Pingshuo in Shanxi Province.

China is the world's fifth-largest producer of oil. The Chinese have opened up potentially large oil tracts to foreign exploration and production, including

Figure 2-6. One of the world's largest open pit coal mines in Fushun, Liaoning Province, Northeast China. China mines over 1.2 billion tons of coal annually. More than 5 million people are employed in coal mining. By the year 2020 China will replace the United States as the largest source of waste gases being pumped into the atmosphere. From the chimneys that puncture the haze of China's industrial landscape, a nimbus of carbon- and sulphur-based gases billows into the atmosphere. China's coal industry death rate is among the highest in the world. In 2003 4.7 Chinese miners were killed for every 1 million metric tons of coal produced. (Photo: Robert Beatty.)

the Tarim Basin in Xinjiang. This area of far-western China could have reserves as big as Saudi Arabia's, or at least Alaska's North Slope. China is wooing foreigners because it can't get its oil out of the ground fast enough to meet growing energy demands. Until recently, foreign oil companies had been restricted to the role of hired hands in China's most promising fields in the northern and western interior. They had been allowed to engage in the potentially lucrative exploration and production business only in the relatively oil-poor southern and offshore areas. In 1983, the Atlantic Richfield Company, based in Los Angeles, discovered commercial quantities of gas off the Chinese coast and became a partner with China and with Kuwait's national oil company in the development of a gas pipeline. In 1992 Amoco, with headquarters in Chicago, signed a contract for onshore oil exploration in far west China.

The Tarim Basin, like the Alaska North Slope, is extremely inhospitable. This is an area about the size of the state of Texas, situated in the Xinjiang Uygur autonomous region. The Tarim Basin is an intermontane basin—one ringed on all sides by mountain ranges. Here an Exxon-led consortium will explore for oil and gas. It is one of the harshest and most remote deserts in the world. In ancient times, caravans following the old Silk Road skirted around the Tarim Basin rather than go through it. Marco Polo wrote, "This desert is the abode of evil spirits which lure travelers to their destruction." Roads traverse the Tarim today, but petroleum operations will represent a formidable challenge.

A visit into the wastelands of Taklamakan, home of the Tarim Basin oil fields, offers a glimpse of the trouble that lurks in the desert (its name in the local Turkic language means: "You go in but you do not come out"). The only passable road from the capital of Urumqi to the vast area opened to foreign bidding is dangerous. The big question is how to move out the millions of barrels of oil a year from the Tarim Basin. Sand dunes up to 150 feet high are blocking progress in China's road-building efforts to its biggest prospective oil field, Tazhong, in the center of the desert. Often the road is obliterated within 24 hours when the winds reshape the dunes.

China is believed to have one of the world's greatest hydropower potentials. A number of hydropower projects are underway to fully tap this potential, including the world's largest dam at the Three Gorges site on the Chang Jiang (Yangtze River). The Chinese have built a number of nuclear power plants using indigenous technology, including one near Guangzhou and Quinshan (south of Shanghai).

China is the world's fourth-largest power producer, but the average Chinese consumes less than 650 kilowatt hours—barely enough to burn a 75-watt light bulb year round—and about 120 million rural Chinese—one-tenth of the population—live without electricity in their houses or villages. Building a modern electrical power system for the 1.2 billion Chinese is critical for sustaining economic growth and maintaining political stability. With modern economic growth, China's current generating capacity is not adequate to meet the demand for electricity from thousands of new factories, office towers, and shopping centers. The demand for power is outpacing the current generating capacity by 30 percent in the fast-growing coastal provinces and by 20 percent nationwide. Blackouts plague the largest industrial centers such as Shanghai, and shortages cut deeply into productivity.

LAND USE, AGRICULTURE, AND FOOD SUPPLY

China, a country with only one fifteenth of the world's arable land, has been praised for its ability to feed its people, more than one-fifth of the world's population. When the People's Republic of China was founded in 1949, only about 0.2 hectares (ha) of land per capita were cultivated. With rapid population growth, this figure dropped to 0.1 hectares in the late 1970s.

In 1990, nearly 30 percent (or 286 million ha) of China's total land area (960 million ha) was in pasture and grassland. Nearly 15 percent (or 140 million ha) was cultivated land; forest land occupied 13 percent (or 124 million ha). Settlements and related built-up areas covered nearly 5 percent (or 467 thousand ha). Inland water bodies constituted about 3 percent (or 287 thousand ha). An estimated 11 percent of the land (or a little over 100 million ha), which is now occupied by low-quality grassland, bushes, marshes and wetlands, could be used after improvements. The remaining 23 percent of the land constitutes high cold desert, gravel desert such as the Gobi, and snow and icefields.

Wetlands ecosystems compose about 7 percent of China's land area. Wetlands—coastal and inland marshes and mudflats—are viewed as wasteland to be converted to agricultural or industrial use, overlooking their ecological and economic benefits such as natural flood protection and improved water quality. Some of the coastal wetlands in eastern China in Jiangsu, Zhejiang, Fujian, Guangdong, and Liaoning have been converted to grain, cotton, and sugarcane fields during the last three decades.

Most of China's labor force is engaged in agriculture even though only 15 percent of the land is used for cultivation. Virtually all of the cultivated land is used for crops; China is the world's largest producer of rice, potatoes, sorghum, millet, barley, peanuts, tea, and pork. The major industrial crops include cotton and other fibers and various oilseeds. Agricultural exports provide China with a large share of its foreign trade revenue.

To cope with increasing food demand during the period of rapid population growth in the 1950s and 1960s, the Chinese government instituted collective farming and a government-operated grain procurement policy in rural areas in addition to a food rationing system in urban areas. But China paid a high price for these policies. The collective farming system was detrimental to work incentives, and the grain procurement and marketing policies fragmented the national grain market into thirty self-sufficient regions. The result was that, despite sharp increases in modern inputs in the 1960s and 1970s, grain production in China barely kept pace with population growth.

In 1979, thirty years after the socialist revolution, China's leaders, frustrated by their inability to raise living standards substantially, initiated a series of sweeping reforms in agriculture. The most important reform was the creation of the household responsibility system, which made the individual household, rather than the collective team, the main unit of agricultural production. Although China's population grew by 1.4 percent per year between 1978 and 1984, the net value of agricultural production grew by 7.7 percent annually and that of grain output by a 4.8 percent. The success of the household responsibility system reform was the main factor behind this phenomenal growth in agricultural production.

Reforms allowed the revival of rural farms and private markets, encouraged the formation of rural enterprises, and will gradually phase out compulsory state purchases of grain, vegetable oil, cotton, and other agricultural items over which the state formerly exercised a monopoly control. The move to create a market economy in food, initially by freeing prices for most food except grain and eventually by abolishing the agricultural communes as the unit of production and replacing them with what were basically family farms, was a spectacular success. Output rose sharply. More significantly, so did productivity. The farming output per head in China did not go up at all between the mid-1950s and 1978. During the first half of the 1980s, real value added in agriculture increased by 7 percent a year while the number of people working the land decreased. It laid the groundwork for the sustained growth of agricultural output and generated a surplus of rural savings needed to finance the industrialization of China. The genius of the reforms was that they captured this surplus not by milking the countryside, as many developing countries' industrialization drives did, but by making the farmers richer (Figure 2.7).

The agricultural sector as a whole continued to perform well after 1984. The average annual growth rate reached 5.4 percent in the 1984–1994 period. However, grain production in China stagnated for several years after peaking in 1984, and in 1994 per capita grain output was 5 percent lower than in 1984. The stagnation and slow growth of grain production after 1984 were mainly due to the fact that reforms in food policies lagged behind reforms in farming institutions.The household responsibility system provided only a one-time boost to peasants' work incentives, and the effects had been realized by 1984. Although individual households were given more autonomy in agricultural production, farmers were still required to meet government grain quotas at below-market prices, and grain market transactions were heavily regulated by the government. The profitability of grain production was much lower than that of other crops and nonfarm activities. Farmers began to allocate resources to more profitable activities such as the production of fruits and aquatic products and township or village enterprises. In 1993 both the procurement and sale prices of grain were decontrolled. Nevertheless, farmers were still required to meet grain quota obligations.

Figure 2-7. Agricultural reforms have led to the revival of rural farms and markets. This farmer in Hubei Province near Wuhan raises pigs and sells them in the open market. On market day the muddy streets of his village are filled with pigs, chickens, and livestock salesmen. (Photo: P. P. Karan.)

Recently, the question of whether China will be able to feed itself in the future has been the focus of worldwide attention. While China's demand for food grain is increasing, its capacity to produce food is shrinking due to the massive conversion of cropland to nonfarm use. China has only 7 percent of the world's arable land and 22 percent of the world's population, which is growing by about 14 million each year. Even this limited farmland is disappearing so rapidly to make way for industry and development that China could once again face the nightmare of food shortages. The total farmland in the country, about 370,000 square miles, has declined by nearly 20 percent since the late 1950s. If the experience of Japan, South Korea, and Taiwan can be used as a measure, China may be expected to average a 48 percent loss of cropland over the next forty years. The problem is most serious in the booming coastal provinces such as Guangdong, which has recorded double-digit economic growth for years because of its proximity to Hong Kong. In the provincial capital of Guangzhou (the city known in colonial times as Canton) downtown land prices equal those of some West European capitals. The city has been turned into one vast construction site, with building cranes rising every few hundred feet along the gray waters of the Pearl River.

The land of the Guangdong Province is prized by farmers for its fertility. But its value to farmers cannot compare to its value as the site of clothing factories, soft-drink bottling plants, or luxury hotels, all of which have recently risen there on what used to be agricultural land. Although the government has issued orders to preserve the farmland in Guangdong Province, as elsewhere in southern China, the huge profits from land sales tend to overwhelm any fears of the central government. With the prospect of millions of dollars in profits on even a small plot of land, the developers and corrupt officials are often willing to take the risk of ignoring instructions from the central governent. Near the booming towns of southern China, superhighways such as the $1 billion highway linking Guangzhou to Hong Kong, and smoke-belching factories have destroyed the quiet farm landscape.

As incomes rise in China, the consumption of meat is increasing even more quickly than the population, placing an ever-greater demand all along the food chain. When China's economic reforms were launched in 1978, only 7 percent of the grain was used for animal feed. By 1990 it had increased to 20 percent, most of that increase to produce pork. Now the demand for beef and poultry is also climbing. More meat means more grain for the feed lot. The potential grain deficit is raising a most difficult question: Who will feed China?

Rice yields in China are starting to level off at around four tons per ha, suggesting that the potential for raising yields further is limited. No country has been able to push the rice yield per ha above five tons. Further dramatic boosts in rice yields in China may not be possible without a new technological breakthrough. With wheat, China's other food staple, the rise in yield is also slowing after jumping 83 percent from 1975 to 1984 with the initiation of economic reforms. Neither is there much prospect of any large gains from the further use of fertilizer, which has been one of the keys to raising yields since the agricultural reforms. After climbing from 7 million tons in 1977 to nearly 29 million tons in 1993, fertilizer use is leveling off as farmers encounter diminishing returns from further applications.

Food production in China is also influenced by several environmental factors such as soil erosion, waterlogging and the salting of irrigation systems, air pollution, and global warming. Soil erosion is common on the half of

China's cropland that is not irrigated. The Huang He (Yellow) River that drains much of Northern China derives its common name from the 1.6 billion tons of ocher-colored topsoil that it annually transports to the ocean. Water-logging and salting are reducing productivity on an estimated 15 percent of China's irrigated land. Air pollution and acid rain are intensifying, too—largely as a result of the increased burning of coal. The result lowers crop yields and forest productivity, not only in China but also in Korea and Japan. Finally, there is the potentially enormous toll of global warming. A rise of 3 degrees Fahrenheit in an average summer temperature would markedly reduce rice yields.

Water scarcity is another factor hindering China's ability to increase its crop productivity. Although roughly half of the total cropland is irrigated, some of this land receives only a fraction of the water needed to maximize yields. Three hundred Chinese cities are already short of water. As the problem worsens, it is likely that urban dwellers will win the struggle to control the water supply and farmers in surrounding rural areas will be denied sufficient water. The result is likely to be greater use of acquifers that will eventually become depleted, causing water tables to fall. This has already occurred in an area of northern China the size of Hungary.

When the loss of farmland to development, the increased demand for grain for the feed lot, and environmental factors are considered, it appears likely that China's grain production will fall by at least 20 percent by 2030, according to Lester Brown of America's Worldwatch Institute. Scholars from China's World Development Institute concede that there will be a deficit but do not agree with the assertion that domestic grain production will decline by 20 percent by 2030. In any case, the deficit will be huge. China's grain yield declined in 1994 to 450 million tons from 456 million tons the year before. Only modest rises have been recorded since 1987. Increasing industrialization will also divert scarce water supplies from fields that already suffer drought in many areas of the country. The same is true of labor. Already tens of millions of Chinese peasants have left the land to contribute to, and profit from, the nation's fast-paced industrialization.

The Chinese Academy of Sciences has observed that if the nation continues to squander its farmland and water resources in a breakneck effort to industrialize, it may have to import massive amounts of grain from the world market. China's only option amounts to a delicately balanced combination of conserving land to minimize the loss in agricultural productivity, investing in water efficiency by pricing water at full cost, and stabilizing its population. These are monumental challenges.

Problems in China's Rural Areas

China's farmers are increasingly discontented. More than 170 instances of unrest by Chinese farmers complaining of the "tyranny" of local government officials have been reported across several provinces. The farmers' complaints are deep rooted, stemming from a distrust of the Communist Party and the local governments. In Sichuan Province angry farmers attacked rural post offices when they would not cash money orders. In Renshou, about 100 km from Chengdu, and in Fujia, about 20 km from Renshou, there were violent protests. There have been peasant demonstrations in the provinces of Heilongjiang, Jilin, and Anhui. The nub of the complaints is that the peasants have once again fallen to the bottom of the economic pecking order.

Rural incomes have failed to keep pace with inflation. Even worse is the fact that because so much local government money has gone into setting up economic development zones and building hotels and offices, local authorities keep running out of money to pay farmers cash for their grain.

During the first half of the 1980s, farmers were the first to benefit from economic reforms when they were given responsibility for their land plots and allowed to sell their produce on the free market. Now that the gap between the prices of industrial and agricultural products has widened, the farmers' incomes have only slowly risen and their financial burden has been too heavy. Out in the heart of the countryside, many peasants are scraping a living from the soil while they see or hear of China's new entrepreneurs getting rich quickly.

Official estimates are that nearly one quarter of farmers' incomes are eaten up by taxes, which cover anything from irrigation works and road building to the use of tractors. The farmers have been hit with charges for a range of expenses, from training the militia to carrying out social welfare projects. The farmers suspect that much of this money simply ends up in the pockets of corrupt officials. All of this means that the reputation of the Communist Party in the rural areas is very poor. Local party officers are for the most part seen as corrupt, and the central government is thought to be ineffective.

The low status of women in China, the rapid shift to market economy, and the easy rural availability of pesticides have led to high rates of female suicide in rural China. Some 56 percent of the world's female suicides—about 500 a day—occur in China, according to a study based on Chinese vital statistics by the World Bank, Harvard University, and the World Health Organization. Most victims are young rural women. In China there are three times as many suicides in the countryside as in the cities. It is the only country where more women than men die as a result of suicide each year: twice as many in the age group under 45. Among rural women lack of sense of their own worth is one of the major reasons for the outbreak of suicides. When the World Bank researchers compared rates in different countries, they found that the overall suicide rate in China (the World Bank put the rate at 30.3 per 100,000 deaths annually) was about three times the average of the rest of the world and that the rate among women was five times that of other countries.

Wary of rural discontent, the central government has launched a campaign to reassure the farmers. In Anhui Province, the campaign has netted more than 300,000 government officials—one fifth of the province's public servants—who were caught stealing or misusing 826 million yuan (about $95 million) in public funds. They spent it on houses and fancy furniture, education for their children, gambling, and visits to prostitutes. Local officials have been ordered to scrap dozens of fees and quotas that have incensed the farmers. The central government agencies are banned from collecting money for 37 kinds of activities, from rodent eradication to movie screening to water improvement. Local officials are forbidden to demand money for 43 kinds of projects, from improving public toilets to building police stations. The sheer scope of fund-raising activity now banned indicates how badly farmers have been squeezed by officials—apparently there was a charge for just about every public service imaginable. Officials are also forbidden to confiscate grain, livestock, or furniture as part of fund-raising activities. Still, there is skepticism in the Chinese countryside over the government's efforts, with some farmers convinced that local officials will just do as they please.

INDUSTRIALIZATION

SOEs and TVEs

The agricultural reforms initiated in 1978 worked so well that China proceeded to change the centrally planned economy to a market system. To begin with, goods were made available through the market rather than through administrative allocation. In 1992 the market rather than the plan distributed 60 percent of the country's coal, 55 percent of the steel, and 90 percent of the cement. The prices of most of the raw material inputs are now market-set and not subject to price controls. The spread of competition was encouraged through foreign trade and investments, and interprovincial rivalry was released by the decentralization of economic power. Every Chinese province has been transfixed by the success of Guangdong, where the real GDP has grown by an amazing 13 percent per year for the past twenty years. Guangdong has had the advantage of being next to Hong Kong, but the province also has a pro-business government.

The biggest spur of all to competition has been the growth of industries, mainly in the countryside, that are not owned by the central government but are not exactly privately owned either. These industries, known as "township and village enterprises" (TVEs), are controlled by units of the local government: counties, townships, or villages. Managers are answerable to local officials and to householders who started the business or invested in it.

Some TVEs' profits go into the local infrastructure such as roads and schools, some are retained for investment, and some are paid as dividends to individual households.

In 1978 there were 1.5 million nonstate industrial firms, employing 28 million people. By 1991 there were 19 million TVEs, employing 96 million people. The output of these firms has been growing by an average of nearly 30 percent per year for more than a decade. By the early 1990s TVEs accounted for nearly 40 percent of China's industrial employment, more than 25 percent of the industrial output, and nearly 25 percent of the exports. The provinces where TVEs are strongest—the coastal belt stretching from Guangdong in the south to Shandong in the east—have been the source of China's economic miracle.

In 1978, just before the reforms began, state-owned enterprises (SOEs) accounted for 78 percent of China's industrial output. The state share has fallen by more than 2 percentage points per year. It was estimated to decline to 25 percent by the year 2000. SOEs in China and in other countries have not functioned well because they are geared toward the bureaucracy that gives them orders rather than toward the customers who buy from them, toward output rather than profit, and toward the social welfare of their employees rather than toward efficiency. In 1991 the losses of Chinese SOEs grew to 55 billion yuan.

SOEs range from airlines to steel producers and bicycle manufacturers. Some firms such as Shanghai Automotive Industries, Deqing Petroleum, and Anshan Iron and Steel are among Asia's largest companies. SOEs employ 110 million workers—almost equivalent to the entire American workforce. They are running at a loss. Many are undercapitalized and crippled by debts, both to each other and to China's banks. State-owned industry accounts for nine tenths of outstanding bank loans (5 trillion yuan or $600 billion) in China, equivalent to about 70 percent of the GDP. At least one third of the workers at state enterprises are nonproductive because of overmanning. SOEs also provide a wide range of social services to workers. Some are self-contained communities that feed, house, and care for employees and their families from the cradle to the grave. Nearly 6 percent of a typical SOE's costs and 40 percent of its wages are absorbed by social services. In addition, the TVEs are providing increasing competition to the SOEs in such industries as consumer goods and textiles.

In 1997 China announced its intention to convert state-owned enterprises to private ownership. China's leaders have been talking about separating government from business, but have been stymied by the difficulty of pursuading officials and workers schooled in old communist ways to adapt. Wary of the Russian record in trying to shock the system into sudden privatization, China wants to make the switch more gradually through a combination of mergers, shareholding systems, and public listing of shares. The legal framework to set up the most basic guidelines for a new corporate system will need to be developed. Today (as in the 1980s) roughly one Chinese adult in five works for the state, where only a small portion of enterprises turn a profit. China has been able to afford to carry its unprofitable state sector because the business sector outside the state has been growing rapidly.

The major areas of industrial concentration are in the Shanghai-Nanjing area, the Beijing-Tianjin region, the Anshan-Shenyang area, and the Guang-zhou region. During the 1960s industrial development was promoted in the interior cities, resulting in several major centers of industrial activity such as Baotou, Lanzhou, Chengdu, Chongqing, and Kunming.

The Anshan-Shenyang area lies in China's industrial heartland, where large-scale communist industry was born of exuberant idealism in the 1950s and is now flailing for life. As the government in 1998 started drastically pruning thousands of bloated, money-losing state industries, workers were laid off by the millions all over China. But nowhere are the effects more severe than in rust-belt northeastern cities such as Harbin and Shenyang, where many experts believe (there are no reliable published data) the unemployment rate exceeds 20 percent. Harbin No. 1 Tool Factory laid off 2,000 of its 10,000 workers in 1998. Here and around the country, one third of China's 100 million state workers must be laid off if surviving companies are to pay their own way.

The extent of serious suffering from unemployment is hard to gauge. Like those in the Harbin area, many laid-off workers have found new ways (Figure 2.8) to make money, though often by working in competition with the rural migrants who have streamed into China's cities to work as day laborers or peddlers or nannies, and in jobs without the accustomed security or health and retirement benefits. It is not clear what the effect will be as more industrial workers begin to compete for these same lowly positions. For China's vast hinterlands, low-end work in the cities has been a vital safety valve.

Some of China's manufacturing industries continue to export prison-made goods to the United States by disguising their origins and mixing prison products with legitimate exports, according to a study by the Laogai Research Foundation in June 1993. The Chinese gulag is known as the *laogai,* or reform-through-labor, prison system. American businesses take advantage of cheap, forced labor from China. For example, one American company, Columbus McKinnon Corporation of Amherst, New York is reported to be the sole agent for chain and lever hoists manufactured by the Zhejiang Province No.4 Prison, which publicly goes by the name of the Hangzhou Wulin Machinery Plant. Prisons in the northeastern city of Shenyang produce half of China's rubber vulcanizing accelerators, or chemicals, and millions of pairs of rubber boots for export. An estimated 10 million Chinese are incarcerated in China's prison system, which is said to generate some $100 million in exports annually.

Figure 2-8. Changchun City, Jilin Province. In this city in China's industrial northeast, laid-off workers supplement their meager pensions by working as bicycle guards in front of a large department store. The unemployment rate in this region is increasing because of the lay-offs by money-losing state-owned industries. As the overhaul of China's moribund state industries enters a decisive phase, public protests by displaced workers are becoming larger. Economic reforms have yanked away from employees of the state companies the lifetime social safety net known as the "iron rice bowl"; 26 million have been laid off in recent years. Corruption thrives in the Communist Party, and crime is rising on the streets. Although its economy is opening, China remains a police state. Dissenters and followers of "unauthorized" religions are arrested. (Photo: Robert Beatty.)

Industrial Restructuring and Foreign Investment

Direct foreign investment by Hong Kong, Taiwan, Japan, the United States, and the Western European countries has played a major role in China's development and industrial restructuring. A large part of direct foreign investment in China has been directed toward the manufacturing and service sectors. Foreign investment in China has been motivated by its immense market potential and the attractiveness of an abundant, inexpensive labor force.

Following the adoption of the Joint Venture Law in 1979 by the China's People's Congress, foreign firms began to enter into joint ventures with Chinese businesses. The first and still largest wave of foreign investment came from what China calls "compatriots" in Taiwan and Hong Kong. These investors set up joint ventures with the TVEs to produce textiles and goods for export. Hong Kong and Taiwan account for over three fifths of the foreign investment. Between 1983 and 1998, China, Taiwan, and Hong Kong have become one integrated economic region, but the investments and economic ties have not eliminated the political rivalry between China and Taiwan. Economics is clearly the engine driving these entities into an increasingly close economic relationship. Business services, including finance, advertising, communications, and most corporate headquarters, remain in the Hong

Kong central business district, whereas most manufacturing has moved toward the periphery located in Guangdong and Fujian and has spread northward along the China coast. The United States is the largest market for the products of this economic region, and Japan is the largest supplier of capital goods and technology.

The economy of this region is formulated on the so-called Taiwan model. China opens her vast, cheap labor market and allows foreign capital and technological know-how to set up factories for export-oriented products. The low-cost, labor-based exports earn China a large sum of foreign currencies. China in turn uses these earned foreign currencies to subsidize its ailing but vast state-owned industries. An important measure in this Chinese structure is closing their domestic market. The major outlet for this low-cost product is traditionally the United States. United States trade deficit with China has increased as the Chinese economy and exports have expanded. Japan and Europe have carefully guarded against the inflow of the products of this low-cost, labor-based sector. Unfortunately, when China buys low-level and medium-level technologies, it turns to Japan. When Taiwan and Hong Kong enterprises open factories in China to manufacture export-oriented goods, they buy machines and other things from Japan.

The first joint venture between China and Japan was set up in Tianjin in early 1981 by the China Medical Industry Corporation and Japan's major pharmaceutical firm, the Otsuka Pharmaceutical Company, as a 50-50 partnership. Shortly after Otsuka, Hitachi established a TV manufacturing venture with the Fujian Industrial Investment Corporation and the Fujian Electronics Import and Export Company. By mid-1985 there were 102 Sino-Japanese joint ventures, and Japan ranked second only to Hong Kong in foreign investment. Investment from Japan, initially localized in north coastal Shandong and Liaoning provinces, is growing and spreading southward.

The Japanese ventures in China differ in many ways from those of the United States and other countries. The Japanese have invested a much smaller proportion in manufacturing. Out of 466 cases, only 337 (66 percent) were directed to production, compared with 83 percent by the United States and about 73 percent by other countries. Compared with the United States, only a few Chinese industries—textiles and garments, wood and furniture, and precision machinery—have attracted a large proportion of Japanese investors. Except for precision machinery, the number of Japanese ventures in the machinery industry is much lower than the number of United States ventures in that industry. Chemicals, ceramics, and cement have drawn more investments from the United States and fewer from Japan. On the other hand, the service industry, real estate, commerce, and construction are sectors where a larger share of Japanese investment was made compared with the United States. In terms of a sectoral composition of direct foreign investment in China, Japan and the United States stand at the extreme ends and the other countries as a group fall in the middle.

Geographically, the bulk of the foreign direct investment is located in China's coastal provinces (Guangdong, Fujian, Jiangsu, Liaoning, and Shandong) and the three municipalities (Beijing, Tianjin, and Shanghai). Japan's direct foreign investment in China is largely concentrated in the three municipalities; as much as 41 percent of Japanese ventures went to one of the three major cities, compared with only 35 percent of the U.S. ventures. The coastal provinces received 51 percent of the Japanese investment, and 47 percent of the U.S. investment. Japan invested only 7 percent in the eighteen inland provinces, but the United States directed as much as 17 percent to that area. The coastal province of Guangdong is the most favored location for investment by both the Japanese and the Americans.

CHINA'S ECONOMIC GROWTH AND THE ENVIRONMENT

China's economic revolution might be dotting the countryside with new factories and electricity plants, but it is also having unintended effects: the air and water in some of its leading cities are heavily polluted, and China is contributing to global warming faster than any other major country.

The enormous human and environmental toll of China's rapid development is not only an unintended side effect but also an explicit choice by business executives and officials who tolerate deaths and environmental degradation as the inevitable price of progress. Most industries do not spend much money to treat industrial toxic wastes. For example, Taizhou's main industrial area (Yantou) in Zhejiang Province (south of Shanghai) lies on the East China Sea. Here, several Chinese companies produce drugs based on foreign investment and international partnerships with American companies such as Drug Store and Eli Lilly. These companies release 3.6 million tons of water laden with organic and inorganic compounds that receive little or no processing. Yantou's shoreline is edged with sludge. Inland, the air is sulfurous. Polluted seawater causes the hands and legs of local fisherman to become ulcerated. Elevated rates of cancer and respiratory diseases among residents have appeared in national environmental reports. The Medical Information Institute in Zhejiang Province found a correlation between children born with birth defects and the chemical pollutants, yet one of the comparative economic advantages for Chinese industry is that it does not have to spend much on anti-pollution systems.

Most countries have become increasingly aware that the warming of the earth could cause climatic changes and rising sea levels. Even the United States, which contributes more to the greenhouse effect than any other country, is considering putting curbs on the gases that are thought to cause global warming. But in China there is little awareness of the problem. China burns increasing amounts of coal.

The rate of growth in China's carbon dioxide emissions is far greater than any other major emitter in the world. Burning coal produces carbon dioxide, the most significant greenhouse gas, but coal is China's main source of energy and thus an essential element of its strategy to catch up with the industrial world. During the wintertime, plumes of black smoke rise from the chimneys of millions of homes that burn coal for warmth. In major cities, where few homes use gas heating, a typical family might burn nearly half a ton of coal during the winter. Three quarters of China's energy comes from coal, and power generators and industrial boilers pump hundreds of thousands of tons of carbon dioxide into the air each year. Each year China mines more than a billion metric tons of coal, more than any other country in the world. By the end of 2000, the country was producing 1.4 billion tons each year, almost all of which it will burn at home. By the year 2020, it could mine 2 billion tons a year—half the world's production.

China is aware of the pollution that unrestrained coal burning can cause, aside from the risks of global warming. But the government has made its position clear: it will not sacrifice development for the environment. At last count, in 1989, China produced 9.1 percent of the gases that contribute to global warming, ranking third in the world. The United States produced the largest amount, 17.8 percent; the former Soviet Union produced 13.6 percent. On a per capita basis, China does not even rank in the top fifty countries; each American released nine times as much greenhouse gas as each Chinese. But if China's gross domestic product grows 8.5 percent a year for the next three decades—which is improbable but not impossible, since China's economy grew by 9.7 percent per year in the 1980s—then by 2025, the amount of carbon dioxide released could be three times the amount released by the United States. The International Energy Agency in Paris predicts that the increase in greenhouse gas emissions from 2000 to 2030 in China will nearly equal the increase from the entire industrialized world.

As China surpasses the United States and other industrial countries as the largest single producer of climate-warming carbon dioxide, China itself may face serious consequences from global warming as rising sea levels inundate coastal zones. Researchers at the Chinese Academy of Sciences believe that global climate changes during the next thirty to fifty years could cause a 1-meter rise in sea levels which, when magnified by storm tides, would inundate an area the size of Portugal on China's coastal plain, including the important manufacturing centers at Shanghai and Guangzhou, forcing 67 million people to abandon their land and homes. Equally vulnerable is China's straining agricultural base, which must nearly double its harvest to feed more than 1.6 billion Chinese who will live in the country thirty years from now.

Though uncertainties abound in these projections, profound concerns about the potential impact of global climate change have mobilized China's scientific community. But for China's Communist Party leaders, the question of who should bear the burden of reducing the enormous volume of warming gases draws a fiercely nationalistic response and quickly turns to the question of whether the West is seeking to limit China's emergence as a great power.

Many Western and Chinese scientists believe that despite China's dependence on coal for the foreseeable future, China's emissions of carbon dioxide could be held to a doubling instead of a tripling of output during the next thirty years by increasing efficiency and investment in alternative energy sources. But that would require a huge mobilization of capital, technology, and political commitment. With its huge reserves of coal, China sees any energy alternative that costs more or requires more capital as a threat to its development. Much of China's coal is produced from small coal mines. There is no sorting, cleaning, or washing, and this kind of coal generates a tremendous amount of pollution. The decentralization of economic power in China has made it more likely that boilers for heat, steam, or electrical generation will become even smaller and less efficient.

A chemical analysis of acid rain in Japan indicates that the problem in Japan stems from emissions in China. Acid rain during the winter in Niigata Prefecture, which is on the coast of the Sea of Japan, contains a mix of sulfur and sulfer oxides consistent with emissions from the burning of Chinese coal. Acid rain in Niigata contained the same quantities of the sulfur isotopes S32 and S34 that are found in Chinese emissions. Sulfur oxides, nitrogen, and other substances that cause acid rain originate from the burning of fossil fuels such as coal and oil. Because the mixture of sulfur oxides and sulfur isotopes varies according to the type of fossil fuel consumed, it can be used to trace the origin of polluted air. The burning of coal in China produces emissions with S34 concentrations; these are more than three times as high as that found in emissions from factories in Niigata Prefecture itself.

To get a comprehensive view, scientists checked for S34 in rain and snow in Nagaoka, Niigata Prefecture, during 1991. The results showed that quantities of the acid rain–related substance rapidly increased during the months of January, February, November, and December of 1991, when seasonal winds from the Chinese mainland blew across the Sea of Japan. China's massive consumption of coal, which is causing the acid rain problems in Northeast Asia, is certain to become a global problem in the near future. China refuses to allow any joint monitoring of its acid rain problem, insisting that it is a domestic issue.

Coal burning and wind-blown dust from the Loess Plateau are the major sources of air pollution in cities of northern China such as Beijing, Shenyang, and Benxi, where pollution is compounded by poor air dispersal and low-level temperature inversions. In southern China, acid precipitation is a growing problem, especially in Sichuan, Guangxi, Hunan, Jiangxi, and Guangdong (Figure 2.9).

Development over the past twenty years has led to rapid growth in the number of cars and motor scooters without any pollution control technology on the roads, increasing the emission of hydrocarbons. China is already the

Figure 2-9. China's industrial regions, cities with severe air pollution, and potential nuclear hazard zones (based on Global Environment Monitoring System).

world's fastest-growing car market, with sales up 73 percent in 2003. General Motors predicts that China will account for 18 percent of the world's growth in new car sales from 2002 through 2012. If China can sustain this growth, then the next big growth area in greenhouse emissions is likely to be cars. Air pollution, including cigarette smoke, is responsible for serious health problems in China and accounted for 26 percent of all deaths in 1988. Some cities such as Benxi are switching to natural gas and have launched clean-up efforts based on the polluter-pays principle, in which factories that create pollution are required to finance the cost of clean-up. Sichuan Province plans to impose taxes on polluting inputs such as coal to encourage conservation and use of coal with less sulfur and ash. The installation of pollution control technology and price reforms on domestic coal (the bulk of which is sold below the cost of mining) can be effective mechanisms to control air pollution in Chinese cities.

About 80 percent of urban river water in China is polluted with ammonium nitrate, volatile phenol, and oxygen-consuming organic matter. About one-third of the industrial wastewater enters rivers, lakes, and seas without treatment, causing damage to marine resources and human health. Urban drinking water is generally poor. The widespread practice of boiling water reduces some contamination but does not eliminate the toxins.

The large number of widely dispersed and small TVEs, which are responsible for China's industrial boom, use outdated pollution control technology and discharge most of their industrial effluents into the environment. The bulk of the TVEs' pollution comes from the brick and tile, porcelain and pottery, cement, and paper and pulp industries.

A recent World Bank study estimates that if China does not improve its environment, its urban residents face 600,000 premature deaths and 5.5 million cases of chronic bronchitis a year by 2020 because of exposure to fine particles in the air. Moreover, a report released in Kyoto at the Global Climatic Change Conference in 1997 by the Washington-based World Resources Institute says that the use of fossil fuels releases tiny particles that carry toxic heavy metals that can infiltrate the bloodstream through the lungs.

GROWING INEQUALITY AND CORRUPTION

China's fast economic growth has raised several concerns. With increasing urbanization and industrialization, more and more farmers, who produce food for China's 1.2 billion people, are quitting their jobs. Corruption and crime are rampant, making it more difficult to steer the country. The supply of steel, cement, and other raw materials has been insufficient to meet the demands created by rapid growth, pushing up their prices by more than 10 percent. Extreme inadequacies in the transport infrastructure have created serious problems.

China's shift from a planned economy toward a market economy involved the dismantling of old controls but not their replacement with new ones. As noted earlier, in rural villages, accelerated economic development has rapidly decreased the amount of farmland. Discontented with their relatively unprofitable occupations, a growing number of farmers are abandoning their land and moving to other areas. The Chinese government blames the expansion of new economic zones for the rapid contraction of farmland and has blocked the establishment of such zones. Since the latter half of the 1950s, the amount of farmland has continually shrunk, depressed by urbanization and industrialization. Farmland is now shrinking by an average of 400,000 ha each year.

Another problem stemming from China's shift to a socialist-style market economy is a sharp growth in crime and corruption at the local government level. The situation is extremely serious in the southern investment enclaves. On January 9, 1993, a Guangdong Province court simultaneously handed down verdicts to about 1,200 defendents, about 300 of whom received sentences of death or life imprisonment. The largest corruption case in the nation's recent history, involving $6.72 million in bribes, was uncovered in a Hainan Province special economic zone.

Corruption is widespread and flagrant at the township, county, and even the provincial level. An anticorruption drive was instituted in 1994, with mass public trials and summary executions. Although this may be enough to strike fear briefly into the local cadres, the higher ranks of the Communist Party are still untouched. The depth of corruption within the Party is impossible to gauge but easy to guess at—just count the stolen limousines with smoked-glass windows that cruise the boulevards of China's cities. So completely has the culture of money saturated the Party that anything done in the name of securing wealth, save for the crudest bribery, seems permissible. Entrepreneurs and bankers in China and Hong Kong flock to present foolproof deals to the sons or daughters of leaders, hoping for favors in return. Big money from China, some of it hot, is conspicuous in Hong Kong's property and share markets.

The rapid development has spawned a small but all-too-visible class of super rich—known as "princelings"—who have acquired wealth and power not because of their business skills but because of their bloodlines. The princelings are the sons and daughters of the Communist elite. The princelings are a potent issue because, for all of China's economic success, much of the vast country is still either desperately poor or suffering from the excesses of runaway capitalism, or both. The divide between rich and poor is growing. Consumption, particularly of cars, including luxury sedans like BMWs, is soaring in big cities. Still, peasants can occasionally be seen riding mules on the outskirts of Beijing. Some of those cast off by the new economy have vented their anger in protests. Many demonstrations are small and peaceful, but some are large and violent.

A major effect of rapid development has been the strengthening of the position of cities and provinces, shrinking the Party's power to plan the economy from the center. Although rapid development is giving many more people previously unheard of freedoms, including the choice of where to live, work, and spend money, the relations between the central government, on the one hand, and China's twenty-two provinces, three metropolitan areas and five autonomous regions, on the other, are troubling the Party. The extreme case is Guangdong, which leads China in trade and inward investment and is largely self-financing. It pays little of its tax revenues to the central government and receives little central-government investment in return. In 1994 the central government was trying to bring China's growth rate down to 9 percent from the 13 percent rate in 1993, but Guangdong did not respond. It continued to profit from its inflow of foreign investment. Shenzhen, next to Hong Kong, grew by 30 percent in real terms in 1993 and has no plans to grow by a piffling 9 percent anytime soon. With Guangdong setting its own economic policy, there is schism between a big provincial Communist Party and the central authority. Rapid growth has created regional rivalries among the provincial governments which are hungry for new revenues. They speculate in property and invest in light industries and service businesses that they hope will bring quick returns, but neglect investment in infrastructure.

China's economic growth has brought unparalleled affluence to many Chinese, but misery to others. In the past, communist ideals of equality and the superiority of the working class largely prevented abuses in the workplace. But these ideals have eroded after twenty-five years of economic reforms. Reports of worker abuse have been surfacing with increasing frequency as economic reforms have also infused society with greed and a get-rich-at-all-costs mentality. Young women, particularly peasant women, are most vulnerable to unscrupulous employers. They generally don't know their rights, and they make up the bulk of the workforce in small, private establishments such as restaurants and dance halls and in foreign factories turning out toys or shoes. Peasants eager to leave their farms for city jobs also have fallen victims to scams.

Heavy emphasis on raising production has placed a relatively low priority on safety in the workplace. Accidents took the lives of 11,500 workers during the first nine months of 2003, an increase of 9 percent over the corresponding period a year earlier, according to China's State Administration on Work Safety data. Death in the workplace in China is far disproportionate to workplace fatalities in other countries. Coal mines continue to be the most dangerous places to work. A record number of 4,620 coal miners lost their lives in accidents between January and September of 2003, a reduction of 1 percent from the corresponding period in 2002. The modest improvement came as a result of intense efforts to shut down illegal mines. The other industries that contribute to the spike in workplace deaths are construction and fireworks, both of which rely heavily on migrant workers who receive little or no training. China's socialist laws theoretically protect workers even as the country embraces capitalist ways. But the authorities crush efforts to set up independent unions because they are perceived as a threat to the Communist Party. Often the sole legal state-run union is a charade, a feckless bureaucracy that makes only a pretense of representing the proletariat.

The migration of staggering numbers of peasants from the countryside to wealthier cities threatens to create an urban underclass. Pollution and environmental degradation are appalling. Neglect of industrial safety kills thousands a year in mines and factories. The growing disparity of wealth is creating bitter divisions, triggering unrest from Shenyang to Sichuan.

To address some of the negative effects of development and solidify the market economy, the next round of reforms in China would require enormous political courage. China would need to reform the dangerously over-extended financial system to allow banks to become real lending institutions rather than funnels of credit to bloated, state-run companies (SOEs). But if inefficient SOEs were allowed to go bankrupt, an estimated 30 million workers employed in state-owned enterprises would be laid off without a social safety net, resulting in more painful dislocation.

POPULATION IN THE PEOPLE'S REPUBLIC

China's historical population data start with the year 2 A.D.; the Chinese reportedly numbered about 60 million at that time. Some twelve centuries after the birth of Christ, when the Mongols were driven out of China and the Ming Dynasty was founded, the population was again reported at around 60 million, despite the fact that in the interim there were periods when it was reported at over 100 million. During the Manchu period from the middle of the seventeenth century, the population generally increased until the devastating Taiping Rebellion in 1851. That rebellion, and a series of smaller, more localized revolts, resulted in millions of deaths, not only from the civil wars but also from floods, famines, and epidemics that followed. The population declined from a recorded high of over 430 million just prior to the Taiping Rebellion to a figure usually estimated at between 375 and 400 million, when the empire fell in 1911. In 1949 the population was estimated at 541 million.

After the Communists assumed power, a census was organized in 1953. According to this census the total population on the Chinese mainland was 582 million. In 1983 China's population was 1,025 million. The 2001 national census recorded the population at 1,260 million. Some analysts believe that the census figure underestimated the population and the annual growth rate (1.07 percent). Counting China's massive population is extremely difficult, and is made more so by its one-child policy; tens of millions of people with extra children are thought to have hidden them from census takers for fear of being punished. During the period 1953–2003, China's population doubled. The basic task confronting China has been to feed, house, educate, and employ this vast population.

Intense family planning efforts since the 1970s, which merged into the 1978 campaign limiting each family to one child, have propelled China through a demographic transition. The pre-1949 era was characterized by a high birth rate, high death rate, and hence low rates of population growth (Figure 2.10). A dramatic decline in mortality in the 1950s and 1960s, combined with high fertility, triggered the population explosion. Improvements in water supplies, food production and distribution, sanitation, and medical care had a very beneficial effect on reducing mortality levels. Between 1949 and 1957 China's death rate fell by about 20 points, from about 38 to 18 per thousand. The demographic success was temporarily reversed by the demographic disaster of 1998–1962. At the height of the disaster the death rate exceeded the birth rate and China's population went into decline. Between 1958 and 1961 China had some 25 to 30 million more deaths and experienced 30 to 35 million fewer births because of the nationwide famine arising from the

Figure 2-10. China's demographic transition (based on official Chinese data).

political mismanagement of the Great Leap Forward and a consequent decline in grain production.

In the 1970s the government engineered a spectacular decline in fertility. By the end of the decade, a combination of late marriages, the adoption of modern forms of contraception by almost 70 percent of married couples, and the considerable use of induced abortion reduced the fertility rate substantially. In 1978 came the one-child policy, aimed not only at reducing the growth rate, but also at eventually reducing the size of China's population. By the 1980s the relatively low birth rate, low death rate, and small family size reduced the population's growth rate to modest proportions (Figure 2.11).

To pursuade couples to accept the one-child policy, China adopted a system of financial rewards and penalties. One-child families get a wide range of benefits. These vary, but can include monthly subsidies, higher retirement pensions for the parents, a greater allocation of land, lower grain taxes, and easier access to good schools. A fine for a child born out of the plan can be up to two year's income, but villages tend to set their own fines. Some even offer installment plans for families that cannot pay the fine in one lump sum. The government also uses pressure tactics, aimed at making people feel guilty if they breach the one-child policy. The incentives are linked to an efficient monitoring system—which includes about 13 million volunteers—intended to detect pregnancies as soon as possible. Villages and townships keep lists of all women of childbearing age, and oblige them to undergo gynecological check-ups every three months—apparently to ensure that no one conceals a pregnancy.

One of the most effective methods of preventing unauthorized pregnancies is the obligatory sterilization of couples who have already had two or more children. But it is common for mothers to flee their villages when they are

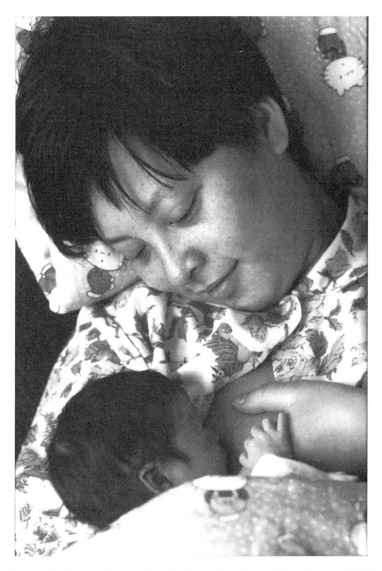

Figure 2-11. A mother breastfeeds her baby at the International Peace, Maternity and Child Hospital in Shanghai. Population growth is a pressing concern for China, but the one-child family policy and maternal-child health services have reduced the pace of growth. (Photo: UNICEF by Roger Lemoyne.)

summoned for sterilization or when they are expecting a baby outside of the plan. The most common reason for couples to breach the policy is that they want a son, to continue the family name and ancestry. In the Chinese tradition, daughters are married out of the family, but sons remain to care for their parents in their old age. Thus, parents often keep having children until they have a son.

The one-child policy has been successful in cities but has fallen short in rural areas, where the majority of couples still want a larger family. In the countryside, population control has caused a mixture of anger, support, frustration, enthusiasm, deviousness, and pain. Many Chinese intellectuals endorse the policy and believe it has given new hope for their country's long-term development, but it has also ruined marriages, intensified sexist attitudes, and led to murder, bribery, abandonment, and countless battles between mothers and daughters-in-laws. Women often become emotionally disturbed when pressured to have abortions. There have long been criticisms abroad of China's one-child policy because the program is coercive. However, the family planning policy has made substantial progress over the last twenty-five years. The one-child policy is being relaxed now because of the government's growing concern over the reverse demographic pyramid that confronts China (there will be too few young people to take care of older generations). Thus, it is now acceptable for couples in which both the husband and wife are from families that had only one child to themselves have two children.

Children from China's mandatory one-child families are often referred to as "little emperors" because they are spoiled and passive. Their parents shield them from household chores. Now parents are sending their spoiled only children to camps for toughening. In recent years a number of summer camps have developed where children from one-child families are taught to fend for themselves. Far from their coddled lives at home, they march in the Gobi Desert, herd cattle and sheep in the grasslands, and train with army units. Nearly one million children went to summer camps in 1994, an increase from a few hundred thousand in 1993. The voluntary camps are mostly financed by the government and donations from parents and sponsors. They are run by the Chinese Young Pioneers, the communist youth organization.

The soaring population and insufficient farmland are major problems in China, but the country has come to grips with the problems, giving its present and future generations a greater opportunity to rise above poverty. Most urban Chinese now accept the idea that they can have only one child, and even in the countryside people want fewer children than their parents had, although they still frequently want more than the government allows.

The demographic transition has presented China with a great challenge to the traditional method of supporting the elderly. By 2004, China will have 130 million people over the age of 60, accounting for 10 percent of the country's population. Over the next fifty years, China's aging population will increase by 3 percent per year. Old people have been looked after by their families for centuries. As the country becomes more urbanized, more rural youngsters are rushing to the city, making it harder for them to care for their parents in the countryside. The decline of the extended family, coupled with the rise of the nuclear version, has also weakened the support systems. As more of China's one-child-family children get married, those couples will find it hard to support two sets of parents with no help from siblings. As people live longer, there is a greater incidence of families of four generations, and the breadwinners have to support their own children, their parents, and their grandparents. As a result of these changes, the method by which China switches from family-based care to a social insurance system is becoming a very significant issue.

The Urban Population

In 2000, China had 668 designated cities with a total population of 376 million, comprising 30.9 percent of the country's population. Thirty-four cities had populations of more than one million each. Of the eleven cities with more than 2 million people, the largest were Shanghai, Beijing, Tianjin, Shenyang, Wuhan, Guangzhou, Harbin, Chongqing, and Nanjing; they accounted for nearly one quarter of the total city population of China. A characteristic feature of these "extra large cities," as they are called by Chinese writers, is their widely dispersed pattern of geographic distribution. Except for Tianjin and Nanjing, which are located close to Beijing and Shanghai, respectively, all of the largest cities are separated by distances of between 500 and 1,000 km (300 to 600 miles), reflecting the long-standing primacy of the traditional regional centers.

In the early 1950s, the rural-to-urban migration was fairly free and cities grew rapidly. Since the mid-1950s, the national policy has been to restrict urban growth by controlling the rural-to-urban migration and by encouraging the industrialization and growth of small and medium-sized cities. China's urban population growth was heavily affected by the state's development policies and was controlled by direct and indirect administrative restrictions on migration. The commanding position of the state in the centrally planned economy gave the government much greater power and a more effective means of controlling migration than that existing in market economies.

With the implementation of the new economic reforms in urban areas, government controls on rural-to-urban migration were relaxed. China's strict residence-registration system disintegrated. In 1984 a new policy permitted farmers to move permanently to officially designated towns or market towns and to engage in nonagricultural activities. In 1985 the state further relaxed its control on migration to cities and towns by permitting migrants to become temporary urban residents. Changes in government policy have made it increasingly easy for peasants to migrate to towns and cities. The massive influx of rural Chinese to the cities—as many as 100 million by one estimate—is a major challenge confronting the government. Known colloquially as *mang liu,* or "blind flow," this migration is changing the face of China (Figure 2.12). Workers in the cities earn nearly three times as much money as those in the countryside, and they send much of it home, sometimes supporting entire villages.

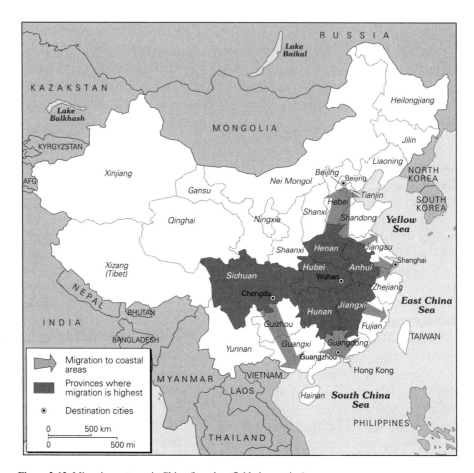

Figure 2-12. Migration patterns in China (based on field observation).

MIGRATION FROM POORER RURAL PROVINCES TO CITIES
AND PROSPEROUS COASTAL REGIONS

The man camped outside the Guangzhou station had arrived ten days earlier as part of a thirteen-member group from his village in Henan Province. It was their first time in Guangzhou. They had spent the day perched on huge sacks containing their belongings, hoping someone would offer them jobs. But none had yet found any work.

Under a nearby tree, a farmer from Hunan Province lay on his back, legs crossed, reading a paperback love story. It was his first visit, too, and he was not sure how to look for a job. A group of thirty from Sichuan Province was more fortunate; it was their third year back in Guangdong Province and they were returning to the site of past jobs—building a sea-wall in a coastal town.

The Guangzhou station forecourt and the surrounding streets have become an open-air jobs bazaar. Red posters stuck on trees and concrete posts advertise work in textile factories and on building sites. Nearly 90 million people are streaming from the rural provinces such as Sichuan, Anhui, Henan, Jiangxi, and Hubei to the booming coastal cities. Some return to existing jobs after the annual holiday, but up to half may have set off with no firm destination after hearing tales of lucrative urban opportunities or because of the lack of work at home. The migrants head for the strong economies of the Pearl River Delta cities.

Migrant rural girls head for Beijing to work as nannies and maids, a burgeoning market. Some are attracted to jobs in Shanghai's huge Pudong development zone. Most of the migrants from Sichuan and rural Hubei Province travel through Wuhan, the communication hub of China, either by train or on the Yangtze ferries.

The tidal wave of migrant workers was first noticeable in 1987. It fell back around 1990 because of China's austerity program, which reduced casual work, but in recent years it has grown rapidly. Peasants used to be tied down by the strict household registration system which specified their place of residence and made it difficult for them to obtain food and lodging in the cities. These days farmland can be contracted out and train tickets bought without a permit. The economic reforms mean that food and lodging can be bought without government coupons or permission.

Although new freedoms provide opportunities, many people are now leaving rural life because they have to. The surplus labor on farms and in rural state enterprises is huge; wages are low and a big income gap is opening up between the countryside and the city. Many migrants are poorly paid for doing lowly, unwanted jobs. They are emerging as an urban underclass and living in poor accommodations–though they could still be better off than at home.

At the top of the urban hierarchy in China are the three independent municipalities with provincial status: Shanghai, Beijing, and Tianjin. Guangzhou, the largest extended metropolis in South China, is also a national urban center. These are followed by smaller municipalities controlled by the provinces which, in turn, are followed by a large number of towns.

Beijing: Development and Urban Structure

Beijing, which was founded about 1000 B.C., became the capital of the territory ruled by the Zhou dynasty. It lies at the junction of hilly northeast China and the North China Plain, which favored the growth of the city. Beijing became the capital of the Ming Dynasty (1405). The city covered an area of 62 square km within a city wall and contained nearly one million people. Despite many political changes, the urban outline of Beijing remained intact until 1949, when the People's Republic of China was founded.

Historical sentiment and the traditional belief in geomancy influenced the choice of Beijing as the capital in 1949. Historically, Beijing seemed always to symbolize a powerful dynasty with numerous military conquests and immense territorial expansion, though it was a capital of alien rule, as exemplified by the Mongol Dynasty. According to traditional geomancy (*Feng-shui*) any structure placed by man on the landscape must harmonize perfectly with local physical features. For a walled city, a site backed by a hill or mountain and facing the water was ordinarily considered good. Since the Gulf of Chihli is enclosed by the Liaodong and Shandong peninsulas, this more or less symmetric physical arrangement was often thought to have had a favorable influence on the location of the capital city of Beijing.

Since 1950, the urban development of Beijing has grown outward from the city center to the suburban areas. Core government offices are located in the old city and new housing districts have developed in the peripheral areas outside it. Because some of the housing in the old inner city has been replaced by new offices, the urban land use structure of the old city has changed. Many large factories were also constructed, mostly in the industrial district located to the east of the city center. Factory labor is drawn from the rural areas of the nearby provinces and from the old city. The middle-size and small factories are located toward the north and northwest areas of the inner city. The industrial growth around Beijing has caused serious environmental problems, particularly in the eastern and southern suburbs.

To the northwest of the old city, a new office district with many central government institutes has developed. Residential districts were developed near these facilities to house the people who work in the area.

Since the economic reforms of the 1980s, retail and commercial enterprises have increased rapidly. The major shopping centers are situated around the Forbidden City and Tiananmen Square, which is the center of the city.

Three distinct residential areas can be identified, based on the various urban development periods. The old inner city, which was built before 1949, is distinguished by old houses and a high-density population (reaching 57,400 per square km in some areas). The peripheral residential belts developed during the 1950s are occupied by the staff of government institutes, factories, and other enterprises. Surrounding this zone are modern residential areas, built mostly since the 1970s.

Based on the internal structure of the city, five zones may be identified in Beijing.

1. **The city core.** This area consists of the Forbidden City, the old city center, and the new buildings surrounding the core which house offices of the central government. It also contains three large shopping and service centers. People living in the city core neighborhoods work in the office, commercial, and service sectors.

2. **The inner city residential zone.** This is one of the most crowded areas in Beijing, with very old housing. Residents of this zone work in the commercial, service, official, and manufacturing sectors.

3. **The periphery belt of the inner city.** This area has mixed land use with residential, industrial, commercial, and service functions. Residents living in this zone are employed in the manufacturing, retailing, and service sectors. High-rise housing and offices have grown rapidly in this zone.

4. **The new development zone.** This area has developed mostly since the mid-1970s and contains housing and offices; the latter comprise a large area.

5. **The outer zone.** This area lies at the rural fringe of the city. The agricultural land in this area is being rapidly converted to urban use.

The uncontrolled flow of rural workers into the cities has resulted in teeming underclass enclaves of migrant laborers on the outskirts of Beijing. The outsiders, or *wai di ren*, now make up 14 percent of the population of Beijing. De facto ghettos have sprung up, grouped by the inhabitants' place of origin and profession. The Anhui village is home to young women seeking work as nannies and cleaners. Muslims from Xinjiang village peddle kebabs. The Zhejiang village laborers sell leather goods and clothes. Many other immigrants do the dirtiest jobs for the lowest pay—collecting trash, cleaning sewers, and working in sweatshops that churn out apparel and toys for U.S. stores. Others are carpenters, food vendors, or construction workers who build the roads, office towers, and hotels that are transforming the city.

The availability of cheap migrant labor is at the expense of social control. Migrants account for one in eight of China's births, above the official one-child-per-family quota. Babies go unregistered and unvaccinated. In Beijing outsiders account for 80 percent of total criminal offenders. Reacting to a flood of workers moving into the capital, Beijing's municipal authority announced regulations in 1994 to impose a fee for the privilege of living in the city. It is not clear how the city government could enforce these regulations. The city left plenty of maneuvering room to grant exemptions, because most of the construction work in Beijing is in the hands of government construction companies where the migrants are employed.

Shanghai: Financial Center and Service Hub

European, U.S., and Japanese colonial powers built one of the first commercial enclaves in China on Shanghai's waterfront. They carved out sections of the city and made them exempt from Chinese law, with exclusive parks and gentlemen's clubs. Hundreds of international banks and trading houses opened in Shanghai, with the most prestigious occupying the stately European-style buildings on the Bund, the famous riverfront boulevard. During the time between the two world wars, tens of thousands of European refugees fleeing Bolshevism and Nazism flooded the area, as did Chinese refugees fleeing civil strife and the Japanese invasion.

In the decades before the 1949 Communist Revolution, Shanghai was called the Paris of the Orient. It was China's most cosmopolitan city and a hub of free-wheeling capitalism. While Shanghai's high society thronged to cabarets, dances, and greyhound races, its vast underclass endured slave labor, opium addiction, and starvation. East Shanghai's dope-dealing gangsters such as Du Yuesheng ("Big-Eared Du") and Huang Jinrong ("Pockmarked Huang") dominated Shanghai's underworld in the 1920s and 1930s.

After four decades of stagnation and decay under communism, Shanghai is trying to regain the glory it once enjoyed as a center of international finance and trade. The city is reviving its international vision in a political climate that, for the present, encourages foreign investments of capital and technology.

The city is wooing foreign investors and spending massive amounts of money on public works in an effort to build a glittering nexus of commerce on old Shanghai's faded ruins. The local government wants the city to rival Asia's modern urban centers such as Hong Kong and Singapore within the next two decades as the nation converts from state planning to free enterprise.

More than seventy big shopping centers opened their doors between 1994 and 2000, but consumer demand has not kept apace. The shopping centers all target the same customers—the city's 700,000 richest people, or 5 percent of the population. Local and foreign developers have rushed into the market, only to find themselves competing for customers.

Nowhere is this crowding more apparent than in the vicinity of Huai Hai Road, Shanghai's main shopping drag. Here eight foreign stores—including the first Japanese Isetan—jostle for space and attention. Some, such as the Pacific Department Store, which has Taiwanese investment, have resorted to year-round discounting. The specter of a shake-out looms over Shanghai's retailing sector.

The Chinese companies that left Shanghai after 1949 are streaming back with an eye to tapping its burgeoning markets and employing China's best-educated workforce at wage levels that are rock-bottom by world standards. The Chung Shing Textile Company, whose founder fled Shanghai for Taiwan, has formed a joint venture with the Shanghai apparel factory it had owned before the plant was nationalized by the communists.

Multinational corporations from the United States, Europe, and Japan have poured billions of dollars a year into factories, offices, bank branches, chemical plants, and distribution facilities. American firms such as AT&T, Du Pont, Merrill Lynch, Bristol-Myers Squibb Company, Citibank, Morgan Stanley & Company, Hilton, and Sheraton have made their way to Shanghai, joining Volkswagen, Unilever, Toshiba, Hitachi, Matsushita, Pilkington Glass of England, and many others.

Tax laws have been changed to entice foreign-funded ventures, and $17 billion worth of infrastructure projects are nearing completion in the city, including power generation plants, wastewater treatment facilities, and two bridges over the Huangpu River, which connect the city's western and eastern parts for the first time. A second group of projects—including a new airport, subway, road system, and ocean container terminal—has been completed.

China's high-powered economy has remade Shanghai into a glittering citadel. Across the city, soaring office towers and apartment blocks have supplanted two- and three-story wood and stone residences dating back to the early twentieth century. In 2003 the city boasted more than 100 skyscrapers that reach more than 330 feet into the murky gray air. Since 1991, an outstanding 299 million square feet of outdated residential space has been demolished. A second wave of development now underway will demolish old dwellings over an additional 100 million square feet. The human dislocation is equally breathtaking. At least 640,000 households have been moved to make way for new development. An additional 80,000 to 100,000 families will be displaced each year. In Shanghai most of those uprooted accept the deal and move on; those protesting relocation policy have been arrested.

The construction of gleaming apartment towers to replace old multifamily homes epitomizes both the best and worst of contemporary China. In Shanghai and dozens of other cities, swiveling construction cranes and wrecking balls are creating more comfortable dwellings with modern amenities, visible proof of the better life the Communist Party promises. But as the economy leaps ahead, China's political system stagnates. The Party's prickly response to complaints about low compensation to residents forced out of their old dwellings, complaints about the relocation policy, allegations of irregularities by rich developers with ties to municipal officials to circumvent land use regulations, and fraudulent land deals spotlights the shortcomings of China's political and legal structures. Between 2001 and 2003, 88 percent of 479 Shanghai land parcels were sold without the required public bid, according to *China Business*, a Beijing-based biweekly publication.

The most dramatic development in Shanghai is taking place in a section of the city on the eastern bank of the Huangpu River, which remained mostly farmland and villages while the western bank was urbanized. In this area of the city—the Pudong—several hundred foreign-funded ventures are either completed or under way (Figure 2.13). These include a giant department store backed by the Hong Kong retailer Yaohan, a spandex-manufacturing venture bankrolled by Du Pont, and an air conditioner factory established by Japan's Sharp Corporation. By 2000 Pudong's skyline boasted numerous high-rise buildings, including a financial center that houses China's main stock exchange, commodities exchanges, and currency trading operations. On the western bank of the Huangpu, some of the most prominent buildings on the Bund (Zhongshan Road) are being leased to their original occupants, such as the Hong Kong & Shanghai Bank, American International Group, and Bank Indosuez.

The port of Shanghai handles more than 160 million tons of cargo a year through loadings and unloadings along the 40 miles of wharves on the Huangpu River. The freighters and other ships come from around the world, leaving the East China Sea for the Yangtze River, and then the Yangtze for the Huangpu, past the container terminals and the shipyards.

Shanghai's comeback offers a bold challenge and a key test of China's ability to deal with urban problems. Shanghai, China's largest city, encompasses nearly all of the nation's most troublesome economic problems: poor transportation and distribution systems, inefficient state enterprises, poorly defined property rights, and an imperious bureaucracy. Years of neglect have left an infrastructure that was designed for a population a fraction of Shanghai's size. Most families sleep three to a room in tiny, dilapidated apartments, sharing kitchen facilities with two or three other families. Nearly 3 million Shanghainese work for SOEs, which are losing money, but authorities are reluctant to allow extensive lay-offs that would enhance efficiency. Foreign

Figure 2-13. Across from the Huangpu River is Pudong, the new financial center that is Shanghai's splendid city of the future. Calm and quiet reigns in Pudong. Life is proper and well-ordered. Despite the appearance of affluence, many of Shanghai's 17 million residents live in poverty. (Photo: P. P. Karan.)

companies complain that bureaucrats, eager to fill municipal coffers, are demanding very high rent for property leases, a development that threatens to cool investors' enthusiasm.

Shanghai has the advantage of location; it is situated at the mouth of the Yangtze basin, the largest and most productive river basin in China. Shanghai is emerging as the domestic financial center of China, but it cannot replace Hong Kong as a regional or international financial center unless the Chinese currency can achieve convertibility on the capital account. Given the corrupt, inefficient, and immense bureaucracy in China, developing an efficient international services center will be difficult. In addition, the silting of the Yangtze River allows ships over 50,000 tons to enter Shanghai (or any other port along the Yangtze) only at high tide.

REGIONS IN TENSION: COASTAL AND INTERIOR REGIONS

Major regional tensions have arisen as a result of the widening gap in economic development between the rapidly developing coastal and the lagging inland regions. Much regional tension has been generated because the inland provinces feel that the coastal provinces and regions have received favorable treatment. In the coastal areas, state policies have encouraged foreign investments and have developed infrastructure by building docks, factories, roads, and rail links. As a result of the encouragement from official government policies and inherent locational advantages, coastal regions have emerged as the wealthiest industrialized rural areas. These include Guangdong, south Jiangxi and north Zhejiang, and parts of Fujian, Shandong, and Liaoning. Guangdong has become immensely wealthy, due to the special powers it gained under the "Open Door" policy, which introduced more foreign trade and investments.

In 1985 four coastal cities—Shanghai, Dalian (Dairen), Tianjin (Tientsin), and Guangzhou (Canton) in the Pearl River Delta—were designated "open" cities for overseas investment. Both the Pearl River Delta and Yangtze Delta, together with some coastal areas of Fujian, are also open zones. The local and provincial authorities in these areas now have more economic decision making power with which to mobilize capital for industrial and commercial development and to search vigorously for overseas investments.

The provinces, particularly the coastal provinces (the main beneficiaries of the new economic order), are now very powerful. They maintain a great pressure for continued reform, whatever the conservatives at the center may think. For the coastal provinces, the condition of continued rapid growth is expanding reforms, moving toward a full market economy. But the center leadership moves very slowly, trapped between those who say what happened in June 1989 was due to an excess of reform, and those who argued it resulted from the failure to reform enough.

China's sprawling interior lags behind the rich coastal provinces. The gap is vast, whether measured by personal income or economic output. The gap has created problems. Among the poorest area are those populated by non-Han minorities—the Tibetans, Muslims, and Mongolians. They look with envy at their rich compatriots in Shanghai, Jiangsu, and the rest of the coastal provinces. By 1996 China's leaders began to perceive a threat to social (and political) stability, and urged rectifying regional imbalances. Foreign businesses were urged to invest in the hinterland. Local governments in the interior were authorized to do more business on their own, and to offer tax and other incentives.

CHINA'S ECONOMIC FRONTIERS: THE TWO DELTAS

Two major economic regions have emerged in China during the last decade: the Pearl River Delta and the Yangtze Delta. The Pearl River Delta was China's economic miracle of the 1980s. In the 1990s the Yangtze Delta emerged as a major economic frontier, with nearly as much foreign investment as the Pearl River. For the first part of the 1990s, economic growth in the Yangtze was a third higher than in China as a whole. Between 1990 and 1993, industrial output in the Yangtze grew, in real terms, by 67 percent, according to official figures. The Yangtze Delta region now accounts for one third of all China's output. But the Pearl River Delta sends abroad a much higher proportion of its product than does the Yangtze. Shanghai, the delta's principal port, is notable mainly for its bulk cargo of raw commodities, rather than for exports of finished goods. The industrial revolution and economic transformation of both deltas thrive by marrying foreign capital with cheap Chinese labor.

The Pearl River Delta is a southern Chinese region of fish farms, toy factories, and private bars, with a knack for free-market communism that has made it one of the fastest-growing economies in the world. It is China's greatest success story, and already it is becoming an international manufacturing center for such products as Mickey Mouse toys, Wendy Walker dolls, Adidas sweat pants, Yashica cameras, Accord watches, and a cornucopia of sweaters, brassieres, purses, and shoes. In some ways it recalls the early years of the "four dragons": Hong Kong, Singapore, South Korea, and Taiwan. Chinese leaders have recently praised it as a national model and called upon Guangdong Province, where the Pearl River Delta is located, to become Asia's fifth "dragon."

Guangdong is a symbol of aggressive restructuring, a place where people go to Paula Abdul concerts instead of Marxist study sessions and where entrepreneurs outnumber ideologues. This is China's economic frontier, a magnet that draws the ambitious and restless from all over the country, and it is becoming a more important force than Beijing in shaping the values, fashions, economic understanding, and social problems of the entire country.

What is the basis for this extraordinary growth? Key factors were the reform of the rich, well-watered agriculture of the delta region, the increased prices of agricultural produce, the restoration of the local markets, and the rural industrialization program encouraged by the government. Other factors involved the coincidence of three factors: first, Hong Kong's rising wages along with strict immigration controls, which forced employers to search out new locations for the kind of manufacturing that depends on cheap labor; second, the long expansion of the United States economy with a radical dependence on increasing manufactured imports; and, third, the Chinese government's deliberate encouragement of foreign investments, creating a framework to assure foreign businesses that they could manufacture their products without facing expropriation or predatory taxation.

For someone arriving from northern China, the towns around the Pearl River Delta do not feel like those in a communist political system. Guangdong still has political prisoners, but fewer than does Beijing. There is also less surveillance here, less intimidation, less political indoctrination, and less of the state sector. One prosperous township, which is brimming with new companies, is Houjie, located about half-way between Guangzhou and Hong Kong. Houjie has an official population of 75,000, mostly peasants who used to wade through the surrounding rice paddies. Some twenty years after it began attracting billions of dollars in foreign investment, Houjie and the surrounding province of Guangdong have become the world's largest and most dynamic manufacturing region, making everything from shoes to Sony PlayStations. Most of the textile, apparel, computer accessories, toys, and sporting goods manufacturers are within a 100-mile radius of Hong Kong. Houjie is also a temporary home to more than 80,000 migrant laborers who work on assembly lines in the township's over 900 factories.

The region's success depends on an endless turnover of migrants from the hinterland, who rarely become full local residents and are effectively prohibited from bargaining for a share of the profits. Though the Pearl River Delta has maintained a double-digit rate of economic growth during the past decade, wages for the migrant workers, adjusted for inflation, have fallen during the same period, according to research by the Institute of Contemporary Observation in Shenzhen. Base pay often falls below legal minimums, and overtime hours often exceed regulated maximums.

No country has more potential workers eager for jobs paying $2 a day than does densely populated rural China, where economists estimate that the number of unemployed people in rural areas exceeds the entire United States labor force. The prospect of competing with such a vast and inexpensive workforce in the two deltas has alarmed developing countries. But China's ability to produce fabrics and garments cheaply has especially alarmed workers and companies in U.S. states such as North Carolina. Democratic and Republican U.S. lawmakers, responding to the closing of manufacturing plants in their districts, have introduced legislation to impose import restrictions.

U.S. labor organizations have charged that Guangdong factories are inhuman sweatshops that frequently employ children. Although some teenagers do work in the factories, most are in their late teens and their dormitory living conditions are often better than those they left behind in their villages. Wages are low by U.S. standards, but extravagant by Chinese terms: $50 to $60 a month, which is more than some university professors earn. Almost all of the workers are women, who are regarded by factory managers as more responsible and more adroit with their hands than men, and they typically work six days a week for up to about 10 hours a day. The women say this is far preferable to sloshing around the rice paddies. Flexible Hong Kong businessmen have shifted almost all of the former British colony's low-end processing just across the border into the Pearl River Delta to take advantage of the cheap land and labor.

The Yangtze Delta—comprising Jiangsu, Zhejiang, and Anhui provinces, plus Shanghai—holds nearly 200 million people: 16 percent of China's population on 3.7 percent of its land. The region is equivalent in population and output to Indonesia, which is itself the world's fourth-largest country. At least 35 cities in the delta have populations of one million or more. With abundant labor pouring off the land, and with little regulatory oversight, new township and village enterprises (TVEs) thrive by churning out all manner of low-tech goods. In the Yangtze Delta TVEs account for about half of the industrial output, as opposed to 30 percent for the state enterprises (SOEs), despite the state sector's dominance in Shanghai. Economic transformation in the Yangtze Delta is being driven by these township and village enterprises.

Two high growth corridors anchored by Shanghai are emerging in the Yangtze Delta. One runs south through Hangzhou to the port of Ningbo. The other runs west through Suzhou and Wuxi to Nanjing. These two corridors account for two-fifths of the delta's population. The Delta "megalopolis" is a mighty concentration of purchasing power and production, and a profitable site for foreign investment. Poor infrastructure as compared with the Pearl River Delta is a problem. The central government has given priority to linking the Yangtze Delta with its distant hinterland, Sichuan province and beyond, before linking together the disparate, rapidly growing coastal centers in Guangdong and Fujian provinces, along the Yangtze Delta, north along the Bohai gulf, and in Manchuria.

PEOPLES IN TENSION: THE HAN MAJORITY AND ETHNIC MINORITIES

Although China is often regarded commonly as a homogeneous nation, some 8 percent of the population is made up of members of fifty-five minorities (Figure 2.14). Most of them live in the border regions, and their homelands comprise more than half of the country's territory and much of its deserts, steppes, and mountains. The national minorities, as they are called in China, differ from the predominant Han Chinese in one or more of the following ways: language, customs, historical development, religion, and race. The integration of non-Han people has always presented problems. Comprehensive policies for minorities issued after the Communist Revolution included limited regional autonomy and special privileges to co-opt the minorities into the system. Outside of Xizang (Tibet) and Xinjiang (Sinkiang), where separatist movements are strong, China's policy toward minorities has been quite effective. Members of the ethnic minorities grumble that the fundamental problem is that many Han are arrogant and look down on other people.

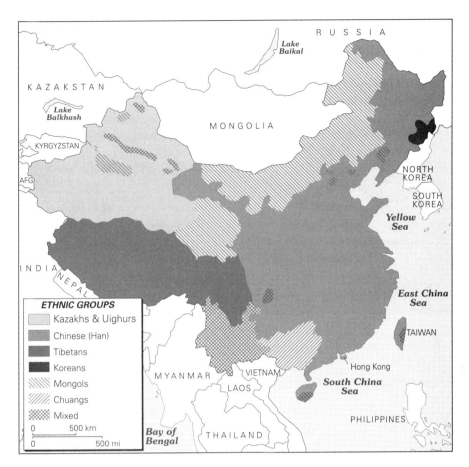

Figure 2-14. China: Ethnic Groups

This is a problem, but there is also increasing intermarriage between the Han and the minorities, which indicates developing mutual respect.

The largest ethnic minority are the Chuang, with a population of 15.5 million concentrated in southwestern China, but the Chuang have been partly assimilated and do not cause any problems. The Chuang share common linguistic roots with the Dai (ethnic kin to the people of Thailand). But unlike the more remote Dai (Figure 2.15), the Chuang have had a close relationship with the Han for centuries. So, too, have the Bai (rice farmers from villages in the high plains of Yunan), whose ancestors were among the original inhabitants of the region. Scattered in small stockaded villages in the rugged mountains of Yunan, the Yao raise rice, maize, and sweet potatoes by slash-and-burn farming.

One reason for the relative contentment among the ethnic minorities in Yunan is the preferential treatment given to members of minority groups. Typically, ethnic minorities are allowed to marry earlier than are members of the Han ethnic majority, and, most important, are allowed to have more children. Their children can also get into universities with lower examination scores than are required of Han students, and model members of minorities

Figure 2-15. Girls of the Dai ethnic group smile during class in a village school in Jing Hong county, Yunan Province. Yunan has more ethnic groups than any other region of China. Each has its own language (although not always with a written form) and its own cultural heritage. Virtually all groups are farmers who live in small villages and produce dry rice, corn, and buckwheat, except in the river valleys where wet rice is predominant. (Photo: UNICEF by Roger Lemoyne.)

are chosen to fill permanent government posts. Because of the affirmative action policy, some families that in the past had tried to assimilate into the Han majority are now applying for declarations that they are members of a minority and not Han, so that their children will have a better chance of getting into the universities. Some Han complain that preferences are unfair, but there is little noticeable resentment against the affirmative action policies in China.

Dispersed from southern China across northern Vietnam, Laos, and into Thailand are the Miao (Hmong) people. Forced southward by the Han, often despised and exploited, many settled in distant mountains, raising millet and buckwheat by slash-and-burn farming, their diet supplemented by animals raised domestically and those felled through hunting.

Some minorities have been so assimilated that their status as separate people is nearly lost. For example, the Tujia people who live in southeast China were not recognized until the 1950s. The Tujia farm rice and corn, gather fruit, fell trees for lumber, and are adept at handicrafts. The She, who now speak mainly Chinese, may be descended from the Yao, who retreated to the west 500 years ago under pressure from the Han expansion. To the northeast, the Manchus—once herders and hunters who conquered China in the seventeenth century—were gradually assimilated and are now found in all trades across the northeast, though little remains of their ancient customs or language. China's 1.9 million Korean inhabitants, most of whom immigrated decades ago from North Korea, are concentrated in the hilly region just inside China from North Korea. The Koreans, who have risen to positions of real national power in the country, are probably the most successful ethnic minority in China.

The 4.8 million Mongols have also been politically quiet. Fewer than 10 percent of Inner Mongolia's people are Mongol today, but their population is increasing. Livestock, coal, iron, salt, steel, and grain are economically important, yet many Mongols remain seminomadic. They follow their flocks in the summer, covering great distances and living in felt tents called yurts.

The minorities who live in Xinjiang and in the Tibetan highlands are, on an average, poorer and less educated than the Han, and some—such as the Tibetans and various Muslim ethnic groups of Turkish origin—have tense relations with the Han and complain that the Han look down on them. In Tibet and the far western region of Xinjiang, ethnic tensions have led to clashes with the Chinese authorities and to independence movements. The Silk Road, which threads through Xinjiang's deserts and mountains, carried China's trade westward and eventually opened the way for Islam's expansion eastward. The Muslim minorities of the area speak Turkic languages and for centuries used the Arabic script. The Uighurs raise fruit, wheat, cotton and rice by extensive irrigation. The Kazak, renowned for their horsemanship, and the Kirgiz, who keep Bactrian camels, have reduced their pastoral wanderings as herders of sheep and goats. Growing Han Chinese immigration and colonization of Xinjiang has intensified local Muslim resentment. Anti-Chinese riots occasionally erupt in some cities, where Han Chinese reap the most benefit from economic development via oil exploration, coal mining, and tourism.

China would never willingly surrender Xinjiang, or even loosen its grip on the place. It has strategic importance in Central Asia and is rich in oil and gas. China has vowed to crush any who dare to revive the notion of an Eastern Turkistan Republic, the name under which Xinjiang briefly had independence between 1944 and 1949. A bomb blast by a Xinjiang separatist in Beijing in March 1997 shattered the notion that China's capital city could remain insulated from the ethnic troubles seething in the western part of the country. The Uighurs make up about 7 million of Xinjiang's 16 million people, most of the rest being Han, the dominant ethnic group of China.

Xinjiang is designated an "autonomous region," as are Tibet and Inner Mongolia, home to two other ethnic minorities that lack enthusiasm for Chinese rule. The government says that the Uighurs receive numerous benefits, including cash subsidies, preferences for jobs and school places, and exemption from China's one-child policy. The Uighurs say there are restrictions on their religious practices and that the best jobs created by new investments go to the Han who have been encouraged to migrate to the region. In 2003 China declared four Xinjiang Muslim groups as terrorists: the Eastern Turkistan Islamic Movement, the Eastern Turkistan Liberation Organization, the World Uighur Youth Congress, and the Eastern Turkistan

Information Center. Critics have argued that China is using the pretense of a campaign against terrorism to legitimize its harsh treatment of the Muslim Uighur minority that is peacefully seeking a separate state in the province of Xinjiang to maintain their ethnic and cultural identity.

Herders of yaks, sheep, and goats, and landowners who farm barley, peas, and tubers, the Tibetans sparsely inhabit a high, desolate region surrounded by mountains and barricaded on the east by the canyons of the Yangtze, Mekong, and Salween rivers. The advent of Buddhism in the seventh century led to a theocratic state intermittently controlled from China from the thirteenth century onward. Here nationalism is forging a significant challenge to the Chinese leaders 1,600 miles away in Beijing. This was Deng Xiaoping's Lithuania, and if China ever crumbles, Tibet is likely to be the first piece to break off. Discontent and repression have been pervasive for many years, and the mood of the Tibetans suggests a dangerous cascade of bitterness that overwhelms the land that inspired the notion of Shangri-La.

STATUS OF HUMAN RIGHTS

The state of freedom, rule of law, and movement toward democracy in China have become important questions in the world. Never in their long history have the Chinese been as free to earn, to invest, and to move about their country building networks of commerce and industry. Peasants are taking part in village elections, and China's rubber-stamp parliament is beginning to assert itself. Yet the Chinese are far from free and far from satisfied about the state of their liberties. They yearn for a system in which their voices would be heard, and their grievances addressed. They see the over the corruption and inequities that flourish. Thousands of political offenders languish in prisons and labor camps for challenging the corrupt or arbitrary acts of countless local Communist Party chieftains.

In a country where all policy is made at the top by the Politburo and the Communist Party Central Committee, the significance of village elections at the bottom of the system is not that they are liberating the peasantry, but that they provide for improved local leadership and a measure of participation. Village elections have done little to relieve the average peasant's burdens or eliminate arbitrary government intrusions. County governments levy taxes and fees and county family planning officers relentlessly enforce the one-child policy, while township and county police officials crack down on religious practice and unsanctioned political activity.

The new economic freedoms are very visible today in major cities and along China's bustling coastline, but the bleak landscape of political repression and human rights abuse are always less visible than commerce. There are few if any basic protections against arbitrary arrest and imprisonment. There is no freedom of the press nor any prospect for freedom of expression in the arts, film, or news media. In 2000, more than 1,300 "counter-revolution-ary" political prisoners were being held in jail, according to the Ministry of Justice. Countless thousands of other political and religious prisoners of con-science are in labor camps and mental institutions. In a heavily policed soci-ety, little has changed since 1979, when young intellectuals such as Wei Jingsheng and Xu Wenli pasted up on Democracy Wall their call for reform. That stretch of masonry was dismantled in 1980, and in 1982 big character posters were outlawed. Wei went to prison, where he remains. In 1986 and again in 1989, pro-democracy movements erupted on the streets of Beijing, and each time the government cracked down—most brutally on June 4, 1989.

According to Amnesty International, 1996 was a record year for death sentences and executions in China. More than 6,100 death sentences and 4,367 confirmed executions were recorded; more people were executed in China than in the rest of the world's countries put together. Executed prisoners are the main source for organ transplants, according to Human Rights Watch-Asia, a private group that promotes human rights and monitors abuses. Chinese doctors participate in pre-execution medical tests, matching the donors with recipients, and surgeons are commonly present on execution grounds to perform on-site removal of vital organs. In some cases, kidneys are removed from prisoners the night before executions, and some executions are deliberately botched to keep the bodies alive longer and improve chances of organ transplant success. The transplantation program began in the 1960s and now includes the harvesting of kidneys, livers, hearts, lungs, and corneas. Although Chinese law stipulates that convicts must consent to any transplants, the Human Rights Watch report says that prisoners are rarely informed and relatives are coerced to sign documents.

China, Tibet, and Human Rights

Tibet, now an autonomous region, was invaded or liberated—the term depends on the speaker—by Chinese troops in 1950. The Dalai Lama was the supreme figure in a theocratic government, and even though he fled to India in 1959 after an abortive uprising, his influence is felt everywhere (Figure 2.16). After his flight China consolidated its hold on Tibet, which had been claimed by all Chinese governments since the fall of the Qing Dynasty in 1911, although the western two thirds of Tibet had been effectively indepen-dent since 1912.

Since the Chinese occupation, the economy of Tibet has improved, but the beneficiaries are largely Chinese migrants, now so numerous as to have reduced Tibetans to a minority in Lhasa and other major towns and, possibly, in the whole of Tibet. Chinese businessmen are the dominant force in the lucrative tourist industry, and local industries are being overwhelmed by cheap imports from other parts of China.

Figure 2-16. The Potala, former palace of the Dalai Lama, lies in Lhasa. For the millions of Tibetan Buddhists, the Dalai Lama is the fourteenth reincarnation of their patron god. To the People's Republic of China he is a leader-in-exile of forces trying to drive out the Chinese and reestablish Tibet's independence. Tibet has been part of China since it sent troops into the country on October 7, 1950, citing its rule of Tibet since the seventh century as a pretense for invasion. (Photo: P. P. Karan.)

Anti-Chinese protests have been violently suppressed, with police firing on crowds of demonstrators around the Jokhang Temple in Lhasa. By official count, there are slightly more than 100 people now imprisoned for engaging in illegal separatist activities, but independent estimates are higher. China denies that those persons imprisoned have been tortured, but most Tibetans say that physical abuse is routine. A comprehensive report in 1990 by Asia Watch, a U.S. human-rights organization, detailed the treatment of prisoners, which included attacks by trained dogs, assaults by electric cattle prods, suspension by ropes, scalding with boiling water, and the raping of nuns.

A broad spectrum of Tibetans are resentful of Chinese domination (Figure 2.17). As China's leaders try to win over the Tibetan population and earn the appreciation of local residents, their challenge is compounded by economic difficulties. Despite enormous subsidies from Beijing—some of which go to pay the salaries of Han Chinese officials rather than to benefit local Tibetans—industry in Tibet has grown by only 6 percent per year over the last decade, compared with about 12 percent annually in the rest of China. The economic gap between Tibet and coastal China is growing, not diminishing, and that adds to the perception of neglect and mismanagement of the local economy by China.

Figure 2-17. Tibetan refugees from China in Bhutan. Thousands of Tibetans have fled their homeland to escape persecution for political and religious activities. Cases of torture have been reported from Tibet. Persons arrested for "counter revolutionary" activities are often beaten to death in Tibet. (Photo: P. P. Karan.)

There is growing evidence of the Chinese cultural and economic presence in Tibet, especially in Lhasa. In the 1990s, much of the old city—by some estimates as much as two thirds—was torn down and replaced by modern Chinese structures. Bars and shopping arcades abut traditional Tibetan buildings in what formerly was one of the most architecturally distinctive cities in the world. In Tibetan schools, children who continue their studies beyond elementary school are required to speak Chinese in all classes except Tibetan language courses. The Dalai Lama is emphasizing now that Tibet's identity is being imminently overwhelmed by China's long-time policy of settling the ethnic Chinese.

Between 1994 and 1998 Chinese authorities carried out a careful campaign to tighten control over Tibetan monasteries, which China has come to see as nests of opposition to Chinese rule over this starkly devout region. The number of monks allowed to enter monasteries has been sharply cut back, and entrance to one of these centers of Buddhist learning is now strictly vetted. All monks are required to swear patriotic allegiance to China, even though many see China as an occupying foreign power. Monks have also been required to declare formal opposition to the Dalai Lama, the exiled leader whom Tibetans revere as a god and a king and Chinese consider a bitter enemy.

LAOGAI: INTEGRATION OF PRODUCTION AND POLITICAL EDUCATION

Laogai, or reform through labor, is a central feature of the Chinese prison system. The *laogai* began to appear in 1949 to reform counter-revolutionaries and other criminals through labor. It is designed to integrate punishment and thought reform and serve both the objectives of production and political education. According to the Laogai Research Foundation, there is a vast network of prison camps stretching across the country, holding an estimated 16 to 20 million prisoners. Inmates in the *laogai* are not only forced to perform hard labor to atone for their crimes; they are also required to abandon their "incorrect" beliefs and attitudes and conform to the standards set by the Communist Party.

One of the functions of the *laogai* has been to provide free prison labor for large-scale infrastructure projects such as road and railway construction, mining work, land reclamation, and massive irrigation programs, especially in the less-developed regions of the country such as Xinjiang and Tibet. During the 1960s the *laogai* began to expand into all areas of industrial and agricultural production. Under the economic modernization policies initiated in 1978, the *laogai* became independent commercial enterprises responsible for their own financing, production, sales, and cost accounting. Camps are expected to make a profit for the state, and this has driven some camp managers to seek joint ventures with foreign companies.

Laogai camps are spread all across China (Figure 2.18). In 1949, when China incorporated the Tibetan region of Amdo into the country, it renamed it Qinghai Province. This cold and remote plateau has one of the major concentrations of *laogai* prisoners. There are twenty-eight recorded *laogai* farms and factories spread across northern Qinghai, including Haomen Farm, with an area of 30 square kilometers; the huge Tanggemu Farm, which is 70 km across; and at least five or six major camps in the town of Xining. Tanggemu Farm, also known as Qinghai Province No. 13 Labor Reform Camp, is a vast prison-farm complex in Gonghe County with an estimated inmate population of up to 20,000 engaged in the production of rape-seed, vegetables, and high-land barley.

Qinghai also receives prisoners under forced job placement (*jiuye*), a practice in which prisoners who have completed their sentences are forced to remain and continue working in the *laogai*. Many dissidents sent to Qinghai are not allowed to return to their homes, and instead their families are "encouraged" to resettle with them. Between 20 to 30 percent of the population

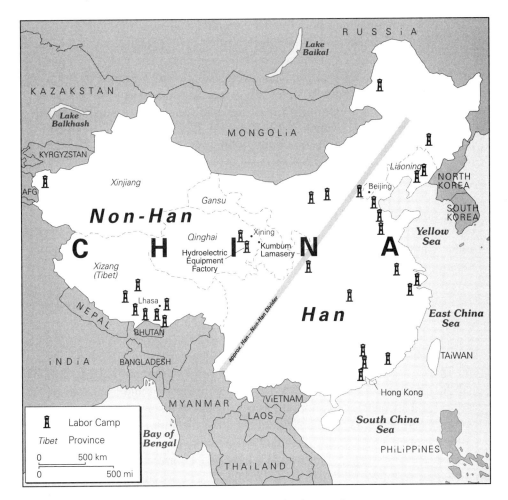

Figure 2-18. Chinese labor camps. (Based on Amnesty International Reports.)

of Qinghai Province is made up of *laogai* inmates. The aim of this policy is to build up the population of the region, enabling more rapid economic development. The result has been to increase the proportion of ethnic Chinese in northeast Tibet to such an extent that they have come to outnumber the indigenous population.

The *laogai* is less extensive in Tibet than in Amdo, with only fifteen camps documented by the Laogai Research Foundation. Some 60 to 70 percent of the inmates in the *laogai* system in Tibet are ethnic Tibetans, most of whom have been imprisoned for their belief in Tibetan independence, although religious observance and possession of literature written by the Dalai Lama have also led many to *laogai*. There is more emphasis on punishment than reform inside the Tibetan *laogai*. Tibetan prisoners are often allocated more dangerous or menial tasks, and Chinese inmates are given skilled and semi-skilled jobs. Cruel, inhuman, and degrading treatment and torture are widespread in Tibetan *laogai*. *Laogai* camps in Tibet include Shigatse Prison, Garza Prison, and the Drapchi Prison, where nearly 2,000 monks were held after the 1959 uprising; 1,400 of these died from starvation over the following two years. The Sangyip prison complex in Lhasa contains five separate detention facilities.

In recent years the commercial aspect of the camps has assumed great importance, due to the enthusiasm of China to offer the produce of the camps for foreign export. Because *laogai* production amounts to slave labor, some countries have looked into enforcing legislation banning the import of *laogai* produce.

CHINA'S DISSIDENT MOVEMENT

Several years after its defeat by the army at Tiananmen Square, China's dissident network is reemerging to challenge the ruling Communist Party with a call for greater political freedom. Dissidents in Beijing and Shanghai have issued bold appeals for freedom of speech. They are also seeking to represent workers and peasants, who are proclaimed the backbone of the Communist Party but often have been left behind by China's sweeping economic changes.

Dissidents work in tiny pockets and have yet to form a broad-based movement. They work alone or in small groups. Some are disgruntled workers; others are angry peasants who feel a responsibility to make their voices heard. Their renewed activity reflects a growing discontent with many of the same issues that sparked the 1989 protests: unemployment, rising inflation, a widening income gap, and corruption. The efforts by dissidents to organize Chinese workers are of great concern to China's leaders, who have long feared the emergence of a worker-based movement like "Solidarity" in Poland, which ultimately defeated the communists. The dissident movement poses a major challenge to the idea that economic reform must not be accompanied by political change and that everything must proceed under strict Communist Party control.

The growing economy and increased social mobility have led to rising expectations, but not always to improved conditions for all Chinese. The dissidents are trying to take advantage of a growing disaffection in their society, including peasants who make up the vast majority of China's population. Peasants, angry over excessive levies and lagging incomes, have banded together to fight local despots. In the cities, workers are unhappy because failing state factories often cannot pay their salaries. In the central city of Wuhan, several thousand elderly men and women staged a sit-in to demand higher retirement benefits. The poorer the place, the more serious the discontent.

The widening rifts in Chinese society between the new class of entrepreneurs and plodding state workers who are losing their guaranteed wages are becoming a fertile breeding ground for the dissident movement. The focus of the dissidents on specific grievances is a change from the abstract calls for democracy that characterized the student-led movement that was crushed by the Chinese Army on June 4, 1989. For a ruling party that has for decades called itself the dictatorship of the proletariat, the dissidents' focus on workers and peasants strikes at the heart of the Party's grip on power. Because of the fear of reprisal, dissidents are unable to create a formal organization or call regular meetings. But they have core cadres in various places throughout the country.

Dissident political and religious groups and individuals continue to operate despite crackdowns on their activities. As China's computers multiply, China's democracy movement has entered the information age, and dissidents can organize without meeting.

In 1998 the year-end secret trials of several peaceful political activists, culminating in long labor-camp sentences signaled a return to a harsher political climate. By sentencing two of China's most prominent democracy campaigners to long prison terms, China took its harshest steps yet in its crackdown on organized political opposition. Xu Wenli—at 55 the dean of the dissident movement, and a man who had already spent twelve years in prison, most of them in solitary confinement, for advocating democracy—was sentenced to thirteen years. Xu's alleged crimes included helping to organize a new political party, calling for an end to Communist rule, and calling for independent labor unions. Xu edited an influential dissident journal in the Democracy Wall movement twenty years ago. In 1989 Jampel Changchub was sentenced to nineteen years in prison for translating U.N. human rights document into Tibetan. Dr. Hu Shigen, a physician, received a twenty-year prison term for suggesting that China should permit press freedom and trade unions.

Also sentenced to eleven years in prison was Wang Youcai, 32, founder of the China Democracy Party. Wang was tried on subversion charges in the eastern city of Hangzhou. His trial, along with the trials of hundreds of lesser-known individuals who tried to organize the Party, appeared to spell the effective end of the China Democracy Party. The dissidents had set up China Democracy Party branches in fourteen provinces and cities and tried to register the party with authorities as required by law. At least thirty members of the party have been detained. With the sentencing of the democracy movement's leaders, China's Communist government has silenced its most energetic critics and those who had given their life to the cause of democracy.

CHINA'S PROSPECTS: STABILITY AND COHESION

The economic and geopolitical policy makers are focusing their attention on the Pacific Basin. In most places it is taken for granted that China will be a superpower in the future and will challenge Japan and the United States by its economic dynamism, military power, and geopolitical claims. The scale of the military and political ambitions of China today is certainly clear, and the continuation of China's rapid economic growth is a defensible assumption. However, China is in the midst of profound economic and social change that is leading to growing strains that threaten to undermine the country's stability and cohesion. Regional disparities, mass rural migration, rising unemployment, frictions between central and provincial governments, and simmering ethnic discontent are some of the most serious problems confronting China. At the same time, the authority and reach of traditional organs of political power such as the Communist Party have steadily declined in the 1990s.

Can China's Communist leadership maintain stability and hold on to power in the face of numerous challenges? To meet the challenge, China has been stepping up political repression and building up the capabilities of its vast internal security apparatus. It is stressing nationalism as the ideological glue to hold the country together as Communism becomes increasingly irrelevant in a market-oriented economy and society. Although nationalist sentiments are strong among the population, the Communist leadership has been less effective in using them as a means to bolster its own political legitimacy.

A principal challenge to China's stability will continue to come from deep-seated social discontent among groups left behind by economic reforms. The incomes of up to one quarter of the urban population, especially state workers and pensioners on fixed incomes, have shrunk because of spiraling living costs. In less-developed parts of the country such as Sichuan Province, as many as one out of every three people are losing out in the economic reforms. Friction is also rising, as discussed earlier, between prosperous coastal areas and underdeveloped inland regions over the uneven distribution of income and resources. Coastal provinces have enjoyed special economic privileges that have helped to attract foreign and domestic investors to finance their development. Inland regions have received only a trickle of investment, however, and they have been left behind by the economic reforms.

HONG KONG

Hong Kong's teeming population of 6.8 million (2004) is crowded into an area of 398 square miles to the east of the Pearl River Delta. Hong Kong includes the island of Hong Kong (ceded to Britain by China in 1842), the Kowloon Peninsula (ceded in 1860), and the New Territories, which include part of the mainland, all of which were leased to Britain in 1898 for a period of ninety-nine years. Sovereignty over the entire territory reverted to China in 1997. Under this arrangement, Hong Kong is to enjoy an autonomy that will be maintained for at least fifty years. The fine anchorages between the capital of Victoria on the northern shore of Hong Kong island and Kowloon, provide an ideal situation for the growth of one of the world's leading entrepot ports.

Hong Kong is mostly hilly and stripped of natural vegetation. Flat land and agricultural land is scarce everywhere. Land reclaimed from the sea is being used for building purposes—housing and factories—and for the extension of the runway of Hong Kong's old airport. A new international airport, built on reclaimed land at Chek Lap Kok Island, opened in 1998.

Hong Kong has experienced extraordinary growth in population. Between 1841 and 1941 the population increased from 2,500 people to 1.5 million. The quiet colonial life ended in 1949, when prosperous Chinese fled the communist revolution, settled in Hong Kong, and transformed the city into an industrial hub. Refugees became the bedrock of Hong Kong's current prosperity. Many were country peasants, happy to arrive in Hong Kong and eager to start anew beyond the fledgling bamboo curtain. Former industrialists from Shanghai and other cities arrived with ambition, dreams, and a wealth of knowledge about business. Their background in textiles was the foundation from which the colony's exports grew. In the 1950s the colony thrived on low-cost manufacturing, with waves of cheap labor constantly arriving from China. Now that kind of manufacturing has moved into China itself. Financial and business services have overtaken manufacturing in economic importance in Hong Kong. Hong Kong is Pacific Asia's main financial center outside Japan, reaping wealth from the boom in China. The territory is seen as one of the great economic miracles of the modern world, where a hodgepodge of refugees and riffraff have created one of the world's most powerful economies.

Hong Kong's major factories—producing Cabbage Patch dolls, Mutant Ninja Turtles, fishing rods, neckties, and other goods—have moved a few dozen miles north to Guangdong Province in southern China, attracted by lower wages. The Hong Kong companies still design the toys, manage the manufacturing, package the dolls, and ship them abroad. Hong Kong has now become like a company's corporate headquarters, housing the bosses, the accountants, and the planners; China has become the factory site. Hong Kong and Guangdong are quickly integrating. There is little doubt that the continuing prosperity of Hong Kong has been built on its economic links with China.

Increasingly, businessmen and geographers are thinking in terms of a southern China growth triangle on the southeastern coast that includes Hong Kong, Taiwan, and the four Special Economic Zones (SEZs) of Shenzhen, Zhuhai, Shantou, and Xiamen.

The huge investment of U.S. capital and people means that Hong Kong and its future will remain one of the central U.S. policy concerns in Asia. Hong Kong's continued prosperity depends to a considerable extent on its way of life continuing as it has. If China allows the territory and the city to retain its entrepreneurial spirit, fair judiciary, free press, civil liberties, open markets, low tariffs, and freewheeling capitalist system, it will assure a stable Hong Kong (Figure 2.19).

Although most American companies believe that business will continue as usual under Chinese control, this optimism does not mean that there are no concerns. The number of visitors to Hong Kong declined following the transfer of territory to China, and Hong Kong's economy eroded by 2 percent in early 1998, the first negative growth in thirteen years. The economy, which at the time of the hand-over to China seemed resilient and growing, slipped

Figure 2-19. People march in front of the Hong Kong City Hall to protest restrictions aimed at curbing political rights. In the 1995 election for Hong Kong's legislature, the Democratic Party and pro-democratic independents won 29 of 60 seats. After China's resumption of rule over Hong Kong in July 1997, the elected legislature was replaced with a body chosen by China. Now the public votes directly for only two-fifths of the Legislative Council, while business leaders and the executive branch play a large role in selecting the rest. Pro-democracy parties are in the minority in the Council, but a huge pro-democracy march in July 2003 forced local leaders and China to retreat from introducing a stringent internal security bill that set stiff penalties for sedition, secession, treason, and other offenses. (Photo: P. P. Karan.)

into recession in 1998. Unemployment was at its highest rate in fifteen years. Stock market and property values in 1998 were half of what they were in 1997. Hong Kong was plagued by a series of weird disasters, from the chicken flu that forced the destruction of every hen in the city to tens of thousands of fish wiped out by a killer red tide. In 2003 hundreds of SARS (severe acute respiratory syndrome) cases crippled the economy.

As the Chinese government presence in Hong Kong grows, some fear that mainland Chinese individuals will buy large interests in successful Hong Kong businesses, bringing with them the same potential for abuse and corruption that has occurred in China itself. Hong Kong has now ended its colonial period of British political patronage and cronyism, but it may simply usher in Chinese patronage and cronyism in its place.

Environment and Development in Hong Kong

To maintain sustained economic growth, Hong Kong faces a number of constraints on development posed by the environment. To avoid further overcrowding, Hong Kong limits migrants from China (Figure 2.20). The expansion of Hong Kong has caused increasing pressure on developable land, resulting in urban development on uphill slopes. Space for development is a major environmental constraint on future expansion because of the steep and mountainous nature of the territory. The scarcity of flat land and the competition for space have generated very high land prices. The need for additional land has also prompted reclamation of land from the sea.

One immutable legacy that British colonialism has left is the radical reshaping of the harbor that separates Hong Kong from Kowloon. This reshaping through land reclamation took place at an accelerated pace in the colonial government's dying days. Over the last hundred years, nearly 21 square miles of land have been reclaimed from the sea around Hong Kong, including some along the harbor front. The harbor, which in places is more than a mile wide, is to shrink to a narrow channel. The serrated, twisting shoreline has been smoothed and straightened. The current plans to reclaim 5 square miles from the harbor for broad new highways, towering office buildings, housing, and some park land have drawn growing concern from legislators, urban planners, and environmental groups, who are deeply worried about the vanishing harbor.

Another environmental constraint on the development of Hong Kong is the lack of an adequate water supply. The territory has no sizable rivers or lakes, and groundwater resources are limited. Variations in annual rainfall and seasonal distribution of precipitation cause further difficulties in water supply. The seasonal rainfall requires storage of water to maintain supplies during the dry period from November to March. Since 1960 China has supplied a major proportion of Hong Kong's water. A further constraint on the development of Hong Kong is water pollution. The sea around Hong Kong receives virtually all of the urban, industrial, and agricultural liquid pollution load. Continued

Figure 2-20. Migrants from China are not allowed to reside in Hong Kong without valid permits or ID. A mother without her ID looks after her own children and those of her friend who was sent back to China by Hong Kong authorities. Although Hong Kong has one of the highest per capita incomes in Asia, many live in urban slums without adequate sanitation and water supply. (Photo: Shin-ichii Asabe.)

pollution of the marine waters will eventually threaten their use. In recent years Hong Kong has upgraded facilities for the collection, treatment, and disposal of wastes.

The industrial and commercial areas of Hong Kong suffer from serious air pollution. Fossil-fuel-fired power stations and vehicles are major sources of air pollution. Over 12,000 tons of particulate matter was emitted in 1995, of which industrial fuel combustion and emissions from vehicles were the principal sources in industrial areas. Industrial pollution problems are of considerable concern in Hong Kong because of the high density of chimneys built on multistory industrial buildings in close proximity to residential buildings. Hong Kong undoubtedly needs an effective air quality management program to deal with the close proximity of residential and industrial areas.

MACAO

Macao, about 6 square miles in area, lies on the western side of the Xi Jiang, opposite Hong Kong. Taken by Portugal in 1557, Macao was not merely the first European colony in China; it was Europe's and, later, America's first gateway to Japan and Taiwan, as well as China itself. A rental was paid by the Portuguese until they declared the independence of the port in 1849. Portuguese sovereignty was not recognized by China until 1887. Macao continued throughout the eighteenth century as the chief entrepot center for European trade with China, but declined in the nineteenth century due to the rapid development of Hong Kong and the inadequacy of Macao's harbor. It was the last foreign colony to revert to China's control, in 1999, two years after Hong Kong.

After the Second World War, the emergence of energetic, pushy British Hong Kong reduced the Portuguese colony of Macao to a lethargic and charming backwater territory; it has always looked like a second-rank Mediterranean fishing port rather than an imperial outpost. Its postwar development was mostly as a center for weekend gambling for Hong Kong's Chinese merchants. More than 6 million visitors entered Macao in 1990—an overwhelming number for a territory with less than half a million residents. Of these, 4.5 million came from Hong Kong. Of the remaining 1.5 million, about a third came from Japan, Korea and Taiwan, demonstrating the growing trend toward intra-Asian tourism.

In the 1950s Macao also profited from smuggling refugees from China into Hong Kong and embargoed goods from Hong Kong into China. More prosaically, its chief manufactured products were matches and firecrackers. A century and a half of decline has now ceased. In a frenzy of expansion, yellow construction cranes hovered busily over Macao's new high-rises and over the beaches of its still bucolic outer islands (Taipa and Coloane) as it became a fitting bride—or sacrifice—to China in 1999.

Aside from renewed ambitions and the end of gold trafficking, the essentials of Macao are unchanged. The chief sources of income and amusement are still gambling and girls. The gamblers, who contribute a third of Macao's gross domestic product of about $3 billion, were still the chief source of revenue in 1999. This may continue if the puritanical Chinese authorities allow gambling, which they officially abhor as a debilitating national vice.

TAIWAN

Offshore from the Asian land mass lies Taiwan, the largest island (13,885 square miles) between Japan and the Philippines. Due to the mountainous character of the island, only about one-third of the area is cultivable; arable land is found mainly in the broad western coastal plain, and the mountainous core is mostly forested (Figure 2.21). With its population of 23 million (2004), Taiwan is almost twice as big a market for U.S. exports as the People's Republic with its 1.2 billion citizens.

Taiwan is one of the most densely populated countries in the world. In 1991 it had an average density of over 1,400 persons per square mile. There are also highly concentrated populations in the cultivated parts of the western plain, where densities reach an average of 3,000 per square mile. It is also a country with the world's second largest foreign-exchange reserves and East Asia's fourth-largest GDP (after Japan, China, and South Korea).

The original inhabitants of Taiwan were people of Malayan descent. Chinese settlements were established in the fourteenth century. Large numbers of Chinese from the densely populated coastal provinces of Fujian and Guangdong settled on the island. In 1895 China ceded Taiwan to Japan. In 1945, after half a century of Japanese rule, the island was restored to China. In 1949, when the communists gained control of the mainland, the Nationalist Government of China moved to Taiwan. The Nationalist Chinese Government

Figure 2-21. Spring plowing in Taiwan. The lowlands of Taiwan, the North China Plain, the plains of the middle and lower Yangtze, Sichuan Basin, and the lowlands of tropical South China are regions of intensive land use. These are areas of high agricultural productivity and industrial development and represent the "key economic areas" of the Chinese cultural realm. (Photo: Kwang Hwa Mass Communication.)

in Taiwan once spoke of "gloriously recovering the mainland," but it is questionable whether Taiwan will ever take back China. Taiwan's leaders seem to be pushing reunification into the distant future. These days some dissidents want Taiwan to declare itself the independent Republic of Taiwan.

Curiously, the diminishing enthusiasm for reunification comes as Taiwan rapidly expands its economic links with the mainland. Taiwan business people started going to China in the mid-1980s as economic and political policy relaxed on each side. Now, Taiwan business people can be found in every major mainland city, both as private investors and as resident representatives of multinational companies. In July 1996 Taiwan's state-run Chinese Petroleum Corporation teamed up with its mainland Chinese counterpart to jointly exploit oil and natural gas fields in the South China Sea. Taiwan is gradually being transformed from mainland China's bitterest rival to its greatest economic partner. Although political relations between Taiwan and the mainland remain tense, most of Taiwan's shoe-making industries have moved their assembly lines to the mainland. Garment workers and sports equipment manufacturers are also relocating factories. Nearly one million Taiwanese visit the mainland each year. Taiwan's future economy will depend a great deal on mainland China. Taiwanese firms, buffeted by rising labor costs and growing public concern for environmental protection, are moving their operations to the Chinese mainland to secure stronger international competitiveness. In 1998 Taiwan had sixteen business groups, 372 large enterprises, and 1,752 small or midsize companies operating on the mainland. Aside from diplomatic huffing and puffing that Taiwan is an "inalienable part of the motherland," China is also steadily expanding business ties with Taiwan, which is increasingly seen by the mainlanders as a model for how to do business more efficiently and profitably.

The new generation of Taiwan-born leaders is often considered more sympathetic to eventual independence than are the mainland emigres, whose rule is gradually being replaced by native Taiwanese. In the 1993 election of mayors and county magistrates, the Nationalists did poorly, winning just 47 percent of the vote. In 2000, for the first time, a president was elected from a party other than the Nationalist Party. Although many people in Taiwan feel that all of China should one day be united, virtually no one wants to be ruled by the communists from Beijing. For the 21 million people of Taiwan and their government, the more immediate problem is not how to achieve ultimate reunification but rather how to maintain their de facto independence. A large faction within the Democratic Progressive Party believes that Taiwan should remain permanently free of mainland control, and that in order to do this, it should proclaim itself to be the independent Republic of Taiwan. China has repeatedly threatened to use force if Taiwan declares itself independent. In addition to obvious damage from the war, any fighting between Taiwan and China would have serious economic costs to both countries, which have close trade relationships despite their immutable political stances. And any fighting would surely cause serious strains for the United States, which has ties to both countries.

There has been no explicit declaration from the Taiwan government of a move toward independence, an act the government still regards as precipitous and unnecessarily inflammatory. Instead, Taiwan tries to demonstrate the island's distinction from China in political, economic, and social spheres. It is doing all it can to create de facto independence for Taiwan by fostering new political, economic, and cultural links with the world. In Taiwan's schools, textbooks that devoted most of their pages to China are being replaced by books focusing on Taiwan. People boast of their Taiwanese roots, and outside Taipei are more likely to speak the local Taiwanese dialect than the Mandarin dialect favored by Chinese from northern China. There are increasing and deliberate attempts to forge an identity distinct from that of China. The United States and virtually all other countries recognize China's claim over Taiwan through the "one-China" policy that is embedded in treaties and resolutions.

Much of Taiwan's sense of identity and purpose comes from its extraordinary economic growth. In two decades Taiwan has managed to transform itself from a backwater into a dominant economic presence in Asia with the world's nineteenth-largest economy. With the economic power has come a surging confidence that buttresses Taiwan's claim to a greater stature in Asia, and fuels increasingly aggressive moves toward international recognition. The most visible sign of this policy is Taiwan's continuing effort to regain admission to the United Nations, from which it was ousted in 1971 when the mainland took over the China seat. As Taiwan pumped up its economic muscles—the country's per capita gross national product was $13,925 in 2000, four times what it was a decade ago—it also embraced a tumultuous democratic politics unknown in the Chinese-speaking world. In March 1996, for the first time in Taiwan's history, the country's president was popularly elected. Taiwan's nascent democracy coupled with newfound economic strength has infused the island with a sense of distinct national identity. Taiwan has produced a prosperous, growingly democratic society of its own, separate in political practice and desire from the mainland.

It is the fear that today's freedom and prosperity would be lost under China's harsh authoritarian rule that fuels Taiwan's quest for a separate identity. China has made no secret of its concern that Taiwan is drifting toward independence and, according to reports in 1996, has completed plans for a limited military attack on Taiwan. China would do better to address the fear of the people of Taiwan with political and economic reforms at home rather than threatening the use of force across the Taiwan Straits. China has lost sight of one of the basic understandings underlying improved Chinese-American relations since the Nixon administration: that Taiwan's future status must be settled by peaceable means.

The rapid development of Taiwan over the past twenty-five years is legendary. With a per capita GNP of over $13,000, the International Monetary Fund labeled Taiwan as an advanced economy in 1997. (The World Bank currently uses an annual per capita income of U.S. $10,000 as its minimum threshold for high-income economies.) The country's initial conditions—the economic infrastructure from Japanese colonialism, entrepreneurial talent from mainland China, and U.S. aid—were important to its success. But its rapid industrialization owed much more to domestic policies. In addition to the early success of land reform in bringing about a remarkable equity of income and wealth, policies for macroeconomic stability, domestic investments, and industrial development were highly effective. In the 1980s Taiwan placed more emphasis on liberalization and export development, resulting in the generation of massive payment surpluses and the means to invest elsewhere in the region on a scale rivaling that of Japan. Taiwan today is the United States' seventh-largest trading partner, and has one of Asia's highest living standards. Taiwan's free-market prosperity must not be disrupted, and its new democracy should not be threatened by force from China.

Four cities—Taipei, Taichung, Tainan, and Kaohsiung—contain the bulk of Taiwan's industry. Taipei has the heaviest concentration of industry. It is the political and economic center of Taiwan and is the largest city. It has one major disadvantage: it is located in a basin, which restricts the amount of land available for industrial use. Many industries have moved to flatter areas in Taipei and Taoyuan *hsien* in the suburban areas. The growth of Taichung is related to major government investments in infrastructure projects, which include the Taichung International port and industrial estate at Wuchi, two Taichung industrial estates, and an export processing zone at Fengyuan. The increase in industrial activity at Tainan is related to the redevelopment of the port area. Kaohsiung, the third-largest container port in the world, remains a major of industrial activity. Keelung is Taiwan's second-busiest seaport.

In the last quarter-century, Taiwan has become a major manufacturer of electronics and other high-technology products (Figure 2.22). It has dramatically upgraded the technological foundations of the manufacturing industries and the quality of its technical and engineering workforce. At the root of its success lies a developmental state, able and willing to increase the competitiveness of Taiwanese companies in the world economy by providing necessary support in the form of industrial and communications infrastructure, labor training, credit, trade policies, and science and technology. The government-supported technological and scientific research institutes and centers have been indispensable in Taiwan's high-technology industrial development.

A government-led technological center started operation in 1980 at Hsinchu, on the west coast of Taiwan, 40 miles south of Taipei. Hsinchu Science-based Industrial Park includes industrial, residential, and research zones. It epitomizes Taiwan's drive to develop high-technology manufacturing. The goal is to attract 150 to 200 high-technology firms and to create between 30,000 and 40,000 jobs. Nearly 100 firms, mostly Taiwanese but also some U.S. firms of ethnic Chinese origin, have located in the Park. A major government research institute,

Figure 2-22. Taiwan's future lies in its electronics industry, especially now that the manufacture of labor-intensive goods—the foundation of recent wealth—is being driven by high wages to cheaper locations in Southeast Asia and mainland China. The microchip industry operates in high-tech industrial parks such in Hsinchu, the island's Silicon Valley. (Photo: Kwang Hwa Mass Communication.)

Industrial Technology Research Institute at Hsinchu, played a critical role in the location and development of the Park. There has been significant technology transfer from foreign companies attracted to Hsinchu. Most of these foreign companies were owned or managed by Chinese Americans who had interests in linking up with the booming high-technology sector in Taiwan. By developing linkages with firms in Taiwan and overseas, Hsinchu Park, and the national development-oriented policies, Taiwan has modernized and upgraded its industrial structure to become a major competitor in high-technology trade in international markets.

A light foreign-debt burden, better banking regulations, and improvements in the efficiency of firms have helped Taiwan escape the economic turmoil that faced South Korea, Thailand, and Indonesia in 1997–1998. Unlike the Thai or Indonesian firms, Taiwanese companies are prevented by strict controls from taking on cheap foreign-currency loans for speculative projects. And unlike South Korea's giant conglomerates, most Taiwan firms are small and have stuck to just one line of business.

MONGOLIA

Mongolia, a vast, reawakening land larger than all of Western Europe, lies in central Asia between China and Russia. Scattered across one of the most sparsely populated areas in the world, nomadic herders account for about two fifths of Mongolia's 2.7 million people. Mongolia is struggling to adjust to democratic ways as the nation leaves behind seven decades of communism.

It is trying desperately to leapfrog over centuries of cultural stagnation and economic sloth—from the glorious dreams of Genghiz Khan and the Utopian promises of Karl Marx to democracy—and the process is, understandably, a bewildering one. It is not easy to discard centuries of customs, tradition, and superstition in one clumsy, monumental effort to catch up with the rest of the world. But Mongolia is making the effort—largely because her sense of national pride, extinguished six centuries ago after the disintegration of the Mongol Empire, has once again been ignited. Mongolians feel themselves to be a nation, for the first time in centuries, even though, theoretically, they have been independent since 1921.

Mongolia is a land of extremes. Sometimes its beauty is breathtaking, when splashes of sunlight bring the dark green face of a mountain to life; at other times its ugliness is painful, when duststorms turn the Gobi into a swirling inferno.

Geographically, Mongolia has five regions. In the west are the Altay Mountains, where peaks covered with snow rise to over 15,000 feet. To the east of this lies a great depression dotted with lakes. The north-central part of the country is occupied by a mountain complex, enclosing the relatively fertile and productive agricultural Selenge-Tuul Basin. To the east again lies the high Mongolian Plateau reaching to the Chinese frontier, and to the south and east stretches the Gobi Desert. Animal herding, the traditional occupation of the people, is still the mainstay of Mongolia's economy.

Today only a minority of Mongols live in the independent Mongol state. Most live in the Inner Mongolia autonomous region of China and in adjacent Russia. Mongolia is wary of China. Many Chinese consider what they call Outer Mongolia to be part of China, as Inner Mongolia is. Mongolia's self-imposed servitude to Russia during the communist period was endured partly on the ground that it was preferable to becoming another Tibet. Now that Russia is no longer the protective power, Mongolia keeps a watchful eye on its southern neighbor.

Mongolia is still only at the threshold of modernization after decades of a Soviet-style economy. In 1990 a new government was elected. Mongolia's transition to the market economy has been painful, but the economy is now growing, unlike those in Mongolia's ex-Soviet neighbors in Central Asia. Improved infrastructure will speed economic growth.

Mongolia's economy took a severe knock with the end of subsidies from the Soviet Union. But the country adopted a privitization policy as part of the larger push for economic change. In 1994 the GDP grew by about 2 percent. After growing by 3.9 percent in 2002, Mongolia's economy is expected to grow by 5 percent in 2004. All small enterprises formerly owned by the state are now privatized, but some large ones are still in the state's hands. Mongolia is trying to deal with the social problems following the introduction of market economy. Poverty and unemployment did not really exist before, but about 22 percent of the population of 2.3 million now lives below the poverty line. Unemployment stands at 9 percent.

In the national election of 1996, when many herdsmen rode on horseback for miles to vote, a clear majority chose the young and untested democratic party, Democratic Union, which held just 6 of 76 seats in the previous legislature. Voters were fed up with the ruling Mongolian People's Revolutionary Party, whose former communist leaders clung to power after the democracy arrived in 1990, but failed to undertake serious changes.

A determined, but young and inexperienced, group of politicians from the Democratic Union Party set up the first non-communist government in Mongolia in 73 years, and has begun to carry out a detailed plan for radical reform. An important tool of the election campaign was Mongolia's contract with voters, which promised a slash in government spending, a sharp reduction of aid, and top to bottom transformation of the government. The new government has already reduced the central government from thirteen ministries to nine, drastically raised the prices of many essential goods, and begun fiscal reforms to avert a collapse of the central government.

The development of Mongolia will be determined not only by the amount of help the country receives from the outside and the degree of energy, skill, and imagination with which this is exploited, but also by important long-term factors such as the severe climate, the short growing season, the difficulties of transport over long distances, the country's remoteness from world markets, and above all, the shortage of skilled and unskilled workers.

Mongolia's big problem is its isolation. To reach Mongolia from a seaport there are two options. One could take goods to Vladivostok in Russia, then risk robberies along the 1,000-mile track through Siberia and northern Mongolia, until one reaches the Mongolian capital of Ulaanbataar. Alternatively, one could arrive in the Chinese port of Xingang and take the train through northern China and Inner Mongolia before changing railway gauges at the Mongolian border and crossing the Gobi Desert. In both cases the journey takes three days.

Throughout Mongolia, the beginnings of a religious revival are becoming apparent, and this has profound implications for neighboring China and its troubled province, Tibet. Mongolia is, more than any other communist state, recapturing its traditions. It is a linchpin of the Tibetan religious world, a country with such strong cultural ties to Tibet that it took the bold step earlier in the twentieth century of recognizing Tibet's independence from China. Now, with Tibet back firmly under China's control and its religious ruler, the Dalai Lama, in exile in India, Tibetan Buddhism's tenuous rebirth in Mongolia gives the Dalai Lama a new ally. Whereas the Dalai Lama previously had no country in the world where Tibetan Buddhism was the main religion, one is now reappearing.

Tibetan Buddhism, which embraces the Russian territories of Buryatia and Tuva, forms an arc that almost encircles China's western regions, adding powerfully to the Dalai Lama's stature at a time when China is trying to crush his influence in Tibet (Figure 2.23). Tibetan Buddhism still has a long way to go before it regains the dominant position it had before 1937. Then, Mongolia's

Figure 2-23. Lhasa, Tibet. One of the major challenges facing China is the integration of minorities, particularly Muslims and Tibetan Buddhists. The outstanding development in the post-1950 era is the standardization of urban form and the establishment of new standardized structures for housing, commerce, and industry throughout China. The most common type of new building is multistory concrete structures with uniform facades and plans based on simple rectangular units, as seen in this view of Lhasa. Substantial changes in urban form have brought Lhasa closer to China in terms of urban development and morphology. Buildings, traffic circles, and other structures seen in Lhasa today resemble those in other Chinese cities. But the residential pattern remains largely segregated; Han Chinese reside mostly in the western part of Lhasa and the Tibetan population is concentrated in the older eastern section of the city. Residential segregation does not facilitate closer social and cultural interaction between the Han and Tibetan groups. (Photo: P. P. Karan.)

brutal dictator Choibalsan, under orders from Stalin to stamp out Mongolia's historic religion, had 17,000 of the country's 110,000 monks executed and all but a handful of its 746 monasteries burned to the ground. Whether Mongolians ever return to the Buddhist life they knew before the communist revolution is doubtful, but they are enthusiastic about their rediscovered roots. Throughout this sparsely populated land of 2.3 million nomadic herders, ruined temples are being rebuilt.

In 2003 Mongolian army soldiers joined the roster of thirty-four nations serving in Iraq. Mongolia's decision to send troops to Iraq reflects a desire to bolster geopolitical ties with the United States and to return their long-eclipsed name to the world stage. Mongolia is the only nation in Asia where there is widespread support for sending troops to Iraq. Russia glowers, China appears neutral, and Japan and South Korea have sent troops despite public protests at home. Mongolia is rapidly embracing the United States in an effort to develop a balance to its dangerous neighbors, China and Russia. After centuries of Chinese rule, Mongolia won independence only in 1921 with Soviet support. It has a deep, if rarely voiced, fear of becoming another Tibet. The United States has provided the Mongolian military with peacekeeping training, English lessons, and for the Chinese border areas, patrol radios and engineering work. In 2002 Mongolia's trade with the United States was only $180 million, but it has proposed a free trade pact. Such a pact would not have any impact on the United States, which in one year trades less with Mongolia than it trades with Taiwan in twelve hours.

FURTHER READINGS

Becker, Jasper. 2000. *The Chinese*. New York: Free Press.

Blum, Susan D. and Lionel M. Jensen, eds. 2002. *China Off Center: Mapping the Margins of the Central Kingdom*. Honolulu: University of Hawaii Press.

Brown, Lester R. 1995. *Who Will Feed China?* New York: W.W. Norton.

Buoye, Thomas, et al. 2002. *China Adopting the Past: Confronting the Future*. Ann Arbor, MI: The University of Michigan Center for Chinese Studies.

Chan, Ming K. and Alvin Y So, eds. 2002. *Crisis and Transformation in China's Hong Kong*. Armonk, NY: M.E. Sharpe.

Chang, Sen-dou. 1998. Beijing: Perspectives on Preservation, Environment and Development, *Cities* 15(1):13–26.

China in Transition. 2002. *Social Science Japan*, 24 October.

Copper, John F. 1995. *Taiwan: Nation-State or Province?* Boulder, CO: Westview Press.

Croll, Elisabeth. 1994. *From Heaven to Earth: Images and Experiences of Development in China*. New York: Routledge.

Edmonds, Richard Louis. 1994. *Patterns of China's Lost Harmony: A Survey of the Country's Environmental Degradation and Protection*. New York: Routledge

Fan, Cindy. 1997. Uneven Development and Beyond: Regional Development Theory and Post-Mao China. *International Journal of Urban and Regional Research* 21(4):620–639.

Fan, Shenggen, Linxiu Zhang, and Xiaobo Zhang. 2002. *Growth, Inequality and Poverty in Rural China*. Research Paper 125. Washington, D.C.: International Food Policy Research Institute.

Gamer, Robert E., ed. 1999. Editor. *Understanding Contemporary China*. Boulder, CO: Lynne Rienner Publishers.

Gaubatz, Piper. 1995. Changing Beijing. *Geographical Review* 85(1):79–96.

Gaubatz, Piper. 1996. *Beyond the Great Wall: Urban Form and Transformation on the Chinese Frontiers.* Stanford: Stanford University Press.

Gladney, Dru. 1997. *Dislocating China: Muslims, Minorities, and Other Sub-altern Subjects.* London: C. Hurst.

Goldstein, Melvyn C. 1997. *The Snow Lion and the Dragon: China, Tibet, and the Dalai Lama.* Berkeley: University of California Press.

Gong, Ting. 1994. *The Politics of Corruption in Contemporary China.* Westport, CT.: Praeger.

He Bochuan. 1991. *China on the Edge: The Crisis of Ecology and Development.* San Francisco: China Books and Periodicals.

Hansen, Hette Halskov. 1999. *Lessons in Being Chinese: Minority Education and Ethnic Identity in Southwest China.* Seattle: University of Washington Press.

Hessler, Peter. *River Town: Two Years on the Yangtze.* New York: Harper Collins.

Huang, Chun-chieh and Erik Zurcher, eds. 1995. *Time and Space in Chinese Culture.* Leiden, The Netherlands: E. J. Brill.

Karan, P. P. 1976. *The Changing Face of Tibet: The Impact of Ideology on the Landscape.* Lexington, KY: University Press of Kentucky.

Karan, P. P. 1989. Perception of Environmental Pollution in a Chinese City. In *Urbanization in Asia.* Honolulu: University of Hawaii Press, pp. 111–138.

Klintworth, Gary. 1995. *New Taiwan, New China: Taiwan's Changing Role in the Asia-Pacific Region.* London: St, Martin's.

Kristof, Nicolas D. and Sherry WuDunn. 1994. *China Wakes: The Struggle for the Soul of a Rising Power.* New York: Times Books.

Mackerras, Colin. 1994. *China's Minorities.* Hong Kong and Oxford: Oxford University Press.

McElroy, Michael B., Christopher Nielsen, and Peter Lydon, eds. 1998. *Energizing China: Reconciling Environmental Protection and Economic Growth.* Cambridge: Harvard University Press.

Ming, Ruan. 1994. *Deng Xiaoping: Chronicle of an Empire.* Boulder, CO: Westview Press.

Orleans, Leo A. 1991. "Loss and Misuse of China's Cultivated Land," in U.S. Congress Joint Economic Committee, *China's Economic Dilemmas in the 1990s: The Problems of Reforms, Modernization, and Interdependence.* Washington, D.C.: Government Printing Office.

Richardson, S. D. 1990. *Forest and Forestry in China.* Washington, D.C.: Island Press.

Ross, Lester. 1989. *Environmental Policy in China.* Bloomington: Indiana University Press.

Rubinstein, Murray. 1994. *The Other Taiwan, 1945 to the Present.* Armonk, NY: M. E. Sharpe.

Schell, Orville. 1994. *Mandate of Heaven: A New Generation of Entrepreneurs, Dissidents, Bohemians, and Technocrats Lay Claim to China's Future.* New York: Simon & Schuster.

Skeldon, Ronald, ed. 1994. *Reluctant Exiles? Migration from Hong Kong and the New Overseas Chinese.* Armonk, NY: M. E. Sharpe.

Smil, Vaclav. 1993. *China's Environmental Crisis.* Armonk, NY: M.E. Sharpe.

Stockholm Environment Institute and the United Nations Development Program China. 2002. *China Human Development Report 2002: Making Green Development a Choice.* NY: Oxford University Press.

Sullivan, Lawrence R., ed. 1995. *China Since Tiananmen: Political, Economic and Social Conflicts.* Armonk, NY: M. E. Sharpe.

Wu, Harry Hongda. 1992. *Laogai—The Chinese Gulag.* Boulder, CO: Westview Press.

Chapter 3

Japan and Korea

What is Japan like? Who are the Japanese people? Their characteristics collide: democracy and hierarchy, formality and chaos, overfed wrestlers and bonsai trees, traditional skill and daring modernity, permissiveness and restrictiveness. In form, Japan is a parliamentary democracy. Yet a single party, the Liberal Democrats, was in power for all but three of the past fifty years. Again, in form, Japan is a capitalist, free enterprise society. Yet bureaucrats, businessmen, and politicians seem to collude with one another for the greater glory of Japan. Is this real democracy? A real free enterprise society?

How do we meet such a culture? Where did the Japanese come from? Where are they going? In this chapter we explore Japan's social, economic, and political structure. We will try to understand its environment, culture, and economy within the context of geography, and provide explanations that clarify much of what seems so contradictory about Japan and the Japanese.

THE GEOGRAPHY

Japan is a predominantly mountainous and hilly island country (Figure 3.1). Its four major islands—Hokkaido in the north, Honshu in the middle, Shikoku in the southeast, and Kyushu in the south—cover a total north–south distance of over 1,150 miles. The southern chain of the small Ryukyu Islands extends over 700 miles. The northernmost part of Japan lies in the same latitude as Maine, and the southern areas lie in the same latitudes as southern Alabama. The Ryuku Islands run south of the Florida Keys and central Mexico. Japan's land area is about 148,000 square miles (373,000 sq km), slightly smaller than the land area of France, but somewhat larger than that of the United Kingdom or Italy.

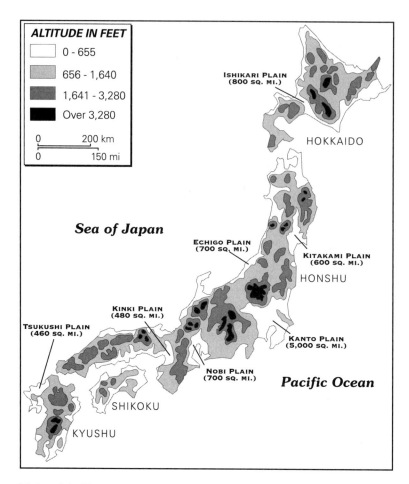

Figure 3-1. Japan's landforms.

Japan lies on the edge of the Asian continental shelf, and the Korean Strait between Japan and Korea is only 150 feet deep. On the eastern edge of Japan, the sea bottom drops away quickly to form one of the greatest ocean depths in the world—the Japan Trench or Tuscarora, at 35,000 feet deep. The Japanese archipelago was created by crustal movements involving four major tectonic plates: the Pacific Plate underlying the Western Pacific, the Eurasian Plate beneath the Asian land mass and Sea of Japan, the North American Plate in the north, and the Philippine Plate to the south (Figure 3.2). The lines of collision between the plates are marked by ocean deeps. The intermittent sliding of the ocean bed along the deeps results in earthquakes and tidal waves called *tsunami*. The friction of movement deep beneath the western plates melts the surrounding crust, which spews forth as volcanoes which run along the entire island chain. The volcanic zones, many of which contain hot springs, have considerable value as tourist attractions.

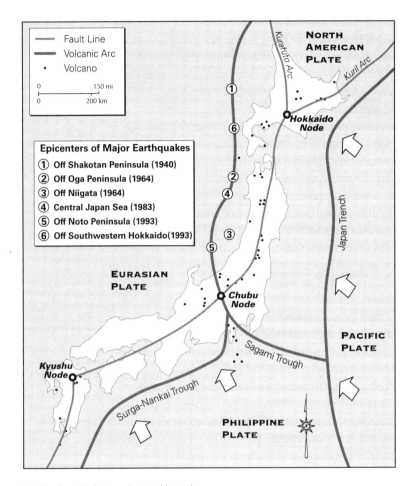

Figure 3-2. Continental plates and natural hazards.

In the traditional East Asian belief, the onset of a new historical era is marked by catastrophes. This was true for Commodore Mathew Perry's opening of Japan. Just months later, Japan was hit by major earthquakes and tidal waves. The earthquakes in the Tokai region in 1944 and the Mikawa area in 1945 caused massive destruction and loss of life. But the two great urban quakes of the twentieth century occurred on September 1, 1923 in Tokyo and on January 17, 1995 in Kobe.

The Great Kanto Earthquake of 1923 was the deadliest quake in Japanese history, killing more than 100,000 in an urban population of 2.5 million. Quakes centered in the Kanto region are caused by movement of the Pacific Plate, but the Philippine Plate under the Tokai region is stronger and more active. The Great Kanto Earthquake struck at 11.58 A.M. on September 1, 1923. It reduced much of Tokyo and Yokohama into a wasteland in an instant. A few hours later, a strong southwest wind whipped up the tongues of small blazes, which soon merged into a massive firestorm, more than 500 meters wide. Unstoppable, it steadily consumed everything in its path.

The disaster was the "death of old Tokyo and Yokohama." In the immediate aftermath of the earthquake and fires, people wandered aimlessly through the rubble and corpses, searching hopelessly for their separated relatives and friends. As the days progressed, many dramas of self-sacrifice and courage unfolded. People who were buried under heaps of bricks were rescued in the nick of time, just before fires consumed them. Captains of ships, in a show of daring seamanship, maneuvered their vessels out of the blazing harbor set afire by spilled oil.

While such valiant relief and rescue operations were taking place at a frantic pace, corpses were being collected and cremated by the thousands under sheets of corrugated iron. Looters seized the opportunity to pocket the contents of many safes lying unsecured in the midst of rubble. But these crimes paled in comparison to the atrocities committed against the Koreans. Police rounded up Koreans by the droves and tied them to telegraph poles, executing others. Vigilante groups were founded in response to unfounded rumors claiming that the fires were lit by Koreans and that they were poisoning wells. As a result, as many as 8,000 Koreans are thought to have died in the great quake's aftermath, after having escaped the natural cataclysm.

To the southwest of Yokohama, below Suruga Bay, lies the epicenter of the overdue Tokai earthquake which will badly jolt the Tokai region of central Japan. The epicentral area has been ominously quiet for too long, though the coastline has been sinking. The tension is expected to break with a quake of over 8 on the Richter scale, to be followed by a tsunami 3 to 4 meters high. The Tokai region suffers major seismic upheaval roughly every 130 years. The last big quake was in 1854. In 1979, 170 municipalities in the Tokai region, including 75 in Shizuoka prefecture were designated areas for disaster relief measures. With scientific prediction, equipment, and countermeasures, Shizuoka plans to minimize the damage by the quake. The earthquake proof wharves at Shimizu will keep the port open to receive food and other aid sent by sea.

Few will ever forget what happened to Kobe and its surrounding areas at 5.46 A.M. on January 17, 1995. No other event in twentieth-century Japan, save for the Great Kanto Earthquake and World War II, claimed so many lives and shattered so many hopes in a few seconds. Registering 7.2 on the Richter scale, the quake was centered on a fault near Kobe. The earthquake began at a depth of 12.4 miles. The Philippine Sea plate moved in a northwest direction near Kobe, striking the Eurasian plate and causing that plate to buckle. The buckling resulted in a twist ing motion that caused the destruction in Kobe. It killed more than 5,300, injured nearly 27,000, and left 300,000 homeless. The temblor struck a crucial economic zone that encompasses Kobe, Japan's sixth-largest city and a major commercial hub, and Osaka, the nation's second largest city and a financial center.

Many elevated expressways, bridges, and buildings collapsed because of flaws in engineering design. The Japanese rely on brute strength in structural engineering. Support columns, especially those used to hold up roadways and train tracks, tend to be huge and brittle. When the ground shakes, the columns are meant to stand firm and resist collapse. In the United States support columns are smaller and more flexible; they may deform under stress and sustain damage, but they do not collapse. Newer Japanese buildings incorporate the American approach, but those built before 1983 and most elevated roadways followed the brute strength approach. The Japanese approach works as long as ground motions occur in a range that has been anticipated, but the ground motions in the Kobe earthquake were twice as large as expected.

Like the Great Kanto Earthquake, in the Kobe (Hanshin) quake the minorities and the poor suffered heavy losses. Although nature was democratic in that the temblor rattled rich neighborhoods and poor neighborhoods equally, the consequences of the quaking were not equal. Frequently, it was the poorer people's homes that collapsed and burned their owners in the rubble. Niigata Ward, a gritty industrial center just west of downtown Kobe, suffered among the worst damage and fires. Here, old traditional Japanese wooden houses with heavy tile roofs easily collapsed in the earthquake. Kobe's largest minority group, the Koreans living in this area, absorbed a disproportionate share of the disaster.There are about 700,000 ethnic Koreans in Japan, many living in the region around Kobe and Osaka. About half of Kobe's 20,000 Korean residents lived in Niigata. The industry the Koreans dominated and which employed a majority of people in Niigata—shoe production—was nearly destroyed. The shoe industry is not likely to be rebuilt to its prequake level, and may wither to a fraction of its previous size, causing hardship to the Koreans. The scale of the disaster in Niigata Ward fell hard on another minority, a group known as *burakumin*. The *burakumin* were Japan's official outcasts for more than a century, given jobs that were considered unclean, such as butchering and leather work. Many of Kobe's *burakumin* were clustered in Niigate Ward, and many relied on the small shoe workshops for jobs.

The earthquake zone in the Kobe region included some of the wealthiest parts of Japan such as Ashiya, to the east of Kobe, where $5 million ranch-style homes peek from behind stone walls. Here, many of the homes came through unscathed. Ashiya was the setting for the novel *The Makioka Sisters,* Junichiro Tanizaki's portrayal of the life of a rich family in the 1930s. The sturdy homes of the wealthy withstood the shocks much better than did the poorly constructed homes of poorer people. In the wealthy neighborhoods such as Ashiya, residents have built newer homes and have spent more money on better-quality construction. The affluent also tend to have larger rooms and often sleep on beds; poorer people sleep on futons on the floor of tiny rooms, where a falling wardrobe is almost sure to hit them.

The major mountains are the dissected Hida, Kiso, and Akaishi ranges, which run across the entire length of Honshu. The mountains form parallel chains separated by numerous steep-sided intermontane basins. They run together in central Honshu, near a great structural depression or rift valley called the Fossa Magna, which extends across Honshu from the Sea of Japan to the Pacific Ocean. Within this depression, partly filled with volcanic material, lies Japan's highest peak, Mt. Fuji (12,461 feet or 3,776 meters). South of the Fossa Magna the parallel lines of mountains continue until they are broken by faults and subsidences in which the Inland Sea and Lake Biwa have formed.

Within the complex mountain framework there are small areas of habitable land generally confined to the coastal margins. Among these areas of relatively level land are the Kanto Plain around Tokyo, Ishikari in southeast Hokkaido, Echigo on the west coast of Honshu, Nobi around Nagoya, Kitakami north of Sendai on the Pacific coast of Honshu, Kinki or Settsu around Osaka at the eastern end of the Inland Sea, and Tsukushi surrounding Kurume in western Kyushu. These plains consist of separate sections of alluvial lowland with finer material which blankets the downstream part of the plains, followed by degraded alluvium or diluvial upland which flank the mountains.

The alluvial lowland portion of the plain is valuable for paddy cultivation and as the site for urban or industrial development. Intensive agriculture with rice as the major crop occupies about half of the lowlands (Figure 3.3).The diluvial upland portion of the plain consists of coarse materials forming porous dry areas with a deep water table. With the water shortage and porous soil, the upland is used for orchards and nonirrigated crops such as wheat, barley, and vegetables. The margins of uplands are used for tea growing. The higher areas flanking the mountains are covered with forest, varying from broadleaf trees in the south to pines in the north. Lumbering is a major activity.

The extreme scarcity of level land is one of the salient features of the geography of Japan. In a country where the population is currently 125 million, only 16 percent of the total land area is cultivable. Thus, the small areas of lowland, which contain not only most of the cultivated land but also all the major concentrations of population and industry, are of vital importance.

The large latitudinal extent of Japan, the sheltering effect of the mountains, and the monsoonal air stream produces considerable climatic differences between north and south and between the western Sea of Japan side and the eastern Pacific side of the islands. Summer along the Pacific coast is hot and humid, and the winter is generally dry and cold. Along the coast of the Sea of Japan the summer is relatively dry and there is heavy snowfall in the winter.

Figure 3-3. Rice paddy fields and snow-capped Mount Iwakisan (5,231 feet), 40 miles south of Aomori, Japan. Most of the country is mountainous, and level areas are limited to intermountain basins such as this one or alluvial plains along the coast. Less than 15 percent of the country is suitable for agriculture, settlement, or commercial and industrial use. Lowland areas are intensively used. (Photo: Cotton Mather.)

The cities of Niigata and Kanazawa receive their peak precipitation in December in the form of snow, often as much as 25 inches. The northward passage of the *sakura zensen*—the cherry blossom front—in late March or early April, marking the onset of spring, is widely publicized in the media and weather forecasts in Japan. It is the time when millions flock to public parks, ostensibly to view the blossoms, but in practice to enjoy the many hours of song and drink.

Hanami. Cherry Blossoms, The Messengers of Spring

In Japan, the harbinger of spring is the blooming of the sakura—cherry blossoms. As the days grow longer and the sun begins to warm in late March, the tight flower buds of the cherry trees begin to open. The buds are quite unnoticeable until the pink petals begin to show here and there. Perhaps three or four days pass without much happening. But then, one day, all the cherry trees suddenly bloom. In fact they blossom so abruptly that you wake up one morning, surprised to find that your neighborhood is filled with the pink, hazy clouds of cherry blossoms.

The sensational moment when the cherry blossoms open completely is eagerly anticipated by the Japanese. People watch weather forecasts far in advance (often one or two weeks ahead) to try to gauge exactly when the sakura will start blooming. Indeed, information on the *sakura zensen*, or the cherry blossom front, is crucial for planning the exact timing for a *hanami*, or flower-viewing party. Why? Because the flowers begin to shed their petals just a few hours after they reach full bloom. If you do not plan properly, you are apt to be too early. Worse still, the flowers could all be gone by the time you begin your party.

In addition to all the planning and preparation, it is important to consider finding space—someone must set out early in the morning to find the best cherry tree under which the *goza*, or straw mat, should be spread. Here again, skill is required to find the best location because these *goza* mats will become the temporary livingroom rugs that will hold all the food, drink, people, and, perhaps, *karaoke* sets.

Hanami parties sometimes start early in the morning and last until evening sets in. Some people begin in the evening, when lanterns are lit among the cherry trees, and continue late into night. Many stalls selling *yakitori* (barbecued chicken), *yakisoba* (fried noodles), and drinks augment the crowd. This added activity intensifies the already tense excitement and fervor of the people.

Cherry blossoms often arouse very typical Japanese sentiments among the people. Sometimes recalling scenes from Buddhist teachings, the fragile beauty of the cherry blossom is said to represent the brevity of life. This idea leads to the conclusion that "life is too short for worries, so you might as well enjoy it now," a sentiment that aptly fits many people at *hanami* parties. At other times, the cherry blossom is used to represent something that is short-lived. This is why couples in Japanese soap operas often pose under cherry trees—it is an indication that their love is almost over. *Harakiri* scenes in Japanese dramas are also frequently performed under cherry trees. Here again, these delicate flowers are used as a subtle reminder that life is often short and empty.

HISTORICAL AND CULTURAL ROOTS

What are the historical and cultural roots of the Japanese? When did they begin to inhabit the Japanese archipelago? Archaeological evidence indicates that a rich Paleolithic culture existed in Japan, and the islands may have been inhabited for as many as 50,000 years. During the ice ages of the later Pleistocene period Japan was linked to the Asian land mass. Paleolithic hunters crossed what is now the Korean Strait from Korea to Japan. Similar prehistoric movements took place from Siberia to Hokkaido on land bridges which disappeared when the great glaciers melted and sea levels rose.

Evolution of the Yamato Cultural Core

Over many thousands of years there was gradual movement from a Stone Age culture through a pottery-making (Jomon) culture, and then to a metal-using agricultural society (Yayoi period). From around 300 A.D. the physical and cultural landscape was transformed by the appearance of great tombs centering on the Yamato region at the eastern end of the Inland Sea. The greatest concentration of large tombs (Kofun) is in the Osaka-Nara area; they are associated with the Yamato rulers, ancestors of the present imperial line. The rulers of Yamato, perhaps a confederation of tribal chieftains, claimed descent from Sun Goddess and extended their power westward and eastward from the Nara-Kyoto-Osaka region. By the fifth and sixth century a single kingly line seems to have developed within Yamato.

Throughout these early centuries of the Yayoi and Kofun periods there were intermittent but close connections between clans in Japan and people in China and Korea. In the middle of the sixth century the Japanese society was transformed by a new cultural element from the continent: Buddhism (Figure 3.4). Buddhism found its way to Japan through immigrant communities. Gradually, Buddhist temples replaced the great tombs as the places of ritual burial for the ruling groups in Japan. When Buddhism was introduced in Japan, the Japanese already had their own system of spiritual beliefs and ritual practices called Shinto, which touched every aspect of Japanese emotional experience and shaped Japanese responses to nature, life and death. Shinto, Buddhism, Confucianism, and to a lesser extent Taoism and Christianity, have all exerted a profound influence on Japanese culture and the spiritual life of individual Japanese.

Buddhism settled into an easy complementary relationship with Shinto practices, and Japan was transformed in the seventh and eighth centuries from a clan society headed by a great chieftain to an imperial state rules by a heavenly sovereign, based on the Tang model of China. The transformation was based on the importation of Buddhism and a whole series of Chinese administrative and legal institutions. Until the establishment of Buddhism, which brought in its wake a clear governmental structure and a code of laws, Japan

Figure 3-4. Sensoji Buddhist Temple, also called Asakusa Kannon, Tokyo. The statue of Boddhisatva in the temple was found, according to folk tradition, in the Sumida River in 628 by two fishermen. The temple was rebuilt during the Kamakura period (1185–1333) after many fires. The temple is the site of many events throughout the year, and is visited by large numbers of Japanese annually on New Year's Eve. (Photo: P. P. Karan.)

was still a loose confederation of clans in tenous balance, with the imperial clan precariously at its head. The mechanics of rule and succession were undefined, creating violent conflicts. In addition, due in part to a Shinto belief that death was a source of ritual pollution, each time a new emperor took the throne the palace and capital were moved to a new site.

With the ascendancy of the imperial clan, supported by religious, court, and bureaucratic structures based on Chinese models, the need for a capital on a grand scale could not be ignored. The Chinese precedent required a permanent capital, laid out according to an orderly plan. The new capital was built at Nara in 710. All the arts that had made their way from China and Korea had gradually taken root in Japan—architecture, sculpture, painting, calligraphy, music, lacquer, and silk making—and came into play in creating the temples and palaces of the capital (Figure 3.5). In 794 the capital was moved to Kyoto (Heian-kyo, the capital of peace and tranquility), which remained the capital of Japan until the emperor moved his court to Tokyo in 1868. The new capital was modeled on Chang'an (modern Xi'an or Sian in China) with a grid pattern of avenues and streets and the great palace to the north of the city. The residences of the aristocracy were close to the imperial palace, followed by those of petty officials, artisans, store-keepers, and commoners (Figure 3.6).

The Shogun, Daimyo, and Samurai Culture (1185–1868)

The feudal culture of Japan from the twelfth to the nineteenth century (1185–1868) was dominated by *daimyo*, regional magnates who ranked below Japan's shogun rulers and above samurai warriors. Castle towns served as the center of the *daimyo*'s domain. The martial society of Japan's middle ages began about a century after the beginning of Europe's feudal era and lasted well into the Victorian period. Japan's feudal social structure was similar to Europe's hierarchy of kings, lords, warriors, and vassals, but while Europeans allowed their cultural traditions to remain dormant until the Renaissance, the Japanese *daimyo* nurtured art forms such as painting, poetry, drama, and ceremony. The goal of the *daimyo* was to maintain balance between the arts of combat, or *bu*, and the arts of peace and culture, or *bun*. The embodiment of *bu* was the sword, which the samurai saw as an object of spiritual significance. Although mastery of the *bu* discipline was essential for the *daimyo* to survive and hold on to land, many regional lords also became patrons and even practitioners of the arts. Literature, painting, and sculpture were all cultivated, but perhaps the most profound of the *bun*-related traditions was the tea ceremony, a disciplined and beautiful event first used to achieve the relaxation of Zen meditation. Another expression of *bun* was the *Noh* plays which, like the miracle plays that preceded Elizabethan drama in the West, taught moral lessons in the context of entertainment.

Figure 3-5. Itsukushima Jinja at Miyajima, near Hiroshima, is well known as one of the most scenic places in Japan. The large torri gate (525 feet) out in Hiroshima Bay marks the sacred space and symbol of the shrine. Much of the shrine is constructed over water so that when the tide rises Itsukushima Jinja appears to be floating on water. (Photo: P. P. Karan.)

The idea of a full-scale warrior government, headed by a shogun and detached from the imperial court, was firmly established in the feudal period. The imperial court was enfeebled and reduced to a ritual and legitimizing role, but it was not stripped of sovereignty. Japan had admitted European traders and Christian missionaries, but evicted them and closed her doors after observing what was happening everywhere in Asia where Europeans had been admitted. Introduced into Kyushu in 1540s, Christianity spread rapidly. Francis Xavier, who landed in Kagoshima in 1549, preached in Hirado, Hakata, Yamaguchi, Kyoto, and Shimabara. Jesuits, Franciscans, and Dominicans strove to convert both *daimyo* and commoners. The expulsion of missionaries in 1587 and relentless persecution of Christians after 1612 by the early Tokugawa shoguns eventually crushed missionary effort in Japan. The few Christians who clung to their faith did so secretly.

By the mid-eighteenth century the teeming garrison city of Edo (Tokyo) began to assume the intellectual and cultural primacy over Kyoto, which had been the cultural pacesetter in Japan. The presence of shogunal court and

Figure 3-6. Kumamoto Castle is (with Osaka and Nagoya castles) one of the three most famous in Japan. Designed by Lord Kato Kiyomasa (1562–1611), it is noted for the spectacular long wall fronting the Tsuboi River, and the famous *mushagaeshi* (enemy-repelling) wall. During the civil war of 1877, the last major armed uprising against the Meiji government and its reforms, the castle withstood forty days of bombardment and seige by the rebel army. (Photo: Cotton Mather.)

daimyo residences, temples, shrines, and a large population created a huge demand for goods, services, learning, and entertainment. Edo merchants had the wealth and confidence to patronize culture.

Over 80 percent of the population of Tokugawa Japan lived on the land. The Tokugawa shoguns compartmentalized Japanese society into four hereditary status groups: samurai, farmers, artisans, and merchants, with outcasts (*eta*) and non-people (*hinin*) below them. In the Tokugawa status hierarchy farmers ranked immediately after the samurai in importance. Their valued function in Confucian economic theory was to sustain society through their labor. *Daimyo* squeezed as much tax from the peasants as possible. By 1640 Japan was closing in on itself commercially; trade with other countries was restricted to Nagasaki.

The Tokugawa shogunate survived until 1867, and during this long period of peace and stability a uniquely Japanese cultural style developed. Land surveys to assess the land in terms of rice productivity (*kokudaka*) were completed. It became the basis for setting land tax, village size, and allotment of *daimyo* domains, samurai stipends, and feudal obligations. Thus, one characteristic of premodern Japan was that rice production became the standard for everything, as indicated by the expression *komedate* (rice-based calculation). *Daimyo* had their own domains and castles and were served by samurai vassals. Entrusted by the shoguns with the registers of lands and peoples in their domains, they enjoyed the right to govern the territory and collect annual land taxes.

Emergence as a Great Power (1868–1914)

In 1853, eleven years after the Treaty of Nanking opened up China, an American navy commodore, Mathew C. Perry, steamed into Tokyo Bay and so overawed the Japanese that they opened their ports to shipwrecked American sailors and to American trade. The alert Japanese were much impressed by the technological superiority of the Americans. In 1868, just fifteen years later, a group of forward-looking young Japanese overthrew the existing government and began reorganizing the Japanese government and society along modern Western lines. Taking what they considered best from the various Western nations, they patterned their business methods after those of the United States, their legal system after the French, and their navy after the British. But it was Bismarck's Germany that impressed the Japanese most. They built a military machine and an authoritarian government and education system on the model of the German Empire.

In an incredibly short time Japan became a modern industrialized military power. In 1894 Japan attacked China, and forced it to pay a large indemnity and to give up Korea (which Japan annexed in 1910) and the island of Formosa (Taiwan). Japan attacked Russia in 1904 and defeated it on land and sea. Japan took the southern half of Sakhalin Island and Russia's railroad and port concessions in southern Manchuria, thereby becoming the dominant power in East Asia. By 1914 Japan was a first-rate power—industrialized, militaristic, and imperialistic. It participated in World War I on the side of the Allies and received Germany's island possessions in the Pacific north of the equator as her reward. Japan gained a military monopoly in East Asia and the western Pacific.

The Triumph of Fascism

In the 1920s Japan stood at a crossroads: the country could use its great energies and skills either to develop its own institutions and raise standards of living or to become a predatory military state. At the same time, liberal democratic trends were being overshadowed and weakened by aggressive nationalism. Japan's quickly built industries had overexpanded during the wartime prosperity, and postwar deflation and sharp competition from the former allies brought severe economic stresses.

Three divergent groups competed for the leadership of Japan in the 1920s. The dominant group was made up of the great industrialists. Seventy-five percent of Japan's industry and capital was concentrated in the hands of five great families, called the *zaibatsu*. These industrial giants had such a stranglehold on the Japanese economy that they were able to control the government. The *zaibatsu*, enjoying this economic and political monopoly, wished to see no fundamental change in Japan. They advocated peaceful economic penetration of Asia.

The liberals were the second group, comprising mostly university professors and students. This group set out to broaden suffrage, which was restricted to the well-to-do, to encourage the more effective unionization of labor, and to diminish the power of the military. In 1925 suffrage was broadened and liberal political parties emerged. There were periods of growing democratic impulses. The young Emperor Hirohito, who ascended the throne on December 25, 1926, adopted the name Showa (meaning "enlightenment and harmony") for his reign. But the long tradition of passive submission to authority on the part of the masses made liberal reforms difficult.

The third group, the professional military, was determined to strengthen its own traditional power. In the early 1930s Japan's growing international isolation—resulting from its aggression in China and Manchuria, war fervor, and patriotic hysteria—combined to undermine the authority of the parties and reassert the power of the military. Once in power, the military destroyed all democratic processes of government and civil rights. The *zaibatsu* were corrupted and won over with lush military contracts. By 1940 the strengthened militaristic and authoritarian tendencies in Japanese policy put it on the brink of war with the United States. A surprise attack on Pearl Harbor by Japan on the morning of December 7, 1941, started World War II in the Pacific. The attack failed in Japan's strategic aims of totally destroying the U.S. Pacific fleet and shattering the American will to fight.

Reform, Reconstruction, and Emergence as Economic Superpower

Japan emerged from World War II defeated on sea and land, the shocked victim of history's first two atomic bombs used for military purposes. Japan surrendered on September 2, 1945. With the cessation of hostilities, all administrative powers of the Japanese government were placed in the hands of General Douglas MacArthur. From September 1945 to April 1952 the Japanese government was officially responsible to an American occupation force. The U.S. government followed a four-point policy for postwar Japan: (1) Japan was to be limited to the four "home" islands and some small ones in the vicinity; (2) Japan was to be completely demilitarized; (3) civil, political, and religious rights and liberties for the Japanese people were to be restored; (4) Japan's economy was to be developed for its peacetime needs. A democratic constitution was drawn up and educational and land reform programs were implemented.

During the 1950s and 1960s Japan made an outstanding economic recovery. In rebuilding its ruined industries Japan adopted the most modern and scientific labor-saving devices. By the mid-1960s Japan was the third-greatest industrial power in the world, outranked only by the United States and the Soviet Union, and her people were enjoying a prosperity and a standard of living such as they had never known before. In the 1980s Japan emerged as an economic superpower in the world.

Since the 1960s high-growth era, Japan's economic policy has had two major features. First, government agencies cooperated with big business to enhance the international competitiveness of strategic industrial sectors. Market-conforming instruments nurtured new technologies, ensured stable domestic markets, and promoted exports. As Japan became a first-rank industrial power, a subtle shift occurred from state-guided industrialization to network capitalism. This form of capitalism involves constant consultations and cooperation between the economic ministries and the major corporations to manage both domestic and international market trends. It helped establish privilege for large firms and condoned preferential trading practices among firms in a particular *keiretsu* (business network). Second, while promoting internationally competitive sectors, the Japanese government compensated the economically weak sectors such as agriculture and small business, especially the retail sector. This policy was implemented through import quotas and tariffs, price supports, subsidies, tax breaks, and protective regulations. Its purpose was to prevent rapid industrial change from aggravating socioeconomic inequality and uneven development. The policy sacrificed economic efficiency and aggregate productivity gains to sustain societal cohesion.

Japan's political economy based on government–business cooperation and consultations, compensations for weak economic sectors, and employment security for workers made it possible for the country to respond to changes in world markets and in technology while minimizing the dislocative effects on domestic society. This Japanese-style capitalism has been termed a "developmental state," in which consensus is forged among government, political parties, corporations, and the key societal groups. It promoted Japan's development enormously, but it tended to export the social costs of economic adjustments to Japan's more liberal trading partners, especially the United States.

In the 1990s Japan's developmental corporatism came under severe challenges. The collapse of the bubble economy (asset inflation, or speculative and inflated wealth in securities and land in 1986–1989), excessive productive capacity, and bad debts threw Japan into the throes of one of the worst economic recessions since the end of World War II. Many Japanese banks are saddled with heavy debts. Even if Japan's economy fully recovers from the recession, long-term growth rates in early twenty-first century are likely to be low. Unfortunately, neither the fragmented ruling party, a disorganized group of opposition parties, nor the Japanese electorate has a sense of how Japan should reform itself.

How did the Japanese economy get into such terrible shape in the late 1990s, and what accounts for Japan's inability to recover from its economic problems? To solve Asia's economic crisis, it is important to reestablish Japan as an engine of regional growth, but how can the country kick-start its economy? The Japanese economy got into poor shape because upheavals in the financial system since 1990 were producing a deflationary impact on the economy. Values of Japan's assets were contracting. Under these circumstances, household spending of the Japanese people was falling. For all of 1998, household spending fell 2.2 percent, the sixth straight annual decline and the worst drop in twenty-four years. The decline in consumer spending, which accounts for about 60 percent of total demand in the Japanese economy, has caused profits to plunge at manufacturers such as Toyota Motor Corporation and Matsushita Electric Industrial Co., and pushed others such as Nissan Motor Co. and Hitachi Ltd. into the red. Unemployment stood at 5.4 percent in 2002. Industrial output fell in 2001 as demand fell in Japan.

There are several reasons for Japan's inability to recover from its economic problems. First, banks and other creditors are immobilized by huge losses (estimated at $575 billion) from the collapse of the speculative bubble in land prices in the early 1990s. While banks battle with debts, they have cut back on new loans to business, contributing to a credit crunch. Japan's unwillingness to write off bad loans, and the inability of creditors to pursue their claims through courts have prolonged the loan crisis. A strong legal system and new bankruptcy laws are needed to replace the "informal" guidance by the bureaucrats who have dominated the country since the Meiji era (1868–1912). Second, bureaucrats at the center are dictating national policy. Regions need to stand on their own in the next five to six years so that they can produce new and competitive industries. Third, there is a need for change from the webs of relationships that misallocate resources and a parliamentary system that hugely over-represents the rural parts of the country. Japan has not lost many of the key ingredients for growth, such as social stability, high literacy, skill, know-how, technology, and capital. Reforms are needed to stimulate the economy.

Japan can kick-start its economy by boosting economic demand through government intervention. Intervention through lower taxes and lower interest rates (the Keynesian model) does not make much sense in the Japanese context. Japanese interest rates are already very low, and lowering taxes leads to a rise in the savings rate. High savings is a rational choice in a society where social provisions are not underpinned by the state. So how could the Japanese be persuaded to spend? In Japan the state should spend for the public. Taxes may be raised and the money spent to boost economic demand by expenditure on "soft" infrastructure such as the creation of social provisions, more housing, better health care, and social welfare. In the past, Japan has spent vast sums to feed the concrete and construction industry, helping political cronies rather than the economy.

JAPAN'S POLITICAL SYSTEM

Racked by scandals and controlled by one party from 1955 to 1993, Japan's weak political system contrasts sharply with its economic system. Although Japan adopted the formal structure of democracy—a constitutional government, universal suffrage, and multiple political parties—the way the political system operates in practice is often far removed from the ideals of liberal democratic government. The weakest link in the chain is the party system, which enjoys little popular respect and has consistently failed to implement badly needed reform.

In the early 1950s, to prevent the Japanese left from impeding economic growth, the private sector got together with conservative politicians and government bureaucrats to shape the political system in their favor. The result was the formation of the Liberal Democratic Party (LDP) in 1955, by a merger of conservative forces. In return for keeping the left from power, corporate Japan agreed to fund the new party on a massive scale and give it whatever other support it needed. In turn, the LDP offered to provide voters with economic prosperity. For forty years, until 1993, there had seemed to be no real alternative to the LDP, which was supported by the business and bureaucracy and preached economic expansion and alliance with the United States.

Many Japanese favor political reforms and changes in the electoral system, which discourage mass participation and preserves the status quo. The medium-sized multimember constituency system makes political campaigning extremely expensive and discourages the development of new parties. Many traditional forms of political campaigning such as door-to-door campaign, signature drives, parades, and candidate-produced literature are not allowed. Candidates send out government-produced postcards, place posters on official signboards, and make several television and radio announcements. To get around these laws, politicians spend most of their time doing favors for constituents, attending weddings and funerals, and generally trying to secure as much patronage as possible for their home districts.

For electoral purposes, Japan is divided into 129 districts which elect 511 representatives. Each district chooses two to six representatives by single, nontransferable voting. Under this rule voters can vote for only one name, though the districts elect more than one representative. In 1994 a new law was passed by which 300 representatives would be chosen by a single-member district plurality system and 200 would be chosen separately by a regional proportional representation system with a party-decided list of candidates. For elections the country is divided into eleven areas (Kinki, Kyushu, Minami-Kanto, Tokai, Kita-Kanto, Tokyo, Tohoku, Chugoku, Hokushinetsu, Hokkaido, and

Shikoku). In the regional proportional representation system, the voters simply vote for a political party and the party chooses the representatives. The apportionment of representatives in Japan is unfair. The 1994 election reforms correct this unfair representation system a little, but not completely.

When the electoral boundaries were drawn up after the war, Japan was primarily rural. Now Japan is primarily urban, but the seats have never been adequately redistributed. Even though the courts have encouraged redistribution, they have no power to enforce their will, and so urban Japan is under-represented by at least sixty seats. This helps explain the political delicacy of the rice import issue and also why urban salaried employees end up paying most of the taxes in Japan.

Failure to pass a package of political reform bills led to the fall of the LDP government in mid-1993. Between 1993 and 1995 there were three successive governments in Japan. The 1996 election in Japan was held under the new election reform law. Japanese voters endorsed the conservative Liberal Democrats, but it did not get a clear majority. The Liberal Democratic Party secured only 233 seats in the Lower House in the 2000 election and formed a government through coalition with smaller parties. In the 2003 election Japan's ruling coalition won by a slim majority. The end of the one-party dominance in Japan is likely to produce a prolonged period of political fluidity and weak governments, thereby impeding timely decisions for dealing with the changing international and domestic issues.

As Japan pursues its quest for a cleaner, more open political future, three common themes run through the people: (1) a revulsion against corrupt politicians, (2) a skepticism that real change will occur, and (3) a sense that the public is powerless. The ruling Liberal Democratic Party suffered a major loss in the 1998 election for the upper house. It relied too much on an ineffective civil service demoralized by mistakes and scandals. The LDP continues to receive giant contributions from construction companies, real estate developers, and farm organizations who benefit from public works projects and arcane government regulations.

TERRITORIAL DISPUTES WITH RUSSIA AND CHINA

The territorial dispute with Russia involves four Kurile Islands: Etorofu, Kunashiri, Shikotan, and Habomai. Czarist Russia and Soviet Union (until the end of World War II) recognized the islands as Japanese. The Soviet Union unilaterally broke its neutrality pact with Japan three days after the atomic bombing of Hiroshima, and attacked Japan one week before it surrendered in 1945. The Soviets retook the southern Sakhalin lost in the Russo-Japanese War, and grabbed the four disputed islands north of Hokkaido for good measure. Due to the illegal occupation of Japanese territory by Russian forces, there is no peace treaty between Japan and Russia.

A second territorial dispute involves a tiny chain of islands in the East China Sea. The Japanese call them the Senkaku Islands and the Chinese refer to them as the Tiaoyutai Islands. They are uninhabited and consist of five tiny rock islands and three reefs 100 miles notheast of Taiwan and 250 miles east of China. Japan has long asserted sovereignty over the Senakaku Islands, but since they were returned by the United States to Japanese control along with nearby Okinawa in 1971, the nation has never taken steps to press its claim. China and Taiwan have also long asserted sovereignty. The seabed around the island group is thought to be rich in oil reserves and maritime resources.

GEOGRAPHIC REGIONS

A major feature of the geography of Japan is the tremendous variety of landscapes compressed into a small space. Over centuries, the human impress on the land has accentuated the variety. Certain areas have long been recognized as possessing a distinctive regional personality stemming from a composite of environment, cultural history, and development. These regions are Hokkaido, Tohoku, Kanto, Chubu, Kinki, Chugoku, Shikoku, Kyushu and Ryukyu or Nansei Islands (Figure 3.7).

Hokkaido

Hokkaido, northernmost of Japan's main islands, is the nation's last frontier. Here, stretch the virgin forests and open wilderness that give the island its unique character. Several mountain ranges cross Hokkaido, and these are separated by a series of basin areas. To the west of these mountains lies the Ishikari Plain. To the southwest of the plain is a long peninsula which is the area closest to Honshu and the first part of the island settled by the Japanese. The climate is colder and drier than in the rest of Japan. It forms about one fifth of the total area (32, 247 sq mi or 83,520 sq km) of the country, but is home for only one twentieth (5,667,024) of the nation's population.

Hokkaido was inhabited by the Ainu until Japanese settlements were established in the southwest corner during the Edo period (1603–1867). Development of Hokkaido began during the Meiji period (1868–1912). People were encouraged by the government to settle in Hokkaido. The early settlers had to struggle against a harsh environment, but they persevered, and now the results of their pioneering efforts are visible in the well-developed agriculture, forestry, and fishery. About 10 percent of the area is cultivated, and the most important crops are rice, oats, and wheat. The region has large dairy farms, and vegetable farming also is important.

Ishikari Plain (Ishikari Heiya) is the most productive farming area in Hokkaido. Wetlands along the river Ishikarigawa have been converted to

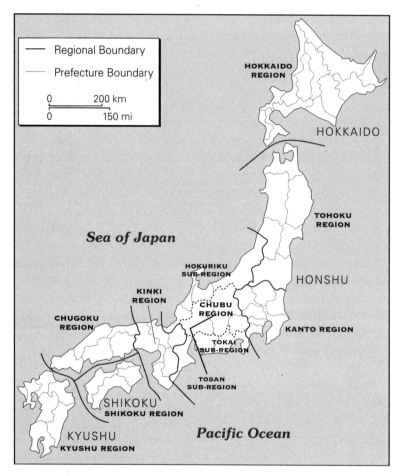

Figure 3-7. Japan's geographic regions. Ryukyu (Nansei) Islands lie Southwest to Kyushu.

agricultural use, providing fertile land for rice, vegetable, and dairy farming (Figure 3.8). The establishment of Sapporo in 1869 and the subsequent arrival of the colonist militia (*tondenhei*) contributed to the agricultural development of the region. The Meiji government established the Hokkaido Colonization Office in 1869 in Sapporo. In 1873 the government adopted a plan in which former samurai in the northern prefectures (many of whom had been unemployed since the Meiji Restoration of 1868) were encouraged to settle in Hokkaido. By 1882 more than 2,400 people had been resettled. Around 1890 Japan intensified its presence in Hokkaido by recruiting some 40,000 people, commoners as well as samurai, to settle in the area. With increased population the *tondenhei* system of settlement was abandoned in 1904.

The rural landscape of Hokkaido is unique within Japan, with large farms, pastures, and barns. The urban centers reflect modern layout and structure. Much of Hokkaido's mountainous interior comprises national parkland. With more than 70 percent of the area under forest, lumbering is a key industry.

Figure 3-8. The Ishikari Plain, formed by the meandering Ishikarigawa in Western Hokkaido, is one of the most productive farmlands in Japan. Nearly 1,500 square miles in area, it is intensively used for agriculture. Farms in Hokkaido are much larger than those in the rest of the country. The settlement of the region followed the establishment of Sapporo in 1869 and the subsequent arrival of the colonist militia, or *tondenhei*. (Photo: P. P. Karan.)

Hokkaido produces a quarter of the nation's annual lumber production. Kushiro is a major center of the lumber and fishing industries. There is a major coalfield in the Muroran area, which is the basis of an important iron and steel industry. In recent years biotechnology industries have developed in Hokkaido.

A distinctive activity in Hokkaido is thoroughbred horse breeding, with breeding farms concentrated in the Iburi and Hidaka regions. The farms, much smaller and less manicured than those in the bluegrass region of central Kentucky, rarely include training facilities (Figure 3.9). Although many of the breeding operations are modeled after Kentucky horse farms—a farm near Lexington's sister city of Shizunai was christened Lex Stud by its owners—they look more like Wisconsin dairy farms than any of Kentucky's blue-ribbon horse operations. Most of Japan's horse farms are small, family-run operations. Shadai Farm, Japan's biggest at 1,680 acres, is divided into four locations in Hokkaido. Shadai's facilities are superior, but it cannot escape the long cold winters. Because of the space shortage, training facilities are another problem. The Japan Racing Association has constructed a massive new 3,500-acre training facility for yearlings in the Hidaka region.

Hokkaido has three large wetlands near Kushiro, Lake Kutcharo, and Lake Utonai. Large areas of the wetlands have been reclaimed and turned into

Figure 3-9. The Northern Horse Park, near Tomakomai, Hokkaido. Thoroughbred horse farms are concentrated in this area of Japan. The British and American residents of Yokohama introduced Western-style horse racing with betting to Japan in the early 1860s. The horse farms in Hokkaido are much smaller and less manicured than those in the Bluegrass Region of Kentucky. (Photo: Cotton Mather.)

factory and residential sites, garbage disposal lots, or other developments. However, a multitude of plants and creatures inhabit wetlands in a complex ecological system. The Kushiro Marsh, some 18,290 hectares in area, provides a safe nesting habitat for the rare Japanese red-crowned crane. The present size of the marsh represents less than two thirds of its original size. Although 26,861 hectares of wetland in this area was designated as National Park in 1987, nothing protects the periphery from developers of homes and leisure facilities, or from the local paper industry's desire to fell more trees. All of this peripheral activity affects the water table and the ecological integrity of the adjacent wetlands. National park land in Japan is classified into three categories, two of which permit development (in varying degrees). Only 6,490 hectares of the Kushiro National Park lies in the area where development is prohibited, and only 7,726 hectares have been registered by Japan under the Ramsar Convention on Wetlands of International Importance. Between 1980 and 1985 nearly 3,000 hectares of Kushiro Marsh were lost to development, posing a threat to the splendid giant cranes that depend on it for their existence.

The modern settlement and colonization of Hokkaido has also led to the disappearance of the unique culture developed by the Ainu. By the end of the fourteenth century the Ainu, an indigenous people, had developed a culture based on hunting and fishing. They built communities, called *kotan*, along rivers. They sailed to Kamchatka and the far reaches of the Amur River to barter bear fur and deer skin for other commodities. Extensive contact between the Ainu in Hokkaido and the people in Honshu began in the twelfth century, giving rise to increasingly serious conflicts. After the 1669 Battle of Shakushain—believed to be one of the largest Ainu uprisings against the Japanese—the Ainu and their land were placed under the virtual control of the Matsumaehan, a feudal clan in northern Japan. Their lifestyle and living conditions then began to crumble, due to over fishing, over hunting, and exploitation by Japanese traders.

During the Meiji era, the Ainu people were brought under the control of the central government. In the 1890s, when many Japanese were migrating to the north to settle in Hokkaido, an 1899 law required the Ainu to abandon their hunting and fishing rights in exchange for farmland. Since that time rapid assimilation of the Ainu into Japanese society and intermarriage has reduced the number of pure-blooded Ainu to about 25,000, or less than 0.5 percent of the Hokkaido population. Ainu maintain that the 1899 law impugns their dignity, and the Hokkaido Ainu Association has sought to replace the law.

Ainu have also protested the building of the Nibutani Dam (now completed) to supply nonpotable water to an industrial complex built east of Tomakomai. It submerged an Ainu *chinomishiri*, or holy site, when the downstream dam was completed.

Tohoku

Encompassing the entire northern part of the island of Honshu, the Tohoku region consists of six prefectures: Aomori, Iwate, Miyagi, Akita, Yamagata, and Fukushima. The area is largely mountainous. The frontier of Japanese settlement passed through the area between the seventh and ninth centuries. Remote from centers of Japanese culture and political life, much of Tohoku retains its rustic character and is relatively less developed. The main areas of settlement in Tohoku follow the wide intermontane valley between the Ou and Kitakami ranges, in other small mountain basins, and along the Pacific and Sea of Japan coastal plains. The climate is highly seasonal, with short summers and long winters. The region, comprising an area of 25,835 sq mi (66,912 sq km), has about 10 million people, nearly 8 percent of the nation's population.

During the Edo period development took place in some of the feudal domains. Cottage industries developed in castle towns such as Morioka (iron ware), Yonezawa (silk weaving), and Soma (pottery). After the Meiji Restoration (1868) the development of Tohoku was not emphasized. Following World War II, improvement in agriculture in Tohoku was emphasized to increase food production. Tohoku has now become an important rice producing area. The southern part of the Tsuguru Plain, around Hirosaki, is Japan's leading apple producing area. Many Tohoku farmers migrate to Kanto and other regions of Japan during the long winters to supplement their incomes when there is little agricultural activity in the area.

South of Sendai lies the Joban coalfield. The Joban-Koriyama area is recovering from the decline of its traditional coal mining industry. A new port has been constructed in Sendai to encourage the development of new industries. Akita, on the west coast, has petroleum refining and metallurgical industries. There are minor industrial areas in larger cities. Tohoku is not favored with large coastal industrial regions. Its dominant role traditionally has been food production.

Kanto

Located in east central Honshu, the Kanto region consists of Tokyo, Chiba, Saitama, Kanagawa, Gumma, Ibaraki, and Tochigi prefectures, with an area of 12,504 sq mi (32,385 sq km). Kanto began to develop when the Tokugawa family made it the base of their power. They raised their mighty castle at Edo, present-day Tokyo, the capital of Japan and one of the largest cities in the world. After the Meiji Restoration (1868), Kanto became the center of Japanese politics, economy and culture. Now the most densely settled region in Japan, it is home to about 41 million people, about one third of the nation's population.

Kanto Plain occupies more than half of the Kanto region. The western two thirds is low diluvial upland. The eastern third contains alluvial areas and deltas of the rivers Tonegawa, Arakawa, and Tamagawa. There are numerous lakes and swampy areas. Divides between the major streams in the center and east are generally tongues of diluvial terraces extending toward the center from the west. The center and east of the plain is particularly flat and liable to flooding. Many of the rivers flow between levees and dikes. The Tone River, which flows through Kanto, was diverted eastward to its present course into the Pacific Ocean during the Edo period (1603–1867) because of frequent floods in Saitama Prefecture and downtown Edo (Tokyo). A number of dams have been built on the upper reaches of the Tone River for flood control and water power development. The Tama River was the principal source of domestic and industrial water supply for Tokyo. Water is now diverted from the Tone River to Tokyo by the construction of the Great Tone Dam at Gyoda to meet the increasing demands of the urban area.

The region is undergoing rapid change as land is reclaimed in Tokyo Bay and as the hills are turned into residential areas for the swelling Tokyo metropolitan area that includes Tokyo, Yokohama, Kawasaki, and their suburbs (Figure 3.10). The Tokyo-Yokohama urban area in the center of the Kanto region is Japan's leading commercial and industrial area.

Figure 3-10. New urban subcenters on Ariake and Daiba sites in the Tokyo Bay have been developed on reclaimed land. Reclamation projects continue to be implemented in Tokyo Bay at the Outer Central Breakwater through landfill. In addition to residential flats, the development includes blocks of high-technology buildings, sport and leisure facilities, and international conference centers. (Photo: P. P. Karan.)

Although Kanto is one of the most urbanized areas in Japan, agriculture plays a declining but important role in the region. Rice is an important crop on the alluvial lowlands and coastal plain. Nonrice crops such as barley, vegetables, sweet potatoes, beans, and potatoes or orchards are common on the diluvial uplands. Intensive truck farming of vegetables and flowers, poultry, and dairy cattle has spread to the Boso and Miura peninsulas. Summer cabbage, fruits, and vegetables are grown in the Gunma prefecture. The expansion of Tokyo and its suburbs as well as the other towns has used most of the arable land of Kanto. Coastal fishing in the Pacific and Tokyo Bay has declined because of vastly increased catches by deep sea fishing trawlers and because of increased pollution and land reclamation in Tokyo Bay.

Chubu

The Chubu region, with an area of 25,783 sq mi (66,777 sq km) and a population of 21 million, comprises Niigata, Toyama, Ishikawa, Fukui, Yamanashi, Nagano, Gifu, Shizuoka, and Aichi prefectures in central Honshu. The region is steeped in history and ensconced in natural surroundings. The Chubu region produced three men—Oda Nobunaga (1534–1582), Toyotomi Hideyoshi (1537–1598), and Tokugawa Ieyasu (1542–1616)—who had an indelible impact on the formation of premodern Japan. Oda Nobunaga was a military genius known for his extraordinary foresight. No mere warrior, Nobunaga devoted himself tirelessly to encouraging commerce and culture. The son of a poor farming family, Hideyoshi in 1590 completed the work of national reunification begun by Oda Nobunaga. Ieyasu, the first shogun or generalissimo of the Tokugawa Shogunate, ushered in a 265-year period of peace in Japan, starting in 1603.

Chubu is geographically divided into three subregions: the Hokuriku on the Sea of Japan side, the Central Highlands or Tosan, and the Tokai on the Pacific seaboard. This largely mountainous region is dominated by the Japanese Alps and contains numerous volcanoes, including Mt. Fuji (Fujisan). Some of Japan's longest rivers, the Shinanogawa, Kisogawa, and Tenryugawa, flow through the Chubu region.

Due to the central location of Chubu, the region has served as a corridor linking the Kinki and Kanto regions. Historical highways such as the Tokaido and Nakasendo connected Kyoto with Edo (Tokyo), and the Hokurikudo joined Kyoto with Tohoku. During the Edo period (1603–1867) many stage towns (*shukuba-machi*) developed along these roads. Today the corridor-linking function of the region remains important, with fast trains along the Tokaido and Tokaido-Sanyo lines, and the Nagoya-Kobe and Nagoya-Tokyo Expressways.

The Hokuriku area along the Sea of Japan receives heavy snowfall in winter and has high temperatures in summer. This area is Japan's principal single-crop rice production area. Many of the fields in the lower course of the Shinano River on the Niigata Plain were formerly swampy and poorly drained. Irrigation and drainage channels were constructed and pumps were installed, resulting in high yields of rice. Both hydroelectric and nuclear power plants are located here. Japan's worst nuclear-power accident took place at the plant in the town of Mihama in Fukui prefecture in 1991. An estimated 20 tons of radioactive water leaked from the plant, contaminating the water in the steam generator. Several other small accidents at nuclear plants have fed a growing antinuclear movement. The accidents embarrass the government, whose plans called for more than doubling the nation's thirty-nine nuclear plants in 1990.

Heavy chemical industries are important in Hokuriku. Toyama and Takaoka have chemical fertilizer, synthetic fibers, and aluminum industries. Petroleum refining and the petrochemical industries are important in Niigata. Among the traditional products of the region are lacquerware in Wajima, and silk weaving in Ojiya and Fukui.

The Central Highlands or Tosan consists of three mountain ranges extending north to south: the Hida Mountains (also called the Northern Alps), the Kiso Mountains (Central Alps), and the Akaishi Mountains (Southern Alps) with several peaks over 10,000 feet. Nestled among the mountains are important basins such as the Takayama, Nagano, Matsumoto, Suwa, and Kofu basins (Figure 3.11).

Figure 3-11. The Nagawado Dam on the Azusagawa, near Mount Norikura, west of Matsumoto Basin. There are over 2,471 dams in Japan; 1,475 of these are irrigation dams, 436 are multipurpose dams, and 36 are hydroelectric dams. (Photo: P. P. Karan.)

The weather in the mountains is often cloudy, and one can go an entire day seeing no further than 50 meters. On a clear day, though, you can witness the creation; the rising sun lifts entire ranges out of darkness, the peaks dividing light and shadow like prisms separating colors. Over the morning cloud the vertebrae of ranges—the Northern, Central and Southern Alps—form an archipelago that ranges nearly as far as the prominent cone of Fuji.

Takayama Basin is set deep within the mountains of Gifu Prefecture. Rice is cultivated along the Miyagawa River, and fruits and vegetables are grown along the highland slope. The major city is Takayama, which developed from 1586 as a castle town, and the chief industry is lumbering and carpentry. Nagano Basin consists mainly of alluvial fans and the floodplain of the river Chikumagawa. This long, narrow basin is known for the cultivation of rice, apples, and apricots. Nagano, the major city in the basin, developed as a market and one of the post-station towns on the old historic road. Today it is a commercial center with electrical machinery, food processing, publishing, and printing industries. Matsumoto Basin is flanked by the Hida and Chikuma mountains. It consists of piedmont alluvial fans below the fault scarp and river terraces. The area is known for horseradish (*wasabi*) and rice. The city of Matsumoto has one of the best-preserved feudal castles in Japan. Suwa is a graben basin (bounded by faults), spread around Suwa Lake in Nagano Prefecture (Figure 3.12). The basin is noted for the production of raw silk and precision instruments. The city of Suwa developed as a castle town. The traditional silk-reeling industry was replaced after World War II by precision instruments, *miso* (bean paste), and woodworking industries. Kofu Basin lies in central Yamanashi Prefecture, bounded by the fault scarps of the Akaishi and Misaka mountains. The basin is made of piedmont alluvial plains of the upper reaches of the Fujikawa. Rice is grown on the floodplain, and grapes and peaches are grown on the slopes. Kofu developed as a castle town and post-station town during the Edo period. Food processing, textiles, wine, and crystal ware are major industries.

Throughout the Tosan district there are a number of ski resorts and hot springs, making this region one of the major tourist area in the country. Skiing has been taken up by the Japanese with the kind of enthusiasm they used to reserve for exporting video recorders. Modern ski resorts in Tosan are indistinguishable from their American counterparts, except for the language and the fact that cafes serve bowls of noodles and green tea instead of chili and hot chocolate.

The Tokai lies along the Pacific coast between the Kanto and Kinki regions. The Tokai area has a mild climate, and mandarin oranges, green tea, and vegetables are important products grown in this area. Since the Meiji period the area has undergone heavy industrialization. Hamamatsu has pharmaceutical, musical instruments, and motorcycle industries. The paper and pulp industries dominate Fuji and Fujinomiya. Food processing industries are

Figure 3-12. Suwa Basin is graben in central Nagano prefecture in Chubu region. Spread around Lake Suwa, the area is noted for the precision-instrument manufacturing, *miso* (bean paste), and woodworking industries. Before World War II, the silk industry was important. (Photo: P. P. Karan.)

important in Shimoda, Yaizu, and Shizuoka. Shimizu in Suruga Bay has petroleum and aluminum refining industries.

On the Izu peninsula, inns and hot springs coexist with snack bars and crowded beaches. The 35-mile-long peninsula begins about 65 miles south of Tokyo. Its wrinkled western coast, jutting southward into the Pacific, is an array of dramatic cliffs and fishing villages nestled in coves. The mountains, which once hid political exiles, are dotted with natural hot springs that have been channeled into soothing baths at traditional inns. Izu is also well known for its excellent seafood and, in the wooded interior, pheasant and wild boar. Over it all towers the graceful symbol of Japan: the perfect cone of Mount Fuji, just a few miles across Suruga Bay.

Izu, like much of the Japanese countryside, is irritatingly commercial, over-built, and jammed with people, particularly on the more popular east coast, which has miles of sandy beaches and some golf courses. The towns are often clogged with souvenir shops and snack bars. Neon-lighted motels carry names such as "L'Auberge des Blue Marlins," and stand near beaches that can become packed with sun worshipers. In short, Izu has some of the best and worst of the Japanese countryside. It exemplifies the jarring experience that people undergo when they try to square the nation's sophisticated aesthetic heritage and splendid natural setting with the poorly situated power lines, industrial plants, and tacky commercial strips that mar parts of the country.

At the southeast tip of Izu Peninsula is the heavily commercialized resort of Shimoda. This is where the United States established its first consulate, in 1856, after Commodore Mathew Perry forcibly opened Japan with his imposing black ships. The one enduring memory of that episode seems to be the tragic fate that befell Tojin Okichi, a woman the Japanese offered as a mistress to Townsend Harris, the first American consul. As the story goes, Harris, a New Yorker who had helped found what became City College, returned Okichi after three days. She became dissolute, wandered for years, and eventually drowned herself, a result, according to legend, of the humiliation she suffered at the hands of the barbarian. Her memory is preserved at one temple, Hofuku-ji, with placards depicting the sacrifice she made for her country.

To the west, on the Nobi Plain along the Pacific coast, is one of the most densely populated and industrialized areas in Chubu. The Chukyo industrial region, centered on the city of Nagoya, extends east to Toyobashi in Aichi Prefecture, north to southern Gifu, and west to northern Mie Prefecture. The major industries are chemical fibers in Gifu and Okazaki, automobiles in Toyota, petroleum refining and petrochemicals in Yokkaichi, and steel and machinery in Nagoya. There is considerable agricultural development on the Okazaki plain, with emphasis on vegetable growing for the Nagoya market.

The Chubu region (Hokuriku, Tosan, and Tokai) has launched an intensive drive to become the country's most influential region internationally with a number of major projects meant to improve its industrial and cultural infrastructure. There are a number of projects planned on transportation, industrial technology, and urban development. The Chubu International Airport Construction Promotion Council has been established to promote an early opening of the Chubu International Airport, to be built off the coast just 30 km south of Nagoya. The 500-km Chuo Linear Express (a magnetically levitated train which will provide a one-hour connection between Tokyo and Osaka via Nagoya) and the second Tomei and Meishin expressways are among the other transportation projects that are considered key to further development of the region. Although Chubu holds its own against other regions of Japan in economic development, there is concern about the lack of labor in the region. In March 1993 the job opportunity ratio in Aichi was 1.28, compared with the national ratio of 0.88. The figure translated into 128 jobs for every 100 job seekers. The region attracted foreign workers from Peru, Brazil, Iran, and other Asian countries. Since the mid-1990s the region, like the rest of Japan, has been in recession.

Kinki

The Kinki region is the original heartland of Japanese culture. With an area of 12,767 sq mi (33,075 sq km), it comprises Osaka, Hyogo, Kyoto, Shiga, Mie, Wakayama, and Nara prefectures. It is a mountainous region with a population of 22 million concentrated in many small basins and coastal plains on the Inland Sea, Osaka Bay, and Kii Peninsula. The northern part of Kinki faces the Sea of Japan and is colder than the rest of Kinki, with snowfall in the winter. The southern Kii Peninsula receives heavy precipitation and is relatively warm in winter.

The Kii Peninsula exemplifies Japan's religious roots and striking natural landscape with the wilderness of its forests, waterfalls, and rushing rivers. At the center of the peninsula is Koyasan, a small plateau resting atop some steep slopes rising from the heavily wooded interior of the Kii Peninsula and surrounded by a cluster of slightly taller peaks. A temple complex, one of the most sacred in Japan, is stretched atop this relatively flat, elevated area, often shrouded in mountain fogs and, for most Japanese, shrouded in the mysterious mists of legend and myth, associated as it is with a powerful religious sect, influential priests, religious wars, and some of the country's greatest warriors and rulers. Koysan is the headquarters of the Shingon sect of Buddhism, which was founded with an imperial blessing on the 3,000-foot peak in 816. Its central place in Japanese history and culture is evident in the famous necropolis, in which some of the most well-known figures in the country's legends are buried. Koysan remains an active destination for religious pilgrims. Robed monks with shaved heads stroll the streets and the Buddhist monasteries. South of Koysan lie more rounded mountains and canyons sculptured by several rivers dotted with pleasant and isolated *onsen*, or natural hot spring resorts. To the east, along the Ise Bay lies an agricultural area that produces some of Japan's finest green tea, and Ise, which is home to the holiest Shinto shrine. Over the centuries, Ise has remained a magnet for pilgrims. Every year more than 6 million people visit the shrine. Here, the sun goddess Amaterasu is revered as the ancestral goddess of the imperial family and guardian deity of the nation. Her shrine is no opulent palace, but a humble, unpainted structure made of cypress wood with reed-thatched roofs, mirroring the Japanese love of simplicity. Following ancient rites, in 1993 white-robed priests symbolically transported the sun goddess Amaterasu through towering cypress trees to her new home at the Grand Shrine of Ise. Every twenty years a new shrine is built nearby and the sun goddess is moved from her old sanctum and resettled in the new one. The ritual takes place at regular twenty-year intervals, and the 1993 move marked the sixty-first recorded divine "house moving."

The Kyoto-Nara area was the political and cultural center of Japan in ancient times, but it lost its political significance after the capital was moved to Tokyo in 1868. Osaka developed as the center of commerce and industry during the Edo Period (1603–1868). Today the Osaka-Kobe area is the center for industry and commerce in western Japan. This area, called the Hanshin industrial region, is dominated by chemical and heavy industries.

Osaka, a port for trade with China during the seventh and eighth centuries, developed around the Osaka Castle built in the late sixteenth century by

Toyotomi Hideyoshi, the national unifier. Osaka served as the entrepot for goods, especially tax rice, for the entire nation during the Edo Period. Osaka is the third-largest city in Japan, after Tokyo and Yokohama.

A major boost to the economy of the Osaka region should come from the new Kansai International Airport, built on a 1,300-acre artificial island in the waters of Osaka Bay. It is Japan's first 24-hour airport, allowing leeway on arrival and departure times for flights connecting with locations in different time zones in Europe and North America. Out of deference to local residents, the airport at Tokyo is closed from 11 P.M. to 7 A.M., and the old Osaka airport is closed from 9 P.M. to 7 A.M. The new Kansai Airport is able to avoid this problem by routing all take-offs and landings over the sea—well away from the residents of Osaka, Kobe, and surrounding communities. Built at a cost of $14 billion, it is the most expensive airport in the world. To cover the cost the airport charges the highest rents, food prices, and landing fees in the world.

The airport is involved in a nasty conflict between the central government bureaucrats and the local business community. The question is who should pay for running it. The locals say the central government should pay because the project is expected to attract a great deal of commerce, and thus tax revenues. Nonetheless, the government—especially the Finance Ministry—has insisted that the users must bear the costs. Despite this dispute, there is at least one thing everyone agrees on. It is Japan's most elegant architectural wonder.

In 1992 a special law was enacted for the development of Osaka Bay. The law is designed to ensure systematic development of business, academic, housing, and leisure facilities in the area, while giving full consideration to environmental protection. In addition to boosting the local economy, the development plan of Osaka Bay is expected to become a model of well-balanced development of national lands and serve as a first step toward decentralization of power and cooperation among local governments. Centralization of government functions in Tokyo has been under fire for decades. The experiment with decentralization of power and cooperation among seven prefectures in the Osaka Bay and the surrounding area is most appropriate because the region contains many areas of historic, cultural, and economic importance. It also contains major cities known for their independent spirit such as Kyoto, Osaka, and Kobe. The prefectural governors are required to work out development policies in consultation with local organizations such as the Osaka Bay Area Development Organization, which comprises local governments, businesses, and academics. This means that the governors will seek a broad regional view for growth and development beyond the narrow boundaries of a single prefecture.

Kobe ranks second in importance as a port, after Yokohama. It is one of the largest container ports in the world. Overlooking Osaka Bay and sheltered on the north by the Rokko Mountains, Kobe has developed as a major urban area. Only limited space is available for development, and residential areas have developed on the steep slopes at the foot of the mountains. Kobe built the massive Rokko Island to meet the land shortage that makes building huge islands in the sea seem sensible. During World War II Kobe was laid waste by fire bombs, and was hurriedly rebuilt in a hodgepodge of cul de sacs, winding alleys, and tiny homes and shops. Kobe began planning for transforming the heavily industrialized city in the 1970s, when it became clear that the steel and shipbuilding industries were destined to decline. Kobe built an 8.75 mile conveyor belt to transport to the bay earth and stones from mountains flattened for inland suburbs. Port Island, a 1,076-acre reclamation project finished in 1981, was developed to provide land for housing, government offices, and modernized port facilities. About 40 percent of Kobe's revenue still comes from activities related to shipping. Kobe's 1,432-acre Rokko Island includes a water amusement park, moderate and luxury housing, a five-star hotel, and a shopping center. Rokko Island opened in 1992. Most of this area was severely damaged in the 1995 earthquake, and massive reconstruction is continuing.

Nara, located in a basin, was the site of the Yamato Court which unified Japan from the fourth through the seventh century. The city of Nara was the country's capital between 710 and 794. Nara has a population of 365,000 inhabitants, but because the boundaries of the city include 81 square miles, it embraces rice fields, orchards, small mountains, and part of a national park in addition to temples, shrines, and dwellings. The gentle hills of Yamato surrounding Nara today have embraced a thousand years of Japanese art and literature. Vermillion-pillared, tile-roofed temples rose by the score within the orderly grid of streets. The new imperial capital, planned along the lines of the Chinese capital at Ch'ang An, blossomed 1200 years ago into a metropolis of 200,000 inhabitants, of whom perhaps 20,000 formed an elite society centered on the imperial court. Among Nara's most impressive structures is the great temple of Todaiji, completed in the mid-eighth century. The dedication of the Great Buddha image, 71 feet high, established Buddhism as the state religion over the Shinto faith. Todaiji's Great Buddha Hall, though rebuilt in 1700 to only two thirds its original size, remains the largest wooden building in the world.

But it is not, in the end, the monumental Nara that is most appealing. Nearly 15 million tourists visit Nara each year. Probably most of its inhabitants rely, directly or indirectly, on tourism for a living. In the narrow, quiet streets and lanes away from the Todaiji temple with its crowded tour buses, the hundreds of schoolgirls in identical navy blue uniforms and white socks, and the souvenir shops selling pagodas and miniature Great Buddhas, Nara becomes a small town quietly going about its own small business.

Although Nara's history is ancient, the town as we know it today took shape during the sixteenth century, the layout and names of districts and streets probably fixed when the Tokugawa Shogunate established an administrative office here in the first half of the seventeenth century. Although doubtless rebuilt many times since then, the old houses with their smoky grey, cracked walls, tiled roofs, and rusticated fences of unstained and aged wood (these seem to be typical, maybe unique, to Nara) recall an earlier time more poignantly than do Kyoto's perfect, and thus somehow exclusive, housefronts. The ancient capital region of Nara is more than the sum of its many great and small temples, graceful pagodas, and parks. It is, more than anything, a sense of quietness that pervades the narrow streets, the gravel-covered precincts of a small temple surrounded by rice paddies and persimmon orchards, shifting sunlight on a worn and mossy stone Buddha.

Today the problem of how to reconcile the 1300-year history of the city with the modern appetite for growth is gripping Nara. Visitors—people from outside Nara—expect the city to remain old and traditional. But some of the residents expect modernization and growth. Some fear that Nara will be ruined by a chaotic mixture of contemporary buildings and traditional architecture. Nara Machi, an area dominated by more than thirty temples and a row of old stores and houses, has been labeled a preservation district, and residents receive subsidies to help maintain the wooden front entrances to their homes. But new modern buildings are coming in a development zone around JR Nara Station, which may ruin the city's skyline.

Serene and contemplative, Kyoto is the heart of Japanese Buddhism, the site of hundreds of Shinto shrines, and an irrepressible fountainhead of art and artisanship. For more than a thousand years, from 794 to 1868, Kyoto was the imperial seat of government. It was called Heian-kyo, the capital of peace and tranquility. Living up to its name centuries later, it came through World War II unscathed. Though no longer the capital, Kyoto still reflects the peculiar aura that surrounded the throne.

Lacking a harbor and surrounding open land, Kyoto was slow in developing industries. It has electrical, machinery, and chemical plants. But Kyoto is primarily a cultural and educational center. The city has been divided into three districts for planning purposes, and new developments are rapidly transforming Kyoto. The Kyoto municipal government designated its northern section as a preservation area, its central zone as a redevelopment area, and its south as a development section.

Public opinion is divided over two major development projects completed in the southern section—the JR Kyoto Station and Kyoto Hotel—and the city must choose which way to go: modernization or preservation (Figure 3.13). In addition to functioning as a key railway station, the new Kyoto Station building also serves as a complex offering public space, a hotel and convention hall, a shopping center, an auditorium, and a parking lot. Everything is housed in a 60-meter-high, 470-meter-wide box-shaped building. Some people are worried that Kyoto's traditional landscape has been destroyed by the new complex. The cityscape dispute between the municipal government and Kyoto residents began in 1964 with the construction of the Kyoto Tower, which stands in front of the JR Kyoto Station. Many citizens were against the construction of the 130-meter-high tower because they felt it would deprive

Figure 3-13. Kyoto's historic character is being altered by a wave of ultramodern architecture. The high-density development in front of the Kyoto Railway Station is dominated by Kyoto Tower, a 130-meter-tall structure meant to look like the candles in the Buddhist temples—but with a circular restaurant and observation deck. The tower has sparked controversy over the scale of buildings and the extent to which their features harmonize with traditional structures. A coalition of Buddhist priests, architects, planners, and housewives has been organized to save the city's skyline from huge glass and steel structures. (Photo: P. P. Karan.)

them of a view of Kofuku Temple's five-storied pagoda, which is nearly as high as the tower. The city went ahead with the project, and a series of high-rise apartments and office buildings were constructed in the 1980s. The building rush triggered land price inflation and prompted residents to move out, leading to the creation of what are called "hollow" districts. Kyoto municipal office has given consent to the construction of buildings up to 45 meters tall in the development area.

The conversion of the Kyoto Hotel into a 60-meter-high structure is another major issue. The Kyoto Buddhist Association is against this development. It feels that the construction of high-rise buildings will dull people's senses, particularly the sense of aesthetics. Most business leaders and city officials believe that high-rises will lead to prosperity and revitalize the local economy. Many people feel that the new Kansai airport, which opened in 1994, will spur development in Kyoto, Nara, and Osaka, and all construction projects in the area are being built with the new airport in mind. What should Kyoto preserve? What is necessary to Kyoto? These are questions the people of Kyoto and the rest of Japan must consider seriously.

Chugoku

The entire western tip of Honshu comprises the Chugoku region. It consists of Hiroshima, Okayama, Shimane, Tottori, and Yamaguchi prefectures, with an area of about 12 thousand square miles (31,790 sq km) and a population of 7.7 million. It is a mountainous region with many small coastal plains and basins. The Sea of Japan side of the region is called San'in, and the area facing the Inland Sea is known as San'yo.

Communications between the San'in and San'yo areas of Chugoku remain poor. Economically, San'in is among the least-developed parts of the country. Shimane prefecture in San'in was thirty-sixth among Japan's forty-seven prefectures in terms of per capita income in 1984. In national tax payments, it ranked forty-third per capita. Despite its poverty and relative isolation, Shimane ranked first in new public works construction projects financed by the national government. It had more museums and art galleries per capita than all but one other prefecture. This peripheral area had strong leverage in the political world in the late 1980s with the most powerful members of the Liberal Democratic Party in the Lower House of the Diet, including Takeshita Noboru. Because of its remoteness, Shimane and Tottori have remained predominantly agricultural. The Tottori Plain, formed by the floodplain of the river Sendaigawa, is a rice producing area; pears are cultivated on the surrounding foothills and along the coastal sand dunes. Other industries include fishing, forestry, and food processing.

San'yo, comprising Hiroshima, Okayama, and Yamaguchi prefectures, has a modern industrial economy. Its strategic location between western Honshu, Kyushu, and Shikoku led to its early development. Industrial areas have developed along the Inland Sea coast. Although agriculture, fishing, and forestry have declined in recent years, industrial growth has been rapid in the coastal cities. Major industries include shipbuilding, chemicals, steel, machinery, automobiles, textiles, petrochemicals, and food processing. The waters off the coast were once among Japan's richest fishing areas, but catches have declined because of industrial pollution. The most heavily populated areas are along the Inland Sea, around the cities of Hiroshima, Okayama, and Shimonoseki.

Shikoku

Shikoku, the smallest of Japan's four main islands, is 7,262 sq mi (18,808 sq km) in area, with a population of 4.1 million. It consists of Kagawa, Tokushima, Ehime, and Kochi prefectures. The island is largely mountainous, which limits agricultural area. The northern half of the island has a long, narrow plain along the Inland Sea; the southern half has a wider plain facing the Pacific Ocean. Three newly constructed bridges linking Shikoku to Honshu are expected to bring new industries to the island.

In the Kochi Plain facing the Pacific Ocean, the warm climate allows two rice crops in some areas. However, since the postwar era and rice subsidies from the government, two crops have not been allowed. The area still grows a lot of rice, but is making more money by growing vegetables in vinyl houses (to keep off the salt spray). In the Matsuyama Plain, located in central Ehime Prefecture, rice is cultivated in the lowlands and mandarin oranges in the surrounding hills. Many of the industries in Shikoku such as the textile manufactures are moving overseas. Manufacturers of traditional product have been expanding their business in China and other Asian countries. Materials and labor are cheaper in China, so industries such as Asahi Senshoku Company, an Ehime towel manufacturer, are able to produce items at lower cost. In 1991, Asahi Senshoku established a $2.1 million subsidiary in Dalian, China. The subsidiary, Dalian Asahi Senshoku Company, exports towels to Japan, and its annual sales are reaching $8.5 million.

Kusubashi Mon-ori Company, another Ehime Prefecture towel company, began in 1988 to invest in Raja Uchino Company in Bangkok, Thailand. Towel manufacturers in Ehime Prefecture will stop manufacturing in Shikoku within a few years. Ehime manufacturers will survive by establishing joint companies or subsidiaries in Asian countries. Shifting the production base to foreign countries has weakened the island's industrial base.

Kyushu

Kyushu, including the southern Nansei Islands, consists of Fukuoka, Nagasaki, Oita, Kumamoto, Miyazaki, Saga, Kagoshima, and Okinawa prefectures. The region has an area of 17 thousand square miles (44,420 sq km) and a population of 14.5 million. Kyushu has a mountainous interior with many small coastal plains, volcanoes, and hot springs. The climate is subtropical, with heavy precipitation.

Northern Kyushu, with the regional capital of Fukuoka, is one of the major areas of industrial activity in Japan. Kitakyushu was the site of Japan's first Western-style steel mills, built in 1901 by the government-operated Yawata Iron and Steel Works (now Nippon Steel, a private corporation). Kitakyushu was proud of its slogan: *Kemuri wa hanei no shirushi*—"smoke is the symbol of prosperity." The industrial area based at Kitakyushu grew rapidly after 1901, because of its proximity to the Chikuho coalfield and the availability of iron ore resources imported from China. Its importance declined after World War II, when these imports ceased. Other factors contributing to the industrial decline were the switch from coal to oil as an energy source and a shift in the industrial structure away from the dominance of heavy industries such as iron, steel, and cement. In recent years, iron and coal have been imported from Australia and other countries. At present the steel, chemical, machinery, ceramics, food processing, and electrical applaince industries are concentrated along the 19-mile coastline of Kitakyushu from Moji to Tobata. Increasingly, information-intensive high-technology industries are replacing the traditional manufacturing muscle.

Southern Kyushu is relatively less developed and more agricultural. Historically, the eastward extension of Japanese civilization began from southern Kyushu and later set the foundations of the Yamato Court in the Nara Basin of the Kinki region. Reflecting its close proximity to the Asian mainland, Kyushu has been the principal gateway through which outside influences entered Japan from very early times. In 1549 Christianity was introduced in Japan with the arrival of St. Francis Xavier at Kagoshima. When Japan adopted a policy of seclusion from the rest of the world, between 1639 and 1835, Nagasaki was the only port through which foreign influences trickled into the country. Nagasaki maintains a strong cosmopolitan atmosphere resulting from its long contact with the outside world. After massive destruction caused by the atom bomb at the end of World War II, Nagasaki has been completely rehabilitated to its former status of Kyushu's leading ship-building port and center of Catholicism (Figure 3.14).

Figure 3-14. Nagasaki, Kyushu, is a major port city. Overseas trade centered in the port of Nagasaki from the first arrival of Portuguese ships in 1571. During the period of national seclusion under the Tokugawa Shogunate, the Chinese and the Dutch were permitted to trade at Dejima, an artificial island in Nagasaki harbor. Nagasaki was completely destroyed by an atomic bomb in 1945; the city has recovered since then as a center of shipbuilding and other industries. (Photo: P. P. Karan.)

Kumamoto Plain, in western Kyushu, extends from the diluvial uplands on the slopes of Asosan, where fruits and vegetables are grown, to alluvial lowlands that border Shimabara Bay, where rice is the major crop. The city of Kumamoto has emerged as a principal center of the semiconductor industry. Kyushu, sometimes called "Silicon Island" for its concentration of companies similar to those in California's Silicon Valley around San Jose, is quiet and clean. The semiconductor industry has been attracted to this area by the relatively dust-free environment (10 particles to a cubic foot of air), land availability, local government policy and labor supply, and excellent transport facilities for the shipment of raw silicon chips to markets in China, South Korea, and Southeast Asia. Kyushu now produces 40 percent of Japan's integrated circuits—a tenth of the world's market. In the past decade hundreds of corporations, Japanese and foreign, have set up factories here, tapping the island's reservoir of cheap land and well-educated workers and counting on its proximity to the rising economies of Asia to pull them into new global markets.

Tsukushi Plain, located in Fukuoka and Saga prefectures, borders the Ariake Sea. It consists of the floodplain and delta of the river Chikugogawa and has extensive alluvial fans. It is an important rice producing area in Kyushu. Krume, the major city on the plain, is a center for the rubber industry in Japan.

Along the Miyazaki coastal plain in eastern Kyushu, vegetables and mandarin oranges are grown on upland terraces, and rice on the lowlands. Plastic tunnels act as greenhouses for sweet potatoes and other crops in Kagoshima and Miyazaki prefectures. Japan places a premium on Kyushu's stretches of level land for agriculture.

Kyushu's most enduring challenge is what the Japanese call *kaso*—or depopulation. A large percentage of the island's high school graduates still leave their native towns and villages for work off the island. But local governments are now encouraging their return to Kyushu's "technopolis" centers such as Kumamoto. Kyushans refer to return migrants as "U-turn" persons—a growing number of young and middle-aged professionals who eschew the higher salaries and prestige of jobs in Tokyo and Osaka for a chance to return to the more relaxed ways of their native Kyushu.

Ryukyu (Nansei) Islands

South of Kyushu lies a chain of some sixty islands generally referred to as the Ryukyu Islands. Okinawa is by far the largest in terms of size, population, and economic development. The people of Okinawa have developed outside the framework of Japanese state for much of their history. After the Meiji Restoration (1868) Japan claimed formal sovereignty over the Ryukyu, but it was not recognized by China until the conclusion of the Sino-Japanese War in 1895. During World War II Okinawa was the site of some of the bloodiest battles.

The islands were administered by the United States from 1945 to 1972, when they were returned to Japan. Nearly 60,000 American military personnel and their families still live on Okinawa (Figure 3.15). Since the reversion, Okinawans have lived quietly, if not happily. Now that is changing. Acceptance of military personnel is turning to anger, an anger that is directed more at the central government in Japan thlong felt like Japan's second-class citizens; not Japanese enough to be accepted by Japan, over-influenced by American culture, and unable to fully revive their native culture.

Okinawa has been largely left out of the economic boom that propelled the rest of Japan to remarkable heights. And conservatives in Okinawa—previously the most strenuous advocates of the American presence—are now talking in resentful terms about how Japan abandoned Okinawa to a foreign power. Much of Okinawa, including prime agricultural land, has been occupied by American military bases. Superficially, the debate has centered on a series of clashes between local people and American forces. But the context for these controversies is Okinawa's sense that it is once again Japan's political pawn, that little has changed since Emperor Meiji forcibly brought the islands under Japanese control in 1879. That sense was reinforced in 1989an the United States. Okinawans have when evidence emerged that Emperor

Figure 3-15. A residential section of the U.S. military base in Okinawa. There are over 100 U.S. military bases in Japan. The U.S. military has provided employment for local people, supplies and services. The infusion of dollars into the local economy accelerated economic recovery in Okinawa after World War II. However, the destruction of rural homes and agricultural land to expand military facilities such as the military housing seen in the photo has generated conflicts between the local people and the U.S. military. The national government favors the presence of the U.S. military forces in Japan, which serves to protect the country. North Korea's firing of missiles over Japan in 1998 gave a fresh sense of urgency to defense planning for Japan. Japan and the United States have decided to develop a joint TMD (theater missile defense system), which would intercept missiles through the use of reconnaissance satellites to guide sea- and land-based counter-missiles. (Photo: P. P. Karan.)

Hirohito—never a popular figure on the only Japanese island to suffer invasion—invited the United States to continue the occupation of Okinawa long after the four main islands returned to Japanese sovereignty.

For Okinawans, most of whom were born long after soldiers battled each other with flame throwers and destroyers blew up after hitting mines in the bay, the import of the emperor's message seems remote. But older people say it is unthinkable that the emperor would have invited a foreign nation to permanently occupy one of Japan's four main islands to the north. Americans here, even those on the receiving end of the anger, say they understand the way Okinawans feel.

Okinawa lacks political muscle in the central government. Most pork-barrel projects in Okinawa are for Japan's support of the American troops, not the natives. No Okinawan has served in the cabinet. The unemployment rate is the highest in the country and per capita income is among the lowest.

POPULATION AND DEMOGRAPHIC TRANSITION

Japan's population of 127.4 million (2002) is the seventh-largest in the world. The course of demographic transition in Japan can be divided into five phases: (1) premodern Japan before 1868 with high birth and death rates and a stable population; (2) from 1868 to 1920, when population began to grow more rapidly, from 34.8 million to 55.9 million; (3) 1920 to 1950, with a rapidly declining death rate and slowly declining birth rate, when the population increased from 55.9 million in 1920 to 83.2 million in 1950; (4) 1950 to 1980, characterized by a major decline in the birth rate and continued decline in the death rate; and (5) the period since 1980, with both low birth and death rates (Figure 3.16).

According to the demographic transition theory, the population during a preindustrial period usually remains stable through the balance of high death and birth rates. The excess of birth over death, if any, is almost always either small or negligible. In the later stages mortality declines rapidly through the broadly perceived development process, which includes industrialization and urbanization. The rapid decline of mortality without the concomitant decline of fertility results in rapid rates of population growth. It is only after a certain period of adjustment for the new socioeconomic conditions and standard of living that the birth rate begins to fall to a low level, making it possible to stabilize again at the new balance of low birth and death rates.

From the early eighteenth century to the middle of the nineteenth century, when both birth and death rates were high, the population of premodern Japan remained almost stable at a level of approximately 30 million. With the shift from a feudal to modern society in the Meiji Era (1868–1912), the population began to increase rapidly: to 40 million in 1887, 50 million in 1911, and 55.9 million in 1920. As Japan began to modernize, it passed through a phase in

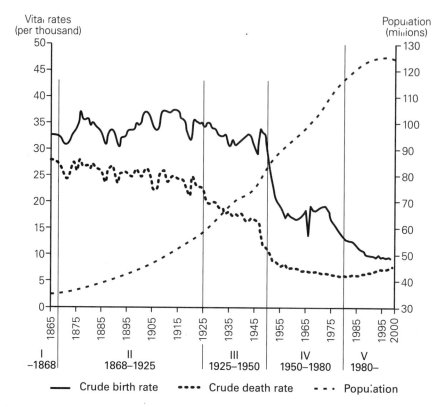

Figure 3-16. The demographic transition of 1868–1998 (based on official Japanese data).

which population rose rapidly as the death rate dropped sharply and the birth rate remained stable or fell very slowly.

Japan's first population census was held in 1920. The population reached 60 million in 1926, 73 million in 1940, and exceeded 83 million in 1950. The rate of population growth was higher in the 1920s and 1930s than in the previous decades. The only exception to the general growth of the population was during 1944 and 1945 in the latter part of World War II, when the population declined by 2.3 million. Nevertheless, the loss of population was more than offset by rapid increases after the end of the war, with an annual growth rate of 3.1 percent between 1945 and 1950.

There was a reduction in the rate of population growth after 1950. The population increased by 33 million between 1950 and 1980. During this thirty-year period the average annual growth rate was about 1.1 percent, which was lower than the average rate experienced during the last century. Since 1980 population growth is the lowest ever recorded. Because of the low birth rate the average family size is shrinking, and there is a shortage of young people entering the workforce. In addition, because the Japanese have the longest average life span in the world (78.32 years for men, 85.23 for women), the percentage of elderly in the population is increasing rapidly. Japan's demographic changes in the future will have a profound impact on the economy and serious policy implications for the government.

Declining birth rates are a feature of all modern industrial societies, including the other rapidly developing nations in the Asian Pacific region where work opportunities are opening up for women and social security systems are taking the place of children caring for their aging parents. But no other country in the world has experienced the steady and rapid drop in birth rates that Japan has seen over the last twenty years (Figure 3.17). The causes of the drop in the birthrate, not to mention the concerns it has provoked, offer a lesson in how increasing wealth has not brought increasing happiness among the Japanese. Today, two thirds of the men and a third of the women do not marry until they are over thirty years of age. Only in Sweden do people marry later; but unlike Sweden and other places, Japan is a country where unmarried couples almost never live together. Young women are more interested in careers, education, and the attractions of a single lifestyle. They complain about living in tiny apartments, about the drudgery of marriage to demanding husbands who do not help at home, and about the near impossibility of mixing work and motherhood.

Population Distribution and Migration Patterns

The uneven geographical distribution of Japan's population is related largely to regional differences in the level of development. Since early times, a major proportion of the country's population has resided in coastal plains, inland basins, and flat lands along river valleys which are suitable for agricultural and fishing activities. In the past, the western part of the country (especially the Kinki region), which was more developed, was more densely populated than the eastern part. During the Meiji Restoration the promotion of developmental activities in Hokkaido resulted in new settlements and, consequently, in an increase in population in the northeastern part of the country.

Industrial development since 1872 has led to the concentration of the population in a few urban areas while many rural areas experienced population declines in the modern period. During Japan's post–World War II recovery and the period of high economic growth since 1960, employment has shifted from primary industries to secondary and tertiary industries. These shifts in employment were accompanied by a massive concentration of the population in urban areas. The population of three large urban regions—Tokyo, Osaka, and Nagoya—increased from 30 million to 50 million between 1955 and 1975.

The southern part of the Kanto region, which includes the Tokyo metropolitan prefecture, has had the largest share of Japan's population since 1950. It has 8.7 percent of the total land area of the country, but contains nearly 25

Figure 3-17. Child and mother in Yatsushiro, Kyushu. The falling birth rate in Japan has become a cause for much concern because of its relationship to problems such as the shortage of young workers and the unbalanced age structure, which is aggravated by the increasing size of the elderly population. The drop in the birth rate is related to the rise in the average marriage age of women, accompanying recent changes in lifestyles, and the progress of women in the workplace. It is estimated that 2.08 children must be born per mother in Japan for a stable population; at present only 1.57 children are born per mother. (Photo: P. P. Karan.)

percent of the national population. The second-largest concentration of population is in the western part of the Kinki region (about 14 percent of the country's population), which includes the Osaka and Kyoto metropolitan prefectures. The Tokai region, with Nagoya city, has the third-largest metropolitan area, with 12 percent of the nation's population. Thus, over half of the country's population is concentrated in the densely populated areas in and around the cities of Tokyo, Osaka, and Nagoya. These areas face a number of problems related to overcrowding, such as environmental pollution and housing shortages.

Since 1950 some nonmetropolitan regions such as Tohoku, Hokuriku and Tosan, Shikoku, and Kyushu have experienced a decrease in the absolute number of their population as well as in their share of national population. The continuing flow of people from nonmetropolitan to metropolitan areas—particularly to the three major metropolitan areas of Tokyo, Osaka, and Nagoya—has been conspicuous since the early 1950s. The Minami-Kanto (south Kanto) region receives about 55 percent of its migrants from northeast Japan (the Hokkaido, Tohoku, Kita-Kanto or north Kanto, Hokuriku, and Tosan regions). The Nishi-Kinki (west Kinki) region receives its migrants from western Japan, especially from east Kinki, Shikoku, and Shokoku. The Kyushu region sends out a third of its migrants to Minami-Kanto and another third to Nishi-Kinki. The Tokai region (Nagoya metropolitan area) receives about 30 percent of its migrants from Kyushu and another 24 percent from Minami-Kanto.

There are two major focal points serving as destinations for migrants: the Tokyo and Osaka metropolitan areas. Tokyo has a nationwide attracting influence, but the influence of Osaka is limited largely to western Japan. The Nagoya metropolitan area, situated between Tokyo and Osaka, serves only as a minor focal point for migrants.

Japanese rural regions and communities have changed remarkably since the 1950s, as a result of the outflow of labor from rural areas brought about by rapid economic growth. Many farm laborers have begun to work in the urban industrial sector. Part-time farmers have increased in number, and the worker-peasant phenomenon has become widespread. As economic conditions in rural areas have stagnated, farmers have made efforts to get more stable off-farm employment, such as working in the public sector or for large companies. As a result, nonfarm occupations have become so important for farmers that they pose a detriment to efficient farm management.

The overwhelming concentration of population in the Tokyo metropolitan area and declining population in the countryside has prompted the government to begin relocation of certain administrative functions from Tokyo to other regions. In recent years, attempts to revitalize industries such as biotechnology and semiconductors in Kyushu have had some success in attracting young people back to depopulated rural areas from the big cities.

Minority Groups in Japan

Nearly 4 percent of the Japanese population consists of minorities, who suffer discrimination resulting from psychological and cultural factors. These groups comprise *burakumin*, Koreans, Ainu, and Okinawans, representing respectively, indigenous, foreign, aboriginal, and conquered minority population groups.

About 2 to 3 million former outcasts are called *burakumin*. Nearly 40 percent of *burakumin*, and the bulk of the Koreans, are in the Kinki region. People who practiced occupations centering on death acquired an outcast status as *burakumin*. The Shinto association of pollution with death was linked with the Buddhist teaching against the killing of animals. Those who were engaged in work dealing with the dead and the slaughtering of animals were considered polluted and were called *burakumin*. Contacts with these people were shunned, and a pattern of residential segregation of *burakumin* has emerged in major communities. Despite occupational changes, their outcast status has continued as long as they live in segregated areas known as *buraku*. Some *burakumin* try to hide their outcast identity from their friends by getting off at bus stops or train stations some distance from their *buraku* homes. Japan's elaborate system of "family registers"—a permanent, official record of each person's ancestry—makes it almost impossible for *burakumin* to conceal their origins, and therefore to work for a major company or marry outside the caste.

Discrimination against *burakumin* persists in many aspects of social life. Parents routinely investigate the background of their children's prospective marriage partners. A pending marriage between a *burakumin* and a person of non-*buraku* origin may be broken up by strong objections from the latter's family. There has been an increase in the number of incidents of harassment against *burakumin*. There is no law in Japan prohibiting incitement to discrimination, and there are no effective ways to cope with such incidents of discrimination.

The presence of a large Korean ethnic minority, which also faces social discrimination, is mainly a legacy of Japanese colonialism. During World War II, Koreans were brought to Japan as forced laborers. In 1990 there were over 688,000 Koreans living in Japan. Most of these are Japanese-born second- and third-generation Koreans, but they are legally aliens because birth in Japan does not legally assure Japanese citizenship unless one parent is a Japanese national. There has been recent improvement in their legal status, but many Koreans in Japan still face discrimination in their daily lives.

Foreign workers, attracted to Japan during the economic boom of the 1980s which led to severe shortages of labor, especially in construction and service industries, form another minority group in the country. Most of them come from Brazil, the Philippines, China, Bangladesh, Pakistan, and Iran. Most of the Brazilians are descendents of Japanese who had sought opportunity in South America earlier this century, but bias is an obstacle even for these ethnic Japanese; native Japanese can often tell they are Brazilians just from the way they dress or act, even before they open their mouths. They suffer discrimination in stores and restaurants. Many of the Asians come to Japan on tourist visas and remain illegally while the immigration authorities look the other way.

Rural Settlements

Villages or *mura* comprising clustered houses are the dominant form of rural settlement in Japan. Separate farmhouses scattered in the field are found only in Hokkaido. Dispersed settlements are also found in mountain regions of central Honshu. Agriculture in Japan has been associated with much communal activity, especially for the allocation and organization of irrigation facilities, which has favored the development of clustered rural settlements. Most Japanese villages are loose agglomerations of houses without a definite street pattern, separated by small fields, and connected by winding narrow lanes.

There are four types of villages in Japan, based on their origin or historical method of formation. *Jori* settlements are nucleated villages laid out on a rectangular or grid system under a system of land division in the seventh and eighth centuries. Tracts of land were divided into squares measuring one *cho* (358 feet) to a side. Villages, roads, canals, and fields in the Kyoto-Nara-Osaka region retain the dimensions of the ancient *jori* system. *Goshi* settlements were developed by country gentlemen (*inaka no shinshi*) from manorial estates in the outer domains of the empire rather than in the Kanto and Kinki heartlands of Japan. The low-ranking samurai who lived in the countryside supported themselves from these holdings. *Shinden* villages developed on new lands reclaimed by feudal lords during the Tokugawa Shogunate. The opening of new lands to cultivation and the conversion of dry fields to paddy during the Edo Period (1600–1868) was one of the most active periods of land reclamation in Japan (*shinden* refers to reclamation of new lands for paddy). The Tokugawa Shogunate and *daimyo* encouraged land reclamation to increase the base for their major source of revenue, the annual land tax. *Tondenhei* settlements were developed by the colonist militia, soldiers recruited to open up and defend new farmland in Hokkaido. They were pioneer settlements in Hokkaido laid out in grids, like the *jori* pattern.

AGRICULTURE IN JAPAN

Agriculture has played an important role in Japan's transition to a leading industrial nation. It not only provided the country with food and export goods (such as silk), but also accounted for 91 percent of tax revenues during the early Meiji Period, around 1880. Until fairly recently Japan had a rural-based economy. Agriculture provided employment for 73 percent of the workforce and yielded 45 percent of the GDP in 1885. The figures were 39 and 21 percent, respectively, in 1955. The relative importance of agriculture diminished rapidly as economic development gathered momentum in the 1960s.

Agriculture and rural regions in Japan began to change rapidly from 1960 onwards. In 2000 the total cultivated area in Japan amounted to 4.91 million hectares, about 6 percent of the working population was employed in agriculture, and agricultural output accounted for a mere 1.1 percent of the gross domestic product. Nearly 54 percent of the cultivated area was in paddy land. Japan's self-sufficiency in grain is only 28 percent, and for foodstuffs on a caloric base is about 40 percent. Among the industrial countries, Japan's dependence on foreign countries for agricultural products is high.

The shift in employment from agriculture to nonagricultural industries, a drop in birth rate, and the increasing tendency for more nuclear families have caused a decline in farm households. In addition, the number of younger farmers is dropping. The age of the core workforce in agriculture is gradually increasing, and the shortage of agricultural workers is expected to increase as more farmers in their sixties begin to retire. In 2003, the number of full-time farmers decreased to 2.8 million, down from 12 million in 1960. The average cultivated land per farm household was very small, only 1.2 ha. Accordingly, farmers have had to depend heavily on off-farm jobs; only 18 percent of their income was derived from farming in 1989. As of 2000, on the average, there were fewer than 1.1 farm workers per household, and two thirds of them were female. Regionally, the basic pattern is a low proportion of full-time farmers in central Japan and a high proportion in eastern and southwestern Japan.

Low income is the main reason for the continuing decline of new workers in farming. Per capita productivity in agriculture is roughly one fourth that of manufacturers. One reason for the low productivity may be the government's policy of low-priced agricultural products. The average area of tillage for rice cultivation in Japan is 0.7 hectares. Expansion of this size is needed for Japan's rice cultivators to compete internationally. But land reform legislation of 1945–1946 set a ceiling of 3 hectares (12 ha in Hokkaido) on land owner-ship, which prevents farmers from increasing their holdings. A sweeping redistribution of land largely eliminated tenancy by 1949 and resulted in 90 percent of the cultivated land being farmed by owners. Land reform of 1946 was most successful in bringing about basic changes in Japan.

In less than a generation Japan's traditional labor-intensive agriculture has been transformed into a highly mechanized capital-intensive farming system. Yet agriculture faces several problems. First, production costs, especially for rice, are very high, and Japanese agriculture requires heavy subsidies. Most farms are too small for maximum use of land and capital. Therefore, small-scale, relatively unproductive farms still predominate. Second, much of Japan's food supply is imported, and self-sufficiency in food continues to decrease. This is partly because it is less expensive to import food than to grow it domestically. Third, urbanization and industrialization, coupled with steep land prices, are steadily reducing the amount of land available for farm-ing. Finally, there is a chronic shortage of agricultural labor due to the gradual decrease of farm households and shrinking size of farming communities.

Agricultural Policy

As Japan's rapid postwar economic growth continued in the 1960s, progress achieved in industry consistently superseded advances in agriculture, and income derived from industrial employment began to exceed that obtained by farming. As a result, the Japanese farming community began to be relatively impoverished. To deal with this problem of structural changes in the economy, the Agricultural Basic Law was enacted in 1961. It authorized the government to protect and support agriculture and farmers' income. Under this law, farm subsidy and agricultural import protection became major elements of Japan's agricultural policy from the early 1960s.

Many Japanese citizens empathize with their country's agriculturists because an extremely high proportion of the citizenry is only one or two generations removed from the land. People are well disposed to agricultural subsidies and import restrictions, especially if they have the effect of enhancing employment and income-generating facilities for the aged. The implicit social security benefits of agricultural protection are visible in the Japanese countryside, with viable rural communities maintaining good environmental conditions.

The production of agricultural products is promoted and protected. On an individual crop basis, import protection has been particularly high for food grains such as rice, wheat, and barley but low for feed grains used as fodder for the cattle industry. With rising incomes, Japanese households are changing their diets; they are consuming more meat, dairy products, and fruits, and less rice. The government therefore has taken measures to promote the production of livestock, fruits, and vegetables. Import restrictions in the form of quotas are imposed on beef, fruits (particularly oranges), dairy products, flour, beans, fish, shellfish, and processed foods. High protection (i.e., low quotas) is given to final consumer agricultural goods to encourage their domestic production or processing. Imports of needed raw materials or products such as feed grains for livestock, wheat for flour and flour products, and soybeans for soy products are given low protection.

Japanese farmers have been lavishly bestowed with direct subsidy payments. The ratio of general subsidies to agricultural output has been nearly three times higher in Japan than in Europe. Subsidies amounted to 49 percent of the total agricultural budget in 1960, 61 percent in 1980, and 66 percent in 1991. They are paid to growers of a large number of agricultural items, and many farmers benefit from these payments; this has been politically important to the Liberal Democratic Party. Although farm subsidies and protection have raised rural incomes, they have hindered rationalization of the agricultural sector, have been excessively costly, have penalized consumers, and have failed to enhance Japan's food self-sufficiency.

The politically powerful farm block organized under the agricultural cooperatives supports protection and subsidies and promotes farmers' interests in Japan under the political leadership of Zenchu (Central Union of Agricultural

Cooperatives), the nation's most powerful farm lobby group. In 1988 an agreement was reached between Japan and the United States that allowed American beef producers to increase their exports to Japan. The agreement also increased United States exports of citrus products. Liberalization of rice imports has not yet been achieved. In 1993 Japan agreed to substitute tariffs for quotas on all agricultural products except rice. Over time the government has committed to a lowering of agricultural tariffs. The liberalization of agricultural trade has thus far had little impact on domestic output.

Rice and the Japanese

Japan has been a rice growing society for over 2000 years. Rice planting and rice harvest rituals are crucial elements of the nation's culture, tradition, and the indigenous religion, Shinto. Rice is grown widely in Japan from Hokkaido to Okinawa. Despite the wide range of latitude, high average temperatures in summer combined with the development of rice varieties adapted to low temperatures and the use of special techniques in the north have made it possible to grow rice throughout Japan. The distribution of major rice growing areas has been influenced by three factors: (1) the size of the alluvial plains, (2) the availability of water, and (3) government policy. Principal rice growing areas are located in Niigata, Kitakami Plain, Ishikari Plain, Western Kanto, Nobi Plain, Tsukushi Plain, and to lesser extent in the inland basins. Koshihikari and Sasanishiki, both grown in the northeast, are among the most popular types of Japanese rice, and they command high prices. In 1990 rice was grown on over 2 million hectares, and the production was 10.4 million metric tons. Producer prices were over six times those of U.S. rice growers.

Rice prices in Japan have been regulated by the national government for many years. Although free marketing of a certain portion of the rice crop has been allowed since 1969, farmers must sell most of their rice crop to the government through giant agricultural cooperatives (Zenchu) at a price set by the government. The rice is then distributed to authorized retailers, who sell it to consumers at a lower price, established by the government. Thus, rice prices in Japan have been determined by political considerations and not by free market forces. Both prices are kept artificially high and the result is that the Japanese pay about eight times more than the world price for rice. The giant agricultural cooperatives—the government-sanctioned monopolies that profit from the huge subsidies of about $5 billion annually—prefer to maintain the status quo. The rice subsidy is a welfare program for the cooperatives. The subsidies and tax breaks for rice are more than most part-time farmers can resist. As a result, Japan is covered with tiny, inefficient rice farms—more than 80 percent are only a few acres—that have been producing far more rice than the country could consume.

In the 1980s rice, the import of which was prohibited, became a symbol of Japan's closed market. In 1993 Japan dropped its resistance to rice imports by a small opening of its rice market; it would import 4 percent of its rice in 1995, rising to 8 percent in 2001, and 10 percent in 2003. The government's decision to begin opening the rice market is in effect a recognition that Japan's future lies more with its globally competitive automobile and electronic companies than with its uncompetitive farmers. Limited rice imports in some sense also signify the end of decades of Japanese history in which farmers have wielded power far out of proportion to their numbers. That power resulted in policies that favored farmers at the expense of urban consumers, most notably protection from foreign products that kept the price of rice far higher in Japan than elsewhere in the world. Farmers were favored because they were a pillar of support of the Liberal Democratic Party, which governed Japan for thirty-eight years until it was voted out of office in summer of 1993 as corruption scandals spiraled around its leaders.

As Japan became urbanized in the last three decades of the twentieth century, electoral districts did not change quickly enough, leaving farmers over-represented in the Parliament (Diet). And the farmers often act with a single voice because of the role of powerful agricultural cooperatives, which have a wide influence over the business and political life of farming villages. The farmers are still a political force to be reckoned with, but there has been erosion of the farm bloc influence due to the shrinking of farm households from 6 million in 1960 to less than 3 million in 1992 as farmers abandon a business that is often unprofitable despite government subsidies. Most farmers now till the soil only part time and earn the majority of their income from jobs in factories and stores.

Wet, cool weather destroyed much of the 1993 rice crop in Japan. To cope with the bad harvest, retailers were required to package or blend domestic rice with imported varieties. This was a stunning change in a country that has maintained a "not one grain" policy against imported rice. Part of the problem foreign importers face is the traditional leeriness about imported products that bedevils many foreign companies trying to sell to the Japanese. This is compounded by the seriousness with which the Japanese take rice. People in Japan pride themselves on being able to distinguish among high-grade brands of rice the way wine connoisseurs distinguish among vintages. Nevertheless, California-grown rice proved highly popular during the first days of 1994's spring foreign rice sales, because it is short-grain like Japanese rice and closely resembles it in flavor and texture. But Chinese and Thai rice often remained unsold, after unfavorable publicity.

Although rice is bound up with Japan's most ancient mythology (rice and sake and the wine fermented from it, are offered to Shinto gods and pounded rice cake, *mochi*, is a common offering in Buddhist temples), meat and dairy products have replaced rice as the mainstay of Japanese diet. In a 1993 study that reflects the continued Westernization of this traditional non-Western Asian society, Japan's Agriculture Ministry reported that meat and dairy replaced rice as the chief cash crop of Japanese farmers in 1991. The ministry predicts the dominance of meat and dairy and the decline of rice in the coming years. The report reflects a fundamental change in the Japanese diet. It is a transformation visible each day at noon in every Japanese city, as tens of millions of people turn away from the traditional lunch of rice balls wrapped in seaweed to form long lines in front of places like MacDonald's and Kentucky Fried Chicken, which now rank as the first and second most popular restaurants in Japan.

Virtually every Japanese home has a *denkigama*, or electric rice cooker, and most housewives still make a full pot of rice in it every morning. But more and more the rice is a supplement to meals of meat, vegetables, and bread with margarine that would look familiar on an American table. The traditional Japanese breakfast—rice and seaweed, pickled vegetables and soybean-paste soup—has been replaced almost everywhere by something called a "morning set": toast, cereal, scrambled eggs, and tossed salad (a breakfast item people here think they learned from the United States). This is so common that some hotels now actually advertise that they offer a Japanese breakfast in addition to the expected Western version.

Some experts on Japan argue that this ancient society is highly resistant to change; others maintain that Japan is becoming more like other Western industrialized countries all the time. Dietary trends in Japan support the latter view.

URBAN SETTLEMENTS

The development of urban centers in Japan can be traced back to the eighth century, when the capital cities of Nara and Kyoto were established. Other urban centers developed to serve political and military purposes. Osaka developed to serve the needs of travelers. When the central authority of the military government declined in the fifteenth and sixteenth centuries, towns developed around castles built by regional warlords, *daimyo*, to defend their petty fiefdoms. The castle towns continued to grow in size and stability during the seventeenth and eighteenth centuries. The castle town of Edo (modern Tokyo), with a population of over 1 million by the mid-eighteenth century, was the largest city in the world at that time.

Classification of Towns

In addition to castle towns, or *jokamachi*, post-station towns (*shukuba machi*) developed along the five radial roads (*gokaido*) which extended from the shogunate capital of Edo (Tokyo). These towns catered to the needs of travelers along major roadways. *Daimyo* and their retainers stopped in special inns in *shukuba machi* en route to fulfilling their obligation of alternate-year residence (*Sankin Kotai*) in Edo. Alternate-year residence in Edo was a device developed by the shogun to maintain control over the more than 260 *daimyo* who were autonomous feudal rulers of four fifths of Japan. The *daimyos* had to maintain residential estates in Edo, where their wives and children were permanently detained by the shogunate. *Shukuba machi* facilitated the national integration of Japan through efficient regulation of movement across the country.

Monzen machi, or religious towns, developed along roads to popular temples or shrines. Today *monzen machi* are valued primarily as historic and religious sites. Another group of Japanese towns developed as *ichiba machi,* or marketing centers. These market towns established a link with urban life for residents of nearby villages and served as the trading place for merchants. Trading centers that developed around seaports are known as *minato machi,* or port towns. Many towns such as Hakata (now part of Fukuoka), Sakai (in Osaka Prefecture), Nagasaki, and Hyogo (now Kobe) flourished as *minato machi*. During the seclusion policy of the Tokugawa Shogunate, domestic trade continued at the port towns of Osaka, Shimonoseki, and Niigata on major sea routes.

Resort towns at hot springs, or *onsen machi,* have developed at famous hot springs in Japan. Visiting hot spring spas has become one of the nation's popular leisure activities. In 2000 over 143 million people visited hot springs in Japan.

Urban Development

Modern urban growth is related to changes that took place in Japan's economy during the Meiji Restoration (1868–1912). The shift of economy from agriculture, fishing, and forestry to manufacturing led to the migration of people from rural areas to towns. The population living in towns of 50,000 or more increased from 8 percent in 1868 to 16 percent in 1912. Urban population was 18 percent of the total population in 1920, 37 percent in 1950, and 76 percent in 1980. The influx to the country's three big conurbations—Tokyo, Nagoya, and Osaka—slowed in the 1980s. Prefectures located in the commuter belts of the big urban centers are gaining the most population in the 2000s. Saitama, northwest of Tokyo, showed the largest increase, followed by Chiba, Nara, Shiga, Ibaraki, and Kanagawa prefectures in 2000.

The axis of the greatest concentration of cities in Japan extends from Kanto to Kinki and along the Inland Sea to northwest Kyushu. This belt forms the Japanese megalopolis, with six great metropolitan areas: Tokyo, Yokohama, Nagoya, Kyoto, Osaka, and Kobe. By 2004 the Tokyo metropolitan region (Tokyo and the surrounding seven prefectures) had a population of over 41 million, a concentration of 32 percent of Japan's total population in 10 percent of the land area.

Massive urbanization prompted the enactment of urban planning law in 1968 to guide urban growth in Japan. Land use, maintenance of city facilities (such as streets, railways, parks and plazas), and urban development projects (such as land regulation projects or residential development projects) are regulated to provide orderly growth of cities. The law applies only to city planning areas designated by prefectural governors, and divides urban areas into growth promotion and growth control areas. The development activity in the urban areas requires prior approval from the prefectural governor. The law has established an approval system for city planning projects. The decision making authority for city planning is delegated to the mayors, the prefectural governors, and the minister of construction.

Tokyo Metropolitan Region

The Tokyo metropolitan area called *Shutoken* comprises the region within a 150 km (93 mile) radius of central Tokyo (Figure 3.18). It extends into the surrounding Saitama, Chiba, Kanagawa, Ibaraki, Tochigi, Gumma, and Yamanashi prefectures. This region is the economic, political, and cultural center of the nation.

Urban Tokyo contains 12 million people living in twenty-three wards of the city. The city grew around Edo Castle, the present site of the Imperial Palace, with the samurai residential district on the castle's western side. To the east, marshland was reclaimed and a commercial and industrial area developed, taking advantage of river and canal transportation. The city grew rapidly as merchants and artisans moved to Edo. The population reached 1 million in 1720. With the Meiji Restoration, Edo was renamed Tokyo, and the imperial family moved to Edo Castle in 1869. It grew steadily as the political, commercial, and financial center of the country. In 1923 an earthquake destroyed most of the city, and during World War II, it was destroyed by bombing.

During the period of economic recovery after World War II, most of the large Japanese corporations selected Tokyo as the center for their business operations. The population of the city increased from 6.3 million in 1950 to 9.7 million in 1960, and by 1965 had reached 10.9 million, resulting in serious housing shortages, environmental problems, and skyrocketing land prices. A further rapid spiral in land prices since the mid-1980s has put home ownership beyond the means of most Tokyo citizens. Land prices in Tokyo average $8,500 per square meter (10.76 sq ft). The Ginza district stands on the most expensive plot of land in Japan, according to Japan's National Land Agency land price report: one square meter of land there is valued at about $345,000. Although land prices in Japan's largest cities have fallen in recent years, the average price in Tokyo's most expensive districts has risen.

Figure 3-18. Tokyo's skyline. Tokyo city has a population of about 12 million; the Tokyo metropolitan area, which extends beyond the administrative limits of the city, has a population of over 30 million. The urban region is viewed as a single entity for the formulation of development plans. (Photo: P. P. Karan.)

Along the Tokyo Bay, waterfront land has been reclaimed for a number of development projects. Along the waterfront in Yokohama, a new city with hotels, parks, a convention center, housing, and attractive commercial buildings has been developed as part of the Minato Mirai 21 project. It is designed to attract more business from the Tokyo area. Japan's tallest building, the seventy-story, 296-meter Landmark Tower, opened in 1993. During its 134-year history, Yokohama has usually been a place verging on its future. An insignificant village with ninety households, Yokohama was established as the first treaty port in 1859 under the Japan–U.S. Treaty of Amity and Commerce. Though devastated by wars and earthquakes, Yokohama has developed into one of the world's great ports, and is Japan's second-largest city, with a population of 3.2 million.

At the other side of the Tokyo Bay, on a bustling plot of landfill, is the Tokyo Disneyland and DisneySea. With 25 million visitors in 2003, each spending on average about $200, the park less than 10 miles from downtown Tokyo has surpassed the original Magic Kingdoms in the United States in attendance (Walt Disney World, Florida, had 12 million; Disneyland, Anaheim, California had 11.4 million).

Functional Areas of Tokyo

Tokyo consists of a series of densely built neighborhoods or districts, each centered around a train station or subway. Many of these districts retain their traditional character; others have evolved into commuter service centers. A number of distinct functional areas can be identified in the city.

The Central Business District On the eastern side of the Tokyo Railway Station is Nihombashi, the financial and commercial district, lined with department stores, shops, and restaurants. Nihombashi has been the banking center of Japan since the Edo period, and is today headquarters of most important Japanese financial concerns, including the Bank of Japan and the Bank of Tokyo. In 1896 the Bank of Japan opened its headquarters in Nihombashi. The bank was joined by stock traders and other financial enterprises, and today the Tokyo Stock Exchange, one of the world's largest, is in Nihombashi.

The commercial area extends south toward Ginza, famous for elegant and expensive shops. Ginza is Tokyo's most famous shopping area, with many fashionable and expensive boutiques and department stores. The streets of Ginza are crowded day and night. At night, Tokyo businessmen come here, often on expense accounts, and business relationships are forged over the dining tables of Ginza.

To the west of the railway station is Marunouchi, headquarters of major Japanese corporations. The Meiji-Era brick building of the Tokyo station was built in 1914; there is dense commercial development under the station. Marunouchi has come to be Japan's most prestigious commercial address. Since the early days of the Meiji Restoration, trade and business have been carried on here, and when Tokyo station was built, here the importance of Marunouchi was strengthened.

The Cultural Core Ueno district, with museums, art galleries, Tokyo University, bookshops, temples, and the zoo, forms a major cultural core. It has been a popular area for outings and excursions since the Edo period. In addition to its many cultural attractions, it has also developed into a major shopping district. To the east of Ueno is the oldest temple in Tokyo, Asakusa Kannon (Sensoji), in the heart of the Shitamachi area, along with many shops selling traditional handicrafts. Asakusa reflects more of the old character than any other Tokyo neighborhood. It epitomizes the old merchant-artisan area and has prospered as the gateway to the Sensoji Temple. Asakusa is fast losing its old neighborhood character as traditional buildings are torn down and replaced with modern gray brick and glass apartment buildings.

To the south of Ueno are Kanda, renowned for its bookshops and universities, and Akihabara, famous for its discount stores selling electronic and electrical appliances. Kanda has become known primarily as a student quarter because of the many educational institutions clustered in the Surugadai section, and as a center for secondhand bookstores, publishing houses, and printers, most of which are concentrated in the Jimbocho area.

The Wholesale Food District In the south, near the port of Tokyo, lies the wholesale food and fish market. Tsukiji is the principal fish market. Thousands of wholesalers and retailers use the market each day. Buying and selling starts before the sun comes up, and the area is dotted with seafood restaurants that offer, of course, the freshest fish in town.

The Port District South of the commercial and business district lies the port of Tokyo with several wharves and terminals. Tokyo's port has four major wharves: Harumi, Shinagawa, Takeshiba, and Shibaura. Harumi is the largest, and is used mainly for the Okinawa and overseas trade. Takeshiba is used mainly for the Izu Islands, and Shinagawa for Kushiro (Hokkaido).

Major projects are underway to develop the waterfront area. A 1,106-acre Teleport Town development has been completed in Tokyo Bay. The development, begun in 1987, provides homes for 60,000 people, offices for 110,000 workers, and leisure facilities for the entire city. Financing problems brought about by the fall in real estate prices in 1992 and difficulty finding tenants have delayed the schedule of some waterfront projects.

The Manufacturing District The manufacturing area extends along the Sumida River and into Shitamachi. Concrete warehouses and factories with rusting metal roofs line the river. Industrial areas now extend into Kawasaki and Yokohama, forming the Keihin Industrial District of Japan. Large plants along the waterfront include manufacturers of electrical machinery, precision apparatus, fertilizer, iron and steel, and petroleum refining. Publishing and printing businesses are concentrated in the city.

Residential Areas Residential areas are generally mixed with business or commercial use in Japanese cities. In the 1950s the city expanded beyond the wards into neighboring prefectures. Large housing complexes developed east and north of the city. The Akasaka-Aoyama, Shibuya, and Meguro have expensive residential districts. Among Tokyo's neighborhoods, Akasaka is perhaps the most sophisticated and expensive. To the west of Akasaka is Aoyama, one of Tokyo's major fashion centers. Here remnants of old Japan are tucked between modern Western shops. There are sophisticated boutiques and stores with elegant and expensive silk kimonos next to tiny shops filled with tea caddies and handleless Japanese porcelain cups. Italian, Korean, Chinese, and Japanese restaurants sit amicably beside Parisian bistros.

Since 1965 large-scale development of new towns in peripheral areas has taken place to relieve the congestion in Tokyo. Satellite cities such as Tama New Town, west of Tokyo, and Tsukuba City, northeast of Tokyo have been developed to relieve overcrowding.

Urban Subcenters A number of commercial and business centers have developed in Tokyo at the intersection of railroads radiating outwards from the city and the circular railway loop around the city. These urban subcenters, forming a multiple nuclei pattern, are spaced in a ring a 4-mile radius from Tokyo Central Station. These subcenters consist of department stores, markets, amusement and cultural facilities, restaurants, banks, and high-rise office and apartment buildings. Ikebukuro, Shinjuku, and Shibuya are major subcenters of Tokyo.

Ikebukuro district centers on Ikebukuro Station in the central part of Toshima ward of Tokyo. During the Meiji (1868–1912) and Taisho (1912–1926) periods, Ikebukuro grew from a farm village into a suburban rail terminus. With the development of residential communities along the suburban rail lines in the period after World War II, Ikebukuro rapidly expanded into one of the biggest centers in the Tokyo metropolitan area.

Shinjuku was a post-station town on the Koshu Kaido (Koshu Highway) during the Edo period (1600–1868). It developed rapidly during the 1920s, and is today one of the major business and commercial centers of Tokyo. To the west of the Shinjuku station is one of Japan's largest concentration of skyscrapers, including the new Tokyo Metropolitan Government Offices. To the east of the station is a busy shopping and entertainment district.

Shibuya lies on the higher southwestern area of Tokyo called Musashino Plateau. The area around the Shibuya station has become one of the major commercial and amusement centers of Tokyo, although the district is primarily a high-quality residential area. Streets radiate from the station in all directions, with shop windows filled with youthful clothing and accessories. Close by is Harajuku, which draws young Japanese in pursuit of designer apparel.

DEVELOPMENT OF THE MODERN JAPANESE ECONOMY

In comparing the economic modernization of Japan with that of the West, several important differences stand out. In the first place, the process of economic modernization took place over a much longer period of time in the West. Western capitalism first appeared about 500 years ago, then the Industrial Revolution occurred in Britain starting about 1750, and finally industrial corporate capitalism started to appear in the second half of the nineteenth century. In contrast, Japan changed from a traditional commercial agrarian economy in a single generation. The *zaibatsu* were the central institution in this transformation, and understanding of the history of the *zaibatsu* is essential in understanding how Japan developed as a modern technological society.

Industrialization began after the arrival of Commodore Perry in Edo Bay in 1853. Spurred on by this military and industrial threat from the West, Japan began a concerted effort to transform its antiquated economic system. In contrast to the West, where industrial capitalism evolved from the ground up, Japan's leaders decided to impose industrialization from the top down by using the power of government and government bureaucracies to import Western technology and Western know-how to build a modern industrial base.

In contrast to countries such as Canada, which relied heavily on foreign capital to industrialize, Japan's leaders decided to use Japanese capital and Japanese economic structures as much as possible. They did this because they were not simply seeking to modernize Japan; rather, they were determined to build a strong economic base, owned and controlled by Japanese private and public interests, to protect the nation's political and economic autonomy. Thus, while Japan's nineteenth-century leaders vigorously imported Western technology, they did not encourage Western corporations to enter Japan's domestic market in force to build Japan's new economic infrastructure.

What exactly were the *zaibatsu* and how did they contribute to Japan's economic modernization? A *zaibatsu* is a group of diversified businesses owned exclusively by a single family or an extended family. *Zaibatsu* existed in a variety of sizes, ranging from the enormous Mitsui, Mitsubishi, and Sumitomo to medium-sized and small business groups. The *zaibatsu* form was not unique to Japan, but the huge scale and the number of *zaibatsu* formed in the course of industrialization were distinctively Japanese phenomena. Of the ten major *zaibatsu*, Mitsui and Sumitomo, originated during the Tokugawa Shogunate, and the other eight (Mitsubishi, Yasuda, Asano. Furukawa, Fujita, Okura, Nakajima, and Nomura) during the first half of the Meiji era.

Initially, the Meiji government had to take the lead in industrialization, directly managing a variety of enterprises ranging from arsenals and shipyards to telegraphs and mines. When the government found entrepreneurs willing to cooperate in its industrialization program, it forged close connections with them and supplied generous assistance, thereby creating a new type of political merchant. In the 1880s, when the government turned over the industrialization of the country to private individuals, the families that undertook this task played a significant part in, and profited from, the government's initial efforts. Many of these families moved from finance and mining to shipping, shipbuilding, and metal making. Some of then formed trading companies both to export their products and to import the new materials and technology necessary for industrialization. Simultaneously, they established banks and insurance companies to support their industrial and trading activities. By the turn of the century, these mutually supporting multibusiness groups had become a continuing source of capital for the ongoing transfer of modern industrial technology. Gradually, family members withdrew from all but the highest positions in their *zaibatsu* and were replaced by trained managers who were much more versed in engineering and technical skills, as well as in foreign languages.

During World War I and in the 1920s, the *zaibatsu* provided pools of capital and managerial skills needed to bring Japan the more technologically advanced science-based industries such as chemicals, electrical equipment, electrical machinery, and improved metal making. In the 1930s the military had a major impact on the operations and investments of *zaibatsu* enterprises. Following World War II, the Supreme Commander for the Allied Powers dissolved the *zaibatsu* and prohibited holding companies.

Most scholars believe that technological societies could develop within any one of the three main political ideologies: liberal capitalism, Marxist communism, and national socialist historicism. Japan offers a fourth alternative, which might be called *bureaucratic capitalism*. The development of Japan's industrial society and its economic modernization offer an example to many non-Western nations in Asia and Africa, particularly in the way old traditional wealth was transformed into modern industrial capital and the way in which government and private capital were able to achieve high levels of economic growth and development without sacrificing Japanese autonomy.

Economic Development, 1945–2003

The economic development of Japan since 1945 can be divided into several distinct periods: (1) 1945 to 1952, the period of Allied Occupation characterized by land reforms, dissolution of *zaibatsu*, and establishment of a new constitution; (2) 1953 to 1973, the period of high economic growth led by exports; (3) 1973 to 1989, a period of stable growth with low inflation, low unemployment, and low interest rates, leading to asset inflation and a speculative bubble economy during 1986–1989; (4) 1989 to 1990, the burst of the bubble and the fall of stock and property markets; and (5) 1991 to the present, a period of recession and restructuring.

At the end of the Allied Occupation, in 1952, Japan ranked as one of the less-developed countries. During 1953–1973 the economy grew with unprecedented rapidity and Japan became the first less-developed country in the postwar era to move up to developed status. The structure of the Japanese economy changed from an emphasis on primary activities to an emphasis on secondary and tertiary sectors. Several factors such as the Korean War, full access to the United States market, and the Japanese government policy contributed to rapid growth during this period. Rapid industrial growth led to major environmental problems.

In the 1950s, the large corporations that belonged to the *zaibatsu* prior to their breakup revived the old *zaibatsu* corporate names. However, these postwar corporate groups were not owned exclusively by a single family. The new groups, often called *keiretsu*, characterized by mutual shareholding among their constituent firms and consultation among the group members' top managers, came into being in the postwar period. They are much looser groupings than the old prewar *zaibatsu*. The *keiretsu* include the Mitsui, the Mitshubishi, and the Sumitomo. Coordination of *keiretsu* activities is achieved through periodic meetings of the presidents of the most important companies in each group. General trading companies and *keiretsu* banks also serve a coordinating function in these groups. Sanwa, Fuyo, Toshiba, Matsushita, and Dai-Ichi are among the other large *keiretsu*. To some extent, members appear to show a preference for purchasing products from other members of the group, and this preference is stronger in the case of helping out fellow firms with the introduction of new products such as supercomputers.

Japan's continued export-led growth in the 1970s and 1980s led to trade frictions with trading partners in Europe and the United States. Partly in response to protectionist threats, after 1980 Japan launched a program of foreign direct investment in the United States and Europe to manufacture goods in the major markets and protect its market share. From a modest $4.7 billion in 1980, foreign direct investment rose to $22.3 billion in 1986 and to a peak of $67.5 billion in 1989. During this period Japanese automakers and consumer electronics firms set up plants in the United States and Europe. Environmental legislation passed in 1967 and revised in 1973 led to improvements in environmental conditions in Japan.

Japanese businesses were raising capital for expansion and speculation in property and stock markets from 1986 to 1989 at extremely favorable terms due to low interest rates and financial deregulation, which lead to the development of the bubble economy. The bursting of the bubble in 1989–1990 led to the collapse of land prices and property values, and Japanese banks were left with mountains of debt. An economic recession followed in 1991, from which Japan was still recovering in 2004, but there was economic surge toward the end of 2003.

In the 2000s Japan is facing problems of recession and financial and industrial restructuring. Government has introduced several financial packages to restore the economy, but they have failed to address the banking crisis and tax reforms to move the economy to a reasonable growth path. In addition, Japan faces a shortage of labor with its aging population, an export-based economy with dependence on foreign markets, and industrial restructuring involving adjustment to declining industries while fostering growth industries. There is also the problem of how to resolve the conflicts between economic development and environmental preservation.

Industrial Regions

Most of Japan's principal industrial regions have developed around ports, chiefly because Japanese industry depends heavily on imported raw materials. Also, the bulk of the manufactured goods are exported to foreign markets. There are five major manufacturing regions in the country (Figure 3.19).

Figure 3-19. Japan's manufacturing regions and urban centers.

The Keihin Region

This region extends along Tokyo Bay and the nearby inland areas, with major concentrations in Tokyo, Kawasaki, and Yokohama. Manufacturing activity now covers parts of seven prefectures—Tokyo, Kanagawa, Saitama, Chiba, Ibaraki, Tochigi, and Gumma prefectures. It ranks first in Japan in the value of industrial goods produced. Proximity to the large consumer market, labor force, and the ports of Tokyo and Yokohama have contributed to the growth of this manufacturing region.

The heart of this industrial region is the coastal belt between Tokyo and Yokohama. Between Kawasaki and Yokohama are large steel mills, oil refineries, petrochemical plants, shipyards, food processing plants, and thermoelectric plants. A little further inland are the automobile plants, electric machinery, secondary food processing, and precision machine industries. In recent years overcrowding, congestion, pollution, and a shortage in the water supply have led to the movement of industries to the interior of the region.

Chukyo Industrial Region

This region is centered on the city of Nagoya, and extends east to Toyohashi in Aichi Prefecture, west to southern Mie Prefecture, and north into Gifu Prefecture. The major industries are chemical fibers in the cities of Gifu and Okazaki, automobiles in Toyota, petroleum refining and petrochemicals in Yokkaichi, and steel and machinery in Nagoya.

Tokai Industrial Region

This industrial area lies between the Keihin and Chukyo industrial regions, along the Pacific coast in Shizuoka Prefecture. Industries include musical instruments, motorcycles, paper, processed foods, and textiles. Shizuoka, Shimizu, and Hamamatsu are major centers of manufacturing.

Hanshin Industrial Region

Hanshin industrial region extends along Osaka Bay, with Osaka and Kobe as principal manufacturing centers. In recent years the industrial area has expanded in the west to Himeji and in the northeast to Kyoto and Otsu. Industrial areas now extend south to Wakayama. Sometimes this larger industrial area (Osaka-Kyoto-Kobe) is called the Kinki industrial belt. The principal manufacturing industries in this region are metals, iron and steel, electric machinery, textiles, chemicals, and food processing. The industrial structures in the Kobe area suffered major damage from the January 1995 earthquake; rebuilding is progressing gradually.

Setouchi Industrial Region

This area comprises the southern part of the Chugoku facing the Inland Sea and the northern part of Shikoku. The principal industrial centers are Hiroshima and Okayama on the Chugoku side of the Inland Sea, and Takamatsu and Matsuyama on the Shikoku side of the Setouchi. Sanyo, the north side of the Inland Sea, is relatively more important in manufacturing than the southern part in Shikoku. The major industries are iron and steel, chemicals, transport machinery, oil refining, and petrochemicals.

Kita Kyushu Industrial Region

This industrial area is located in northern Kyushu and the western part of Yamaguchi Prefecture in Honshu. The principal industries are iron and steel, cement, chemicals, fertilizers, glass, ceramics, and metals. Availability of local coal from the Chikuho field and raw materials from China led to the rapid development of industries in this area after 1900. The shift of Japan's industrial structure from heavy industries such as steel and cement has led to the relative decline of industries in this area.

Other industrial centers in Japan include cities in Hokuriku along the Sea of Japan, with concentrations of manufacturing activity at Fukui, Kanazawa, Toyama, and Niigata; southern Hokkaido, with principal activity at Muroran (steel) and Tomakomai (paper); Hitachi city in northeastern Ibaraki Prefecture; and Kamaishi in southeastern Iwate Prefecture, an important steel producing center since 1858 which is now in decline.

Postindustrial Japan

Since the mid-1970s, when manufacturing employment began to decline, a major transformation has been ushering Japan from the industrial to the postindustrial era. The passage into postindustrial society is marked by structural shifts from the production of goods to services, and the growing importance of technology and information as factors in production. The most obvious characteristic of economic life in postindustrial society is that the majority of the labor force is no longer employed in agriculture or manufacturing, but in services. In 1990 the service or tertiary industries (retail and wholesale trade, banking, finance, real estate, business services, personal services, and public administration) accounted for nearly 61 percent of the country's output and employed 59 percent of the national labor force. So wide is the range of services provided in contemporary postindustrial Japan that it is useful to distinguish the physical services of transportation and utilities in the tertiary sector; the financial services, including trade, insurance, and real estate, in the quaternary sector; and quinary sector idea and information services. The growing size of the quinary sector in Japan is the most important indicator of the progression of the country into a postindustrial society characterized by a prosperous service-and-technology oriented, information-and-research based society.

High-Technology Industries

High-technology industries are knowledge-intensive industries such as microelectronics, optical fiber, mechatronics (industrial robots and medical electronics), semiconductors, new materials, aerospace, and information and communication systems. The success in attracting high-technology industries to an area depends to a large extent on access to research and development centers such as universities and research institutes to constantly collect up-to-date information to enable businesses to cope with the rapidly evolving technology. Living conditions are also important and include both high-quality physical and cultural environments.

Integrated circuits (microchips and silicon chips) form the heart of electronic products from microwave ovens to weapon systems. Most U.S. weapon systems depend on Japanese-made chips. Another high-tech industry is the computer industry (Fujitsu, Hitachi, NEC). Several U.S. companies procure parts in Japan, and Japan has a large share of the world's silicon chip market. Japan also has a major lead in robotics (Matshushita, Toshiba, Kawasaki, and Hitachi). Of the world's top high-tech companies, six are Japanese.

Japan's semiconductor industry got its start through the acquisition of U.S. technology in the early 1950s, when Kobe Kogyo imported transistor technology from RCA and Sony imported similar technology from Western Electric. The technology gap between the United States and Japan was closed in the 1970s. In contrast to the U.S. semiconductor industry, which achieved its development primarily in industrial machinery, the semiconductor industry in Japan centered on consumer products. In the United States venture-business specialty firms that started out as small enterprises form the heart of the semiconductor industry. In Japan the industry is based in large corporate manufacturers such as NEC, Toshiba, Hitachi, and Fujitsu (Figure 3.20).

The high-tech industries in Japan are concentrated in three areas. In general, most factories are concentrated in and around the Tokyo metropolitan area, which includes Tokyo, Chiba, Saitama, and Kanagawa prefectures. Factories in this area manufacture products that require close contact and information exchange between users and makers, and they depend on universities for basic research. Tokyo and Kanagawa prefectures have over 37 percent of the private research institutes and 39 percent of the scientific researchers in Japan. At the Hirayama Industrial Complex in Hino, western Tokyo, about fifty high-technology companies and research institutes have assembly plants or laboratories. A second concentration of high-tech industries is in the Osaka and Nagoya metropolitan areas, which also contain a large number of research institutes.

The third concentration is in Kyushu, where factories produce standard goods. It is not important for these factories to have contact with research and development sources. These mass-producing factories require a large, high-quality labor force, a large land area, and clean air and water. These factors have induced them to locate in Kyushu and other smaller cities. During the last two decades Kyushu has become a major area of high-technology industries. Local government policy, availability of industrial sites, ample water supply, and low-cost female labor are major factors attracting the industry to Kyushu. (Photo: Cotton Mather.) Technology-intensive high value-added products can bear high transport costs, which has facilitated the location of high-tech plants near airports in local areas. The handicap of distance has been overcome by the development of communication technology.

Figure 3-20. A NEC silicon chip plant in Kumamoto. NEC Corporation (Nippon Denki) is a world leader in the high-technology industry. Incorporated in 1899 as Nippon Electric Company to manufacture telephone and switching equipment, the company is now a major manufacturer of electronic products. NEC companies have 25 plants in 14 countries, employing over 158,000 workers worldwide.

Restructuring of the Japanese Economy

Ever since the early 1950s, when the Korean War stimulated the Japanese economy and the U.S. promoted Japan as a bulwark against communism, Japan's economic and business policy has been based on high growth rates. Many features of Japanese corporate behavior, including the priority given to market share over profits and the system of lifetime employment, can be sustained only if business is in a period of long-term expansion. Primed by access to the vast U.S. market and by cut-rate prices for Western—mostly U.S.—technologies, the Japanese economy expanded at double-digit rates from the 1950s to the mid 1970s. In the latter half of the 1970s it slowed to about 5 percent, then to an average of 4 percent in the 1980s. The surge in the late 1980s was an aberration fueled by cheap credit and the unprecedented boom in land and stock values. The price of the excess, shown by a growing number of bankruptcies and a weakened financial sector, will continue to be paid for several years.

When Japan faced other economic crises, such as the oil shocks of the 1970s and the *endaka* (or high yen shock) in 1985, there was always a way to respond that allowed it to preserve its traditional practices and its hard-to-penetrate domestic markets. The oil shocks were overcome by high manufacturing productivity and a surge in exports. When *endaka* arrived, Japan leveraged its new wealth in real estate and stocks into an asset-buying spree at home and abroad. But now there appears to be no way to escape, except by making changes in the system. With Japan's trade surplus hitting a record $140 billion, it is clear that the export escape route is closed by political reality.

Japanese companies are discovering that many of their usual advantages have been eroded. Manufacturing, for example, the leading force in Japan's global expansion, is in trouble because rivals have become more competitive. Another advantage Japan has lost is its free ride in technology. For most of the postwar period, Japan paid little for technologies that were important to its industrial development. Most U.S. companies simply underestimated Japan's potential, and the U.S. government was more concerned with security than with economic issues. Both these conditions ended with the Cold War.

Japan once verged on global technological dominance. Now it is conceding leadership in many key emerging commercial technologies, chiefly to a resurgent United States. Japanese industry is floundering in a creativity crisis, and has lost market share—even in strongholds such as semiconductors, automobiles, and computers. America's Intel Corporation has replaced Japan's NEC as the world's largest semiconductor maker. North American automakers are making a comeback, and U.S. computer firms—despite their many problems—are expanding their market-share lead. More tellingly, Japan is missing out as U.S. companies forge new markets and seize control of key technologies and standards expected to yield the highest profits in the future. Control of the most profitable computer markets—microprocessors and operating systems—continues to elude Japanese companies. The memory chips they produce so well, in contrast, yield only modest profits and are available from many competing companies. Other traditional Japanese cash cows such as cars, audiovisual equipment, and VCRs now face saturated markets and low profit margins. Little distinguishes one company's products from another's.

Even in long-lost markets such as consumer electronics, U.S. firms are winning technological leads in new areas such as multimedia, high-definition television, and handheld electronic communicators. By setting the technical standards, U.S. computer, software, and semiconductor manufacturers can control the markets and profit from patent royalties.

The same corporate and government structures that nurtured Japan's industrial growth in the past share part of the blame for the current situation. The system created to catch up with the West is ill-equipped for moving ahead with original technology. Much of Japan's technological development has involved catching up with, and then perfecting areas of, technology invented elsewhere. Among Japan's recent hit products, for example, compact discs were proposed by Philips of the Netherlands, VCRs were developed by Ampex, and liquid crystal displays by RCA.

Japanese companies hesitate to move into uncharted technological waters. Instead, they continue to do what they have done so well in the past—honing new technologies often developed abroad and finding inexpensive applications in consumer products. Japan's own attempts to pioneer new technology have not dazzled. Projects for magnetically levitated trains, nuclear and superconducting chips, advanced rockets, and high-definition TV have been plagued by unexpected snags. Japanese companies failed to take over the technological lead during the boom years in the 1980s because they did not pursue original research.

Increasingly, Japan will have to pay more for intellectual property; it will also have to increase spending on basic research, which, unlike its investment in applied research, remains far below that of the United States and Europe. In the twenty-first century Japan faces a new world, and Japan, a mature economy is beginning to reinvent itself.

The changes are by no means bad for the Japanese. In time, they should result in a greater emphasis on domestic consumption over investment, perhaps making Japan a more comfortable place to live. The changes could further open the Japanese economy to foreign companies, offering its people greater selection at lower prices. And Japanese companies that survive the shakeout will emerge as more efficient competitors both at home and abroad.

Across the country, people realize that Japan cannot recover from economic stagnation without drastic change. But there are formidable obstacles in implementing the change. The system that helped Japan catch up with the West after World War II is unable to function now that the nation has matured economically. It was a great system (with close relationships between government, industry, and banks) for rapid development and industrial takeoff. But once Japan caught up with the West, the system failed to make the transition to a market economy. Instead, it reinforced import protection, cartels, and a bank-centered financial system to operate its economic policy.

Japan's strict seniority system stifles entrepreneurial ideas. Consensus-oriented management reacts too slowly and too meekly to a rapidly changing world. And too many government regulations needlessly raise the price of doing business. Also, Japan's capital market shuns corporate bonds or venture-capital funds for a system of cross-ownership in which banks and their largest corporate clients own each others' stock. Such a system has led to collusion, and funding decisions often are made on the basis of corporate loyalty rather than on objective calculations of potential return on investment. This corporate funding system makes it almost impossible for young firms to raise the funds they require to succeed in a new enterprise. So a system of bureaucratic guidance and business loyalty that once helped pick strategic winners now coddles a raft of economic losers. Japanese banks have made loans to old, tired companies and enterprises, even though these old firms were hiding huge losses. In the process Japanese banks' overhang of bad loans has swelled to an estimated $1 trillion, or more than 12 percent of the GNP. Japan kept funding the past for traditional and cultural reasons, rather than funding its future. Once the pillar of prosperity and stability in a confident Asia, Japan is now feared for its economic stagnation and the harm its ailing economy might do to the rest of Asia and the world.

There is need for change, but the old system holds vast sway over domestic politics. Is Japan really ready to permit bankrupt companies to collapse, for example, even if doing so leads to massive unemployment in what once had been considered a "full employment" society? By Japanese standards 4.1 percent unemployment in 1998 was considered scandalously high. Would Japan accept hostile takeovers and real voting rights for corporate shareholders if this meant giving courts, lawyers, and outsiders real power over corporate governance?

Japanese businesses are beginning to embark on a full-scale economic restructuring, prompted most basically by slowing growth rates, technological change, and intense competition. The result is a move away from the ingrown business practices that have characterized its economy since World War II to a more open system more like that of the Western nations.

All across Japan today factories are being forced to restructure operations, doing things they would have never considered just a few years ago, such as cutting payrolls and capital spending and bailing out of unprofitable businesses. After thirty years and more than 10 million cars, Nissan Motor Company decided to close its main plant at Zama, south of Tokyo, in 1995. It transferred car production from Zama to a newer, more efficient factory halfway across the country. The end of auto production directly affected 2,500 of Nissan's 4,000 Zama workers who were transferred to other facilities. Nippon Steel Corporation banked the last blast furnace operational at its Hirohata, Hyogo-ken, Works in June 1993 and withdrew from unprofitable lines such as personal computers. It will cut the personnel at its iron and steel division by 4,000 people or 15 percent. Nippon Steel closed its blast furnaces in Kamaishi in 1989. At Toshiba Corporation, structural reform includes retraining employees and shifting them to the information, communications, and multimedia divisions where there is growth potential. The aim of restructuring at Nissan, Nippon, Toshiba, and others is the same: survival in the face of a more serious than anticipated decline in consumer spending and capital investment and a surge in the value of the yen, which makes Japanese products more expensive in relation to those produced in other countries.

Companies are rethinking long-standing relationships with local suppliers and buying more components abroad. NEC is switching its purchases of components away from captive suppliers in high-cost Japan to cheaper suppliers of products such as computer motherboards in Taiwan, China, and other low-cost countries. This will produce profound changes among the legions of subcontractors and local businesses that rely on the factories for their customers

Businesses are also streamlining product lines. For example, Ajinomoto has reduced its number of products from 4,000 to 2,500. Kikkoman Corporation has reduced its products from 5,000 to 2,500. The number of products at

Ricoh has been cut from 7,000 to 6,200, and unprofitable lines such as printers have been curtailed.

A large change effort involves rethinking the sacred commitment of lifetime
employment and other management practices that Japanese companies thought
were the basis of their competitive strength. Big Japanese companies traditionally have guaranteed lifetime employment for workers, but the recession has
strained—and sometimes broken—those paternalistic ties. Some companies
are encouraging workers to leave voluntarily or take early retirement. Minolta
Camera Company reduced its workforce by 1,700 by getting employees to
leave voluntarily, and Nippon Telegraph and Telephone reduced its workforce
by 15,000 by the same method.

These changes are the inevitable consequences of the 1980s economic boom.
A slowing Japanese economy in recent years and the resulting sharp decline in
corporate profits have prompted some of the changes in business practices.

DEVELOPMENT AND ENVIRONMENTAL
DEGRADATION

Environmental degradation in Japan has accompanied the development of
modern industry since the Meiji period. Environmental problems caused by
drainage from the refineries at Ashio Copper Mine in Tochigi Prefecture,
operated by the Furukawa company, go back to 1878. The pollution in Ashio
is of such long standing that it is referred to as the origin of Japan's environmental problems. The acid wastewater polluted large areas of agricultural
land in the lower reaches of the Watarase River, damaging farm products,
killing fish, and doing serious damage to the health of residents along the
river. About 12,000 hectares of land was deforested by sulfurous acid gas
from the refineries by 1893. The mining was closed in 1973, when the copper seam was exhausted, but refineries continued operating, using imported
ore, until the early 1980s. Although the efforts to restore the environment in
the area have been under way for nearly forty years, it is still a long way
from full recovery.

The discharge from chemical industries polluted coastal areas around
Tokyo Bay after 1920. The use of coal as the major source of energy for
industry caused widespread but localized air pollution. However, environmental degradation as a devastating side effect of rapid Japanese development
has occurred only since the 1950s.

Since the 1950s, concern over environmental problems has gone through a
series of distinct stages. Until the mid-1960s there was widespread apathy
concerning the environment on the part of the government as well as the public. Although the pollution-related Minamata disease caused by mercury from
Chisso Corporation plant was reported in 1956, until the mid-1960s Japan's
major industries succeeded in primary capital accumulation by forgetting the

diseconomies of environmental pollution by spending the larger portion of profits on new production equipment (Figure 3.21).

By the late 1960s, awareness of environmental degradation began to strike the national consciousness. The pollution of air and water became serious in major industrial areas, and many respiratory diseases were named after the industrial cities where they frequently occurred, such as the Kawasaki asthma and Yokkaichi asthma. Environmental pollution in Japan was at its worst between 1965 and 1975. Inadequate disposal of industrial waste led to widespread contamination of the environment and the emergence of various diseases related to air and water pollution. Rapid urbanization and industrialization, a lag in the construction of capital facilities such as sewerage systems, and a public policy that heavily favored economic growth over public health and a clean environment contributed to the emergence of serious pollution problem. Bays, inland seas, lakes, and other water areas such as Tokyo, Ise, and Osaka bays and lakes Biwa, Kasumigaura, and Suwa suffered considerable pollution from organic substances and industrial wastes.

Calls for the government and industry to take responsibility for environmental protection led to the passage in 1967 of the pollution control laws. These laws were successful in the removal of toxic substances from the water and the reduction of sulfur oxides in the air. Photochemical smog first

Figure 3-21. Chisso Chemical Corporation Plant in Minamata, Kyushu, is a manufacturer of chemical products, including synthetic resin, fibers, and chemicals. Effluents from the Chisso acetaldehyde factory in Minamata led to serious mercury poisoning of hundreds of residents of the city. The company was found guilty of negligence in 1973. (Photo: Cotton Mather.)

appeared in Tokyo in July 1970. The Environmental Agency, attached to the Prime Minister's Office, responsible for environmental conservation and pollution control was established in 1971. However, the oil crisis of 1973, the decline of industries such as shipbuilding and textiles, a slump in the steel industry, and other economic issues subdued the public pressures for a clean environment by the late 1970s. The right of the victims of pollution-related diseases to compensation was established in cases such as the Niigata Minamata disease (1971), Yokkaichi asthma (1972), and Kumamoto Minamata disease (1973). In the 1970s Japan adapted the "polluter pays principle," in which the polluting enterprises have to accept financial responsibility for damages they have inflicted on the community. A Nature Conservation Law was passed in 1972 to serve as the basis for all legal measures to protect the environment.

The national government sets general standards for environmental protection, but much of the implementation of the policies is done at the prefectural or municipal level. Local governments and citizen groups then negotiate with industrial firms to establish standards for specific facilities. These standards are invariably stricter than the national standards, and permit a great deal of local citizen involvement. This involvement strengthens a community's willingness to accept a new facility and supports a healthy industry–community relationship.

Although some areas in Japan face serious environmental problems, the thrust of public environmental concern shifted in the 1980s. New environmental issues such as groundwater contamination by organic solvents in the effluence from high-tech semiconductor factories, the pollution of rivers and streams from agricultural chemicals used to maintain golf courses, and acid rain attracted major public concern. Extensive land reclamation schemes, often in coastal areas renowned for their scenery, and the development of housing and industrial complexes such as the western Tokyo's Nishi-Tama plan aroused concern among environmentalists. The large number of visitors to national parks, and the conflict between economic demands and the need to preserve areas of natural wilderness have led to a keen awareness among the public of the effects of overdevelopment on the environment.

Acid rain in areas facing the Sea of Japan comes from China and Korea. Dead trees resulting from acid rain have been observed in areas facing the Sea of Japan, especially in Shimane and other nearby prefectures. In recent years the construction of golf courses has caused environmental concern. The use of huge amounts of underground water for sprinkling the greens has caused land subsidence, and drying up of ponds, marshes, lakes, and springs. Chemicals used for the growth of grasses contaminate the water supplies. The Live Tree Trust Movement, a conservation group, has used tree rights to halt the construction of golf courses in Gifu Prefecture. Under the law, land and tree rights can be sold separately, which means that developers buying land for golf courses must get permission from both the land and tree owners.

Nowhere else in Japan is concern for the environment more intense than it is in Ryukyu's tiny Ishikagi Island, 1,200 miles from Tokyo. This island is called the Galapagos of the East, and for good reason. On this tropical island with its sparkling emerald-green reef below—a rare sight in a country whose scenic coastlines tend toward oil storage tanks and factories—Japan melts invisibly into Southeast Asia. This remote corner of Japan became a center of conflict between development and environmental protection in 1979, when the Okinawa government announced plans to build a modern airport with a 2,500-meter runway projecting into the sea, on landfill that would cover much of what appears to be the world's largest stand of rare blue coral. The existing runway does not allow large aircraft to land to develop tourism, which is essential for the economic future of Ishigaki and the surrounding islands. Environmentalists argued that precious coral reefs could be destroyed during building, and that in the long run the airport would do irreversible damage to the environment. To environmentalists, the Ishigaki coral reef is a symbol of Japan's awakening consciousness to an issue that has long been at center stage in the politics of other industrialized countries. Most reefs in the Ryukyu have died as construction projects have changed the flow of currents and sent sediments into the sea.

The island's balmy climate and natural beauty make it a prime vacation spot for Japanese citizens armed with an increasing amount of vacation time and income. More than 250,000 visitors come annually to the small, uncrowded Ishigaki Island of about 46,000 residents and some gentle mountains. The new airport will allow 1.6 million visitors a year to fly direct from Tokyo. Farming, the islands' main occupation, is on the decline. Young people are leaving for the mainland in search of work. Some residents backed the idea of airport construction, but the majority of the residents of the fishing village of Shiraho, the site of the proposed airport, were opposed to the idea. In the face of mounting opposition, the local government abandoned its plan to build the airport in 1989.

In Japan, the challenge is to find a balance between the need for development and the preservation of its precious natural beauty and environment, designing and carrying out a strategy for environmentally integrated development. In various parts of the country local citizens have started grassroots environmental movements to save the environment and the quality of life of their local areas (Figure 3.22).

DIVIDED KOREA

The Korean peninsula, between China and Japan, served as a land bridge by which Chinese ideas and institutions entered the Japanese islands. In modern times, Korea provided the base from which Japan could embark upon military expansion into the rich lands of Manchuria and north China.

Figure 3-22. Major Japanese environmental disasters (1955–1965) and grassroots environmental movements (based on field observations).

The total area of Korea (85,266 sq miles) is roughly equal to the area of the United Kingdom. From 1910 until the fall of the Japanese Empire in 1945, Korea was a colony of Japan. The Japanese modernized Korea's transportation, communications, and industrial infrastructure, but most resources from

Korea were sent back to Japan, and Koreans enjoyed no democratic freedoms. Nationalist feelings ran strong, and in 1919, a group of Korean leaders met in Seoul and declared the nation independent. In response, an estimated 2 million peaceful pro-independence demonstrators filled the streets of the capital. Thousands were arrested, wounded, or killed in the brutal Japanese crackdown. During World War II, Japan drafted thousands to join the Japanese forces or to work in factories. The Korean language was banned. Koreans were forced to worship at Shinto shrines and adopt Japanese names.

After 1945, the Soviet occupation of Korea north of the 38th Parallel and the U.S. administration of the zone to the south led to the emergence of two rival republics in the peninsula—the communist Democratic People's Republic (population 23 million in 2003) in the north, and the Republic of Korea (population 48 million in 2003) in the south. In 1950 North Korea launched a military attempt to unify the peninsula, capturing the South Korean capital and pushing so far south that the South Korean forces and the U.N. troops were left holding only a small area of the peninsula around Pusan. U.N. forces then moved north and captured the North Korean capital and later reached the Yalu River. An armistice, though not a peace treaty, was signed in 1953. Total casualties of the Korean War are estimated at 2.9 million; the United States lost 54,200 persons. The 1953 cease-fire line, which for the most part runs slightly to the north of the 38th Parallel, has formed the boundary between the two Koreas (Figure 3.23).

An uneasy peace reigns across the 2.5-mile demilitarized zone buffer strip that separates North and South Korea. About 1 million soldiers face off against each other along the 150-mile-long demilitarized zone that cleaves the two countries. In recent years North and South Korea have talked about reunification. However, the North's alleged development of nuclear weapons and apprehension about the problems a sudden reunification might cause have made South Korea much less sure about a speedy reunion.

Rugged upland, typically blanketed in either pine forest or scrub, predominates throughout the peninsula. Cultivated lowland forms only 20 percent of the combined area of North and South Korea. Most of the mineral deposits are concentrated in the north, where large-scale mining operations were started by the Japanese before the Second World War.

The nearly four fifths of Korea that is too high or has slopes too steep for the traditional system of agriculture is sparsely settled. Settlement is confined almost wholly to the alluvial valleys and basins, with their fertile, well-watered soils and superior communications, and to the lower slopes. The long and intricate coast is also densely settled wherever sufficient level space is available. There is a strong contrast between the heavily populated southwestern Korea, with its warm climate and subdued landforms, and thinly settled northeastern Korea, with its harsher climate and rugged topography. Along the southwest coast there is a continuous zone of dense settlements reaching into the interior valleys. The least populous tracts are in

Figure 3-23. The Korean Peninsula.

north-central and northeastern Korea and in the region of high ridges behind the southeast coast.

Nearly 61 percent of the population of North Korea and 74 percent of the population of South Korea lives in urban centers. The cities of old Korea had their origins as administrative and local marketing centers. Under Japanese control, not only did the older towns increase in size and take on new functions, but a fairly large number of new cities appeared around major rail junctions, mines, industrial plants, and some of the strategically located harbors. All Korean cities occupy lowland sites, the majority at river mouths or confluences and other key points. Rapid economic development in South Korea during the last four decades has led to phenomenal urban growth. Seoul has a population of over 12 million.

South Korea

Three decades ago the average South Korean earned around $100 a year, less than the average Indian or Ghanian. Today South Korea's GNP per head is $8,500, thirty times India's and twenty times Ghana's. Two decades ago the streets of the capital, Seoul, were empty but for a few government cars; neon signs were an extravagance. Now the streets are clogged with cars, and neon illuminates the night. Seoul is full of glamorous people, trendy bars, and department stores as overstuffed with merchandize as are their Japanese equivalents (Figure 3.24). New cities have appeared on the map which are

Figure 3-24. A view of Central Seoul, South Korea. With a population of nearly 10 million, it is the commercial, industrial, and cultural center of South Korea. The city suffered extensive damage in the Korean War (1950–1953) and has largely been rebuilt since 1953. Although the city now boasts high-rise buildings, twelve-lane boulevards, and urban problems to match, the centuries-old royal palaces, temples, pagodas, and imposing stone gateways remain timeless and elegant. Seoul has twenty-two urban districts (*gu*) and 494 neighborhoods (*dong*). (Photo: Tae Kim.)

now exporting goods to far-flung countries. For example, Ulsan in the 1960s was just a small town. Today, with one of the world's biggest car plants, Ulsan's dry docks are a sculpture park of arched steel and tall cranes.

South Korea's economic success is breathtaking. It stands as proof that a country held down for most of this century by brutal colonization (by Japan, from 1910 to 1945) and civil war (against communist North Korea, from 1950 to 1953) can leap from poverty to affluence in one generation. It is proof, too, that a lack of natural resources need be no obstacle to development. South Korea's development model has much in common with Japan's. Like Japan in its period of fast development (roughly from 1950 to 1980) South Korea discouraged inward foreign investment and import of consumer goods. South Korea focused on exports. Like Japan, it combined world-class manufacturing with much less developed agricultural and service sectors. South Korea's government, more than Japan's, directed firms to develop specific industries and held prices to fit in with its industrial policy.

Armed with a literate and hard-working workforce, a sense of common purpose, and the fierce nationalism that had kept Korea independent and united for twelve centuries, South Korea managed to condense a century of growth into three decades. South Korea's growth was export-driven development. Much of its export success was due to the nation's business conglomerates which dominate the economy. South Korea's business conglomerates, or *chaebol,* are large groupings of firms owned and controlled by a single entrepreneur and, usually, family members. Some of the nation's largest *chaebol* such as Hyundai, Daewoo, and Samsung have built worldwide reputations and now sell everything from supertankers to microchips. They wield enormous power, in part because the conglomerates are controlled more as family concerns than as stockholder-owned companies. Much more than most other countries in Asia, South Korea is dominated by its large companies. By some estimates, forty conglomerates control half or more of the country's industrial output, and there are periodic calls for the government to help smaller businesses instead.

The *chaebols* are the progeny of miscegenation between business and government. They were set up in the 1960s when the government called on entrepreneurs to launch ventures in industries targeted for development, and they helped South Korea leap from poverty to affluence in one generation. Now the *chaebols* represent a disturbing concentration of market power. Taken together, the four biggest *chaebols*—Hyundai, Samsung, Daewoo, and LG Group—employ 3 percent of the workforce and account for almost a third of the total sales of South Korean companies. These four alone ship nearly 60 percent of the total exports. The concentration of ownership is tighter still: the families that founded the top thirty *chaebols* still own perhaps 60 percent of their combined equity. Their intimate relations with government also invite graft.

Several cultural and historical factors unique to South Korea have also influenced the country's development. Among these are (1) the role of Confucianism, (2) the influence of Japan, (3) the effect of the Korean War, (4) the effect of the North–South division, and (5) the role and influence of the United States in South Korea's development. The strict discipline in the tradition of Confucianism has been conducive to the emergence of the strong authoritarian government which took the lead in development. During the 1960s and 1970s Japan had considerable influence on South Korea's development. Many of South Korea's senior policymakers received their education under the Japanese system, internalizing Japanese values such as respect for honesty and integrity. The Korean War tended to destroy social barriers and increase social mobility, which facilitated the adoption of outward-looking development strategy in the early 1960s. The division of the country forced South Korea to pursue two goals at the same time—increasing the wealth of the country and strengthening its arms.

Over the past thirty years or more, the United States has affected South Korea's development in many ways. The U.S. military presence has enabled the country to devote a greater amount of resources to development. The U.S. aid contributed to development, and by making its market available to South Korea, facilitated the export-driven development strategy.

The government's supercharged development policy has led to environmental degradation which is now causing the nation a lot of anguish. In the scrubby valley formed by the Naktong River, the "industrialize at all costs" policy has created severe industrial pollution. For years, South Korea has been lax about what is dumped into the air and water, and the absence of environmental regulations made investments in industry attractive. A phenol leak in Kumi polluted water in Taegu, South Korea's third-largest city, 120 miles southeast of Seoul. Kumi is jammed not only with Korean companies but also with Japanese and American joint ventures. Along the 326-mile Naktong River there have been illegal discharges of toxic waste. The intense reaction against environmental degradation in South Korea has underscored the growing conflict between industrial companies unaccustomed to being questioned and a public that got its first taste of real political power a few years ago.

South Korea has a reputation as one of the most corrupt countries in a region known for corruption. Bureaucratic controls are so widespread that bribes are the most efficient way for a company to get some breathing space. South Korea has cracked down on bribes in the last few years since the first civilian president came to power in 1993. In 1995 several executives of conglomerates such as Samsung and Daewoo were indicted for giving bribes.

South Korea's Economic Crisis

South Korea's postwar economic development has been the envy of developing countries. By using the Japanese model of high savings, close cooperation between government and business, and export-oriented growth, South Korea quickly transformed itself from a poor, war-torn nation to an industrial and technical powerhouse. After starting at $200 in 1960, by 1996, the GNP per capita in South Korea, had risen to more than $11,500.

But rapid development had a dark side. The system of close government–business cooperation ended up fostering a web of insiders and a system of corruption and speculation. Business, protected from the harsh rules of the market, continued to invest in the old target industries of electronics, steel, and shipbuilding—often without regard to profitability. Korean companies borrowed huge sums of money and began amassing large amounts of debt. In 1997 the giant conglomerate Hanbo went bankrupt with a $6 billion debt. Hanbo's chairman was convicted of bribing government officials and bankers in a futile attempt to keep the group afloat. The Hanbo crisis exposed the inherent corruption and poor lending practices within the system. For years, merchant banks were used as private coffers by the conglomerates that often owned them. The Hanbo scandal caused banks to scrutinize their portfolios and recall loans from the more indebted firms, creating a domino effect of corporate failure.

The free floating of Thailand's currency in July 1997 caused panic in South Korea and several Asian countries, because in export-dependent Asian countries it meant cheaper Thai exports compared with other countries such as South Korea. To stay competitive in export markets, the value of the won (South Korea's currency) also needed to fall. The devaluation of the won hurt many South Korean companies, which had gone abroad to borrow money and subsequently found their debts increasing. To stem the crisis, South Korea received a huge bailout from the International Monetary Fund which has insisted that the aid be paired with reform in South Korea's financial system.

North Korea

North Korea's economy is only 8 to 10 percent the size of the south's. The arable land is concentrated in the relatively flat western provinces. Development has taken place under successive economic plans since 1953, but the North lags behind South Korea. With the loss of subsidies from Russia and China, its supporters during the Cold War, North Korea's economy shrank by a quarter between 1990 and 1994. Dissidents escaping to South Korea report food shortages in North Korea's countryside. In 1994 North Korea came to terms with the death of Kim Il Sung, the "Great Leader" who ruled the country from 1945, when the Korean peninsula was divided.

In the mid-1990s, successive years of floods devastated crops in the coastal areas. The conditions, coupled with the inefficient controls on agriculture by the government, created severe food shortages throughout the country. By 1997, the U.N. was forecasting that maize production would be reduced by some 1.25 million tons. In the case of rice, losses would amount to

340,000 tons. The general breakdown in the North's state-controlled and centrally planned system compounded the food crisis. The fall of the Soviet Union in 1991—which had caused the loss of valuable subsidies, petroleum supplies, and a major export market—was already wreaking havoc on North Korea's fragile economy. The situation was aggravated by North Korea's limited ability to buy food from abroad. To help stem the crisis, the U.N's World Food Program launched an appeal in 1998 for more than $378 million to avert famine in North Korea.

The economy of North Korea has been helped by infusions of foreign aid delivered in exchange for its promise to halt the production of plutonium from which nuclear bombs can be made. But in 2002 North Korea admitted it has an active nuclear weapons program in defiance of the 1994 agreement. The United States called North Korea part of an "axis of evil" (with Iran and Iraq under Saddam Hussein) for developing weapons of mass destruction. North Korea received equipment to process highly enriched uranium from Pakistan in exchange for a North Korean–designed missile called the Nodong. North Korea has acquired nuclear arms to protect itself from being overrun by South Korea, a fear that pervades everything from government propaganda to children's textbooks.

Ever since communism collapsed around the world, the expectation seemed to be that North Korea's regime would follow shortly. But lumping North Korea with other communist regimes may be a mistake. North Korea is based not so much on Marx as on an intense sense of nationalism. North Korea turned Marxism into an indigenous creed with its own texts and icons. In place of Marxist theory, North Koreans study Kim's philosophy of *juche,* or self-reliance. Instead of statues of Marx or Lenin, North Koreans have built monuments to their own leader, who liberated the country from Japanese rule and defended it from American invasion. This nationalism is reinforced by comparison with the South, whose leaders collaborated with the Japanese and whose territory still plays host to the U.S. army. Self-reliance seems to be a source of genuine pride in North Korea. Communism may be dead, but nationalist emotion is strong.

North Korea's gross national product, which at nearly $22 billion (2001) is about equal to the annual revenue of Bank of America or GTE, has been shrinking at an estimated 5 percent a year. Factories are idle for lack of fuel. Since the collapse of the Soviet Union, North Korea no longer gets cheap oil and other economic supports. Some experts fear that North Korea could collapse, sending millions of refugees streaming to South Korea, China, and Japan. Or, a desperate regime might start a war to divert public attention from internal problems.

To encourage development, North Korea established a free trade zone at Rajin-Sonbong in 1996 to help growth of the area around the Tumen River, where the borders of North Korea, China, and Russia meet. As in China, the opening of the first North Korean free trade area could lead to economic changes. The hope is that combining the natural resources of eastern Russia and Mongolia, the labor of China and North Korea, and the capital and technology of South Korea and Japan could make northeast Asia the world's next growth area. Most investments are coming from Chinese companies or from Hong Kong business executives, many of whom have also played an important role in developing China.

The 288-square-mile zone, bigger than Singapore, does have some strengths. If its port, built by the Japanese occupiers in the 1930s, can be modernized, Rajin is ideally positioned to serve northeastern China, Siberia, and even Europe by the Trans-Siberian Railroad. Already some earth movers, steel, and other products are being shipped from Pusan in South Korea to Rajin, where they are carried by rail or truck into northeastern China. The rugged coast and wooded hills could attract vacationers if there were easier ways to get here. Rather than the next Shenzhen, some people think the free trade zone will become the next Macao, the Portuguese-controlled playground near Hong Kong.

Tensions between North and South Korea have kept South Korean companies, which would be the most willing investors, out of action. South Korea, wanting to avoid a collapse of North Korea that would overwhelm their own economy, relaxed restrictions on doing business in the North in 1994. But since then only one project—light manufacturing by the Daewoo group in the port of Nampo—has been approved. As for U.S. companies, the restrictions on doing business with North Korea were supposed to be gradually lifted under a 1994 agreement in which North Korea agreed to give up its suspected nuclear program. But so far, few rules have been relaxed—in part because North Korea has refused to talk with South Korea, as is also called for in the agreement.

North Korea's Nuclear Program

Although little is known about North Korea's nuclear history, much of the country's nuclear program is believed to have grown out of technology developed in the former Soviet Union, during the Cold War. North Korea's nuclear capability centers around the city of Yongbyon, about 60 miles north of the capital, Pyongyang. Here the country is reported to have several nuclear facilities (atomic reactors and plutonium reprocessing plants) with the potential to produce nuclear weapons. North Korea has reportedly also developed missiles capable of delivering nuclear warheads. In 1993, North Korea tested a SCUD missile with a range estimated at 600 miles, able to hit both South Korea and part of Japan.

During the early 1990s, the United States and South Korea tried to engage North Korea in talks designed toward securing the country's adherence to treaties such as the Nuclear Non-Proliferation Treaty and other denuclearization agreements. But the North rebuffed U.S. and international demands for inspections. North Korea rejected the request for inspection of nuclear waste sites at Yongbyon, and threatened to withdraw from the non-proliferation treaty in 1993.

In 1994 North Korea agreed to suspend efforts to build nuclear weapons and dismantle its existing graphite nuclear-power reactor. In exchange, North Korea would receive two light-water nuclear reactors, with fuel that is more difficult to convert to weapons use. North Korea would also receive 500,000 tons of fuel oil each year. In 1997, North Korea broke ground on the $5 billion nuclear energy project. The country continues to be short on fuel. Despite pledges to honor the nuclear accord, in 2002 North Korea confirmed that it was operating a secret nuclear weapons program.

In August 1998, North Korea fired over Japan the Taepo Dong-I, a ballistic missile that may herald a time in the not-too-distant future when improvements in the third stage of the missile would enable it to reach the United States. If North Korea developed technology to attach small nuclear devices, or biological or chemical weapons to its missiles, the situation could pose a great threat in the Pacific Rim. North Korea already possesses biological and chemical weapons but has not perfected the technology that would allow missiles with these payloads to hit their targets with accuracy. The United States has responded by pursuing research and development of a National Missile Defense (NMD) system and Theater Missile Defense (TMD) system to defend Japan and South Korea, and possibly Taiwan. At the same time, the United States is also pursuing a policy of engagement with both North Korea and China. In the coming years, the most delicate problem in international relations will be how to negotiate the end of the crisis in North Korea.

Reunification

The future of the Korean peninsula is dependent on national reunification and the development of a single national ideology. The bringing together of the two diverging forces in North and South Korea into a single force would not only create a bright future for the Korean people, but would contribute to the peace and stability of East Asia. Unification would create a population of nearly 70 million, big enough to create a major domestic market. It would combine the North's resources and the South's agricultural and industrial strength and open the door to trains from Pusan to Paris, direct flights to Europe, and highways extending into the heart of the Asian continent.

Both Korean governments have repeatedly affirmed their desire for reunification of the Korean peninsula, but until 1971 they had no communication or contact. After several meetings in 1972, the two sides agreed to work toward reunification and an end to hostilities. The process broke down a year later. Tension between North and South increased dramatically in 1983 when North Korean agents tried to assassinate the South Korean president in Burma. North–South relations further worsened after North Korean agents bombed a

South Korean airliner in 1987. In 1988 South Korea called for more efforts to promote exchanges, family reunification, and inter-Korean trade. South Korean firms began to import North Korean goods soon afterward and direct trade began in the fall of 1990. In 1997 North Korean negotiators sat down with U.S., South Korean, and Chinese officials for the first substantive peace talks in forty years.

In 2000, after forty-seven years of uneasy truce, leaders of North and South Korea convened an inter-Korea summit. They agreed to economic cooperation, cultural exchanges, and cross-border visits for relatives separated by the Demilitarized Zone. These initiatives sprang from South Korea's Sunshine Policy of engagement with the North. Yet acrimony between North Korea and the United States, South Korea's strong ally, complicates efforts for North–South reconciliation.

In the end, unification is bound to come. Korea's tradition of political unity stretches back much further than Germany's, a country that was finally reunited after its World War II division. Koreans feel just as strongly as Germans do about their shared language and culture. North Korea may shut out foreign influence for a long time, but its walls will eventually leak. Given time, South Korean firms may gain access to the North to create pockets of industry which may reduce the cost of unification, which are estimated at $1.2 trillion, or four times South Korea's GNP.

FURTHER READINGS

Abe, Hitoshi, Muneyuki Shindo and Sadafumi Kawato. 1994. *The Government and Politics of Japan.* Translated by James W. White. Tokyo: University of Tokyo Press.

Atlas of Japan. 1990. Tokyo: Teikoku-Shoin.

Beasley, W. G. 2000. *The Rise of Modern Japan.* 3rd ed. New York: St. Martin's Press.

Dore, Ronald P. 1993. *Shinohata: A portrait of a Japanese village.* Berkeley: University of California Press.

Eberstadt, Nicholas. 1995. *Korea Approaches Reunification.* Armonk, NY: M.E. Sharpe.

Gordon, Andrew. 2003. *A Modern History of Japan: From Tokugawa Times to the Present.* New York: Oxford University Press.

Jansen, Marius B. 2000. *The Making of Modern Japan.* Cambridge, MA.: Belknap Press of Harvard University Press.

Karan, P. P. and K. Stapleton, eds. 1997. *The Japanese City.* Lexington: University Press of Kentucky.

Lo, Jeannie. 1990. *Office Ladies/Factory Women: Life and Work at a Japanese Company.* Armonk, NY: M.E. Sharpe.

Mather, Cotton, P. P. Karan and Shigeru Iijima. 1998. *The Japanese Landscapes.* Lexington: University Press of Kentucky.

McClain, James J., John M. Merriman, and Ugawa Kaoru. eds.1995. *Edo and Paris: Urban Life and the State in the Early Modern Era.* Ithaca, NY: Cornell University Press.

Organization for Economic Cooperation and Development (OECD). 2003. *OECD Economic Surveys: Japan 2002.* Washington, D.C.

Porter, Michael E., Hirotaka Takeuchi and Mariko Sakakibara. 2000. *Can Japan Compete?* Basingstoke, U.K.: Macmillan.

Reischauer, Edwin O. 1989. *The Japanese Today.* Harvard University Press.

Robertson, Jeniffer. 1991. *Native and Newcomer: Making and Remaking of a Japanese City.* Berkeley: University of California Press.

Seldon, Kyoko and Mark Seldon. 1990. *The Atomic Bomb: Voices from Hiroshima and Nagasaki.* Armonk, NY: M.E. Sharpe.

Totman, Conrad D. 2000. *A History of Japan*. Malden, MA.: Blackwell Publishers.

Varley, H. Paul. 1984. *Japanese Culture*. Honolulu: University of Hawaii Press.

Yagasaki, Noritaka. 2002. *Japan: Geographical Perspectives on an Island Nation*. 3rd ed. Tokyo: Teikoku-Shoin.

Yoda, Yoshiie and Kurt W. Radtke. 1995. *The Foundations of Japan's Modernization*. Leiden, The Netherlands: E. J. Brill.

Chapter 4

Southeast Asia

GEOGRAPHICAL SETTING

Southeast Asia is a collective name for the lands lying to the east of the Indian subcontinent and to the south of China. Its regional unity derives in the main from its transitional character between the two great demographic and cultural foci of India and China. It consists of the Asian mainland and fringing islands, with a population of nearly 552 million. Southeast Asia has great diversity in its population, resources, and political and economic patterns. Perhaps no area in the world has been swept by so many tides of military, mercantile, and cultural influence as Southeast Asia, and few areas preserve the relics of those influences in such astonishing and appealing variety.

Due to its peninsular and island character and the deep penetration of the interior by great rivers such as the Irrawaddy, Red, and Mekong, Southeast Asia enjoys a high degree of accessibility. The accessibility through the sea facilitated Chinese and Indian influences in ancient and medieval periods, and the integration of most of the area into commercial, then colonial empires of the Western European powers in the eighteenth and nineteenth centuries. Today, Asia's three giants—China, Japan, and India—loom over the region.

Physically, Southeast Asia comprises frayed-out ends of mountain ranges separated by lowland areas. The mountains are remains of old massifs, with gently rolling topography, and zones of much younger fold mountains characterized by steep slopes and diversified by active or extinct volcanic cones (Figure 4.1). These younger folds, interrupted by the sea, provide the backbone of the Indonesian and Philippine island groups, linking up with the great belt of mountains that rims the Western Pacific. These upland mountain areas are occupied by diverse tribal groups frequently dependent on shifting agriculture. When Southeast Asia was parceled out between European

Figure 4-1. The volcanic peak of Mount Batur, Bali, Indonesia, lies in one of the most active volcanic regions in the world. The village in the foreground lies at the edge of the old crater. (Photo: P. P. Karan.)

colonial powers, the frontiers were drawn through these sparsely settled upland mountain areas.

From the human and economic viewpoint the most significant areas are the alluvial lowlands of the Irrawaddy, Menam, Mekong, and Red rivers and coastal lowlands of the Indonesian islands. These alluvial areas form a series of favored ecological niches. In the past they were cradle areas of some of the mainland peoples—the Burmese, the Thai, the Khmer, and the Vietnamese. Today these areas are the mostly densely populated zones of Southeast Asia, with intensive, irrigated rice farming. Each of the major political units of Southeast Asia consists of a lowland core region inhabited by the majority group and an upland periphery inhabited by the minority groups.

The cultural geography of Southeast Asia has been characterized by constant convergence of peoples, resulting in a great diversity of peoples, languages, and religions. In the earliest period the mainland was dominated by peoples speaking languages of the Mon-Khmer group, and the islands by peoples speaking Malayo-Polynesian languages. This pattern was changed by migration into the area of peoples speaking languages of the Sino-Tibetan group: the Burmese, Thai, and Vietnamese. These peoples pushed the earlier Mon-Khmer peoples into the forested uplands so that today, with the exception of Cambodia, all the major lowlands of mainland Southeast Asia are dominated by peoples speaking languages of the Sino-Tibetan group; the peoples of the islands and peninsular Malaya remain, by contrast, solidly

Malay in their speech, though many dialectal variations have emerged. In the late nineteenth century Indian and Chinese immigrants were drawn into Southeast Asia by the European-sponsored economic development. Indian merchants and money-lenders settled in Burma, and Chinese merchants into all the territories around the South China Sea. Development of tin and rubber in Malaya, based on Indian and Chinese indentured labor, created an entirely new ethnic situation in western Malaya, in which the Malayans found themselves overwhelmed by these two immigrant groups.

A major element of diversity in Southeast Asia is in religion. Hinduism and Buddhism were diffused widely throughout the region, including the islands, during the phase of Indianization in the early centuries of the Christian era. An amalgam of animist, Taoist, and Confucian ideas spread south from China into Vietnamese lands during the long period of Chinese control and left a lasting imprint on the social and political systems of easternmost Southeast Asia. Islam reached the area in the Middle Ages. Its advance on the dominantly Buddhist mainland was confined to the Malay peninsula, but it displaced Hinduism in the Indonesian islands (except Bali) and its advance into the northern Philippines was checked only by the Spaniards, who had succeeded in establishing there an outpost of Spanish Catholicism. Buddhism, Islam, and the Catholicism that Spanish and French missionaries brought to the Philippines and Vietnam have been factors of considerable political importance in several countries during recent years.

SOUTHEAST ASIA BEFORE WESTERN DOMINATION

Southeast Asia was subject to powerful external influences before the Western domination of the area. Two major waves of Malaysians spread through the mainland and western two-thirds of Indonesia before the Christian era. Around the dawn of the Christian era, Indian cultural colonization brought a decisive change leading to the foundation of a string of Indianized states in favored localities along the sea routes to China. Thus arose Java and Funan in the Mekong delta, probably in the first century. They were soon followed by Champa, based in coastal Indo-China, and lesser settlements along the Gulf of Martaban, east Sumatra, and other areas. During the early Christian era, the Indian culture also spread in southern Siam along with intensified activity in the earlier centers in Burma, Champa, and Cambodia. The first Indianized Kingdom of Sri Vijaya, established near Palembang, rose to a commanding position during the fifth and sixth centuries. This was followed by the rise of the rival Indianized empire of Majapahit, based in central and east Java, in the fourteenth century. The Indian colonial civilization extended in a broad belt latitudinally across the region.

The Tibeto-Burmans migrating into the Irrawaddy valley established the Burmese dynasty in central Burma in the eleventh century. Farther to the east, as a result of many centuries of Chinese pressure in Yunan, the various peoples of this area—Lao, Shan and Thai—were forced southward into the Menam valley, where they established the new state of Siam, and also onto the plateau country that surrounds it on the landward sides. The Annamites in eastern Indo-China were absorbed into the Chinese Empire in 111 B.C., and remained part of China until 939 A.D. Chinese cultural influences, the art of dike building, and intensive rice cultivation spread in the Songkoi (Red River) delta.

In the late thirteenth century, following the Muslim invasion of India, Islam began to be propagated in Southeast Asia. Like the Buddhist and Hindu predecessors, Islam followed the commercial route, first to northern Sumatra, then to Malacca (1414), and thereafter to Java and other islands. Malacca became the major center for diffusion of Islam in Southeast Asia. Although the Buddhist states of the mainland (Burma, Thailand, Cambodia, Vietnam, and Laos) never accepted Islam, the Malay-speaking people, with the exception of the Balinese, became Muslim. The spread of Islam was checked by the Roman Catholic missionaries in Luzon late in the sixteenth century.

European influences began to reach Southeast Asia with the occupation of Malacca by the Portuguese in 1511. Later, the Dutch established their principal settlements in Java, at Bantam (1600) and Batavia (1619). The Philippines was administered by Spain as a dependency of its American empire. British and French interest in Southeast Asia arose from the desire to participate in the China trade, which was dominated by the Dutch during the seventeenth and eighteenth centuries. Penang was acquired by Britain in 1786, and Singapore was annexed in 1819 to ensure the access of British shipping to the South China Sea. The need to buttress the eastern frontier of the Indian Empire led to the British occupation of Burma. The French sought to tap the China trade, first by the Mekong and later by the Songkoi valley (Red River). France established its control over the two deltas in Indo-China. In a joint convention of 1896 France and Britain agreed to preserve Siam as a buffer state between their respective colonial territories. In 1898 the Spanish-American War led to the annexation of the Philippines by the United States. This process completed the Western colonial domination of Southeast Asia.

Topography played a role in the pattern of political units imposed by the Western powers in Southeast Asia. The Netherlands Indies (Indonesia) coincided with the archipelago that had been the medieval empire of Majapahit. The historic state nuclei such as the Irrawaddy valley (Burma), Menam valley (Thailand), Tonle Sap basin (Cambodia), and Mekong and Songkoi deltas (Vietnam) remained cores around which new political units were integrated.

CONTEMPORARY PATTERNS

Once the arena of rival Western colonial powers, Southeast Asia in the 1980s and 1990s experienced robust growth in Singapore, Malaysia, Thailand, and Indonesia (Figure 4.2). But in late1990s, the once-roaring Southeast Asian economies were falling into recession or slumping in that direction. Thailand, the first Southeast Asian country to fall, has been in recession since 1997, when its economy shrank to one percent from its 5.5 percent growth in 1996. Next was Indonesia, which experienced negative growth. Malaysia and Singapore also experienced economic slow downs.

During the 1960s phase of the Cold War there was widespread belief in the United States and Europe in the domino theory, which postulated that the fall of South Vietnam to communist rule would lead to the fall of other states to communist rule. Vietnam was divided along the 17th Parallel in 1954 after the defeat of France at Dien Bien Phu. North Vietnam, with the support of China, sent arms to Viet Minh, communist guerrillas operating in South Vietnam. Between 1965 and 1975 there was war between North and South Vietnam. The military forces of the United States and other Western nations were involved in the conflict in support of the South Vietnamese government and to contain the spread of communist rule in Southeast Asia. In April 1975, when North Vietnam successfully gained control of the southern part of the country, the Socialist Republic of Vietnam was established.

Figure 4-2. The Menam Chao Phraya at Bangkok. The hypergrowth of the city in the late 1980s and 1990s is reflected in the construction of new hotels such as the one on the Chao Phraya. (Photo: P. P. Karan.)

After South Vietnam fell to the communist North, the Khmer Rouge, in mad pursuit of agrarian revolution, emptied Cambodia's cities and butchered its middle class; and the communist Pathet Lao declared a people's republic in Laos. Meanwhile, Myanmar (Burma) entered a self-imposed, near-absolute isolation. In the mid-1980s changes began. In November 1986 Laos introduced its "new economic management" program; the following month Vietnam approved a policy of *doi moi* (renovation); and in 1988 Myanmar announced an "open door policy." Even Cambodia, under Vietnamese dominance but locked in civil war, joined the trend, emphasizing the private sector in its five-year plan of 1986–1990 and writing laws for foreign investment in 1989. There were several reasons for the liberalizing tendency in Indochina. One was the sheer difficulty of exporting communist politics to other countries of Southeast Asia. Internal security forces cracked down on any symptoms of Marxism in Thailand, Indonesia, and Singapore. At the same time, Southeast Asia's various treaties with the West, and U.S. bases in the Philippines, ruled out military action. There was a growing communist insurgency in the Philippines, but it could never develop enough popular support to topple the government. Another factor was the diminishing power of the Soviet Union, Indochina's superpower patron. After 1985 the Soviet Union became less willing to support decrepit economies. Soon it became not just unwilling but unable to do so.

The biggest reason for the failure of the domino theory was the simplest: the ever-increasing and ever more obvious prosperity of Southeast Asia's market economies led by Singapore, Malaysia, Thailand, and Indonesia. The gap between the fast-growing market economies and the ones held back by socialism and central planning grew wider as the capitalist countries collectively doubled the size of their economies in the 1970s, and again during the 1980s. By the mid-1980s even the most conservative members of Indochina's ruling parties could not fail to notice the economic miracle in the capitalist countries and the stagnation in the socialist road to reconstruction and development.

TWO GROUPS OF NATIONS : LEADING AND LAGGING STATES

The political and economic changes that have taken place during the last twenty-five years have led to the emergence of two distinct groups of countries in Southeast Asia. The capitalist countries of Southeast Asia in the first six-nation ASEAN (Association of South-East Asian Nations)—Indonesia, Malaysia, the Philippines, Singapore, Thailand, and Brunei—have experienced rapid economic growth; the others—Cambodia, Laos, Vietnam, and Myanmar—are economically lagging, with Vietnam (the seventh nation to join the ASEAN) exhibiting signs of a new economic resurgence (Figure 4.3).

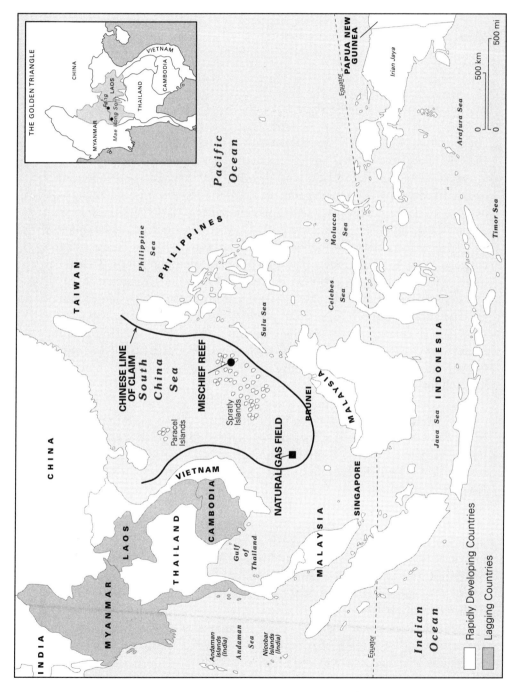

Figure 4-3. Southeast Asia's rapidly developing and lagging states.

Although often spoken of as a single group, the Southeast Asian economies are, in fact, remarkably diverse. The region includes some of the richest and poorest of the world's developing countries, some of the most populous, and some with virtually no population. Moreover, despite its steady growth, in the 2000s Southeast Asia is still grappling with serious challenges, including environmental degradation, infrastructural bottlenecks, and financial crisis.

Rapidly Developing Countries

For the people of ASEAN, economic growth means that fewer people live in what the World Bank calls "absolute poverty," which means that they manage to ingest fewer than 2,150 calories a day. In 1970 three fifths of Indonesia's people lived below this poverty line, by 1980 the proportion was down to 29 percent, by 1990 it was down to 15 percent, and to 12 percent in 2000. For Thailand the equivalent figures were 26, 17, 16, and 14 percent (a leveling off that reflects the persistent inequality between Bangkok and the rest of the country). Even the Philippines managed to reduce its figures from 35 percent in 1970 to 30 percent in 1980, 21 percent in 1990, and 15 percent in 2000. The investment boom of the late 1980s transformed the Malaysian economy and triggered a double-digit GDP growth. Today, it is one of the largest makers of microchips and a leading producer of TV sets. It is also one of the largest producers and exporters of rubber, palm oil, and tropical timber. Growth was at a rate of 5 percent in 2004. Singapore's rapid development has led the Organization for Economic Cooperation and Development (OECD) to classify it as a developed country since 1996.

The economic stars of the region—Singapore, Thailand, Malaysia, and Indonesia—have followed a distinctive path to development with an export-based growth strategy, human resource investments, and an outward orientation. Their development strategy differs from Japan's and South Korea's in one major way. These Southeast Asian countries are more open to foreign direct investment than Japan, South Korea, and Taiwan have been. But like Japan and South Korea, bureaucrats have been agents of development in Southeast Asia. In Indonesia, Malaysia, Thailand, and Singapore, bureaucrats, party officials, political leadership, and businesses have worked hand in glove for the development agenda. The close crony relationship between business and government has led, in part, to financial crises in some of the countries in the region.

In the wake of these financial crises, Thailand, Malaysia, Singapore, and Indonesia face domestic political and economic challenges. Although Singapore, Thailand, and Malaysia have relatively strong political systems to cope with these challenges, it will be years before Indonesia regains political stability. Singapore, well-managed and with relatively strong financial institutions, has not been as badly affected by the economic crisis as other

Southeast Asian countries. However, because of its location and size, Singapore is substantially affected by developments in Indonesia and Malaysia. Singapore is stable politically, but there are questions about how the nation will fare in the long term in a technocratically, tightly managed system. Economically, Singapore has ambitions of becoming the financial center of Southeast and East Asia, but it is doubtful whether Singapore has the human resources and freedom to achieve that goal. With only 4.3 million people, Singapore's main challenge is to stay competitive as a regional and global city.

Far more serious are the problems facing Indonesia. Elections there have not produced a strong, stable government that can undertake necessary economic policies. The needs to restore political stability and make progress on political and judicial reforms are major challenges confronting the country. The role of the military and whether Indonesia's political system will remain a unitary state or move toward a federal system with more powers given to the provinces are other serious problems facing Indonesia. The country is a mosaic of ethnic and religious groups that came together under Dutch rule and then formed as Indonesia in the post-Dutch period. So Indonesia is very much the nation-state in its formation process. Many of the challenges Indonesia faces today are the result of problems ignored while Indonesia was experiencing economic growth. Indonesia has made slow progress in restructuring its banking sector and offshore debt to facilitate recovery from the economic crisis that has afflicted the country since the second half of 1997.

In Malaysia and Singapore political development accompanied economic development. In the case of Indonesia, there was economic growth and development, but there was no political development. It is important for a country that political and economic development go hand in hand.

1. Malaysia

Malaysia, established in 1963, comprises two geographically discrete units: West Malaysia, which includes the eleven states of the former Federation of Malaya, and East Malaysia, which includes the two former British Crown Colonies of Sarawak and Sabah in northern Borneo. West Malaysia and East Malaysia are separated by several hundred miles of open sea and exhibit major contrasts in their population and culture.

The physical separation between West and East Malaysia is appreciable, as was the case with West and East Pakistan, and distances range between 600 and 1200 miles. West Malaysia is more advanced than East Malaysia in terms of overall economic and sociopolitical considerations. The western unit is quite obviously the more prestigious in terms of historical perspective, civic grandeur, religious fervor, and international recognition. The East sector is the poor relation of the West. However, East Malaysia exceeds West Malaysia in area by around 33 percent, but the aggregate population of the East is far lower than that of the West.

West Malaysia is densely settled, particularly on the west coastal zone; East Malaysia is relatively sparsely populated. In West Malaysia the population is dominantly Muslim Malays, with substantial numbers of Indian and Chinese ethnic origin. In East Malaysia, Malays and other Muslim peoples are confined mainly to the coastal zone, and are considerably outnumbered by indigeneous animist and Christian peoples. There is also a large Chinese element in the population of East Malaysia. The contrast between the two parts of the country shows up most sharply in urbanization. West Malaysia has a number of urban centers, including Kuala Lumpur, the national capital. East Malaysia has only one, Kuching, the capital of Sarawak, and the largest town in Sabah is Kota Kinabalu.

For hundreds of years Malaysia was an important crossroads for the great civilizations of China and India. A quirk of geography—the country's strategic position just north of the equator, between the Indian Ocean and South China Sea—made it a historic meeting place for traders and travelers from west and east. This mix of cultures is reflected in the country's eclectic architecture, especially in Kuala Lumpur, Malaysia's most developed city. Kuala Lumpur is filled with Moorish buildings out of North Africa, colonial and Tudor structures from the English countryside, Chinese temples, Buddhist pagodas, and Muslim mosques. Also influential are the Southern Indian and Mogul styles, with exuberant domes and minarets, introduced by the British in the late 1890s.

During the last thirty years the skyline has shot skyward with an amazing variety of supermodern architecture. Even here, however, the international influence is mitigated by necessary solutions to the tropical climate. Many of the later buildings are also now striving for a more Malaysian identity—bringing back large overhanging roofs, verandas, and columns.

The Malaysian government's policies of rapid development based on export-oriented industrialization to address the country's poverty and unemployment have achieved many successes. The development of free trade zones, first around Penang and then Kuala Lumpur, drew thousands of people from the surrounding agricultural areas into the booming industrial sectors. One of the outstanding manufacturing sectors is electronics and electric products. The world's leading consumer electronics and semiconductor firms from Japan and the United States have moved their lower-value-added, labor-intensive, end-of-production work offshore to Malaysia in search of increasing profits. Accommodation to the needs of foreign companies has been the hallmark of the Malaysian government's industrialization program, including the tax-free status of "pioneer" industries, protection from the threat of national unions, and refusal to set a legal minimum wage. The process of rapid development has unfortunately brought about environmental damage, political and labor repression, social dislocation, and recently financial crisis.

Malaysia's problem is that it grew very quickly during the 1980s through foreign investments and the export-based growth strategy. But much of the investment that it has been able to attract both from abroad and at home has not always been on productive areas. It often has been in the areas of hubris and prestige—the big towers, the big roadways, highways, development projects—much of which does not contribute to the productivity and performance of the Malaysian economy. These projects may add to the lifestyle and the general social conditions but they do not add necessarily to the productivity of the economy. That's the problem—so much of the investment has been wasted, particularly in the property areas, and the banks continued to lend rather furiously to sustain this level of projects and construction to the point that in 1998 Malaysia had bank credits at 160 percent of its national output, by far the largest in Southeast Asian region. Malaysia's economy has slowed considerably. The economic downturn has severely dented gross fixed investment, which fell from 43.1 percent of the nominal GDP in 1997 to 23.2 percent in 2002. The reduction was caused by lower foreign direct investment and lower private domestic investment. A growth rate of about 5 percent is estimated for 2005.

2. Thailand

Formerly known as Siam, this country occupies the center of the Southeast Asia mainland. Unlike all the other states of Southeast Asia, Thailand never came under Western colonial rule. The heirs of an ancient civilization, the Thai are descendents of tribes who in the thirteenth century were pushed out of Yunan in southern China by the Mongol hordes of Kublai Khan, and who then overran the Khmer and established a new nation. Thai history is easily traceable everywhere throughout the country, primarily through temples and relics.

Thailand had fairly consistent and rapid growth between 1955 and 1996. It emphasized private sector development, an outward orientation, and an export-based growth strategy. Between1965 and 1995 the economy of Thailand averaged over 7 percent growth a year, supported by high levels of foreign investment. The government made things easy for business by drafting a liberal investment code. But even where regulations exist, they are often breached. Orderly graft and corruption in Thailand provide a welcome way of cutting through red tape for foreign investors (in contrast to the unpredictable, chaotic corruption of Indonesia). There is continuing focus on stimulating economic growth, and the real gross domestic product is expected to accelerate in 2004 as private investment picks up.

From 1960 to 2000, Thai trade shifted from dependence on agricultural exports to manufactures and sex tourism. The share of manufactures in the total exports rose dramatically from a mere 2.4 percent in 1961 to over 80 percent in 1990. Rapid industrializarion increased manufacturing's percentage of the country's gross domestic product to almost three times that of agriculture.

New or expanded factories were springing up at the rate of about 300 a year, turning out canned and frozen foods, computer parts, televisions, automobiles, motorcycles, air conditioners, refrigerators, shoes, ready-to-wear clothes, microwave ovens, and hundreds of other consumer goods. These products fed an export market that has doubled to 30 percent of Thailand's GDP since 1980. Until the financial crisis and recession of 1997, the country was expected to continue growing at an annual rate of 7 to 8 percent through the year 2000. The recession exposed the weakness of Thailand's development policy and lack of government oversight of banks and financial institutions. By 1995 Thailand had built up a huge amount of borrowing through its banks—offshore banking centers—which provided a lot of cheap capital for investment. As long as Thailand was able to export more and increase its growth as a result of that investment, there was no problem. But in 1995, as Thailand's currency appreciated (with the appreciation of the U.S. dollar), its exports got more expensive. The decline in exports, combined with financial scandal, left behind bankrupt corporations and failed financial institutions. Thailand is attempting to enhance economic stability and lay the foundation for a sustained economic recovery.

In 1980, 1.8 million tourists spent $700 million; by 1986 the number of tourists increased over 50 percent to 2.8 million and spending almost doubled to $1.5 billion. In 1990 the number of tourists increased to over 5 million while spending increased to $4.5 billion. The sex industry now accounts for about 10 per cent of Thailand's GDP, only $500 million less than income from all agricultural exports. Within the tourist sector, sex tourism is the most important component. About 13 percent of the total female labor force is directly or indirectly employed in sex tourism, including 2 millon prostitutes (Figure 4.4).

With a significant part of Thailand's growth occurring in and around Bangkok, a key goal of the Thai government is to decentralize industrial development away from the city. The intent is to attract greater private investment in rural economies still plagued by poverty, while simultaneously easing demands on Bangkok's infrastructure. Applications for development in provinces remote from Bangkok tripled in 1993 from the previous year. For example, Teijin Polyester (Thailand) Ltd., has opened a joint venture polyester and fiber plant near the old capital of Ayutthaya. The company finds incentives for expanding outside Bangkok especially important because of rising business costs in Thailand's maturing economy.

The scope of growth and change in Thailand is significant, but the capital city of Bangkok dramatically reflects both the endurance of traditional Thai customs and the profound impact of new industry and commerce in daily life. Along with its 400 Buddhist temples, decorated in dazzling golds, reds, and blues, Bangkok's famous open-air markets and stalls numbering in the tens of thousands continue along streets and canals. While the street markets continue their busy trade, towering construction cranes operating far into the night have

Figure 4-4. Thai girls at a bar in Bangkok. Tolerance of prostitution has translated into a sex industry serving intercontinental clientele. The specter of AIDS stalks the nation. Prostitution, drugs, deforestation, pollution, and overcrowding all can be traced to the yearning for quick money. (Photo: Shin-ichi Asabe.)

become fixtures in the ever-changing skyline (Figure 4.5). New construction in Bangkok, a city of 5.6 million, tends toward high-rise condominiums and huge shopping complexes featuring department stores, supermarkets, restaurants, and movie theaters. One of the city's newest developments is Seacon Square, a mega-mall containing 300 stores and 500,000 square feet of space. The mall, which opened in 1994, is one of the world's five largest shopping centers. Residents of Bangkok now earn on average around $4,000 a year. The number of households is growing by a steady 2 to 3 percent a year. The expanding middle class has more than enough disposable income to make the trip to the mall a feasible alternative to a visit to a pollution-choked park.

One secret of Thai growth is its dominance in an economic activity that is very profitable and has a specialized niche in the global market place—prostitution, the child sex trade, and child labor. It is based on the impoverishment of peasants and intensive exploitation of labor; peasants are indebted, and incomes plummet as prices decline, forcing many into low-paid industrial and "service" employment. The social costs of this pattern of development—child prostitution, incurable diseases, and virtual enslavement of large segments of the female labor force—far exceed those of the worst period of the nineteenth-century industrial revolution in the West. The operation of thousands of brothels,

Figure 4-5. Old buildings are making way for high-rise structures in Bangkok, whose official population count is 6 million; the actual population may be twice that. Bangkok is experiencing many of the problems facing large Asian cities. (Photo: P. P. Karan.)

massage parlors, bath-houses, bars, clubs, teahouses, and even barber shops that serve as fronts for the selling of sex has resulted in cultural decay. Violence, drugs, and commercial sex have replaced intimacy and social solidarity. On a per capita basis, the Thai murder rate is one of the highest in the world, twice the U.S. rate and ten times that of Japan. With a rich cultural past, Thailand has become a country of cultural anomie. In the new international division of labor in this interdependent global economy, the Thai state functions as the pimp and procurer for the leisure world of advanced capitalism. Thai activists campaigning against child prostitution are seeking international support from human rights and women's organizations.

The social, political, and environmental consequences of explosive growth make Thailand a kind of laboratory of change. What strikes anyone returning to Bangkok is the physical transformation. But the social transformation is more important. A country of peasants is becoming one of industrial workers and entrepreneurs. It is also a development that is perpetuating poverty and poor working conditions; undermines human decency, particularly of women and children; is destructive of the natural environment; and has widened inequalities between people, between rural and urban areas, and between regions.

To boost regional investment and cross-border trade in Southeast Asia, Thailand is advocating a bold plan to cut a canal across the narrow part of southern Thailand between the Gulf of Thailand and the Andaman Sea. The project would be a tool to stimulate regional economies hit hard by the current financial turmoil and promote economic unity in Asia in the long run. The approximately 60-mile-long Kra Canal would help accommodate the annual 2 billion tons of maritime cargo that currently passes through the Malacca Strait, and get multinational companies involved in utilizing local resources and building industrial and residential complexes, telecommunications infrastructure, petroleum refineries, and petrochemical complexes. The Kra Canal would cost more than $10 billion and require ten years to complete.

3. Indonesia

Indonesia lies along the equator between the southeastern tip of the Asian mainland and Australia. It is the world's fourth-most populous country. It is a diverse society, rich in both culture and natural resources. This territory is divided between some 3,000 islands of highly varied size and character. Java and Sumatra have been the two most important islands in Indonesia. Java's greatest single natural asset has been the possession of an exceptionally fertile and accessible core area capable of producing an abundance of rice and hence of supporting a large population.

Sumatra has been lacking in any comparable nuclear region. For although the whole eastern side of Sumatra consists of a vast lowland, the seaward half consists of ill-consolidated swamp, which bars the way to the better-drained—but not particularly fertile—inner plains flanking the eastern slopes of the island's mountain backbone. The mountains rise steeply from the west coast, and present a continuous obstacle to east–west movement throughout the entire length of the island. Sumatra as a whole has supported a much lower density of population than has Java, and no single dominant group, comparable to the Javanese, has emerged to give its name to the island as a whole. Instead, the Sumatran peoples have comprised a series of relatively small and widely separated ethnic groups that, owing to their continuing mutual isolation, have preserved their mutual distinctiveness. One of these groups, the Acehnese on the northern tip of Sumatra, is fighting for a separate state.

Sumatra's earth is crammed with oil and coal and other minerals, lush forest covers half of its territory, and the land is fertile. Its population of 39 million occupies an island the size of California and more than three times the size of Java, which is home to 112 million people. This is why Sumatra has a higher income per person than Java, whose hard-pressed farmers till smaller lots. But Sumatra has never had the clout it thinks it deserves. Java has been the first choice for foreign investors. Land rights, legal complexities, labor unrest, and educational inadequacies are among the hurdles Sumatra must leap before it can attract substantial investments. Nevertheless, Medan, in the north, Sumatra's capital and home to just under 2 million people, is attracting investments and is dotted with new office buildings and factories.

Northern Sumatra could become part of a growth triangle, with northern Malaysia and southern Thailand as the other corners. Penang, the thriving

Malaysian light industrial and electronic center, would be the hub; it has air and sea links with Medan, which is building a larger airport. Although northern Sumatra has an affinity with Malaysia, the south is more Javanese. Lampung, Indonesia's fastest-growing province in the 1980s, is beginning to attract Javanese industry. For the rest of the south, though, growth is based on natural resources. Palm oil production is booming. Plywood, pulp, and paper mills are growth industries.

Kalimantan (formerly Borneo) has 10 million people in an area the size of France and Germany combined. Much of Indonesia's timber exports, which make up 20 percent of the country's exports and account for 7 percent of the GDP, are from Kalimantan. Inland Kalimantan has few roads and is home to dozens of tribes, known collectively as Dyaks. The Dyaks are predominantly agricultural and Christian, maintaining a distinctive culture and system of land rights that has survived for centuries. They have suffered from the encroachment of the loggers, who have powerful connections with the central government. Tribes living near Samarinda, a provincial capital, have protested and pleaded with the provincial government to halt logging locally. Such protests are increasing in frequency. Indonesia has tough forestry laws, but enforcing them is a different matter. Many forests are cut illegally.

Kalimantan is potentially rich. In addition to timber, it has oil, natural gas, gold, and diamonds. These assets benefit Indonesia as a whole, and have fueled growth in east, west, and south Kalimantan. Kalimantan is growing more quickly than the rest of the country; only central Kalimantan lags, though it has a growth of 6 percent a year. East Kalimantan is the fastest-growing of Indonesia's twenty-seven provinces, with growth reaching 13 percent in 1992. The coastal cities hum to the sound of new construction, motorbikes, and karaoke. Inland life moves at a slower pace, but ultimately, the cities' prosperity depends on the riches of the interior. Managing them well is Kalimantan's challenge.

Irian Jaya (formerly Dutch West New Guinea) came under Indonesian control in 1963. It accounts for 22 percent of the land area of Indonesia, but just 1 percent of its population. Indonesian control of Dutch West New Guinea climaxed the long struggle of Indonesia to oust the Dutch from the last of their East Indies colonies. For Indonesians it seemed to matter little that the people of New Guinea belonged to the Melanesian culture of the South Seas—that they had animist beliefs, a pig-based economy, a tradition of head hunting and cannibalism, and hardly anything in common with the Asian, predominantly Muslim culture that prevailed throughout the rest of Indonesia.

Irian Jaya, the western half of the largest tropical island in the world, is a realm of rainforest, swamps, and cloud-covered mountains reaching heights of 16,000 feet. It is the last great wilderness of the Asian Pacific Rim. The population is sparse (only 1.9 million), and some 250,000 of them are recent migrants from other parts of Indonesia. More than a million of the others are tribal inhabitants, collectively called Papuans, from a Malay word meaning "frizzy haired." Many Papuans still live as hunter-gatherers or subsistence mountain farmers, grouped in small clans.

The indigenous Irianese people did not embrace their new rulers. In the 1970s and 1980s the Indonesian Army crushed an independence movement; thousands of Irianese died. A small band of separatist guerrillas, the Organisasi Papua Merdeka or Free Papua Movement, still operates near the Papua New Guinea border, some of its members armed only with bows and arrows. Indonesia exerts iron control; political dissent is a criminal activity. But a deep-seated cultural conflict festers.

With its growing economy and the world's fourth-largest population, Indonesia views the province as a huge depot of natural resources, not as one of the world's last sanctuaries of biodiversity. Rainforests, with their valuable timber, blanket 85 percent of the territory. Rich deposits of copper and gold have been found in the mountains, and pockets of oil in the lowlands. With more than half of the nation's population jammed onto the island of Java, one of the world's most crowded places, the Indonesian government has already moved at least 200,000 settlers to transmigration camps in Irian Jaya. Some 50,000 other migrants have come on their own. It has become Indonesia's "wild east"—a land of opportunity where, more often than not, the local native people are found to stand in the way. Large areas of rainforest have been cleared for the transmigration program. To ease overcrowding on the islands of Java and Bali, the government offers five acres, a year's worth of rice, and a one-way air ticket to anyone who will move to an undeveloped region. The old-growth forest is coming down in Irian Jaya to feed Indonesia's export-driven timber industry.

The last three decades have brought profound change to the remote Irian Jaya, the inhabitants of which have recently abandoned the stone axe. The Indonesian government has carried development to the interior largely on the back of Christian missionary efforts to reach isolated areas, and the missionaries have scored some successes in replacing spirit worship with the Christian gospel. But Indonesia has difficulty convincing the tribes of the benefits it can offer. A drive to speed up development in eastern Indonesia has brought more money to Irian Jaya in recent years. Priorities are infrastructure and migration, a policy designed to relieve crowding on other islands and open up new areas. Although thousands of Indonesians from overcrowded parts of the country have been resettled in the province, migration remains a controversial way of developing Irian Jaya. Locals tend to regard it with suspicion. The majority of the migrants are simple farmers who bring few skills with them. Skilled migrants, who have come to Irian Jaya independent of the official scheme, also worry the locals. Native people have found it hard to compete for jobs. Education will help to narrow the gap between local people and outsiders. But for the time being, the Irianese feel marginalized by a development process that often excludes them.

Other major Indonesian islands include Celebes or Sulawesi (Figure 4.6),
Madura, Bali, and Moluccas Java, Madura, and Bali form the core region of

Figure 4-6. Sulawesi, Indonesia. Four long peninsulas radiate from the central mountain arc of Sulawesi.
Its geography is dramatic—from rice fields to rainforests, and from mountains to hidden bays. The Sulawesi
Paddy Land Development project aims to increase the cultivated areas and crop yields on the island through
land clearing and complementary investments in infrastructure and land development. (Photo: International
Fund for Agricultural Development by G. Mintapraja.)

Indonesia, with less than one thirteenth of the total area of the country and almost two thirds of the population.

Nearly 800 miles north of Jakarta on the Natuna island a huge natural gas field was discovered in 1973. Natuna field is located in water 470 feet deep, requiring platforms reaching sixty stories above the seafloor. The field is estimated to contain 210 trillion cubic feet of gas. The Natuna field is being developed by Indonesia in stages consistent with market demand. There are enough reserves in the Natuna field to produce about two billion cubic feet per day of gas for more than thirty years. It will become a major long-term supplier of liquefied natural gas to the Asian Pacific market.

Coastal peoples throughout western Indonesia are Muslims, with the solitary exception of the Balinese, who follow Hinduism (which formerly predominated over all the more advanced parts of western Indonesia). Java peoples in the interior of all the islands are animists, though some in recent times have adopted Christianity. In the eastern third of the country the narrow coastal fringe is Muslim, the interior is predominantly animist; in some of the islands the Muslim element is almost entirely absent, and in others Christianity has made deep inroads (Figure 4.7). In Sulawesi communal conflict between Muslims and Christians has raged for several years. A hard-line Muslim cleric associated with Jemaah Islamiyah, a terrorist organization, was responsible for bomb explosions in Bali in October 2002, damaging the tourist trade that accounts for 3 percent of Indonesia's gross domestic product (Figure 4.8).

An Islamic revival is under way in Indonesia, which is the world's largest Muslim country, with an estimated 87 percent of the nation's 212 million people calling themselves Muslims. On the streets of Java, which has traditionally adhered to a moderate blend of Islam, a growing number of women now venture out in their *jilbaba*, the Arab-style head wear that covers all but a small oval of the face. Attendance at mosques is reported to be surging. Muslim political parties, including the Justice Party, have substantial representation in the parliament. The goal of the Justice Party is to impose the traditional Sharia or Koranic law on this secular nation.

In the past, Indonesia was not a fertile ground for foreign investment outside the oil, raw materials, and banking sectors. But a more hospitable business environment in the 1980s lured investors from Indonesia's Asian neighbors and, increasingly, from the United States. General Motors has invested in a new assembly plant outside Jakarta, lured by the prospect of 5 to 7 percent economic growth, abundant natural resources, and an emerging middle class of consumers. Citibank opened the first drive-up automated teller machine in Indonesia. Amway began to peddle perfume and honey-glycerine soap. A crowded McDonald's in central Jakarta operates 24 hours a day. Procter & Gamble, Avon, and Levi-Strauss are also doing business. Indonesia also became a low-cost manufacturing base for shoemakers like Reebok and for toy maker Mattel. In 1994 Indonesia allowed foreign companies to own 100 percent of their businesses for the first fifteen years in which they do business

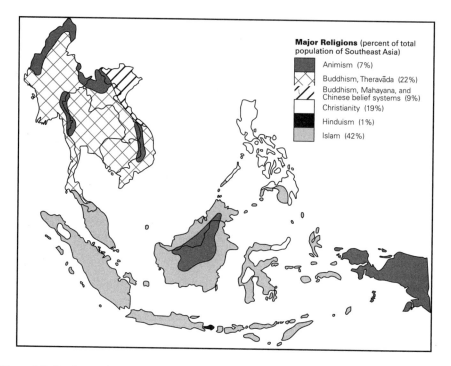

Figure 4-7. Southeast Asia's major religious groups.

there. Bimantara Citra, a wide-ranging Indonesian conglomerate, has emerged as one of the major business houses in the country. Its businesses range from infrastructure projects such as gas and oil pipelines to chemicals, hotels, and financial services. Bimantara is controlled by Bambang Trihatmodjo, former President Suharto's second son. Bimantara's partners include Japan's NEC and Sumitomo; America's Hughes Aircraft, Ford, and Union Carbide; France's Alcatel; Germany's Deutsche Telekom; and Switzerland's Nestle.

Family ties bind much of the growth in Indonesia. From hotels, taxi cabs, and cellular phones to television shows, auto dealerships, banks, and factories, businesses are controlled or owned, in whole or in part, by relatives of former President Suharto. And Suharto's close friends such as Mohammad Hasan control vast business empires. Hasan's main business is timber: his Kalimanis Group controls over 7,700 square miles of prime concessions in Kalimantan, the Indonesian half of Borneo Island. It also dominates the saw milling and plywood operations, and heads the cartel (Apkindo) that regulates Indonesia's plywood exports. The Apkindo plywood cartel is associated with Indonesia's dismal record on the environment.

If Indonesia, like many developing countries, wants to get to the next rung on the ladder of development, it must change. Ubiquitous nepotism, corruption, and favoritism threaten future development. Apprehension about the future swelled as the country began to face a serious financial crisis in

Figure 4-8. Unlike its Muslim neighbors, Bali is Hindu. Women with baskets filled with fruit offerings walk past a Hindu temple. Hindu culture came to Bali as early as the ninth century; by the fourteenth century the island was part of the Hindu Majapahit Empire of east Java. When that empire fell to the Muslim invaders, Majapahit aristocrats, scholars, artists, and dancers fled to Bali, consolidating Hindu culture and religion on the island. (Photo: Cotton Mather.)

1997–1998. The deadly student riots in May 1998 led to the fall of President Suharto's nearly thirty-two years of authoritarian rule. Indonesia's climb from brutal poverty toward the lower tier of middle income nations during the last three decades has not come without heavy costs and lingering problems. Among these is the widespread and deepening perception that the economic benefits of growth are unequally shared. Thousands of low-paying, low-tech factories, producing clothing, shoes, electronics, and toys for export, are at the core of Indonesia's recent growth. But their day is almost done. Countries with even lower labor costs such as Bangladesh, Cambodia, China, and Vietnam are attracting international manufacturers. What's more, the economy is plagued by a large foreign debt and inflation.

The contrasts and contradictions of Indonesia are sharpest in Jakarta. The inner city is a cluster of new high-rise banks, offices, and apartments. There are shopping malls lit with neon signs where the rich can shop in air-conditioned comfort. In the streets, buses, cars, and motorcycles fight through traffic jams to transport the continous flow of people. Besides many large roads are rows of street vendors selling everything from food to engine parts, although in the streets around the center of the city all vendors have been banned since late 1994. There are also beggars, and children trying to sell food, newspapers, and other small objects. Of the 13 million people living in

Jakarta, it is estimated that half are poor. As the economy grows, the gap between rich and poor is growing too (Figure 4.9).

Outside the center of the city are rapidly expanding manufacturing areas such as Pluit and Tanggerang, where hundreds of factories are situated behind walls topped with barbed wire and with guards at the gates. With some 1,100 strikes in Indonesia annually, and 500 of these in the areas around Jakarta, factory owners clearly feel the need to keep close control over their employees. Nearby these huge industrial estates are equally large communities of living quarters of workers. It is common to find only one or two toilets for a community of fifty to one hundred workers, and no clean water supply, so that workers are forced to buy expensive bottled water. Pluit is one of the most overcrowded and polluted of these areas. In the nearby harbor area, which looks like a huge open sewer, the water is black and a smell of rotting garbage fills the air. Pluit itself has a certain resemblance to descriptions of workers' conditions in Europe during the Industrial Revolution. The streets are extremely narrow, and in front of the houses run open drains that seem to be filled with raw sewage. Small, roughly built houses crowd together, their

Figure 4-9. High-rise buildings and impoverished slums in Jakarta. An estimated 25 to 50 percent of the urban inhabitants in developing countries in Asia live in impoverished slums and squatter settlements, with little or no access to adequate water, sanitation, or refuse collection. In such situations, both environmental quality and human health are at risk. Founded in 1619 by the Dutch merchants, Jakarta was formerly called Batavia and became the headquarters of the Dutch East India Company. It became capital of Indonesia in 1949. Despite rapid economic growth in the 1980s and 1990s, Indonesia did not spend much in developing adequate housing and safe water supply in urban areas. (Photo: UNICEF by Thomas Sprague)

balconies, draped with washing, sagging over the streets. Women wash clothes in doorways, and hundreds of children play in the dirt, often climbing into the drains to use them as toilets. Many have rashes or the big, glazed eyes of malnutrition. The new generation of factory workers, migrants from rural areas, do not earn enough to send money back to their families, and must work overtime for more than a month to afford to visit their families for the Muslim holiday. The traditional village extended family has been destroyed for this generation.

One of the greatest changes in Indonesia has been the emergence of an urban middle class, now estimated at betweeen 14 and 15 million people—a small portion of the nation's population of 224 million, but a conspicuous consumer elite nonetheless. They are a product of Indonesia's recent growth and economic prosperity. They work in the sleek office towers, moving money and managing markets. They carry cellular phones, they surf the Internet, and they travel abroad. They can be found late in the evening at trendy discos in Jakarta. And they seem uninterested in politics or in changing a military-led authoritarian system that many see as the force behind their economic success. These affluent urban Indonesians are complacent because they benefit financially from a system in which personal connections matter more than legal contracts and it is commonplace to ignore weak government institutions.

The deepening gap between rich and poor, widespread official corruption, peremptory land seizures, and a disruption of traditional rural society have led to convulsions of violence against two minority groups in this overwhelmingly Muslim and ethnic Malay nation: the Chinese and Christians. The Chinese minority, about 2 percent of the population, controls as much as four fifths of the private economy and has for years been the target of animosity and violence. Among Chinatowns of the world, Jakarta's is unique. It has many smashed and burned-out buildings, and not a Chinese character in sight. The Chinese community, the most successful of Indonesia's ethnic groups, is battered. Long a target of jealousy for their perceived wealth, the role of ethnic Chinese in the economy grew during the now-disgraced rule of former President Suharto. Alongside Suharto's own family, a handful of ethnic Chinese dominated the companies and banks that flourished under his rule. Suharto gave preferential treatment to the few ethnic Chinese, but the Chinese community as a whole lost its political and social rights. Under Suharto, Indonesian Chinese were barred from the military and civil service and the government outlawed the teaching of Chinese in schools. Even the use of Chinese characters in public was banned. When the Suharto government began to crumble in May 1998, the Chinese became the target of violence that swept Indonesia. The homes and shops of many ordinary ethnic Chinese were destroyed and scores of their women raped. Christianity is also viewed as a symbol of wealth in parts of Indonesia. Four Christian churches and a

Christian elementary school near Jakarta were smashed or gutted by fire in 1997. Tension between Muslims and Christians continues.

Increasing environmental degradation is forcing Indonesia to make political commitments to natural resource conservation. The government has designated 25 percent of the country's lands as protected areas and legislated an impressive array of laws for protected areas management. But the country's institutional capacity to actually manage its protected areas is weak. A successful resource conservation and development policy must (1) integrate conservation activities into Indonesia's plan for economic development; (2) ensure that the vertically structured Directorate General of Forest Protection and Nature Conservation (PHPA) develops horizontal links with local agencies, district heads, and resource users; (3) establish regional coordination mechanisms for land use planning and spatial planning; (4) include local communities in the planning and zoning of protected areas and their surroundings; (5) promote private sector involvement in the management of protected areas; (6) create an agency to coordinate the management of marine and coastal areas by the various government agencies; (7) establish zones around protected areas in which traditional land use is sanctioned and regulated; and (8) establish an independent unit, consisting of university researchers, local and national government representatives, and nongovernmental organizations (NGOs) to monitor Indonesia's protected areas.

In the twenty-first century, politically and economically, Indonesia continues to be of concern. Its transition to democracy is fraught with danger, and the rise of Islamic militancy poses a severe threat to political and economic stability.

4. The Philippines

The Philippines first became a single country under Spanish rule (1565–1898). The islands were discovered 475 years ago when Portuguese explorer Ferdinand Magellan was trying to find a new route to the Spice Islands, and instead bumped into the Philippines. He claimed the land for the Spanish because his expedition was paid for by King Philip II of Spain. A subsequent expedition named the islands after the king. Legacies from the Spanish colonial era include the concentration of land ownership and political and economic power in the hands of a small number of families.

In 1898 Spain and America went to war over Cuba, which ended with Spain ceding Puerto Rico, Guam, and the Philippines to America. The new colonial masters promised independence after a suitable custodial period of political and economic development.

During World War II, thousands were killed by the Japanese. Eventually, the Philippines became an independent republic in 1946. After independence and a communist insurgency, it was pillaged by an indigenous dictator, Ferdinand Marcos, who imposed absolutist rule from 1965 to 1986. He ruined an economy that had been one of Asia's richest, while its Southeast Asian neighbors were speeding towards prosperity. A "people's revolution" forced Marcos into exile in 1986 and the new government moved to broaden democratic freedoms.The last two decades were punctuated by a civilian coup backed by the military, earthquake, volcanic eruption and flood, and economic problems. The one-time dreams of democracy and prosperity are beginning to fade before the dreary reality of a persistently weak economy, some of the world's worst pollution, rampant urban crime, and corruption.

The Philippines' colonial legacy vested land and political influence in a small number of powerful families. Some were Spanish (often owners of vast *haciendas*), some Filipino, and some ethnic Chinese, who now make up a large part of the Philippines' newly rich. The elite guarded their interests, dominating the legislature either by holding office themselves or by patronage. The system made the country parochial and inward-looking with crony capitalism. The country is still an oligarchy ; its politics and economy have been run, since the Spanish introduced a rigid landholding system, by a few rich families. But that has started to change, as the government's policy of liberalization has introduced competition into an oligopolistic economy.

The two large islands, Luzon in the north and Mindanao in the south, account for 67 percent of the territory. The central lowlands of Luzon provide by far the best major food-producing region within the country. Rice forms the most important item in the agricultural system, but partly because of cultural links with Latin America, maize is the leading food crop.

The greater part of the population is concentrated in a relatively small part of the total area and, particularly in the lowlands of central Luzon, the resultant pressure is now a serious problem. The great majority of the population shares a common culture which is much influenced by Catholicism. In recent decades an attempt has been made to develop Tagalog, the language of central Luzon, as the national language, though English is widely used among the elite. The only large indigenous group is the Muslim Moros inhabiting the southern and southwestern peripheries of the country.

The population of the Philippines increased from 20 million in 1950 to nearly 84 million in 2004. Although the rate of growth has declined from the 1950s, the large proportion of young people and increasing numbers of women in their childbearing years ensure that the Philippine population will continue to grow rapidly for some time. Under the influence of the powerful church, the government has done little to curb population growth through education, family planning, and availability of low-cost contraceptives. As the country has grown more crowded, it has grown ever poorer, with 40 percent of the population living on less than $1 a day (Figure 4.10). Jobs, food, and farmland are increasingly scarce, and urban slums are teeming.

The growth of the "upland" population in the Philippines is of increasing concern. The upland areas are defined as lands with an 18 percent slope or higher. They are the home of the public forest lands and approximately 18 million people. Many of these upland dwellers live in forested areas and

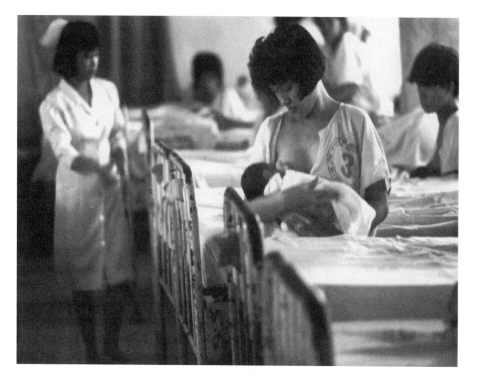

Figure 4-10. Over 50 percent of births in the Philippines were attended by trained personnel in facilities such as the Jose Fabella Memorial Hospital in Manila. Major improvements in health facilities are important to promote development in the Philippines, where more than 30 percent of the country's estimated 70 million people live below the poverty line. (Photo: UNICEF by Sonny Yabao.)

depend on the land and its resources for their survival. The upland population is considered to be the most impoverished in the Philippines.

Increasing population growth will lead to continued migration to upland areas, conversion of forest lands to agricultural use, and cultivation of marginal lands. New migrants to upland areas cleared about half of the total forest area between 1960 and 1985. The destruction of forest cover results in soil erosion and other environmental effects, including flooding and sedimentation. The ultimate effect of environmental degradation is the reduction in crop capacity, which will threaten the ability of the Philippines to feed its teeming population.

Coastal areas also face serious environmental problems that are associated with population pressure: the destruction of the mangroves; the pollution of freshwater lakes, swamps, and rivers; and the deterioration in the quality of marine, brackish, and fresh water through increased sedimentation and industrial pollution. The basic causes and effects of land and water resource degradation in the Philippines are high population growth, poverty, ineffective government controls, and greed. These are the problems that must be tackled to achieve sustainable development. Equally concerned with alleviating poverty is the Catholic Church. The extent of real progress in Philippine family planning will depend on how far the Catholic Church and the state, given their positions on population-related issues, can work together in their common pursuit of sustainable development as an effective means of easing poverty.

Growing population and unemployment in the Philippines has forced large numbers of its citizens to find work abroad. Filipinos have been seeking work overseas since the 1920s, when they labored in the sugar and pineapple plantations of Hawaii, at that time a U.S. colony. In recent decades more Filipinos have gone abroad to work because of lack of opportunities at home. The Philippines now is the world's largest exporter of labor, with an estimated 4.5 million of its people working abroad. Their earnings from laboring on building sites in Saudi Arabia, nursing in the United States, washing floors in Hong Kong, singing in Tokyo nightclubs, or crewing ships have provided the country with a lifeline. In 2000 remittances by Filipinos living abroad soared to over $5 billion; with money coming through more informal channels the estimated total comes to more than $7 billion. In recent years more and more of those going overseas are women, working mostly as domestic helpers, nurses, or entertainers. Large families have two or more daughters working overseas, and probably a son as well. In poor villages such families are instantly recognizable by their well-to-do houses. Some Filipinos endure harsh conditions abroad and are physically abused. Many work below their potential: about a third of the Filipino maids in Hong Kong have had some form of college education.

Industrialization will have to play a large part also in any solution to poverty. But it will be years before the industry provides enough work to soak up surplus rural labor. Other things have to be tried. Raising agricultural productivity rather than just distributing scare resources is the obvious way to go. That means breaking the kind of vicious cycle into which small farmers are locked. Their problem starts with the diminishing size of the average farm, from 24 hectares when homesteaders first gained ownership in northern Mindanao in the 1950s to the couple of hectares now. Crop yields are falling and rains are erratic. They need to invest in fertilizers and more expensive seeds, but they are unwilling to take the risk, fearing that a failed crop could land them in permanent debt. They are locked into subsistence farming on ever-smaller and less-productive plots of land (Figure 4.11).

Much of the Philippines' recent industrial growth has been concentrated in a series of industrial parks and enterprise zones that have been springing up all over the country. Some of the industrial estates provide perks for exporters, but the main attraction is that they come with a working infrastructure in place. The government is encouraging their spread because they help to decentralize the economy away from Manila.

Throughout the Philippines, graft and abuse of power have corroded public institutions, from local governments to security forces to the top levels of the administration and the judiciary. Widespread corruption also afflicts other Southeast Asian nations, notably Indonesia, Thailand, Cambodia, and

Figure 4-11. Negros Occidental Province, the Philippines. Feeding the ever-larger population predicted for the future will require an agricultural system that keeps pace with population growth. People in Negros Occidental Province have cleared more land to grow food crops. However, most high-quality agricultural land is already in production, and the environmental costs of converting remaining upland habitats to cropland can be severe. (Photo: UNICEF by Jim Wright.)

Vietnam. But the Philippines is unique. As a former U.S. colony, its institutions were modeled on those of the United States and once represented a showcase of U.S.-style democracy in Asia. In many ways, this country of 84 million people has become a case study of what can happen when democratic institutions deteriorate. The result has been a breakdown in the rule of the law in many areas. Corruption and graft has taken a heavy toll on the Philippines development process. There is also growing concern over terrorism from the militant Islamic network, particularly the Abu Sayyaf terrorist group, which has established connections with Jemaah Islamiyah, a radical network with Al-Qaeda connections that seeks to create an Islamic state across Southeast Asia.

5. Singapore

Singapore is an independent republic of 4.3 million people whose skills and hard work have made their country an economic powerhouse in the non-Western world. Modern Singapore's founding father was Sir Thomas Stamford Raffles. In 1819, he established a British settlement and trading station on the island through treaty with its Malay rulers. Raffles recognized Singapore's strategic and commercial significance, situated as it is at the southeast end of the Strait of Malacca, the vital waterway connecting the Indian and Pacific Oceans. It is a gateway to the world's largest land mass.

Singapore also offered early traders one of the finest natural deepwater harbors in the world. After 1869, steamships transiting from Europe to the West Pacific through the new Suez Canal made Singapore their prime refueling and supply port, as well as the principal trading center for Southeast Asia. When the Malay States' rubber and tin industries were developed in the last decades of the nineteenth century, Singapore became the main rubber-exporting center of the world. During the latter half of the nineteenth century Singapore became one of the world's nearly unparalleled conveyor belts. It handled the pooling and transhipment of such primary products as tin and spices, and a wide range of oriental textiles and craft products. At the same time it became the principal port undertaking the sorting and distribution of fabricated goods from the West to a wide scattering of entry points around the land areas of Southeast Asia.

In February 1942 the great British imperial fortress and naval base at Singapore was surrendered to Japanese forces almost without a shot being fired. The fall of Singapore dealt an enormous psychological blow to the integrity of the British Empire and was a significant turning point in the process of European imperial decline. The contempt with which the Japanese treated the tens of thousands of European troops who laid down their arms so meekly at Singapore shattered Britain's imperial prestige in Asia.

After World War II the British sought to reestablish their colony as a commercial and military base. But the urge for self-determination and eventually total independence from colonial rule had taken firm root. By 1959 Singapore had won full internal self-government, but Britain still controlled foreign affairs and defense. In September 1963 Singapore entered into a political and economic union with Malaya, Sarawak, and North Borneo (now Sabah) to form the new state of Malaysia. However, on August 9, 1965, Singapore separated from Malaysia and became a sovereign and independent nation.

In the early years of independence, Singapore promoted itself as a place in the Asian Pacific region where multinational corporations would be welcome, and where a high-quality, low-cost workforce was available for hire. Industrial estates were created and factories built for quick start-up by companies locating there. The strategy worked so well that by the 1970s, Singapore shifted its focus to capital-intensive businesses—especially knowledge-based industries—and those in the service sector such as financial, medical, and computer-related services.

Singapore's economic development formula has been (1) to leverage its strategic location by establishing world-class transportation and material-handling facilities; (2) to extend the concept of such "hubbing" by setting up a similarly sophisticated communications and information technology system;

(3) to upgrade continuously the skills of its workforce to keep up with the more challenging demands placed upon it; and (4) to monitor closely and absorb relevant global technological developments as rapidly as possible. A small island with few natural resources, Singapore has invented itself as an efficient and orderly society, and it continues to try to reinvent itself for the changing times.

Today, Singapore is the world's busiest container port. Roughly 700 ships are at the quays or anchorages on any given day. At least half of them take on fuel. Singapore's lifeblood is trade, and perhaps more than any other country, it depends on the movement of goods for its survival. In the United States, by contrast, trade accounts for only about 15 percent of the GDP. But Singapore is an island of only 246 square miles, a little smaller than New York City. It has no resources (even its milk is imported from Australia) other than its population of 3 million people. As real estate speculators are fond of saying, Singapore has three great advantages: location, location, and location. It sits midway between the Middle East and Japan on the prime sailing route of most ships, making it a natural port of call. Along with a beautiful natural harbor, location was what presumably attracted Sir Thomas Stamford Raffles when he acquired the island for the British East India Company. Because of its location, Singapore also became a service center for shipping itself, an undertaking that has since blossomed into a major ship repair business. The multinationals have been attracted to Singapore for many reasons, but good infrastructure led the list. There is a world-class airport and probably the best telecommunications system in the world.

Between 1873 and 1913, Singapore attracted thousands of immigrants seeking work and a better life. They came principally from China, India, and Sri Lanka. The language of administration in Singapore is English, inherited from 136 years of British rule. However, as befits the nation's multiracial and multireligious society, Mandarin Chinese, Malay, and Tamil also are recognized as official languages.

The Singapore landscape has been transformed by a thirty-year building boom. Along with factories, industrial estates, refineries, and shipbuilding/repair and other port facilities, Singapore has built miles of new highways, and scores of commercial skyscrappers, luxury hotels, and shopping centers. In addition, a new $3 billion rapid-transit system was constructed.

Vast new self-contained suburban communities have been built by the government or private developers, and government apartments have been made available at low cost to nearly everyone. Today, some 87 percent of Singaporeans live in government-built apartments, and of these, 80 percent own their residences. The city is clean and safe. Singapore's tough police methods and harsh punishments are responsible, the government says, for its social order and one of the highest material standards of living in Asia. But the strong-arm policies have also helped perpetuate a one-party state, a cowed press, and flagrant abuses of individual liberty. There are few clearer demonstrations than Singapore that free-market prosperity does not automatically bring respect for human rights.

The government exercises tight control over society with extensive curbs on individual freedoms. Family size and timing of household formation and child birth are regulated by the government. It also requires citizens to save one-fifth of their income. Since 1996 citizens must financially support their parents in old age. Residential location and tenure are regulated by the state. Access to the free press is constrained by controls on circulation of foreign news publications. Local media are controlled by the government. Political debate is allowed only through government-controlled agencies. The ruling People's Action Party (PAP) enjoys more opportunities than other officially registered parties. Labor union activity is government controlled through affiliation with the National Trade Union Congress, which is headed by a government minister. As much as anything, Singapore is famous for its edicts: do not jaywalk; do not throw garbage from rooftops; do not chew gum, spit, or urinate in elevators; do commit "spontaneous acts of kindness."

Nothing, however, is more ephemeral than power. Yesterday Singapore epitomized the *Pax Britannica*. Today she expresses the very essence of resurgent Asia, a bustle of modern Asian enterprise. She presents the feeling of a confident economic power on a dateline of history, standing between the yesterday of one era and the tomorrow of another. Furthermore, Singapore's development has demonstrated the force of imagination and endeavor over environmental considerations. If only the advocates of environmental determinism could see Singapore now, the ranks of the possibilist school would be swelled by many a convert.

Singapore and Hong Kong have been arch-rivals in their long-running battle for the coveted status of Asia's No. 2 financial center after Tokyo. Given the Asian Pacific's time zones in relation to Europe and New York, the region can support only two first-rate financial centers: Tokyo and either Hong Kong or Singapore. Hong Kong had been Asia's de facto second financial hub, but its economic difficulties following the Asian financial crisis have given Singapore room to challenge. The battle for supremacy between Singapore and Hong Kong began in 1998 in the securities industry. Trading of Hang Seng index futures on the Singapore International Monetary Exchange marked the official start of the battle. A Singapore government package of cost-cutting measures has boosted the city-state's competitiveness. On a comparative study of cost competitiveness of the two cities in wages, rent, interest costs, utilities, and service costs, Hong Kong comes up short. The average manager in Hong Kong earns double the salary of a Singapore manager. Rentals for a small two-bedroom apartment in Hong Kong averaged U.S. $6,400 a month in a "good area," compared with U.S. $2,000 for a comparable apartment in Singapore. Singapore is also ahead of Hong Kong in reforming its financial sector in the midst of the Asian financial crisis. Some of the world's biggest companies are putting their faith in Singapore, including

Caltex Petroleum Corporation, which announced in 1998 that it would relocate its headquarters from Dallas, Texas. But Singapore's competitive advantage may be slowly eroding as some of the international businesses move part of their operations to Hong Kong to be closer to China's fast-growing economy.

6. Brunei

The Sultanate of Brunei occupies a small territory of over 2,000 square miles facing the South China Sea along the coast of Borneo. It is one of the world's tiniest nations, a place the size of Delaware, cut out of the rainforests. It was a protectorate of the British crown for nearly a century before gaining independence in 1984. On its landward side it is surrounded and split into two separate units by Sarawak. The greater part of the territory is a low coastal plain. Apart from agricultural land adequate to feed its population of 400,000, its major resource consists of oil from the Seria field close to the Sarawak border and from the offshore field at Ampa.

Brunei seems less a country than a place built on an oilfield. The question is how long the world's richest man—the Sultan of Brunei—and his 400,000 subjects can keep living off a diminishing supply of oil and natural gas. Partly out of benevolence and partly to keep political peace, over two decades the Sultan has turned this country into the ultimate welfare state. Almost everyone (except the Chinese merchant class) works for the state. All medical care, old-age pensions, and education are provided by the government, and the personal income tax rate is zero percent.

Brunei's famed water villages keep alive traditional style houses on stilts over the water. Ten miles upstream from the mouth of the Brunei River, close to the tiny capital of Bander Seri Begawan, lies the water village of Kampong Ayer. In Kampong Ayer, not only homes but medical clinics, mosques, fire and police stations, shops, schools, and markets line the suspended maze of stilt-supported wooden walkways. Beneath them run metered water mains and electrical power lines. Kampong Ayer enjoys modern luxuries, including washing machines, televisions, cellular phones, and fax machines. But fishing lines and gill nets are still strung from the pilings, and boats are moved into the cool shade underneath the houses. Kampong Ayer's vernacular architecture is supremely adapted to the tropical environment of Brunei. Before the discovery of oil at the turn of the century, each neighborhood of Kampong Ayer specialized in a craft: silver and gold work, brass casting, or the weaving of brocades. But now, few craftsmen are found. Young residents now prefer to become doctors, businessmen, motor mechanics, bus drivers, plumbers, teachers, or computer programmers rather than artisans. People of Kampong Ayer have integrated village life with changes brought about by the oil economy of modern Brunei, but the residents remain united by a strong sense of community and by their unique setting.

Oil, first struck in 1929, has been exploited in earnest since independence from Britain in 1984. By 1991 Brunei's oil industry was producing a billion barrels a year. Then natural gas was discovered, most of the 5.8 million tons exported going to Japan. Beneficiaries of one of the highest (roughly U.S. $17,000) average annual incomes in the world, Bruneians are not inclined to truculence, and the sultan's absolute power goes largely unchallenged. The country's Islamic austerity (alcohol is banned, female dress is conservative, and dating couples are chaperoned) might strike outsiders as fairly oppressive. That is not something the leadership loses sleep over. Tourism is limited; a rich country need not bend over backward to please tourists. Nor need it ravage the environment to survive. Logging, despoiler of substantial swaths of Borneo's rain forests, has no place in Brunei's economy. Consequently, the jungle that surrounds 90 percent of its territory remains pristine—an unspoiled Amazon in miniature.

Lagging States

While some countries in Southeast Asia have shown economic progress, some have not. In Myanmar and the countries of Indochina the economies have remained stagnant.

1. Myanmar (Burma)

Myanmar is a green and pleasant land with glistening, golden-roofed pagodas. Geographically, it falls into three well-marked divisions: the western hills, the central belt or Burma proper, and the Shan Plateau in the east, with a southward continuation of highland in Tenasserim. The western hills run along the India–Bangladesh border, southward to the coast as Arakan Yoma, west of the lower Irrawaddy. The hills are sparsely peopled by tribes such as the Chins and Nagas. Along the coast, in Arakan, some of the rivers have built up small lowlands which are densely populated. The central belt, the heartland of the country, consists of the valleys of the Irrawaddy, Chindwin, and Sittang. They have a general north–south direction with the important exception of the great east–west bend of the Irrawaddy from Mandalay to the Chindwin confluence. The area around the great bend of the Irrawaddy is known as the dry zone with only 20 to 40 inches of rain. Irrigated rice paddy is the major crop in the dry zone, with settlements located around the waterpoints. The lower Irrawaddy and the delta form the key agricultural area of Burma, with rice paddy as the leading crop. Rural villages in the delta are sited on embankments and small rises.

East of the central belt lies a great tableland of massive limestone and crystalline rocks, most of which is occupied by the Shan states. The tableland is

deeply dissected by the Salween and its tributaries. The forested ranges
of Tenasserim run north–south. Further south, the route from Mergui to
the Gulf of Siam was one of the most important trade routes up to the eighteenth century.

Rangoon (Yangon) in the delta and Mandalay in the dry zone are the two
major cities of Myanmar. Built largely by the British, Rangoon is a city of
broad streets and squat Victorian buildings mixed with a few dog-eared edifices in a semimodern style. Rangoon looks outward to the sea, but landlocked Mandalay, the ancient capital, has always looked inward. Northeast of
Mandalay, the main road served as a gateway to the famous Burma Road of
World War II, a vital supply line through the jungle for war material shipped
by the United States into China for use against the Japanese. Today, the rutted,
two-lane highway is still being used to transport armaments, but the flow has
reversed. Chinese-made weapons are coming south on Japanese-made trucks
at the behest of the military government of Myanmar, which uses some of the
arms to help keep its restive citizens under strict control.

For nearly five decades Myanmar has remained one of the world's most
isolated, repressive countries. There are few signs of the former grandeur of
Burma, which was once called the richest nation in Southeast Asia. It was a
major oil and mineral producer and the world's largest rice exporter. British
rule was replaced by an ineffective and increasingly chaotic government
under the politician U Nu. He was overthrown in 1962 by General Ne Win, an
intensely xenophobic military commander who cut Burma off from the
outside world and wrecked its prosperous economy with a socialist system. In
1988, Ne Win officially retired after an explosion of street demonstrations
demanding democracy, but the military returned to power later that year after
a chaotic summer in which more than 2,000 demonstrators, most of them
students, were killed by soldiers. Thousands more fled to Thailand, where they
continue to dwell in refugee camps along the border (Figure 4.12). In 1992
General Than Shwe took over as chairman of the ruling junta. Than Shwe
announced a timetable for making a transition to civilian rule by 1996. The
May 1990 elections, in which the National League for Democracy, headed by
Aung San Suu Kyi, won an overwhelming majority, were a humiliating fiasco
for the military. It has since gone about meticulously altering the results—at
least 113 elected members of Parliament are in jail, have fled the country,
have been disqualified, or are dead. Suu Kyi, who won the Nobel Peace Prize
for her campaign to bring democracy to Burma, was released in May 2002
after house arrest and confinement by the nation's military junta. More than
1,200 political prisoners remain in jail, many of them elderly and sick.

While Western governments continue to express concerns about human
rights in the country, it is the sad condition of the economy that is most troubling for most ordinary Burmese. Government statistics put Myanmar's per
capita income at 1,225 kyats a year, which at the unofficial rate of exchange is
only $10. Even at the official exchange rate it is just $200 a year, a figure that

Figure 4-12. A harassed Burmese student dissident refugee along the Thai border. Authoritarian regimes from China to Burma have persecuted political dissidents. A large number of Burmese dissidents live along the Thai border as refugees in fear of their lives. During the first decade of independence, Burma (or Myanmar) was a parliamentary democracy; since 1958 it has been ruled by the military. The country's economic and social problems have increased during the last thirty years. (Photo: Shin-ichi Asabe.)

would still rank Myanmar as one of the world's ten poorest countries. Luckily for the government, 80 percent of Burmese live in rural areas and are essentially divorced from a cash economy, bartering agricultural products for whatever goods they need. Foreign aid from most Western countries was suspended after the 1988 massacres and has not been resumed. In 1990 Japan provided more than $61 million in aid to Burma despite its ruthless supression of democracy and systematic human rights violations. In 1991, after the military junta provoked international condemnation for disregarding the elections, Japan actually increased its aid to nearly $85 million. Myanmar has also been coddled by its neighbors. Brushing aside concerns over human rights abuses, the Southeast Asian economic bloc (ASEAN) agreed to admit Myanmar as a member in 1997. The United States imposed economic sanctions on Myanmar in 1997, citing a continued record of "severe repression" by the military government. The economic and political support Burma gets from other Southeast Asian states and from China has effectively annulled attempts to induce domestic political change through international pressure.

Burmese–Chinese ties warmed in 1988, when other nations cut off weapons supplies and economic aid to Myanmar to protest the junta's brutal crackdown on democracy demonstrators. As other nations isolated Myanmar, the Chinese stepped in. China is now the main arms supplier, providing the military with enhanced capabilities for suppressing dissent and intensifying campaigns against armed opponents. The growing Chinese trade is changing the face of Mandalay, the site of Burma's most sacred religious shrines and the former capital of Burmese kings, made familiar to westerners by Kipling. Flashy concrete villas are springing up at every turn in Mandalay's grid-patterned streets, nearly all of them owned by the Chinese. Trucks trundling in from China via Lashio bring Chinese goods for sale in Mandalay's markets. Chinese engineers are developing the railway from Mandalay to Myitkyina, near the Chinese border, and the line from Mandalay to the capital.

Regional separatist feelings have persisted in Burma for several decades. In the heartland, the Irrawaddy valley, government authority is reasonably firm. But even near Rangoon, in the Irrawaddy delta, dissident elements are strong. In the western hills, government troops hold sway only as long as they are physically present. Once they move on, rebels take over once more. To the northeast, the Shan tribesmen largely run their own show. The Shans are Burma's single largest minority. They have never been terribly fond of the ruling Burmese, feeling closer to the Thai, with whom they have cultural and linguistic affinities. The Kachins, in Myanmar's far north, share the Shan's dislike for the Burmese central government, as do Chins in the Western Hills

Of all the minorities, the Karens, who live along the Thai–Myanmar border, are by far the biggest, about 3.4 million. They are mainly Christians in an overwhelmingly Buddhist country. The Karen National Union is the largest of a score of rebel outfits that have fought for more autonomy (Figure 4.13). The Karens have never reached cease-fire with the government, though their long-time capital, Manerplaw, was overrun in 1994. They have shifted to guerrilla tactics and they operate from about 300 mobile bases along the frontier.

Since Myanmar won its independence from Britain in 1948, the army has been at war with a welter of insurgent ethnic minorities—Christians, Buddhists, and animists—as different from one another as they are from the ethnic Burmans who dominate the government and military. The 8000-soldier Kachin Independent Army is the strongest of the armed insurgent groups. Many of the 1.5 million Kachin are Christians, a legacy of the generations of Western missionaries who once flocked to this predominantly Buddhist land. The decades-old insurgencies help explain why Myanmar, despite vast natural resources, is today one of the poorest and most backward countries in Southeast Asia.

The war with the Kachin appears to be ending because of the realization by both the rebels and the Myanmar Army that this is a war that neither side can hope to win. Several other ethnic groups—the Wa, the Kokang, the Palaung, and the Shan—already have made peace with the junta.

Myanmar's ruling junta, the State Law and Order Restoration Council, or SLORC, is one of the world's most brutal and least legitimate regimes. It seized power by massacring democracy demonstrators in the streets of Rangoon. Since then it has ignored elections, cooperated with drug lords, and waged relentless war against democratic political leaders, university students, Buddhist religious activitists, and ethnic minorities who make up more than a

Figure 4-13. A boy from the Karen ethnic minority living in a refugee camp in Myanmar (Burma). Ethnic conflict, civil war, and economic circumstances generate refugee movements. The minorities in the Southeast Asian hill country are often Christian or animist, embrace cultures that set them apart from the majority population, and follow distinct livelihood strategies, which have resulted in their exclusion from the mainstream of national life in various countries. (Photo: Shin-ichi Asabe.)

third of the country's population. This grim dictatorship is being courted by countries eager for new economic opportunities in the world's rapidly growing region. To the east, Thailand makes refugees fleeing the SLORC's repression feel unwelcome. To the north, China provides military aid, consumer goods, and diplomatic support.

2. Cambodia

Cambodia, which in the heyday of Angkor ruled over vast territories in mainland Southeast Asia, and in more recent times formed part of French Indochina, now occupies a relatively small and compact area of about 66,000 square miles between Thailand, Laos, and Vietnam. The greater part of the country consists of a shallow lacustrine basin centered on Tonle Sap, which was formerly much more extensive. This lowland drains eastwards to the Mekong, which flows through the eastern part of the lowlands from north to south.

Throughout its course through Cambodia, the Mekong averages over a mile in
width, but is interrupted by rapids and waterfalls along the Laotian border.

With relatively good alluvial soils and abundant irrigation water, Cambodia
has considerable agricultural potential and could support a greater intensity of
cultivation to feed its present population of nearly 13 million. However, the
decades of war have ruptured the delicate irrigation system of Cambodia,
sown its fields with land mines, and killed of professionals who would have
speeded its recovery (Figure 4.14).

Cambodia's economy, long held hostage to violence, radical politics, and
ideology, has teetered on a knife's edge. After decades of bloodshed at the
hands of autocratic leaders and a fourteen-year civil war, the country is struggling with serious economic problems (Figure 4.15). Industry makes up just

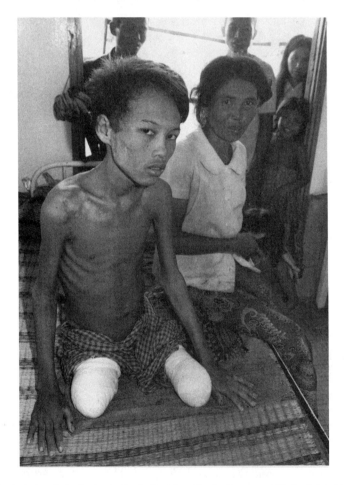

Figure 4-14. A victim of a land mine in Cambodia. Many Cambodians were killed or injured by land mines
planted by forces fighting the civil war in the country. The plight of the Cambodian refugees—the real
victims of the country's geopolitical instability—remains largely unaddressed. (Photo: Shin-ichi Asabe.)

Figure 4-15. A girl pumps water from a well installed with international assistance in Okoi village in the province of Kompong Speu. Available supplies of safe water are scarce in rural areas of Cambodia and many other Southeast Asian countries. Provision of clean, safe water is essential for human resource development and environmental health. (Photo: Shin-ichi Asabe.)

16 percent of gross domestic product, and this figure is sliding. The country also lacks a modern financial system to support investment.

When the Khmer Rouge took power on April 17, 1975, they forced the country's educated people to work alongside farmers on huge rural communes where many people were killed or died of hunger and disease. By 1979, when a Vietnamese invasion ousted the Khmer Rouge, more than one million of Cambodia's people had died. Though the power of the Khmer Rouge is waning, guerrillas continue to battle the government troops and to haunt the memories of those who survived their rule.

The peace pact signed in Paris in October 1991 by the country's four main factions offered a chance for Cambodia to pull itself out of poverty with the help of international aid. The four factions include the Khmer Rouge, which ruled Cambodia from 1975 to early 1979 with Maoist zealotry. The government that was installed by the Vietnamese army after it deposed Khmer Rouge leader Pol Pot also killed many civilians. The other two factions are small, noncommunist groups supported by the West but lacking large military resources. The Khmer Rouge opted out of the peace process altogether, and the other three factions accuse each other of violent attacks and of failing to create a safe and democratic atmosphere for the polls. The 120-seat constituent assembly, elected in May 1993 in U.N.–organized polls, established a power-sharing interim government, formally ending fouteen years of civil war. Stable government is important to boost the economy.

Along Cambodia's long, semicircular border with Thailand, stretches of what had been dense tropical jungle now resemble a strip mine. In this bleak, slate-gray landscape, fanatical guerrillas of the Khmer Rouge have managed to survive and even prosper. When they controlled the central government in the 1970s, the rebel group's Maoist-inspired leaders punished free-market commerce by death. Today, the Khmer Rouge functions to a large degree as a business venture, granting lucrative concessions to companies—most of them from Thailand—involved in gem mining and logging. The cross-border timber trade is barred, but it has been difficult to monitor compliance with the lumber ban in Khmer Rouge–held areas, where the United Nations does not have access. The moratorium on logging is intended to halt the ravaging of Indochina's forests. Large flatbed trucks head across the Cambodian border bearing tons of tropical hardwood bound for lumber mills in Thailand. Thai military leaders are widely believed to profit personally from the timber exports, sometimes as secret partners in the logging companies. There are no sanctions on gem mining, and each day thousands of Thai cross the border into Khmer Rouge–held areas to mine for precious gems. Khmer Rouge businesses are believed to earn the rebels millions of dollars a month, which has allowed the rebel groups to survive for years without any other assistance.

From the air, Phnom Penh looks like a well-ordered and pleasant city, which in many ways it is. Its major landmarks, such as the Bassac River, the National Museum, and the Hotel Cambodiana, are easily picked out as the plane banks for a bumpy touchdown. The dominant colors are yellow, ochre, and sahara brown. Twenty years of conflict razed much of Phnom Penh's beauty, but the visitor is taken in by the charm of a quintessentially Asian city gone French. It is a generally successful melange in which raised pedal cyclos are just as much a part of the scene as are the circular traffic stands in the middle of intersections, once used by gendermes to direct the low throb of traffic that flows along the ample boulevards and tree-lined avenues that enhance this city at the confluence of the Mekong and Tonle Sap rivers. The city's well-laid-out streets, with their elegant median strips, seem to have instilled a degree of order and symmetry in the Phnom Penhois, who have factored the town planner's sense of unity into their neat storefronts and market gardens. The smidgens of French, Khmer, and to a lesser degree,

Chinese and Vietnamese influences are visible in the royal administrative and commercial architecture.

The gracious old French villas in Phnom Penh, built to house three or four people, now accommodate extended families of ten or twelve who let their chickens and pigs forage where colonial residents had once cultivated their hibiscus borders. Although there are unavoidable reminders of the days of Pol Pot, such as the Tuol Sleng Museum of Genocide and Choeung Ek, principal site of the Killing Fields, there are also uplifting ones such as Wat Phnom (pagoda) and the Royal Palace complex. The survival of so many opulent buildings such as the Royal Palace, given that the Khmer Rouge dismantled much of the city, is one of the surprising things about Phnom Penh. The Royal Palace complex appears to be completely unscathed. Walls along the nearby cloisters delicately depict scenes from the Ramayana—dancers, courtesans, messengers of the gods; but even among this sunny imagery, the dark side of the Cambodian universe appears time and again in purgatorial scenes of interrogation and torment. The tyranny of demons is a recurrent theme here, reflecting the violence that seems to have run eternally beneath the surface of the culture.

In spite of the present bleak economic situation, the country has a number of advantages. The most important of Cambodia's assets is its location in the middle of one of the growing regions in the world. In addition, the country could have a trade surplus if logging and gems in areas controlled by the Khmer Rouge were taken into account.

3. Laos

Laos, along with Vietnam and Cambodia, made up the former French colonial territory of Indochina. During nearly seventy years of comparatively indulgent and negligent French rule, the aristocracy acquired a veneer of French education but was undisturbed in its traditional semifeudal status. The country is mainly an agglomeration of rural dwellers who lead a life of bucolic simplicity. They are simple peasants and isolated tribal peoples scattered through a spoon-shaped, monsoon-swept expanse of lush, tropical valleys and jumbled mountains in a country about the size of Kansas. Clustered in the lowlands of the Great Mekong River and its tributaries are the Buddhist Laos, who are charming and unassertive. They make up about half of the population and are the dominant people of the country.

The other half of the population comprises a score of tribal groups living in the forested hills. All the people of Laos are called Laotians, but only the "superior" valley dwellers, who scorn the hillmen, are known as Laos. The thousands of valley Laos villages are huddles of thatch-roofed shacks on stilts flanked by rice fields and shaded by clumps of bamboo. The rural Laos live by cultivating rice, fishing, raising chickens, and growing tropical fruits. They make elegant silk and cotton textiles, basketry, and Buddhist artifacts, with skills that are slowly dying out.

Lao men and women exert themselves during the rice-growing monsoon season and take it easy during the dry months. Dressed in colorful sarongs, they stage numerous festivals with dancing and games held in compounds of gilt-roofed temples. These fetes coincide with the harvest cycle or with Buddhist holy days and cremations. The Laos were made unaggressive and passive by the Buddhist emphasis on contemplation and fatalism, their isolation from the rest of the world, lack of education (French policy was to keep them "unspoiled"), and a history of conquest and invasion. Neither Laos nor the hill people have an aptitude for business. It is carried on their country, as in most of Southeast Asia, by Chinese and Indians.

Each tribe has its own distinctive culture. Some practice slash-and-burn agriculture, setting fire to all vegetation in a hillside plot, digging holes for seeds with sticks, reaping a pitifully thin harvest, and moving on. But many weave highly sophisticated textiles and baskets, with bold and beautiful designs and colors. Among these mountain tribesmen are the Hmong, who migrated to northern Laos from China in the last century. Before the United States entered the Vietnam War, they were slash-and-burn farmers living in isolated hamlets. Then, recruited by the CIA to fight the "secret" war in Laos, Hmong became some of the United States' most loyal allies in Southeast Asia. With the U.S. pull out, Vietnam and Laos fell to the communists, and Hmong fled to refugee camps in Thailand and Malaysia. For many, that exodus ended in the United States. Today, half of the Hmong refugees live in California, mainly near Fresno.

The lowlanders—and the French before them—have consistently discriminated against, scorned, and neglected the hill people. With divisions between lowlanders and hill people, and lingering regional loyalties, Laotians do not have much of a sense of national identity. The lack of communications hampers cohesion.

Cambodia's natural resources are extremely meagre. Successive Laotian governments composed of the traditional elite have made some progress in economic development, but they have done far too little to cope with the wants and stirrings among both lowlanders and hill peoples. Laos has been intermittently at war, and during the Vietnam War, Lao territory was used as the supply route from North to South Vietnam, which became known as the Ho Chi Minh Trail.

In their constant search for low-cost production locations, sportswear giants Nike and Adidas have added the tiny Laos to their list of worldwide suppliers. With low wages and a pliant workforce, Laos has become an attractive investment destination for international manufacturers. The weak kip (Laos currency) has been a boon to garment exporters, who now employ thousands of young women in the capital to produce sportswear and garments for the top brand names, including Nike, Kappa, Adidas, and JCPenney. Although garment exports are still small—about $90 million, or 9 percent of export revenue in 2000—the textile and garment sector had attracted foreign investments worth more than $72 million. In the factory operated by Trio (Laos) Export Company, about 1,200 workers cut, stitch, and embroider apparel for Nike, Adidas, and other international brands, in a well-lit, air-conditioned facility that boasts staff dormitories and piped pop music.

Workers earn on an average less than a dollar a day for an eight-hour shift and work six days a week. They can increase their wages by 30 percent per month by working overtime of up to 40 hours. Though their wages seem meager by world standards, these women can earn three times as much as a Lao government worker. One reason Lao people are popular with foreign firms is because of their gentle nature, being devout Buddhists for whom confrontational behavior is unacceptable.

4. Vietnam: An Economy in Transition

The Socialist Republic of Vietnam is one of the poor nations in the Asian Pacific region. The territory of Vietnam is slightly smaller than the state of California, but its population of about 80 million is more than a quarter as large as that of the United States. It is the world's thirteenth-most and Asia's fifth-most populous country. Its territory is elongated along a north–south axis that extends from China to the Gulf of Siam. Only about a quarter of Vietnam is good farmland. Most of the ethnic Vietnamese, who make up 85 percent of the population, live in two small core areas of the Red River delta and the city of Hanoi in the north and the Mekong River delta and Ho Chi Minh City (formerly Saigon) in the south. These two concentrations of population are linked by a long, thin band of coastal plains along the South China Sea. Most of the central portion of Vietnam is mountainous and is inhabited by ethnic minorities.

Vietnam does have natural resources, including oil, which make up 25 percent of its exports by value, and its potential for tourism is strong. But it is in people—human capital—that it is strikingly rich. The Vietnamese are better educated and healthier than could reasonably be expected for a nation with such low income. Over four fifths of the population (82 million) in the country and almost all those living in towns and cities can read and write, the pay-off from state money poured into primary schools (Figure 4.16). Health spending likewise has produced the welcome result in so poor a country of an infant mortality rate of 36 per 1,000 live births and an average life expectancy at birth of sixty-seven years.

As nations go, Vietnam is old. The cultural hearth of the Viet ethnic group, the delta of the Red River in northern Vietnam was first settled more than three millenia ago. Throughout its recorded history, the delta has had continuous and progressively more intense human habitation. The movement outward from the cultural hearth put the Vietnamese in contact with both new environments and other peoples, and as a consequence the national territory today features great ecological differentiation, ranging from the intense wet-rice agriculture of the lowlands (especially the Red River delta) to extensive swidden (burned clearing) exploitation of large parts of the upland territories. Land-hungry

Figure 4-16. Education is the beacon that offers the opportunity to escape from poverty and stagnation. Vietnam is emphasizing basic education, especially education of girls, to promote economic and social development. To encourage children to continue their studies even if they need to work to supplement their parents' income, the government has initiated a program of alternative basic education with the support of aid from international agencies. Alternative basic education classes are held in the afternoons and evenings at the Nguyen Hue School in Ho Chi Minh City (Saigon); children attend classes after their workday is over. (Photo: UNICEF by Emily Booker.)

Viets spilled out of the crowded Red River valley around Hanoi before the fifteenth century. Having defeated the Cham people on the central coast, they colonized the south in the seventeenth and eighteenth centuries. A Vietnamese sense of identity was honed in resistance to French rule (1883–1954), to U.S. support for the government of South Vietnam (1965–1975), and to China's ever present attentions and interferences. Chinese cultural influences also shaped Vietnam. These included Confucian, "male" values—respect for hierarchy, order and rules, a taste for learning, a sense of decorum, and a regard for sincerity, courage, and perseverance—and balancing Buddhist, "female" values—compassion, flexibility, and a feel for equality.

Compared with many countries in the non-Western world, the Vietnamese have a strong sense of national identity. Despite civil war, partition, conquest, regional disparities, and growing differences in wealth, its national identity endures. It may be the test that makes a nation rather than just geographical entity. Some countries, for example, Pakistan, break up for good. Others, Turkey for example, teeter forever. A third sort are both impossible as a whole and impossible in pieces, such as Afghanistan or Somalia. A fourth kind lasts: China, India, Egypt, Korea, Japan, and Vietnam.

Vietnam was split into two in 1945, when the job of disarming Japan's army in the north was given to Nationalist Chinese troops and in the south to British ones. After the defeat of the French in 1954 Vietnam was divided at the 17th Parallel into the communist Democratic Republic of Vietnam (north) and the U.S.-backed Republic of Vietnam (south). Both north and south speak one language and share a common history and culture.

The Vietnam War between North and South Vietnam and supported by the United States, scarred the landscape and devastated the economy of the country and left more than 2 million Vietnamese soldiers and civilians dead on both sides. Even today, twenty years after Communist North Vietnam defeated U.S.-backed South Vietnam and forcibly reunified the country, Vietnamese are being killed or maimed by unexploded bombs. But for the Vietnamese this war was little more than a blip on the screen of the country's 2,000 years of recorded history, which is a saga of recurrent strife, turmoil, invasion, occupation, and hardship.

Ignorant of Vietnamese history and culture, the United States failed utterly to understand the dedication and staying power of North Vietnam. The United States misconstrued the relationship between China and Vietnam, failed to appreciate the intense nationalism of the Vietnamese, and never grasped that Vietnam, as a largely agrarian society with a subsistence economy, could not be crippled by bombings. U.S. bombing never seriously threatened North Vietnam's capacity to wage war, and the U.S. ground operations never established any real, lasting security in the South Vietnamese countryside. About 58,000 Americans died in Vietnam. The American people were not fully committed to the war, sensing that their leaders did not know what America was fighting for. U.S. leaders could not grasp the appeal of Vietnamese nationalism. It was a failure of intellect, not will. It was an easy mistake for the United States to make. The United States' leaders saw themselves as defending freedom and democracy against world communism. It did not register until too late that most Vietnamese might put up with communism to protect nationalism.

Today, as always, it is China, this country's large neighbor to the north, that preoccupies Vietnam. China dominated Vietnam for 1,000 years, repeatedly invading and occupying it but never managing to assimilate it. The main streets of Hanoi are named for ancient Vietnamese heroes who vanquished Chinese invaders centuries ago, honing the guerrilla tactics later used against the French and Americans. The last Chinese incursion came in 1979, when the two nations fought a brief border war. Vietnamese remain distrustful of their historic adversary. China claims islands in the South China Sea that Vietnam considers its territory, and the country worries about Chinese economic domination. With China's economy booming, cheap manufactured products are flooding across the border and driving many Vietnamese factories out of business. One of the ironies of the United States' intervention in Vietnam was to contain Chinese communism. The misguided effort ignored centuries of enmity and pushed North Vietnam and China into a temporary partnership that broke up when the war was over.

Although there is still much trauma in Vietnam, and the Communist Party of Vietnam still rules the country, its old Marxist-Leninist doctrine has been trashed. The values of Western capitalism prevail. The communists won the war, but lost the peace. The policy of *doi moi,* or renovation, adopted in 1986, led to the abandonment of central planning and control, and eager pursuit of a free market.

Lack of infrastructure, poverty, the constantly changing legislation and differing perceptions of priorities are restraining advances in Vietnam. The National Assembly has passed many pieces of legislation liberalizing the economy, but the middle-ranking bureaucrats remain a problem. Between 1998 and 2002 Vietnam achieved 6.2 percent growth in gross domestic product, and saw industrial and agricultural production increase substantially. But without the proper infrastructure, Vietnam cannot meet the requirements of foreign investors. In addition, Vietnam in 2004 looks nowhere near as attractive to foreign investors as ASEAN did in the 1980s, when the market economies of Southeast Asia received investments worth $38 billion (the largest share coming from Japan). Vietnam now has one of the most liberal laws on foreign investment, yet it has not been able to garner high levels of foreign investment. Three-quarters of the investment is in the south, where commercial tradition has much deeper roots than in the north.

The Indochinese subregion offers key raw materials for industries—wood, coal, oil, natural gas, minerals, and precious stones—cheap labor, and a huge market. Japan resumed its Overseas Development Assistance to Vietnam in 1992. The United States lifted its embargo on trade and investment with Vietnam and established diplomatic relations in 1995, two full decades after the fall of Saigon. There are two major considerations in the U.S. recognition of Vietnam. One is U.S. business, which is eager for its share of the riches that Vietnam, its talented people, and its offshore waters seem to promise. The other is the United States' geostrategy, which views Vietnam as an important asset as the United States seeks to counter Chinese influence in Asia.

The delay in establishing relations with Vietnam was the difficulty in accounting for U.S. soldiers still carried on military rolls as missing in action; there are 2,302 of them in all of Southeast Asia, and 1,618 in Vietnam. Far more Americans are listed as missing in the Korean War (8,170) and in World War II (78,750). A few years after World War II, the United States was engaged in huge rebuilding efforts in Germany and Japan, even though Germans had killed millions of Jews and Japanese had tortured prisoners on a vast scale. The real reason for the delay in normalization of relations with Vietnam lay deeper in the national consciousness of America. The difference between Vietnam and other wars is that the United States lost in Vietnam. It is never easy for a world superpower to shake hands after losing the fight to a little country, especially when the superpower has never lost before. The open wound of defeat and resentment over the loss, combined with the unresolved controversy over the purpose of the war itself, made it hard for the United States to restore full political and economic relations.

The Vietnam War wreaked havoc on the country's natural environment, but the years since have seen even greater destruction. The population has doubled since the country's unification in 1975, and the population is expected to reach 82 million by the end of the century. In the last two decades, Vietnam's forest has shrunk from 51 million acres to 22 million acres, due to population growth. Fewer than 1 million acres were destroyed during the war with the United States, but 13 million were destroyed due to population pressure during peacetime. If people continue to cut down more forest, practicing their slash-and-burn methods, it will be a catastrophe for Vietnam. Soil erosion, dwindling mangrove forests, mudslides, and a weakening harvest combined with a heavy monsoon will prove an ecological disaster worse than the war.

Vietnam is making the transition from a planning economy to a market economy. Farming accounts for over a third of output, industry for just a quarter. Three quarters of Vietnam's workforce of 34 million are in the countryside. The policy of economic change known as *doi moi* (literally, "new change") was approved in 1986, implemented in 1988–1989, and confirmed in 1991. Under the new policy, trade was liberalized and foreign investment encouraged, mainly in the form of joint ventures with wholly or partly state-owned enterprises. In 1988 collective farms were scrapped and food prices freed. The first phase of the economic reform benefited both the farmers and the city-dwellers. The social costs of closing state industries have not been as devastating in Vietnam as in the former communist economies of Eastern Europe because of Vietnam's rural economy. State firms are being turned into joint ventures with foreign participation. The second phase of economic transition, in which Vietnam must create a modern infrastructure and institutional framework for a market economy, is more difficult. Vietnam has a strong party, but too weak a state bureaucracy to fine-tune development policy.

Taiwan, Hong Kong, South Korea, Malaysia, Singapore, France, Australia, and Japan have contributed most of the foreign direct investment since 1993. The atmosphere in Vietnam in 2004 suggests the early stages of an economic transformation, from the cellular phones and beepers worn by members of the new entrepreneurial class to the television aerials sprouting from peasants' thatched huts in the countryside. Vietnam's gross national product has been increasing, and two thirds of the GNP is created in what used to be South Vietnam.

Ho Chi Minh City and Hanoi and the Urban–Rural Divide The inter-linked processes of reform, growth, and internationalization that Vietnam is experiencing are making a major impact on the landscape, economy, and society in a remarkably uneven manner. Changes are heavily concentrated in and around the urban centers of Ho Chi Minh City, Hanoi and, to a lesser extent, Da Nang-Hue. In this respect the Vietnamese experience closely mirrors that of Thailand, where rapid economic growth, closely associated with the influx of foreign investment, has been heavily concentrated in the Bangkok metropolitan region and its immediate environs, largely bypassing the remainder of the country and the bulk of the population. Over 89 percent of the foreign investments are located in Ho Chi Minh City and Hanoi and their immediate adjacent provinces, compared with 79 percent in the Bangkok metropolitan region.

The economies of Ho Chi Minh City and Hanoi are both growing at around 20 percent a year, providing new opportunities for people who are migrating from the rural areas in search of work. There is worry about the prospect of a flood of indigent job-seekers overwhelming services and housing in the cities. Ho Chi Minh City's population is growing by over 7 percent a year and Hanoi's schools are struggling to cope with an unexpected influx of children.

The growing gap between the cities and the countryside also has uncomfortable implications. Vietnam's economic reforms were designed to benefit rural areas first, by allowing private enterprise in agriculture. That made political sense, because over 80 percent of the population lives outside the cities. But now that economic growth in the cities is fast outpacing the gains in farming, the poverty of rural Vietnam is coming into sharp focus.

Ho Chi Minh City, the former Saigon, where U.S. influence is strongest, has witnessed the greatest surge in investment. This is also the area where Vietnamese enjoy the highest standard of living. Ho Chi Minh City, a city of at least 8.5 million people, swirls with humanity and commerce. Vietnam's new free enterprise is everywhere. On many streets, every building has a shop on the ground level, and more stalls line the sidewalks, selling odorous dried fish, Pepsi and 7-Up, Heineken beer or half a dozen other brands (all brewed in Vietnam), straw baskets, plastic furniture, flowers, textiles, lottery tickets, and *pho*, the ubiquitous and tasty Vietnamese noodle soup. But the entrepreneurship of southern Vietnam goes far beyond street commerce. Huge new industrial enterprises are beginning to sprout up—firms such as the Huy Hoang Company.

Huy Hoang's mammoth garment factory covers more than 5 acres on the Bien Hoa Highway that used to connect Saigon to the huge U.S. air base at Bien Hoa and the Army base at nearby Long Binh. The first Huy Hoang garment factory opened in 1989 with 100 employees. In 2000, over 3,000 employees worked in two shifts, six days a week, sewing stylish clothes for export to Japan and other foreign markets. They are paid piecework rates and earn about $55 a month, big money in a country where the per capita income is still less than $250 a year. Coping with growth will not be easy. In Ho Chi Minh City, government officials fear becoming another Bangkok, where unplanned growth has choked a giant city and left it virtually unlivable for many of its residents. But there is no indication that the costs of headlong economic development will deter Vietnam from its course of aggressive growth.

In southern Vietnam, high-profile incidents of physical abuse against employees at factories working under contract to the U.S. footwear giant Nike have fueled charges that foreign companies exploit Vietnamese labor. For their labors, employees at foreign-owned factories earn about 20 cents an hour, the minimum wage set by a government keen to attract foreign investment. The rural–urban divide and exploitation of labor in cities—and the unsettling social consequences that go with them—are likely to widen. Sustained 8 percent growth would virtually abolish poverty in Ho Chi Minh City over the next decade. But in the poorest provinces of Vietnam, 70 percent of the population would still be classified as poor.

DEVELOPMENT OF THE MEKONG BASIN

The Mekong a mighty, venerated river, has sustained the livelihoods of fishermen, boatmen, rice growers, and slash-and-burn farmers for many decades. The basin covers six countries (China, Myanmar, Laos, Thailand, Cambodia, and Vietnam) through which the river flows. From its source in Tibet, the river cascades and flows for 2,600 miles before it reaches the sea in Vietnam. Since the 1950s, at least six overlapping committees and forums have discussed plans for the development of the Mekong Basin. The first one was the Mekong River Commission in the 1950s. The Asian Development Bank launched the Greater Mekong Sub-region initiative in 1992 with a series of studies on cross-border projects and issues. A Japanese initiative known as the Forum for Comprehensive Development of Indochina concentrates on jobs and infrastructure, with a private sector advisory group. Another group, AEM-MITI, links Japan's Ministry of Trade and Industry with economic ministers from ASEAN (Brunei, Indonesia, Malaysia, the Philippines, Thailand, and Vietnam). It concentrates on the transition to a market economy, with a "working group" on Cambodia, Laos, and Myanmar. The ASEAN Mekong Basin Development Co-operation was set up after ASEAN's summit in Bangkok in 1995. Pushed by Singapore and Malaysia, it has discussed development of railways. Another development commision known as Quadripartite Economic Co-operation joins Thailand, Myanmar, Vietnam, and Laos. It is also called the Golden Quadrangle, and is not doing as well as the Golden Triangle, a smaller part of the same area that specializes in narcotics production.

With China's Yunan Province, the countries through which the Mekong flows are home to over 230 million people. Many live in poverty. Cross-border links such as roads and railways are often rudimentary, where they exist at all. The region's economies are growing, and have complementary strengths and weaknesses. By improving transportation links, telecommunications, and electricity, prosperity may spread throughout the Mekong Basin.

The Mekong can become a channel of commerce and prosperity—Southeast Asia's Danube.

The development of the basin has been hampered by war for much of this century. And now that peace has arrived, geography and underdevelopment have conspired to make the improvements of infrastructural links an expensive undertaking. Priority projects include an improved road linking Bangkok, Phnom Penh, and Ho Chi Minh City; a railway from Kunming through Laos to Thailand and perhaps even Singapore; and hydroelectric dams on the Mekong and its tributaries.

For China, the Mekong offers a link with Southeast Asia, and a chance to develop Yunan, one of its poorer provinces. A dam is being built at Jinghong in Yunan, to be joined by transmission lines across Laos to Thailand. For the poor countries, the development of the Mekong Basin offers a dream of prosperity, although the poorest of all—Laos—is more cautious, fearful that its natural wealth will be carved up by overbearing neighbors. Thailand, the strongest economy in the region, needs resources. Already Thai businesses are cutting down forests in neighboring countries. The potential for both mutual benefit and suspicion is seen most clearly in the plan for the river. The countries (Thailand and Vietnam) with the biggest demand for electricity are not those with the greatest hydroelectric potential (Yunan in China, and Myanmar). Many environmentalist have opposed the dams because of problems ranging from the intrusion of saltwater into the delta, to the loss of fish and rare mammals, to floods and deforestation.

The cost of the Mekong Basin development may exceed $40 billion. The Asian Development Bank may contribute up to $1 billion, which leaves a big shortfall. Private investors are needed, but they may prefer to wait and see.

CENTRIFUGAL FORCES

In every union or federation of states there are forces that tend to weaken the central government, which we will call *centrifugal forces*. These may be ethnic differences, economic problems, political factors, or physical factors such as distance that make it difficult to achieve complete unity. For a union or federation to survive there must be unifying forces—or *centripetal forces*—strong enough to overcome the opposing forces. In Southeast Asia the centrifugal forces are numerous. Following is a discussion of how some of these are affecting Southeast Asian governments in the first decade of the twenty-first century.

Ethnic Struggle in Malaysia

When Britain granted independence to Malaysia in 1957, the country enjoyed ample natural resources of tin, rubber, teak, and palm oil, and—unlike some of its neighbors—more than adequate living space. The main drawback was the communal divide: the mainly rural and poor Malays outnumbered the more prosperous and urban Chinese and Indians. Religious conflict also existed between Islam, to which most Malays adhere, and the Buddhism, Christianity, and Hinduism practiced by the rest.

During the past three decades, Malaysia has crafted an impressive national affirmative action program to ease ethnic tension. The government effectively segregated the economy between the indigenous majority, known as *bumiputras* or "sons of the soil" and non-*bumiputras*—primarily ethnic Chinese who dominated the economy for generations.

By subsidizing the *bumiputras* and restricting the others, the government aimed to deliver a third of the economy into *bumiputra* hands by 1990 and avoid the kind of ethnic frictions that led to bloody riots in 1969. Laws were passed to favor *bumiputras*, who account for 60 percent of the population. Companies seeking listing on the local stock exchange are required to have a *bumiputra* shareholding of at least 30 percent. The policy has reduced poverty and helped integrate and harmonize a potentially volatile population.

Ethnic Chinese, who make up about 30 percent of the population, were not interested in investing in *bumiputra*-controlled companies, and Chinese companies were not favored in government contract bidding. Many of Malaysia's non-*bumiputras* tolerated the restrictions as a small price to pay for social stability. Overall, *bumiputras* have been strengthening their grip on the economy at the expense of non-*bumiputras*. It is estimated that *bumiputra* companies account for almost 20 percent of corporate equity, up from 2.4 percent in 1971, while the Chinese share has declined to 41 percent from almost 50 percent. Some of Malaysia's *bumiputra* businesses owe their success to government patronage that favored them for their ethnicity more than their business skills.

Now, however, the program is in trouble. The economy has been hit by a one-third drop in the value of the currency and by a slide in exports, which has exposed the unintended side effects of the pro-*bumiputra* policy. After a generation of entitlements, Malaysia is littered with clunky conglomerates, debt-saddled banks, and crony capitalists. Companies are so desperate for cash that the government in 1998 announced that it might repeal the spirit, if not the letter, of affirmative action by permitting non-*bumiputra* companies to acquire a substantial or a controlling interest in *bumiputra* companies. Structural inefficiencies resulting from excesses of the affirmative action program, concealed for years by decades of rapid expansion, are becoming apparent as growth recedes. The weaker economy is exposing the cost of creating a *bumiputra*-dominated Malaysian economy. Malaysia's three decades of grand social experiment to ease ethnic conflict is the casuality of too many politically correct business decision and bank loans made to *bumiputra* companies that those companies are now unable to repay. Economic decisions were made on the basis of a company's place in the *bumiputra* hierarchy rather than on its credit worthiness or the viability of the business. The political reverberations of the ethnic struggles are likely to be felt throughout Malaysia for years to come.

Religion-Based Movements in Indonesia, Thailand, and the Philippines

The concern over the potential for violence from religious upheaval remains high in the Indonesian archipelago of 224 million people—the world's largest Muslim nation. Crowds of radical Muslims, reacting to what they charge is excessive proselytizing by Christians, have attacked or burned several Christian churches or homes on Java and Sumatra. More than 10,000 activists tore down and burned the home and church of a self-styled Pentecostal preacher outside Pasuruan, East Java, in November 1992, to protest anti-Islamic materials he had allegedly distributed. The large number of attacks on churches or other Christian property have been attributed to radical right-wing Muslims who have been encouraged by government efforts to win favor with Islamic groups.

Although Indonesia has vigorously promoted a nondenominational philosophy called *Pancasila*, it has also stressed the Muslim roots of the country and has courted Islamic groups. With political groups and news media under tight constraint, Islam is seen as the main outlet for opposition sentiment in Indonesia. A country with nearly 13,700 islands and 300 distinct linguistic groups, the world's largest archipelago and fourth most populous nation is also susceptible to ethnic division.

Religion is a volatile element (see Figure 4.7). Up to 87 percent of Indonesia's population is Muslim, with Christians accounting for about 10 percent. Hindus and Buddhists make up the rest. Many Muslims adhere to pre-Islamic beliefs based on Javanese mysticism.The Indonesian government has indicated a readiness to crack down on militant Muslims who seek to create divisive centrifugal forces.

The largely Christian and traditional-religion population of Irian Jaya (West Papua) provides another case of the role of religion in defining the separatist movement in predominantly Muslim Indonesia. Over the years, the Free West Papua Movement in Indonesia has survived as an irritant to Indonesian rule in Irian Jaya. The movement has been weakened by recent internal divisions, by the departure of a number of its leaders, and by the vastly superior military capacity of the Indonesian government. Apart from the concern of church-related human rights organizations, the Christian church has not shown the concern for the plight of the largely Christian population in a predominantly Muslim country that the international Muslim community has shown for Muslim minorities in non-Muslim countries.

Dusty monuments of the Christian cross and the Islamic crescent, common in the landscape of the Philippines, stand as reminders that Christians and Muslims once lived together there in harmony. But increased incidents of terrorism and crime, a protracted separatist war, refugee migration, and a resurgence of religious fervor in other parts of the world now threaten to divide communities such as Zamboanga, on the island of Mindanao more than 780 miles from Manila, which is known for its divergent cultures. Roman Catholics—comprising 70 percent of the city's population of 440,000—have coexisted with Muslims in mutual tolerance and acceptance. Muslim extremists allied with separatist rebels in Basilan have started a series of terrorist attacks on Christians. In nearby Basilan Province, soldiers bombarded villages that were suspected to be sheltering a Moro National Liberation Front group that ambushed and killed marines. Armed Tausug tribesmen in motorized boats kidnapped two Spanish nuns on Sulu Island in early 1993. They were later released, but the kidnappers reportedly intended to force one of the nuns into marriage. Most of Zamboanga's Muslims are Tausugs.

An Italian priest and a Protestant pastor were assassinated in 1990 in Zamboanga in two separate incidents—both in cold blood and before horrified witnesses in broad daylight. The murders were motivated by extremist religious beliefs. In summer 1992 the city's holiest Catholic shrine—the Lady of the Pillar—became a terrorist target. A grenade was thrown into the huge crowd of worshippers there, killing four and wounding many people. The tension has damaged Christian–Muslim relations in the Philippines.

The Malay Muslims in Buddhist Thailand offer another example of religion-based separatist movements in Southeast Asia. The Malay Muslims (as distinct from a smaller non-Malay Thai Muslim group centered around Bangkok) inhabit the four southern provinces of Thailand in what was once the kingdom of Patani. The Patani court officially adopted Islam in 1457. The area fell under Thai control in the late eighteenth century and thereafter experienced alternating periods of independence and subjugation to the Thai. The emergence of the present Patani separatist movement had its beginning in a political reorganization in the first decade of this century, in which the Malay provinces of Kedah, Perlis, Kelantan, and Trengganu were ceded to Britain (eventually becoming part of independent Malaysia) and the neighboring area that now comprises the Thai provinces of Pattani, Narathiwat, Yala, and Satun came firmly under Thai control. The Thai government embarked on a strenuous campaign to assimilate the Malay people into Thai Buddhist society. Among other things, the government replaced the Islamic *shariah* with Thai laws, imposed compulsory attendance at Thai primary schools to undermine the traditional Islamic schools, and promoted the use of Thai over the Malay language. The Malay resisted Thai integration, and several new underground groups emerged in Patani to press for Malay Muslim separation.

A sense of grievance remains and provides the basis for the continued existence of the Patani movement.

The Geography of Hate and Human Rights

From brutal conflicts in Cambodia, Indonesia, and Myanmar violence has taken root between people who share the same terrain but differ in ethnicity, race, language, or religion. Although some of these conflicts have long histories, many have been fanned by deliberate government policies to divide and conquer opponents, justify repression of separatist movements, or fend off calls for democracy.

In Myanmar guerrilla warfare by at least four insurgent groups has killed about 6,000 since 1988, including Muslims in the west fleeing into Bangladesh and Karens in the east along the Thai–Myanmar border. Government offensives against minorities living along borders with Thailand, China, and Bangladesh have killed unknown thousands. Torture is widespread and extrajudicial executions are still common. In August 1990 a group of about twenty schoolchildren, ages 12 to 15, gathered in front of the American Embassy in Yangon (Rangoon), vowing to continue the fight for democracy. Seven were arrested on their way home and have not been seen since.

Mostly Muslim Indonesia fought a separatist movement among the mostly Roman Catholic East Timorese population. Up to 200,000 died from 1974 to 1980 after the Indonesian Army invaded, occupied, and quickly annexed the region. The sufferings of this poor, parched, and distant place have faded from the world's memory. In Dili, the principal city in East Timor, Muslim Indonesians were settled in large numbers and small mosques were built, angering the deeply Roman Catholic Timorese, who lived under Portuguese rule for more than 400 years. Despite Indonesia's considerable efforts at development, the Timorese remember the harsh years after the invasion of December 7, 1975, when thousands of peasants fled to the parched mountains and tried to survive helicopter gunships, free-fire zones, the burning of their crops, and a military that suppressed all resistance. In September 1999, an Indonesian military–backed militia ransacked the province of East Timor. The destruction was triggered by the referendum of August 30, when the East Timorese voted overwhelmingly in favor of independence, ending Indonesia's unilateral occupation dating from 1975. The conflict destroyed much of East Timor's infrastructure, burning 70 percent of the capital city of Dili and laying much of the province to waste. A U.N. peacekeeping force arrived in late September 1999. Shortly thereafter, an interim government was established to bring order to the territory and prepare an orderly transition to a democratic government.

Militant Islam is also unsettling most of Southeast Asia as Islamic fundamentalists mount aggressive campaign for separate states and strict adherence to religious laws. The countries most concerned are Indonesia, with the rise of radical Islamic parties; the Philippines, with an intractable separatist insurgency in its partly Muslim southern islands; and Malaysia, where radical Muslim groups are taking advantage of a time of political flux. Worries also exist in Thailand, which has a small but persistent separatist movement on its southern border with Malaysia. The surge in peaceful Islamic fundamentalism as well as violent extremism is viewed as one of the most serious threats to the stability of Southeast Asia, an area whose shipping lanes, low-cost manufacturing, and emerging markets make it important to global economy.

Oil rich Aceh, in northern Sumatra, is another area where a separatist movement has raged on and off for more than twenty-five years, leaving thousands dead. Acehnese have an illustrious history of independence. They never reconciled to Dutch rule, and they are still opposed to rule by a central government in Jakarta. Very little of the huge wealth generated from the development of a gas field in Aceh has filtered down to the local people. In 2003 the government broke off peace talks, declared martial law, and sent in 40,000 troops. Acehnese separatism began as a struggle for political and economic autonomy. But now the war is about the war—Acehnese join or support the guerrillas because of the army's brutality. Measures to control the behavior of troops and protect civilians have no powerful constituency in Indonesia, but they are crucial to pursuading the Acehnese to abandon separatism and the guerilla war, and to negotiate an agreement that will keep them part of Indonesia.

The explosion of violence is the paramount issue facing the human rights movement in Southeast Asia, and containing the abuses committed in the name of ethnic or religious groups is a major challenge. The conflicts of the future in Southeast Asian countries are between people rather than states over issues related to culture, ethnicity, or religion.

Singapore, Malaysia, and Indonesia have dissented to the application of the concept of universal human rights to all countries. These free-market countries have achieved impressive economic growth in the past two decades, but heavy-handed "benevolent authoritarianism" and repression of freedom of expression have been hallmarks of their political regimes. In Southeast Asia, qualifying the application of democratic freedoms with a concern for cultural diversity serves merely as a pretext for repression by the state.

The United Nations Universal Declaration of Human Rights, adopted in 1948, offers a common standard against which the nations of Southeast Asia and other countries can measure the treatment of their citizens. The fundamental rights and freedoms found in the Universal Declaration, in effect, propose limits on the powers of governments to compel or control the behavior of individual citizens. The Universal Declaration also lists social and economic "rights," but they are dependent on and, indeed, arise from, satisfaction of the basic political, civil, and human rights of a truly free and democratic society. The data for the period 1988 to 2003 in the annual

Country Reports on Human Rights Practices by the U.S. Department of State, Amnesty International (London), and Human Rights Watch (New York) reveal that human rights remain circumscribed in most countries of Southeast Asia. Many of these countries have authoritarian governments in which a single party backed by the army retains dominant decision-making authority. Severe repression of all forms of political dissent characterizes the situation in Myanmar. There a military government had allowed free elections and then refused to accept the outcome, thus rejecting the overwhelming desire of the people to return to parliamentary democracy. In Indonesia and Malaysia, areas of human rights abuse included the killing and physical mistreatment—sometimes torture—of civilians by military and police; significant restrictions of freedoms of speech, press, and assembly; and persistent discrimination against ethnic Chinese.

THE GOLDEN TRIANGLE: MYANMAR, THAILAND, AND LAOS

The Golden Triangle of Southeast Asia (see Figure 4.3 inset) offers an interesting example of the internal and external political and economic factors that led to the emergence of one of the three major areas for cultivation of coca and opium in the world. (The other two areas are the Golden Crescent in Afghanistan, Pakistan, and Iran; and Colombia, Peru, and Bolivia in the Andes.) These crops offer farmers low-cost entry into the cash economy in parts of the world receiving little or no state support or resources. In addition, the crops are low-bulk, nonperishable, and easily stored and transported. The farmers are assured of market access and traffickers make advance payments.

Although the growers know it is illegal, for the most part they are not fully aware of the future uses or ramifications of their harvest after it is transformed into heroin and cocaine. In their own environment, opium and coca ease the symptoms of illness, relieve hunger pains, and comfort the aging. They cannot fathom how the narcotics trade fits into world commerce and power politics.

The Golden Triangle of Southeast Asia in 2000 was one of the largest sources of heroin coming into the United States, with production levels rising sharply. In 1987, only 18 percent of the heroin in the United States originated in Southeast Asia; in 1990 the figure was 45 percent. In 1984, only 5 percent of the heroin in New York City was Southeast Asian; in 1990, according to the United States Drug Enforcement Administration, the figure was 80 percent. The increase is a result of many factors, ranging from unrest in Myanmar to a decision by some drug smugglers to bypass Latin America, which has gotten increasing attention from government authorities, and seek safer routes.

The changing patterns of heroin supply have brought new and unwanted attention to Thailand as the main smuggling and shipment center for heroin from the Golden Triangle, where Myanmar, Laos, and Thailand meet. Although Thailand has sharply reduced the amount of opium poppy cultivation on its territory, the rapidly developing communications and transport systems of its booming economy are also being used for shipping the increasing amounts of heroin being produced in Laos and Myanmar to Europe and the United States. The large growth in Thai exports and in tourism provides more options for smuggling, ranging from individual couriers to large shipments hidden deep in legitimate exports moving through container-ized ports. The amount of money at stake makes the problem of corruption among the Thai police, army, and customs officials, none of whom are paid very well, a growing concern even for a well-intentioned Thai government that cooperates with Western law-enforcement authorities.

The Golden Triangle produces about 70 percent of the world's opium.The major areas of opium cultivation are in Myanmar and Laos, two of the world's most isolated countries. At least 3,000 tons of raw opium are produced annually in the Golden Triangle, which would yield 300 tons of heroin. Out of this, nearly 2,600 tons are usually produced in Myanmar. Loas generally produces an estimated 300 to 400 tons. Thailand is estimated to produce about 50 tons. With the increase in heroin production, Thailand's role of regional entrepot has become very critical. It is also becoming a focus for well-armed and well-financed drug syndicates that might threaten the stability of the state in the future.

Heroin produced in Myanmar has also swept into the neighboring Yunan Province of China. It has brought with it the companion plague of the human immunodeficiency virus (HIV) to Yunan, which is rapidly spreading among China's population of intravenous drug users. Officially, China's Ministry of Public Health has reported 2,428 cases of HIV infection nationwide. But few people have been tested and health officials privately estimate that China has as many as 100,000 carriers of the virus. More than half are believed to be in Yunan Province, which shares the border with the Golden Triangle states of Myanmar and Laos. In Yunan both needle sharing by drug users and sexual intercourse are spreading the disease.

SOUTHEAST ASIA'S DISAPPEARING RAINFORESTS

Southeast Asia's rainforests, the most bountiful in the world, are disappearing (Figure 4.17). Rainforests, which girdle the world's equatorial regions, once covered 10 percent of the earth's surface, nurturing its richest cornucopia of plants and animals. Now the total area has been reduced by one-third. In much of Southeast Asia the rate of destruction has been faster than elsewhere. There were 2.49 million square km of virgin forest in the region outside of Papua New Guinea in 1900, but only 602,222 square km remain. The three countries with the smallest expanse of remaining forests—Vietnam, the Philippines, and

Thailand—are also those where deforestation has been the most rapid during the last twenty-five years. In the 1980s Malaysia chopped down more tropical trees than any country except Indonesia and Brazil.

Southeast Asia has cut more of its forests than either Africa or Latin America. The rate of forest clearance has roughly trebled in Southeast Asia since the early 1960s and is still rising. The United Nations Food and Agricultural Organization reported in 1993 that Southeast Asia had (with Central America) the world's fastest rate of deforestation. Illegal logging by timber companies is a particularly serious problem because of the scale and sophistication of their operations. Indonesia is estimated to have 109 million hectares of forests, about 56 percent of its national land area. All the forests are government owned, but the country is losing about 1.3 million hectares of first-growth forest each year. Because forestry is vital to Indonesia's economy in terms of both of securing jobs and earning foreign currency, the task of balancing the imperatives of industry against pressure to conserve the rainforest is a difficult one.

In the Philippines some 60 percent of the land was forested forty years ago; now 10 percent is forested. Poorer countries such as Laos and Myanmar have barely started exploiting their forests. Somewhere between these two groups

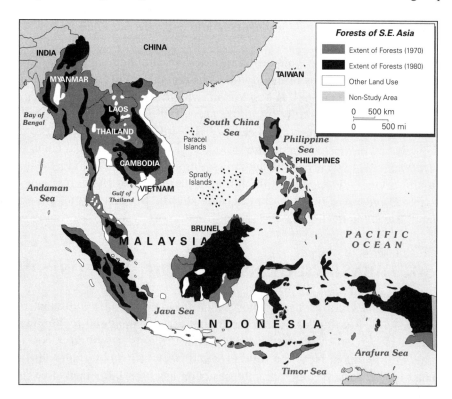

Figure 4-17. Geographic patterns of deforestation in Southeast Asia. (Compiled from the Asian Development Bank data and reports from individual nations.)

lie Malaysia and Indonesia. Logging continues there, but both countries still have vast areas of forest left.

Two forces drive deforestation. One is hunger for land. A slice of the remaining forests in Southeast Asian countries is earmarked for conversion into plantations, farmland, and building sites. The other force is a booming demand for timber. However, international agencies and the Southeast Asian government departments identify traditional shifting cultivation as the main culprit of deforestation. Although some groups do practice predatory forms of shifting cultivation, the majority do not. Land pioneering by nonminority peoples who often rely on slash-and-burn cultivation—or hire tribal people to do it for them—is a major factor in deforestation. The land pioneers destroy the forests and replace them by permanent agriculture, but shifting cultivators through traditional swidden agriculture often contribute to the regeneration of tropical forests.

Just as the rate of degradation of the world's rainforests has reached record levels (about 200,000 square km are destroyed or degraded every year), evidence is accumulating that they are assets the world needs. Only recently have we begun to tally the consequences of deforestation. The genetic pool, for instance, is rapidly diminishing. Biologists estimate 10,000 species vanish each year. The chances of breakthroughs in medicine resulting from the use of jungle plants vanish too.

Then, there is the weather. Scientists believe deforestation has contributed to the current gradual warming of the earth's atmosphere, partly caused by an increase in levels of carbon dioxide. Trees are one of the main agents for removing carbon dioxide from the atmosphere, giving out oxygen in return. When rainforests burn, there is a double jeopardy. Burning trees give off carbon dioxide, and burned-out forests can no longer remove it.

There is also more obvious and localized havoc. Loss of forest cover can cause erosion, sparking floods and mudslides and the silting of rivers. In November 1988, villages in southern Thailand were washed away in flash floods or buried in mud and logs. Rainforests have a remarkable capacity to absorb rainfall. Steep hillsides without forest cover become unstable. Replanting often ends in failed crops or crops washed away by heavy rains. Often, alternative uses of the forest—especially cash crops—have not produced the yields envisioned by government planners. In parts of Kalimantan and the Philippines there are examples of forest conversion for agriculture where the investment to promote and subsidize agricultural settlements has surpassed the yields. Often, this is because the soil beneath tropical forests is thin and lacks nutrients.

There are also direct economic losses. People who depend on the tropical forests for their livelihood suffer when forests dwindle. Meanwhile, tropical forests generate millions in export revenues each year, but from a rapidly dwindling resource. Already, Thailand has gone from an exporter to an importer of timber, and the Philippines timber trade is down to a trickle.

In September 1994 a haze blanketed much of Malaysia, Singapore, and Indonesia. The haze came from massive fires on the Indonesian islands of Kalimantan and Sumatra. The smoke from the fire trapped the by-products of the region's development—car exhaust and industrial fumes—close to ground level. As a result, the usual pristine cities of Singapore and Kuala Lumpur were breathing very unhealthy and hazardous air for more than a month. The Indonesian government blamed traditional seasonal slash-and-burn farming for the fires. It also reported that fires were started by people opposed to the government's timber-concession programs. Many native Kalimantese are opposed to the government's transmigration program, under which Javanese are granted timber concessions in Kalimantan. Nongovernmental organizations blame plantation and logging companies which start the fires to clear land for palm oil plantations.

Deforestation has many causes, and slowing the deforestation requires global and national actions. Sweeping structural changes are needed to increase the price of timber products to reflect their replacement cost rather than their extraction costs and create financial incentives for conservation. Tropical countries also need to reevaluate land use decisions. There is a growing consensus that producers have undervalued their forests and must change their policies, especially those regulating the timber industry. Agroforestry has the potential to halt deforestation in some areas and improve the livelihoods of poor inhabitants. Yet agroforestry depends on people's rights to plant and use trees, rights established by the prevailing system of land and tree tenure. Without clear property rights, there are few incentives to preserve natural resources and to invest in trees, because benefits would not accrue to those who manage them.

Tropical countries (in theory, at least) can choose to leave their remaining forests untouched. Few, if any, actually have this luxury, for the land transformed to other uses can provide cash, jobs, and homes for an ever-growing populace. Or forests can be cleared, the timber turned into immediate cash, and the land turned into agricultural plantations. Or countries can follow a middle course; extracting economic value from their forests through logging, but conserving them at the same time. However, this requires long-term planning by countries and a willingness to enforce strict logging rules to keep settlers out of production forests. At present, very little forest is under sustainable-yield management in Southeast Asia. The best examples of better-managed forests in Southeast Asia are found in areas of Peninsular Malaysia. Other places that are particularly successful include Mae Poong forest in Thailand; the Jengai Forest Reserve in Trengganu, Malaysia; Sabah Foundation in Sabah, Malaysia; Nasipit Lumber Company in Nasipit, Philippines; and operations of Padeco in Sumatra, Indonesia.

Traditionally, governments in Southeast Asia have viewed the jungle as valueless in its natural state; a rubber plantation or widescale planting of other cash crops seemed a better use of land. In Indonesia and Malaysia it was the colonial agricultural system that first transformed large swathes of forest into tree-crop plantations. More and more of the jungle was needed as the population soared. Conversion to agricultural uses—both conversion instigated by government master plans and informal conversion by migrants—remains the main cause of deforestation. Poverty drives the landless agriculturist migrants onto the forest. They burn trees and squat on the cleared land, and when that land is exhausted they burn some more. In areas where the population pressure is minimal, such as Sarawak or Sabah, encroachment may be prevented, but in parts of the Philippines it may not be politically feasible. Migrants often follow the logging roads and find degraded forests easier to clear.

In Southeast Asia forest and logging operations are dominated by politics. Rosters of those with interests in logging companies in Sarawak, Sabah, and Kalimantan read like a roster of who's who in the political elite. In Thailand many cabinet ministers have been involved in timber-related businesses, and a large number of parliament members are bankrolled by provincial timber interests. This makes it difficult for forest departments to enforce the rules for sustainable management of the rainforest. In addition, forest use practices by concessionaires, developers, migrants, and local populations, particularly near roads and urban centers, are responsible for rapid degradation.

Throughout Southeast Asia, but more spectacularly in Kalimantan and Sarawak, the scars of development appear among the tumultuous greens of the tropical rainforest: the felled trees, the bulldozers, the bright orange mud of the logging roads, and the smudges of smoke alongside, where slash-and-burn farmers have followed the loggers in. But there are also some signs of conservation and reforestation as governments begin to enforce environmental laws. Striking a balance between development and preservation is particularly difficult, especially with millions of young people seeking jobs every year in countries such as Indonesia where underemployment is a severe problem. Indonesia has announced its intention to reforest 50 million acres of devastated land. There are new projects to create buffer zones for shifting cultivators and to allow farmers to grow pepper and cloves amid the young trees, tending the trees at the same time.

Traditional communities have a thorough knowledge of forest ecology and regenerative processes based on centuries of experience with long-rotation agriculture. Traditional wisdom combined with more recent scientific experimentation can help regenerate forests under the stewardship of local communities.

Malaysia and Indonesia have instituted policies to conserve forests. In Indonesia the government requires those who are granted logging concessions to replant where they fell. Even so, a World Bank report indicates that harvests are running at 50 percent above the sustainable level. Indonesia had 565 forest concessions in 1989, most of which were in East Kalimantan. The number dropped to 500 in 1994 after the government revoked many of the concessions because of violations. In Malaysia the federal government has been trying to discourage deforestation; in 1993, for instance, the police and the army got new powers to round up illegal loggers and impose much higher fines. Occasionally, these powers are actually being used.

Both countries are keen to curb illegal logging because they want an industry that uses the wood rather than one that simply sells the unprocessed logs. In Malaysia a ban was imposed in 1993 on the export of logs from the state of Sabah, where illegal logging is rampant. Indonesia, Asia's largest logger, has an official ban on log exports.

ENVIRONMENTAL IMPACTS OF DEVELOPMENT

In Southeast Asia's breakneck race to development—an effort that produced impressive 8 to 10 percent growth rates in the last decade—the environment has become a principal casualty. Southeast Asian cities such as Kuala Lumpur, Bangkok, Manila, and Jakarta have boomed with flashy new shopping malls, office skyscrapers, trendy eateries, and discos. But they also are clogged with traffic, choking on exhaust fumes, and sorely lacking open green space. People in these cities continue to breathe in a toxic cocktail of carbon dioxide, carbon monoxide, lead from gasoline, and sulfur dioxide from power plants and refineries. In some industrial areas such as the Kelang Valley around Kuala Lumpur factory smoke and vehicle emissions blanket the skies.

For most governments around Southeast Asia, the imperative of rapid economic development and concern for the environment have seemed like contradictory goals. And in most countries, except Singapore, environmental protection movements are small, weak, and barely effective in raising public consciousness. In the Philippines, for example, the push for foreign investment has brought a spate of new Taiwanese, Korean, and other factories to specially designated economic zones in places such as coastal Cavite province outside Manila. But Cavite fishermen say the new industries have dumped increasing amounts of toxic chemicals into Manila Bay, polluting the waters, causing the deaths of thousands of fish, and depriving traditional small-scale fishermen of their livelihood. The Manila industrial area annually generates an estimated 6.5 million tons of waste, but the Philippines lacks any treatment facilities.

In Thailand, a decade of rapid growth and construction produced an insatiable demand for timber that has virtually depleted its forests. Thai logging firms now are turning to the forests of neighboring Cambodia and Burma. In the capital, Bangkok, the air—laden with factory emissions, construction-site dust, and vehicle exhaust—is so bad that health officials estimate it costs each resident $65 per month to treat pollution-related health problems (Figure 4.18).

Within the non-Western world, environmental problems could be summed up in three categories, depending on each country's level of development: (1) poverty problems, such as the lack of basic sanitation, particularly in

Figure 4-18. A Bangkok slum. Major urban centers of Southeast Asia are growing at a rapid rate, in part due to massive migration of people from rural areas. Many of these migrants live in slums such as this one along a canal in Bangkok, near the railway station. Urban environmental deterioration seems to worsen by the year. People discard their garbage and waste in the canal, creating environmental problems and huge health risks. (Photo: P. P. Karan.)

urban areas; (2) the problems associated with early industrialization, as in noxious factory emissions; and (3) the more sophisticated pollutants found in more mature industrial societies. Southeast Asia suffers from all three types of environmental problems.

In many places, there are laws protecting forests and prohibiting burnings, for example. But these are too often inadequate, or rarely enforced, when large financial interests of agribusinesses are at stake. Indonesia, for one, has had a law since 1995 banning the burning of forests to clear land. But satellite photographs show most of the fires have been started on palm oil plantations, as the industry eagerly expands to keep up with the growing international demand for palm oil products, worth about $1 billion to the Indonesian economy.

Malaysia's environment department similarly has approved a Clean Air Action Plan to, among other things, control vehicle emissions by limiting the number of cars on the streets. But the plan has been stalled by the government's cabinet committee, where officials voiced concerns that the impact on Malaysia industries would prove too onerous. Among other things, protecting the environment might require a change in lifestyle, such as the newly affluent urban middle class giving up their cars—something that they may not be willing to accept. The car has become the status symbol for the growing middle class, with a car craze fueled in part by homegrown auto industries in Malaysia (the Proton car) and in Indonesia (the Timor). The cars are not equipped with the catalytic converters that would make them burn fuel more cleanly.

The combined new vehicle sales in ASEAN's Big Four markets—Indonesia, Malaysia, Thailand, and the Philippines—in the first nine months of 2003 totaled 1.02 million. Car sales in Malaysia jumped nearly 150 percent between 1992 and 1996, from 138,831 to 345,134, and to 434,856 in 2002. The car in many ways has become a necessity because governments have invested little in public transportation. Buses and public minivans are jampacked. Malaysia only recently began building a subway system for Kuala Lumpur; in Bangkok politicians have been arguing over a mass-transit rail project for nearly a decade. In Kuala Lumpur, there are an estimated 1.3 million vehicles—cars, trucks, taxis, buses, and motorcycles. The city's population is only 1.5 million. Over 70 percent of the city's air pollution comes from vehicle emissions.

Only the tiny city-state of Singapore has strict environmental protection policies that, among other things, restrict the number of vehicles allowed in the city center at peak hours and impose high taxes and licensing fees to dissuade people from driving. Singapore also has a modern and efficient subway system that closely resembles the Metro system in the Washington, D.C. metropolitan area.

Malaysia stands as a classic example of a country in a hurry to develop, with a slew of prestige-enhancing megaprojects underway, but where environmental concerns have been given a relatively low priority. The government has pushed ahead with a massive $6 billion Bakun dam project on Borneo, despite conservationists' concerns over the displacement of 8,000 indigenous people and the loss of habitat for 800 plant types, 104 fish species, and 229 mammal and bird species. Malaysia is home to one of the world's tallest buildings, the twin Petronas Towers, but they were constructed on land designated for recreational use.

Rapid industrial growth and coastal tourist developments such as the one at Phuket, Langkawi (West Malayasia), Bandaneira (Banda Islands, Indonesia) have brought conflicts between development and use of coastal resources, in addition to potential negative impacts on the environment (such as pollution and beach erosion), society (such as increase in crime rates and the demise of local traditions), and the village-level economy (such as cost of living increases). Tourism development often over-exploits the environment. Development of infrastructure frequently spoils the natural beauty of the area and sometimes destroys ecological systems. This causes a variety of problems as areas are often left with lasting damage in exchange for short-term profits. In Indonesia, tourism development has been particularly damaging to the coral reefs and their environment. For example, in several coastal areas of Bali and many of the other islands of Indonesia, accommodation facilities were developed on the coastline. This development damaged coral reef habitats, which in turn destroyed coastal habitats. Coral reef damage is clearly evident in the Seribu Islands (north of Jakarta), Anyer beach, and the Pangandaran-Pananjung Nature Reserve (both in West Java). Much of the destruction is caused by coral "mining" for souvenirs for visitors. Still worse, coral is often used as foundation stone for lodging facilities. Kelor Island of the Seribu Islands no longer has reefs because coral was either stolen or destroyed. The island is now exposed to heavy waves and other ecological problems.

In September 1994 Southeast Asia had an unpleasant lesson on the consequences of deforestation and factory building. Severe air pollution kept people in their homes and threatened to close schools. Two ships collided in poor visibility off Singapore, killing two people. Kuala Lumpur's main airport reported two "near misses" in less than a month. Just about every major city in Southeast Asia is covered by a brownish pall of smog, visible from a distance. The smog is caused by unregulated or little-regulated industrial processes based largely on fossil fuels. Jakarta, Bangkok, Kuala Lumpur, and Manila are among the cities where the air contains more particulate matter or dangerous sulfur dioxide—or both—than the amounts recommended by the World Health Organization. At ground level, waterways have also become reservoirs of pollution. Less than half of the urban populations and few living in rural areas of Indonesia and the Philippines have access to safe drinking water (Figure 4.19).

These problems have been growing for several years. But three specific factors are producing changes in Southeast Asian industry's approach to the environment. New government regulations in the United States and Europe have forced the region's high-technology industries, in particular, to adhere to sound ecological principles in order to keep exports flowing to their major markets. Southeast Asian governments themselves, increasingly aware of the damage that pollution can cause, are now promulgating their own environmental regulations. And, slowly, Asian industry is realizing that cleaning up can save them money.

Government encouragement of environmental protection is most evident in Singapore. One imaginative scheme helped Singapore companies to deal with the CFC problem preemptively. In the early 1990s the government started to auction permission for companies to use specific quantities of CFCs. As soon as they realized the cost of successful bids, the island republic's electronic companies started to change over to substitute products and techniques. It is not just the elctronics industry that must follow strict government regulations in Singapore. Companies wishing to enter the Singapore Science Park must satisfy the park committee that, among other things, their work will not cause pollution or abuse land.

Figure 4-19. Threshing the rice harvest in Bali, Indonesia. Over the next several decades, Southeast Asia and the rest of the non-Western world will face growing pressures on its land, water, and food production systems. The principal driving force will be population growth and its rising food demand. So far, gains in food production can be traced to policies that emphasize national food self-sufficiency at the expense of sustainable resource management. A critical challenge for Indonesia and other non-Western countries in the next few decades will be to adopt integrated land and water strategies, good management practices, environmentally sound technologies, and better policies to support food production increases without putting potentially disastrous stresses on land and water resources. (Photo: P. P. Karan.)

Environmental Degradation and Loss of Indigenous People

Environmental degradation, particularly deforestation, has placed indigenous peoples such as the Penan, a cultural minority in Sarawak, in danger. Indigenous people differ from the rest of the population because they live closer to the soil and remain distinct from the dominant cultures. Most consider themselves caretakers, not owners, of the land. They have a large, perhaps pivotal, role to play in sustaining the earth as guardians of critical habitats and biological riches.

The Penan in northeastern Sarawak number about 7,600, of whom about 25 percent are settled. The remainder are semi-settled or nomadic and depend on the rainforest for most of their needs. Of an estimated 100,000 indigenous peoples who once roamed the forests of Sarawak at the turn of this century, only the nomadic Penan remain. As hunters and food gatherers, they moved through the immense wooded uplands in the headwaters of the Baram River in Sarawak's Fourth Division. Isolated groups of Penan ranged east into Indonesian Kalimantan and north into Brunei. The rainforest habitat of the

Penan, one of the world's oldest living terrestrial ecosystems, remained undisturbed for millennia. Until the twentieth century, human impact was slight. The Penan view the forest as an intricate living network, with the forest landscape linking the past, present, and future generations.

Today the Penan and their Dyak neighbors face a major threat to their society from deforestation and degradation of their habitat. Between 1963 and 1985, 30 percent of the forested land of Sarawak was logged. Another 60 percent of Sarawak's forested land is held in logging concessions. The banks of the Baram River are lined for miles with stacked logs awaiting export. The assault on Sarawak's forests started in earnest about a decade ago. Since then, the rivers have turned brown from topsoil runoff, the fish have disappeared, and the weather has become drier. Jungle animals the Penam depended on have been driven off by deforestation and the noise from the logging equipment.

The destruction of the local environment means that the Penan have to depend more on packaged goods from the outside, brought to them by the very logging roads that are responsible for their problems. Large areas along the Kemena River are totally devastated from extensive clearcut logging. Whole valleys have been stripped of trees and the stumps and underbrush burned off by villagers for rice production. The streams are brown with topsoil and clogged with logs and dirt.

Japan depends on Malaysia for 85 to 90 percent of its tropical wood imports. In 1992, a Japanese environmental group, the Sarawak Campaign Committee, staged a sit-in in front of Marubeni Corporation's office in Tokyo urging the company to suspend massive timber imports from Sarawak, Malaysia. The action was also a protest against the suffering of Sarawak's indigeneous people, the Penan, from commercial logging for Japanese general trading companies.

Marubeni imported the largest amount of tropical timber—845,000 cubic meters—of the Japanese trading companies in fiscal 1990. Japan, as the world's number one consumer of tropical hardwood logs, imports more than 10 million cubic meters annually. Of that, 64 percent come from Sarawak in the Penan homeland. The Penan are threatened with hunger because of the destruction of the rainforests they live on. Their proud culture and way of life that is built on the forest and land are being destroyed by the lack of sustainable forest management.

The Ecological Disaster of 1997

The haze, as the phenomenon is known in Southeast Asia, has been called the world's most widespread ecological catastrophe, wreaking havoc on a region already battered by environmental problems. The area affected by the smog extended over more than 2,000 miles east to west, covering parts of six countries (Malaysia, Thailand, Indonesia, Singapore, Brunei, and the Philippines) and perhaps 70 million people. It was an ecological disaster of huge dimensions and one that left environmentalists gasping at the political, legal, and diplomatic failures that allowed it to happen. The smog contained more than just wood smoke. It served as a kind of atmospheric lid to contain all the lead, carbon monoxide, sulfur dioxide, and particulates that the industrializing countries of the region pump relentlessly into the air.

The haze was produced by the massive forest fires in Indonesian Borneo and Sumatra, where small-scale farmers and some large agribusinesses have long practiced the slash-and-burn method of clearing land. Normally the annual monsoon rains douse the flames, but in 1997 the prolonged drought brought about by the unforeseeable consequences of El Niño has been blamed for the catastrophe. Though it is true that drought contributed to the fires, El Niño is a recurring event that has been documented for a century, and never with such terrible ecological consequence in Southeast Asia. Poor forestry practice is at least partly responsible for the fires and the haze. Moreover, most of the fires were deliberately set. Some were lit by farmers, slashing and burning as thay always have done, but most were lit by plantation workers employed by companies.

The fires are set on land that has already been logged. Fire is the cheapest and fastest way to clear the ground of misshaped and scrubby trees, together with undergrowth. It is then turned into plantations growing palm oil, rubber, and fast-growing trees for the booming pulp-and-paper industry. Setting the fires is supposed to be illegal. The practice was outlawed in 1995 after a previous bout with smog in 1994. Indonesia's failure to enforce its own laws worries its neighbors. In the worst-affected countries—Malaysia and Indonesia—political opposition is weak, and complaints about government inaction and complacency are easy to brush aside.

For environmentalists, the smog highlights several weaknesses in the region's societies. Many of the plantation owners are breaking the law, but enforcement is weak and susceptible to bribery and political influence. Political systems are often too rigid or undeveloped to make such widespread vandalism impracticable.

The long-term damage from the smog to human health could be enormous. The smog is heavily laced with polycyclic aromatic hydrocarbons, which are carcinogens. Small children are especially at risk. In the cities, where smog mixes with already dirty air, the atmosphere is even more dangerous. Many people are likely to die prematurely. The wildlife at risk ranges from insects and frogs to tigers, elephants, and orangutans, whose habitats and survival already were threatened by forest clearing. In the southern Philippines, birds were reported to be dropping dead from the sky. Some of the direct economic costs of the disaster included lost production at factories that were closed when the air became too dangerous to work in, the disruption brought by closed airports and seaports, and a sharp decline in revenues from tourism.

SOUTHEAST ASIA, CHINA, JAPAN, AND THE UNITED STATES: SHIFTS FROM GEOPOLITICS TO GEOECONOMICS

The strategic reordering of the world, underway since the end of the Cold War, is producing highly complex changes in the geopolitical structure of Southeast Asia. An essentially benign regional security environment in Southeast Asia is leading to a significant reduction of forward-deployed U.S. air and naval forces in the region. An important implication of this draw-down has been the acceleration of indigenous defense build-ups among all the ASEAN states, designed not only to protect national territories but also to project forces into disputed areas such as the South China Sea. For example, China, Malaysia, Vietnam, the Philippines, and Brunei all claim portions of the Spratly Islands. Even those countries that do not contend for ownership of the Spratlys (Thailand and Indonesia) still have overlapping 200-nautical mile exclusive economic zones with others that must be resolved if harmonious economic exploration and exploitation are to take place.

China has become a major arms supplier to Myanmar and has been aggressively marketing its deadly wares among other countries of the region. The Chinese also are building a huge naval base at Hainggyi island in Myanmar. Thailand is a big buyer of the Chinese missiles. The Indonesian navy has expanded with the acquisition of thirty-nine warships from the former East Germany. It is also buying a number of Hawk Trainer planes from British Aerospace, and is eyeing the United States for additional F-16 fighter jets. Meanwhile, tiny Singapore is buying more F-16s and is in the midst of upgrading its fleet of A-4 Super Skyhawks and F-4 Phantom jets. Neighboring Malaysia, which bought twenty-eight Hawk trainer and fighter jets, has also acquired thirty MiG-29 frontline jets from Russia.

Japan views Southeast Asia as a potential market, and needs Southeast Asia to achieve sustainable economic growth. Japanese business executives have taken it for granted that they should play the central role in the Southeast Asian economy, which they regard as part of their business territory. Southeast Asia has been a major recipient of Japanese manufacturing investment in the 1980s (Figure 4.20). The volume of investment is high in Singapore and the four ASEAN countries (Indonesia, Malaysia, Thailand, and the Philippines). The investment has been motivated by the Japanese desire to develop a division of labor in producing lower value-added products in the Asian countries where labor costs are lower.

Electrics and electronic machines compose the largest sector of manufacturing investment in Southeast Asia. Six Japanese companies are making video-cassette recorders in Malaysia. Hitachi has shifted its production of some electric motors to Thailand. Mitsubishi Motors, and the leader of its huge industrial group, Mitsubishi Corporation, have invested in the automobile

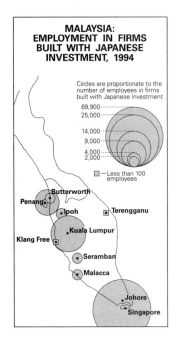

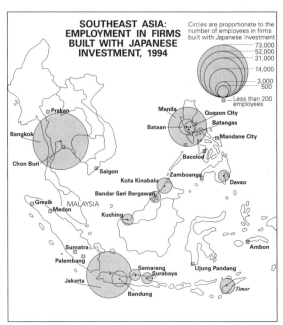

Figure 4-20. The pattern of Japanese investments in Southeast Asia: employment in plants built with Japanese investments. (Based on data from *Comprehensive Directory of Japanese Overseas Business,* 1994.)

industry in Malaysia. Mitsubishi's network of auto suppliers is setting up joint ventures with local companies.

Malaysia and Thailand are Japan's main manufacturing outposts in Southseast Asia. The outskirts of Bangkok and Kuala Lumpur are dotted with factories producing Japanese brand refrigerators, auto parts, televisions, and computer components. The factories enable Japan's highly paid workers to concentrate on manufacturing high-tech, higher value-added goods in Japan. In addition, goods shipped abroad from these foreign factories are not counted in Japan's trade surplus. As Thai and Malaysian labor costs rise, Japanese companies are scrambling for access to Indochina, especially Vietnam.

In part, Japan has been successful in Southeast Asia because its companies are willing to tread lightly. Japanese do not insist on majority ownership. They seem less fazed by occasional political instability. Almost all the countries in Southeast Asia attracting Japanese investment are run by authoritarian-leaning governments. Many consider stability essential to staying focused on economic development. For Japan the surge of investment in Southeast Asia offers an answer to labor shortages at home, and gives it a presence in the fast-growing markets and possibly a way around trade barriers in the West. For the nations of Southeast Asia, Japanese investment has helped fuel economic growth and brought them advanced technology that they can use to improve living conditions or make better products themselves.

Although Japan has been quick to invest tens of billions of dollars in the region, primarily in manufacturing facilities, it has lagged in integrating with local economies by promoting non-Japanese to top positions, listing on domestic stock markets, and setting up research and development centers. Likewise, Japanese manufacturers have been slow to source many components locally, instead of importing them from Japan. Matsushita Electric group shifted its product development to a new research and development center in Malaysia and stopped purchasing parts from Japan by 1997. Corporate Japan is watching Matsushita, which has appeared more politically sensitive to local demands than other Japanese companies. The degree to which other Japanese-owned concerns follow suit will help determine whether future trade relations thrive or turn sour. Still, fundamental technology development will stay in Japan. Even in Singapore, which has been particularly successful in attracting Japanese corporate research centers by offering foreign companies certain incentives, there are few examples of the transfer of cutting-edge technology.

Despite Japan's major role in the economy of Southeast Asia, its geopolitical role remains constrained because the specter of Japanese militarism in the region during World War II is deeply rooted in Southeast Asian emotions. There is fear of Japanese rearmament. However, the fear of Japan's rearmament for aggressive purposes fails to take into account the present geostrategic realities. The situation has changed so much over the last half-century that a remilitarized Japan would be in no position to repeat its territorial conquests of the 1930s and 1940s. The region is dominated in demographic and military terms by China, which has nuclear weapons and has embarked on a major program to modernize its conventional forces. It would be extremely difficult for Japan to dominate Southeast Asia by military means. Such action by Japan would be counterproductive, threatening its vital trade lifelines and access to resources.

Japan may be viewed as a potential partner, not as an historical adversary for Southeast Asian nations. It is a valuable source of trade, investment, aid, and technology for Southeast Asia. It could also be a countervailing power to China's growing military might. But recent reports that the former Imperial Japanese Army forcibly recruited 100,000 to 200,000 women from Southeast Asia, China, and Korea to serve as "comfort women," or prostitutes, in military brothels in occupied areas during World War II has further caused resentment in the region. Citizens' groups in Malaysia, Thailand, and the Philippines have compiled a list of victims for compensation from Japan.

The United States reduced its military profile in Southeast Asia with the withdrawal of forces from Clark Air Force Base and Subic Bay in the Philippines in 1992. However, U.S. policy objectives in Southeast Asia to ensure stability, trade, and investment access remain firm. In 1990, in a modest but symbolic expansion of the U.S. military presence in Southeast Asia, the United States and Singapore agreed for Singapore to serve as a base for increased U.S. training missions, visiting warships, and Air Force and Navy personnel. As a Pacific power, the U.S. forces will remain in forward deployment in Southeast Asia, but in a different form, to respond in an ad hoc fashion. And it will continue to pursue its basic interests of stability, trade, access, and democracy. In 2002, the United States sent nearly 2,000 troops to the Philippines in a combat role to fight militant terrorists alongside Philippine forces.

China has shown in the recent past that it is not afraid to use its military advantage in Southeast Asian territorial disputes. In 1988, China conducted raid and occupation missions on a number of the disputed Spratly Islands in the South China Sea. One such raid resulted in the deaths of 100 Vietnamese sailors. Such raids have stopped and China has said that it will put the Spratly Island dispute on the back burner until other issues such as reunification with Taiwan and its relationship with ASEAN are settled. Yet fluctuation in China's policy toward the Spratlys continues. In 1995 Chinese warships steamed up to the Philippine-claimed Mischief Reef, one of the Spratly Islands, and planted a Chinese flag; the raid came as a rude shock. At the same time, China has laid separate claim to some of Indonesia's Natuna gas field. The Spratly Islands, with the sea around them, are probably worth quite a bit in oil resources and mineral deposits.

China has added new fuel to the dispute over who controls the islands and resources of the South China Sea by awarding an oil exploration contract to a U.S. company, Crestone Energy, in an area near the Spratly Islands. Vietnam has given a similar contract to the Mobil Oil Corporation for an exploration area that overlaps Crestone's. This China–Vietnam dispute comes as Taiwan is asserting its own claim over the Spratly (Nansha) Islands, located some 800 miles from Taiwan. Taiwan maintains a military base on the largest island in the group, Taiping. Cooperation would seem a much more fruitful course than the current sharpening of tensions between Vietnam and China, with the possibility of face-offs between military forces protecting rival oil companies.

Two countries, China and Taiwan, now lay claim to all the Spratly Islands. Four others—Vietnam, the Philippines, Malaysia, and Brunei—claim parts of them. China's assertion of claims all over the South China Sea with greater force will destabilize Southeast Asia. The Chinese threat may force a new collective security arrangement upon Southeast Asian countries.

Many of the Southeast Asian nations also see China as a rival for investment. China's fast-developing coastal region is becoming more attractive for labor-intensive investment than Indonesia, Thailand, the Philippines, Vietnam, and Malaysia. The lure of gaining direct access to China's market of 1.2 billion consumers and huge pool of cheap labor is drawing investment away from Southeast Asia. To remain competitive with China, Southeast Asian nations will have to liberalize and deregulate more quickly, and move more quickly into higher value-added production. Several Southeast Asian nations are moving in this direction. Malaysia is considering tax-free benefits to attract investment in projects that will upgrade the country's industries. Others are gearing toward encouraging a transition to capital- and technology-intensive industries that have higher added value.

FUTURE PROSPECTS

The growing economies of Southeast Asia followed Japan's development model (close ties among government, industry, and banks) and Japanese experience after World War II. Malaysia's "Look East" program of the 1980s, for example, urged Malaysians to look to Japan for inspiration instead of the West. Among the lessons Southeast Asia learned from Japan was a secret to turbo-charged growth: discourage bond markets and keep savings in banks, which can better be trusted to lead businesses that support national ambitions in such industries as textiles, steel, shipbuilding, electronics, and automobiles. Like Japan, the rapidly developing nations of Southeast Asia often protected banks by restricting growth of bond markets through stringent regulations. The model was designed to support growth, the national ideology.

The big risk, playing out in Southeast Asia in 2004, is that healthy capital markets—particularly bond markets—did not emerge to support stable, long-term growth. Southeast Asian nations lag in channeling money into capital markets. Much of the nation's capital resources are in the hands of a limited number of banks. In Thailand, four banks accounted for nearly half of the lending. Southeast Asian bankers often gave dangerously low rates to poorly conceived projects just because borrowers were well connected. A developed bond market better avoids excess because the market forces decide who gets money and at what rate.

Japan was successful when it used banks to direct capital in industries such as automobiles and consumer electronics, but partly because Japan was the first to do so. Southeast Asian bankers funded similar ambitions. Even though the region has higher savings rates, capital markets failed to meet the capital needs, and companies relied on financing from abroad. Such foreign borrowing widened Southeast Asian capital deficits in 1997, and contributed to the collapse of local currencies and declines in foreign investment.

With their booming economies weakened by financial mismanagement, the future rapid growth of Southeast Asian economies has been thrown into doubt. Thailand, the hardest hit by the financial crisis, received a bailout package from the International Monetary Fund. Indonesia also has received help from the Fund and has been asked to swallow bitter economic medicine. And the Philippines, which has been hurrying to catch up with its neighbors, has been left struggling not to collapse. Malaysia has been forced to put some of its grandiose projects on hold. Singapore's economy is in line for a long-awaited upturn with the recovery in the global economy, and the gross domestic product is expected to accelerate an average of 4.9 percent in 2004–2005.

Of all the Southeast Asian economies, it was Thailand's that grew most quickly and was most at risk. It borrowed most heavily in foreign currency to finance its growth, indulged the most in vanity projects such as four-star hotels, golf courses, and ill-conceived business ventures; and extended loans most profligately in an overbuilt property market. Each of the affected nations has its own story: the heedless spending of Thailand, the careful management tainted with corruption in Indonesia, the overambitiousness of Malayasia, the stirrings of growth in the Philippines. As the foreign money poured in, all of them, to one extent or another, squandered their new wealth through inefficiency and self-indulgence. Thailand demonstrates most vividly the costs of the downturn: collapsing banks, stalled construction sites, empty new office buildings and half-empty hotels, rising prices, spreading joblessness, and an increasingly restive public.

If Southeast Asian nations take some tough steps to make their economies more efficient, the resource-rich area from the vast Indonesian archipelago in the south to Myanmar, Laos, and Vietnam in the north could emerge as one of the world's most dynamic political and economic regions. The free-market economies of Southeast Asia can move ahead again with economic growth. The command economies of Myanmar, Laos, and Vietnam have no choice but to change and liberalize. There is hope that foreign investments may revive their transitional economies. Terrorism and religious and ethnic mistrust between Muslims and Christians, Malay and Thai, and Khmer and Vietnamese will hamper growth. There could be more conflict, and sovereignty over the Spratly Islands in South China Sea is disputed among several Southeast Asian nations and China. Against this background Southeast Asia could find economic development and integration major challenges not only for regional prosperity but also for peace and stability in the twenty-first century.

FURTHER READINGS

Bresnan, John. 1994. *From Dominoes to Dynamos: The Transformation of Southeast Asia.* New York: Council on Foreign Relations Press.

Canoy, R. 1987. *The Quest for Mindanao Independence.* Cagayan de Oro City: Mindanao Post Publishing Company.

Che Man, W.K. 1990. *Muslim Separatism: The Moros of Southern Philippines and the Malays of Southern Thailand.* Singapore: Oxford University Press.

Davis, Wade and Tom Henley. 1993. *Penan: Voice for the Borneo Rainforest.* New York: Pomegranate Press.

Duiker, William J. 1995. *Vietnam: Revolution in Transition.* Boulder, CO: Westview Press.

Dutt, Ashok K, ed. 1996. *Southeast Asia: A Ten Nation Region.* Norwell, MA: Kluwer Academic Publishers.

Gregor, James. 1989. *In the Shadow of the Giants:The Major Powers and the Security of Southeast Asia.* Palo Alto: Stanford University Press.

Karan, P.P. and Chris Jasparro, 2000. Geographic Pattern of Japanese Foreign Investment in Southeast Asia. *Reitaku International Journal of Economic Studies* 8:13–30.

McNamara, Robert. 1995. *In Retrospect: The Tragedy and Lessons of Vietnam.* New York: Times Books.

Pluvier, J. M. 1995. *Historical Atlas of South-East Asia.* Leiden: E. J. Brill.

SarDesai, D. R. 1994. *Southeast Asia: Past and Present.* Boulder, CO: Westview Press.

Steinberg, David Joel. 1994. *The Philippines: A Singular and a Plural Place.* Boulder, CO: Westview Press.

Truong, Thanh-Dam. 1990. *Sex, Money, and Morality: Prostitution and Tourism in Southeast Asia.* London: Zed Books.

Ulack, R. and G. Pauer. 1988. *Atlas of Southeast Asia.* New York: Macmillan.

Chapter 5

The Indian Subcontinent

Stretching from Pakistan to the borders of Myanmar (Burma), from the Himalaya to the Indian Ocean, the Indian cultural realm embraces seven nations and more than a fifth of humankind. It presents a number of perplexing contrasts and problems. For example, there is on the one hand a sense of overriding unity throughout the whole sweep of long history, and on the other there is a baffling degree of local and regional variation. Within this area one encounters a rich and bewildering diversity of peoples, the ever-changing manifestations of four and a half millenia of civilization and interaction between indigenous and foreign peoples. The abiding heartland of Hinduism and the cultural hearth of Buddhism, the Indian subcontinent also includes more Muslims than the whole of the Islamic Middle East and approximately 25 million Christians. Not only in religion, but also in philosophy, mathematics, astronomy, art, architecture, music, dance, literature, psychology, and medicine, the contribution of the Indian cultural realm to our common human heritage is enormous.

The Indian subcontinent's huge emerging market represents one of the last untapped economic frontiers in the world. India's middle class alone has nearly 300 million people and is growing by 5 percent per year. This rivals the total population of the United States. Strong institutional and legal framework, an English-speaking professional and entrepreneurial class, and impressive scientific and technical skills are additional advantages for Americans, Europeans, and Japanese doing business in the region.

Both fundamanetal unity and internal diversity accurately characterize the Indian subcontinent. It is unique and distinct from other great cultural regions of the world in the same sense that Europe or China is unique and distinct. The cultural frontiers of this region are closely defined and have remained remarkably constant, partly because the physical frontiers are clearly marked.

To the northwest, north, and northeast, massive mountain ranges, including some of the highest peaks in the world, separate this cultural area from the rest of Asia. To the south, southeast, and southwest, it is effectively contained by the wide expanses of ocean. The Indian subcontinent is comparable in size to western Europe (Figure 5.1).

Yet despite its size and importance, the Indian subcontinent remains little understood in the Western world. Furthermore, much of what most Americans know is incorrect, largely because classical tradition, modern romantic authors, Hollywood films, television, and the popular press have combined to portray India in extreme terms of stunning wealth or abject poverty, of unbridled violence or pacifism, of gross sexuality or spiritualism—and sometimes all of the above. How many of us know that India is the world's most populous democracy, has the third-largest pool of scientific and technical personnel, ranks among the ten leading industrial powers, and produces more feature-length films than any other country? How many recognize the intellectual debt of Emerson and Thoreau to the Upanishads, of Gandhi to Thoreau, and of Martin Luther King to Gandhi?

Figure 5-1. Darjeeling, located at an altitude of 7,500 feet in eastern Himalaya, lies in the backdrop of the Great Himalayan Range with fine views of Kanchenjunga peak, the third-highest peak in the world. Dominating the entire northern borders of the Indian subcontinent, the Himalaya stretch for over 1,500 miles from the Pamirs in the northwest to the borders of Burma in the northeast. The Himalaya provide dramatic barrier between the subcontinent and the Tibetan region of China. The scale of the Himalaya is unparalleled anywhere in the world; of the 94 mountain peaks above 22,000 feet, all but two are in the Himalaya. (Photo: P. P. Karan.)

For centuries there have been strong economic, political, and strategic ties between the Indian subcontinent and the West. The lure of India's wealth provided the impetus for the Age of Discovery and the riches extracted from India helped sustain England's Industrial Revolution. Always renowned for its handicrafts, India now has a highly diversified industrial base. It is expected to increase substantially its share of the world's manufacturing output in the coming decades and is becoming an attractive field for Western investment and an expanding market for Western goods.

Politically, the stability of Indian democracy provides a model for other developing nations. Over the past half-century millions of Western tourists, business people, and students have visited the countries of the Indian subcontinent. More than a million from the subcontinent have, in recent years, become citizens of the United States, greatly enriching its social and cultural milieu. Their professional attainments, creativity, and industry are epitomized by the fact that Indians currently have the highest per capita income of any ethnic group in the United States. Astrophysicist (and Nobel laureate) Subrahmanyan Chandrashekara, geneticist Har Gobind Kohorana (also a Nobel laureate), orchestra conductor Zubin Mehta, and writers Anita Desai, Kamala Markandaya, Gita Mehta, Jhumpa Lahiri, and Bharat Mukherjee are but a few among many Americans of Indian origin who have achieved eminence in their respective fields.

ENVIRONMENTAL DIVERSITY

Lying between two distinctly different types of environments—the arid and semi-arid lands of southwestern Asia and the rice-producing, wet monsoon lands of Southeast Asia—the Indian subcontinent exhibits physical and economic characteristics of each. Until 1947 this entire area was under British colonial rule or hegemony. At that time the former British Indian Empire, which had existed for nearly 190 years, was brought to an end. The new nations of India, Pakistan, and Sri Lanka came into being, and the older nations of Nepal, Bhutan, and Afghanistan (all under British influence) emerged from isolation. In 1971 Bangladesh was formed in the area previously called East Pakistan, as a result of the defeat and surrender of West Pakistan forces.

Three major geographic regions exist in the Indian subcontinent: (1) the central and southern uplands of Indian peninsula, (2) the northern mountain system comprising the Himalaya and associated ranges, and (3) the Indo-Gangetic alluvial lowland between peninsular India and Himalaya (Figure 5.2).

The surface of peninsular India is made up of plateaus seldom rising more than 2,000 feet. Several hills rise from the plateau surface to heights of more than 3,000 feet, and in the south the Nilgiri Hills rise to an elevation of more than 8,000 feet. To the west of the plateau are the Western Ghats, an

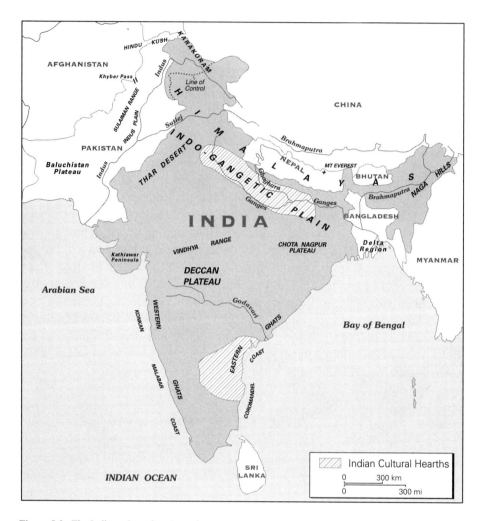

Figure 5-2. The Indian subcontinent's environmental setting and historic core areas.

unbroken chain of hill-ranges extending south of Malabar. On the eastern side of the peninsula is the broken and discontinuous line of hilly country called the Eastern Ghats. The northernmost part of the peninsular highlands is formed by the Aravalli Range, which terminates south of Delhi. To the northeast the Chota Nagpur Plateau of Bihar forms the eastern extremity of the peninsular highlands. The island of Sri Lanka comprising complex hill land with broad coastal lowland has many characteristics similar to the uplands of peninsular India.

Centuries ago, the southern part of peninsular India was the center of old Hindu empires and a civilization that, in many pockets, never fell under the control or influence of the Islamic conquerors from the Northwest Frontier or their descendants, who conquered most of India. This is a land of Dravidian temples, old towns where fresh spices perfume the evening air, tropical beaches, and shaded inland waterways. Though predominantly Hindu, it remains a successfully polyglot region spiritually and linguistically. Strong and growing Christian churches were established well in advance of the arrival of foreign missionaries. According to history that slips into legend, St. Thomas the Apostle brought Christianity to India in the first century, long before most Europeans practiced the new faith. Jewish settlements sprang up too. The British Empire in India began here in the seventeenth century, with the establishment of a trading post in Madras, now renamed Chennai.

The second geographic region, the mountainous area of the Himalaya, comprises a series of several more or less parallel ranges intersected by enormous steep-sided valleys and gorges. Their width is between 100 and 250 miles, comprising many minor ranges, and the length of the central axial range, the Great Himalaya is about 1500 miles. The Great Himalaya and associated ranges form one of the most formidable topographic barriers to communications in the world. Although crossed by numerous caravan routes, the highest passes are nearly three miles in height; new highways now pierce the mountain wall from Tibet to Nepal, and Sinkiang to Pakistan. The mountains are continued to the west in Pakistan and Afghanistan. In Afghanistan the Hindu Kush mountains comprise a complex, rugged region close to the borders of the Republic of Tajikistan. South of the Hindu Kush is the narrow alluvial plain of Kabul River, in which the city of Kabul, the capital of Afghanistan, is located. Beyond this, to the south, lies the complex mountainous region of Hazara. The famous Khyber Pass (3,450 feet) in the mountains provides the route between the city of Kabul and the plains of Pakistan.

The third geographic division, the great alluvial plain of the Indus, Ganges, and Brahmaputra, stretches from the Indus delta in Pakistan in a contiguous belt across northern India to the Ganges-Brahmaputra delta in Bangladesh. Covering an area of about 300,000 square miles, this region is of great historic and economic importance; it has been the principal theater of Indian history and its cultivated land supports the bulk of the population of India, Pakistan, and Bangladesh. In the west the Indus, born of five mighty tributaries (Sutlej, Ravi, Beas, Jhelum, and Chenab) streaming out of the Himalaya, flows southwest to the Arabian Sea. Fed by rivers from both the Himalaya and peninsular India, the Ganges flows eastward to the Bay of Bengal. It shares a common delta with the Brahmaputra River, which rises in Tibet and enters the plains of India through a deep gorge in the Himalaya (Figure 5.3).

Everywhere in the Indian subcontinent the climate is dominated by the seasonal shift of winds—an inflow of warm, water-saturated winds from the Indian Ocean in summer and an outflow of cold, dry winds from the land in winter—which determine the seasonal rhythm of rains known as the monsoon. The region alternates between luxuriant green during the monsoon rain from mid-June to October and drab brown of the dry season (March to May). The latitudinal range from south to north provides broad temperature differences, and the east–west extent affects the influence of the Arabian Sea and Bay of Bengal as sources of moisture for rainfall. The northwestern part

Figure 5-3. The Brahmaputra Valley, Assam, nearly 500 miles long and 50 miles wide, forms the eastern part of the northern alluvial plains of India. Generations of farmers have practiced agriculture in the Brahmaputra Valley with enormous subtlety and sensitivity to their environment. The boundary between the valley and the Himalayan ranges is a zone of continuing violent earth movements with earthquakes common from the western borderlands of Pakistan, through India, Nepal, and Bhutan to the Brahmaputra Valley. (Photo: P. P. Karan.)

of India and Pakistan have the least rainfall (varying from less than 10 inches in the Thar Desert to 15 inches in some favored areas), and much of Deccan Plateau of peninsular India receives an average of only 20 inches annually. The Indira Gandhi Canal, which taps the water of the Sutlej, was completed in 1987 to irrigate 1.4 million hectares of cultivated land in the Thar Desert of India along the India–Pakistan border. Rains in excess of 80 inches a year fall in the Ganges delta of Bangladesh and eastern India, along the west coast of India, and in southwestern Sri Lanka.

HISTORICAL EVOLUTION

Indus Valley Civilization (2500–1500 B.C.)

The Indian subcontinent has an unbroken literary heritage of thousands of years dating back to the time of the *Rig-Veda* (mid-second millennium B.C., the oldest literary work in any Indo-European language) and an even longer record of high civilization, beginning with the Indus culture which flourished as early as the mid-third millennium B.C. At about that time a sophisticated urban culture rapidly arose, hinged on the two cities of Harappa (near Lahore) and

Mahenjo-daro (near Larkana in Sind) and extending from Rupar in the present Indian state of Punjab (where the Sutlej emerges from the hills) to the Arabian Sea, Gujarat, and the Gulf of Cambay. The cities were laid out in grid patterns with efficient drainage systems, writing was practiced in a script as yet undeciphered, and trade was carried on by sea with Sumerians of ancient Iraq.

The Indus Valley or Harappan culture lasted for about a thousand years, in a state of apparently static prosperity. Toward the end of this period there are signs of decay, but the end seems to have come as suddenly as its beginning. Natural upheavals such as floods may have played a part, but the main cause may have been violent overthrow by more vigorous invaders. These were the Indo-Aryans, a complex of tribes speaking prototypes of the Aryan family of languages. At this time, in the second millennium B.C., they were on the move and were about to enter Europe as the Greeks, Asia Minor as the Mitanni, Persia as the Iranian-speaking Avesti, and India as the fair-skinned Aryans.

Aryan Period (1500 B.C.–1206 A.D.)

Blue-eyed, fair-skinned, tall and vigorous Aryan peoples probably came in migratory waves. A pastoral people with an aristocratic organization, they spread over Sind, the Punjab, tending their cattle; they celebrated their arrival by composing hymns to the nature deities they worshipped, now enshrined in the oldest Aryan literature, the *Rig-Veda*. They moved through the Punjab and into the Ganges Valley. Physical and cultural mixture with the local population took place, agriculture began, and cities appeared, but not on the old sites of cities.

North India thus entered on the epic or late Vedic period, historically obscure but culturally rich. It was during this time, from about 1200 to 600 B.C., that the core of the two great epics, the *Ramayana* and the *Mahabharata,* were probably composed. The center of settlements had moved eastward to around the upper Jamuna and Ganges. The river capitals were Delhi (Indraprastha) and Hastinapur. The pastoralists of the Punjab had now become agriculturists, centered on capital cities with palaces and temples. They drove chariots to battle, they had begun to admit gods connected with earlier tradition to their pantheon, and they were developing the caste system. The Indo-Aryans had become Hindus.

About 600 B.C. the clash of cults produced a series of universal religions, and organized kingdoms began to develop into empires. In reaction to the ritualism of the Brahmins, Jainism of the sage Mahavira (died c. 467 B.C.) appeared, and the religion of Gautama, the Buddha (died about 487 B.C.). Hinduism itself, in response, underwent radical changes that produced a religion based on Upanishads and the Bhagavad Gita.

The first historical kingdom of Magadha appeared, and it is at this point that India and Europe had their first encounter. Alexander the Great's invasion from 327 to 325 B.C. was brief, but it opened the way for contact with the West through Persia.

The first pan-Indian state, the empire of the Maurya, was founded in 320 B.C. Chandragupta defeated Seleucus, the Greek successor to Alexander in the east, and established a bureaucratic empire vividly described by the Greek ambassador Megasthenes. His grandson was the famous Asoka (reigned 273–232 B.C.) who promoted Buddhism and preached nonviolence. The second great Indian empire, that of the Guptas in the fourth and fifth centuries A.D., stretched from the Bay of Bengal to the Gulf of Cambay and far into the northwest. It was an age of achievement and consolidation. Indian literature reached its peak with the poet Kalidasa; art, science, philosophy, and law all flourished.

In the seventh century A.D., north and northwest India emerged under new rulers, the Rajput chiefs. A network of chiefs with clan ties built up empires by personal prowess and lost them again through wars and revolt. This was the age of Rajput chivalry, a gallant, colorful, restless, and rather futile age which lasted with little change until the Muslim Turk invasion at the end of the twelfth century.

Muslim Period (1206–1757)

In 711 the Arab invasion of Sind started the Muslim penetration of India. But it was not until 1206 that a Muslim military empire, known as the Delhi Sultanate, was founded. South India remained under the Hindu empire of Vijayanagar. The Delhi Sultanate was overthrown after two centuries, and India, except for the south, was parcelled out into a number of successive kingdoms, militant and unstable. It was during this period that a Muslim community in India took form as a result of large-scale conversion of the local population to Islam. In 1498 Vasco de Gama sailed to India, and discovered the sea route. The founding of the Mughal empire in 1526 ended the organizational confusion. It's third ruler, Akbar, organized a stable, efficient, bureaucratic system of government.

Internal decay and lack of a vigorous governmental machine in later years led to the fall of the Mughal empire. The Marathas' power gave the empire mortal injury. It was on this scene of confusion that Europeans entered India.

British Period (1757–1947)

The British East India Company, founded in 1600, intially came to buy spices and silk, but soon took over the country. It intervened in Bengal against a rash and unstable Mughal governor. The resulting battle of Plassey in 1756 ended with the company's take-over of the rich provinces of Bengal and Bihar.

During the following decades the British control or hegemony of India extended up to Punjab (1849) and Sind (1843), while to the east Burma was absorbed in three stages between 1824 and 1886.

Prosperity for the common man remained elusive during British rule. The appalling, unparalled poverty and low economic level during the colonial period have been extensively recorded. Around 1900, the per capita annual income was "30 rupees or 3 pounds" according to Viceroy Lord Curzon's budget speech of 1901. In the frequent famines between 1871 and 1897, about 15 million people perished. Indian economic growth, in terms of per capita income, was almost stagnant during the Bristish period. Between 1860 and 1900, it grew at an average annual rate of .40 percent, and between 1900 and 1948 at a slightly higher .48 percent. At that annual rate per capita income would double in 160 years. By and large, colonial policy let the industrial revolution simply bypass India. As late as 1948–1949, India's share of modern "mining and factory establishments" in the net domestic product was merely 7.1 percent, with employment in those sectors at 4 percent of the total labor force.

Colonial exploitation and the arrogance of the British led to the formation of the Indian National Congress in 1885 to demand a share in the administration of the country. After World War I Indian political consciousness entered a new phase with demands for self-determination. The 1919 massacre at Amritsar, in which British troops killed 387 Indians, marked a watershed in the national movement. M. K. Gandhi carried the Congress into a nonviolent, noncooperation campaign against British rule. He extended the national movement from the middle classes to the masses. Gandhi also embarrased the British on their moral rectitude. The British had always prided themselves on building a righteous *raj*, but they were challenged on the vulnerable ground of conscience. The nonviolent technique of opposition also perplexed the British, for it seemed to put them in the wrong even when they thought they were right. In 1942 Gandhi devised the "Quit India" slogan. Indian independence was ushered in in 1947, along with the partition of the country into India and Pakistan.

The Partition

Communal riots following the Muslim League's "direct action" movement to secure the goal of the creation of Pakistan led to the massacre of millions of Hindus, Muslims, and Sikhs (Figure 5.4). It was in this environment of fear and hatred that the decision was made to partition British India to create a separate homeland for Muslims on the subcontinent.

There are two schools of thought on the partition of India. The first is that the partition of the subcontinent was not inevitable; it created many problems and solved none. It was an impractical and reactionary solution to the Hindu–Muslim problem. Not all Muslims chose to move from India to Pakistan. As a result, there are over 140 million Muslims in India today, making it one of

Figure 5-4. The partition of the Indian subcontinent in 1947 and conflicts following the division led to one of the largest refugee movements in the world across the borders of India and Pakistan involving an estimated 12 million people. Into India came nearly 8 million refugees. Two thirds of them came from Pakistan, the rest moved westward from former East Pakistan (now Bangladesh) in a prolonged and steady stream of migration. Refugees flood the road near Bagha on the border of East Pakistan. (Photo: UNICEF by Jonathan Weinberger.)

the countries with a large Muslim population. The partition created new problems, which in turn caused hostility and even war between India and Pakistan. Each has spent more money on its defense than on social services for its masses. The whole of the Indian subcontinent has turned into a trouble spot. The partition benefited none except a small section of middle-class Muslims who found new avenues of power in politics, commerce, and industry in Pakistan.

The second school believes that partition was inevitable because Muslims and Hindus had lived as distinct and separate communities. Muslims would not have lived in an India dominated by the Hindus after the withdrawal of British power. But if the partition of India was the only solution for the Hindu Muslim problem, then how do over 140 million Muslims still manage to live and work together with the Hindus in the villages and towns of India?

Since independence and partition from India in 1947, Pakistan for most of its troubled history has been plagued by coups and repressive military rule. The last coup took place in 1999 when a military general seized power from an elected government. In return for Pakistani support for the U.S. campaign in Afghanistan, the United States has given Pakistan large amounts of economic and military aid on the condition that it curb terrorism and make progress toward democracy. As Pakistan enters the twenty-first century, the situation is fragile. It is a country of impoverished multitudes, presided over by rival elites—the military, the Islamic clergy, the feudal landlords, the business leaders—all of whom distrust each other.

Post-Independence Period (Since 1947)

In the post-independence period all the countries in the subcontinent share the serious problems of poverty and over-population. Poverty is widespread in India, Pakistan, Bangladesh, and Nepal, with millions of people living below the poverty line in each country. About 25 percent of India's population lived below the poverty line in 2002. Nearly 35 percent of Pakistan's population of 149 million lives below the poverty line. Pakistan has a population growth rate of 2 percent a year, among the highest in Asia. The other annual population growth rates are 2.26 percent in Nepal (26 million), 2.06 percent in Bangladesh (138 million), 1.47 percent in India (1,027 million), and 0.83 percent in Sri Lanka (19.7 million). These growth rates operate over a very wide population base, resulting in huge population increases.

Regional separatist movements based on ethnicity, religion, or language continue to be a problem in India, Pakistan, Bangladesh, and Sri Lanka. Terrorist attacks in India's Kashmir; demands for Sindhu-Desh, Azad Baluchistan, and Free Paktunistan in Pakistan; a Buddhist Chakma state in Bangladesh; and the Tamil Ealam in Sri Lanka provide a bewildering diversity of regional movements for autonomy or separation. At bottom, all the movements revolve around a single issue: identity. In one way or another, most of the subcontinent's population will have to figure out how diverse groups of people can come together under common political structures. This question also confronts other areas of the non-Western world in Africa, the new republics in Central Asia, and western China. In India, the regional separatist issue emerged earlier than it did in other countries of the subcontinent because India has had a democratic system for over fifty years and, in a way, the issue of identity lies at the heart of democracy.

The survival of each nation in the subcontinent depends on peace between various religious, linguistic, and ethnic groups. India has changed political leadership in peace through several general elections, despite religious and nationalist passions that tear it apart. The hardheaded, canny Indian electorate have rejected politicians and those politicians have stepped out quietly. The world takes this for granted; so does India. But nowhere else in the world has a nation fragmented under colonialism not only come and stayed together in independence, but done it under political democracy. In Asia and Africa the leaders of other newly independent countries betrayed freedom, dragging their people from foreign colonialism to domestic tyranny. In too many countries, dictators cite poverty, corruption, and social diversity as excuses to avoid elections. In India, those ills spur democratic electoral change. What distinguishes a democracy is the people's right to reject those in power. In India, the world's largest and the non-Western world's most durable democracy, voters have done that over a dozen times since independence. They vented their anger at incumbents for corruption, inequality, religious discord, and a variety of local failures by voting them out of office.

The United States and India have two important things in common. One is political democracy and the institutions of liberty such as the free press and free speech. The other is the belief that diversity and freely chosen unity can strengthen each other. That idea built America and has allowed India to grow in freedom. It is now catching on in a number of other non-Western countries. One reason Americans find India different from other countries in the non-Western world is the vitality of its democracy, the vigor of its free press, and the freedom with which different groups defend their interests and press their claims. Major decisions have to be worked out over time because the nation must take into account how decisions will affect various groups of farmers, workers, and businesses. All citizens have and exercise their right to vote. The governing party has to consider also how its policies will be interpreted by the opposition party.

Fifty-Five Years of India and Pakistan

Widespread deprivation has persisted in India and Pakistan even though their first leaders set social progress as a national goal. Jawaharlal Nehru, in his memorable midnight address to India's constituent assembly on August 15, 1947, called for "the ending of poverty and ignorance and disease and inequality of opportunity." A day earlier, Mohammad Ali Jinnah had urged Pakistan's assembly to "wholly and solely concentrate on the well-being of the people and especially of the masses and the poor." It has not turned out that way. Successive governments have pursued other priorities at the expense of basic needs. Both countries greatly neglected investment in mass education and health.

India long focused on achieving what the British had not permitted in their bejeweled colony: building an industrial base and educating what is today one of the world's largest pools of scientific and technical experts. Pakistan concentrated on industry too—and on an expensive military for defense against its much larger neighbor, with which it has fought and lost three wars. Both tested nuclear weapons in 1998. Both also launched successful efforts to become self-sufficient in basic foodstuffs.

For all the similarities between India and Pakistan, there are significant differences between their economies. Initially critics doubted that Pakistan would be a viable country with two parts (West and East Pakistan) separated by the Indian territory. After the loss of East Pakistan, which later became Bangladesh, Pakistan's economy has grown more quickly, at an average of about 5 percent a year (compared with more than 3 percent in India). Pakistan's more rapid growth resulted mostly from U.S. influence on what was a major regional ally, which kept its economy more open to foreign trade and investment. India, on the other hand, chose a path closer to Soviet-style central planning. India's government took direct control of 40 percent of the economy, rationed business licenses to set up private factories, and restricted trade to protect domestic producers from foreign competition. India and Pakistan liberalized their economies at about the same time in 1991, but even now Pakistan's economy remains more open.

Agriculture remains the biggest employer in both countries, but India's economy has grown more stable and diversified so that industry and service sectors contribute three fourths of the gross domestic product while agriculture contributes less than one fourth. India has also surged ahead of its smaller neighbor in high technology, churning out customized software and launching satellites. To drive its economy, Pakistan continues to depend on a good cotton crop. Heavy defense spending has represented a major threat to solvency. Defense and payments on loans taken largely to finance the military have soaked up more than 60 percent of the government's annual budgets. In 2002, Pakistan spent 4.6 percent of its gross domestic product on defense, twice the percentage (2.3) India spent. Pakistan has emerged as the intellectual and trading hub of a loose network of nuclear proliferators involving Iran, North Korea, and Libya.

Since 1947 both countries have reduced poverty rates, to about 35 percent in Pakistan and 25 percent in India, based on their own standards. India launched waves of antipoverty programs. Many have been loosely targeted, inadequately funded, and dogged by corruption. In the 1980s Prime Minister Rajiv Gandhi complained once that politicians and bureaucrats gobbled up more than 80 percent of every Indian rupee the government allocated to help the poor. Pakistan's antipoverty strategy differed. Officials believed that higher economic growth would alleviate poverty, but the benefits scarcely have trickled down in a society still dominated by feudal landlords with large ancestral holdings. By comparison, India lessened the dominance of its rural landlords by imposing ownership limits in the 1950s. As a result, income appears to be more evenly distributed in India, which has more of a middle class. At least 250 million Indians belong to a middle class that Western corporations spotted as an attractive market after the economy opened wider.

Wages have been held down by large supplies of surplus labor, a result of galloping population growth. Since 1947, India's population has almost tripled, leaving it the world's second-most populous country. The population of Pakistan—which in 1947 was West Pakistan, the less-populous half of a split country—has quadrupled in a half-century to 149 million. Pakistan's population growth rate of 2 percent a year is among the highest in the non-Western world. India, one of the first developing countries to adopt a family planning program, has brought its annual growth down slightly to 1.47 percent. Pakistan's efforts to control population have been weaker; at times, they have also lacked credibility. When two-time prime minister Benazir Bhutto waged her political campaign in 1988, she urged families to have two children, a voluntary limit her government later promoted with the slogan "Two Children, Happy Family." But by the time Bhutto returned to office in 1993, she had delivered her third child. Her second government dropped the two-child campaign.

Longer life spans have contributed to the population growth in both countries. The life expectancy of Indians, for instance, has risen from 32 years in 1947 to 63 years in 2000. Greater illiteracy partly accounts for Pakistan's faster population growth. Research conducted in India has shown that primary schooling of girls for even a few years reduces their birth rates because it improves their understanding of birth control information (Figure 5.5). In half

Figure 5-5. Major declines in fertility rates have occurred in countries that have recorded improvements in educational levels of girls and women. With 82 percent female illiteracy, Nepal has one of the highest fertility rates in the Indian subcontinent. In the town of Nepalganj, in western Nepal, a volunteer woman teaches girls to read. (Photo: UNICEF by Shehzad Noorani.)

a century, India has increased literacy from 14 percent to 59.5 percent; about 48 percent of Indian women can read and write. Pakistan's literacy rate is 45.7 percent overall and 30.6 percent for women. In both countries, population growth has been spurred by family demands for wage-earning boys as security for parents in their old age. Women keep bearing children to have more sons. Girls are treated as burdens not worth educating and to be married off quickly so they can move in with the husband's family. In India and Pakistan, girls marry at an average age of 18.

In both countries, devaluation of females has taken more deadly forms at times: killings of Indian brides whose families deliver an insufficient dowry, fatal stonings of suspected adulterers in Pakistan, deliberate underfeeding of both Indian and Pakistani infant girls. As a result, India and Pakistan are among the few countries in the world populated by more males than females. For every 100 females, there are 108 males in India and 111 in Pakistan. Each year hundreds of women in Pakistan's western frontier areas are killed by family members on the grounds that the woman's behavior (adultery or marriage without the family's consent) has damaged the family's honor and reputation.

The compounded effects of social deprivation in India and Pakistan make it difficult for either country to compete fully in the global economy. India, included on the U.S. Commerce Department's list of big emerging markets, likes to compare itself to fast-growing China rather than to Pakistan, but China's great economic advances have been built on a solid workforce that is better educated and healthier than India's.

But in contrast to China, there are profound democratic political changes taking place in India's hundreds of thousands of villages where most of the nation's 1,027 million people live and vote. The low castes, the poor, and the illiterate have been voting and joining political parties in growing proportions, as have women, who were on the fringes of the nation's political life. Many of these voters are flocking to the caste-based and regional parties that more directly reflect their own identities and interests and that now hold the power to make and to break governments. Remarkably, the poorest Indians are now more likely to vote than the richest ones. This turns on its head what was true in India only a quarter of a century ago, and what is still true of the U.S. and European democracies, where the prosperous are more likely to vote than are the disadvantaged.

The 1990s witnessed increased voter turnout, rising membership in political parties, and a deepening faith in democracy itself among the people at the bottom of India's deeply inequitable social structure. The percentage of people from formerly untouchable castes (Dalits) who are members of the political parties rose from 13 percent in 1971 to 19 percent in 1996, while the percentage of upper castes who belonged to a party declined from 36 percent to 28 percent. Politics has given the lower castes the power to claim a share of patronage—everything from housing to schooling to jobs in government.

Politics is providing a route to pride, dignity, and the confidence to fight back against the kinds of indignities the low castes suffered in the past.

CULTURAL DIVERSITY: RELIGIONS AND LANGUAGES

The people of the Indian subcontinent show wide cultural diversity in languages and religion. It is important to consider the lingustic divisions of the people because these, in large measure, form the basis for the current division of the Indian Union into states. The dominant languages of north India, Pakistan, Nepal, and Bangladesh are of the Indo-Aryan family, the most important member of which is Hindi, the language of Uttar Pradesh, Haryana, Madhya Pradesh, Bihar, and Rajasthan. Other Indo-Aryan languages with corresponding states are Bengali, Oriya, Marathi, and Punjabi. In south India the languages are of a quite different family, the Dravidian, and include Tamil in Tamil Nadu, Malayalam in Kerala, Telegu in Andhra Pradesh, and Kannada in Karnataka. There are also tribal languages and Tibeto-Burman languages in the Himalaya.

Religion is in the Indian subcontinent both a divisive and a cohesive force. Communal friction and disharmony are often largely a matter of religion, especially between Hindus and Muslims (Figure 5.6). It was along religious lines that the 1947 partition of the subcontinent into the two political units of India and Pakistan took place. Most of India's peoples are united to a greater or lesser extent by cultural traits and the consciousness of a common heritage, and these derive in very large measure from age-old Hinduism. In addition to the Hindus and Muslims there are other minority groups such as Christians, Sikhs, Buddhists, Jains, adherents of tribal religions, and Parsis. The central challenge of India is to accommodate the aspirations of its different religious groups. The secular ethos—flexible, eclectic, and absorptive—has helped India meet this challenge.

Hinduism

Hinduism, the world's oldest religion, has no beginning; it predates recorded history. It has no human founder. It is a mystical religion, leading the devotee to personally experience the truth within, finally reaching the pinnacle of consciousness where man and God are one. Hindus believe in diverse things, but there are a few major concepts on which most Hindus concur. The following beliefs, though not exhaustive, offer a simple summary of Hinduism.

1. Hindus believe in one all-pervasive Supreme Being who is both immanent and transcendent, both creator and unmanifest.

Figure 5-6. Both Hinduism and Islam have a visible presence in India today. Here in the Middle Ganges Valley city of Patna, Bihar, a Muslim mosque and a Hindu temple (on left back) stand within a few yards of each other. Muslims and Hindus have lived and worked side by side in India, which is home to nearly 140 million Muslims. The intermingling of people of different faiths is evident in the landscape of Indian cities. (Photo: P. P. Karan.)

2. Hindus believe that the universe undergoes endless cycles of creation, preservation, and dissolution.

3. Hindus believe in karma, the law of cause and effect by which individuals create their own destinies by their thoughts, words, and deeds.

4. Hindus believe that all life is sacred, to be loved and revered, and therefore practice *ahinsa* or nonviolence.

5. Hindus believe that a spiritually awakened master or guru is essential to know the Transcendent Absolute, as are personal discipline, good conduct, purification, self-inquiry, and meditation.

6. Hindus believe that divine beings exist in unseen worlds and that temple worship, rituals, and sacraments, in addition to personal devotionals, create a communion with these gods.

7. Hindus believe that no particular religion teaches the only way to salvation above all others. All religious paths deserve tolerance and understanding.

Hinduism is the dominant religion of India and Nepal. For a nonbeliever, Hinduism appears complex primarily because of the vast pantheon of gods and goddesses, and a complex caste system. But the majority of the gods and goddesses are manifestations of one God.

Hinduism shares a number of similarities with Christianity. An orange robe is a symbol of an enlightened person or a saint in India. Jesus is protrayed wearing an orange robe in Catholic churches. Worshipping the Divine Mother (Devi) is a tradition in the Indian culture that is similar to worshipping the Virgin Mary among the Catholics. The third aspect is the use of the bell in churches. The use of the bell is very significant in Hinduism, and most Hindu temples have bells. In a cathedral there are many small altars dedicated for different aspects such as healing, forgiveness, and mercy. In Hindu temples there are different deities with different names said to be different aspects of the same one divinity. The use of rosary, incense, and sacred bread (*parasad* in India) are common in both religions. The concept of the Christian Trinity of Father, Son, and Holy Spirit is comparable to the Hindu Trinity of Vishnu, Brahma, and Mahesh.

The Caste System

In the Hindu social structure there are four main castes: brahmins, the priest caste; *kshatriyas*, soldiers or governors; *vaishas*, tradesmen or farmers; and *sudras*, or menial workers. These are then divided into a myriad of subcastes, with *harijans* or untouchables, who do the most degrading tasks, beneath all of them.

About 14 miles north of New Delhi at Burari there is a tiny brick-enclosed compound called Mukti Ashram, or Liberation House, which is trying to spur a revolution against the deeply embedded forms of caste discrimination in Indian society. It is at the forefront of a growing movement in India to rescue the country's poorest and most vulnerable citizens, who are members of the lowest castes, from stone quarries, carpet factories, farms, and sweatshops, where they are bonded to labor contractors because of inflated financial debts incurred for food, housing, or family crises. Mukti Ashram is training men who have spent their lives as bonded laborers to wage a battle for civil rights. Trainees from Mukti Ashram are returning to their villages across northern India, staging sit-ins at water wells where untouchables are forbidden to drink, and demonstrating for higher wages. Untouchables make up about 20 percent of India's population. Mukti Ashram's staff lead songs, chants, and native dances designed to instill a sense of self-worth in men who have been taught since birth that they have no worth because of their low social status. Mukti Ashram's graduates have met with mixed results when they have taken their new-found sense of justice home. Some have succeeded in opening the village water wells to lower castes and have won better wages. Others have encountered staunch resistance and even violence.

Discrimination on the basis of caste is illegal in India but is widely prevalent in practice, which has ensured that lower-caste people have been deprived of education and good jobs (Figure 5.7). Since 1950, India has followed a policy of reverse or positive discrimination and has reserved over 15 percent of seats in schools and colleges for the untouchables known as Dalits. This has led to some spread of education among the Dalits (whose literacy rate is only half that of the general population). The Indian government also has a policy of reserving jobs for low-caste Hindus and backward tribes. Before 1990 22.5 percent jobs were already set aside for untouchables and the indigenous tribes. In 1990 the government reserved an additional 27 percent of all government jobs for low-caste Hindus. In 1992 the Indian Supreme Court upheld the constitutionality of the 1990 policy reserving jobs, or setting quotas, for low-caste Hindus. The court's verdict in November 1992 led to large-scale student violence in India. Opponents of the job quotas say that the additional reservations, which take half of government jobs out of the reach of upper-caste students, will lead to the promotion of unqualified people and heighten caste tensions.

India's untouchables (Dalits), exploited and oppressed for centuries under the caste system, are now beginning to demand their rights and assert and organize themselves politically. Although the prejudice against them persists, this self-assertion, by a group that comprise 200 million people,

Figure 5-7. Since 1947 federal and state governments in India as well as secular political parties have launched major efforts to fight discrimination based on caste and communalism, which are principal divisive factors in India. A sign on a public building in Patna, Bihar, by a political party calls for fighting these divisive forces in the social structure of India. Obvious forms of social discrimination based on caste and religion have largely disappeared in urban areas, but communal feeling remains an extremely important element in Indian social structure. (Photo: P. P. Karan.)

holds the potential to transform India's society and politics in a more egalitarian direction. India, for the first time, elected a Dalit as president in 1997; the election had immense iconic significance, and will further boost Dalit self-assertion. Many Indian states have witnessed Dalit self-assertion. In southern Tamil Nadu, there has been a virtual uprising on the part of a Dalit caste, the Devendrakula Vellalars, who have long been dominated by more numerous and powerful higher-caste Thevars. The Vellalars are now refusing to be hired by the Thevars for low wages. In Uttar Pradesh, India's biggest state and the world's sixth-most populous territory, a Dalit woman held the office of chief minister.

Traditionally, Dalits were not allowed to live within the boundaries of the Indian village, nor allowed to eat or drink with caste Hindus. They were forced into menial occupations, prevented from learning, and made to perform degrading functions such as flaying dead animals. This is gradually changing, but prejudices and discriminatory treatment remain, ideologically legitimized by social traditions and customs.

Hinduism today faces the problems of the liberalization of Indian society. The incidence of marrying outside one's caste and religion are both on the increase, and tensions are growing between Hindus and Muslims and Hindus and Sikhs. Economic growth would ease the tension, but tolerance must be pursued by all groups. Secularism is the basis on which mostly Hindu India set out at independence to build a democracy. Secularism in India is not a rejection of any religion; it is an assertion of the freedom of the individual to follow whatever path the person chooses to reach the ultimate good.

Buddhism and Jainism

Buddhism and Jainism had their origin in Bihar in the sixth century B.C. Jainism is practiced by only a very small population in India. Buddhism spread over a large area in Asia, but it is practiced by only about five million people in India.

Gautama Buddha, the founder of the religion, was born in 566 B.C. (624 B.C. according to tradition in Sri Lanka) at Kapilvastu in the Nepalese *tarai*, about 12 miles (20 km) from the Indian border town of Nautanwa. He came from a ruling family of the Sakya clan. He had an intense desire to find a way out of the sufferings that afflicted people. In his twenty-ninth year he gave up wordly life and wandered about in search for the Truth. At last his enlightenment, the Truth, came as he meditated under the bodhi tree at Bodh Gaya, India. He first preached his doctrine at Sarnath, near Varanasi, India. He died at the age of eighty.

Buddha advocated following the Middle Way, avoiding the two extremes of indulgence in luxuries and hard physical austerities. The Middle Way comprised a disciplined life with the bare necessities of life and the practice of the Eightfold Path, which included ethical teachings, mental control, and the acquisition of knowledge or realization of the Truth. The observance of Five Precepts, the essential basis for mental control and the realization of the Truth, is the primary condition for all Buddhists. These precepts are abstinence from killing, stealing, speaking falsehood, immorality, and intoxicating drinks.

True knowledge, or realization of the highest truth, is centered on three watchwords: suffering, impermanence, and the substancelessness of all beings. Suffering includes the desire that becomes a source of pain. Impermanence arises from the dynamic nature of all wordly beings and objects. Substancelessness means that a consituted being has nothing that is without decay. Nirvana is eternal, unchangeable, without origin and decay.

Buddhism, during its early period, was introduced from Kalinga (modern Bihar) to Andhra. Buddhism had the support of the Kusana king, Kaniska, who helped the propagation of the faith in Central Asia. There are two schools of doctrine in Buddhism: Theravada or Hinayana, and Mahayana. The fundamental difference between Hinayana and Mahayana is the latter's denial of the real existence of matter, the fleeting existence of which is admitted by the Hinayanists. Extreme altruism is one of the features of the Mahayana system: a Mahayana seeks the happiness and emancipation of others before his own. During the eighth century, Tantric Buddhism appeared. It prescribed five gradual steps for spiritual culture—rites and ceremonies, meditational practices for external and internal purity, finger gestures and physical postures, utterances of spells, and yoga—by which the human body could be transformed into a divine state. Meditation was the most important of these means. By meditation the Tantrics made the mind force rise to the center of the eyebrows, along three nerves in the backbone. When the mind force reached the eyebrows, the meditator realized the truth of the oneness of wordly forces. Hinayana Buddhism is now dominant in Sri Lanka and Southeast Asia; the Mahayana and Tantric Buddhism prevail in the Himalaya, Tibet, and Central Asia.

Sikhs

The name Sikh is derived from a Sanskrit word meaning disciple. The Sikhs are disciples of Guru (teacher) Nanak, who lived from 1469 to 1539. He was born a Hindu, but devoted most of his life to traveling and preaching brotherly love. He attacked the fanaticism of the Muslims and the Hindu emphasis on ritual.

Nanak was followed by nine other gurus who gradually molded their followers into a community with its own religion, language, and traditions. The fifth guru, Arjun, who lived from 1563 to 1606, compiled the writings of the gurus and Hindu and Muslim saints into a book of more than 6,000 verses known as the *Granth Sahib*. This is the Sikhs' sacred scripture, their only guru since 1708, and their source of prayer. In many Sikh homes, portions of it are read every day, just as devout Christians read the Bible. Sometimes it is read completely by a continuous relay of readers, a process that takes two full days.

The basic Sikh belief is that there is only one God and that he represents the abstract principle of truth. The Sikhs shun idol worship and give no special status to their priests. Their temples, in which the *Granth Sahib* is the central object, are called *gurdwaras,* or gateways of the guru.

A close kinship has persisted between Sikhism and Hinduism. Many of their festivals, customs, and observances are virtually the same. Until recently, many Hindu parents of northwestern Punjab brought up at least one son as a Sikh or found a Sikh husband for a daughter. Despite the gurus' contempt for Hindu casteism, the Sikhs have divided themselves into three hereditary groups: farmers, nonfarmers, and outcastes. Although the Sikhs—unlike the Hindus—do not revere the cow, they usually protect it zealously, as do the Hindus, and refrain from eating beef.

A main difference between Hindu and Sikh is in physical appearance. The last guru, Gobind (1666–1708), made his followers take an oath to wear their hair uncut, to carry a comb (which is usually beneath the turban), to wear a thin steel bracelet on the right wrist, to wear undershorts, and to carry a dagger. In addition, Sikhs are exhorted not to use tobacco or drink alcoholic beverages and to avoid the meat of an animal that has been bled to death. Many Sikhs have drifted away from these customs and are clean-shaven. This disturbs the conservative Sikhs, who feel that such unorthodoxy robs Sikhs of their distinction. Yet, on the whole, orthodoxy appears to persist more among Sikhs than among other religious groups.

The traditional Sikh occupation is farming the golden wheat fields of Punjab. But hundreds of thousands of Sikhs have moved to cities all over India. They have shown a flair for almost anything mechanical. In Delhi and Calcutta, they have nearly a monopoly on driving taxis. In the Indian capital, they are considered the best plumbers, electricians, and carpenters.

When the British ruled India, they found the Sikhs a prime source of military manpower. The Sikhs have been a militant community since the seventeenth century, when they reacted strongly to severe persecution by the Mughals. They have won many medals for gallantry, have been prominent in the Indian Army, and have dominated the country's athletics.

In the early twentieth century, many Sikhs migrated abroad. They make up the cream of the Hong Kong police force and the watchmen in Singapore. Others have thrived as businessmen in England, as lumbermen and railway workers in British Columbia, and as farmers in Southern California.

Guru Gobind gave his followers the surname Singh (lion). Today there is a Singh in the name of every male Sikh, and a Kaur (lioness) in the name of every female. Some Sikhs, however, have appended to the Singh the name of ther village. Their given names are determined by opening the *Granth Sahib* at random. A given name must begin with the first letter of the first word on the page. The name can be bestowed on a boy or a girl, however. This means that only the Singh or Kaur tells the person's sex. The title Sardar, which most male Sikhs use, is the equivalent of Mister.

There are four famous holy places of Sikh pilgrimage in India: Akal Takht in Amritsar, Punjab; Sri Kesgarh at Anandpur, Rupar District, Punjab; Takht Janamsthan (also known as Takht Sri Harimandirji, Patna Sahib), Patna, Bihar; and Takht Hazur Sahib, Nanded, Maharashtra). Each of these four sites is historically associated with Sikh gurus. The fourth guru laid the foundation of Amritsar in 1574 and excavated the famous sacred tank there three years later, and the fifth guru constructed the Golden Temple in the center of the tank. Anandpur, with the Sutlej flowing by and the Siwaliks in the backdrop, was founded in 1664 by Guru Teg Bahadur, the ninth guru of the Sikhs. Patna is the birthplace of the tenth guru, Gobind Singh, and Nanded is the site where the last guru was assassinated on October 7, 1708. The Sikh temples (or *gurudwara*) at Amritsar, Anandpur, Patna, and Nanded receive wide attention as sacred spots with inspiring traditions and legends associated with them, and they attract crowds of Sikh pilgrims from various parts of India and abroad.

Islam and the Hindu–Muslim Hostility

Islam was first introduced in the Indian subcontinent by Arab traders, who established their settlements on the western coast of India and obtained permission to practice their religion. Sind was conquered by the Arabs early in the eighth century, and northwest Punjab by the Turks in the eleventh century. The Delhi Sultanate was established in 1206. The invading armies of the Arabs, the Turks, and the Mughals were very small, and there is no record of Muslim immigration on an extensive scale. The large number of Muslims on the Indian subcontinent is doubtless due to conversion. The establishment of Muslim government was followed by the construction of mosques, which became centers for religious and social activities. The entire territory under Muslim rule was gradually covered with mosques.

The word *Islam* means submission to the will of God. Its basic doctrines are few and simple. There is one God, omniscient, omnipotent, the creator of the universe, of time, and of space, whose law governs all that exists. The Koran (Qu'ran) is the word of God, revealed to His messenger, the Prophet Muhammad, to lead mankind to the right path. Muslims believe that there will come the Last Day when God will judge all mankind, and give to each person the reward and the punishment due to him or her according to his or her actions. The basic commands of Islam are prayer five times a day, fasting during Ramadan (the ninth month of the Muslim lunar year), pilgrimage to

Mecca, and *jihad*, or striving in the way of God. War against aggressive enemies of Islam and the Muslims is one important aspect of *jihad*. The social precepts of Islam include the observance of the principles of equality and brotherhood among Muslims, of generosity and charity toward those in need, and of earning one's livelihood through personal labor. The totality of beliefs and practices is called *sharia,* or the path of Islam. The ruler was responsible for enforcing the *sharia*.

The vast majority of Muslims in the subcontinent are Sunnis. They insist on practice and strict adherence to the Sunni Hanafi, a code of jurisprudence; special emphasis on *sunnah*, the example of the Prophet; emphasis on the Koran as the real and immediate source of guidance; and belief in the khalifas of the Prophet.

The other sect of Islam is Shia. There are Shia Muslims on the subcontinent, but they form a minority. *Shia* means supporter or partisan of the claims and cause of Ali. They believe in the twelve imams (Ali, Hasan, Husain, Zain al-Abidin, Muhammad Bakr, Jafar Sadiq, Musa Al-Kadim, Ali al-Rida, Muhammad al-Taqi, Ali al-Naqi, Hasan Askari, and Muhammad al-Mahdi) as the rightful successors of the Prophet. Shias disassociate themselves positively and fervently from the khalifas of the Prophet, who, according to them, were responsible for depriving Ali of his legal and spiritual rights as a successor or imam after the passing of the Prophet. A basic difference between Sunnis and Shias is that Shias consider imams to have been chosen by God, like the Prophet, and to be infallible interpreters and exponents of the faith. There are relatively large number of Shias in Uttar Pradesh (Oudh, Rampur, and Muzaffarnagar) and Hyderabad in Andhra Pradesh. Ismaili, a sect of the Shias in India, believe that the succession stopped after the seventh imam. The major groups among the Ismailis are Khojas, whose religious head is the Aga Khan, and the Daudi and Sulaimani Bohoras. The Khojas are found mainly in Bombay, Poona (Pune), and Gujarat. Bohoras are also concentrated in Bombay and in Hyderabad.

The partition in 1947 gave Muslims a home in newly created Pakistan. But two fifths of the Muslims chose to remain in India. In 1951 Muslims accounted for 9.9 percent of India's population. They now constitute about 12 percent of the population. The Muslim population is increasing at a faster rate for several reasons: their mullahs claim birth control is against Islam; illegal immigration from Bangladesh is swelling Muslim numbers; Muslim women are held back by Islamic traditions; and Muslims are poorer and less literate than Hindus. Poverty, illiteracy, and Islamic tradition go together with high birth rates. More Hindus than Muslims practice contraception. In 2000 nearly 46 percent of the Hindus used some form of birth control, compared with 34 percent of Muslims.

What is the root cause of Hindu–Muslim hostility in the Indian subcontinent? One view is that, ideologically, Muslims everywhere feel it is their destiny to rule. They do not feel they can discharge their religious obligations except in an Islamic state, the Dar-ul-Islam. This notion has the sanction of the Muslim religious law, the *sharia*. It imposes a responsibility on the Muslim community living in a sovereign Muslim state to go to the aid of Muslims who live outside the community, especially in neighboring states under non-Muslim rule.

Although most of the Muslims on the subcontinent are converts from Hinduism and belong to the same races and speak the same languages spoken by other Indians of the region in which they live, their customs and way of living differ in some respects. A Muslim child is given a distinctively Muslim name such as Mohammed Ali. Sikhs and Hindus of northern India, particularly Jats, Rajputs, and Gurkhas, often have similar names: for example, the surname, Singh. Even Christians in most parts of India retain their Hindu names; only conversion to Islam requires a change.

The dietary laws of Hindus and Muslims are different. Hindus revere the cow. The Muslims eat it. Hindus, if they are not vegetarian, eat pork. Muslims are seldom vegetarian and, like the Jews, consider the pig unclean. Muslims eat the flesh of only animals slain by being being bled to death. Hindus prefer to decapitate their goats, and Sikhs consider eating the meat of an animal slain in the Muslim fashion to be sinful.

There are certain differences in the style of dress of the two peoples. Hindus wear dhotis; Muslims wear loose-fitting pajama trousers. Hindu women wear saris and sport a little red dot on their foreheads. Muslim women prefer the *salwar-kameez* or the baggy *gharara*. Muslim women are often veiled. Hindu women never veil themselves.

Hindus worship a multiplicity of gods, read many sacred texts, and venerate innumerable avatars. Muslims worship the one and only Allah, honor Mohammed as His one and only Prophet, and read the Koran as the only true revelation of God. Hindus go to many places of pilgrimage and wash off their sins in India's many sacred rivers. For the Muslims the only places of pilgrimage are Makkah and Medina, or for Shia Muslims, Karbala in Iraq.

When a Hindu falls ill he consults a Hindu *vaid* learned in the ayurvedic system of medicine. When a Muslim falls ill he consults a Muslim hakeem, learned in the *yunani* system of medicine. When a Hindu dies, he is cremated and his ashes immersed in a river or the ocean. When a Muslim dies, he is buried with his face turned toward Makkah.

In every Indian city there is a Muslim locality distinct from the Hindu. Even villages where the two live groups together are more often than not known by their religious character as a Muslim village, Hindu village, or Sikh village.

History casts a long and dividing shadow between Hinduism and Islam, and the shadow is a division of religion, not of race or language. Arab traders are known to have come to India from time immemorial. After the Prophet Mohammed converted the Arabs to Islam, these traders introduced their new faith into India. The amicable relationship between the Hindu and the Muslim changed when, instead of the peaceful Arab trader, India began to be invaded by Muslim armies. Early in the eighth century, the 17-year-old Mohammed Bin Qasim overran Sind. From 1080, Mahmud of Ghazni began his invasion of India. He destroyed Hindu temples as centers of satanic idolatry. He put thousands of Hindus to the sword and made a pastime of raising pyramids of skulls of infidels. Mahmud's destructive zeal reached its full frenzy in Somnath in Gujarat, reputed to be the richest temple in India. Mahmud slew its Brahmin priests, smashed the idols with his own hands, and looted the temple coffers of their silver, gold, and diamonds. Mahmud of Ghazni was only the first of a long line of Muslim idol breakers. His example was followed by other Muslim invaders and rulers. They killed and destroyed in the name of Islam. Not a single Buddhist, Jain, or Hindu temple in northern India escaped their iconoclastic zeal. Some temples were converted to mosques; idols and figurines had their noses, breasts, or limbs lopped off; wall paintings were charred beyond recognition.

Even the Mughal dynasty, which ruled India for 200 years and gave it its most beautiful monuments such as the Taj Mahal at Agra, had its quota of Hindu-baiters. Baber, who conquered India in 1526, raised a ghoulish mountain heap of 60,000 heads of Hindu Rajputs he had defeated in battle. He reputedly destroyed the temple of Ram Janmabhoomi—Rama's birthplace—at Ayodhya and built a mosque on the site known as as the Babri Masjid, 300 miles southeast of New Delhi. The site is the center of a bitter dispute between Hindus and Muslims as Hindus demand that the mosque be replaced with a larger temple. The Hindu campaign helped topple the central government in India in 1990. On December 6, 1992, the Babri Masjid was destroyed by Hindus. For most Hindus it stood as a symbol for a host of ancient religious grievances in a country where the overwhelming Hindu majority feels oppressed.

There were peaceful interludes in the two centuries of persecution by Mughal rulers, the most notable being the reign of Akbar, 1556–1605. Akbar abolished discrimination against subjects of different faiths, elevated Hindus to high positions, and entered into matrimonial alliances with Hindu Rajput princes. But the last ruler of the dynasty, Aurangzeb, is reported to have ordered governors of provinces to snip off the pigtails of Hindus and send them to Agra to be weighed. He imposed a tax, the *jiziya*, on all his non-Muslim subjects and forced many to be converted to Islam.

It is little wonder that the Hindus began to look upon Muslims as tyrants. It took many years of suffering and humiliation before the Hindus were able to hit back. One Hindu who struck back was Sivaji, the Mahratta. He defied the Mughals in central and southern India and ultimately triumphed over them.

Before the Sikh and Mahrattas triumphed they had to suffer at the hands of two more Muslim invaders. In 1739, the Persian Nadir Shah looted Delhi and massacred more than 100,000 men, women, and children. He took with him the Peacock Throne, India's famous diamond, the Koh-i-Noor (which means "mountain of light"). The Afghan Ahmed Shan Durani followed Nadir Shah and sacked Delhi more than once. Twice he blew up the Sikh temple at Amritsar and filled the pool surrounding the shrine with the entrails of cows. The Sikhs returned the compliment by defiling mosques. They forced the Afghans they had taken prisoner to wash the floors of the mosques with the blood of pigs.

The British rule in India encouraged Muslim separatism. Under the guise of neutrality the British gave Muslims more privileges in services such as the police and army than their numbers entitled them to. The British encouraged separate educational institutions; Islamic schools and colleges were matched by Hindu and Sikh schools and colleges. In public places such as railroad stations there were separate restaurants for Hindus and Muslims. Even drinking water booths bore signs labeling them as Hindu water or Muslim water. The British government set the scene for political separatism when it gave Muslims and, later, other religious minorities separate electorates in the election to legislative bodies. This policy encouraged political parties that represented only the interests of their communities, and kept the Muslims from joining the nationalists.

There is little doubt that secular India has done better by her religious minorities than Islamic Pakistan and Bangladesh. Indian Muslims have held and now hold positions of eminence. Muslims have been elected as presidents of India. There are now Muslim cabinet members, governors of states, ambassadors, generals, and senior civil servants in India. Pakistan's and Bangladesh's record on this score is a very dismal one.

DEMOCRACY AND HUMAN RIGHTS IN THE SUBCONTINENT

Given the fate of democracies in much of the non-Western world, the Indian subcontinent is a success story. Even though there have been setbacks for elected governments in Pakistan and Nepal, a majority of the world's democratic citizens live in the region. In recent years, the subcontinent's two oldest democracies, India and Sri Lanka, have shown remarkable resilience by surviving political assassinations, secessionist struggles, and violent insurgencies.

India is the world's biggest democracy, and its general elections, with over 640 million voters, are the largest organized activity in the world. Yet, possibly with the exception of India, the future of democracy in the region is by no means assured. Parliaments in most of the countries function less as deliberating bodies than as arenas for political warfare and manipulation. Political parties are mostly undisciplined and often appeal to narrow ethnic or religious interests. Judicial independence is inadequately safeguarded. All governments share a colonial legacy of overcentralized administration. People of the region are generally neither complacent about the future of their democracies nor unaware of the many challenges they confront. So far, the Indian subcontinent has shown that democratic politics is not dependent on high per capita GNP levels, but rather on cultural roots, tradition of tolerance and social equity, respect for law, and experience in operating democratic systems. A key feature of the push for transition to democracy among India's neighbors is that the pressure for change has come from the populace.

Institutional and legal bases for the protection of human rights are relatively strong in most countries of the Indian subcontinent. Systematic or widespread human rights abuses are rare, though violations of many kinds often occur. Nongovernmental organizations (NGOs) have been playing an increasingly active role in human rights issues, primarily through educational activities and the investigation and reporting of abuses. These organizations face considerable obstacles from suspicious governments, but have nonetheless made impressive strides in fostering an awareness of human rights conditions in their respective countries.

In India, human rights abuses have taken place in Kashmir and the northeastern states, areas where the government has suppressed secessionist movements. The Border Security Force, not the Indian army, has been blamed for the majority of human rights violations in the context of these ethnic conflicts. Relative peace in the Indian Punjab and Kashmir has reduced a major source of common human rights violations in India.

The ethnic conflict in Sind Province is the main source of human rights violations in Pakistan. Arbitrary detention and arrest, torture, and other abuses reportedly continue in the region, though some decline in extrajudicial killings has been reported in recent years. Paramilitary security forces, the army, and private death squads operating in the province have all committed violations. Human rights violations in Sri Lanka also stem largely from the country's ethnic and civil conflicts.

The abuse of political rights has declined considerably with the spread of democracy in the subcontinent. All the countries today have moved toward greater freedom of expression, the press, and organization. Still, given the rough-and-tumble character of the subcontinent's politics, violations of political rights do occur. Police abuses are also a problem, particularly in rural areas, but as with violations of political rights, they do not appear to be systematic. Rather, they stem from poverty, illiteracy, and local disputes. Efforts are being made to investigate and punish such abuses more stringently.

Throughout the Indian subcontinent women are subject to discrimination (Figure 5.8). By any standard—educational level, employment, or legal protection—women are subordinate to men. The lack of access to education for women, apart from being discriminatory, has negative effects on population planning and on social development. In addition to educational and social discrimination, women are often victims of practices such as bride burning and female infanticide. The use of prenatal diagnostic tests to abort female fetuses has contributed to sharply lower female sex ratios in a number of areas.

Figure 5-8. Gender inequality is a major problem in the non-Western world. In most of the non-Western world, women's status has not improved substantially. Promotion of education for girls and improvement of primary health care for women are important to increase equality of opportunity for women. A volunteer teaches English to a girls' class at the Raza Mustafa Child and Youth Welfare School in Karachi, Pakistan. With one of the highest population growth rates in the world—3.6 percent annually—and 84 percent female illiteracy in low-income urban areas, particular attention is focused in Pakistan on improving the situation of girls and women, so they have the opportunity to participate fully in their society. A fundamental reexamination of current social and political institutions with the goal of giving women equality with men is a major development challenge. (Photo: UNICEF by John Isaac.)

At the same time, some women on the subcontinent have long enjoyed opportunities not readily available to women in many other societies. Urban middle-class and upper-middle-class women gained at least limited access to professions such as law and medicine well before many of their Western counterparts. Women have been active in politics and government for decades, as is reflected in the fact that four of the seven countries have had women as heads of government, three of them more than once. Educated women have taken the lead in forming local and national NGOs that address a variety of women's issues and raise awareness in the broader society of the need for action.

Governments in the Indian subcontinent have moved to address human rights concerns, albeit slowly and partially. India has established a Human Rights Commission with power to investigate abuses of all kinds. India has also allowed a team from the International Committee of the Red Cross to visit Kashmir and invited Amnesty International to meetings in India. Sri Lanka, Bangladesh, and Pakistan have maintained ties with nongovernmental organizations investigating human rights abuses.

POPULATION AND DEMOGRAPHIC CHANGE

Within the Indian subcontinent, the huge population is distributed according to the availability of water. The well-watered Ganges-Brahmaputra Valley and coastal areas, having good soil and abundant rainfall, are densely populated. The drier parts of peninsular India and the arid west are relatively sparsely populated except in the canal-irrigated areas of the Indus Valley. Most of the population of Sri Lanka lives in the wetter southwestern part of the island; in mountainous and arid Pakistan, the Indus Valley with its irrigation agriculture is the main populated area. The population distribution and density is a graphic expression of the regional's varied natural endowments, and of the unequal agricultural potential of the Indian subcontinent.

The northern part of the subcontinent has higher fertility rates, lower life expectancies, and faster population growth than the south and west. The Indian state of Uttar Pradesh is the most populous, with 166 million inhabitants in 2001; it contains more people than Japan or Bangladesh, and nearly as many people as Russia. Fertility and mortality are also high in the eastern part of the subcontinent. The southern and western states of peninsular India are more developed economically and have lower fertility and mortality rates.

REPUBLIC OF INDIA

Demographic Transition

Since the first census (1871) the population of India has risen from 203 million to 844 million in 1991, and 1,027 million in 2001. About 16 percent of the world's population is in India, but the country accounts for only 2.4 percent (3.28 million square km) of the earth's surface.

India's population development since 1871 can be divided into several phases (Figure 5.9). The first phase (1881 to the 1920s) shows fluctuating, but higher, birth and death rates. The reasons for the high death rate were famines, diseases, and epidemics. Between 1893 and 1901 and 1912 to 1921, the high death rate lead to a population decrease amounting to no less than 41 million. The devastating influenza epidemic of 1918 cost 18.5 million lives. Until the 1920s India remained in the first phase of a preindustrial agrarian society, which was characterized by high values for natality and mortality. This resulted in insignificant population growth.

The second phase (the 1920s to 1960s) was characterized by the lowering of the death rate, but the birth rate remained relatively high. Improvements in public health service, hygiene, nutrition, and education resulted in a distinctively regressive death rate. This proved to be a major factor in the large growth of population during this period. Population more than doubled, from

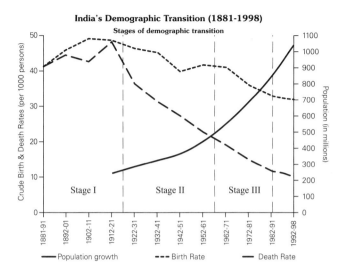

Figure 5-9. India's demographic transition: 1881–1998 (based on the Census of India data).

251 million in 1921 to 548 million in 1971. India's relatively rapid population growth during the second phase of demographic transition is identical with the experience of most other countries.

In the 1970s the demographic transition process entered its third phase, which brought with it a noticeable decrease in the birth rate, accompanied by a further drop in mortality. As a result, the decadal population growth rate declined slightly from 24.8 percent in 1971 to 24.6 percent in 1981, and 23.5 percent in 1991. India is experiencing a decline in birth rate; the total fertility rate has dropped from more than six children per woman in 1950 to 2.9 children in 2003, but is still above the 2.1 rates that would stabilize a population that already exceeds a billion people. The transition is occurring as India experiences extraordinary economic growth spawned by economic reforms introduced since 1990. India's fertility decline has been obscured by a corresponding decrease in mortality rates that have led to life expectancy rising from about 50 years in the early 1970s to 63 years in 2003. In the 2000s fertility is declining faster than mortality, and overall population growth is expected to slow down.

India's national family planning program had a vital role in lowering the birth rate, as did social and economic changes including later marriages, increased literacy, urbanization, industrialization, and the communications and technology revolution. However, the low status of women tends to work against the trend toward lower birth rates. Marriage customs and many other cultural traditions perpetuate the subordination of women. A reflection of the low status of women can be found in the wide gap between male and female literacy; nearly two-thirds of wonen cannot read or write, compared with just over one third of men.

India is now at the beginning of the fully effective third phase of demographic transition, in which the regressive birth rate dominates. Attaining the following phases of the demographic transition process (phases four and five) is at present a merely hypothetical matter so far as Indian population development is concerned. It seems improbable that India will pass quickly through the present third phase and enter the fourth phase, which is characterized by very low birth and death rates manifesting in small increases in population.

The recent successes in lowering the birth rate must be acknowledged, but continuing and increased measures are needed for reducing the births. Family planning was introduced in India in 1951, but has had little success. Noticeable success in Indian family planning has come only in recent years. In 1990 it was estimated that 41.9 percent of couples (139 million) in the reproductive age bracket used some form of contraception, averting nearly 106 million births. However, this has not resulted in a substantial lowering of India's population.

On a main New Delhi boulevard, next to a huge advertisement for a brand of condoms with the unerotic name "Obstruction," there is India's population clock. Its green, digital numbers glow with the arrival of a new baby every 1.5 seconds. By the time the boulevard traffic light has changed a minute later, another thirty-five babies have been born. A similar clock in Beijing would count thirty-three births a minute, while in New York you might miss the green light waiting for the birth of an American.

Unless India slows its birth rate drastically, its population, currently standing at over one billion, is expected to top the 2 billion mark in 2035, exceeding China's. This could be the worst nightmare for India's planners and developers. Comparison's are inevitably made between India and China. Beijing's authoritarian regime has been able to curtail population growth ruthlessly. The one-child campaign, started in 1979, led to extensive human rights abuses, with many women dragged into clinics for forced sterilizations and abortions. Female infanticide arose. These draconian methods did, however, reduce population growth. India's goal was to have two children per family by the year 2000, but that has not materialized.

What worked in China cannot succeed in democratic India. When the former Indian prime minister Indira Gandhi and her son, Sanjay, tried forced sterilizations under the 1975 emergency laws, international health organizations may have been relieved that India was, at last, doing something about its population explosion, but the Indians were outraged. They voted Mrs. Gandhi out of office. Press censorship was imposed as stories emerged of police stopping buses at roadblocks and herding men, aged 17 to 70, at gunpoint into tents for sterilization. This harsh exercise failed to dent population growth at all, and it gave people a lasting suspicion of the government's family planning program.

India is now struggling to balance its democracy with its demographic pressures. The national mood favors a tougher approach, and Indian states, free to adopt their own population policies, are experimenting with laws mandating a two-child norm for members of the village councils and civil servants. States are also increasingly turning to incentives—pay raises, or access to land or housing—for government employees who choose sterilization after one or two children. A move is gaining steam to revive a national bill limiting members of the parliament and state legislatures to two children. Critics point out that countries and Indian states that have most successfully limited population growth have done so by increasing education and work opportunities for women, improving health care, and providing a wide range of contraceptive choices. A decade ago, India embraced the conclusions of a 1994 United Nations conference on population in Cairo, which called for abandoning contraceptive targets, improving education and health for women and children, and offering multiple voluntary contraceptive choices.

Population experts talk of offering "cafetaria choices" in birth control. This means that Indians in rural areas should have access to condoms, the pill, the coil, and other contraceptive devices. A plane with condoms could fly over India and dump them across the countryside, but that wouldn't help if the people down below didn't have a clue what the condoms were for. The best long-term contraceptive is not the condom or the IUD; it is female literacy and the empowerment of women. Enhancing the educational, political, and economic opportunities for women is perhaps the surest way to curb further population growth. It is intuitively right to assume that women, as bearers of children, are in the best position to slow birth rates and that, if given greater opportunities, they will forgo continuous childbearing. Beyond intuition, there is empirical evidence. The state of Kerala in India, though poor, has reduced its fertility rate to replacement levels, thanks in large part to high levels of female literacy and education and growing economic opportunities for women. Couples living in high-literacy states such as Kerala tend to have only two children, while in the more populous states where fewer can read, families have more than five children. However, the population clock in New Delhi is not going to stand still while India dithers over educating its poor.

India's rate of population growth, stuck at around 2 percent per year for four decades, dropped to 1.4 in 2003, and experts expect it to decline further in coming years. Population growth is likely to fall to 1.3 percent by the year 2005. Why this breakthrough? The answer lies in relative movements in the birth and death rates. At the beginning of this century, the death rate was almost as high as the birth rate, so the population grew slowly. As health services improved, the death rate fell from 45 per thousand in 1941 to 8.4 per thousand in 2003. The birth rate also began to decline, thanks to higher incomes, more education, better health, and a government family planning program. It dropped from 45 per thousand in 1941 to 29 per thousand in 1991 and 23 in 2003. Since this decline was offset by the declining death rate, the population grew steadily.

KERALA: A DEVELOPMENT ENIGMA

India's southern state of Kerala, with a population of 30 million and per capita income of $298-350 a year, represents a development paradox. It is poor, but the male life expectancy is 70 years (compared with 72 in the United States), literacy is 100 percent, and the birth rate hovers near 18 per thousand (compared with 16 per thousand in the United States) and is falling fast. Despite poverty, Kerala has achieved the kind of social progress that characterizes advanced industrial nations.

Development experts use an index they call PQLI, for "physical quality of life index," a composite that runs on a scale from zero to 100 and combines most of the indicators of a decent human life. In 1981, Kerala's score of 82 far exceeded all of Africa's, and in Asia only the incomparably richer South Korea (85), Taiwan (87), and Japan (98) ranked higher. And Kerala has kept improving. By 1989, the score had risen to 88, compared with 60 for the rest of India.

Kerala has managed all this even though it is among the most densely crowded places on earth, holding the population of California squeezed into a state the size of Switzerland. Not even the diversity of its population—60 percent Hindu, 20 percent Muslim, and 20 percent Christian—a chronic source of conflict in the rest of India, has stood in its way. It undercuts maxims about the world we consider almost intuitive. Rich people are healthier, rich people live longer, rich people have more opportunity for education, rich people have fewer children. We know all these things to be true, and yet here Kerala is the counter-case.

An odd mixture of influences has been responsible for Kerala's social advances in education and health. In British colonial India, royal rulers, Christian missionaries, and a Hindu reformer promoted a social emphasis in development policy that has continued since independence in 1947 under successive state governments, beginning with an elected communist government in 1957, one of the world's first. Kerala's spending priorities have been social. One result of social priorities in Kerala is that its quality of life in some ways rivals Western standards.

Kerala remains the agricultural producer it has been since helping create India's ancient allure as the land of spices—cardamom, pepper, turmeric, and ginger. About 75 percent of Kerala's produce is unprocessed commodities, including coconuts, black pepper, and seafood. Amid unemployment that approaches 30 percent, one major export has helped maintain social peace: workers. Hundreds of thousands of Kerala's people work outside India, mainly in the Persian Gulf states and as teachers and nurses in Africa and Europe. Since India opened its economy wider in 1991 to foreign investment and trade, Kerala, with its predominantly leftist politics and aggressive labor unions, has discouraged prospective foreign investors. Quality of life is high, but there are limited opportunities.

How can the Kerala model (high quality of life without rapid economic growth) spread to other places? How might its successes be repeated in places like Vietnam and Mozambique? But Kerala also may offer a significant lesson for richer countries. Kerala is one large human population on earth that currently meets the sustainability criteria of simultaneous small familes and low consumption. Kerala suggests a way to manage not only the classic development goal of more material consumption, but also the goals of living lightly on the earth, using fewer resources, creating less waste. Kerala demonstrates that a low-level economy can create a decent life, abundant in the things—health, education, community—that are most necessary for us all.

The fertility rate is already at or below replacement rate in three states: Goa, Kerala, and Tamil Nadu. This is also true of many towns in other states. But fertility remains particularly high in four states in the Indian heartland:

Uttar Pradesh, Bihar, Madhya Pradesh, and Rajasthan. These states account for almost 40 percent of the population. Education and social services such as health and housing in these states are poor, and incomes are low. Still, all the factors affecting fertility—literacy, infant mortality, poverty, age of marriage, and acceptance of family planning—also have improved in these states in the past decade. In Bihar, long regarded as the slough of despond, infant mortality has fallen to 72 per thousand, less than the national average and comparable with China's 69 per thousand in 1970. In the four laggard states, the fertility rate in towns is one-third lower than the rate in rural areas. The people of the towns will eventually influence those in the countryside.

Rural and Urban Population

Nearly 72 percent of India's population is rural, living in over half a million villages (Figure 5.10). The average population of a village was just over 1,000 in 2001. The rural nature of the country has been sustained by the fact that 46 percent of the land area is used for cultivation. Agriculture is the mainstay of the economy. India's situation contrasts sharply with that of China, where only 11 percent of the land area is arable, but where the bulk of the population lives in rural areas.

The remaining population, one of every four Indians, resides in urban areas of various sizes. There are twelve cities with over a million people. There is a rural-to-urban population shift occurring, with major migration to cities and towns. Rural overpopulation, fragmentation of the fields, and the lack of employment opportunities in rural areas have led to increased out-migration from villages to the cities, particularly to larger cities. The attraction of the large city for the migrant lies in the hope of finding a job and, linked with it, social mobility. However, for most of the migrants the reality of the Indian city turns out to be the very opposite of their expectations: disappointment, unemployment, and destitution. Many of these migrants wind up living in the rampant slums of the larger cities.

The greater part of the urban population now lives in large (Class 1) cities. The urban population has shifted from small and medium-sized towns to large cities. The four large cities of Calcutta, Bombay (Mumbai), Delhi, and Madras (Chennai), each has grown from colonial stronghold to major commercial and industrial center. Each of these four cities has more than five million people, led by Bombay with 12.57 million, Calcutta with 10.86 million, Delhi with 8.38 million, and Madras with 5.36 million. Two southern cities have grown significantly over the past ten years: Hyderabad, from 2.2 million to 4.27 million, and Bangalore, from 2.9 million to 4.1 million.

In urban India, particularly the large cities, air pollution from industry and motor vehicles has created serious environmental health problems. Many urban areas also have inadequate sanitation services. Poorly maintained

Figure 5-10. The bulk of the population on the Indian subcontinent lives in villages such as this one in Haryana State, northern India. Some of the biggest disparities in living standards in the Indian subcontinent are between rural and urban areas. Typically, incomes per person are lower in rural areas and the incidence of poverty far higher. The village, in most areas, is a compact cluster of dwellings. Rural families keep their cattle outside, but adjacent to the dwelling. Rural electrification and agricultural improvements, cattle breeding, access to clean water, and educational and health services are among the major goals of Indian development planning. (Photo: P. P. Karan.)

drainage and sewage facilities contaminate piped water and cause serious health hazards. Safe drinking water is in short supply in most Indian cities.

India has enacted a series of environmental and sanitation laws designed to protect the health of citizens. However, these laws and regulations are not strictly enforced and have not prevented extensive pollution of air, water, and land. The Indian civic authorities, like their counterparts in many cities, find it extremely difficult to provide adequate public services for their growing urban populations.

Form and Morphology of Cities

There are differences in the morphology and forms of cities in different culture areas. A majority of Indian cities have checkered historical antecedents. They grew as politico-economic centers of kingdoms or as principalities of local chiefs. Owing to the fear of invasion, they were built on commanding situations or defensible sites on the river banks. Houses were huddled together in a compact area, and in many cases towns were fortified with walls, resulting in greater compactness and irregular patterns of streets, structures, and activities. The focus of such a town is usually the fort of the king or chief (similar to the castles in Japanese castle towns), around which the city was built. Some ancient towns such as Varanasi (Benares), located on the bank of the Ganges, possess great religious importance and contain a large population of worshippers. Their shrines and temples are visited by thousands of pilgrims annually. Sentiment and tradition have favored their continued growth in modern times.

The development of modern economic and political systems has led to the growth of several Indian cities such as Bombay, Calcutta, and Jamshedpur. They differ considerably from the classical cities of ancient India. The differences are not only confined to architecture, physical morphology, and layout, but also to the very reasons for their existence. Traditional cities of India are characterized by an absence of clear-cut functional zones, although a central zone called the "business section," containing a bazaar (market) and residences, may be distinguished in many towns. This business section comprises the general bazaar, the specialized bazaars for grain and other products, and vegetable and brassware markets. This commercial core of the Indian town is similar to the retail merchandising section of small midwestern U.S. market towns, but it has a completely different atmosphere and appearance. Surrounding the business section are primarily residential zones with small markets and retail shops scattered in them. Industrial areas are not distinct, although modern factories are generally, but not always, located on the outskirts of the town.

Quite distinct from but adjacent to the town proper are the civil lines—the new settlements added to many towns during the British colonial rule. Civil lines are mainly administrative and residential in function, containing government offices, courthouses, post and telegraph offices, public gardens, parks, clubs, and bungalows of officials strung along the pitched shady roads, often in separate gardens. In civil lines all the buildings are brick-built, generally constructed in a Western style with some modifications such as the addition of a verandah and courtyard to suit the local climate. The density of dwelling in the civil lines is low as compared with the older sections of the town. With extensive lawns, broad shady avenues, and a generally flattish skyline broken sometimes by the spire of a church or high government building, the civil lines present a distinctly modern appearance, forming an outlandish neighbor to the older section of the town.

Also located outside the confines of the town proper is the railway colony, a distinct functional zone in towns that are important railway centers. The railway colony lies adjacent to the railway station on the other side of the town. The railway track is an important cultural divide in Indian towns, because the older part of the city invariably lies on the "other side of the track." Military cantonments, built adjacent to the older parts of the town

during the British rule, are also quite distinct functionally and morphologi-
cally. Streets in the civil lines, railway colonies, and cantonments are broad
and lined with shady trees. In contrast, streets in the older part of the city are
narrow and irregular. The domes and minarets of mosques and pinnacles of
temples are prominent in the skylines of the older section. Here on the streets
cars and bullock-carts go side by side.

All of India's metropolitan areas have been the subject of major planning
exercises, though none of them can claim a large degree of successful
implementation of the urban plan. There are three general weaknesses that
characterize urban plans in India. First, the dynamic processes of urban growth
are never examined in any detail, and consequently the implications of alternative patterns of growth are not examined. Second, the economic processes of
growth also generally go largely by default. All metropolitan cities have
economic influence well beyond their limited hinterlands. Much of the
approach to urban planning sees the city simply as a problem, rather than also
viewing it as a center of opportunity. Unless planning attempts to take account
of this wider role and understand the processes through which it is fulfilled, it
is almost inevitably doomed to failure. Finally, urban planning in India is
apolitical. Urban planning problems posed by rapid growth, inadequate
services, and extremes of wealth and poverty ultimately revolve around political questions which cannot be resolved simply by reference to technical criteria. In the meantime, the urban landscape of many large and mid-size cities is
changing. One sign of change is the proliferation of malls. India's first mall
opened in 1999 and its second in 2000. By the end of 2004, it will have 150.

Cities of the Subcontinent: A Cross Section of Cultural History

The cities of the Indian subcontinent reflect the long cultural history of this
area. In the following section, five cities—Varanasi (an ancient town), Calcutta (a city that owes its origin to modern commerce and industry), Cochin (a
city that provides a cultural history of the Indian Jews), Madras (a town that
developed along a fort built by the East India Company), and Hyderabad (a
city that exemplifies the blending of Hindu and Muslim cultures in addition to
the cultures of north and south India)—are discussed as examples of the varied cultural mosaic of the subcontinent.

Varanasi

Varanasi, Benares, and Kashi are all names of the same city which, to every
Hindu, symbolizes the ultimate destination, the holiest of the holy cities. Each
year more than a million pilgrims visit this ancient city. They pay homage to
the Hindu gods and goddesses in its 1,500 temples. And they wind their way
down the many *ghats* (steps leading to the water) lining the banks of the
Ganges River, to bathe in the holy waters of "Mother Ganges."

Today, the former maharaja of Benares continues to hold a mythical grip on the psych psyche of the city. Standing on the breeze-filled verandah of the Ramnagar Fort, his royal residence built on the banks of the river, he looks out over the Ganges. Stripped of his title and power, the maharaja looks like an ordinary man dressed in a white, hand-spun cotton coat. But it is the cap of ochre and gold, that touch of brocade, casually resting on his head like a forgotten crown, that lends him an air of distinction. And his gentle, solitary, lived-in eyes are those of a man who has reflected on the experiences that have been a part of his life. "Benares is not a city but a state of mind," he says, gazing distantly at the river. "If one has reached this terminal city one cannot go anywhere else; one cannot be reborn. When the river washes away the good and the evil, there is no rebirth. Once one knows this one can abandon himself or herself to the freedom."

Varanasi is decaying, the river is polluted, and the people are decrepit, says a family patriarch who, having made his fortune, has retired to preside over a large white house tucked in a narrow, dark city lane. It is a city where trucks honk all night, where streets are filled with nothing but shops whose keepers haggle and sell at all hours, where women buy too many saris, and men do nothing but chew the betel leaf.

The women of his household, dressed in nylon saris, speak pidgin English and sit in wicker chairs on the verandah, looking urbane. The river in this house commands no reverence, just a massive indifference. What does the city mean to them? "Nothing," they say, looking bored. Do they bathe in the holy river? "No. We take the children to swim when we go for picnics in the summer on the other—the cleaner—side of the ghats."

"We want the city to become modern," says the eldest daughter-in-law, deemed the most "modern" in the family. She runs a factory that produces the famed Benaresi silk saris, but chooses to wear only synthetics made in Japan. "We have started a ladies club," she continues, her voice betraying a sense of mission. "The club arranges swimming classes in the Ganges." Do the ladies of Benares wear the swimming costume, I ask. "No," she giggles, embarrassed with the image of semi-nude women. "We have taught them to wear blouses and half-pants."

As I say goodbye, I ask the family patriarch if he ever leaves Benares. "I am an old man and I don't want to go anywhere lest I die in another place and miss out on my *moksha* [liberation]," he says with a laugh. His words trail out of the large house and follow me through the dark lane that leads me back to the ghats and the holy river.

Varanasi symbolizes the energy of ancient Hindu learning and art. Situated on the confluence of the Ganges and the Varana rivers (from which it gets its most common name), Varanasi is one of the few cities in the world that still lives by its ancient traditions, which date from the sixth century B.C.

Calcutta (Kolkata)

If New York has a twin city in the language of urban despair, it is Calcutta. Any American deploring beggars and filth, crime and homelessness, almost reflexively invokes the warning name of India's huge and hopeless city. Yet in some ways the comparison is uninformed and, in Calcuttan eyes, cruelly unfair.

It is true that Calcutta's problems are appalling and seemingly insoluble. But its streets are friendly rather than mean, and murder and violent crimes are a rarity; it has thus far been immune to the communal strife now rending much of India. This is a matter of stubborn pride not just to a communist-led local government, but also to business leaders and a conservative opposition press. Their fierce patriotism is as unexpected as the flowers that improbably abound even in squalid slums.

Calcutta's population is reckoned at about 11 million, triple the figure of 1950. Some 300,000 Calcuttans live on the streets, and nearly half of the city's families are crammed into squatter huts or slum settlements known as *bustees*. The state-run power plant operates at 37 percent of capacity, and blackouts occur daily. The air is blue with pollution, and the roads choked with traffic.

Not all these evils are of Calcutta's making. Like New York, Calcutta has had to absorb millions of newcomers (many of them Bengali refugees from what is now Bangladesh) but pays out more in taxes than it gets back from the central government. The resulting hostility to New Delhi helped spur the rise of the 25-year-old Left Front government in West Bengal, of which Kolkata is capital. Yet in this urban purgatory the homicide toll averages less than a hundred a year, compared with New York's record of more than 2,200 in 1990. Calcutta's 21,000 police are mostly unarmed; none have been killed on duty in the last five years. Purses, not persons, are the target in petty thefts. Reported rapes numbered 27 in 1989 and 23 during most of 1990. There has been no outbreak in Calcutta of communal violence between Hindus and the Muslim minority.

Neighborhood solidarity helps explain this low incidence of criminal violence. Amazingly, for all its seeming anarchy, Calcutta consists of a network of relatively homogenous subcultures. And in this there lies hope for mitigating the decay and shabbiness that pervade slum neighborhoods, notably in north Calcutta.

North Calcutta is a maze of alleys lined by impressive remnants of Calcutta's past as the imperial capital (until 1912) of British India. The warren of narrow lanes winds around the astonishing hidden palaces of the *babus* and *boxwallahs*, the Indian clerks, officials, and businessmen of wealth and social staus who thrived at the edge of British India while nurturing the classical Indian arts and a deep Bengali nationalism. The British called the north Calcutta neighborhood, several square miles in area, the "native town" and rarely went there. Here Eastern and Western styles collide in Mughal arches on corinthian columns, or medieval half-timber overhangs and shuttered, French-style windows on houses in the shadow of Asian mosques. The alleys and twisting lanes sometimes open into small squares that create breathing space and centers of activity. The squares and lanes also provide a ventilation system, and this part of Calcutta is noticeably cooler than the rest.

Most houses have a courtyard flanked on two sides by verandas and an anteroom at the other side. The Bengali courtyard, entered through an arched gateway to the street, traditionally has a Hindu temple at one end for family use, and living accommodations along the other three interior walls. Courtyards can be used for cultural performances, meetings, or family gatherings.

These open spaces ventilate the family compound, drawing cool air in from damp, dark alleys, and letting heat rise above the verandas.

The hundreds of old Bengali palaces and stately houses of north Calcutta are polyglot in style or inspiration, but they serve a cohesive neighborhood of proud Bengalis. In the colonial days the Bengalis would escape here to a cultural environment not spiritually or intellectually diluted by the British town. Some homes became salons of sedition, drawing together early advocates of independence.

A small group of young conservationists is now trying to preserve many of these eighteenth- and nineteenth-century homes, temples, and business houses of north Calcutta. Their regenerating work is as much a part of Calcutta as are the amply publicized efforts of Mother Teresa and her Sisters of Charity in aiding the destitute and dying. Other local landmarks are the Metro, an eight -stop subway that is the pride of Calcutta. The fare is a nickel. It is scrupulously clean, and its passengers are not importuned by beggars.

An interesting cultural legacy of British rule is the gentleman's club, a peculiarly British institution. As one of the oldest and largest centers of British influence in India, it was hardly surprising that Calcutta proved a fertile plot for such clubs. Many of them are alive and flourishing in this vibrant Indian city today. The Tollygunge Club is a green and ordered oasis in the chaos of downtown Calcutta. Its 100 acres contain a golf course and riding stables. The Royal Calcutta Golf Club is another green and pleasant place and another magnificent building. The club is the fifth-oldest golf club in the world and the oldest outside of Britain.

The original Calcutta Club was started in 1882. It is a stately place with bearers in immaculate livery always on hand. The club president, an Indian barrister, commands immediate respect by wearing a three-piece suit even in the clammy Calcutta heat. The library and reading room are full of rather grand-looking ladies reading *Punch* and glaring over the top of the magazine at intruders. Ladies have been admitted to the ground floor of the club since 1957, when their annex was turned into a swimming pool.

Then there is the Calcutta Ladies Golf Club. It claims to be the only golf club in the world run entirely by ladies, and is probably the only one to share its nine-hole course with herds of goats and packs of footballers, and to have a moving clubhouse. The club exists on the Maidan, a huge expanse of parkland in the middle of Calcutta, which belongs to the army. The army insists that the clubhouse, which is on wheels, be moved every year. One year it is pushed one foot to the east; the next it is pushed one foot to the west.

There is also the Saturday Club and the city's oldest surviving club, the Bengal Club (1827), where there is excellent choice of Indian and European food. The Royal Calcutta Turf Club (1847) is a good antidote to doubt and uncertainty, with its teak paneling and the sort of leather armchairs and sofas that invite repose with dignity. Racing is a very important part of Calcutta social life and it causes high emotion. Indians had little problem adapting to clubmanship because Indian society has built-in social stratifications. "Indian" India does not seem to penetrate past the club gate; the language and mannerisms of the clubs are still well-modulated, if occasionally eccentric, English.

Cochin

This city on the west coast of India provides a fascinating cultural history of the Jews in India. The origins of the Jewish community in India are as ancient as they are obscure. Jews migrated to Kerala State between 2,000 and 2,500 years ago. Official records indicate that 10,000 Jews settled in Cranganore, a port 20 miles north of Cochin. They quickly took their place alongside other residents, prospering in a variety of sea-related trades. Quite remarkably, they also were granted an independent principality by a Hindu king, according to an ancient decree inscribed on copper plates that are now kept in the Cochin synagogue. The king appointed a Jewish leader as sovereign prince, and his rule was handed down to his descendants, who governed for more than 1,000 years.

In 1341 a massive flood silted up Cranganore's port. Most of the city's Jews journeyed south to Cochin, where the same flood had created an enormous natural harbor. When the British seized control in 1798, social and economic pressures led to a gradual weakening of the Cochin Jewish community. Lured by prospects in such rapidly industrializing cities as Bombay and Calcutta, thousands moved north, where they were assimilated into other Jewish settlements. So great was their migration that by the end of British rule in 1947, only about 300 Jews remained in Cochin.

Today, Cochin's Jew Town, as it is called by everyone, remains a throwback to medieval times. The pungent aromas of cardamom, cloves, and pepper still waft through its narrow, cobblestone streets. Embellishing the pastel-colored homes that line Synagogue Lane are stars of David and menorahs (Jewish candelabras), now joined by Muslim crescents, Hindu images, and Christian crosses.

Four hundred years ago, the Paradesi Synagogue was founded in Cochin, ordered by royal decree to abut an ancient Hindu temple. Although the arrangement may seem startling to Americans, to Indians it is a way of life. Since the Jews' arrival in India, the sounds of mantras have comingled with Hebrew chants in the coastal city of Cochin. Yet the tranquility of this Old World charm belies deep concern over Jews leaving for Israel. Emigration has decimated this proud community. The Jews are a highly educated, secure, and prosperous group. With no experience of persecution other than for a brief period during Portuguese rule, Jews found in India a haven in which their traditions flourished and developed unique forms. But many of Cochin's Jews have opted for a harsher life in Israel.

Madras (Chennai)

Madras, now called Chennai, may be India's most attractively situated large city, strung along a wide Bay of Bengal beach from Fort St. George at the northern end of town to the estuary of the Adyar River near the south. The buildings of the fort complex, the oldest dating to 1650, now house government and military offices. The British Empire in India took root here in the settlement built by functionaries of the East India Company about the same time the Pilgrims of New England were carving the first Thanksgiving turkeys.

The first British (Anglican) church in India, St. Mary's, was built in the fort in about 1678. Still home to an active congregation, it displays many historical plaques, one commemorating Elihu Yale, the founder of Yale University, who worked in Madras as an East India Company clerk and worshipped here. Records show that the first marriage at St. Mary's, in 1680, was that of Catherine Hynmers and Elihu Yale.

At Adyar, one of Chennai's greenest residential suburbs, the world headquarters of the Theosophical Society is set in extensive grounds, both arboretum and bird sanctuary. The society—founded by an American Civil War veteran, Col. Henry S. Olcott, and the Russian-born mystic, Helena Petrovna Blavatsky—lures students of New Age religions as well as theosophists from all over the world.

Chennai also had a few early brushes with American technology and capitalism. A young fellow from Boston named Frederic Tudor came here in the 1840s selling ice from New England's winter ponds. Someone—no one knows for sure who—built a grand, arched and colonnaded ice house on the Chennai waterfront to receive and store this unusual cargo, which arrived packed in sawdust and apparently still in shape after a four-month journey.

Chennai is a town of bungalows in gardens, grouped in neighborhoods with distinct characters based on their different histories. As Chennai changes and grows, taxing its fresh water supply and its social harmony, it also confronts political issues with national implications. Some intellectuals in Chennai, a city of at least 4 million people that is primarily Hindu with a strong Christian minority, have become part of what is being called a Brahman backlash. (Brahmans are Hinduism's highest caste.) In Tamil Nadu State, of which Chennai is the capital, 68 percent of all places in schools and colleges are reserved for lower-caste children, part of a large-scale affirmative action program. Brahmans, traditionally the educated class, say they are suffering unusual discrimination over several generations. They have begun to support private education for their children, which other Indians regard as elitist. Intercommunal violence is often easily proved in India and all efforts are made to keep arguments about caste out of the public eye. But the Tamil Brahmans Association, which has pursued its campaign peacefully, is attracting attention in other parts of the country where Indians charge that affirmative action programs have created new elites that are themselves discriminatory.

Hyderabad

Hyderabad is a graceful city of two cultures. The north and the south meet in Hyderabad, as do the Hindus and Muslims. Situated on the burnished Deccan Plateau, the city is in the center of India. With a skyline of white domes and minarets, the city sprawls among the smoothly sculptured rocks of the plateau and straddles the Musi River. At its commercial heart is Char Minar, a magnificent 400-year-old granite triumphal arch with four soaring minarets and wide arches opening out on all four directions.

After the Mughal empire crumpled, the viceroy in Hyderabad declared himself independent and ruled the area. Its scions, known as the *nizams*, were among the wealthiest people in the world. Seven *nizams* ruled Hyderabad for two turbulent centuries. In 1950, when India reorganized its states on the basis of language, the state of Hyderabad was combined with parts of Madras to form the current Andhra Pradesh, with Hyderabad as its capital.

Although the eighteenth- and nineteenth-century Muslim rulers came from a minority population, their rule has been deemed benign. They often chose Hindus as key officials. The local Hindu lifestyle merged with the Muslim way. This mix is still apparent in the flavor of the cuisine, the Urdu language that is spoken, and its street ethos. Mosques coexist with shrines and temples, reinforcing the city's old synthesis.

Economic Restructuring and Reforms since 1990

From independence in 1947 until the late 1970s, India's economic policies focused on self-sufficieny, import substitution, and state control of basic infrastructure and manufacturing industries. Although this approach led to rapid expansion of India's industrial base, productivity growth was repressed by the lack of foreign and domestic competition. During this period, GNP growth rates seldom exceeded 3.5 percent. A consensus began to develop in the late 1970s, especially after 1984, that India would have to liberalize its economy to reduce poverty rapidly, create adequate resources for social programs, and modernize its infrastructure and manufacturing sector. In 1990 India initiated a major transformation of its development strategy, and vigorously embraced market reforms after three decades of stifling bureaucratic socialism. Radical industrial, trade, and financial policy changes beginning in 1991 have made remarkable progress in liberalizing what was one of the most closed and regulated economies in the world. Regarded by many in the 1950s as a front-runner in the race for development in the non-Western world, India is instead just beginning to catch up now. What went wrong? And what are India's prospects?

India's economic performance prior to the recent reforms was truly dismal. India's weak performance in increasing national and per capita income not only fell below its own aspirations, but also put India behind many developing countries and substantially behind countries of the West Pacific Rim. Recent government estimates suggest that over one-quarter of India's population is considered poor.

India's economic failure must be balanced, however, by its political success. Almost alone among non-Western nations, India remained wedded to democracy in the postwar period, whereas many abandoned it. Indeed, this was what attracted many intellectuals who consistently supported India's developmental efforts in those early decades. Fears that democracy and development would be in conflict were unfounded. Neither the ability to raise savings nor the efficiency of the investments that these savings financed were compromised by democracy. India nearly doubled the savings to over 20 percent of national income between 1960 and the late 1980s. We now also know that democracy usually does quite well in getting the most out of investments; people do not do their best when they lack the freedom that participatory democracy protects.

India's democracy, then, did not cost her the growth that eluded her; the culprit was simply faulty policies. India's misfortune was to choose an economic model that could not and would not work. The major features of these policies were:

- **Rigid controls:** Industrial and trade controls reached Kafkaesque proportions by the mid-1950s.
- **Lack of competition:** India killed foreign competition by controlling imports and domestic competition by regulating the entry of new producers.
- **Discouraging foreign investment:** The sheltered markets for domestic producers also skewed incentives toward the home market and against exports.
- **Poor public sector performance:** Equally dramatic and damaging was the performance of public sector enterprises. These inefficiencies also created problems elsewhere; because these enterprises supplied critical inputs to other industries, public sector inefficiencies hurt them too. The public sector losses, financed by government subsidies, were bad for growth.

India undertook a cascading set of reforms in June 1991. Industrial controls over most investments and over diversification and expansion were removed. Import controls were dismantled. Foreign investment restrictions also ended. Substantial efforts to attract foreign investment are now paying off. Coca Cola and IBM, both virtually forced to leave India earlier, are now back. General

Electric and others are actively investing or exploring investments. New investments in 2003 exceeded $5 billion, a substantial increase over the $100 million annual inflow in 1990–1991, prior to reforms. The acceleration is continuing. Financial sector reforms and privitization are scheduled. The entry of new private sector firms is introducing competition to areas of public sector monopoly and promoting better management and efficiency.

The sense of optimism about India's economic prospects is undeniable. Just over a decade after the Indian economy began shaking off its statist shackles and opening to the outside world, it is booming. The surge is based on strong industry and agriculture, rising Indian and foreign investment, and U.S.-style consumer spending by a growing middle class (nearly 300 million), including people under the age of 25, who make up half of the country's population. Reducing protectionism and red tape, slowly lifting restrictions on foreign investment, and reforms in the financial sector are starting to show substantial results. Companies that stumbled in the face of recession and new competitive pressures in the 1990s have increased productivity and are showing record profits. India is slowly making a name not just for software exports and service outsourcing, but also as an exporter of a wide variety of manufactured goods, including autos, auto parts, and motor cycles. After growing just 4.3 percent in 2002, India's economy—the second-fastest growing in the world, after China—grew 8.2 percent in the year ending March 2004. The growing appetite of the middle class is fueling demand-led growth for the first time in decades. India is now the fastest-growing telecom market, with more than one million new mobile phone subscriptions sold each month. Banks are now making $15 billion a year in home loans, helping to spur spending, building, and borrowing. The potential for even more market growth is enormous, a fact recognized by both multinationals and Indian companies.

The economic reforms in India are expected to endure because they are popular with the vast middle class and others. The major opposition party has carefully kept economic reforms out of its political arsenal. The state-level elections in India have endorsed the reforms fully. The combination of democracy with market reforms gives India a prospect that will outweigh the temporary advantage that economic reforms have given to totalitarian China. To foreign investors, India looks like a politically safe alternative to China: an entrepreneurial treasure trove, with British laws, fairish elections, an emerging middle class, and factory wages of barely $100 a month. The Indian giant is awakening later than the Chinese giant did, but it will step onto firmer ground. The rate of India's growth will not be as explosive as China's. Though India's slow march to prosperity may look less exciting, it may also prove more consistent.

Economic Reforms in India and China: A Comparison

Although much of the Western business in the 1990s was focused on selling to one billion Chinese consumers, it is an Indian market of almost equal size that may well offer the greater opportunity over the next decade. India and China are not the Bobbsey Twins of the developing world. It is their stark differences, not their similarities, that beg for examination. India is a nation breaking loose from the self-imposed shackles of socialism, but doing so without rejecting the richness of its deep and diverse culture. Having rejected both Confucianism and Maoism, China today venerates only the god of rampant materialism.

India is a nation suddenly bursting with economic energy and confidence, but Indians so far have avoided the attitude of arrogance that characterizes both bureaucrats and business partners in China. India is a nation in only the fifteenth year (in 2004) of a determined program of economic liberalization, but more important is its nearly fifty years as a genuine democracy and its three centuries of commitment to a British-based rule of law. By contrast, China, in its second decade of economic liberalization, remains an authoritarian society ruled not by laws but by the whims and anxieties of old authoritarian men.

India is a society in which private property and profit have existed uninterrupted for centuries, thus imbuing the long-established business community with a genuine understanding and respect for both. By contrast, China's twentieth-century history wiped out those traditions, and today's China has little understanding of the basic capitalist concept that business can be a win–win game to enlarge an economic pie. Finally, India offers what in a competitive world may be the most valuable software of all: minds that have been permitted to be open, inquisitive, and creative, and people who are fluent in the global language of business—English.

Despite all this, India, ironically, remains barely on the radar screen for most businessmen. But U.S., European, and Japanese companies are beginning to invest because they are convinced that India's economic reforms, begun in 1991, are for real and are so firmly set in place that they will survive any likely changes in political leadership. Also, the allure of investment in China is fading as China proves either unwilling or unable to keep its commitments to foreign investors, whether Lehman Brothers, McDonalds, or one of the scores of foreign firms whose intellectual property is illegally replicated by Chinese entrepreneurs. Corruption is rampant in China and reaches deep into the army and the government, rapidly eroding public respect for two of the institutions that hold China together. The third, the Communist Party, long ago lost its legitimacy.

Over two decades after Deng Xiaoping launched China's economic reforms, China remains a nation of individuals, not laws. Investors who cross swords with the Chinese increasingly are discovering they have no reliable legal recourse when their businesses are blackmailed or their revenues extorted. So eager are multinationals to be in the China market for the future that few businessmen dare question China's commercial abuses, much less its violations of human rights. The men who rule China continue to believe that they can have their cake and eat it too, that they can have the fruits of economic liberalization without planting the seeds of political liberalization. The history of much of modern Asia, from South Korea to Taiwan to Thailand, indicates that the two go hand in hand—just as they do in India.

On the surface China looks stable, but it is not. On the surface India looks chaotic, but it is stable. Indeed the very diversity and disorderliness of India's pluralist politics provides its underlying strength and stability. Like the United States, India is a polyglot of peoples, religions, and territories held together by free will expressed at the ballot box. Thus, religious riots in Bombay between Muslims and Hindus no more signal the crumbling of India than race riots in Los Angeles foreshadow the demise of U.S. democracy. Although democratic systems like India's or the United States' frequently seem less decisive and act more slowly than authoritarian systems, when policies are vetted and voted they have a durability that authoritiarianism's arbitrary moves can't match.

India's large and long-established private sector includes companies that have been competing worldwide—by global rules—for many years, and the country boasts Asia's oldest and most active stock exchange in the business center of Bombay. Thus, foreign investors can choose among Indian partners or investments with established business records. By contrast, in China investors find themselves choosing among partners who little more than a decade ago were communist cadres, who have now shed the Mao suit but not the mentality.

All that said, India, like China, has a long way to go to become a fully open, stable, and hospitable environment for investment. India's economic growth lags China's; its gross national product is expected to grow by 5.5 percent in 2004, less than half of China's anticipated 10 to 12 percent annual rate. And population in India is growing well above the rate in China, where stringent birth control programs have almost stabilized population. The issue for investors doesn't have to be China or India. Opportunity exists in both. But for the foreseeable future, the tortoise of India is a safer and better bet than the galloping hare to its north. What India has to recommend it is a future based on longer trends; democratic, traditional, commercial, and legal traditions; and more profound tensile strengths. What is happening in India isn't the vision of one man, but the expression of the will of a nation.

In 2003 India had a $500 million trade surplus with China, and Indian companies increasingly see China less as a threat than as an opportunity. Indian companies market everything from steel to pharmaceuticals in China.

Industrial Development

Industrialization's progress over the last fifty-five years has been a major feature of Indian economic development. The process of industrialization was launched as a deliberate policy after independence in 1947. Most of the industries are concentrated in five areas of the country: the Bombay–Pune region, the Ahmedabad–Baroda area, Chota Nagpur, Calcutta–Hooghlyside, and the Bangalore–Coimbatore–Madurai area (Figure 5.11). The large cities of Delhi and Chennai also have attracted a variety of industries. The location of industries is primarily market oriented. The peri-urban areas of metropolitan cities (cities with a population of one million or more) are the favored locations for manufacture of consumer goods, consumer durables, and pharmaceuticals. Even some capital-intensive industries such as the manufacture of motor vehicles are

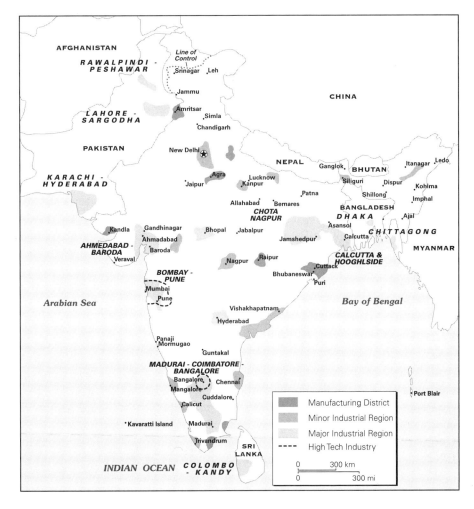

Figure 5-11. The Indian subcontinent's industrial regions.

located in peri-urban areas, and information technology industries also are located close to the peri-urban areas of some cities. The large markets of metropolitan cities and the concentration of entrepreneurs are the principal factors attracting industries to these areas. This locational trend is likely to continue in future.

However, the large industrial plants built with heavy capital investments do not necessarily contribute to the development of a region. Chota Nagpur region of Jharkhand is the site of large steel and mining industries, but it is also the country's poorest region. The benefits of industrialization have obviously not percolated to the entire society. A labor-intensive development program to tackle rampant poverty and unemployment is urgently needed.

Economic liberalization, introduced in 1991, has spurred industrial production and foreign investment, and the growth of high-technology industries. New factories producing computers, electronics, and telecommunications equipment have mushroomed across the nation, particularly in Bangalore, Bombay, Delhi, and Calcutta. A large military buildup, fueled in part by a desire to be recognized as a world power, has accompanied progress in high-technology industries. The government has a multibillion-dollar military research program, aimed at achieving an independent weapons production capability. The latest success in indigeneous research came in 1989 when military scientists test launched India's first intermediate-range ballistic missile.

India's Software Industry

With some 3 million fully qualified scientific and technical personnel, and several million more high school science graduates, India possesses the world's third-largest pool of scientific and technical skill, after the United States and Russia. Its influence is felt as far away as the London Underground, the new networked, interactive time-tabling system of which was programmed by a Delhi-based firm.

India has the second-largest pool of English-speaking technically skilled professionals in the world today, second only to the United States. The fluency of Indians in English, a legacy of British rule, has made India a lucrative hunting ground for U.S. computer firms on the look out for qualified computer manpower. Areas in which Indian software professionals are particularly strong are systems software, CAD/CAM, expert systems, microcomputer software, telecommunications, and applications software development. The German software industry, handicapped by an acute manpower shortage, has switched labor-intensive software engineering work to India. Germany needs about 4,000 electronic data processing specialists, and has filled this gap by using India's skilled and relatively inexpensive workforce.

The Indian software industry is growing at an average rate of 35 percent a year. Indian software exports ($6.2 billion in 2001) registered a healthy growth of 55 percent. The target is to achieve export of $50 billion by 2008. More than 60 percent of Indian software exports are accounted for by the two

Tata outfits—Tata Consultancy Services and Tata Unisys Ltd.—which employ approximately 2,000 professionals in Bombay and Bangalore. Tata Unisys has a collaborative arrangement with Microsoft. There are about 300 Indian firms devoted to software engineering.

The government has already set up technology parks in Bangalore and Pune, with two more expected in Chandigarh and Bhubaneswar, to boost software exports. One feature of these parks is the facility for real-time transmission of software code through dedicated satellite channels to clients in the United States and elsewhere.

About 90 percent of exports are to the United States, where Indian software systems cost half as much as American ones. Two U.S. companies with an eye on available and inexpensive manpower have set up software export units in the southern hill city of Bangalore, India's own Silicon Valley. The $5 million Texas Instruments facility has a staff of thirty-five U.S.-trained Indian engineers and exports software through a dedicated satellite link to its U.S. clients. DEC, in association with Hinitroan of India, exports its software via a Bangalore–Madras–Hong Kong satellite link.

With a climate as dry as California's Silicon Valley's, Bangalore has emerged as a major center for electronic and software industry. Foreign multinationals such as IBM, Texas Instruments, Digital Equipment Corporation, Hewlett Packard, Motorola, Intel Asia, Compaq, Microsoft, Verifone, SmithKline Beecham Pharmaceuticals, and 3M have set up local operations. And the city will soon have a $150 million science park on its doorstep. Workers here are developing new software for Western companies such as Reebok and Nestle. Their terminals are linked to a network that keeps them wired to their customers in Europe and the United States. The workers, all graduates of India's seven institutes of technology, earn around 30,000 rupees ($960) a month: about one-eighth of their counterparts' salaries in the United States. Their employer, Infosys, which now has international sales of $10 million and a market capitalization of $70 million, was started by a group of Indian software workers in 1980. But not all of "the new India" has such recent roots. Wipro Infotech, the software subsidiary of Wipro, a family-owned trading group which was once known best for its vegetable oil, is now trying to focus on technology. Over 80 percent of Wipro Infotech's sales of $80 million come from exports to U.S. high-tech clients such as AT&T, Intel, and Sun Microsystems.

Bangalore has become a symbol of India's business potential. Until July 1991, that potential was limited by the government's command-and-control economic policy. This smothered local businesses in endless regulations and protected them from foreign competition with tariffs and import bans. Since 1991, a policy of economic reforms has slashed tariffs and hacked away many petty regulations.

Studies of high-tech centers around the world have identified seven factors in the success of high-tech industries: the university, large technology companies, small technology companies, federal, state, and local governments, and local support groups. Among these, the university forms the nucleus for the development of high-technology industries. The federal government contributes to their growth through defense spending and sponsored research, the state government through special programs and support for education, and the local government provides infrastructure, competitive rates, and improvements in the overall quality of life. The local support groups help to maintain a long-term nurturing environment for high-tech by lobbying the local, state, and federal governments for financial support, contracts, and regulations. In Bangalore all these factors are present. The Indian Institute of Science was founded in Bangalore by industrialist J. N. Tata to promote excellence in scientific research. It was soon followed by the Raman Research Institute, named after physicist C. V. Raman, who won the Nobel Prize in 1930. These institutions paved the way for the establishment of the Indian Institute of Astrophysics, the Indian Space Research Organization, the National Aeronautical Laboratory, and the Indian Institute of Management. The national government invested heavily in scientific and technological infrastructure for more than forty years, and today the Bangalore region boasts thirty research and development institutes, fifty engineeeering colleges, and 188 industrial training institutes. For the software and other high-tech industries, there is easy access to constant supply of top-grade high-tech talent. The academic institutions, research and development centers, and industries share a symbiotic relationship.

At Bombay's Santacruz Free Trade Zone, Citicorp Overseas Software is generating software for the bank's worldwide use. Hewlett-Packard also has set up a software export unit in India. Recently, Tata Consultancy Services entered into an agreement with Lotus Development Corporation for a whole range of Lotus PC software, and Thapar has a tie-up with Hitachi of Japan for setting up software units. In Noida, a satellite city of Delhi, Moser Baer India, the world's third-largest producer of recordable media such as DVDs and CDs, has built the world's largest production site for such devices.

A dozen cities and states are furiously competing for call centers and software parks that U.S. and Indian companies are opening in India. As tens of thousands of service jobs continue to flow to India from the United States and Europe, small cities such as Chandigarh offer even lower labor costs than India's "first tier" technology hubs—places such as Bangalore, Hyderabad, Bombay, Pune, and Gurgaon, outside New Delhi. In smaller cities, a starting call center operator makes roughly 7,000 rupees or $150 a month. A starting worker in a first-tier city would be paid as much as twice that amount.

Research and Development Centers for High-Tech Companies

Although outsourcing lower-level technical tasks to India has been a practice of U.S. companies for years, the United States technology firms' increasing reliance on Indian research-and-development operations is a relatively new and growing trend. In the process of getting low-end work done in India, multinationals discovered that there are not too many locations with such an abundant high-skilled, low-cost workforce. Thousands of engineers in disciplines as diverse as textile engineering and aeronautics graduate each year from India's engineering schools. They can be hired at salaries beginning at $10,000 a year, even as their peers in the United States earn six times that amount or more. In 2005 the Indian centers of multinational technology companies will double their number of employees from 40,000 in 2003.

The work of these engineers is generating significant amounts of intellectual property for U.S. companies such as Cisco Systems, General Electric, IBM, Intel, Motorola, and Texas Instruments. Their Indian units have filed more than 1,000 patent applications with the United States Patent and Trademark Office. For U.S. technology companies, under pressure to generate quick breakthroughs and develop products while curbing costs, India's big draw is its low-cost, deep pool of well-educated technical talent.

The Indian research centers of Cisco and Motorola are now those companies' largest outside the United States. Intel plans to move into a 42-acre Bangalore campus in 2004 and more than double its number of employees in India to 3,000. The Intel center's rate of innovation compares favorably with Intel's mature development centers in the United States. Texas Instruments and Motorola are expanding research and development operations in India. Nearly two decades ago, Texas Instruments was the first global technology company to set up development operations in India, and the company has reaped benefits in the form of 225 United States patents awarded to its Indian operation, including the world's fastest chip for converting analog signals such as the human voice into digital signals that can be transmitted as data on computer networks. In General Electric's John F. Welch Technology Center, in a Bangalore suburb, 1,800 engineers work on products as diverse as aircraft engines, power and transport systems, and plastics.

The continuing export of high-paying technology jobs from the United States to the research and development centers in India, and its implications for the long-term economy and U.S. standard of living, have become a politically sensitive topic in the United States. But government policy at present is focused primarily on what is best for the corporations. From that perspective, job export and wage compression are good things—as long as they don't get too much high-profile attention.

Agriculture, the Green Revolution, and Food Production

Agriculture provides livelihood to about 67 percent of the labor force, and contributes nearly 25 percent of the gross domestic product (2000). The use of high-yielding varieties of grain along with fertilizers and development of additional irrigation facilities was started in 1966–1967 as a major strategy for increasing foodgrain production. Widely known as the Green Revolution, the area under this program is steadily increasing. Since 1967–1968, in the post–Green Revolution period, agricultural production has grown at a rate of about 2.60 percent per year. Production of foodgrains increased from 95 million tons in 1967–1968 to 208 million tons in 2000, and per capita foodgrains availability went up to 467 grams per day, compared with 395 grams per day in the early 1950s. Through the Green Revolution India has achieved self-sufficiency in foodgrains. Despite the country's record foodgrain production, there are reports of starvation due to the pressing problems of food distribution and unemployment.

Food and energy production are the most critical developmental challenges facing India. Growth in production is essential, and the challenge is to enhance production with minimal environmental damage. Raising productivity on existing lands is the only viable option in the race to keep up with demand for food because there is little room to develop new farmland. Roughly half of India's land mass is used for agriculture. About one third of the cropland is irrigated, the rest depends on rainfall. About 62 percent of the total cropped area is planted with high-yielding varieties, ranging from 44 percent of land planted in maize to 85 percent of land planted in wheat. Although yields of wheat, rice, and sugar cane, to name a few, have gone up spectacularly, the production of pulses—the major source of food protein (including lentils and peas) in a predominantly vegetarian population—has not kept pace.

Several factors affect food production in India. One is the government pricing policy for inputs. Prices are often subsidized, but artificially low prices offer little incentive for more efficient production. Availability of credit or soft loans to buy high-yield seed varieties, fertilizers, and pesticides is another factor affecting food production. Production is also influenced by the vagaries of the monsoon rains. Monsoon rains can set in earlier than expected or end later or earlier than expected; the rains can be copious or sparse, and can vary greatly in intensity. Because of the erratic monsoon in 1991–1992, food grain production was 5.3 percent below that in 1990–1991, when the monsoon was normal. The recent years' seasonal monsoons have been excellent, with normal or excess rainfall in thirty-three of the country's thirty-six subregions. That, in turn, is putting income and credit in rural areas, spurring a run on consumer goods.

In India food production performance is relatively strong and there is moderate improvement in per capita food consumption and food security. Production growth in rice, wheat, and maize are all in excess of 2 percent per year, and production growth for coarse grains is at 1.9 percent. However, with a galloping population now at over one billion, India needs to produce more food and the present growth just barely keeps pace with the population growth rate.

In 2000, e-Choupal, the unique web based initiative of ITC, an Indian corporation, began offering the farmers of India information, products, and services they need to enhance farm productivity. E-choupal allows the farmers to check both futures prices across the globe and local prices before going to market. Farmers can the access latest information on weather, soil testing techniques, and scientific farming practices through this web portal. The concept is taken from the Hindi word (*choupal*) for village square, or gathering place; the *e-* stands for computer and Internet connections for farmers to gather around. ITC selects a lead farmer, or *sanchalak*, to run each e-choupal, which serves three to four villages. In 2003, e-Choupal was serving 18,000 villages, reaching 1.8 million farmers in central India. ITC has plans to reach into most of India's 600,000 villages.

Managing India's Environment

With the growth initiated by the economic reforms superimposed upon a rapidly growing and urbanizing population, there is inevitable pressure on India's air, water, and land resources. Several questions can be raised. Is India addressing the environmental problems efficiently? Is the institutional framework adequate? Is India doing enough to achieve environmentally sustainable development?

Many of India's environmental problems can be traced to distortions in economic policies. Subsidized consumption of power, fertilizers, irrigation water, and diesel fuel encourage wasteful consumption of these resources and thereby contribute to environmental degradation. Subsidies to promote the development of forest industries may inadvertently be encouraging the degradation of forests and protected areas. Reforms to eliminate these distortions would bring two kinds of benefits: reduced economic waste and reduced environmental damage.

Industrial areas near large cities face severe environmental problems (Figure 5.12). For example, Patencheru, 20 miles from Hyderabad, symbolizes the deadly results of an official policy of rapid industrialization without any accompanying political will to control its side effects. Patencheru, once a farming community, is now an industrial development zone, and it has become one of the most polluted places in India. More than 300 factories in the area pollute the air, land, and water. Industrial waste is dumped in public places, fouling the atmosphere. More than 2,000 acres of fertile land has been damaged by chemicals: sulfides, sulfates, nitrates, and phosphorous. The subsoil water is polluted down to 145 feet, but people are forced to drink from wells because there is no other source. Children develop lesions from playing in the dirt. Several boys have died of leukemia, and hundreds of cattle and goats are dying. Women suffer repeated miscarriages. Several children were burned with radioactive waste from the Nuclear Fuel Complex, a government-run uranium enriching plant near Hyderabad.

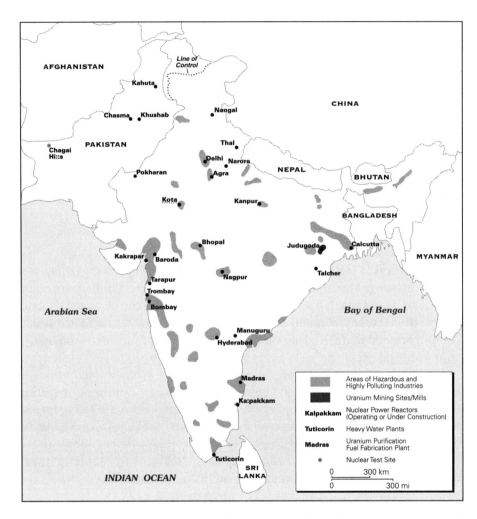

Figure 5-12. The Indian subcontinent's areas of hazardous and highly polluting industries and potential technological hazard zones (based on field research).

The chemical industrial zone near Ankleshwar, Baroda, and Ahmedabad is another example of an area damaged by pollution and environmental degradation. The uncontrolled and unplanned growth of small units producing chemicals, dyes and dye stuff, insecticides, pesticides, drugs, and plastics in this area pose major health hazards to the workers and residents of the region. Many of these factories use chemicals that have been banned in Western countries. Most of the labor employed in the small units is hired on a contract basis and are discharged from work at the first symptoms of adverse side effects. In 1984 a poisonous gas leak from the Union Carbide plant at Bhopal killed and injured thousands of people.

Rapid growth of industries around Delhi has led to serious environmental degradation in the region. Industrial units in the Delhi region increased from 8,000 in 1951 to 125,000 in 1996. Over 98,000 of the units operate in areas not designated for industrial activity. The concentration of sulphur dioxide in the air has risen to 109 percent of the 1989 level and oxides of nitrogen by 82 percent, according to a report prepared by India's Ministry of Environment. Delhi's population is expected to grow to 15 million by 2005. Over 5,000 tons of solid waste are generated in Delhi daily, and this is expected to increase to 12,750 tons by the year 2015. An estimated 67 percent of the air pollution is caused by vehicular emissions, more than half of which comes from 1.8 million two-wheeler motor scooters and motorcycles. The total number of vehicles in Delhi rose from 235,000 in 1975 to 2.6 million in 1996. Even though Delhi forms just 2 percent of the Yamuna River's course, it contributes 80 percent of the river's pollutants, so its flow is reduced to an odious trickle most of the year.

South of Delhi, air pollution is threatening the 350-year-old Taj Mahal at Agra (Figure 5.13). Pollution has already scarred the Indian architectural masterpiece and, despite abatement efforts, environmentalists fear the damage will continue. The monument to love is plagued by sulphur dioxide that comes from power plants, factories, and a nearby oil refinery. The air pollution has dulled the sheen of the once brilliantly white marble monument where Emperor Shah Jahan and his wife are entombed. In recent years, a textured, buff-colored rash has formed in some areas of the Taj. Other portions have been etched an ugly gray by acid rain which is formed when the sulphur dioxide in the air mixes with moisture and becomes sulphuric acid. More than 225,000 saplings have been planted on the 350-acre perphery of the land surrounding the Taj Mahal to save it from air pollution. It is hoped that the green belt will guard the Taj from the discoloring fumes from neighboring industries. The afforestation drive has come amid a campaign by environmentalists to prohibit industries from discharging hazardous waste in the area.

The relentless pollution has caused the slow poisoning of one of the world's great rivers, the Ganges, contaminating the drinking water and destroying the marine life. The river, which has seen the rise and fall of great empires, is considered holy by the Hindus and its banks are home to miilions of people in India and Bangladesh. The Ganges River collects industrial and human wastes from a wide area, and is now one of the most-polluted rivers in India. Most of the towns and cities along the Ganges do not have basic sewage treatment facilities and they discharge waste in the river. At places the coliform bacteria is twenty times the permissible limit, and dissolved oxygen, a sign of marine health, is well below acceptable levels. Millions use the bank of the river as it flows across three Indian states before entering Bangladesh, for bathing and washing livestock as well as dishes and clothes. One source of pollution is the dumping of human corpses into the river by people who cannot afford to cremate them. Near Kanpur, industrial effluents from leather factories have flowed into the Ganges for decades. Litigation by environmentalists forced sixty tanneries in Kanpur to close in the late 1980s. A two-stage

Figure 5-13. The Taj Mahal in Agra, the imperial capital of Mogul kings, and now a thriving industrial center of a million people. Growing air pollution is slowly discoloring the gleaming marble of the world's most extravagant 350-year-old mausoleum. The gray chimneystacks of the state oil refinery twenty miles away, and two power stations belch forth sulfur dioxide, carbon monoxide, and nitrogen oxides into the air. Agra's 250 coal-burning foundries, all privately owned, further add to the pollution. Environmentalists remain baffled by the tenacity of government bureaucrats in refusing to relocate the refinery since it went into full production in 1982. Air pollution has already scarred the architectural masterpiece and, despite abatement efforts, conservationists fear the erosion will continue. A green belt with more than 225,000 saplings has been planted in the last five years on the periphery of land around the Taj Mahal, a world heritage site, under a government campaign to reduce air pollution and preserve the monument. (Photo: P. P. Karan.)

plan to clean up the river and build a network of sewage treatment plants for industrial and domestic waste, known as the Ganga Action Plan, has been set in motion to improve the health of the river. Escalating costs, widespread corruption, inefficiency, and delays have slowed the project.

India's present environmental pollution control strategy combines a big stick (standards and regulations enforced under threat of criminal penalties) with a small carrot (tax breaks on the purchase of pollution control equipment). Despite the progress made in containing air and water pollution, some modification of the present strategy to shift the burden of securing pollution load reductions to economic incentives such as pollution charges could be more effective and efficient.

India's institutional framework for environmental pollution control is well developed. The major challenges in this area are strengthening monitoring and enforcement. Additional legislation is needed to provide a firmer institutional foundation for new approaches such as ecodevelopment and flexible land use arrangements. Environmental assessment is an area that requires closer attention, as illustrated by the controversy associated with the Narmada River Basin Development.

Currently, India's available expenditure on both pollution control and environmental protection falls short of what is needed to implement fully the provisions of current laws and policies. Environment must compete with other high-priority areas such as education and health for limited resources to protect the environment and promote longer-term sustainability of development strategy.

During the last two decades, people in various regions of India have formed nonviolent action movements to protect their environment, their livelihood, and their way of life (Figure 5.14). These environmental movements have emerged from the Himalayan regions of Uttar Pradesh to the tropical forests of Kerala and from Gujarat to Tripura in response to projects that threaten to dislocate people and to affect their basic human rights to land, water, and the ecological stability of life-support systems. They share certain features, such as democratic values and decentralized decision making, with social movements operating in India. The environmental movements are slowly progressing toward defining a model of development to replace the current resource-intensive one that has created severe ecological instability. Similar grassroots environmental movements are emerging in Japan, Malaysia, the Philippines, Indonesia, and Thailand. Throughout the non-Western world, citizenry organizations are working in innovative ways to reclaim their environment.

Even with limited resources, the environmental movements have initiated a new political struggle for safeguarding the interests of the poor and the marginalized, among whom are women, tribal groups, and peasants. Among the main environmental movements are Chipko Andolan, Save the Bhagirathi, and the Stop Tehri project committee in Uttar Pradesh; Save the Narmada Movement in Central India; youth organizations and tribal people in the Gandhamardan Hills whose survival is directly threatened by development of bauxite deposits; the opposition to the Baliapal and Bhogarai test range in Orissa; the Appiko Movement in the western Ghata; groups opposing the Kaiga nuclear power plant in Karnataka; and the campaign against the Silent Valley project in Kerala.

Social and Economic Changes

The Indian economy has been transformed during the last half-century from a dominantly agricultural in which farming contributed more than half of the gross domestic product (GDP) in the mid-1950s to a diversified economy dominated by manufacturing industries and modern services. The latter contributed 75 percent to the GDP while agriculture contributed only 25 percent by 2003.

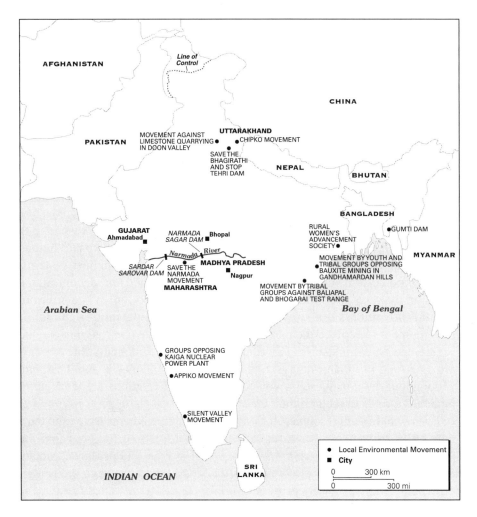

Figure 5-14. Indian environmental movements (based on field research).

India's society is also undergoing major social transformation in response to economic change. Two of the most significant developments have been the emergence of a large and burgeoning urban midddle class and, in the country-side, the growth of politically powerful, wealthy farmers. The introduction of modern technology to farms and heavy government subsidies on seeds, fertilizers, machinery, and farm produce have helped foster economic prosperity in large parts of rural India. A big class of wealthy farmers has emerged from caste groups that traditionally had a low ranking in the social hierarchy.

An educational revolution is underway in both urban and rural areas toward private schools funded by farmers, teachers, landowners, entrepreneurs, and others. The revolution is fueled by parental dismay over the poor quality of government schools. Indian parents are favoring private schools, particularly those with English as the language of instruction, which provide hope for upward mobility of their children. India has neglected elementary education and has devoted proportionately more resources to higher education.

Atrocities against the untouchable landless peasants traditionally have been associated with the Brahmins, the Rajputs, and other upper castes. Now a majority of reported attacks on the landless outcasts involve this new class of socially backward but economically prosperous farmers. Such farmers also have political clout because they make up about one fifth of a typical rural constituency and tend to vote en bloc for a candidate in elections.

The rapid growth of a large, urban middle class is reflected in the mushrooming of fancy beauty parlors in Calcutta, the addition of 10,000 vehicles every month to New Delhi streets, and expensive apartments in large Indian cities. New Delhi's Punjabi-speaking "yuppie" is locally described as a "puppie." He or she drives a gaudily decked-out car, visits a video library daily, and eats dinner in an expensive restaurant. There are so many "puppies" getting married at five-star hotels that wedding receptions yield more profit than room occupancy at some of the luxury hotels.

Some Indian analysts see a link between the "money culture," symbolized by the middle class, and the rapid erosion of traditional values and morality in urban India. Modern technology, meanwhile, is doing wonders to Indian traditions. National newspapers now offer computer matchmaking services to those who advertise in their matrimonial columns, making the task easier for parents trying to arrange the marriage of their children in the Indian tradition. Astrologers, who play an important role in Hindu ritual, are using computers to prepare and analyze horoscopes. As a result, a new elite astrological class of "computer babas" has emerged.

Regional Autonomy and Separatist Movements

Although India has survived more than five decades of independence without territorial losses to regional separatist movements, the cultural diversity of languages, religions, and ethnic groups has played a strong centrifugal role. The growth of regionalism and the increasing assertion of cultural and ethnic identity have led to the erosion of support for the Indian National Congress, the political party that enjoyed support from all communities and regions until the early 1980s. Regional separatist movements are strong in Kashmir and northeast India (Figure 5.15).

Kashmir

A guerrilla war has been waged by Muslim groups in Kashmir, with the support of Pakistan, for the last several years. Some groups say it is a war for independence from India and creation of a liberal democratic state in Kashmir; other groups say it is a war for union with Pakistan and the imposition of

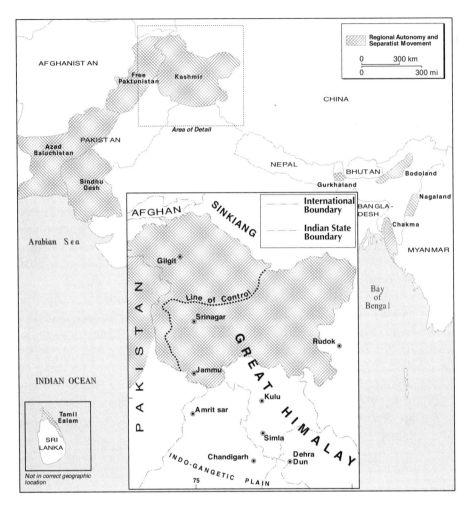

Figure 5-15. The Indian subcontinent's regional autonomy and separatist movements.

a fundamentalist Islamic state. These guerrilla groups—some well armed, others less so, some claiming thousands of members, others only a handful—have ambushed Indian troops, kidnapped government officials, and forced Hindus to leave the state.

Kashmir was a princely state at the time of India's partition in 1947. After Muslim tribal groups from Pakistan invaded Kashmir, the ruler of Kashmir acceded to India. Pakistan was furious, and the two countries have fought three wars over Kashmir. But after a conflict lasting over five decades, nothing much has changed. India holds on to about two-thirds of Kashmir, and Pakistan to a third.

When India complained to the U.N. Security Council about raids by Pakistan tribal groups into Jammu and Kashmir in 1948, the expectation was that the world body would undo the "aggresion." India had also stopped resisting the invaders in the hope that the Security Council would ensure that hostilities ceased. If fighting had continued for a few more weeks, India would have achieved on the ground what it had approached the U.N. to facilitate: the clearance of Pakistani military presence from what has come to be called Azad Kashmir. Cold War politics (1948–1989) intervened to complicate the Kashmir issue and make it virtually intractable.

After the 1971 military conflict in which Pakistan lost its eastern province, now Bangladesh, the Shimla Agreement reaffirmed that any talks on Kashmir could only be bilateral, without the involvement of a third country. The Shimla Agreement of 1972 between India and Pakistan rechristened the earlier cease-fire line as the Line of Control.

Pakistan has repeatedly and unsuccessfully tried to wrest control of Kashmir from India militarily. Since the early 1990s, Pakistan has changed its strategy with the introduction of cross-border terrorism. Pakistan waged a proxy war against India through terrorist infiltration under the assumption that India would not retaliate against a Pakistan newly armed with nuclear weapons. Pakistani-backed jihadi terrorists (trained in Pakistan and Afghanistan) infiltrated across the Line of Control into Indian Kashmir under protecting Pakistan fire to attack civilians, cause breakdowns in law and order, and alienate the population from India.

Three of the largest Pakistan-based terrorist groups—Lashkar-e-Toiba (made up largely of non-Kashmiri fighters), Jaish-e-Mohammed, and Hizbul Mujahideen, all with al-Qaeda links—have carried out operations against Indian troops and civilian targets in Kashmir. The Harkat-ul-Mujahideen Ansar has several thousand armed members located in Pakistan-occupied Kashmir, and in the southern Kashmir and Doda regions of India. It has a core militant group of about 600 to 2,000, mostly Pakistanis and Kashmiris, but includes Afghans and Arab veterans of the Afghan war. The Harkat-μl-Mujahideen is based in Muzaffarabad, Pakistan, and its members have participated in insurgent and terrorist operations in Kashmir, Burma, Tajikistan, and Bosnia. It collects donations from Saudi Arabia and other Gulf and Islamic states. The funding for its militant activities comes from sympathetic Arab countries and wealthy Pakistanis.

The 620-mile long Line of Control separating India and Pakistan in Kashmir is a reminder of the mess created by the partition. India asserts that Kashmir's accession to India in 1947 was legal and final. Pakistan wants the future of Kashmir to be determined by a plebiscite. A UN-sponsored plebiscite agreed to by both countries in 1948 was never implemented because under the terms of the U.N. resolution Pakistani troops were to vacate Kashmir, which they never did. In 2003 the near total ethnic cleansing of Hindus in Kashmir by terrorists rendered plebiscite meaningless.

India maintains an estimated 125,000 soldiers in Kashmir to suppress insurgency and terrorism. The suppression of terrorism has brought charges of killings, torture, and destruction of villages against the army. The Indian government does not have much room to manuever. To agree to give up

Kashmir because of its dominant Muslim population could tear the national fabric and light the tinder of Hindu–Muslim animosity in India, which has over 140 million Muslim citizens.

Deep-rooted hostility and fear remain on both sides. The Pakistanis believe that India has never reconciled itself to the two-nation theory that led to the partition of the subcontinent in 1947. India, in turn, argues that Pakistan has not given up dreams of wrenching away Kashmir by force. Both sides accuse each other of fomenting terrorism. Trade and travel between the two countries, which was cut off after the war of 1965, was resumed in the late 1970s and remains insignificant. In May 1999 India launched a series of airstrikes in its portion of Kashmir to clear several hundred Pakistani armed infiltrators who had crossed the Line of Control into the India territory near Kargil and Dras. A suicide bombing outside the Indian Parliament in 2001 by Pakistani militants working for accession of Kashmir into Pakistan led to increased tensions between the two countries.

India is a democracy and Pakistan is a military dictatorship, but neither country's government could survive a decision to concede Kashmir to the other. There may, however, be a way to solve the conflict based on a permanent partition of the region along the current Line of Control. But this would be possible only after a peaceful environment is created and cross-border infiltration by Islamic militants ceases.

The Most Pressing Issues

Although India's technological momentum seems irreversible, the nation faces several major economic and social challenges. The most pressing issues are poverty, unemployment, population growth, and environmental degradation.

Despite major progress in agricultural and industrial production, a substantial proportion of India's population, nearly 25 percent according to some estimates, remains poor. Unemployment in the countryside is driving hundreds of thousands of poor into the cities every year and creating larger and larger slums. About 20 percent of the urban population lives in slums and under conditions of multiple deprivation. The government had pledged to remove homelessness by the turn of the century, but with no coherent national housing policy, that was widely seen as a hollow promise. The slum-dwellers in Bombay, whose plight was portrayed in the movie *Salaam Bombay,* face a constant struggle to keep their shanties from being bulldozed by the city government.

India's population is still growing relatively rapidly, as was discussed in an earlier section, and the country is poised to overtake China as the world's most populous nation. Contraceptives, sterilization, and abortion are available free of charge, but the backlash triggered by the coercive family planning policy of the mid-1970s still deters policy makers and politicians from advocating tough birth control measures. The new emphasis on improving the educational, political, and economic opportunities for women will curb population growth.

Another problem facing the country is massive environmental degradation in some areas, resulting from developmental activities. India has laws protecting the environment—the most recently enacted one making companies liable for damage—but corruption among politicians and government officials and the power of large industrial corporations, which often defy court orders, make any law hard to enforce. Grassroots environmental movements following Gandhian nonviolent tradition are expanding in India. These environmnetal movements have emerged from the Himalayan regions of Uttar Pradesh to the tropical forests of Kerala and from Gujarat to Tripura in response to projects that threaten to dislocate people and to affect their basic human rights to land, water, and the ecological stablity of life-support systems. These environmental movements differ from the ones in the West in that they are concerned with both environmental preservation and issues of economic equity and social justice. The Chipko movement in the Himalaya, Save the Narmada movement in central India, and Silent Valley movement in the Malabar region of southern India are a few examples of movements that are slowly progressing toward defining a model of sustainable development to replace the current resource-intensive one that has created severe ecological instability.

ISLAMIC REPUBLIC OF PAKISTAN

The Islamic Republic of Pakistan came into being in 1947 as a result of the partition of the Indian subcontinent in an atmosphere of communal violence and hatred. Despite the realization of the dream of a separate homeland for the Muslims of the Indian subcontinent, the Muslim community of the subcontinent was divided into two nations: India and Pakistan. About two fifths of the Muslims of the Indian subcontinent were left behind in independent India. The demand for a separate homeland had been based on the claim that Muslims of the subcontinent were one nation. However, in the success of their movement they got Pakistan but divided the concept of Muslims constituting one nation. Muslims who were left behind in India had generally been the stronger supporters of the Pakistan movement, because they lived in the Hindu majority areas and were afraid of majority oppression. It was often they who had brought zeal to the movement for Pakistan and provided the leadership. In contrast, Pakistan was established in those areas that had been predominantly Muslim and whose inhabitants were therefore not afraid enough of non-Muslims to strive desperately for Pakistan.

Originally, Pakistan comprised two "wings," one in the west (West Pakistan) and another in the east (East Pakistan), separated by Indian territory.

After a brief war with India in December 1971, Pakistani forces surrendered unconditionally in East Pakistan, and East Pakistan became the independent state of Bangladesh.

Pakistan has an area of 310 thousand square miles (slightly less than twice the size of California) and a population of nearly 149 million (in 2004). Much of Pakistan is mountainous or, at any rate, highland. Its northernmost territories consist of the tangled mountains among which the western Himalaya run into the high Karakoram and Pamir ranges. From these the mighty River Indus breaks out through wild gorges to the plains. West of the Indus lies Chitral, a territory of hill ranges, deep gorges, and high plateaus. South of this, along the Afghan border, are mountain arcs such as the Safed Koh, Sulaiman, and Kirthar Ranges, breached by famous passes such as the Khyber and Bolan, and enclosing belts of plateau country. Baluchistan, the westernmost part of Pakistan's territory, is essentially a region of plateaus and ranges which run over the border into Iran.

Contrasting strongly with this mountain terrain is the plain country to the southeast—part of the great Indo-Gangetic Plain of northern India. It consists for the most part of the alluvium brought down by the Indus and its tributaries, of which by far the most important are the five rivers of the Punjab: the Jhelum, Chenab, Ravi, Beas, and Sutlej (parts of whose course lies, however, in Indian territory). Much of Pakistan has little or no rainfall, and without irrigation it would be unproductive agriculturally.

Without the production from the irrigated lands, the economy of Pakistan could not be sustained. Cotton, wheat, numerous small grains, and oilseeds form the major agricultural products of Pakistan. One of the problems that has accompanied the expansion of irrigation is the increase in areas of waterlogging and salinity which has reduced crop yields and made land unsuitable for agriculture. Pakistan's rapid industrial growth is concentrated around the consumer goods industries. The Pakistani government has not been able to attract much foreign investment.

Although the population of Pakistan is Muslim, it is divided by linguistic and tribal differences. Punjabi, Baluchi, Sindhi, and Pashtu are spoken in Punjab, Baluchistan, Sindh, and Northwest Frontier provinces, respectively. Urdu is the main language, but regional ethnic languages are significant. The country is riven by sectarian violence between Sunni and Shi'ite Muslims, and by attacks on the Christians who make up less than 5 percent of the population. In 2001 Christian worshipers were killed by Muslim gunmen in Bhawalpur, and in 2002 worshipers in Islamabad were killed during church services.

The Rise of Islamic Extremism

Since the mid-1980s Pakistan has been pressing a policy of Islamization of society as a means to unify the country. This was done through the introduction of *sharia*, or Islamic law, and the massive development of religious schools called Madrassas, largely funded by Saudi money and teaching an extremely intolerant version of Saudi Islam known as Wahabbi-ism (also espoused by al-Qaeda). With the state education system bankrupted by heavy defense expenditure, these Madrassas have become the schools of choice for many poor Pakistani youth. The hard-line Islamic policy was mirrored by Pakistan's support of the Taliban in Afghanistan. After September 11, 2001, intense pressure by the United States caused Pakistan to abandon its Taliban allies. In the meantime, extreme Wahabii Islam has extended its reach on the ground within Pakistan with the unprecedented election of an extreme Islamic alliance in the Northwest Frontier Province which borders Afghanistan and is believed to be the hiding place of most senior al-Qaeda leaders.

There is apparently some controversy and confusion around the moves to "Islamize" this Muslim nation. This is reflected in the continuing struggle between the traditionists, comprising the mullahs, landowners, and peasantry, and the modernizers, represented by the civil and technical services, the army, and the rapidly growing urban business and professional classes. The struggle continues in the areas of law, education, women's rights, publishing, and entertainment. The Westernized intellectual disdains the growing Islamization. Women have taken their protest to the streets. In 1979 the military government introduced the dreaded *hadd* laws, the most severe, by Western standards, of Islamic punishments. A hand is cut off for stealing; an adulterer is stoned. Yet the laws were never enforced. They continue as a source of often heated debate among the country's eclectic Muslim population, such as Islamic scholars, and even judges on the federal *sharia* court. This court issued a surprise ruling in 1981 accepting a petitioner's claim that stoning, as a punishment, was not sanctioned by the Koran.

The brunt of "social Islamization" has been borne primarily by Pakistan's women, who fear even harsher measures and the loss of hard-won rights. They may no longer dance or sing in public. A dress code for government employees is now prescribed, and the depiction of women on government-controlled TV is forbidden. Television actresses have been ordered to wear veils. Pakistan's female athletes, among the best in Asia, are now barred from participating in spectator sports. But even more frightening is an ordinance which, as feminists here see it, makes it impossible for a women to report, or prove, a case of rape. Women also fear changes in the family-laws ordinance, which protects many of their rights. They fear being segregated in an academically inferior women's university. But most important, they charge that they are being sacrificed to an ill-defined concept of "official Islam."

Western economists doubt the long-term viability of government efforts to make the economy conform with Islam. A 2.5 percent tax on savings deposit, the *zakat* has been used as a major means of aiding the needy and redistributing wealth. There are over 32,000 *zakat* committees throughout the country. Its compulsory collection directly from bank accounts is one of a number of reasons why wealthy Pakistanis are sending their money abroad. Since the tax applies only to savings, rather total wealth, others are now investing in gold, land, jewels, and rugs.

A second Islamic tax, the *ushr*—a 5 percent levy on agricultural produce—was levied for the first time in 1982. Landowners have opposed it, and the provincial governments are critical of *ushr*, which supercedes to a large extent the regular provincial tax, from which they derived a substantial income. Other economic measures, particularly those attempting to mold the banking system to the precepts of Islam, may prove difficult to sustain for long. Non-interest-bearing bank accounts still produce interest, although it is called a "profit-loss sharing project." In November 1991 *sharia* court ruled that regulations governing interest were "repugnant to the Koran." The government, worried that international businesses will shun Pakistan if interest payments are banned, is working to reach a settlement with the court on the issue.

Over the last twenty five years fundamentalist Islamic movements have been expanding their influence, primarily in rural Pakistan where the Friday prayers at mosques give conservative religious leaders a stage for addressing largely illiterate villagers. The largest and oldest fundamentalist party, Jamaat-e-Islami, has received large infusions of money from radical groups in such nations as Saudi Arabia and Iran. Money from Iran has helped finance construction and operation of huge Islamic centers in major cities and hundreds of small facilities in villages.

In 1992 the government introduced legislation that would make the Koran the supreme law of Pakistan and subject all aspects of life, from social behavior to civil liberties, to Islamic tenets. As elsewhere in the Islamic world, this growing Islamization of Pakistan has been fueled by the ballooning social and economic problems of the past decade; a burgeoning population, the long-term burden of millions of Afghan refugees, the loss of expatriate income from the once-booming economies of the Gulf, and endemic corruption and infighting within the secular political system. Ordinary Pakistanis, especially in the villages, remain deeply rooted in Islamic tradition. As in other such traditional societies, where secular political systems were imposed by European colonialism, it has been possible for fundamentalist campaigners to win converts to the idea that secular rule is a foreign idea that has failed a Muslim people.

Weak national governments, fearful of antagonizing influential religious leaders, have catered to them with the proposed constitutional amendment that would give precedence to *sharia* over civil legislation. Sweeping new powers have been given to the federal *sharia* court to try individuals for breaking religious laws. One of the most disputed rulings the court imposed within the last year requires the death penalty for people found guilty of blasphemy against Mohammed. At least thirty have been charged since the stricter penalties were decreed, but none have yet been put to death.

The surge of Islamization is adding to deep religious, social, and economic tensions in Pakistan. The more-educated and Westernized upper classes see the rise in orthodoxy as a giant step backward, saying it is fueling sexual discrimination, religious persecution, and human-rights violations. Business leaders say it will discourage foreign trade and investment, stunting the country's growth and damaging its potential as a trade link between the West and Central Asia.

Economy and Population

Heavily dependent on agriculture, Pakistan has managed to keep its food production barely ahead of population growth. Since 1970 the per capita food production has increased by 4 percent. The flow pattern of the Indus and its tributaries has largely determined the overall intensity of agriculture. The main determinants of agricultural production in Pakistan are water, credit, fertilizer, cultural practices, and price levels. The present system of irrigation on the Indus floodplain began as an imaginative initiative under British colonial rule, but for today it is inadequate because the supply of water is too unevenly distributed for the purposes of either agriculture or electricity generation. It is also inappropriate for dealing with the problems that face Pakistani agriculture as a result of the partition of the Indian subcontinent and the subsequent Indus Water Treaty, which necessitated further dams and canals.

Among other problems facing agriculture are salinity and waterlogging. About 25 percent of the agricultural land is affected by salinity; nearly 8 percent is heavily affected. Local initiatives by farmers themselves, undertaken with local resources such as pumped irrigation, the construction of drainage ditches, and canal clearings, have been successful in sustaining the productivity of agriculture. Irrigation dominates agricultural policy in Pakistan. The focus in the 2000s is on system rehabilitation and increased water use efficiency rather than on system expansion; the emphasis is more on decentralized water management and small farmer participation.

The silt load of the Indus basin system presents problems of a significant magnitude and, along with waterlogging and salinity, it may dominate agricultural development in the future. The management of land and water resources upon which so much depends in Pakistan presents a major development challenge. Resources can be used in various ways: they can be husbanded to maintain productivity at a sustainable level, they can be enhanced to increase productivity, or they can be degraded.

Ecological Crisis in the Indus Delta

From its descent from the Himalaya to its mouth at the Arabian Sea, the Indus and its tributaries support the world's largest system of irrigation canals. The waters of the Indus basin literally underwrite Pakistan's population. But after decades of dam and canal construction upstream, the over-subscribed river carries no fresh water at all in its last 80 miles, instead offering a ribbon of useless saltwater surging up from the Arabian Sea.

The broad, fertile delta of the Indus is suffering ecological catastrophe. Nearly 1.2 million acres of farmland have been covered by advancing sea, and large additional areas are turning to salty desert. Biologically vital mangrove swamps are dying. Millions of villagers have fallen deeper into poverty as empty canals prevent them from planting crops, and even drinking water is scarce. The lush banks of the Indus, which once supported large settlements mixing cattle husbandry and crops, are being deserted. Many have moved to the slums of nearby Karachi; others remain in desolate villages, stunned by the sight of empty canals.

The people of the Indus delta in Sindh Province blame Punjabis, who dominate Pakistan's military and government, for taking more than their legal share of Indus waters. People of Punjab Province in central Pakistan have enjoyed the benefits of large dams and canals and suffered relatively few of the damages. Pakistan is forging ahead with a disputed new canal (Greater Thal) in Punjab which will divert still more Indus water to bring 1.5 million acres of new desert lands in Punjab under cultivation while Sindhi farmlands downstream are famished.

The social and environmental damage resulting from decades of large water withdrawal upstream and reduced water flow downstream is visible in the landscape of the Indus delta: abandoned farmland, salt deposits, and shrinking coastal marshes and mangrove swamps. The problem may be aleviated if more water is released upstream and in seasonal patterns more attuned to ecological needs of the lower basin. An estimated 40 percent of the diverted waters are also lost to seepage from dirt canals and evaporation, losses that can be curbed with investments in concrete and modern irrigation methods.

At the same time, the demands on the Indus have climbed steadily as Pakistan's population has increased from 30 million in 1947 to 145 million in 2003 and is projected to reach 250 million by 2025. The population of Sindh alone grew from 6 million in 1947 to 40 million today. Bitter competition for Indus waters and the ecological costs of that competition seem unlikely to wane.

Population Problems

Population pressure, largely due to rapid population growth, has put increasing stress on resources. The expansion of cultivation into marginal areas, either on flat lands or in the upper watersheds, has contributed to deforestation, soil erosion, sedimentation, and changed hydrologic patterns. Growing urban and rural populations make greater demands on available ground and surface water supplies. A number of cities face growing water supply problems.

The current growth rate is about 3 percent per year. Rapid population growth has been accompanied by rapid growth of large cities such as Karachi, Rawalpindi-Islamabad, Lahore, Hyderabad, and Multan. Infrastructure and services have not kept pace with growth. The concentration of wastes overwhelms the assimilative capacity of natural ecosystems, and human health is threatened by the highly concentrated discharges of pollution in urban areas. Water pollution, air pollution, solid waste management, and inappropriate land use issues require attention in all Pakistani cities.

With a population of about 12 million, and sprawling over a large area, Karachi is the largest and most populous city of Pakistan. Karachi was occupied by the British in 1843 and became a bustling city when Charles Napier shifted the capital of Sind from Hyderabad to Karachi. The town developed as a seaport and a civil and military station. After Pakistan's creation in 1947, Karachi became the capital of Pakistan. In 1960, the federal capital was shifted to Islamabad.

Lahore, a city on the Ravi River, attained its glory under Mughal rule in India. Akbar made Lahore the capital of his Indian Empire from 1584 to 1598. After the Mughal glory there were several invasions, the most notable being the invasion of Ranjit Singh, who ruled the city for several decades. During the British rule from 1849 to 1947, Lahore acquired many fine examples of colonial British architecture—a strange mixture of Mughal, Gothic, and Victorian styles. After the partition of India in 1947, Lahore became the capital of West Punjab. In 1970, after the loss of East Pakistan and organization of the country into four provinces, Lahore became the capital of Punjab Province. Peshawar is the capital of the Northwest Frontier Province. It is situated at the outlet of the Kyber Pass and has been an important center of trade and commerce since historic times.

Rawalpindi and Islamabad are twin cities. Rawalpindi was developed by a Sikh by the name of Rawal nearly 350 years ago. Islamabad is a city that is barely two decades old; it was developed as a new capital of Pakistan.

Asia's Golden Crescent

In the 1980s the tribal belt of Pakistan became a chief supplier of heroin to the entire world, along with the Golden Triangle of Southeast Asia. The Pakistani government has little effective jurisdiction over the region. Wild and sometimes dangerous, Landi Kotal is a place without laws, without courts, without any police. Men's actions are governed by only two things: *Pukhtun-wali* (the code of honor of the Afridi Pathan tribesman) and the search for profit. Women's actions are governed by men. It is a clear-cut way of life.

Experts trace the rise of the heroin from tribal areas of Pakistan to the Iranian revolution of 1979. Before that most of the opium produced both in Pakistan and Afghanistan traveled to Iran to supply that country's estimated 1 million addicts. With the domestic turmoil and breakdown of law and order in Iran after the revolution, however, domestic production soared. The Iranian market was then further closed to outsiders by the Soviet invasion of Afghanistan a year later, which blocked some of the traditional smuggling routes through Afghanistan.

All the opium stockpiling in Pakistan thus posed a major problem for the smugglers by the middle of 1979. Over 800 tons of opium are produced annually in the region, according to some estimates, one-third more than is ever produced in a single year in the Golden Triangle of Southeast Asia. In addition, several hundred tons are produced in Afghanistan and brought east over the border to the tribal areas of northwest Pakistan (Figure 5.16).

With their traditional markets closed and stockpiles overflowing, the relatively unsophisticated tribal traffickers decided to move into the Western market. But opium is not a drug of choice in the West as it is in the East. Addicts in the West prefer the more potent and injectable heroin, which is refined from opium. In mid-1979 tribal entrepreneurs imported a few Southeast Asian chemists to teach the simple conversion process. Soon a network of primitive "bathtub" laboratories sprang up through the tribal belt of Pakistan's Northwest Frontier Province. On the United States' eastern seaboard, probably 85 percent of the total heroin seized is manufactured in the tribal belt of northwest Pakistan.

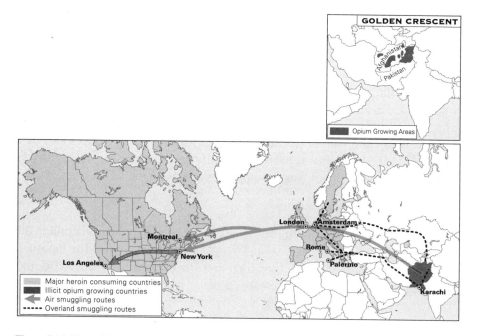

Figure 5-16. The Golden Crescent (based on U.S. Drug Enforcement Administration data).

Regional Autonomy Movements

In Pakistan regional autonomy movements are dominant in Sindh, Baluchistan, and the Northwest Frontier Province. They are based on the articulation of distinct identities of Sindhis, Baluchis, and Pathans, who are dominated by the Punjabi community that accounts for about two-thirds of the population of the country. The Punjabi group is concentrated in the productive irrigated region of the upper Indus Valley, which constitutes the ecumene of Pakistan. Key leaders of the Pakistan Oppressed Nations Movement (PONAM) have asserted that the country will disintegrate if people living in the Punjab Province continue to prosper at the expense of the Sindhis, the Baluchis, and the Pakhtoons of the Northwest Frontier Province.

Sindhu Desh

The Sindhi people have a strong sense of ethnic identity and hold grievances against other Pakistanis, particularly the Muhajirs, a term used for the mostly Urdu-speaking Muslim refugees from India who settled in cities of Sind in the aftermath of partition. The bulk of the Urdu-speaking refugees took the place of urban Sindhi Hindus who left Pakistan. Muhajirs also provided the bulk of the industrial workforce in Sind after partition. Before partition Sind's cities were predominantly non-Muslim; now they are predominantly non-Sindhi. The pattern of urban population has changed further as Pathan and Punjabi workers began to pour into the industrial cities of Sind. Non-ethnic Sindhis constitute the overwhelming majority in the three major industrial conurbations of Sind: Karachi, Hyderabad, and Sukkur.

In Karachi, the capital of Sind, 54.3 percent of the people are Urdu-speaking Muhajirs, 13.6 percent are Punjabi speakers, 8.7 percent are Pushto-speaking Pathans, and those whose first language is Sindhi form a mere 6.3 percent. In Karachi and other urban areas, valuable land has been alloted to Punjabi members of the armed forces or senior bureaucrats. Because of the elaborate network of state control over business, members of the traditional Sindhi business community find it difficult to cope with obstacles put in their way by the government. Their place is being taken by a new class of army-related Punjabi capitalists. Now Punjabis increasingly dominate most positions of wealth and power in Sind. The police force in Sind is almost wholly Punjabi. In the rural areas large tracts of valuable land in Sind, brought under irrigation since 1948, have been alloted to Punjabis, members of the armed forces or their relatives. They tend to be mostly absentee landlords and have brought with them Punjabi tenants or laborers whom they can better control and rely upon than local Sindhis. It is not surprising that Sindhis resent domination by governments, armies, and bureaucrats coming from the Punjab region.

One of the key demands of Sindhi politicians is the right of autonomy and to keep other Pakistanis out of their native territory. The more radical voices favor Sind independence, in a movement called Sindhu Desh. They are followers of G. M. Sayed, the father of Sindhi nationalism, a hereditary *pir* (religious instructor) and guiding force behind the Sindhu Desh movement.

Ethnic and political violence is tearing apart Karachi. The city is ethnically different from the rest of Sind Province and the rest of Pakistan. It took nearly one million Muslim refugees from India on partition in 1947. These Urdu-speaking refugees (Figure 5.17) have their own party, the Muhajir Qaumi Movement (MQM), which is waging an urban guerrilla war of increasing ferocity against the national government in Islamabad. As the heroin smuggling entrepot of South Asia, Karachi is full of urban gangs. Violence claimed thousands of lives during 1994–95; more than 600 people were killed in May and June of 1995. Several middle-class suburbs of Karachi are virtually under seige from urban guerrillas who are armed with automatic rifles, bombs, and rocket launchers. MQM's leaders demand their own province, separated from Sind.

Though Karachi has less than a tenth of Pakistan's population, it accounts for perhaps a third of the country's GNP. Its textile mills are the backbone of the economy. Guerrilla warfare is driving business out to cities such as

Figure 5-17. Urdu-speaking immigrants, who moved from India to Pakistan after partition in 1947, belong to an ethnic political group called the Muhajir Qaumi Movement (MQM) and are concentrated in Karachi and other parts of Sind Province. They seek basic rights of the Mohajirs, such as more jobs and money for development in Karachi. As a result of violence, Karachi's basic services are wrecked. Nearly 60 percent of the population lacks access to water, and over 30 percent live in substandard homes, some of them in slums. (Photo: UNICEF by Bernard P. Wolff.)

Faisalabad and Lahore. Foreign multinationals are shelving plans to invest in Karachi.

Azad Baluchistan

The high mountains and deserts of Baluchistan are the home of 1.3 million Baluchis, who have additional kinsmen in Iran and Afghanistan. Baluchis are divided into dozens of distinct tribes. The Pakistan government has only nominal control of much of Baluchistan. Tribal sardars effectively administer traditional tribal lands. When Baluchis speak of Azad Baluchistan, it is not clear whether they mean an independent nation comprising the Baluchistan province or all Baluchi portions of Pakistan as well as adjoining Iran and Afghanistan. At one time, Iraq, which was feuding with Iran, played host to an Azad Baluchistan movement. In any case, Azad Baluchistan remains something of a mirage. For while the Baluchis are more loyal to Baluchistan than they are to Pakistan, they are also more loyal to their various tribes—Marri, Bugti, Mengal and so on—than they are to any concept of Baluchistan.

Baluchis contend that Baluchistan is being treated as a colony by the Punjabis, and that its wealth and people have long been exploited. Coal mined in Baluchistan, for example, sells for less in Punjab than it does in Baluchistan. Marri tribesmen sell their goats at 40 rupees a head, but they are resold by Punjabis at 200 rupees a head for export.

Free Paktunistan

A more significant and troublesome minority for Pakistan is the Pathan or Pushtu people, who inhabit Pakistan's western border with Afghanistan. The 8 million Pathans in Pakistan are identical in culture to over 16 million Pathans living in Afghanistan. During the Soviet involvement in Afghanistan in the 1980s, and the haven provided for Pathan refugees in Pakistan, the political agitation for the creation of Free Paktunistan was minimal. But in recent years the regional movement for an autonomous state of their own has gained momentum among Pakistan's Pathans.

The proposed state would extend over a vast area stretching from China in the north to Baluchistan in the south and from the Indus River to the borders of Afghanistan and Iran. The state would represent the entire western flank of Pakistan and it would isolate the two remaining provinces of Punjab and Sind.

Pathan nationalists see many parallels between the proposed Pathan state and the secession of the former East Pakistan in what is now Bangladesh. Both Pathans and the Bengalis have been exploited economically and politically by the Punjabis of Pakistan and both speak languages alien to the predominant Urdu of Pakistan.

BANGLADESH

Bangladesh is a country of nearly 140 million people and some 55,000 square miles, largely formed by the floodplain and delta of two major river systems of the Indian subcontinent, the Brahmaputra (called Jamuna in Bangladesh) and the Ganges. In a typical year, about one tenth of the land is subject to severe flooding, and at least one half to some innundation (Figure 5.18). One third of the land area is less than 20 feet above sea level.

In addition to seasonal flooding in the wake of the monsoon rains, much of Bangladesh is affected by the constantly shifting river channels and courses; such shifts can wipe out settlements and complicate the construction of rural roads and other infrastructure development. Cyclones and tidal surges also

Figure 5-18. In recent years the frequency of abnormal flooding in Bangladesh has increased substantially, causing serious damage to lives and property. What really causes the havoc-creating floods and is there a solution to the problem? The heavy monsoon downpour and synchronization of flood peaks of the major rivers are generally considered to be the main causes. Other factors that contribute to the floods are inadequate sediment accumulation on flood plains, river bed aggradation due to siltation and damming of rivers, soil erosion due to unwise tilling practices, deforestation in the upstream region, and excessive development and population growth. Major flood control activity would involve regional cooperation among the riparian nations; a similar example is between India and Bangladesh, which have signed a treaty to share the waters of the Ganges. Extensive annual dredging of the rivers, channels, and creeks in Bangladesh could also increase the water carrying capacity of the rivers. Dredged materials could be dispersed on the flood plains to reduce the severity of floods. (Photo: UNICEF by Jim Davies.)

wreak havoc with settlements and crops, and cause significant property damage and loss of life.

Although the tropical climate does not limit the growing season, there is a distinct dry season, and periodic drought is a problem, especially in the north-west part of the country. Despite the historical expanse of forest cover, many generations of predominantly agricultural land use and expanding populations have reduced the natural forests to less than 6 percent of the total land area.

In response to these environmental factors, the people of Bangladesh have developed diversified and relatively resilient agro-ecological systems which provide for their needs in most years. Intensively managed and densely planted "homestead forests" or gardens containing a large variety of annual and perennial crops are an important source of food and income. Fish are an important component of the Bangladesh diet, and account for a large share of dietary protein, as well as a source of income and livelihood for millions. An extensive system of country boats helps link settlements and supports a large volume of commercial traffic and trade. In recent years, the traditional sail-powered (or towed) boats have been supplanted to a great extent by motorized launches, powered in many cases by the same diesel engines used to pump irrigation water in the dry season.

The Development Challenge

Despite the adaptations and resourcefulness of the people of Bangladesh, the overall economic and development statistics for the country are daunting. With a per capita average annual income of just $224, and 35.6 percent of the people living below the poverty line, government policy is understandably oriented toward poverty alleviation as an overriding development objective. Sixty percent of Bangladesh's households are without sufficient land to produce enough food for their families. Twenty percent of Bangladeshi households do not even have enough land for a homestead.

Some 60 percent of the total land area is cultivated, which is one of the highest percentages in Asia. The annual rate of growth in agricultural production was about 2.7 percent from 1980 to 1986, which was barely enough to keep pace with population growth. Food shortages affect more than half the population, and food imports are rising to keep abreast of demand. Access to clean water is problematic for many households. As a result of contaminated drinking water, gastroenteritis and other waterborne diseases are common.

Population growth is a constant factor in development planning in Bang-ladesh. The present population is up nearly 100 million from 44 million in 1951. The population is expected to reach 160 million by the year 2010. Already, Bangladesh is the most densely populated country in the world (with the exception of city-states like Singapore). If the United States were as densely populated as Bangladesh, the entire population of the world would have to live within the borders of the United States. Even though Bangladesh has made no significant progress in reducing poverty, a vigorous family planning program halved the nation's birthrate between 1975 and 2003. The average number of births for each woman of childbearing age (between 15 and 49) declined from 7 to 3.17.

Much of the success achieved by Bangladesh can be attributed to the fact that the program concentrated from its early days on winning the trust of women (Figure 5.19). Promotion of birth control by women drawn from their own villages has made it more difficult for opponents, including Muslim clerics, to condemn the effort as one foisted on the community by outsiders. The cadre of women counselors, and the independence they have in taking their family planning services to women who are confined to their homes, is the innovation that is chiefly credited with lowering Bangladesh's fertility rate. The number of couples of childbearing age using some form of contraceptive

Figure 5-19. Female group meeting in the village of Balai Khan, Bangladesh. Women meet together regularly to repay loan installments to Grameen Bank and discuss other business. The Grameen Bank project is an innovative credit scheme established in 1976. Landless poor people, who are unable to obtain credit because they lack collateral, receive loans from the Grameen Bank through a system of group responsibility. They use the credit to purchase materials with which they can produce goods for sale. Most of the beneficiaries are women, the poorest of the poor. Collective savings of bank members have allowed whole villages to benefit from new schools and other community services. (Photo: International Fund for Agricultural Development by Anwar Hossain.)

reached 43 percent in 1993, up from 6 percent in 1974. In most Western industrialized countries the rate is about 70 percent.

Few places in the world suffer a greater toll from natural hazards than Bangladesh. Riverine floods, cyclonic surges, tornadoes, earthquakes, droughts, and associated food shortages and epidemics are frequent. During the 1980s, the World Bank proposed spending $6 to $10 billion on the Flood Action Plan (FAP), employing structural measures for the containment of the Jamuna (lower Brahmaputra) River and parts of the Padma (lower Ganges) and Meghna Rivers. The FAP was influenced by planners who dealt with large rivers that do not migrate, such as those in the Netherlands, where an extensive system of dikes and levees is employed. However, the sandy, deltaic terrain of Bangladesh is crossed by international rivers that carry more than a billion tons of sediment a year. Limited flooding is highly beneficial to rice crops in riparian Bangladesh, but levees tend to impound too much water, resulting in crop damage. Indeed, sedimentation of the Padma River leads to rising river bed levels, necessitating ever taller levees, a problem similar to that of Huang He in China. The FAP was modified, but structural approaches are still favored. It would be desirable to start with a flood mitigation plan with a mix of structural and nonstructural approaches, which include planning, land use control, and insurance.

The need to cope with periodic disasters, and a preoccupation with increasing food production and reducing poverty in the face of continued population growth have overshadowed efforts to conserve and manage the natural resources. Serious problems of resource depletion and environmental degradation, if not addressed, could significantly undermine Bangladesh's long-term economic development, and ultimately have a more severe impact than floods and cyclones.

Environmental degradation in Bangladesh is evident in terms of declining soil fertility (particularly deficiencies of sulphur and zinc); lowered water table, especially in the northwest regions; and degradation of remaining natural forests, wetlands, coastal environments, and fisheries by a combination of factors. These factors include a large and rapidly growing population; industrial development without sufficient controls on industrial pollution; improper use of agricultural chemicals and pesticides; poorly designed flood control, drainage, and irrigation works; overcutting and clearfelling of forests, and shortages of alternative sources of household energy in rural areas; urbanization; lack of community control over open-access resources; inadequate land use planning; and institutional weaknesses among the public agencies charged with environmental protection and natural resource management.

The new democratic government's war on the population explosion is meeting with success. They have targeted cutting the annual growth rate (2.08 percent in 2004) to 1.5 percent by the year 2015, which means that about a million Bangladeshis must either begin using birth control or be sterilized each year. It is a formidable undertaking. But Bangladesh's experience demonstrates that reliance on women field workers drawn from the villages where they work can lead to successful family planning.

In recent years clothing has become Bangladesh's most dramatic growth industry. Starting virtually from scratch, and unencumbered by the public sector chaos that blights most Bangladeshi industry, clothing factories employ over 1 million people, mostly women. They account for over 60 percent of total exports. Labor costs are only slightly lower than those in China and Sri Lanka, but Bangladesh is not yet affected by the international quotas that restrict its competitors. Thus, it has attracted buyers from the United States (which takes half the exports), Europe, and elsewhere. Clothing, textiles, and engineering have become the most popular sectors for foreign investment.

Though it is overcrowded and flood-prone country, Bangladesh has some advantages over its neighbors. As a relatively homogeneous nation of Muslim Bengalis, it does not have the ethnic and religious divisions that have turned parts of Sri Lanka and Pakistan into combat zones, and frequently disrupt India. Its Mulims are non-fundamentalist Sunnis. There is no established industrial base, so foreign investors are unlikely to experience Indian-style resistence from vested business interests.The country's quota advantage will fall away as international quotas are phased out in the next few years, so Bangladesh must improve its competitiveness in clothing and diversify its industrial base into other areas that will make use of a cheap, hardworking labor force.

All that requires political will on the part of Bangladesh leaders. The leaders of the two major political parties—the Bangladesh Nationalist Party and the Awami League—are locked in an intense personal feud. Since 1971 Bangladesh has suffered three military takeovers and nineteen attempted coups. Corruption and lawlessness are big problems, and development is thwarted by political wrangling. Bangladesh could export some of its large natural gas reserves to India, but nationalist sentiment and deteriorating relations between the neighbors make this politically unpalatable. Instead, it has spent money on needless military purchases, and has been accused of harboring Islamic terrorists.

THE HIMALAYAN KINGDOMS

The two mountain kingdoms of Nepal and Bhutan are situated between the plateau of Tibet and the Ganges plain. Nepal's southernmost physical region is the Terai, which like the similar region in India, is a belt of low-lying plain. North of it rise series of ever-higher ranges of the Himalayan system, which culminate in the Great Himalaya along the border of Nepal and Tibet. A series of transverse or more complex valleys breaks up the simple pattern of parallel ranges, and one of these, the Valley of Nepal, contains the capital of Kathmandu (Figure 5.20).

Figure 5-20. The Katmandu Valley of Nepal. Until recently, the valley was isolated from the rest of the country. The valley is dominated by Katmandu and a number of other urban centers. Rapid urbanization has led to major environmental problems, particularly air and water pollution. In this 1968 photo the valley looks serene and pollution free. (Photo: P. P. Karan.)

Bhutan has similar elements in its physiography, the Terai belt being known here, as in nearby Bengal and Assam, as the Duars. From them the outermost ranges rise abruptly, followed by a series of successive ranges until, as in Nepal, the snow-capped ranges are reached. There is a series of striking transverse gorges, which are useful as gateways.

Nepal has a population of about 27 (2004 estimate) million and Bhutan has approximately 2.1 millon. Population is distributed in fairly dense clusters and ribbons along the valleys and in the Terai, a scatter of isolated upland settlement, and great empty spaces at high altitude. Both Nepal and Bhutan are the homeland of a number of distinct peoples. Thus in Nepal there are a number of people of mongoloid appearance speaking Tibeto-Burman languages such as the Gurungs, Magars, and Bhotiyas. There are also Gurkhas, Newars in the Valley of Kathmandu, and Indo-Aryan groups in the Terai. In Bhutan Bhutias are the indigenous group, and there are Nepalese settlers in the Duars and southern mountains.

Both the Himalayan kingdoms are among the least-developed countries of the world. In both countries the major natural resources are their arable land, forests, and water. There are small mineral deposits of lead, zinc, and limestone, but they have not been developed commercially on a large scale. The main source of energy is firewood, which, according to some estimates, accounts for nearly 90 percent of the total energy consumption in Nepal. This has caused serious deforestation and erosion problems. In Bhutan the population pressure is not as high as in Nepal, and the environmental degradation is not as severe as in Nepal. There are abundant hydroelectric resources in both countries.

In Nepal the pro-democracy movement of 1989–1990 led to multiparty democracy and general elections in 1991. The establishment of multiparty democracy marked the end of a journey in which Nepal emerged from an insular fief into a modern political state. In 1950 a palace revolt overthrew a century-old government of hereditary rulers who had usurped power from the Shah royal family. King Birendra's grandfather, King Tribhuvan, was restored to the throne with Indian help and shepherded the country through a decade of experimental democracy. King Birendra's father, King Mahendra, however, dissolved an elected parliament in December 1960 and instituted the partyless Panchayat system of tiered village, district, and national councils. The system centralized power in the palace.

Since 1978, Nepal has been buffeted by recurring bouts of protests from educated, and frustrated, urban youth who found ultimate inspiration in the sweeping changes of Eastern Europe in 1989. The general elections in 1991 on a one-man, one-vote basis led to the formation of government by the Nepali Congress, the largest political party in the country. The elections in May 1999 gave the centrist Nepali Congress majority of the votes. On June 1, 2001, the members of the royal family were assassinated by the crown prince, who also shot himself. The brother of the late King succeeded the throne. The king has suspended the elected parliament since October 2002.

Nepal faces major development problems. Just 45 percent of the population is literate; only 15 percent has access to electricity. Nepal has yet to undergo the Green Revolution, and agricultural production is expected to rise only 2.2 percent, about the same as the rate of population growth. That is largely why Nepal's poverty rate is rising, to about 42 percent. Poverty feeds a seven-year-old Maoist insurgency in which over 7,000 people have died. The Maoists have been fighting to overthrow the constitutional monarchy and in 2003 controlled much of the territory outside the Katmandu Valley (Figure 5.21). If many Nepalese did not migrate to the relative prosperity of India, discontent would be more acute.

Bhutan is a hereditary monarchy, and the king is the highest authority. The king relies on institutions set up in the last three decades, namely the Royal Advisory Council, the Council of Ministers, and the National Assembly, which is composed of 150 members, 101 of whom are directly elected. Bhutan is one of the few Asian countries that is not subject to excessive demographic pressure. One of the main constraints on Bhutan's economic development is the shortage of labor.

Although farming involves almost 80 percent of Bhutan's population, just 6 percent of the land area is cultivated. Three quarters of the country is forested, and teak and other hardwood in the south has been commercially exploited. With population increasing at the rate of 2.3 percent annually, new pressures on resources and environments will increase. The government is trying hard to protect the country's indigenous culture and its environment while also encouraging the development processes that challenge these aims.

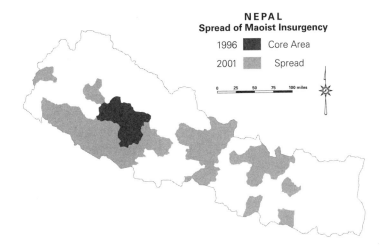

Figure 5-21. The Maoist movement in Nepal.

Tourism is a big business in both Nepal and Bhutan, but is more regulated in Bhutan to prevent environmental degradation. Maoist insurgency has led to the decline of tourism in Nepal.

SRI LANKA: A COUNTRY AT WAR WITH ITSELF

Sri Lanka is an island of some 19 million inhabitants, separated from India by the Gulf of Mannar and the Palk Strait, between which lie, in very shallow water, the string of small islands known as Adam's Bridge, linking Sri Lanka and India. A fundamental geographic division in Sri Lanka is that between the wet and dry zones. The wet zone occupies the southwestern sector of the island, and receives rainfall from both the southwest and northeast monsoons. The dry zone, covering the lowlands of the north and east, has severe drought in the southwest monsoon season and most of its rain comes from the northeast monsoon. Commercial crops such as tea and rubber are almost entirely confined to the wet zone. The wet zone has a dense rural population and also contains the principal urban centers of Colombo and Kandy. Much of the dry zone is still relatively sparsely populated, in spite of considerable colonization.

Sri Lanka has a plural society (Figure 5.22). The majority group, the Sinhalese, speak a distinctive language related to the Indo-Aryan groups of north India, and are mainly Buddhist (Figure 5.23). There are two groups of Tamils: Sri Lanka Tamils, the descendents of Tamil-speaking groups who long ago migrated from South India; and Indian Tamils, comparatively recent immigrants who came over to work on plantations, and their descendents. Both groups are predominatly Hindu. There are also groups of Muslims (called Moors) and Christians (drawn from the Sinhalese, Tamil, and other communities).

Figure 5-22. A health care worker weighs a child as part of a health program for infants in Kalugdollagaya village, Monoragala district, in southeast Sri Lanka, with a dominant Sinhalese population. Improvements in maternal health care and nutrition of children and women have contributed to economic and demographic transition in Sri Lanka, but ethnic conflict has slowed down the development of the country. (Photo: UNICEF by Paul Teixeira.)

Many of Sri Lanka's minority Tamils seek a state independent of the majority Sinhalese. The state, called Ealam, would be based on land once ruled by Tamil kings and still largely Tamil populated. A Tamil colony has continuously occupied the northern Jaffna Peninsula since the medieval period, and newer Tamil migrants came during the past century to work in the island's planatations of tea and rubber. The relative emptiness of the dry zone lying south of Jaffna has long served to insulate the transplanted Tamil culture from the native Sinhalese. However, intermarriages between majority Sri Lankan Sinhalese and minority Tamils have been a common tradition for centuries. The widening rift between the two communities is a relatively recent development.

Since Sri Lanka's independence in 1948 this ethnic confrontation has centered on the question of either autonomy for the island's 18 percent Tamil minority or an independent state. The Tamil Ealam movement had its origins in the mid-1970s when Tamil youth became disillusioned with their moderate leaders for failing to pursuade the Sinhala-dominated government to settle the Tamil question after almost twenty years of peaceful agitation. Since independence in 1948, the Tamil minority has been mistreated by legislation that limited their access to government and university posts and curtailed the use of their language in official transactions, and the government

Figure 5-23. A Buddhist stupa in Colombo, Sri Lanka. Eighteen years of fighting between the Sinhalese Buddhist majority and Tamil Hindu minority in Sri Lanka has claimed over 62,000 lives. People in eastern Sri Lanka—part of the territory rebels claim as the separate Tamil nation they call Eelam—have suffered brutalities committed both by government troops and rebels. In April 2002 the Tamils agreed to a cease-fire, but a terrible anxiety underlies the hope of a negotiated settlement. Most countries in the non-Western world are multiethnic plural societies. For long-term social, economic, and political development it will be essential to reconcile differences and permit full participation of each group in the political process. (Photo: P. P. Karan.)

persisted with the policy of settling Sinhalese peasants in the traditional Tamil homeland. According to the 1980 government statistics, the Sinhalese held 85 percent of all public sector jobs, 82 percent of professional and technical jobs, and 83 percent of jobs in the administrative and managerial categories. Tamils had 11 percent, 13 percent, and 14 percent of these categories, respectively. Tamils contend that they have limited opportunities in education and employment. There is deeply rooted apprehension among the Sinhalese of domination by Tamils. These perceptions have been hardening over the years.

At the outset, groups of unemployed Tamil graduates appear to be prominent in the formation of several militant groups, the most significant of these was the Liberation Tigers of Tamil Ealam. These groups swore to employ violent methods to establish an independent Tamil state, Ealam. By the late 1970s many of them were trained in guerrilla warfare. By 1978 the Tamil Tigers were a significant guerrilla force. In 1983, they ambushed a Sri Lankan Army patrol, killing thirteen soldiers; in retaliation, Sinhalese extremists unleashed an unprecedented wave of violence on Tamils. The conflict developed into civil war, which has continued since 1983. Support for the guerrillas solidified in the north and east after 1987, when Indian troops were accused of human rights abuses in Tamil areas. Indian troops were sent in July 1987, ostensibly to disarm the Tamil separatists under the terms of the India–Sri Lanka Peace Accord. The provisions of the Accord were not accepted by the Tamils because they were not consulted in the drafting of the Accord, and the Accord did not resolve the question of regional autonomy for the Tamils. Soon the Indian troops found themselves battling with the Tamil Tigers in a fruitless conflict that killed 1,155 Indian soldiers and wounded 2,984 of them. After the departure of the Indian troops in 1990, the peace talks between the government and the Tamils collapsed, and the fight was resumed in June 1990.

Founded in 1976, the Liberation Tigers of Tamil Ealam (LTTE)) is the most powerful Tamil group in Sri Lanka, and it uses overt and illegal methods to publicize its cause of establishing an independent Tamil state. The guerrillas of the LTTE are gradually retaking territory across the country's north and east from which they had been driven by Sri Lankan and Indian troops. The LTTE has approximately 10,000 armed combatants in Sri Lanka, and about 3,000 to 6,000 trained cadres of fighters. It has a significant overseas support structure for fundraising and weapons procurement. The Tigers control most of the northern and eastern coastal areas of Sri Lanka. Headquartered in the Jaffna Peninsula, LTTE has established an extensive network of checkpoints and informants to keep track of any outsiders who enter the group's area of control.

In a country at war with itself for nearly two decades, a Tamil guerrilla force pounded by the Sri Lankan military is closer than ever to its goal: domination of the Sri Lankan northeast, the homeland of the Tamil-speaking people. There are indications that the Tamils may be willing to lay down their arms and negotiate a political settlement if the Sinhala-dominated government would be willing to amend the consitution to grant semi-regional autonomy to the Tamil-majority region under a full-fledged federal system of government. Wearied by years of war, Sri Lanka is walking slowly, haltingly toward peace with the Liberation Tigers. Mistrust between Tamil minority and the Sinhalese majority remains strong.

MALDIVES

The Maldives is a nation of over one thousand tiny atolls stretching north–south for nearly 500 miles in a shallow area of the Indian Ocean. It has a population of 214,000, of which 44,000 live in Male, the capital. The island's economy is based on fishing and tourism. Most of the Maldives atolls are only a few feet above sea level. High waves in April 1987 covered two-thirds of Male with seawater. If the worst-case projections of global warming become reality, rising waters could swallow the nation whole within a hundred years.

In the last decade, the Maldivians, who are of mixed Sinhalese, Indian, and Arab stock, have tasted both the blessings and drawbacks of their archipelagic location. Their unspoiled seas and coral reefs are beginning to lure large numbers of tourists, and the shops in the capital are full of imported goods. Always in the background is worry about the rising ocean. With foreign assistance, new breakwaters and sea walls have been built, and the government has passed regulations prohibiting the use of explosives or trawling nets by fishermen. It also has banned the mining of coral for building material around inhabited islands.

FUTURE CHALLENGES ON THE SUBCONTINENT

The countries of the Indian subcontinent face major challenges over the next several decades. One challenge is to speed economic growth, and the other is to reduce population growth. Both development and population growth create many pressures on conserving and improving the environment. But economic growth is essential to improve the quality of life of the poor. All countries of the subcontinent have adopted economic reforms with varying degrees of success. Problems of poverty are closely linked with the status of women, and investment in women's education is also critical to lowering population growth rates. All countries recognize that environment, ecology, and development must be balanced to meet the needs of the society (Figure 5.24). But few have followed sustainable environment and development policies.

Throughout the countries of the Indian subcontinent differences in culture, language, religion, and economic conditions separate people. In several countries the driving force of the government policy is the power of religious beliefs. These forces are stronger and more articulate in some places than in others, but in many places reasoned discourse is being displaced by the intolerance of religious fundamentalism.

Nationalist religious and political organizations have broad appeal in India, Pakistan, Bangladesh, and Sri Lanka. For millennia, Indian Hinduism has been eclectic, embracing, and flexible. Not bound by one diety or text or by a hierarchical clergy or uniform liturgy, it proscribed little and tolerated much. Under centuries of invasion by Muslims, it was astonishingly resilient. But now a less-accommodating Hinduism has become appealing to a large number of Hindus. Just a few years ago, the Bharatiya Janata Party, the Hindu nationalist party, was another minor party. Now it is the largest party in the Indian Parliament.

In Pakistan, a nation created for religious reasons, the forces of fundamentalist Islam have always been strong. In a country where 97 percent of the population adheres to Islam, and where poverty and illiteracy are rampant, the collusion of fundamentalism and extremist politics seems inevitable. The government has turned to Islam to lend religious legitimacy to sometimes

Figure 5-24. Elephants in central Sri Lanka. The expansion of human activities and clearance of wilderness for agriculture and commercial forestry have taken a devastating toll on the elephant population in Sri Lanka. Continued mounting pressure could lead to major losses of its essential habitat. Some countries have identified reserves, which will accommodate human activities such as sustained yield forestry and slow-rotation shifting cultivation that are consistent with elephant conservation. (Photo: P. P. Karan.)

unpopular policies, and to consolidate its control. For the fundamentalists, Pakistan's civil courts are subservient to the religious courts, and the constitution subservient to religious law.

Bangladesh has been battered in the last few years by zealous students and mullahs. Increasingly, religious slogans are mixing with political slogans, and the criterion of truth is religious, not civil. Democracy there is fragile, and there are growing fears of a drift toward authoritarianism.

Nepal's future prospects depend on its capacity to address significant structural problems that have given rise to Maoist insurgency, particularly the lack of law and accountability (especially for the security forces), the failure of economic and social development, and corruption.

For Bhutan, a tiny Buddhist kingdom, conformity in dress, language, and religion is dictated. In fact, Bhutanese forces have driven Nepalese immigrants in the south across the border. Human-rights groups regard Bhutanization as one of the region's most persistent problems.

Sri Lanka struggled in the 1980s with extreme Sinhalese Buddhist nationalism, represented by the shadowy group called the Janata Vimukti Peramuna, or People's Liberation Front. In subduing the movement, government death squads and the army killed hundreds of Sri Lankans. Now, as Tamil separatists persist in their guerrilla war for an independent country, rumors of a revival of Sinhalese nationalism are once again reverberating. Peace talks have remained stalled.

The countries of the Indian subcontinent must cooperate to meet their serious economic, political, and environmental challenges. Even with cooperation it would take many years to solve their pressing problems of poverty, unemployment, and environmental degradation and to promote sustainable development policies. The geography, cultural heritage, and environment they share are not confined within political boundaries. The sooner this is realized, the sooner the entire subcontinent benefits.

FURTHER READINGS

Balk, Debra. 1997. *Change Comes Slowly for Women in Rural Bangladesh*. Asia-Pacific Population and Policy, No. 41. Honolulu, HI: East-West Center.

Bowonder, B. 1988. *Implementing Environmental Policy in India*. New Delhi: Friedrich Ebert Stiftung.

Coll, Steve. 1994. *On the Grand Trunk Road: A Journey into South Asia*. New York: Times Books.

Gadgil, M. and R. Guha. 1993. *This Fissured Land: An Ecological History of India*. Berkeley: University of California Press.

Gregson, Jonathan. 2002. *Massacre at the Palace: The Doomed Royal Dynasty of Nepal*. New York: Hyperion.

Henderson, Carol E. 2002. *Culture and Customs of India*. Westport, CT.: Greenwood Press.

Jones, Owen Bennett. 2002. *Pakistan: Eye of the Storm*. New Haven and London: Yale University Press.

Karan, P. P. and Hiroshi Ishii. 1996. *Nepal: A Himalayan Kingdom in Transition*. Tokyo: United Nations University Press.

Karan, P. P. and Hiroshi Ishii. 1994. *Nepal: Development and Change in a Landlocked Himalayan Kingdom*. Tokyo: Tokyo University of Foreign Studies.

Karan, P. P. 1994. Environmental Movements in India. *Geographical Review* 84: 32–41.

Karan, P. P. 1990. *Bhutan: Environment, Culture and Development Strategy*. New Delhi: Intellectual Publishing House.

Pathak, K.B., Griffith Feeney and Norman Y. Luther. 1998. *Accelerating India's Fertility Decline: The Role of Temporary Contraceptive Methods*. NFHS Bulletin No. 9. Mumbai (Bombay): International Institute for Population Sciences.

Schmidt, Karl. 1995. *An Atlas and Survey of South Asian History*. Armonk, NY: M. E. Sharpe.

Seabrook. Jeremy. 2001. *Freedom Unfinished: Fundamentalism and Popular Resistance in Bangladesh Today*. London: Zed Books.

Srinivasan, K. 1995. *Regulating Reproduction in India's Population: Efforts, Results and Recommendations*. New Delhi: Sage Publications.

Weaver, Mary Ann. 2002. *Pakistan: In Shadow of Jihad and Afghanistan*. New York: Farrar, Straus & Giroux.

Wolpert, Stanley. 1991 *India*. Berkeley: University of California Press.

World Bank. 1995. *Bangladesh: From Stabilization to Growth*. A World Bank Country Study. Washington, D.C.: World Bank.

World Bank. 1995. *India: Recent Economic Developments and Prospects*. A World Bank Country Study. Washington, D.C.: World Bank.

Zurick, David and P. P. Karan. 1999. *Himalaya: Life on the Edge of the World*. Baltimore: Johns Hopkins University Press.

Chapter 6

The Islamic World of the Middle East

The Middle East is a vast region extending from Iran to Morocco and from Turkey to Sudan. The term *Middle East* and other terms such as *Near East* and *Far East* developed in a Eurocentric world. These terms reflect European perceptions of the world and are no longer valid today. But the term *Middle East* is widely used now to refer to the area occupied by Southwest Asia and North Africa, and it has become a useful regional name. The Middle East has a combined population of nearly 530 million, but has a combined gross domestic product less than that of France, which has a population only of 60 million. It is held back by what some observers call a political and economic "freedom deficit" which in some areas has led to a sense of hopelessness and provides a fertile ground for ideologies of hatred. The challenge in this region is to develop a community of nations seeking progress toward greater democracy, tolerance, prosperity, and freedom. With the liberation of Iraq and Afghanistan, there is a special opportunity to transform the Middle East to achieve the region's full potential.

The region is comprised of several large and small states (Figure 6.1), most of them with authoritarian regimes who claim that their power comes from God (Iran), geneology (Saudi Arabia), or the barrel of gun (Libya). But despite these political divisions, the region shares characteristics that give a degree of unity to the region. It is centrally located at the junction of Europe, Asia, and Africa. It has been a gateway from Europe into Asia and through North Africa into sub-Saharan Africa. Because of the central location, some of the world's busiest trade routes have from ancient times crossed this region. Thus, for strategic as well as economic reasons, world powers have at all times been interested in the Middle East.

In terms of climate, the Middle East is a dry land, a vast belt of deserts and dry grasslands. The average annual precipitation is so low (less than 10 inches)

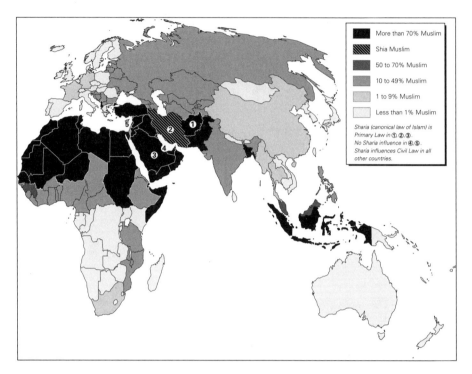

Figure 6-1. The Islamic world.

that major population concentrations are confined to river valleys or coastal areas where water is available for irrigated agriculture. Small groups are confined to oases or thinly scattered as nomadic groups.

The Middle East is the birthplace of three great monotheistic religions—Judaism, Christianity, and Islam—and contains holy places of all three religions. However, the culture of the region today is dominantly Islamic and is deeply penetrated by the Arabic language. Islam is the principal religion in all countries except Israel (Judaism), Lebanon, and Ethiopia (ancient forms of Christianity). All countries have significant numbers of Muslims.

Except for oil and natural gas, the Middle East does not have any natural resources. It contains over 50 percent of the world's petroleum resources, and accounts for about 24 percent of the world's total oil production. Western Europe and Japan remain highly dependent on the Middle East for their oil supplies.

THE EBB AND FLOW OF EMPIRES

The Middle East is a *culture hearth*, a source area or innovation center from which cultural traditions were transmitted to the rest of the world. The culture hearths lie in the Tigris-Euphrates Plain (ancient Mesopotamia) and the Nile Valley of Egypt. Other culture hearths in the non-Western world are in the

Huang He Valley of North China, and the Indus Valley in the Indian subcontinent. The Middle East was one of the places where people first learned to domesticate plants and gather harvests of wheat and barley. They made implements out of bronze, and learned to use draft animals. They employed the wheel, a revolutionary invention, and built some of the world's earliest cities about 5,000 years ago.

Early Civilization

The Nile Valley and Mesopotamia boasted superb cultural achievements at a time when Europeans still lived in rude huts. In Mesopotamia and Egypt 5,000 years ago, men first experimented with systems of writing to preserve spoken languages. In hieroglyphic and cuneiform scripts, symbols represented words and syllables. Out of these early models came one of the world's greatest inventions—the alphabet. Phoenician writing—which recorded only consonants—became the grandparent of all modern alphabets. Greeks added symbols and vowels, an innovation that traveled to the Romans, who developed the Latin alphabet, now used throughout the West.

By 1300 B.C., writing preserved legal codes and calendars captured time. Ambitious Persians extended the first modern empire with a common language and coinage, a postal and road system, and religious toleration. Then, in the first major invasion from the West, Alexander the Great took the entire Persian domain and founded some twenty cities, planting Greek culture (337–323 B.C.). His dream of one world—a unified East and West—was realized by the subsequent Roman Empire (31 B.C.–A.D. 410). Roads, reservoirs, and irrigation works were expanded. Camel caravans and fleets of galleys distributed the papyrus of Egypt, the incense if southern Arabia, the jewels of India, and the silks of China.

Byzantine (330–1453 A.D.) and Sassanid (226–651 A.D.) Empires

As Rome declined, its Emperor Constantine turned to the more prosperous Middle East. In A.D. 324 he founded his New Rome, later called Constantinople, near the Greek colony of Byzantium. Adopting Christianity, he married the new religion to Roman law and Greek culture. Government regulated all aspects of life, from wages to religious rites; heresy was treason. But schisms split off provinces, and Egyptian Copts, Syrian Maronites, and Nestorians formed their own churches, which still survive. Border battles broke out between the Byzantines and the Persians, whose civilization flowered anew under the Sassanid Dynasty. Persian shahs revived ancient Zoroastrianism, with its priests and its sacred fires. Despite warfare, trade and cultural exchanges continued.

Arab Empire (632–1258 A.D.)

The year one in the Muslim calendar, A.D. 622, marked the move of the Prophet Mohammed from Makkah to Medina, where he established the rule of Islam. Soon Bedouin horsemen exploded out of Arabia, wresting empires from the war-weakened Byzantines and Persians. Islam and the Arabic language unified an empire that reached its zenith in a single century. Mohammed's successors, the Umayyad Dynasty, moved the capital to Damascus, adopting Byzantine culture. Grasping power, the rival Abbasids emulated the Persians and, with Baghdad as their capital, brought luxuriant court life and learning to new heights. But the empire fragmented. Seljuk Turks usurped power from the Abbasids. Warfare interfered with Christian pilgrims, helping to trigger the Crusades.

Commanded by the Koran to seek knowledge and read nature for the signs of the Creator, and inspired by a treasure trove of ancient Greek learning, Muslims created a society that in the Middle Ages (the ninth to thirteenth centuries) was the scientific center of the world. The Arabic language was synonymous with learning and science for 500 years, a golden age that can count among its credits the precursors to modern universities, algebra, the names of stars, and even the notion of science as empirical inquiry.

The Ottoman Empire (1290–1922)

The Ottoman Empire expanded from an Anatolian state ruled by the Turkish Ottoman clan to a world power that reached to the gates of Vienna. In 1453 Muslim Turks stormed 1,100-year-old Christian Constantinople and established their adminsitration. Gradually, palace intrigues, corruption, and national revolts sapped the empire. The Muslim lead in science was gradually lost under the Ottomans due to lack of patronage and curiosity among the sultans and caliphs.

European Imperialism

Western nations, vaulting ahead in technology and military power, extended their rivalries to the Middle East. Napoleon's bold invasion of Egypt in 1798 set off a race for influence. Britain soon controlled ports on the sea lane to India. France took most of North Africa and brought in European settlers. Russia annexed the Caucasus and Turkistan. Germany courted the Ottomans, who became her allies in World War I. Britain, in turn, supported the Arab revolt against Ottoman rule, a cause championed by the flamboyant Lawrence of Arabia. Britain and France agreed secretly to dismemberment of the Ottoman Empire, and received Arab lands they coveted as League of Nations mandates.

After World War I and the decay of the Ottoman Empire, Britain and France divided much of the Middle East between them. But they found few natural borders on the vast Arabian Peninsula, home to wandering clans. As a result, boundaries set by British colonial officials were often arbitrary, leading to today's conflicts. The sudden deluge of border bashing is largely coincidental, and each dispute is fueled by its own set of political imperatives. Most of the region's new flash points share common roots. In virtually every case, the skirmishes can be traced to the fuzziness of the borders that the region's British colonial administrators once carved into desert sheikhdoms—borders defined not by rivers, lakes, and mountains but by the location of wandering tribes and armies. Territorial borders are Western ideas imposed on Arab Bedouin states.

ORIGIN AND DIFFUSION OF ISLAM

A Muslim is one who has "submitted" (the literal translation of *Islam*) and committed to God, and has accepted the Islamic creed that "There is no god but Allah, and Mohammed is the messenger of Allah." Submission, to the devout Muslim, means subduing the human ego to a constant consciousness of Allah in daily human life. A common phrase in Arabic is *inshallah*—"if God wills." To the Muslim, *Allah* (the word in Arabic means "the God") made man out of dust, in his human form, and gives him free will to choose between right and wrong. This human being will be judged by Allah on the last day. What the good man does on earth, the Muslim believes, will help him avoid hell and gain a place in heaven. Like Jews and Christians, Muslims are monotheists, and all three groups share in common the prophets of the Old Testament. Muslims accept Jesus Christ as a prophet and even acknowledge his virgin birth, but they do not accept his divinity. Jesus is referred to as *Isa ibn Mariam*—Jesus born of Mary. The Koran records the virgin birth (and omits any mention of Joseph). It mentions that Jesus healed the lame and restored sight to the blind. The Koran records neither the Ten Commandments nor the Beatitudes. Unlike Jesus, but like Moses and Abraham, Mohammed is seen as a temporal as well as a spiritual leader. He led troops into battle, expanded a city-state into a larger domain, and adjudicated disputes. They do not believe Mohammed was divine—to Muslims he is the last prophet through whom God revealed his Word. Judaism rejects both the divinity of Jesus and the idea that Mohammed was the last chosen prophet of God. The Koran in Islam is not like the Bible in Christanity. To a Muslim it resembles the role that an orthodox Christian ascribes to the person of Jesus Christ. The Koran was unfolded to Mohammed in Makkah and Medina, via the angel Gabriel, between A.D. 610–632. The Koran is a long book with 114 chapters (*suras)* and some 6,000 versus. In all, the prophet used ninety-nine names for Allah—wise, benevolent, merciful, and so on.

The fount of Islam is Saudi Arabia, the birthplace of the Prophet Mohammed in the late sixth century A.D. That country has two holy cities: Makkah,
where Mohammed was born and received God's revelations and which is also
the site of Kaaba—the Islamic shrine that incorporates the large Black Stone
that had been holy to Arabs even before Mohammed's era (and to which
Muslims turn in prayer); and Medina (literally, "the City"), to which Mohammed migrated after being initially ostracized in Makkah for preaching the new
Word of God. That migration *(hejira)* occurred in A.D. 622, which is why that
year is used as the first year of the Muslim calendar.

From its roots in the Arab world, Islam spread quickly in virtually every
direction, as far west as the Atlantic Coast of Africa, as far east as Indonesia,
and as far north as the gates to the city of Paris. The historical peak of consolidated Islamic political strength was the Ottoman Empire. The Turks had
accepted Islam in the tenth century, and by the fifteenth century had built an
Islamic empire that virtually ringed the Mediterranean. Ottoman power began
to crumble in the seventeenth century as European colonization picked up
steam, and ended officially in 1923 with the proclamation of the secular
(albeit Muslim) Republic of Turkey. However, the decline of the political
empire was not accompanied by a decline in the number of Muslims; Islam
continued to spread throughout the world.

The core of religious behavior for Muslims is embodied in the Five Pillars
of Islam:

1. The creed (*al-Shehada*) that "There is no god but Allah, and Mohammed is the messenger of Allah"
2. Regular prayers five times a day: at dawn, noon, late afternoon, sunset,
   and early eavening
3. Giving alms or *zakat*, an alms tax of 2.5 percent of savings each year to
   the poor
4. Fasting during the daylight hours of the month of Ramadan
5. Undertaking a pilgrimage (the *Haj*) to Makkah.

Muslims are further bound by the regulation of everyday life prescribed by
the *sharia* (the "way" or "the straight path")—the Islamic law covering both
religious and civil activities (in classical Islam there is no difference between
the two). The *sharia* draws primarily from the Koran (the Word of God as
revealed to Mohammed), the *sunna* and *hadith* (the collection of traditions
and sayings of Mohammed), the *qiyas* (the body of reasoning developed by
jurists over time), and the *ijma* (the consensus of a group of judges representing a Muslim community). Religious courts administer the *sharia*, and in an
officially Islamic nation such as Iran or Saudi Arabia, they are the only courts
in the land. In most Islamic nations, however, there are two sets of laws—secular and religious—governing different but complementary aspects of
people's lives. The fundamentalist movement within modern Islam rests

primarily on the attempt to establish Islamic republics in which the *sharia* is the only governing law.

There are two major Muslim groups—the Sunni and the Shia (Shi'ite Muslims). The origin of their difference lies largely in their belief as to who should lead Islam after the death of the Prophet Mohammed. Sunni Muslims endorse Abu Bakr who was elected caliph ("leader"); he was a faithful friend and the first convert to Islam. Shias believe that Mohammed's son-in-law Ali (also a cousin and close friend of the Prophet) should have been chosen caliph. The majority of Muslims in the world today are Sunnis, but Shia is the major minority sect and forms the majority in the Islamic societies of Iran and Iraq, although in Iraq the minority Sunnis control the government. The 12 million Shias in Iraq are, not coincidentally, concentrated in the southeastern part of the country that borders Iran. Shia Muslims (about 1.3 million) are also a majority among Muslims in Lebanon, but they represent only 30 to 40 percent of the total Lebanese population (which has a large Christian minority).

The Shias attribute political authority to their *imams* (religious leaders), seeing them more in the Christian sense of priests. Shias see their leaders as acting in line with true Islamic authority which, they say, has descended not through the first three *imams* to succeed Mohammed but through the fourth, Mohammed's son-in-law Ali, and through Ali's son Hussein. They count twelve genuine *imams* in all. Hussein, facing greatly superior odds, was killed in battle in A.D. 680. Shias see him as the ultimate martyr and celebrate his death with intense emotion. They see contemporary *imams* as holding power on earth until all twelve *imams* return to earth at a time unknown.

There is no central authority in Islam, and therefore no Muslim hierarchy or bureaucracy. This leaves leadership open to local clerics who may or may not have formal training, but who live among and work with a local community and mosque and may gain considerable prestige and clout. In the Arab world and Iran, the religious leaders are usually called *imam* or sheikh, whereas farther east, in Afghanistan, Pakistan, and India, they are more often called *mullah*, and they hold the title *mallam* in West Africa.

In Islam, as in other religions, the ideal and the practice clash. Westerners see the practice and condemn the ideal. Many Muslims deplore the practice and cling to their own concepts of the ideal. Asian Muslims—in Indonesia, for instance—consider their own form of Sunni Islam to be "purer" than Islam in the Arab world, which they consider adulterated by oil wealth and materialism.

The Koran (accepted by both Sunni and Shia) does not record anything similar to the spiritual account of creation in the first chapter of Genesis. It starts with Allah creating Adam from dust and Eve from his rib. Both were said to have been free from sin. Allah is recorded as having demanded his angels to bow down to them. Iblis (later called Shaitan or Satan) is said to have refused on the grounds that he was made of fire and Adam only of dust. Allah cast Iblis out but granted him the ability to tempt man, and power over all men for all time—unless they believe. It was Iblis, the Koran says, who pursuaded Adam and Eve together to eat the apple from the tree of knowledge. To a Muslim, the devil is very real.

A Muslim sees his human life and belongings as gifts from Allah to be used in God's service and to help others. Suicide is strictly forbidden. So is cremation, since the body must be "given back to God" by being buried. So Islam to a Muslim is both simple (one God, one final prophet) and complex (legalistic, with rules and interpretations for daily life).

Islam is closer to Judaism than to orthodox Christianity in a number of ways: their position on Jesus' divinity and the concept of the Trinity, their legal scholarship, and their dietary laws. Islam agrees with orthodox Christianity on the existence of an afterlife and a final judgment, but believes that Jesus was not resurrected but simply was taken into heaven by God.

POLITICS OF ISLAM

For several centuries Islam was the overwhelming political force in the world. But during the last three centuries, Muslim nations have seen their power eroded by technologically superior Western countries. The majority of Muslims live in numbing poverty. Taught by Islam that they are destined to world preeminence, Muslims often found themselves ruled rather than ruling. That reversal has helped create bitterness and an identity crisis that feeds Muslim hostility, especially in the Middle East. Islam is for many a rallying force against what many Muslims regard as Western imperialism and, worse, Western secularism.

The Prophet and the leaders who followed him stressed that God's way for individuals applied to governments too. That is, government's role was to serve as the arm of Islam to promote God's truth and morality. Those who opposed God's way were agents of Satan; thus the world was largely divided between the servants of God and the infidels, the servants of the devil. In these regards, Islam's founder differed noticeably from Jesus, the founder of Christianity. In the face of persecution, Mohammed organized an army to wage *jihad*, or holy war; Jesus chose to suffer. Mohammed taught that religion and earthly government were one; Jesus said that His kingdom was not of this world. Over centuries, those early differences became integral to the split between Western and Islamic thought. Christianity eventually divided church and state, allowing scientists the freedom to develop technology—and advanced weaponry.

THE PRACTICE OF ISLAM

Islamic practice, as distinct from Islamic principles, varies widely. The principles are endlessly interpreted in light of different national traditions and cultures. The Koran and *sharia* are quoted and requoted to support opposite points of view.

In Saudi Arabia, which uses a strict interpretation of the law called *Hanbali,* king and taxi-driver alike are buried with simple headstones. Yet in Muslim Egypt, whose pharaohs built the pyramids forty-seven centuries ago, families still vie to build elaborate mausoleums unsanctioned by Islam. In Riyadh, a Saudi caught eating in public during daylight during the fasting month of Ramadan can be beaten. In Cairo, an Egyptian can eat or not, as he wishes.

A woman in Saudi Arabia may not drive a car. She is not supposed to travel anywhere without a male member of the family. She does not appear in public without an enveloping floor-length black robe and a black veil pulled over her head to comply with the Koran's injunction that women must be modest in public and avoid what one scholar calls "the lustful glances of men" (Figure 6.2). And several times a day, every day, streets are patroled by bearded men belonging to committees for the propagation of virtue and the suppression of vice. They tap on shop-fronts with canes, closing them down completely for ritual Islamic prayers.

Muslim women across the Red Sea from Saudi Arabia in Egypt walk freely and unveiled. They follow a more liberal intrepretation of the Koran, which says that a woman may maintain a modest appearance by covering her shoulders, arms, and legs. In Indonesia, which is 90 percent Muslim, women are

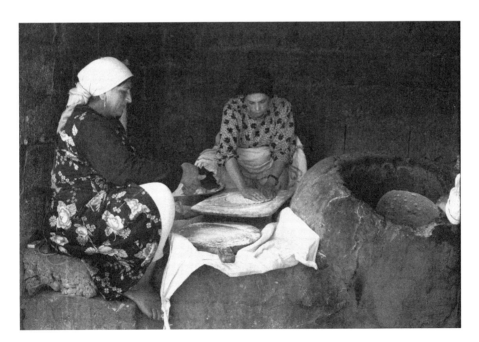

Figure 6-2. Women gather around the neighborhood baking stone to make bread for their families in the village of Akroum in northern Lebanon. Politics of gender and religion have robbed Muslim women of their rights in many countries. Women face many challenges; in some Islamic countries women have created new spaces to negotiate their position. (Photo: UNICEF by Nicole Tautanji.)

unveiled. The Islam that has emerged in Indonesia is very different from the more conservative Islam in Saudi Arabia.

In some countries polygamy is banned by civil law unless the first wife gives permission. Muslim scholars point to another Koranic verse as virtually forbidding more than one wife because it says a man cannot be equal to all his wives, be he "ever so eager." A man is still permitted by the *sharia* to divorce by simple proclamation, but some countries such as Tunisia have placed obstacles in a man's path. Devout Muslims also know that the Prophet is reported to have said that of all actions permitted by Allah, divorce is the least acceptable. As for adultery and theft, such stringent proof of them is required that the death penalty, amputation, and flogging are now rare in many countries, but they do take place in Saudi Arabia. Saudi Princess Misha was shot for adultery in Jeddah in July 1977 and her lover was beheaded.

The Koran specifically forbids the use of alcohol and pork but lays down no legal penalties. Although devout Muslims obey the bans, there are those who do not. The Koran forbids Muslims from doing anything to harm their bodies, so Muslims must make up their own minds about the effects of smoking, which is not mentioned in the Koran.

Islam supports the dominance of males in society, although the *sharia* requires fairness and compassion for females. An Islamic society is patriarchal. The dominance of men is accompanied by their paternalistic attitude toward women and by deep concern for the sexual purity of their daughters and the constancy of their wives. In many Islamic societies, this often leads to the seclusion of women in the home and the veiling of women in public.

Fundamentalist Islam

Decades of political upheaval, along with an increased acknowledgement of religion, gave rise to Muslim fundamentalism. Many Muslims, humiliated by Western domination, trapped by poverty, and abused by corrupt dictators, long for the days when Islam ruled. They represent strands of restless, orthodox, Islamic fundamentalist thinking around the world. They believe themselves to be on the leading edge of a general revival in Islam—a widespread determination to turn away from both communist atheism and Western materialism to a purer Islamic ideal of government. So far Iran is the only country where fundamentalist thinkers have succeeded in overthrowing a secular Westernized leader. The fundamentalists see themselves as closest to the "authentic" Islam of the Prophet Mohammed.

The fundamentalists are forcing some concessions from, and are otherwise worrying rulers in, Egypt, the Gulf States, Sudan, Afghanistan, and Algeria. To fundamentalists in general, the urgent need is to throw off the influences of 200 years of colonial domination. They want to reinstate the kind of Islamic purity that they believe led to the original Islamic surge across the world.

The efforts of fundamentalist groups to alleviate poverty impress many Egyptians, who are often cynical about government corruption. These groups provide funds to the destitute, run clinics, mediate disputes, and patrol against common crime. In many poor neighborhoods, hard hit by the earthquake that struck Cairo on October 12, 1992, the fundamentalists were the only groups dispensing food and blankets for the first few days. There are no grass-roots organizations in many Islamic countries to compete with the fundamentalists, leaving a street-level power vacuum that the fundamentalists have filled.

The consequences of the fundamentalists' rise in power is proving disastrous for some national governments. In Egypt many accuse the ruling National Democratic Party, which has governed Egypt since the 1952 coup led by Gamal Abdul Nasser, of having lost its sense of mission. There is no one leader who dominates the fundamentalist movement in Egypt, but many members follow the teachings of Sheikh Omar Abdul Rahman, 58, a blind theologian who once taught in the university in Assiut and is now held in connection with the bombing of the World Trade Center in New York. Egypt's corrupt and self-perpetuating military autocracy, now in its fifth decade of rule, no longer offers hope for democracy or a better life to millions of desperately poor Egyptian peasants. Islamic fundamentalism, the most potent revolutionary force in the modern Middle East, ruthlessly exploits this vulnerability.

The military-backed government of Algeria is facing mounting armed attacks by Islamic fundamentalists. There is concern that an Algerian fundamentalist government's influence might spread across North Africa, including the West's biggest Arab ally, Egypt. Egypt, which works closely with the Algerian security forces, is shipping in Muslim clerics to try to challenge the fundamentalists on theological grounds. It appears, however, that Algerians' widespread dissatisfaction with their government is rooted in economics, and that the fundamentalists' appeal among Algeria's urban, secularized majority lies more in their reputation for incorruptibility than in their religious conviction. The Islamic Salvation Front, known by its French acronym, FIS, calls for an Islamic state that would reject the political and cultural values of the West. Elections in 1991 gave the Islamic Front an overwhelming majority in the Algerian Parliament. A junta, backed by the army, seized power in January 1992. It outlawed the Islamic Front, and drove it underground. The Islamic movement, denied power through the ballot box, has mounted an armed revolt against the government in Algeria.

In lands such as Egypt and Algeria, fundamentalist Islamic groups have proven to be far better organized and, therefore, more efficient providers of basic services than overburdened governments. Islamic groups opposed to the government provided temporary housing, emergency feeding, and psychological counselors for the bulk of the earthquake victims in Egypt. Egypt's well-intentioned but bureaucratic officials were simply unable to respond quickly. Islamic groups thus secured a double victory. They won the loyalty of the impoverished thousands they helped, and used the government's paralysis to support their argument that "Islam is the solution."

Fundamentalist Islam's appeal is not merely pragmatic or just a form of generational rebellion. Fundamentalist Islam has become, for many young men and women, the favored means of political opposition. Although there are many interpretations of Islam, virtually all fundamentalist versions oppose the nominally Islamic governments even in such religion-minded lands as Saudi Arabia, saying that they are not truly Islamic in law and tradition. They have a powerful argument in the evident failure of many Arab governments to deliver long-promised economic development, social justice, or spiritual dignity.

The Islamic movements draw strength not so much from any surge in religious zeal among the Middle Eastern peoples but from political failure—brutal government, military defeat, economic mismanagement, and corruption. The movements appeal most to those who suffer worst—the people of the shanty towns, bombed villages, and slums of Gaza, southern Lebanon, Algiers, and Cairo. When the government in any of these places fails, support for Islamists grows. The Palestinian Authority's apparent inability to provide better living conditions in Gaza and bring about Israeli withdrawal from the West Bank and Gaza has benefited the militant Hamas.

Al-Qaeda

Al-Qaeda (meaning *the base*) is a terrorist organization based in the Middle East that supports the activities of Muslim extremists around the world. Its founder, Osama bin Laden, is a Saudi-born millionaire. Al Qaeda believes that governments of Muslim countries that fail to follow Islamic law should be overthrown. Al-Qaeda also considers the United States to be a primary enemy of Islam, and supports Islamic militants throughout the world. In 1996 al-Qaeda leaders moved to Afghanistan and lived under the protection of the Taliban, a conservative Islamic government that controlled most of the country (Figure 6.3). The Taliban government fell in 2001 after the United States launched its military campaign against the Taliban following the September 11 terrorist attacks.

Many Muslim militants, including al-Qaeda, regard violent jihad against "unbelievers" as a religious obligation for all Muslims. Islam emphasizes action in the struggle to implement belief, to defend religion, and to spread Islamic society throughout the world. The early Islamic community used the model of jihad for the spread and defense of religion. When Mohammed and his group experienced persecution in Mecca, they emigrated to Medina to regroup and strengthen. Then they began jihad to spread Islam and promote a worldwide Islamic community. Under the leadership of Mohammed and his successors, the Islamic community spread rapidly through conquest and conversion, creating a vast empire stretching from North Africa to India. From

Figure 6-3. The boundary pillar marking the Afghanistan–British India (now Pakistan) border, called the Durand Line, was drawn by Britain in 1893. The boundary runs through the frontier tribal areas of Pakistan and is the stronghold of radical Islamic groups such as the Taliban and al-Qaeda terrorist network that is providing shelter to Osama bin Laden. (Photo: P.P. Karan.)

the seventh to eighteenth century Islam became a global power through the existence of empires and sultanates. The breakup and fragmentation of the Muslim empires by European colonialism reduced the significance of the Islamic worldwide community. During the last half-century the spread of international communication has reinforced the resurgence of Islam, and has produced a wave of radical Islamic movements from Algeria (Islamic Salvation Front, Salafist Group for Call and Combat), Egypt (Islamic Jihad, Muslim Brotherhood, and Jmaat-i-Islami), Israel/Palestine (Hamas, Al Aqsa Martyrs Brigades), Saudi Arabia (the Wahhabi-based pan-Islamic vision), Sudan, Iran, Pakistan (Jamiyat-i-Ulama-i-Islam, Sipah-Sahaba Pakistan, Laskar-e-Jhangvi), Tajiksitan (Islamic Renaissance Party), Uzbekistan (Islamic Movement of Uzbekistan), Afghanistan, Malaysia, Indonesia (Jemaah Islamiyah, Laskar Jihad), and the Philippines (Moro Islamic Front).

The model of jihad for the geographic spread of Islam has guided Muslims throughout the ages, including the al-Qaeda network of the Islamic movement today. Jihad is a defining concept in Islam today as it was in the early years of Islam. It involves efforts to spread Islam and to support the struggles of

Muslims in places such as Israel, Kashmir, the southern Philippines, and Chechnya, and attacking the United States and U.S. interests around the world because they are viewed as a major obstacle in the objective of a global Islamic revolution.

Abdullah Azzam, a faculty member at King Abdulaziz University, a teacher of Osama bin Laden, and founder of Hamas, was an early advocate of a militant global jihad in the 1970s (Cooley, 2000). Azzam maintained: "Jihad and the rifle alone: no negotiations, no conferences, and no dialogues" (Bergen, 2002). The militant Islamic movements conceptualize jihad as global in scope with the objective of reclaiming all the lands that at one time belonged to Islam. Azzam stated that jihad will remain an individual obligation of each Muslim until all lands that were under Islamic empires of the past are returned to Muslims so that Islam will reign again.

The World Islamic Front for the Jihad Against Jews and Christians, an umbrella group of jihadis across the Muslim world, was formed in February 1998 by Osama bin Laden. It trained at least 10,000 potential fighters in eastern Afghanistan. It emphasizes global ideology and agenda, and its geopolitical view conceptualizes the Muslim world as under siege, with their lands dominated or occupied by their historic enemies, Christians and Jews. It underscores the traditional division of the world into the land of Islam (*dar-al-Islam*) and the land of warfare (*dar al-harb*) and infidels.

In the 1990s Afghanistan and Pakistan became primary centers for the globalization of jihad and the culture of jihad through networks of Islamic *madrasas* and training camps for the jihadis. The Taliban government and Pakistan provided refuge and training camps and the base for a network of organizations and cells. Saudi Arabia and Islamic groups in Europe and North America provided the funding for the training camps. In addition, Saudi Arabia finances thousands of Islamic schools and mosques around the world which teach that non-Muslims are inferior to Muslims and must be converted or confronted. Fifteen young Saudis involved in the 9/11 attacks were graduates of Saudi schools and religious classes that justified jihad. An estimated 10,000 to 20,000 young Muslims from around the world trained in bin Laden's camps in Afghanistan in the 1990s.

The al-Qaeda terrorist network is associated with radical Islam and jihad. It represents a form of terrorism that is transnational in its identity and recruitment, and global in its ideology, strategy, and targets, with a network of organizations and economic transactions. A report by the Council on Foreign Relations in New York has stated that al-Qaeda's terror network derives most of its financing from charities and individuals in Saudi Arabia, but the kingdom has turned a blind eye to this problem (Gerth and Miller, 2002).

Since the rout of al-Qaeda in 2001 in Afghanistan and the destruction of their sanctuaries, the followers of al-Qaeda have dispersed throughout the world to reestablish themselves within a loosely knit alliance of like-minded but independent groups. In some cases these groups share planning with operatives of al-Qaeda and receive money from its financial network. But more often the extremists are linked by a common ideology without direct ties to al-Qaeda. Afghanistan was the training ground for a new generation of extremists who have moved their operations into basements, apartments, and remote areas around the world to plan their own attacks. As a result of the broader dimensions of threat, al-Qaeda has evolved into a radical international movement pursuing the United States and its allies. This radical international jihad, with some mid-level al-Qaeda influences, will continue for several years.

In Southeast Asia the primary objective of the Indonesian-based Jemaah Islamiya is the creation of an Islamic state across an arc of Southeast Asia, but it has made the organization available to the global al-Qaeda network for operations against the United States. Jemaah Islamiya began as a religious movement in the 1970s, and made common cause with al-Qaeda in the 1990s. It saw the creation of an Islamic community as the first step toward establishing an Islamic state across an arc of Southeast Asia. Al-Qaeda's senior representative in Southeast Asia, Omar al-Faruq, operated a terrorist network across Southeast Asia and participated in the training camp on Mindanao run by the Moro Liberation Front, which is fighting for an Islamic state in the Philippines. Jemaah Islamiya has a network of cells in Singapore, Malaysia, the Philippines, Myanmar, Thailand, and Cambodia. It resembles al-Qaeda in organization and, like al-Qaeda, operates across international boundaries. This is unlike many other groups affiliated with al-Qaeda, many of which are focused on overthrowing the government of a single country. Jemaah Islamiya has sent people to Osama bin Laden's Afghanistan camps and received money from al-Qaeda. It is believed that Jemaah Islamiya was involved in the blast in Bali in October 2002. Indonesia is an excellent place for al-Qaeda operations. The government has weak control over its far-flung islands, and dozens of al-Qaeda operatives have found safe haven in the world's most populous Muslim nation. Some came here by air, but most sneaked into Pakistan, and then traveled several thousand miles in fishing boats from Arabian Sea ports.

Al-Qaeda-trained terrorists remain in the United States in so-called sleeper cells, awaiting instructions to attack. According to published press reports, law enforcement officials' monitoring of men suspected of ties to al-Qaeda has resulted in a string of arrests and indictments around the country—in western New York, Detroit, Seattle, and Portland, Oregon—of U.S. citizens and others accused of conspiring in terrorist cells to assist al-Qaeda. At least several dozen people now under surveillance in the United States—with different degrees of terrorist training, and with various degrees of loyalty to al-Qaeda—would take part in a terrorist attack if ordered, and they represent a clear threat. Much of the surveillance campaign is centered in Detroit because the region is the home to the nation's largest population of people of Arab descent.

MAJOR TYPES OF SETTLEMENT AND THE ECOLOGICAL TRIANGLE

The Middle East can be divided into three kinds of geo-ecological zones. First is the mountains and uplands zone in Turkey and northern Iran and along the shores of the Mediterranean and in Yemen. This zone gets some precipitation and resembles the alpine region. The second ecological zone comprises the river valleys: the valley of the Nile in Egypt, and the valley of the Tigris and Euphrates in Iraq. The soil there is rich and fertile, with irrigation agriculture and a heavy concentration of population. The third zone is the dry areas. It is the most extensive zone, parched and arid, with rockstrewn or sandy desert landscape. These three kinds of geo-ecological zones have produced varied cultural adaptation patterns resulting in at least three types of settlement patterns.

Nomads

Although the nomads represent a quickly vanishing breed and account for perhaps only about 10 percent of the rural population of the region, they are significant in that theirs is a highly rational adaptation to restricted resources. Although nomadic groups are found in the entire region wherever deserts and mountains form part of the landscape, especially large clusters of them are located in the Arabian, Syrian, and Egyptian deserts. The nomads are the stockbreeders of the Middle East. Their life is dominated by the needs of their animals. They move from oasis to oasis with their herds of camels, or from lowlands to uplands with their flocks of sheep and goats, seeking pasture and water. They supply beasts of burden, meat, milk, and milk products to the villagers and city dwellers. Traditionally, they are also the guardians of the empty spaces in the vast desert. Caravans and desert travelers seek their protection in their long journeys over trackless wastes.

The nomadic way of life has been undergoing changes because the traditional bedouin economy has been undermined. Due to the emergence of the modern nation state, increasing numbers of nomads are being settled in various countries. Most governments have developed comprehensive schemes for the administration of nomads, and the process of sedentarization of nomads and its attendant problems are common in many areas of the Middle East.

There is a continuum of degrees and forms of nomadism, and there are three major categories of nomads, based on the type of animal herded. Each type is limited in area by the environmental requirements of the particular type of animal. The more mobile groups are much further away from sedentarization than the less mobile groups. The first category is the "bedouin of the camel" (*ahl-al-abal*), who dwell mostly on the barren areas. The second category is the less nomadic "bedouin of the sheep" (*ahl-al-ghanam*), who range less widely. They are located near the large markets and in the agricultural areas where they are assured of fodder and more regular water supplies than in the desert. Last, there are the least nomadic and largely settled bedouins (*al-ashn 'ir al mutahaddarah*). They move in a limited area.

Peasants

A substantial portion of the Middle Eastern population lives in village communities. Villages are therefore the foundation of the region's society. Large clusters of village communities are found along the Mediterranean coast, in the Black Sea and Caspian Sea regions, and in the uplands of the Fertile Crescent. Their primary function is farming. They grow wheat, barley, date palms, and other lesser crops. In terms of culture this is where traditional lifestyles find their continuity and stability. Through their function as food producers and through their conventional living patterns they provide continuity to society in the Middle East.

Villages comprise agglomerations of flat-roofed, single-story, rectangular houses along narrow, winding streets. The inhabitants of the villages are grouped spatially by kinship ties and sometimes by religion. Compact agglomerations of 100 to nearly two thousand houses are found in the lowland river valleys. Some villages in central Arabia, Iran, and the Tigris–Euphrates lowlands have defensive walls. Linear settlements stretch along the levees of the Tigris and Euphrates in Iraq and beside the Nile in Egypt. In Iran settlements are generally found around the outlet of a *qanat* or along the side of a water course. *Qanats* are underground horizontal tunnels carrying water to villages. Water is tapped on upper slopes of alluvial fans and brought down by gravity.

In southern Iraq, marshes straddle the lower reaches of the Tigris and Euphrates rivers and their confluence: the waterway called the Shatt al Arab. In this marshy area surrounded by the towns of Amara and Nasiriya and the city of Basra, villages dot the marshes in clusters of anything from half a dozen to 200 dwellings. The Marsh Arabs live in this waterlogged area, and grow rice, wheat, and barley. Fishing is an important part of their economy. They live in intricately designed and well-constructed reed houses.

Urbanites

Nearly half of the population of the Middle East today is urban. The first cities in the region emerged about 4000 B.C. Some ancient towns such as Ur were partially planned. Alexander and his successors established a network of towns throughout the Middle East, notably Alexandria in Egypt. The Romans built a series of fortified towns in Mesopotamia and Syria and in the African provinces. After the advent of Islam, cities became the cornerstone of Muslim culture and civilization.

Like cities elsewhere, Middle Eastern cities were centers of the local economy. Under Islam, the cities acquired distinctive internal spatial patterns marked by the allocation of central space to specific institutions, the development of characteristic patterns of social and economic organization, and the creation of an urban milieu congenial to the practices of Islam. The form and structure of Islamic cities are discussed in a later section.

AGRICULTURE AND WATER IN THE MIDDLE EAST

The Middle East has neither the agronomic capacity nor the environment to efficiently produce enough food to meet the demand generated by population and income growth. The region is composed of oil exporting nations and nations dependent on other than agricultural income to generate economic growth. In the case of the oil-rich nations, consumer subsidies have played a critical role in rapidly advancing diets and improving standards of living. In the case of nations without oil, government efforts aim at improving agricultural output, expanding export crop output, controlling food imports, and minimizing expenditures on subsidies.

In many countries agriculture is of a subsistence type, contributing a very small portion to the GNP; Kuwait, Qatar, Oman, Bahrain, and the United Arab Emirates are in this category. In other countries agriculture is comparatively small, but plays an important role in the country's overall economy: Saudi Arabia and Iraq, for example. For the third set, agriculture is an important sector of the economy, plays a major role in the countries' trade, and employs a large sector of the labor force; Turkey, Jordan, and Syria are examples. In virtually all countries, however, domestic output does not meet growing needs. During the last two decades, food imports have become critical to the food security of these countries. In some countries imports comprise up to 75 percent of the food consumed. Wheat and barley are the mainstays of most of the countries' agriculture. Significant quantities of fresh vegetables, citrus, other fruits, and their processed products are important exports.

Expansion of agriculture in the Middle East depends on availability of more water for irrigation. Drought and pollution have limited the supplies, and war and mismanagement have squandered them. If nations in the Middle East could share both water technology and resources, they could satisfy the region's demand. But in the ethnic and religious rivalries, water seldom stands alone as an issue. It is entagled in the politics that keep people from trusting and seeking help from one another.

Disputes over water rights have been a major feature of the political geography of the Middle East. In 1990, when Turkey built the Ataturk Dam to contain the Euphrates, there were protests from Syria and Iraq. Some Arab commentators have revived old memories of Ottoman rule across the Middle East and view Turkey's action as an effort to subdue Arabs. Ataturk Dam anchors Turkey's Southeastern Anatolia Project which is designed to develop the agricultural potential of the semi-arid plains of the southeast. Full development of the Anatolia Project could reduce the Euphrates' flow by as much as 60 percent. This could severely jeopardize Syrian and Iraqi agriculture.

Syria needs the Euphrates for irrigation agriculture to keep pace with its population growth of 3.8 percent a year. Syria's own large-scale Euphrates Dam at Tabqa has kindled fear of scarcity downstream in Iraq. But Syria sees the great dam as vital to its future security. The nation's rich rain-fed western farmland is already heavily used. The government looks now to its arid eastern steppes, where the Euphrates Dam irrigates 500,000 acres. Syria needs to farm a million more acres in this region to produce sufficient food, and that cannot be done without more river water.

Iraq has adequate river water; its shortcomings are in management, investment, and pollution control. During forty years of wealth generated from oil revenues, Iraq gave its rivers and agriculture low priority. For the ten years of war with Iran, water projects were further set back. Water arrives in Iraq already degraded by salts, agricultural runoff, and chemical pollutants from upstream users, for Iraq sits at the tail end of the drainage. Seasonal floods that once leached and washed the soil have been rare. With over-irrigation and poor drainage, salinization has affected huge areas. In southern Iraq, where brackish marshes surround the Shatt al Arab waterway formed by the confluence of the Tigris and Euphrates, thousands of acres have been glazed with an icing of salt.

Kuwait, the oil-rich nation that Iraq still covets, has little fresh water, but it has the money to make fresh water. To utilize seawater, Kuwait has constructed six large-scale oil-powered desalination plants. The process requires huge amounts of energy and produces a cubic meter of fresh water that costs more than $2, compared with 20 cents in Chicago. Water is heavily subsidized, and consumers in Kuwait pay less than a tenth of the cost.

Saudi Arabia, farther down the Arabian Peninsula, leads the world in desalination. Its twenty-two large plants produce 30 percent of all desalinated water in the world. It is also a leader in the pumping of fossil water—water accumulated in an earlier geologic age—lying deep in acquifers spread under northern Africa and the Arabian Peninsula. Mining nonrenewable water is like extracting oil—someday it will run out. Various estimates of the life span for Saudi fossil-water reserves at the present rate of pumping range from 25 to 100 years. Using such water, Saudi Arabia has exceeded its goal of self-sufficiency in wheat. For drinking water the Saudis will increasingly rely on desalination. They fear only sabotage and pollution, as dramatized by the 600-square mile oil slick that blackened the Persian Gulf during the war against Iraq, threatening to clog desalination intake pipes.

Jordan controls no major rivers, and its acquifers are over-pumped. The Jordan River forms part of its border with Israel, but the Jordan's headwaters rise mainly in the mountains of Lebanon, northern Israel, and the highlands of Syria, and the river is heavily tapped upstream. Jordan depends on the river's main tributary, the Yarmuk, which forms part of the kingdom's northern border with Syria. But the Yarmuk is also crucial to Syria and Israel. Only the small Zarqa River runs within Jordan.

In the 1960s Israel finished its National Water Carrier project, tapping the Sea of Galilee to channel water as far south as the Negev Desert and virtually drying up the southern Jordan River. Jordan and other Arab states were outraged, calling the transfer of water from the Jordan basin a breach of international law. Israel maintains that it has the right to do what it wants with its own water. During the 1967 war Israel captured the Golan Heights and the West Bank, effectively gaining control of almost the entire Jordan River basin. Jordanian farmers in the valley abandoned the east bank, and agriculture shriveled there. In the 1970s Jordan completed the extension of its major project, the East Ghor (King Abdullah) Canal, which runs from the Yarmuk River south, parallel to the Jordan. Agriculture soaks up as much as 73 percent of Jordan's water.

Israel draws 65 percent of its renewable fresh water from two major acquifers: a limestone acquifer under the mountains and a shallower, partly saline one beneath the coastal plain, including the Gaza Strip. The rest comes from the Jordan River and its great storage basin, the Sea of Galilee. Israel has made a major contribution to farming in arid lands by the development of drip irrigation, which brings precisely the right amount of water to each plant through holes in plastic hoses, with minimal waste. Computerized automation has allowed such refinements as high-frequency pulse irrigation. Farmers have more than doubled their output in the last twenty years, with the same amount of water.

Since ancient times the people of Egypt have huddled along the green tendril of the Nile. The delta and the narrow Nile Valley make up only 3 percent of Egypt's land but are home to 96 percent of the nation's population. Here, nearly 58 million people live in an area only slightly larger than Maryland. Every inch of this very narrow strip on both sides of the Nile is cultivated twice, and sometimes three times, a year. Yet to feed it's projected 25 million more people by 2010, Egypt must make better use of the Nile—recycling its waters for multiple use—and pump water from acquifers.

The Nile drains eight other nations: Ethiopia, Sudan, Tanzania, Uganda, Kenya, Zaire, Burundi, and Rwanda—more than 10 percent of Africa. It flows into the Nubian Desert of Sudan and gathers behind Egypt's Aswan High Dam, which has given Egypt's farmers security from destructive floods and drought since its completion in 1971. Lake Nasser spreads south from Aswan High Dam. A hundred twenty million tons of silt settles yearly behind the dam, silt that once replenished the banks and built the Nile Delta.

To compensate, farmers have had to increase their use of fertilizer, which contributes to water pollution. But Lake Nasser has kept Egyptian agriculture stable and the economy from collapse.

Under a "new lands" program, Egypt plans to farm the desert using water from the acquifers. The acquifers that could sustain agriculture in the Western Desert and in Sinai have been identified and drilling programs begun.

FORM AND STRUCTURE OF ISLAMIC CITIES

The design of the great majority of medieval Middle Eastern cities was oval or circular. Those cities had walls and gates that were guarded by military installations. Inside the walls were residential sections for the palace of the ruler and for the aristocracy and other socioeconomic groups. The central mosque also served as the political focus of the city. In and around that mosque the inhabitants gathered to pray, to hear proclamations of the rulers, and to express political sentiments and opinions. The central mosque was also the intellectual and educational focus of a city, because the *ulma,* or learned scholars, met there to discuss and to teach. Many city officials and other administrative personnel came from the *ulma* group.

The commercial area, dominated by a market, or *suq,* was adjacent to the central mosque. Most large cities also had individual market lanes for textiles, books, and various household and luxury goods. The number and types of the shops in a *suq* depended on the size of the city. The *suq* and the area around the central mosque were the only places in Middle Eastern cities where the segregated Muslim and non-Muslim groups came in contact with each other. Because of this social exchange, the market played an important integrating role in a city.

A residential zone surrounded the commercial district. This zone was a mosaic of areas characterized by the segregation of groups according to tribal and religious affiliations, indigenous or immigrant status, social class, and occupation. There was little open space in any of those sections. Houses had inner courts isolated from the narrow streets and alleyways, and buildings were designed to give maximum privacy to their inhabitants. The emphasis on privacy was the result of social mores that required women to withdraw as completely as possible from the public.

Each residential section had coherence and a special character. Among the Muslims, common tribal or village origin was a source of coherence, which was further enhanced by association with a religious school, or *madrasa*, led by a sheikh. A common occupation often distinguished a residential quarter. Each residential quarter contained a place of worship, a school, a public bath, a small *suq,* and permanent workshops, especially for weaving.

A quarter for the Jewish minority was found in most Middle Eastern cities. That quarter, known as *mellah* in Morocco and *hara* in Tunisia and Libya, was often located close to the citadel, perhaps for protection. Jewish quarters emerged in North African and Yemeni cities during the fifteenth century.

Christian Arabs likewise formed their own communities, which were focused on churches. The Christians shared language, economy, and social habits with their Islamic and Jewish compatriots. Cities in Egypt, Lebanon, and Syria have had large groups of indigenous Christian residents for centuries. The Christian population is now widely dispersed throughout most Arabic cities. Some Libyan cities until recently had large numbers of Christian residents, but the government has sought to stop the practice of Christianity.

Land use patterns of the medieval Middle Eastern cities influenced later urban forms in two ways. First, city walls gradually were removed, and new residential districts arose on and beyond the margins of the old cities. Second, satellite communities grew until they abutted the older cities. The new districts attracted residents, especially wealthy families, from the old city, and also drew workshops and *suqs* in need of additional space and a convenient location for customers along access roads. Those moves accelerated the decline of the old parts of the cities.

During the late nineteenth and early twentieth centuries, Europeans built new districts according to their standards of urban design and style. Those districts differed from the Arabic parts of cities in architecture and layout. New residential districts display contemporary international standards of design and style. The ethnic clusters in most Middle Eastern cities are changing. The departure of Jews since 1948 has been followed by the im-migration of other groups. For example, Kurds moved into the former Jewish quarter in Beirut. In Kuwait, government regulations require citizens and non-Kuwaiti residents to live in different districts.

Patterns of Urban Growth

The spectacular recent growth of Middle Eastern cities has been caused by a high rate of natural increase, prolonged im-migration, and annexation of surrounding villages. The rate of natural increase for the Middle East is approximately 2.8 percent, but it is 4 percent for urban areas. The urban rate is produced by a high fertility rate of 45 to 50 live births per 1,000 population and a declining mortality that results from improved sanitation and medical services, particularly in oil-rich countries with small populations.

Net in-migration, partially attributable to labor migration, frequently exceeds 2 percent annually in urban centers such as Benghazi, Cairo, Baghdad, Amman, Jidda, and Riyadh. International labor migration also has been a major factor in urban growth. Before the Gulf War of 1991 large numbers of Yemenis, Palestinians, and Egptians worked in Saudi Arabia and the Gulf states.

The rapid increase in population has created a serious housing shortage that is worsened by the fast-rising prices of land and the costs of construction. There is also the problem of water supply for the urban centers. Large cities such as Kuwait, Abu Dhabi, and Doha on the Gulf depend on desalination of sea water. Water for Jidda, the main Saudi Arabian seaport on the Red Sea, must be brought by pipeline from inland sources. Most Middle Eastern cities must continue to construct large water-supply projects if future demands for urban water are to be met.

Makkah: A Case Study of an Arab City

According to both Islamic tradition and the Bible, Ismail, infant son of the prophet Abraham, and his mother, Hagar, were left in a desolate valley in western Arabia. When their water supply was gone, tradition relates that a fresh-water spring miraculously burst forth at the feet of baby Ismail. Hagar enclosed the spring, which later became a well. As word of the water source spread, Arab tribes began to settle in the area, and so was born the city of Makkah, destined to become one of the most important oases on the spice and incense routes, at the meeting point of the great south–north and east–west caravan trails.

The water of the well, called Zamzam, supplied the tribes that settled there. Makkah's first settlers were nomadic tribes who lived in tents dispersed around the well of Zamzam and throughout the valley. This thriving settlement became a major trade center at the intersection of old caravan routes in the pre-Islamic period.

With the birth of Islam in the seventh century, the flow of pilgrims to Makkah expanded. Some pilgrims decided to settle permanently in the Holy City. The residential area of Makkah continued to grow, fueled by newcomers each year. Today Makkah's metropolitan area stretches about 8 miles from east to west and about 6 miles from north to south along a series of wadis flanked by bare, steep-sided hills. The wadis, major sources of water supply to Makkah, dissect the region and carry ephemeral water flows. Underlying the dry surface of the wadis are important sources of underground water. Makkah receives water from the underground flows of Wadi Naman and Wadi Fatima.

Makkah's urban layout centers around the sacred area of Haram, the center of Islamic pilgrimage, which has exerted a very special influence on the growth of the city. During the early period the growth of the city took place within the inner city core. Political instability limited urban growth and expansion. During the four hundred years of the Ottoman Empire, from 1517 to 1916, the endless disputes among members of the Sharif family (descendents of Hassan and Hussein, sons of Fatima, daughter of the Prophet) left the region unsettled and prevented rapid growth of Makkah.

Following the establishment of the Saudi state, the city has grown rapidly since 1925. Makkah became the social, cultural, and economic center of the newly formed state. Increases in commercial activity and the number of overseas pilgrims led to expansion of the built-up area in every direction. The growth broadly follows the topography and terrain features of the area. To the southeast, the mountains restrict development.

The city of Makkah is organized into twenty-eight *haras* for administrative purposes. The expansion and changes in Makkah's built-up area have influenced the urban morphology and landscape of the city. The Haram district is the focus of pilgrimage and has a status and importance found only in other religious cities. Large parts of the commercial and residential areas originally surrounding Haram have now moved to new areas.

The most densely populated area of Makkah is around Haram. This area has a density of over 400 persons per hectare (2.47 acres). The ground floors of many buildings in this area are given over to commercial use, with only the upper floors used for residential purposes. The population density declines as one moves outward from the inner core. The suburban *haras* located on the outer margins of Makkah have a population density of fewer than 100 persons per hectare. The suburban zone has 51.4 percent of Makkah's total urban land but contains only 8.6 percent of the city's population. In this least densely populated zone of Makkah buildings are a mixture of mansions and villa-type homes that are well spaced. Most of them have their own gardens.

Ethnic Residential Patterns

The residential areas of Makkah are characterized by a marked segregation of various ethnic groups. Generally speaking, ethnicity in Makkah functions like social class does in Western cities as a basis for residential segregation. There is a continuing tendency for some ethnic groups to concentrate in particular quarters, although such clustering is becoming less important than it was in the past. The degree of ethnic concentration weakens as one proceeds outward from the central part of the city. The newly developed *haras* located on the outer edges of the city show a mixture of ethnic populations among their residents.

The Bedouin and Hejazi tribal groups are concentrated in the *haras* located in the northern part of Makkah. The Takarnah (Africans—mainly Nigerians) are concentrated in the western part of the city. Afghani and Iranian groups are concentrated to the north of the city's core. Bukhariyahs from Turkistan are dominant in the southern part. Muslims from Java (Jawah) and other areas of Southeast Asia are dominant in the residential population of four inner *haras* of Makkah. Indian and Pakistani Muslims (Honoud) are concentrated in southern *haras*.

Social divisions along ethnic lines have led to the development of an interesting pattern of social space in Makkah. Each ethnic residential area tends to be a homogenous social space in terms of the perceptions of its inhabitants, which is reflected in the area's particular values, preferences, and aspirations. The spatial differentiations associated with ethnic origin emerge as the most important element in the urban social pattern of Makkah.

PALESTINIANS AND ISRAELIS: PEOPLE TIED TO CONTESTED LAND

In ancient times, when Hebrew tribes left Egypt they settled in Judea. The Hebrews made their home in the area and built the city of Jerusalem. Roman legions entered the region in the second century B.C. and captured Jerusalem in A.D. 70. The Jewish state disappeared. Later, the territory of Palestine passed from Romans to Arabs to Turks. After the disintegration of the Turkish Empire after World War I, Palestine became a British Mandate Territory.

The conflict between Jews and Arabs began in 1947 when the United Nations voted to recommend the partitioning of Palestine into three parts: a Jewish state, an Arab state, and an international zone for the city of Jerusalem, administered by the United Nations. The Jews accepted the recommendation; the Arabs rejected it. Zionism, a nineteenth-century movement, was designed to secure a political home for Jews.

As Britain's League of Nations mandate over Palestine ended, the State of Israel was established on May, 15, 1948. The United States was the first country to recognize it. The same day, five Arab countries—Egypt, Jordan, Iraq, Syria, and Lebanon—declared war and invaded the new nation.

After a marked rise in activities against Israel by the Arab countries, Israel launched a preemptive strike in June 1967 and effectively destroyed the Egyptian Air Force. Israel occupied the area up to the banks of the Suez Canal, then turned on the Syrians in the Golan Heights. When Jordan entered the war, Israel occupied the West Bank and Arab East Jerusalem. When a cease-fire was declared, Israel occupied the Sinai Peninsula and Gaza Strip, East Jerusalem, the West Bank, and the Golan Heights. Israel absorbed East Jerusalem in 1967 and annexed the Golan Heights in 1981. In November 1967 the United Nations Security Council adopted Resolution 242, which called for Israeli withdrawal from "territories occupied" in the June war and for Arab recognition of Israel's "right to live in peace with secured and recognized boundaries."

Jews believe they have a historic and religious right to Palestine. Thousands of Palestinian Arabs also believe they still have a right to their old homes that are now part of Israel. Partition of the former Palestine has always been the obvious solution for the Arab–Jewish problem. It was recommended by Britain's Peel Commission in 1937, and again by the United Nations in 1947 when it voted for the creation of Israel. Tragically, that obviousness never seems to have struck the Arabs and the Jews at the same time. From the 1930s on, the Palestinian Arabs rejected the idea of sharing the land—their land, they felt—and ended up losing all of it. In 1988, with growing recognition of Israel's permanence and of the need to capitalize on Palestinian uprisings, or *intifada,* in the occupied territories, the Palestinian Liberation Organization began to say that it would settle for a separate state alongside a sovereign Israel. The heavy burden of defense and the spirit-sapping *intifada* also pushed Israel toward territorial compromise in 1992. The 1993 Oslo agreement between Israel and the Palestine Liberation Organization (PLO) ushered in a period of negotiations and withdrawal that has left the West Bank under shared Israel and Palestinian control. In 2003 a "road map" for a peace plan was accepted by both parties that requires Palestinians to crack down on terror and Israel to work toward a Palestinian state.

For Palestinians, the chance to govern themselves represents the surest step they have taken toward the statehood that the United Nations promised them nearly half a century ago, but which their own folly as much as the circumstance prevented them from achieving. For Israel, the accord with the Palestinians offers the promise of a successful end to a half-century battle for survival.

In 1994 Israel and Jordan signed a peace treaty, the first peace agreement between Israel and an Arab nation since the treaty with Egypt in 1979. Of the outstanding issues between Jordan and Israel, water was the most far-reaching. Israel had restricted Jordan's access to the waters of the Jordan and Yarmuk Rivers; Jordan is now receiving no water from the Jordan River and only about 100 million cubic meters from the Yarmuk. Israel agreed to divert some 50 million cubic meters of water, or 13.2 billion gallons, a year to arid Jordan. This is a major economic boost for a country that is already rationing water, and where underground water supplies are rapidly being exhausted.

The Occupied Territories

In 1967, Israel captured the West Bank and East Jerusalem from Jordan, the Sinai Peninsula and Gaza Strip from Egypt, and the Golan Heights from Syria. It immediately annexed Arab East Jerusalem, drawing international condemnation. Some Israelis regard the territories as essential to the country's security. Over 3 million Palestinians live in the West Bank and Gaza (Figure 6.4). The population of East Jerusalem is about 300,000, including about 150,000 Jews who have settled there since 1967. In addition, there are about 135,000 Israeli settlers residing in some 150 settlements that have been built in the occupied territories over the past twenty-five years. Various Israeli governments have encouraged Jewish settlement in occupied territories. The presence of Jewish settlers on the West Bank complicates the issue of exchanging land for peace (Figure 6.5).

A striking feature of the economy of the occupied territories is its heavy dependence on the Israeli economy. About one third of the labor force of the

Figure 6-4. Gaza. Rafah Camp (population 70,000) is one of the eight Palestine refugee camps in the densely populated Gaza strip. Within an area of 140 square miles live 800,000 Arabs and 2,500 Jews. The United Nations provides the Palestine refugee community (approximately two thirds of the population of Gaza) with assistance in health, education, relief, and social services. Since the signing of the Peace Accord in Cairo on May 4, 1994, by the Palestine Liberation Organization and the Israeli government, the administration of the Gaza Strip has changed hands and is now officially under the Palestinian Authority. (Photo: UNRWA by M. Nasr.)

Figure 6-5. The West Bank. Palestine refugee pupils at a school in Arroub respond to a question from their teacher. Over two million Arabs live in the small area of the West Bank. Israel has established many Jewish settlements in this area, which has been a source of conflict. (Photo: UNRWA by M. Nasr.)

territories work in Israel (mostly on a daily commute basis), and earnings from these workers account for more than one quarter of the GNP of the occupied territories. Over 90 percent of the trade of the area is also with Israel. Israeli occupation created an economic relationship in which Palestinians are dependent on Israel for livelihoods and supplies. The infrastructure of Gaza and the West Bank is collapsing because Israel made few long-term investments in the territories. The Palestinian administration under the self-rule agreement is in turmoil and does not have the ability to provide basic government services.

The Gaza Strip

One of the most densely populated areas in the world, tiny, 140-square-mile Gaza has over 1 million Palestinian residents, most living in refugee camps. The population is growing rapidly at a rate of 4.4 percent. Gaza, the birthplace of Palestinian uprising, had 25 Jewish settlements in 2004. In September 1993 the Palestinian Liberation Organization and Israel agreed to Palestine self-rule in the Gaza Strip and in Jericho on the Israeli-occupied West Bank. By granting self-rule to the Gaza Strip, Israel has divested itself of a human time-bomb, where thousands of Palestinian families who fled their homes in what became Israel in 1948 are crammed into the narrow strip.

The West Bank

Nearly 2 million Palestinians live here, with the population growing at a rate of 3.3 percent. About 46 percent are young—under the age of 20—and have known only Israeli occupation and military control. By some accounts, Israel had appropriated as much as 52 percent of West Bank land by 1985. Restrictions have been imposed on use of lands still in Palestinian hands. In 1990 over 90,000 Soviet Jews were settled in the West Bank. In all, over 130,000 Jews live on the West Bank. In 2004, according to unofficial Israeli sources, there were 242 Israeli settlements in the West Bank (Figure 6.6).

Infrastructure for the Jewish settlements is fully integrated into the Israeli national system. Water, telecommunications, and electricity grids function as integral parts of the Israeli systems and are operated by the national Israeli agencies. Transport systems built during the past twenty-five years have also been designed primarily to meet the needs of settlements, linking them to metropolitan areas in Israel. For all infrastructure systems, there is an obvious difference in quality between facilities for the Israelis and the Palestinians. In contrast to the generally inadequate and poorly maintained infrastructure for the Palestinian population, there is well-designed and well-maintained infrastructure catering to the needs of the Israeli settlements.

A large number of Israelis feel some form of religious affinity with the West Bank, the Judea and Samaria of biblical Israel. The strands that fasten Israel to the West Bank—the settler interest, the emotional ties to the biblical land, and the security fears—are strong bonds that have become intricately

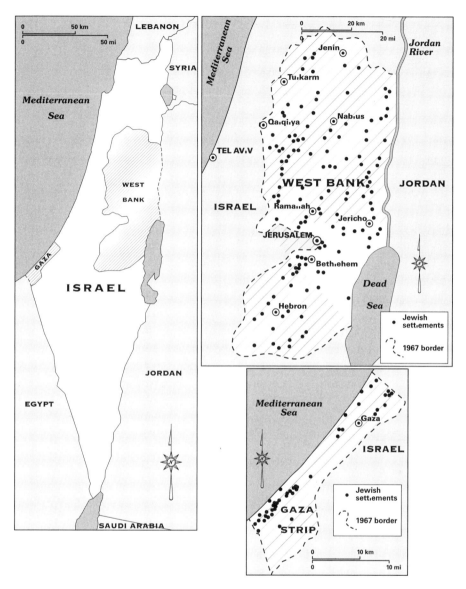

Figure 6-6. Jewish settlements on the West Bank and in Gaza.

woven together. To protect the Jewish settlement from Palestinian attackers, Israel is building electronic fences, concrete walls, trenches, and other obstacles at an estimated cost of $2.5 million a mile. The security barrier will run more than 400 miles on a twisting route through the West Bank. It will put 15 percent of the West Bank land, the most fertile area inhabited by 274,000 Palestinians, on the Israeli side. In some instances, the barrier will separate Palestinian villages from their nearby farmland. In many small Palestinian communities, employees and students must cross the barrier to reach larger cities and towns to work or study. About one quarter of the barrier had been built by 2004, mostly in the northern West Bank and near Jerusalem.

Under the 1993 Oslo accord with the Palestine Liberation Organization, Israel handed 450 smaller towns and villages in the West Bank over to the Palestinian Authority in 1995, but is leaving in place Jewish settlements that have sprouted in the West Bank since 1967, plus a substantial army. Many Israelis are suspicious of the peace process and withdrawal from the West Bank. They are afraid that if Israel gives up the West Bank and shrinks back behind the 1967 borders, it may render the country indefensible. But, if there is to be a lasting peace, Israel will have to leave most of the West Bank. The new West Bank map is a bewildering pacthwork in terms of territorial control. The result is that most Palestinians still need Israeli permission to leave their towns, and Israeli troops still stop the Palestinians' cars on roads between towns.

The unique religious and cultural heritage of the West Bank provides the potential for developing an important tourism industry. The tourist industry was the mainstay of the economy of the area before 1967, but it has suffered serious setbacks since then because of the unsettled political and security situation. With peace in the region, tourism can again become a major strategy for development of the area. However, there are important links between the West Bank and Jerusalem. Decisions concerning Jerusalem would have important implications for development of tourism and other economic prospects for the West Bank because major north–south transportation links in the West Bank pass through Jerusalem, and tourist potential of the region is critically dependent on the ancient religious sites of the city.

The Golan Heights

In 1981, Israel annexed the Golan, where Syrian guns had previously overlooked northern Israel. The annexation of East Jerusalem and the Golan Heights has not been recognized by other nations. In 2004 there were 42 Israeli settlements in the Golan Heights and 29 in East Jerusalem. Israelis are comfortably encamped in the verdant mountains of Golan, enjoying its mild summers and the country's only ski resort. Besides strategic nervousness about topography—the Golan towers over Israeli land—the Israelis are opposed to the Syrian border extending to the Sea of Galilee, which supplies a third of Israel's fresh water. The strongest opposition to returning the Golan comes from the Israeli Jews who live in three dozen settlements there, encouraged by government incentives such as free land. Israel's unwillingness to withdraw from Golan has always been an obstacle to peace with Syria.

The Gaza Strip, the West Bank, and the Golan Heights—three small patches of land—are at the center of the Middle East peace problem. Arab nations have fought for them—and lost. Israeli armed forces and an increasing number of Jewish settlers occupy the West Bank. The 1993 Oslo agreement between Israel and the Palestine Liberation Organization, the 1994 agreement between Israel and Jordan, and the 2003 "road map" for creation of a Palestinian state are major breakthroughs to bringing peace in this area between the Jews and Arabs.

Israeli and Palestinian Water Disputes

The 1993 peace agreement called for continuing discussion on water resources. Palestinians demand recognition of their right over the West Bank's water resources. Israel insists that there should be no change to the present pattern of water use until the issue is resolved at some point in the "permanent status" negotiations due to begin in May 1996.

The present pattern is, in the Palestinian view, grossly unfair. Each year Israel pumps 600 million cubic meters of water (over 30 percent of its supply) from acquifers that lie partly or wholly under the West Bank. Of this, 115 million cubic meters is allocated to the West Bank's 2 million Palestinians and 30 million cubic meters to the 130,000 Jewish settlers. The rest goes to Israel, servicing Jerusalem and greater Tel Aviv. This unequal distribution, according to Palestinians, is booty from the occupation. Israel naturally disagrees.

Why has water become such an issue now? The Yarkon-Taninim acquifer, the largest at issue, lies partly under Israel's coastal stretch near and north of Tel Aviv and partly under the West Bank, notably under the Palestinian towns of Tulkarm and Kalkilya. These are to be transferred to the Palestinian Authority. The Palestinians argue that, since it is about to take over the running of these areas, it should also have the right to drill wells for the water beneath them. It is a demand that fills Israel with dread because it will take away the water going to Tel Aviv.

Israel has agreed to make small concessions that would allow Palestinians to take an extra 80 million cubic meters of water annually from the West Bank's eastern acquifer in the Jordan valley. More than half of the West Bank's Palestinian population is without piped water. Since the occupation began in 1967, Palestinian farmers have been barred from digging new wells or renovating existing ones. If their agriculture is to be developed, Palestinians have to be able to control their own water.

According to Israelis, Israel and the West Bank are basically short of water, and quotas are imposed to prevent over-pumping. This might be convincing if the same restrictions were imposed on Israelis, but they are not. Palestinians, on average, consume 100 cubic meters of water each annually; Israelis—whether in Israel or in settlements—consume four times as much. There is huge disproportion in the use of water, and that, to the Palestinians, is the crux of the water issue. A long-term peace between Israel and Palestinians will depend at least as much on fair allocation of water as of land.

JORDAN AND SYRIA

From ancient times Jordan has been overrun by conquerors. Not until 1921 was a separate emirate named Transjordan created under British mandate by the League of Nations. After World War II, Emir Abdullah of the Hashemite family established a constitutional monarchy called Jordan. In 1948 the United Nations plan for separate Arab and Jewish states in Palestine triggered warfare, joined by Jordan, which absorbed the West Bank. Renewed conflict in 1967 led to its occupation by Israel.

Not rich in resources, Jordan touches Iraq to the northeast; to the south lie the strategic oil fields of Saudi Arabia; and on the western doorstep stretches the West Bank, occupied by Israel, coveted by stateless Palestinians. Despite the attraction of cities such as Amman and Petra, nearly half of Jordan's population still lives off the land even though barely one sixth of the Indiana-size kingdom has water for crops. Along the warm Jordan valley, much of it a thousand feet below sea level, stretches the country's prime farmland. Lacking water, much of this remains fallow.

The 1967 war devastated development plans by splitting the valley. Using portions of the Yarmuk, the East Ghor Canal now waters 57,500 acres in the Jordan valley. Using advanced farming techniques, the Jordan Valley produces 75 percent of the value of the nation's crop on only 10 percent of the cultivated land. The tent-dwelling bedouins, always a minority in the kingdom, form less than 3 percent of the population. Jordan's capital, Amman, has absorbed a flood of rural poor and Palestinian refugees in recent decades. About half of Jordan's 5.3 million population east of the Jordan River now lives in the greater metropolitan area of Amman, including thousands in refugee camps set up after the 1948 and 1967 wars (Figure 6.7).

Syria was host to the empire of the Arab Umayyads, who ruled from Damascus, in the seventh and eighth centuries. From 1516 to 1918, Syria was part of the Ottoman Empire. Following World War I and the breakup of the Ottoman Empire, France assumed a League of Nations mandate. Syria became independent in 1946. After independence, Syria passed through a long period of political instability with more than a dozen military coups. A group of army officers belonging to the Ba'ath Party seized power in 1970. The new government has remained in power since then.

Nearly half of Syria's population (18 million) lives in cities or towns of more than 10,000. The rest are farmers living in smaller towns or villages. Nomads constitute about 1 percent of the population. Damascus and Aleppo, both with populations of more than one million, are principal urban-industrial centers. The major industry is textiles based on domestic cotton from the Euphrates Valley, the Aleppo Plain, and elsewhere to supply the mills. The majority of Syrians are Sunni Muslims, but there are a large Christian minority and several other groups such as the Druze.

Figure 6-7. Amman, Jordan. A school for girls. Education for girls is essential for social and economic development in the Middle East. Female school enrollment in many Muslim countries ranks among the lowest in the non-Western world. (Photo: UNRWA by M. Nasr.)

Like Jordan, cultivation in Syria is completely dependent on irrigation. Agricultural land is concentrated along the Orontes and Euphrates rivers. Wheat and cotton are two important crops. Fruits and vegetables are grown in oases such as the Gut outside Damascus. There is room for further increase in the area under cultivation as a result of the Tabaqa Dam on the Euphrates, but Syria usually imports food now.

Due to heavy military expenditures, Syria has little money left for development projects. In the late 1980s Syria faced major economic difficulties and fell behind in payments of interest on loans from Western banks. Repayment of Soviet military loans exceeding $11 billion posed additional problems. In 1991 Syria departed from the anti-capitalist ideology that marked the Ba'thist rule, and began to encourage foreign investments to develop the country.

THE OIL-PRODUCING STATES

The states located around the Persian/Arabian Gulf contain substantial petroleum reserves and form a major oil-producing region in the world. Oil exists in greater known quantities in the Gulf region than in all the rest of the world's known reserves. Saudi Arabia alone has about one-fourth of the world's known reserves. Kuwait ranks second in the world in reserves. Iran, Iraq, and the United Arab Emirates also have significant quantities.

The region is important to the United States, Europe, and Japan. A quarter of the world's oil flows through the Gulf, and an even higher percentage sustains the economies of European nations and Japan. Therefore, political stability, peace, and freedom from external aggression or internal subversion in the Gulf States are very important.

The world's strategic, economic, and political interests in the Gulf have been challenged in recent years by war and political instability in the region. The eight-year Iran–Iraq war in the 1980s consumed the national energies and resources of both countries. Iraq's invasion of Kuwait on August 2, 1990, and the Gulf War of 1990–1991 revealed how a regional conflict can threaten the interests of many nations in the world.

Petroleum, religious fervor, and tangled international relations have made a deadly brew in the Persian Gulf. A web of often-disputed boundaries overlies the water. Two-thirds of the oil exported by Gulf countries passes through the narrow Straits of Hormuz. Pipelines carry most of the remainder to ports on the Mediterranean and Red seas. Another strategic waterway lies 550 miles away at the head of the Gulf. There the Tigris and Euphrates empty into the 120-mile-long Shatt al Arab, subject of a long-standing border dispute between Iran and Iraq, antagonists with deep-seated differences.

Like a quarrelling family, Gulf countries are both united and divided by their Islamic heritage and mineral riches. Saudi Arabia, Kuwait, Bahrain, Qatar, the United Arab Emirates, and Oman have established the Gulf Cooperation Council to strengthen economic and cultural ties. Security has been a major concern since Iraq's invasion of Kuwait in 1990.

Iran

Iran, a major oil-producing nation, lies at a strategic crossroads of Southwestern Asia. Within this country of 629,345 square miles—as large as the combined areas of Spain, Portugal, France, Italy, Switzerland, Austria, Belgium, and the Netherlands—there is considerable diversity of relief, climate, and natural resources. The terrain is mostly mountainous, with the Elburz Mountains around the southern end of the Caspian Sea and the Zagros Mountains and their continuation along the Gulf. Most of the interior of Iran consists of a series of basins and the desert (Figure 6.8).

Only about 12 percent of the land is suitable for agriculture and pasture. A considerably larger area could be made available for agriculture if water supply were increased. *Qanats,* or underground infiltration tunnels, provide irrigation water to more than half of the irrigated land. Areas around Yezd, Kerman, Teheran, Meshed, Isfahan, and Arak depend on *qanat* water. The leading crop area is from Meshed west to Tabriz and south to Shiraz.

The bulk of Iran's oil resources is located at the head of the Persian Gulf. The first oil was struck in 1908 near Masjid-i-Sulaiman. The fields of

Figure 6-8. Khorasan Province, Iran, along the Afghanistan border. High mountains—often snow-covered—and broad valleys—irrigated in part—make up much of the landscape of eastern Iran and adjoining Afghanistan. The photo shows the Shamsabad Afghan refugee settlement. Civil war in Afghanistan has led to refugee movements into neighboring countries. (Photo: UNHCR by A. Hollmann.)

southwestern Iran are noted for their great production per well and for their very large reserves. Iranian sedimentary basins, in which the environment is favorable for accumulation of oil, cover large area in the southwest, with additional areas beneath the continental shelves of the Persian Gulf and the Gulf of Oman.

Most Iranians are not Arabs, but Indo-Europeans who speak the Persian language. In 1979 religious fanaticism washed over Iran, which is over-whelmingly Shi'ite. A religious mutiny toppled the shah, and the new religious leadership installed Islamic law. The Islamic revolution inflamed the poor with slogans, but the new government run by the *mullahs* (clergy) has not been able to overcome economic hardship. In major cities and rural villages, Iranians are more concerned about how to make ends meet than about going to the mosque. The pumped fists that once wished death to the West are now raised in objection to worsening economic conditions.

Iran's population has swelled from 30 million to 69 (2004) million since the 1979 revolution, while oil revenue has plummeted almost to one-third what it was. Iran's declining economy is drastically undermining the religious leadership's once magnetic quality as protector of the masses and is accenting mismanagement and corruption instead. As poverty and deprivation humble some segments of society, gleaming high-rise office buildings and residential towers are appearing all over Teheran, especially in the affluent districts.

These impressive skyscrapers have been built with capital from private businessmen and the *bonyads*, the revolutionary foundations established by Ayatollah Ruhollah Khomeini to uphold the revolution and care for families of Islamic "martyrs."

Between 1980 and 1988 Iran and Iraq fought a war to control the Shatt al Arab waterway. The war began when Iraq invaded Iran in September 1980, striking refineries and an oil-loading terminal on Kharg Island. Iran responded by taking Iraq's Gulf oil terminals and preventing Iraqi tanker shipments through the Gulf. At the end of the war Iraq returned the captured land and restored the midchannel boundary of the Shatt al Arab waterway.

Iraq

Iraq, a leading oil producer, is remote and landlocked, except for a narrow outlet to the Persian Gulf. Historically, it has been isolated from the rest of the world in a way that seafaring countries such as Egypt, Turkey, or Lebanon never were. This predisposition toward cultural isolation was strengthened by the emergence of the Ba'ath Party, which swept away the Western-educated elite when it seized power and turned Iraq into a one-party police state in the late 1950s and 1960s.

For thirty-five years after the British mandate ended and Iraqi independence was established in 1932, Iraq was riven by tribal strife, riots, and military coups. The last remnants of foreign control were shaken off in 1958 when King Faisal II, a pro-Western cousin of King Hussein of Jordan, was overthrown; that was followed by four leadership changes and several military coup attempts in the next decade. Then Saddam Hussein helped to sweep the Ba'ath Party into power in a bloodless coup in 1968. In 2003 Saddam's government was dislodged, and attempts are being to establish a new democratic Iraqi government.

For Iraq, boundaries have never meant much. Until 1920, when it became a British mandate, Iraq was not even a country. Its borders are artificial lines drawn in the sand by Britain that reflect the interests of the great powers of World War I, not the aspirations of the Iraqi people. As a consequence Turkey and Iran have repeatedly clashed with Iraq over territory; similarly, Iraq's borders with Saudi Arabia and Kuwait have always been in dispute.

Iraq convinced itself of its legitimate territorial claim on Kuwait. In the 1870s, when both Iraq and Kuwait were part of the Ottoman Empire, the Ottomans loosely attached the sheikhdom of Kuwait to Basra, part of which was incorporated into modern Iraq. And in 1961, within days of Kuwaiti independence, Iraq announced plans to annex Kuwait—a move thwarted only by the arrival of British troops on Kuwaiti soil and censure by the Arab League. Along with the tenuous territorial claim were Iraq's distaste for the rich Arab monarchies who had helped bankroll its war with Iran and its obsession with obtaining guaranteed access to the Persian Gulf. During the Iran–Iraq war, Iran had closed Iraq's access to the sea by sealing the Shatt al Arab, the waterway that divides the two countries.

Old cultural and religious differences persist in Iraq, heir to the territory of ancient Mesopotamia. More than half the country's population of 24 million is Shi'ite Muslim, but members of the minority Sunni sect have traditionally ruled. Tribal Kurds from northeastern Iraq have periodically fought for autonomy (Figure 6.9–6.11). The rebellious Shia Muslims living in the southern marshes present another problem. The marshes comprise about a third of Iraq's southern provinces and cover 6,000 square miles including vast banks of reeds, lagoons, and rice paddies. The Shia residents of the island villages have been self-sufficient for thousand of years. In recent years, Iraqi engineers have diverted water from the Tigris and Euphrates rivers, drying up more than half the vast wetlands. The overall aim of Saddam Hussein's government was to wipe out the scattered villages and farms that sustained the Shi'ite rebels. However, the draining of the marshes is decimating the ancient culture of the marsh Arabs, known as the Maadan (Figure 6.12).

Figure 6-9. Sirnak Province of southeastern Turkey bordering Iraq is a complex of rugged mountains and canyons. Here Kurds and Arabs live alongside ethnic Turks. The 1991 Gulf War sent thousands of refugees to this region. This photo shows the Iraqi refugee camp at Isikveren. (Photo: UNHCR by A. Hollmann.)

Figure 6-10. Kurdish refugees at Yekmal Camp along the Turkey–Iraq border after the Gulf War of 1991. Saddam Hussein's government killed an estimated 180,000 Kurds during the 1980s. Iran, Turkey, and Syria—countries intent on dividing and weakening the Kurds to keep their own Kurdish populations from making a move for unity and independence—surround the Iraqi Kurds on other sides. (Photo: UNHCR by Anneliese Hollmann.)

Five Small Oil-Rich States in the Gulf

Five small oil-rich states line the Gulf—Kuwait, Qatar, Bahrain, the United Arab Emirates, and Oman. The governing elites of the Gulf States have been concerned with two questions: how to use their abundant wealth to develop their countries, and how to do so with the least disruption of the existing political structure. The Gulf States share common strategies: they have each decided to share the wealth (but not political power) with their own populations through the expansion of social services and government employment, to diversify their economy by industrial investment, and to erect modern infrastructure such as airports, roads, and communications networks. To pursue these objectives, the Gulf States import workers to construct and operate new facilities and industries and to provide services. As countries with great wealth, low populations, and labor shortages, the Gulf governments have decided against permanent migration. The monarchies of the Gulf States fear the political erosion that might accompany massive permanent migration from countries that have overthrown their monarchies. As small states, they fear being politically overrun by their larger neighbors if they allow foreigners to become citizens. As tribal chieftains—notwithstanding pan-Arab and pan-Islamic

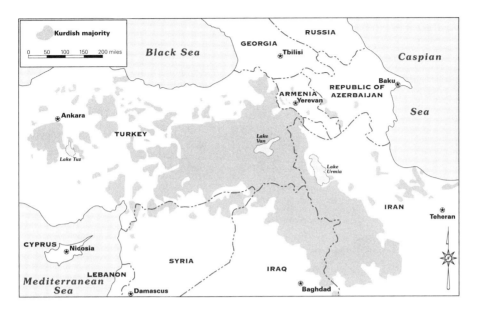

Figure 6-11. Kurdistan.

rhetoric—their first concern is with maximizing the economic well-being of members of their own tribes.

Nowhere else in the world have societies experienced such massive labor shortages satisfied not through open migration, but through the use of temporary imported workers. The United States and Canada, among others, expanded economically and demographically through permanent migrations. Postwar Europe recruited temporary "guest workers" from the Mediterranean countries and the United States has also employed temporary migrants (both legal and illegal) from Latin America, but the size of the labor force in relation to the local population in each instance is small compared with the proportion of migrants in the Gulf States. Moreover, migrants to Europe and the United States from low-income countries have been primarily low-skilled workers, recruited to positions that the local labor force did not want and at wages it would not accept. In contrast, a large proportion of migrants to the Gulf are skilled workers who have entered the modern sectors of the economy in such large numbers that they easily outnumber the local skilled labor force.

As capital-rich, labor-short countries, the Gulf States are not concerned with creating labor-intensive industries to increase employment or with reducing luxury consumption and increasing the rate of savings to stimulate investment; nor are they faced with the problem of obtaining financial resources for delivering medical services, education, drinking water, housing, and sanitation. There is no debate in these countries on the issues of growth versus income distribution, consumption versus savings, industrial versus agricultural development, export-oriented growth versus import substitution.

Figure 6-12. Marsh Arabs of Iraq.

The Gulf States provide an important example of international migration and development.

Dubai: The Persian Gulf's Main Entrepot

Dubai is the Gulf's main trading entrepot and the world's tenth-busiest port. It serves as the major transshipment point between Europe and Asia. Now two completely new ports, one at Salalah in Oman and the other at Aden in Yemen, have opened. The logic behind the development of new ports is that Dubai lies inside the Gulf, three days' extra sailing off the main route from Europe, through the Suez Canal, around the Arabian Peninsula, and on to India and East Asia. Furthermore, with the ever-present risk of war, insurance rates rise slightly for vessels passing through the Straits of Hormuz. Mainline ships that stop in either Salalah or Aden and send Gulf-bound goods on by smaller feeder vessels should thus save time and money. East Africa and the Indian subcontinent are also only a day or two's sailing away. Already, Maersk and Sea-Land, two big shipping lines, have bought stakes in Salalah and they will divert about 300,000 containers a year from Dubai.

The Port of Singapore Authority, meanwhile, is running Aden and has enticed two of its biggest customers, APL and Pacific International Lines, to use the new facility.

Aden and Salalah have disadvantages too. Aden lies in politically unstable Yemen; and Salalah is stuck in the desert hinterland of south Arabia. They have neither Dubai's air and surface-freight links, nor its status as an industrial center.

Kuwait

Kuwait was settled around 1716 by the Utub tribe in a small town called Kuwait (the Arabic word for a fortress built near water). The Al Sabah, the ruling clan of Kuwait, come from a trading family. They invited the British to carry on mutually prosperous trading relations with the Utub tribe during the 1700s. The British protected the Utub tribe from other Arab tribes and from the Persians (present-day Iran). Kuwait became a British Protectorate in 1899. During 1913–1961 Britain provided for Kuwait's defense and carried out its foreign affairs; the Al Sabah family ran domestic operations.

Pearling was once the main livelihood of Kuwaitis. By the 1980s oil wealth allowed Kuwait to provide its residents one of the most complete welfare systems, even though 60 percent were foreign workers rather citizens. The constitution of 1962 stipulates that although a member of the Sabah family will always rule as emir, the country will also have a freely elected parliament that will exercise powers of censure over the government and the choice of cabinet ministers. In 1986 the emir suspended the constitution, dissolved the parliament, and imposed censorship. Until Iraq's invasion, the Sabah family resisted all pressure and demands from various segments of the population to reinstitute the freedoms guaranteed in the constitution. After the liberation of Kuwait in 1991, the Sabah family promised to solidify democracy in Kuwait, but little has been achieved as yet.

United Arab Emirates

Abu Dhabi, Dubai, Sharja, Ras al Khayma, Fujayra, Umm al Qaywayn, and Ajman—the Trucial States, formerly under British protection—became the independent federation of the United Arab Emirates in 1971 (Figure 6.13). It has a population of 2.4 million. The UAE is one of the world's major oil producers, with an installed sustainable production capacity of over 3 million barrels per day. Its reserves of hydrocarbons place it second only to Saudi Arabia in terms of proven oil reserves, and as the world's sixth in terms of gas reserves. The bulk of the oil is in the emirate of Abu Dhabi. Oil production began in Abu Dhabi in 1962. Oil was also discovered in Dubai, the chief commercial center of the Emirates.

The seven emirs rule the internal affairs of their own states; at the federal level authority lies with the Supreme Council of Rulers, with the sheikh of Abu Dhabi as its president. Abu Dhabi has the largest population (about

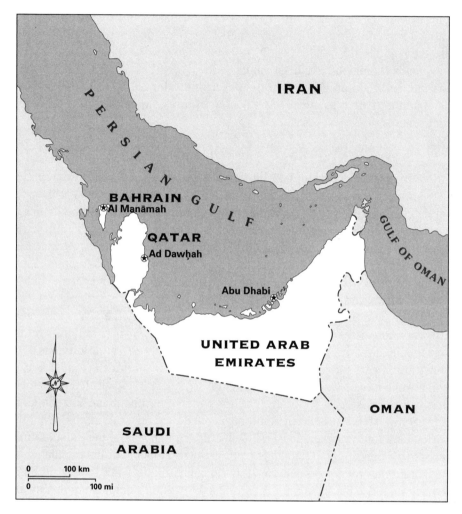

Figure 6-13. United Arab Emirates, Qatar, and Bahrain.

500,000) and it contributes the major portion of the national budget which finances the development work in all states. UAE has a territorial dispute with Iran over the control of three small islands in the Gulf.

The oil revenues have transformed much of the country. Economic activity in Abu Dhabi, the federal capital of the UAE, is surging ahead as government expenditure in the public sector increases. Massive amounts of cash have been injected into infrastructure improvements, civil works, housing, and leisure sectors. One of the biggest projects is the "Lulu" Island leisure complex, a $2 billion development on an artificial island, expected to become a major regional and international attraction. An eighteen-hole championship green golf course is also being built. Locally born citizens now have a per capita income of $128,000 a year—probably the highest in the world, according to one bank director in the city, who estimates that the overall per capita income in the UAE is $29,000. The native-born population is outnumbered about three to one by foreign residents, the bulk of them from India and Pakistan.

The smaller emirates of Fujayra and Ras al Khayma, which do not have oil, grow dates, fruits, and vegetables with irrigation water available from Jabal Akhdar mountains. All the emirates have long stretches of beach, and Fujayra supports a flourishing trade based on the mountains.

Bahrain

Bahrain comprises a group of islands off the coast of Saudi Arabia between the Gulf of Bahrain and the Persian Gulf (Figure 6.14). The largest island is mostly desert, with some gardens and groves near the northern coasts watered by underground springs. Bahrain claims the island of Hawar, near the Qatar coast and the village of Zubara on the shore of Qatar.

Bahrain became a protectorate of Britain in 1861. It became independent in 1971. The emir and his family hold power. An elected National Assembly was dissolved in 1975 and political opposition is not tolerated. A council of "elite and loyal men," mostly wealthy merchants and leaders of important families, provide advice to the emir. Seventy percent of Bahrain's 650,000 population is Shia Muslim; the ruling family is Sunni. Relative poverty, lower-class

Figure 6-14. Bahrain lies off the coastal region of Al-Hasa on the Arabian Peninsula. It is connected with Saudi Arabia by the King Fahd Causeway, 15.5 miles long, which was completed in 1986. (Photo: Bahrain National Museum.)

standing, and perception of discrimination among the Shia population has fueled discontent among the majority population. In October 2002, for the first time in thirty years, the people of Bahrain voted to elect a parliament. The election marked the first time women ran for office and voted in a parliamentary race, making Bahrain the only country in the Persian Gulf to grant women the right to vote in national elections (Figure 6.15).

Diminishing oil wealth has forced Bahrain to diversify into banking and communications (Figure 6.16). The recent expansion of the Aluminum Bahrain (ALBA) smelter marked the dawn of a new era of industrialization for Bahrain, one of the smallest states in the Gulf. Alumina oxide is imported from Australia, and power for the electrolysis process to make the metal is obtained from a new power station using the almost unlimited natural gas from Bahrain's Khuff Field.

Qatar

Qatar is the least-populated country in the Gulf, with 600,000 people, of which 400,000 are foreign workers. It is involved in a territorial dispute with Bahrain over Hawar Island off the coast of Qatar. The ruling family continues to dominate the state, with family members heading the ministries of defense,

Figure 6-15. Women in Bahrain enjoy greater political and civil liberties than do women in neighboring Arab countries. In a region coping with Islamist movements, tiny Bahrain has made a strategic shift toward openness and freedom. (Photo: Bahrain National Museum.)

Figure 6-16. The Standard Oil Company of California discovered oil in Bahrain in 1932; production began in 1933. Extensive oil fields, natural gas, aluminum, shipbuilding, and ship repair industries are dominant in Bahrain. (Photo: Bahrain National Museum.)

interior, and finance. Qatar has many followers of the Wahhabi sect of the Sunni Muslims. It is a key staging area for U.S. military forces in the Gulf, and is the home of Al Jazeera, the Arab world's CNN. Qatar's progressive leadership and its moderate strain of Wahhabi Islam create a friendlier and more manageable environment for the U.S. military than now exists in ultra-conservative Saudi Arabia.

Natural gas deposits in Qatar may surpass oil in importance in the future. The North Shore gas field below the waters of the Gulf ranks as one of the largest in the world, and Qatar ranks third in proven reserves. Energy-intensive industries such as the smelting of aluminum and petrochemical products are important. Qatar plans to become a major producer of ammonia and urea fertilizers in the Middle East with markets in India, China, and Japan. Only about 3 percent of the land is cultivated, which grows vegetables in the winter rainy season.

Oman

The Sultanate of Oman once depended on fishing and farming. Those yields now contribute little to the economy, and oil is the main source of revenue. Flush with wealth from its oil fields, Oman has catapulted from Arabian Peninsula backwater to modern nation. Oil production began in 1967. Until 1970 the country was kept isolated and backward by the current ruler's father. A bloodless coup by the son, the present sultan, deposed the father and turned Oman into a model of development that makes it unique in the Middle East. The country is dotted with health clinics and hospitals, and has one of the highest rates of immunization in the world. A dense network of telephone and paved roads has unified the country creating a cohesive state out of a fragmented tribal society. Oman's transformation from Arabia's poorest country to one of the most progressive is apparent in rural as well as urban areas. Most Omanis are Arab Muslims of the Ibadi sect. Oman controls the Musandam Peninsula along the strategically vital Strait of Hormuz.

Oman—a land the size of Britain and Ireland—has a population of 2.7 million. According to current predictions, its oil wells will be pumped dry in about seventeen years. Considering the fact that oil revenue has helped the country to jump from medieval backwater to prosperity in about twenty-five years, Oman is already beginning to feel the pinch and is seeking to diversify its economy through manufacturing and tourism.

Water from *aflaj* irrigates about 55 percent of Oman's farmed land. The *aflaj* is a system for tapping underground water in the wetter mountain areas and delivering it to flatter areas where agriculture is possible. The *aflaj* have helped to shape the history and settlement patterns of Oman, and they continue even now to tie together each community that draws upon the its flow. Even with oil yielding 90 percent of the revenues, farming, herding, and fishing remain important parts of the economy of Oman. Oman has one of the highest percentages of nomads, with nearly four fifths of the population spending most or all of the year wandering with their herds.

Saudi Arabia: Tradition and Change

An awesome inrush of wealth has brought the Saudi Kingdom—founded on Islamic principles and stern desert ways—to a whirlwind clash of tradition and change. Saudi Arabia guards the cities of the Prophet Mohammed: Makkah and Medina, two of Islam's holiest cities. It also guards the world's greatest supply of oil. Conservative Wahabi Sunnis form the majority of the population which is estimated at 23.5 million. The Shia minority numbers some 500,000 and feels politically isolated.

About the size of the United States east of the Mississippi, Saudi Arabia has not one natural body of sweet water. It contains both the world's largest sand desert, the Rub al-Khali (the "empty quarter"), lying mostly within the country's borders and made up of 150,000 square miles of sand—about as big as Texas; and perhaps the world's largest oasis, al-Hasa. Only 1 percent of the entire nation's land is under cultivation.

Saudi Arabia has about one-quarter of the world's reserves of oil. It is the world's largest exporter of crude oil, and the world's largest producer (since the breakup of the Soviet Union) and a vital exporter of crude and end products to the United States. It is without question a major player in the Organization of Petroleum Exporting Countries (OPEC).

In a daring midnight raid in 1902 on Riyadh's Masmak Fort, Abdul Aziz ibn Saud, who later became king, led a small band of his closest followers to victory. The raid marked the beginning of modern Saudi Arabia. It was not until thirty years later, however, that Abdul Aziz announced a pact between the principal warring factions and declared himself king of Saudi Arabia on September 23, 1932. Six years earlier, he had made himself king of the Hejaz and in 1927, king of the Nejd. The next logical step, which took another five years to accomplish, was to bring the two kingdoms together as one—Saudi Arabia—which has been ruled by the House of Saud ever since. King Abdul Aziz, who died in 1953, was a man of stature and, in addition to being a great warrior king, was a philosopher and statesman who believed in strength through unity and Islam. He laid the foundations for a state that is vast in physical terms—about 830,000 square miles, or the equivalent of the whole of Western Europe. Over the past sixty years, Saudi Arabia has become the most powerful economy in the Middle East. Its oil wealth, now worth about $40 billion a year, has made it a significant player on the world stage.

Since Abdul Aziz's midnight raid on Riyadh, which then had a population of about 30,000, the city has grown to over 2 million. The fort has been restored and much of the old city walls and fortifications have been rebuilt to remind Saudis of their heritage. The present ruler, King Fahd ibn Abdul Aziz, is the fifth Saudi head of the state. King Fahd is gradually introducing reforms. The king named sixty men in August 1993 to the new Shura (consultative) Council, which for the first time will enable Saudis from outside the ruling family to have a voice in the conduct of the oil-rich nation's government. While falling far short of Western concepts of democracy, it was a small first step in a gradual modernization process in Saudi Arabia. The members of the council include specialists in military, health, business, history, and cultural fields and are headed by experts in *sharia* (Islamic law). Saudi Arabia is governed by strict *sharia* law. It executes convicted murderers, rapists, and drug smugglers and enforces the Islamic dress code in public for women.

In the aftermath of the Gulf War, Saudi Arabia was confronted by demands for political change, an independent foreign policy, and a reduction in King Fahd's power. There have been demands by clergymen, scholars, and judges for freedom of speech, equality of citizenship, and freedom of courts. There is demand for accountability by King Fahd and the princes, and the need for real rather than token participation in decision making by Saudis outside the royal family. Saudi Arabia's development plan focuses on manufacturing development through private sector investments in secondary and tertiary industries. Saudi Arabia has used its oil resources to help create a diversified economy, which is now the largest in the Middle East with a total gross domestic product of about $241 billion.

Reacting to years of low oil prices and the high cost of the Persian Gulf War, the ruling house of Saud is learning that even its vast riches can go only so far. It is cutting down on waste, devising unprecedented subsidy cuts for water and electricity, and planning a phase-out of the expatriate workers who make up a fourth of the kingdom's residents. The era of construction at any cost has given way to a period of readjustment, cost cutting, and economic slowdown.

Although the country remains a thoroughly Islamic society where enforcement of morality includes patrols by the religious police, the satellite dishes that crown nearly every roof in the major cities of Jidda and Riyadh freely bring raunchy European and U.S. programs for viewing behind private walls. In a country in which sensors still black out magazine photographs that display too much cleavage, no one in Saudi Arabia seems to be standing in the way of this latest cultural onslaught from the West. With its wide roads, gleaming office buildings, and fancy boutiques, Saudi Arabia has long paired modern trappings with the strict tenets of Islam. But there is no sharper juxtaposition than the pervasive presence of the satellite dishes in a country in which even movie theaters are banned. The technology, almost unknown in Saudi Arabia before the Gulf War, is viewed by many among the nation's religious establishment as an outrage, a vehicle for Western films, music videos, and television broadcasts they regard as devilish.

Saudi Arabia faces critical challenges. A rapidly rising population, eroding oil prices, and rampant corruption have translated into diminishing opportunities and rising discontent. Domestic reforms are overdue. The royal family's absolute power has made few concessions to the twentieth century, let alone to the twenty-first. Women have virtually no civil rights and political rights are denied to both sexes. Because there is no independent judiciary, justice is cruel and arbitrary. A longstanding alliance of convenience between the royal family and fanatical Wahhabi clerics has embroiled the kingdom with terrorist groups such as al-Qaeda and the Taliban. Democracy could be a potent remedy for some of these ills, but thus far no significant Saudi democracy movement has risen.

Yemen: Sheba's Land

The merger of socialist South Yemen and conservative North Yemen in May 1990 led to the establishment of a unified republic of Yemen. The old is very old here, and the new is very new. Sometimes, the collision is painful. The Queen of Sheba once ruled these lands, sending frankincense and myrrh by caravan across Arabia to far-flung Gaza, bound for Jerusalem, Athens, and Rome. Marib was the capital of the ancient monarchy of Sheba.

Yemen and its 20 million people are spread across an arid landscape where intertribal rivalry and conflict abound. Yemen is also the ancestral home of Osama bin Laden, whose father was born in the Hadhramaut region, which straddles the caravan route that connected the Queen of Sheba's realm to King Solomon's court. Key al-Qaeda leaders are reported to be still at large in Yemen.

In response to Yemen's support of Iraq in the first Gulf War, Saudi Arabia expelled the estimated 2 million Yemenis who lived and worked in the kingdom. The burden placed by the returnees had a harsh impact on the fragile economy of Yemen, one of the most populous countries in the region. The payments sent home by Yemenis working in other countries—most of them in Saudi Arabia—totaled about $2 billion a year, and have been the country's largest source of income. Although many returning Yemenis have gone back to their villages, there is little work for them there, and their presence in Sana has prompted already high housing costs to increase further.

Across the Arabian Peninsula, many societies have undergone profound change from feudal ways to a sense of modernity expressed in steel and concrete, largely since the discovery and exploitation of oil. But in Yemen there were no oil funds to pay for development. And here, terrain and the isolationism of its old rulers denied history's unfolding in a land that traces its sense of nation to the days before Jesus or Mohammed.

EGYPT: A THREADBARE ECONOMY BATTLES THE TIDE OF POPULATION

Few spots on earth are as filled with simultaneous contrast as Egypt. Unforgiving desert abuts the ever-fertile Nile Valley. Many of the magnificent marvels from the dawn of civilization are treated with indifference. Napoleonic palaces, suburban skyscrapers, sprawling slums and streets crammed with Mercedes sedans, donkey carts, and three-on-a-bicycle all exist side by side in Egypt. Overcrowding seems hopeless. Yet Egyptians have unbelievable patience, day in and day out, in the chaos at rush hour and in the ramshackle *souks*, or open-air markets.

Socially and economically, Egypt is two countries. One is composed of a small and isolated bureaucratic, business, and military elite centered in Cairo that has enriched itself through the vast patronage network of the million-member bureaucracy and government-owned enterprises. The other Egypt is made up of some 80 percent of the country's 76 million people (2004). The majority has an average income of less than $50 a month, and struggles with unemployment or underemployment of close to 40 percent. Its discontents have fueled the militant Islamic insurgency.

In the thin green line of life along the Nile that stretches through the vast African desert from Aswan to Alexandria live nearly 74 million Egyptians. This is the central economic and political problem of Egypt. The present rate of population growth is 2.7 percent a year, and there already are more than 3,000 people on each square mile of land on which life can be sustained—one of the highest population densities in the world. Birth control is being encouraged by the government. But if the birthrate does not slow, by the year 2025 the population will reach 96 million. Urban sprawl will gobble up more and more of the precious farmland that Egyptians treasure as "the gift of the Nile." Population enters every economic and political decision made in Egypt:

Agriculture

The land is incredibly productive and can be cropped year-round. But the burgeoning population crimps exports and makes Egypt an importer of wheat and other basic foodstuffs. Two out of every five *baladi* (brown loaves of bread), the staple of Egypt, are baked from U.S. wheat. Egypt, once the granary of the Roman Empire, is now dependent on grain imports. The gap between production and consumption has widened alarmingly. Consumption is growing at around 8 percent annually, because there are another 1.2 million mouths to feed every year. At the same time, agricultural production is increasing at only about 2 percent a year.

Revenues

The government's long-time policy of subsidizing basic foods squanders each year the entire earnings from the Suez Canal and tourism. Yet removing subsidies could cause riots similar to those experienced in 1977, when the government tried to raise the price of bread.

Egypt's earnings in recent decades have been gleaned from exporting people to work in oil-rich countries, importing others as tourists, and earning revenues from limited oil exports and the transit fees paid by vessels using the Suez Canal. But now many of the guest workers are unemployed, many tourists have been scared away, and many tankers are idled for want of Iraqi oil to ship.

Unemployment and Poverty

About 85 percent of Egypt's workforce is employed by the government—2 million in the government bureaucracy alone. The average government employee receives $50 a month and many Egyptians take on second jobs, often as taxi drivers or laborers, to support their families. More than 20 percent of the country's workforce is unemployed; another 20 percent are underemployed. What's more, these numbers are expected to rise as a result of attacks by Islamic militants on the tourist industry, which directly or indirectly employs one of every ten working Egyptians. And 500,000 new workers are coming into the job market each year. The political and economic pressures on Egypt come from trying to accommodate these new workers without allowing the public sector to get out of control.

The United Nations Development Program estimates that 23 percent of the population of Egypt lives in absolute poverty. The reality is grim and getting grimmer as Egypt sinks under such pressures as lack of sufficient agricultural land, a shortage of jobs, widespread overcrowding, crushing poverty, and a political system that ignores the aspirations of most of its citizens.

Egypt intends to devote more resources to development of agriculture and industry, and is eager to attract foreign investors and technical expertise for productive industrial projects using Egyptian manpower. But much depends on whether resources get lost in the bureaucracy of unproductive government ministries rather than creating productive economic growth.

Since the Camp David peace accords between Israel and Egypt in 1978, the United States has poured over $30 billion into the country, an amount surpassed only by aid to Israel. Although Egypt's basic services, from roads to water purification plants, have significantly improved, U.S. support has done little to alter the one-party state or dampen dissent despite a grant to help foster democratic institutions.

Islamic militants, by attacking foreign visitors in their armed campaign to topple the government, have wiped out the tourism industry, which once produced more than $2 billion a year. All told, more than 200 people have died in politically related violence, among them government officials, police, Coptic Christians, and intellectuals gunned down in the streets. The government has detained thousands of suspected militants and has shut down mosques, religious schools, and Islamic charity organizations. The Islamic Group, the main militant organization, along with the Muslim Brotherhood and others, has set up a variety of social services. After a devastating earthquake hit Cairo in 1992, Islamic charity organizations were on the streets within hours, handing out food and blankets while the government's relief efforts lagged.

Lebanon: The Search for a Nation

Artificially created by the French in 1920, Lebanon was carved out of Syria after the collapse of the Ottoman Empire. Lebanon has had symbols of nationhood—the poets (the famous Khalil Gibran), the cedars, the proud Mount Lebanon peaks, and the historic ruins of an honorable past—but there is little semblance of a system to back it up. The country's laissez faire attitude made it more of a playground—social and financial originally, military of late—than a nation.

Civil war between Christians and Muslims has ravaged Lebanon since 1975. Rival political parties based on religion, as well as external pressures from Syria, Israel, and various terrorist groups, have devastated the country (Figure 6.17). Shi'ite Muslims are the majority, followed by Maronite Christians and Sunni Muslims. In a country smaller than Connecticut there are now over seventeen major militias in addition to dozens of smaller groups, which range from the so-called Pink Panthers and Green Musketeers to the intensely fundamentalist Islamic Unity gunmen. Lebanon's Christians have enjoyed political, economic, and cultural power since 1920 when the country came into being. In 1975, when they felt this dominance was threatened by the Muslim majority in alliance with the Palestinians, Christians took to arms to defend their concept of Lebanon. After fifteen bloody years of civil war, Christians agreed to the 1989 Taif peace agreement which reduced their power and their share of government institutions.

Under the formula of 1943, the Maronite Christians hold many of the top jobs, with Christians generally having a 6 to 5 edge in all government positions over the Muslims. Sunni Muslims were ranked second and were delegated the premiership. Shiiites were ranked third and were given the post of speaker of parliament. It is a system based on the population strengths of Lebanon's religious communities in 1932, when the last census was taken. The lack of a subsequent census update is partly because Christians feared that a new national tally would legitimize Muslim demands for reform. Estimates now reverse the order of the top three communities. Though Lebanon still has a Christian president, his authority under the 1989 peace agreement no longer towers over the Sunni Muslim prime minister or the Shia Muslim speaker of parliament.

The question is whether the Shi'ites, Druzes, Sunnis, Maronites, and others will be able to humble themselves to bury their differences, end their blood feuds, and for the first time, display a sense of nationalism. In 1990 an oasis of peace was established in Lebanon. Beirut and areas surrounding the capital shook off the rule of various militias and were reunited under the control of a legitimate government and national army. Most of the gunmen departed, leaving a 250-square-mile zone free of private armies for the first time since the first shot was fired in the factional strife nearly twenty-five years ago. The Muslim and Christian areas opened up to each other after the army dismantled the Green Line, which stood as the symbol of partition for many years.

Lebanese government is still a government of greater Beirut, rather than of Lebanon. The major militias have merely withdrawn with their heavy weaponry intact into their Christian and Druze mountain heartlands. Lebanon remains carved into fiefdoms ruled by myriad warlords. Civil war and military invasion have robbed Lebanon of its prized reputation as the Middle East's international marketplace and premier financial center, as the region's educational center and vacation spot, and—perhaps most painfully—as an inspiring example of the peaceful coexistence of differing religions and nationalities. Eager to erase the memories of war, many developers are pressing to rebuild Beirut as a new and glittering modern metropolis.

AFGHANISTAN, TURKEY, AND MUSLIM STATES OF CENTRAL ASIA

Afghanistan and the Central Asian states of Kazakhstan, Uzbekistan, Turkmenistan, Tajikistan, and Kyrgizstan share common cultural heritage

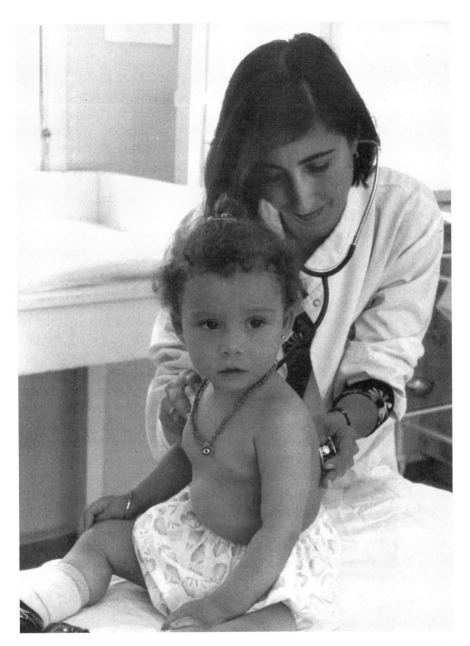

Figure 6-17. Lebanon. A Palestine refugee child receives a medical check-up at a health care center in the Badawi Camp. Thousands of Palestine refugees have moved into Lebanon following the Israeli invasion of 1982 to drive hostile forces from southern Lebanon. Lebanon suffered a great deal during civil war between Christian and Muslim religious factions between 1975 and 1990. (Photo: UNRWA by M. Nasr.)

and history. In this region the interests of the two great empires of the nineteenth century—Britain and Russia—converged. Russia advanced relentlessly southwards, and Britain feared that this advance was aimed at the conquest of India.

A giant area of desert and mountain three times the size of Western Europe, the region extends from Tibet in the east to the Caspian Sea. This vast, empty space lies between five old empires: those of Russia, China, Turkey, Persia, and India. As the former Soviet republics revive as independent countries, Central Asia has again become a place for international rivalry. All the old empires are vying for renewed influence.

Physically, the Muslim states of Central Asia can be divided into four regions: the steppe, consisting of the northern part of Kazakhstan; the semi-desert, comprising the rest of Kazakhstan; the desert region lying to the south of the semi-desert and reaching the Iranian frontier in the west and the Chinese frontier in the east; and the mountain region, of which the main features are the Pamirs and the Tien Shan. Vegetation is sparse, being confined to a belt of wooded steppe in the northeast, the grasslands of Kazakhstan, hardy perennials such as saxaul in the deserts, and a variety of trees and plants along the river valleys and in the piedmont zones. In proportion to the vast areas of desert and mountains, the area of cultivated land and population is very small.

The climate is "continental," with hot summers and cold winters. Precipitation is low throughout the whole region: in the semi-desert most of the rain falls in summer, but in the south most rain falls in March. Heavy snowfalls are uncommon except in the mountainous districts.

Cultivation on a large scale is impossible without irrigation. Simple irrigation was practiced in the area for centuries. During the Soviet rule modern irrigation was greatly extended. Dry farming is mostly practiced in the north. The most important economic asset of the area is cotton, grown mainly in the Fergana and Vakhsh valleys. Cereals are grown extensively in Kazakhstan, and many other crops in the semi-desert and desert regions.

Turkey has the strongest historical and cultural links with the Central Asian states. All but one of the Central Asian states speak Turkic languages. Most of them look to Turkey for a model of how to combine economic growth with modern Islam. Turkish state television is broadcast all over the region, and 10,000 Central Asian students are studying at Turkish universities and high schools. Turkey dreams of fashioning a zone of influence and commerce among the dominantly Turkic-speaking Sunni Muslims of Central Asia. Most big foreign investments in Central Asia have been made by Western companies such as Chevron or Daimler-Benz, but Turkish companies are represented in the region and Turkey is among the largest trade partners of both Kazakhstan and Uzbekistan. Turkey hopes that culture may boost commerce. The Central Asian states have to ship their oil through Russia and are keen to find alternative oil routes. Turkey and Kazakhstan have pledged to study the building of an oil pipeline through Turkey.

In Tajikistan, where Persian is spoken, Iran has influence. China has interests because 6 million Central Asians live in its western provinces which used to be called Chinese Turkistan; many would like to join with their Turkic neighbors to the east. Pakistan perceives itself and Afghanistan as a part of an Islamic bloc along with the Central Asian republics. Pakistan and Iran can provide Central Asian states access to ports and contact with the outside world. Pakistan is already planning to build a network of highways and railways to link the landlocked nations with the Arabian Sea. Iran has been negotiating with Turkmenistan to build a pipeline to transmit Turkmen gas to the Iranian pipeline system that reaches the sea at Abadan. This gives Iran an influence in the region beyond its linguistic cousin, Tajikistan, and will ensure some external support for fundamentalism in other parts of Central Asia. Russia has armies in the republics and 9 million Russians are living in Central Asia.

These states are ethnically divided, and more than 2,000 people have died in interethnic warfare. Mismatched borders have left one million Uzbeks in Tajikistan and one million Tajiks in Uzbekistan (the Tajik areas include Bukhara, a historic center of Tajik culture).

The dominant force shaping the future of Central Asia will be water. The life-giving water system is drying up. The symbol of this environmental disaster is the Aral Sea, once the world's fourth-largest body of inland water, which has lost 60 percent of its volume since 1960 (Figure 6.18). Its level has dropped 15 meters (50 feet) and its main port, Aralsk, now lies 100 kilometers from shore. The problem is that too much of the melting snow from the mountains, which tumbles down along the region's two great rivers (the Amu Darya, or Oxus River, and the Syr Darya), is being drawn off for farming. Every year, to support farming and for other uses, the Central Asian states drain off all but 11 cubic kilometers of the water flowing through their rivers. Those 11 cubic kilometers are not enough even to keep the Aral Sea stable; they merely stop it from dying more quickly than it is dying already (its level is dropping by 30 centimeters a year). By 1993, the Aral Sea's level had fallen by more than 16 meters (48 feet), its surface area had shrunk by nearly half, and its volume by 75 percent. Its salinity had increased more than threefold.

The Aral Sea disaster, which first gained world attention during the final years of the Soviet era, originates from a 1960s' plan that turned Uzbekistan into the world's third-largest cotton producer by diverting two main rivers, the Amu and Syr, which fed the Aral Sea, into a huge desert irrigation project. At the time, a whole people in Uzbekistan—the Karakulpaks—depended almost entirely on the Aral's fresh water and fish. Kazakhstan's Aral Sea port of Aralsk accounted for 10 percent of the Soviet Union's entire fish catch. No longer fed by the two rivers, the Aral has shrunk by half. The fish catch evaporated when the sea's salinization increased threefold, and epidemic-level incidences of tuberculosis and anemia have broken out in the surrounding region of nearly 4 million people straddling Uzbekistan, Kazakhstan, and Turkmenistan.

The shrinking of the sea is destroying the local environment. The Oxus delta was a center of civilization on a branch of the Silk Road leading to the Volga and Eastern Europe. Today little grows on the delta but the cotton that

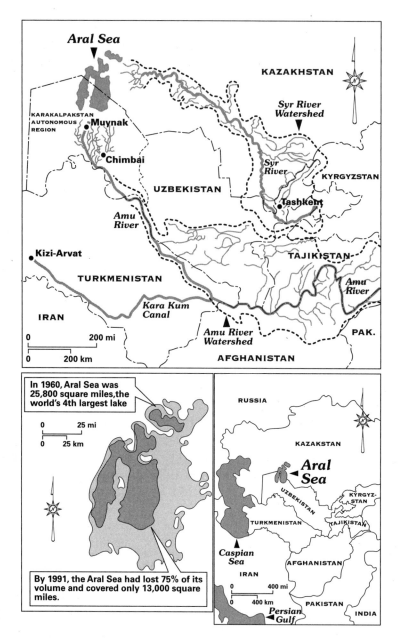

Figure 6-18. The Aral Sea.

the Soviets had decreed for much of central Asia and for which the irrigation schemes were designed. But even the cotton harvest is declining because the smaller sea has resulted in a shorter growing season and frequent dust storms, and the salt blowing off the dry seabed has reduced the soil's fertility. Chemical-happy Soviet collective farms have poisoned the wildlife. The polluted water, in addition to airborne salt and pesticides, is thought to be the source of the region's rampant diseases.

Worse, many of the 4 million people in the Oxus delta of Amu Darya and Syr Darya are being poisoned by drinking water from the two rivers that contains pesticides, defoliants, fertilizers, and raw sewage, purified only partially in the towns by Soviet-era equipment. The air contains salt, dust, and pollutants from the seabed. As a result, there is high incidence of respiratory and stomach problems, typhoid, dysentery, and birth defects.

Uzbekistan, Kazakhstan, and Turkmenistan use most of the river water. They are aware of the Aral Sea problem but have done little to improve conditions for those who live in the area. The republics simply cannot afford to reduce irrigation or to undertake major health improvement projects in the Aral region.

The amount of river water now being used is already too small to maintain current levels of farm output. Nearly a quarter of the irrigated area of the largest farming region in Uzbekistan receives only 70 percent of the water that the main crop, cotton, needs to grow properly. Central Asia has only 0.2 hectares (0.5 acres) of irrigated land to support each person. In arid and semi-arid regions, 0.3 hectares is usually regarded as a bare minimum.

Central Asia has a fast-growing population, increasing at the rate of 3.5 percent a year. At this rate the population will double by 2010, but the supply of water per person will have fallen by half. In short, Central Asia's population is rising, but its capacity to grow food is declining by the fixed or falling availability of water.

These economic pains will increase the attractions of fundamentalism in the area. The Muslim population of Central Asia, at 50 million, is larger than that of any Gulf state. With the collapse of the Soviet Union, Islam's influence has grown dramatically. In 1989 there were only 160 working mosques in Central Asia, and a single Islamic seminary. In 1992 there were around 10,000 mosques and ten seminaries.

Central Asia is a fragile region, politically weak but strategically important. As political corruption took hold, geography and economy joined to make this area a major opium-producing region. With combined surface area that is almost twice the size of Western Europe and some of the most poorly organized and corrupt police forces in the world, Central Asia offers drug traffickers the uninterrupted obscurity they need to flourish. Each of the five countries in Central Asia lacks the resources for effective drug control. In Kyrgyzstan, the 1994 per capita income was $300, 60 percent of what it was in 1991. The figures are only slightly better in Uzbekistan, and anarchy and war have taken root in Tajikistan, which shares some of the best poppy fields with its neighbor Afghanistan.

In the past, opium was always shipped elsewhere to places such as Pakistan for refining. Now there are hundreds of labs spread across the region, although most of them are based in Afghanistan and Tajikistan, the two countries where poppy plantations have grown most quickly. The drugs make their journey by car, truck, bus, mule, and human beings from Afghanistan and Tajikistan to Osh and Bishkek in Kyrgyzstan and Tashkent and Samarkand in Uzbekistan. As Pakistan and Iran have started to get tough on poppy growers and heroin manufacturers, the opium trade is being diverted toward Central Asian republics where places like Osh, Tashkent, and Samarkand have become transit centers for the thousands of tons that are produced each year. This is largely because the commerce carries few risks.

Kazakhstan

The Republic of Kazakhstan has a population of 15 million (2004), of which 40 percent are Kazakhs and the other 40 percent are Russians, and the remainder comprise other ethnic groups such as the Germans, Turks, and Uzbeks. It is the largest Central Asian state, extending from the Volga to the Altai Mountains and from the Siberian plains to the Central Asian deserts. The number of towns and industrial communities in Kazakhstan has increased greatly in recent years. The Kazakh settlement of Baikonur, in the heart of the steppes, is the launching place of the Russian space vehicles. Kazakhstan is Central Asia's state most likely to succeed. The Tengiz oil field, one of the largest in the world, is being developed with foreign capital. State enterprises are being privatized.

During Soviet rule, lethal nuclear testing and tests of all sorts of weapons of mass destruction took place on vast territories of Kazakhstan. There were 467 nuclear tests on the Semipalatinsk test site between 1949 and 1985. In many cases surface tests created radioactive clouds that spread beyond the limits of the test site. Over 500,000 people were exposed to radioactive fallout from these tests. No other territory in the world, or people, has suffered so much from nuclear, chemical, and bacteriological tests as the territory and people of Kazakhstan. The storage of radioactive waste materials from nuclear, chemical, and bacteriological weapons in the Kazakh steppes, the intensive exploitation of the uranium deposits, and the expansion of uncontrolled radioactive pollution of new areas have combined to bring ecological crisis to Kazakhstan.

Tajikistan

Tajikistan is a mountainous region that includes the greater part of the Pamirs. Irrigation systems developed under Soviet rule have improved the land, and cotton farming, grape production, and fruit growing have been developed.

Like Afghanistan, Tajikistan is a patchwork country where Tajiks, Pushtuns, and Uzbeks are slugging it out for control. Months of civil war (between regional groups) among Tajikistan's 7 million people (2004) have left 50,000 people dead and displaced 850,000 more, of whom 150,000 sought refuge in neighboring countries (Figure 6.19). Many villages were substantially destroyed. Much of the recent fighting is simple clan warfare among traditional rivals or enemies in regions that Soviet authorities somewhat lumped together into Tajikistan in the early 1920s. The boundaries created by the Bolsheviks were carelessly drawn and left Tajikistan with internal ethnic fault lines likely to give way under tension. Thousands of Afghan Tajiks have natural ties with their once-Soviet brethren across the 600-mile border, and ex-Soviet Tajiks also communicate easily with the Pushtuns, whose language, like Tajik, is Persian-based. It is possible that Afghanistan's Tajiks may seek to set up a Tajik state in northern Afghanistan and attempt to unite all Tajik areas, including Tajikistan.

Tajiks also comprise about a quarter of the 20 million people in Uzbekistan, Central Asia's most populous state. Most of Uzbekistan's Tajiks live in the south, mainly in the cities of Samarkand and Bukhara, while Uzbeks make up 20 percent of Tajikistan's 5 million people, concentrated in the northern province. Some Tajiks talk of the need for Samarkand and Bukahara to merge into a greater Tajikistan, an area that would correspond to that ruled by the emirate of Bukhara before Samarkand fell to the Russian Empire in 1868.

Mountainous and landlocked, Tajikistan is approximately the size of Greece. Only 7 percent of the area is arable, with agriculture concentrated in

Figure 6-19. During the 1992 civil war in Tajikistan, 60,000 refugees fled to northern Afghanistan. Some 42,000 have since returned home. Civil and regional conflicts arising from ethnicity, the Islamic renaissance, and water disputes have prevented Central Asian countries from realizing social and economic development. The region has encountered pervasive stagnation. (Photo: UNHCR by A. Hollmann.)

the irrigated valleys of the Amu and Syr rivers, which originate in Tajikistan. The different regions of the country are separated by high mountain ranges and are often cut off from each other during winter months. Cotton is the major cash crop, occupying most of the irrigated area. Under the water sharing agreement with downstream riparians of Uzbekistan, Turkmenistan, and Kazakhstan, Tajikistan is entitled to 8 percent of the Syr and 13 percent of the Amu Darya's annual water volume. Most grain is produced on large, rain-fed, state farms. Tajikistan is a large importer of grain.

Tajikistan is well endowed with water-power resources from the streams flowing from the Tien Shan and Pamir mountains. Five major rivers—Pianj, Vakhsh, Amu Darya, Zurkandarya, and Kafirnagan—flow in the southern part of the country. One major river, the Syr Darya, flows in the northern part. The longest river, the Pranz, flows along the border with Afghanistan. Hydroelectric energy is the most important indigenous resource of Tajikistan. Exploitation of this resource began with construction of dams on the lower Vakhsh River, including the Nurek Dam, in the early 1960s. The Nurek hydro-plant (3,000 MW) is the largest power development in Central Asia.

The development of Tajikistan and other Central Asian states is threatened by the lack of environmental considerations. The environmental problems of the Aral Sea, discussed in a preceding section, pose serious policy dilemmas. Industrial plants such as the Vakhsh Nitrogen Fertilizer factory and Leninabad Chemical plant have been responsible for degrading water resources. While large-scale development of hydroelectricity has brought substantial benefits to Tajikistan, it has also resulted in loss of arable land, soil erosion, and reduction in the fish population. Indiscriminate use, over-application, and inadequate storage of pesticides and fertilizers have resulted in considerable contamination of soils, groundwater, surface water, and food products in Tajikistan. The inadequate supply of clean drinking water is the single greatest health hazard. In the Vakhsh Valley, one of the most densely populated areas, about 40 percent of the people get their drinking water from *arycls* (open canals). This has resulted in the high incidence of typhoid, viral hepatitis, and bacterial dysentery. Dushanbe, the capital, is by far the most polluted city in Tajikistan; automotive emissions and the nearby cement factory account for most of the air pollution. The single most significant source of air pollution is the aluminum smelter located in Tursunzade (Regar), near the Uzbek border. The hydrogen fluoride emissions from the plant have been the source of adverse health effects, both to the residents of Tursunzade and to neighboring communities in Uzbekistan

Kyrgyzstan

About the size of England and Scotland combined, Kyrgyzstan is situated at the junction of two gigantic mountain systems, the Tien Shan and the Pamirs.

Modest in size and population, ethnically diverse and difficult of access, the Kyrgyz Republic, independent since 1991, has good grounds for hope of a democratic and prosperous future. Trading skills that go back to the days of the Silk Roads, mineral resources, and scenic natural beauty are among the country's assets, but most important is a hardworking population unified by a thousand-year democratic tradition that reaches back to the days of the nation-builder and folk hero, Manas.

Like the other five ex-Soviet Muslim republics, the boundaries of Kyrgyzstan were artificially carved by Stalin. The country is battling a national identity crisis since the collapse of the Soviet Union. The Kyrgyz government is recalling memories of an unfettered past, when shepherds grazed their animals over immense stretches of the Tien Shan, to give people a feeling of nationalism. In the 1920s many Kyrgyz fled on horseback across the Tien Shan Mountains to China to evade the Soviet colonizers.

Of the five Central Asian republics that were once part of the Soviet Union, Kyrgyzstan has the oldest and most explicit democratic tradition, the most stable social balance, and one of the few heads of state who did not rise through the former political system. In 1993, it became the first of the five to abandon the ruble and establish its own currency—the som—and is now laboring to make the difficult transition to a market economy. Although its economic infrastructure and strong industrial base are still largely oriented to the needs of the former USSR, extensive natural resources and fertile soil offer promise for further development and future prosperity. Kyrgyzstan's natural beauty may prove its greatest asset. Steppes, mountains, desert, glaciers, river valleys, lakes, and forests offer spectacularly varied terrain; Pobeda Peak, in the Tien Shan range, is one of the world's highest mountains, and Issyk Kul, in the northeast, is the world's second-largest mountain lake. As it creates itself, the Kyrgyz Republic taps roots with a depth that gives its diverse people an indomitable cultural strength: years of struggle for unity and independence.

Formerly a colonial appendage of the Soviet Union's centrally planned economy, Kyrgyzstan's economy is plunging toward free enterprise and private ownership. Ninety-four percent of the country's state-owned trading companies have now been privatized, as have 64 percent of those in industry and 39 percent in agriculture. The dislocations of independence have been costly, however, because 80 percent of Kyrgyzstan's trade had been with the USSR.

Kyrgyzstan produces wheat, cotton, grapes, and fruits. Livestock raising is important. Living conditions are hard for most of the country's 4.6 million people. The country wants a rapid transition to the market economy, but faces problems in redesigning its economy. In the old Soviet days, most industry used raw materials from other republics and sent its finished products elsewhere in the Soviet Union. With the collapse of this system, the Kyrgyz find it difficult to get raw materials and have lost their markets. Kyrgyzstan exports hydroelectric power to China, Kazakhstan, and Uzbekistan, but, to fuel domestic growth, it needs to build more dams on its swift rivers to offset its lack of oil and gas.

Oldest and second-largest of Kyrgyzstan's cities, Osh is the capital of a southwestern region that produces more than a third of the country's fruits and vegetables. Once an important trading center on the Silk Road, Osh is still the site of one of Central Asia's largest markets, and a center of the Kyrgyz silk industry. In recent years Osh has emerged as one of the major transit centers of the drug trade. Dissolution of the Soviet Union in 1991, economic and political chaos, civil war, borders that cannot be controlled, and the aggressive anarchy of Afghanistan—one of the biggest growers of opium in the world—have all contributed to propel Osh toward its position as the transit center for thousands of tons of opium produced in Central Asia and Afghanistan each year. Fewer than 300 miles from the Afghan border and less than a day's drive from each of the five other Central Asian countries, the city has become the bustling dispatch point for routes that spin north toward Russia, east to Asia, and west to Europe, through the legendary city of Samarkand, where money was once measured in ounces of silk, not in tons of opium.

Turkmenistan

Turkmenistan is largely occupied by the Kara-Kum Desert, one of the largest Central Asian deserts. Irrigation is of prime importance in this arid land. The Great Kara-Kum Canal, one of the world's longest irrigation and shipping canals, was built by the Soviets. It supplies water for Ashkhabad and irrigates large areas of the desert where long-staple cotton is the principal crop. Oil refining, gas, chemicals, and other industries are based on local resources. Deposits of sulphur are worked in the heart of the Kara-Kum Desert.

Turkmenistan has the potential to be rich. It has probable reserves of more than eight trillion cubic meters of natural gas—among the world's largest. There are only 4.8 million people in the country to share this wealth. While market economies are bringing improvements in other Central Asian republics, the lack of reforms in Turkmenistan has not brought about much progress to combat poverty and unemployment there.

Muslims in Turkmenistan are of the Sunni faith, and do not share the Islamic fundamentalism that has swept Iran and Afghanistan. But tribal loyalty weighs more heavily than does religious feeling. There are five major tribes and more than a dozen smaller tribes and clans spread across the deserts of Turkmenistan. The warring nomadic tribes are reviving the ancient customs and rituals that were papered over during the Russian rule after the Czar's cavalry conquered Turkmenistan in 1881.

Uzbekistan

Uzbekistan lies in the heart of Central Asia. Its population is dominantly Uzbeks, but there are substantial number of Kazakhs, Tatars, Tajiks, and Russians. The city of Samarkand, located on the ancient Silk Road, is one of the major tourist attractions in Uzbekistan. Samarkand became a symbol of Oriental splendor in the fourteenth and fifteenth centuries, after the Mongol conqueror Tamerlane made it the capital of his empire and brought in craftsmen and artists from all over Asia to make it worthy of his name. The architecture thus created had a large influence on later Islamic art, particularly after Tamerlane's descendants established the Mogul empire in India. The great mosques and *madrassas* (Islamic colleges) of the city, and its central square have undergone restoration. Most of the ancient buildings of Samarkand and Bukhara suffer from rising damp from the increased amount of piped water in the city and poor drainage. The damp rising as high as nine feet in the brick walls forms corrosive acids and salts that gradually destroy the masonry, mortar, and decorations.

Uzbekistan has kept most completely the authoritarian style of government. Tamerlane has become an official hero, promoted by the state much as Lenin and Marx once were. He was portrayed as a barbarian warlord in the Soviet era. Today references to Tamerlane in Uzbekistan must be politically correct. He is referred to as Amir Timur (Lord Timur); the historical epithet Timur-i-Leng (Timur the Lame) is not allowed. That he was lame is never mentioned.

Afghanistan

In Afghanistan ethnic identities are sharply etched as a product of the country's mountainous terrain, lack of communication, and tribal traditions. Battles are waging between guerrilla factions, plunging the country into ethnic civil war (Figure 6.20). Afghanistan today is a patchwork of regional fiefdoms, a mesh of shifting alliances, all drawn along fault lines of competing ethnic groups. Across the country, local feudal lords made up predominantly of Pushtus, Tajiks, Uzbeks, Hazaras, and Aimaqs control vast swaths of territory (Figure 6.21). But even among the ethnic concentrations, groups are fractured along sectarian lines or by loyalties to competing leaders.

Decades of Russian and British influence in Afghanistan ended in 1919 when the British relinquished control over the country's foreign affairs. King Zahir Shah ruled the country between 1933 and 1973. In 1978 the Khalq faction of the Communist People's Party of Afghanistan came to power in a coup. Beginning in 1979 the Soviet Union airlifted nearly 115,000 troops into Afghanistan in support of the communist government, which faced fierce resistance from rebel *mujahideen* fighters. Rebel groups were supported by

Figure 6-20. A girl carries water from the village pipe to her home in Bagram, near Kabul. Most of Afghanistan lacks the basic infrastructure of roads, running water, and electricity. Afghans have been waiting for a major reconstruction since the overthrow of the Taliban regime. An international donor community has pledged aid to rebuild the country. Security is the most urgent problem. Afghanistan in 2003 was once again the largest opium producer in the world. One child in four still dies before the age of 5. Women are still harassed and threatened. The provincial warlords battle one another while scoffing at the central government. (Photo: UNICEF by John Isaac.)

Iran, Pakistan, China, the United States, and others. Faced with stalemate and mounting domestic problems, the Soviet Union withdrew its troops in 1989. The collapse of the Soviet Union in 1991 hastened the fall of the Afghan government, and in 1992 rebels proclaimed the Islamic Republic of Afghanistan.

Leaders of the Taliban movement which arose in Kandhar in 1994 cleansed the region of its quarreling factions and gained control of the territory. The Taliban leadership instituted the traditional Islamic laws in Afghanistan. Religious students in their twenties and thirties were the backbone of the Taliban movement. A fair number of Pakistani religious students from the Pathan border region also joined Taliban. They controlled most of the country, including Kabul. The Taliban Islamic fundamentalists were overthrown by the United States military in 2002. The new government in Kabul, the capital, is trying to establish its authority over much of the countryside.

To further its strategic interests and national security, the United States has intervened in Afghanistan twice in less than two decades: first in the fight against the Soviets and then against the Taliban. Now, as Afghans attempt to rebuild, U.S. interests are at stake again. Before the Soviet takeover, Afghanistan was moving slowly toward modernity; its development, impeded by ethnic and tribal divisions, was kept in check by the monarchy's patronage system. Today, the country needs not only a new physical infrastructure but

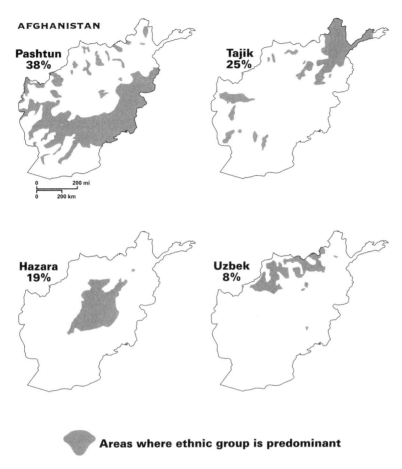

Figure 6-21. Ethnic patterns in Afghanistan.

also institutions that will enable it to function as a modern economy, while politically accommodating its diverse and divided population. Democratization and economic development offer the best hope for stability, and specific steps can be taken to achieve these outcomes, but the country cannot move forward without increased security (Figure 6.22). Warlords contest the authority of the central government, which is itself critically divided. Beyond the issue of security, there is the urgent need for a more active commitment of U.S. resources and influence to the political and economic aspects of the reconstruction effort. In early 2004 Afghanistan adopted a new constitution that guarantees equal political and civil rights to all citizens, clearing the way for its democratic election in the summer of 2004. The adoption of the constitution by 502 delegates came two years after the rout of the extremist Islamic Taliban rule.

Turkey, Iran, and Pakistan all want more influence in Afghanistan and Central Asia. The Central Asians, initially nervous of their southern neighbors, are now keen to strengthen ties to build new trade and transport links.

Figure 6-22. Victims of land mines in Afghanistan. The prolonged conflict in Afghanistan after the Soviet invasion in 1979 to shore up a pro-Soviet government led to a decade-long war between Afghan guerrillas and Soviet and Afghan government troops. After the withdrawal of Soviet troops in early 1989, civil war continued between various factions in the country causing thousands of deaths and injuries. Although some 110,000 land mines have been removed, an estimated 10 million are uncleared. They can remain active for over 50 years. Mine clearance and the building or rebuilding of dams, water pipelines, canals, and water-purification systems will require significant foreign aid. (Photo: UNHCR by A. Hollmann.)

The Soviet Union cut Central Asia off from its historic trading partners to the south, so the countries' only outlets are northwards and are dominated by the old imperial master. This has led to economic disadvantage and political irritation for the republics, which are determined to loosen Russia's grip over them. Central Asia's nearest rail-connected ports are St. Petersburg, 2,000 miles to the northwest, and Vladivostock, 3,000 miles to the northeast. Turkmenistan is making the most consistent efforts to befriend its southern neighbors. With large reserves of natural gas, Turkmenistan is hoping to export gas to Europe. Turkmenistan, Iran, and Turkey signed an agreement in 1994 to build a gas pipeline from Turkmenistan through Iran and Turkey to connect with the European pipeline network. A new railway to Iran is also under construction. Linking Tedzhen in Turkmenistan with Mashad in Iran, it will connect Central Asia's rail network with Iran's, and, through the border town of Zahedan, to Pakistan's. A more direct rail link through western Afghanistan has also been proposed. A road connects Pakistan with Turkmenistan through Afghanistan via Kandahar and Herat. Other possible routes connecting Central Asia with Pakistan lead through China, along the Karakoram Highway to western China. From here roads lead to oil-rich Kazakhstan and to small, mountainous Kyrgyzstan.

Turkey: A Secular State in Transition

Turkey, with nearly 67 million people, has one of the largest populations in the Middle East. It straddles Europe and Asia, and borders the former Soviet republics, volatile Balkans, and equally unpredictable Middle East. During the Cold War, Turkey's frontier with the Soviet Union gave it an indispensable role in NATO strategy. But the Soviet Union is no more, and Turkey shares no borders with a reduced Russia. Its strategic importance now lies in its position as a secular Muslim state bordering fundamentalist Iran. Turkey is seeking closer relations with the European Union, but Muslim Turkey is not likely to be accepted as a full member into the European Union. The resulting sense of Western rejection among the Turks could also strengthen the Islamic revival. A party with Islamic roots won the election in 2002. Turkey needs to do more to improve its human-rights laws, especially those that affect its large Kurdish minority, if the country wants to pursuade the European Parliament to let it enter the European Union.

Rapid urbanization has occurred in the western part of Turkey. Since the 1950s, Istanbul's population has doubled every fifteen years, swollen by migrants from the provinces. Of the 10 million people who live in Istanbul, two thirds are from eastern Anatolia and the Black Sea coast. Not long ago the city was concentrated on the European shore of the Bosporus, where its image was built on the minarets and mosques, the Grand Bazaar and the Ottoman palaces. On the Asian side of the Bosporus, the image of Istanbul is replaced by a sprawl of apartment houses looking out onto bleak hills. Nearly a thousand people arrive in Istanbul every day, and according to government figures, 13 percent of the urban workforce is unemployed. The shift to the cities has created a far broader change in Turkey's demography. When the modern Turkish republic was founded in 1923, only 15 percent of its 13 million people lived in cities. Now two thirds of its 69 million people (2004) are urban. The capital, Ankara, has grown from 2.5 million to 3.5 million since 1980.

The western part of Turkey has a much more diversified economy, but pressure on natural resources has been severe for many years. Deforestation, soil erosion, and air pollution emerged as major problems when the forests of Anatolia were cleared. The growing population and cultivation of marginal areas have worsened the environmental problem.

In the eastern part of Turkey, nearly 12 million Kurds make up a fifth of the country's population. Across the borders of Turkey, another 8 million Kurds live in Armenia, Iran, Iraq, and Syria. With separatist aspirations, the movement for a Kurdish state collides directly with the founding notion of Turkey as a land unified by language, faith, and national identity. The United States has supported autonomy for the Kurds, but has opposed creating a new Kurdish state. That may be a sensible policy. Redrawing borders would invite more trouble and bloodshed in a region that already has plenty. The better solution is to demand decent treatment of Kurds from governments in Turkey and Iraq.

As Turkey's cities bulge beyond control and traditional political parties seem unable to confront the most basic economic and social problems, the main beneficiary from this upheaval is the militant Islamic Welfare Party, which now controls Ankara, Istanbul, and a host of other cities. Islamic revival is familiar from Algeria to the Gaza Strip, from Egypt to Iran. In Turkey it challenges the very secular core of the republic founded in 1923 by Mustafa Kemal Ataturk. And its emergence in this Western-inclined land, with a population that is 99 percent Muslim, has caused tremors of concern among secular Turks. The nation's nonreligious principles, known as *Kemalism*, are at stake. When Ataturk took power, one of his first acts was to dismantle the system of Islamic law that prevailed during the long centuries of Ottoman rule. He introduced new laws based on Swiss and Italian civil codes. He banned the fez as a symbol of backwardness as he sought to propel the nation to the West. He outlawed the use of Arabic in the muezzin's call to prayer. He gave women the vote.

With enforced separation of religion and state, Ataturk laid the foundation of a secularism that has been increasingly depicted as antireligious. Long after his death, some of his edicts were reversed as the government sought to capture what was perceived as an Islamic vote. Arabic calls to prayer were reinstituted in the 1950s. Religious schools were reintroduced. By the early 1980s, the generals who ran the country for two years after taking power in a coup had come to see Islam as a potential counterweight to the communist threat during the Cold War. Throughout the 1980s, the government sought to appease Islamic sentiment by financing new mosques and Islamic education. Turkey now boasts some 400 Islamic schools that turn out many Welfare Party supporters.

Does the rise of the militant Islamic Welfare Party mean Turkey is on the way to becoming an Islamic state? Many secular Turks are concerned. In Istanbul one can sense the new self-confidence among Islamists, and the increased number of women wearing head-scarves and the strong showing of the Welfare Party at the polls presage some kind of change.

COUNTRIES OF NORTH AFRICA

Along the southern shore of the Mediterranean Sea lie the Muslim countries of Morocco, Algeria, Tunisia, and Libya. Mauritania, south of Morocco, is culturally a transitional region, being partly Arab and partly African. After the fall of the Roman Empire, these areas were controlled first by rulers of the Arab Empire, and later by the Ottoman Empire. In 1830 France established influence over Algeria, then secured a privileged position in Tunisia in commercial matters. In 1906 France brought Morocco under its control. Libya fell under Italian rule after the Turkish defeat in the Italo-Turkish War of 1911–1912. The French aimed at rapid assimilation of their possessions in North Africa with the French nation itself. To this end they admitted representatives from their colonies into the French Assembly at Paris. The use of the French language in the schools and administration was an important cultural feature of French policy.

The French encountered a strong nationalist movement in Morocco, Algeria, and Tunisia after 1945. The self-rule and independence was inspired, in part, by the contrast between the poverty of the native Muslim population and the economic prosperity of the French settlers. In 1956 Morocco and Tunisia became independent, and Algeria became independent in 1962. Together these three countries are cut off from central and southern Africa by the Sahara. The high, rugged Atlas Mountains extend through all three and further orient them toward the north. In all three countries economic activities are concentrated largely along the coastal areas. The countries are predominantly agricultural, and much of the farming is based on winter rains and on irrigation waters received from the mountains. Most of the population is a mixture of Muslim peoples of Arab and Berber stocks.

Among these countries, Morocco (population 31 million) offers the best chance of an economic success story in North Africa. Foreign investment is rising, with companies such as the Spanish textile firm Cortefiel moving production to Morocco because labor costs there are at less than 25 percent of European levels. Aware of the fact that fundamentalism has thrived on economic misery in both Egypt and Algeria, Morocco has been trying to open the economy and is pressing for closer links to the European Community. Europe has sharpened interest in Morocco's economic and political stability because of the possibility of Algeria's turning into another Islamic fundamentalist country.

In 1995, Algeria's military rulers permitted the first pluralist presidential vote since independence in 1962. A civil strife began in 1992 when the ruling military generals cancelled elections when it appeared that the Islamic Salvation Front was going to win. Since then the country has been torn by a vicious war. The Islamic forces have launched a terror campaign. When France appeared to support the Algerian military, Islamic militants took their war to the streets and subways of Paris in the summer of 1995. The armed struggle has claimed as many as 40,000 lives. The Armed Islamic Group is waging a civil war to set up an Islamic state in Algeria. With the 1995 election Algeria (population 32 million) has moved tentatively toward a political settlement with the hope for a stable and effective government.

Oil was discovered in the Algerian Sahara in 1956. The known reserves of natural gas are substantial. Saharan oil and gas revenues are of considerable economic significance for the country. Oil earned 87 percent of its foreign currency in 1992, generated 17.7 percent of the GDP, and provided 38 percent of government income. A large petrochemical and refining industry has developed at sites along the coast, to which natural gas and crude are carried by pipelines from the southern fields.

Tunisia has made efforts toward modernization and rapid economic growth, but progress has been slow. Its limited natural resources inhibit prospects for overall development. As with other North African countries, the population (10 million) has grown faster than jobs; many Tunisians work abroad, primarily in France and Libya. Through careful planning, Tunisia has achieved modest development. The potential for further growth is fair. There are areas that could be brought under irrigation. Improved land tenure would also benefit farm production. The existing modern irrigation schemes are not fully and effectively used because of poor rural leadership and lack of incentives for farmers. Tunisia's position as a transit zone for an increasing volume of natural gas moving by pipeline from Algeria to Italy is an added bonus. As with other states of North Africa, the potential will be realized only if political stability can be maintained.

Libya is a land of vast deserts, sparse population (5.6 million), and immense wealth generated by oil resources. Aside from oil, Libya's economic potential is greatly limited by the constraints of a harsh, arid environment. No more than a fragment of the land receives rainfall adequate to support agriculture, and underground water resources are low and declining. Agricultural land is concentrated on the narrow coastal strip. Only 1.2 percent of the country is cultivated, with a further 7.6 percent in pasture. The rest is barren desert. Libya has provided sanctuary to terrorist groups, and tried to develop nuclear weapons with technical help from Pakistan. Early in 2004 Libya pledged to dismantle its nuclear weapons program.

Mauritania (population 3 million), along the Atlantic coast, extends from the delta of the Senegal River in the south to the borders of Algeria and Morocco in the north (Figure 6.23). The landscape of Mauritania is arid and sand desert. Nearly 85 percent of the population is nomadic, semi-nomadic, or seasonally migrating herdsmen. Except for pockets of oasis cultivation in the desert area of central and northern Mauritania, the small amount of cultivated land is almost entirely concentrated in the southern region of the Senegal River valley. Mauritania is a French colonial artifact in which different and potentially antagonistic ethnic groups were thrown together. The majority of the Moorish population and African minorities are divided among themselves. Growth in the economy has been feeble, at about 1.4 percent per year in the last decade. Most economic indicators are adverse, and potential for dramatic economic growth is limited.

Figure 6-23. Fishing has become a major export sector in the economy of Mauritania, an arid and sand desert country on the Atlantic. It is a culturally transitional region between Arab Middle East and sub-Saharan Africa. A former French colony, it became independent in 1960. It started its national life at independence with a very poor and basic economy. (Photo: UNICEF by Jorgen Schytte.)

THE MIDDLE EAST AND THE TWENTY-FIRST CENTURY

To move confidently into the twenty-first century and give their people more of the advantages of the modern world, the Islamic countries of the Middle East must absorb the principles of democracy and accept the idea of gender equality. Only a few countries such as Turkey may be hesitantly called democracies. In Turkey, regular elections have survived three military seizures of power between 1960 and 1980. Too many Muslim countries are non-democracies, and too many of these non-democracies have governments that combine inefficiency and unpopularity.

To avoid being internally divided and using only half of the economic energy available, Muslim countries have to get many more of their women into the higher levels of education, and allow a great many more to take senior positions in industry and the professions. They deserve in practice the equality that the Koran gives them in principle. To accomplish this goal, Muslim countries have to come to grips with the institution that has done most to hold Muslim women back (Figure 6.24).

At a time when Arab countries face far-reaching choices—about economies, democracy, Israel, religion – the region needs most what it lacks most: leaders. Most of those in power seem to "lead" by staying in the crowd,

Figure 6-24. Girls in Bahrain. Recently, women in Bahrain have participated in national election. But in most of the Middle East women do not participate fully in the national life and economy of the country. Opportunities for women are limited by tradition and local culture. In Saudi Arabia, for instance, women cannot drive; only women enveloped in black cloaks called *abayas* appear in public. Religious police, the *mutawwa*, enforce the law. Most unions are arranged by parents, and marrying into wealth and influence often means marrying a relative. The marriage of girls to blood relatives (as many as 70 percent in some Muslim countries) has produced several genetic disorders, including the blood diseases thalassemia, a potential hemoglobin deficiency, sickle cell anemia, and spinal muscular atrophy among children. Social lives are so restricted that it is virtually impossible for men and women to meet one another outside the umbrella of an extended family. Among more-educated Arabs, marrying relatives has become less common, and younger generations have begun to pull away from the practice. But for the vast majority, the tradition is still deeply rooted in culture. (Photo: Bahrain National Museum.)

distracting it when possible, and running around in front of it when necessary. National tumult in countries such as India produced Gandhi and Nehru. America nurtured Jefferson and Madison. But decades of crisis in the Arab world has spawned the likes of Saddam Hussein and Osama bin Laden.

FURTHER READINGS

Abu-Dawoud, A. and P. P. Karan. 1990. *International Boundaries of Saudi Arabia*. New Delhi: Galaxy Publications.

Amirahmadi, Hooshang and Salah S. El-Shakhs, eds. 1993. *Urban Development in the Muslim World*. Piscataway, NJ.: Center for Urban Policy Research, Rutgers University.

Bergen, Peter L. 2002. *Holy War Inc.: Inside the Secret World of Osama Bin Laden*. New York: Free Press.

Braude, Joseph. 2003. *The New Iraq: Rebuilding the Country for Its People, the Middle East, and the World*. New York: Basic Books.

Bregman, Ahron. 2003. *A History of Israel*. New York: Pelgrave Macmillan.

Centre for Research Studies on Kuwait. 1999. *Kuwait-Iraq Boundary: Development and Documents*. Kuwait.

Cooley, John K. 2000. *Unholy War: Afghanistan, America, and International Terrorism*. London: Pluto Press.

Fregosi, Paul. 1998. *Jihad in the West: Muslim Conquests from the 7th to the 21st Centuries*. New York: Prometheus Books.

Fuller, Graham E. and Ian O. Lesser. 1995. *A Sense of Siege: The Geopolitics of Islam and the West*. Boulder, CO: Westview Press.

Fuller, Graham E. 2000. *The Arab Shia: The Forgotten Muslims*. New York: St. Martins.

Gause III, F. Gregory. 1994. *Oil Monarchies*. New York: Council on Foreign Relations Press.

Gerner, Deborah. 1994. *One Land, Two Peoples: The Conflict over Palestine*. Boulder, CO: Westview Press.

Gerth, Jeff and Judith Miller. 2002. Report Says Saudis Fail to Crack Down on Charities That Finance Terrorists. *New York Times* October 17. p. A14.

Held, Colbert C. 1994. *Middle East Patterns: Places, Peoples and Politics*. Boulder, CO: Westview Press.

Hiro, Dilip. 2002. *Iraq in the Eye of the Storm*. New York: Thunder's Mouth Press/ Nation Books.

Hourani, A., P. Khoury, and Mary Wilson, eds. 1994. *The Modern Middle East: A Reader*. Berkeley: University of California Press.

Karan, P. P. and M. Qarami. 1989. Social Geography of Makkah, *National Geographical Journal of India* 35:85–100.

Karan, P. P. 1988. Urban Systems and Urban Regions of Saudi Arabia. *Annals, Association of Geographers, India*. 8:31–41.

Karan, P. P. and Issa Shair. 1979. Geography of the Islamic Pilgrimage. *GeoJournal*. 3:599–608.

Kliot, Nurit. 1994. *Water Resources and Conflict in the Middle East*. New York: Routledge.

Lewis, Bernard. 2003. *The Crisis of Islam: Holy War and Unholy Terror*. New York: The Modern Library.

Lunde, Paul. 2002. *Islam*. New York: DK Publishing, Inc.

Mandelbaum, Michael, ed. 1994. *Central Asia and the World*. New York: Council on Foreign Relations Press.

Ojeda, Auriana, ed. 2003. *Islamic Fundamentalism*. Farmington Hills, MI: Greenhaven Press.

Peretz, Don. 1990. *Intifada: The Palestinian Uprising*. Boulder, Colorado: Westview.

Schofield, Clive H. and Richard Schofield, eds. 1994. *The Middle East and North Africa. World Boundaries*, Vol. 2. New York: Routledge.

Stevers, Eric W. 2003. *The Post-Soviet Decline of Central Asia: Sustainable Development and Comprehensive Capital*. London and New York: RoutledgeCurzon.

Zartman, I. William and William Mark Habeeb. 1993. *Polity and Society in Contemporary North Africa*. Boulder, CO: Westview.

Chapter 7

Sub-Saharan Africa

Sub-Saharan Africa is the ancestral home of millions of Americans and, according to some anthropologists, the cradle of mankind—the birthplace of *Homo sapiens*. From at least the first millennium B.C., elements of Egyptian, Phoenician, Greek, Roman, and Arab culture spread southward into Africa through conquest, trade, and the dissemination of Christianity and Islam. Trade in slaves, gold, copper, salt, spices, and many other items flourished both by sea and, following the introduction of camels in about the third century A.D., across the Sahara.

For a long time, however, easy access to the cultural exchange of the Mediterranean basin was impeded by the vast expanse of desert, causing the peoples of sub-Saharan Africa to develop cultures distinctly their own. Several empires with large cultural centers emerged, but were later destroyed by war or declined following changes in trade patterns. Although European traders had frequented the African coast since the late fifteenth century, knowledge of these empires remained limited until the era of African exploration and colonization in the late eighteenth and nineteenth centuries.

By the early twentieth century, most of Africa had fallen under colonial domination. In sub-Saharan Africa, only Liberia and Ethiopia remained independent. In the decades after World War II, however, the peoples of Africa increasingly rejected foreign rule and demanded for themselves the fundamental freedoms for which they had fought in support of the Allied powers. By the mid-1960s, most African countries had achieved independence. Legacies of slavery, colonialism, imperialism, and racism still haunt the region. It is a region of hope and despair in the non-Western world: hope because sub-Saharan Africa possesses vast resource potential for development, and despair because it continues to be affected by droughts, famines, chronic poverty, disease, and political injustice.

There are over forty-five independent countries in sub-Saharan Africa
and the nearby islands (Figure 7.1). These are among the world's youngest
and poorest nations. Since independence, African countries have experienced considerable political upheaval. The process of forging cohesive
national identities within boundaries drawn by European powers and among
more than 1,000 ethnic groups has been difficult. Except for a few parts of
South Africa, Nigeria, Zimbabwe, Ivory Coast, and Kenya, most of Africa is
still underdeveloped.

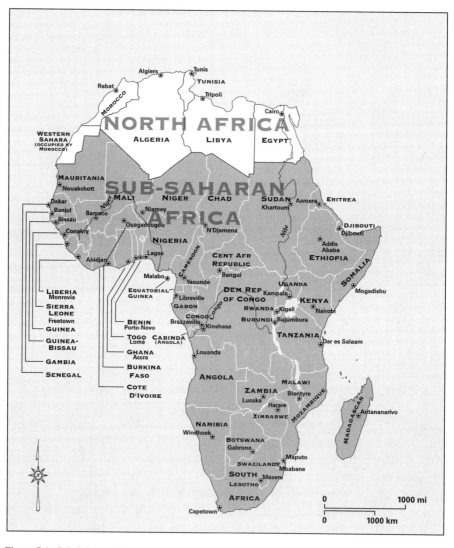

Figure 7-1. Sub-Saharan Africa.

REGIONAL PROFILE

The continent of Africa covers over 11 million square miles—nearly one fifth of the world's total land surface and equal to the combined area of the United States, Western Europe, and India. The sub-Saharan portion of the continent is over 8 million square miles—nearly three times the size of the continental United States—and has a population of about 680 million.

Africa consists of a series of level or slightly undulating plateaus that fall away from a central area of high formations to low-lying coastal zones averaging only 20 miles in width. Many of these plateaus lie at altitudes of anywhere from 3,000 to 9,000 feet in eastern and southern Africa, although in the north and west most of the land is between 500 and 1000 feet above sea level. Massive geologic events in the plateaus have produced ridges that are among the most conspicuous features of the African landscape: the Great Rift Valley of East Africa, one of the deepest fractures in the earth's crust; Mt. Kilimanjaro (19,565 feet above sea level) and Mt. Kenya (17,058 feet) in East Africa are higher than any peak in the European Alps. These changes also produced Lake Chad in Central Africa; the lakes of East Africa, including Africa's largest, Lake Victoria; and the continent's four major rivers: the Nile (4,000 miles long), the Zaire (3,000 miles), the Niger (2,600 miles), and the Zambezi (1,650 miles).

Africa contains the world's largest desert, the Sahara; regions of heavy rainfall and lush forest vegetation; and, between the desert and rainforest, broad savanna grasslands and woodlands. Nearly one half of Africa's total area is desert, 40 percent is partly forested grasslands, and 10 percent is dense forests and thickets. No long mountain ranges rise in Africa to wring moisture reliably from passing air masses. Overall, rainfall patterns reveal extreme contrasts. The equatorial rainforest is deluged during two rainy seasons. Lands to the north, south, and east each have a single wet season, which may deliver insufficient rain to some areas and skip others entirely. Two thirds of Africa loses more water to evaporation than is gained from rain.

Heat overwhelms most of sub-Saharan Africa, which has either a tropical or subtropical climate. Relief from heat comes in the higher altitudes of eastern and southern plateaus and on parts of the west coast, where currents transport seawater from cooler regions. Temperate climates are found along the southern and southwestern areas of the Cape of Good Hope, and on the higher parts of the inland plateaus.

Africa's varied climate has affected vegetation, river conditions, and the incidence of disease; it also has influenced settlement patterns. Africans sought out fertile lands, water, and areas suitable for grazing. Europeans settled near the coasts on the cool eastern and southern plateaus and in the temperate regions. Modern cities, often former centers of colonial administration and trade, usually are located in these areas.

HISTORICAL EVOLUTION

The Negroid group—one of the major physical types of people evolved in Africa—became dominant, learning first to hunt and forage, later to domesticate animals, and finally to domesticate plants. Between 1000 B.C. and 1000 A.D. a Negroid group (known by the linguistic classification of Niger-Congo and Kordofanian or Negritic) exerted control over much of southern Africa, with a major subgroup, the Bantu, nearly eliminating the Pygmoid and Bushmanoid people in the process. Caucasoid peoples from the Mediterranean area first migrated to northeast Africa near the end of the Paleolithic period, and subsequent migrations to northeast and northern Africa occurred in the centuries preceding and following Christ.

Kingdoms and Empires

A number of kingdoms developed in the early days. The Kush Kingdom (700 B.C.–200 A.D.) formed in the area of present-day Sudan. The Axum Empire, established by 350 A.D., comprised much of modern Ethiopia. The Axumites brought Christianity to Ethiopia. Ancient African kingdoms such as Ghana, Kanem-Bornu, Mali, Songhai, and the Hausa states developed primarily in the savanna lands. From their homeland in eastern Nigeria, the Bantu drifted south and east. They gradually adapted their lifestyle to the changing landscapes, assimilated indigenous peoples, and absorbed those peoples' innovations. Thus grew several major states of southern Africa: the kingdoms of Kongo, Lunda, Bunyoro, Buganda, Rwanda, and Munhumutapa. To the east, Bantu interaction with Arabs created the Swahili culture. The city-states of the Guinea Coast—Ife, Benin, Yoruba—date at least to the fifteenth century.

From the tenth to the eighteenth centuries, Muslims continued to settle in eastern Africa from the Horn southward to Zimbabwe. Islam came to sub-Saharan Africa on camel caravans that crossed the Sahara and boats that crossed the Indian Ocean. Today, northern Africa is predominantly Muslim and the south is Christian. In between, the two religions rub shoulders uneasily. Today, Islam in sub-Saharan Africa is growing in size and influence. Islam is spreading faster than any other faith in East and West Africa. Islamic values—emphasis on communal living, clear roles for men and women, tolerance of polygamy—have much in common with traditional African life. Western values such as democracy have been a disappointment in Africa, often producing sham elections, continued misrule, and poverty. Muslims have become an angry, organized force in many African countries such as Kenya, Tanzania, Uganda, Sudan, Chad, Ivory Coast, and Nigeria. In Nigeria, the rise of Islam as a political force has been most explosive and violent.

European Exploration and Colonization

In the early fifteenth century, Portuguese explorers began a gradual build-up of African trade relations with Europe and the Americas, leading eventually to Christian missionary contact with Africa. The Portuguese brought the Christian gospel to western Africa and took home their first sack of gold and their first batch of people. By the mid-nineteenth century, European, American, and Arab slave traders—supplied by African go-betweens—robbed the continent of perhaps as many as 25 million human beings.

Colonial inroads came slowly. The British, French, and Dutch were all trading on the Guinea coast by 1600. In 1652 the Dutch East India Company, vying for the control of the Indies trade, established a resupply station on the Cape of Good Hope. Cape Town mushroomed in spite of company policy restricting the immigration of Dutch farmers, or Boers. Britain won control of the Cape in the early 1800s. The Boers trekked inland and met the Zulu, whom they defeated at Blood River in 1838.

While the general lay of Africa's southern lands was thus learned, much of the interior was unknown as late as 1790. Missionaries, traders, explorers, and adventurers penetrated the heart of the continent beginning in the later part of the eighteenth century. These were the years of such explorers as Mungo Park, who attacked the mystery of the Niger; James Bruce, who explored the Blue Nile; David Livingston, dean of the pathfinders, who mapped the Zambezi and crossed the continent; and John Speke and Richard Burton, who sought the source of the Nile. They were followed, especially after 1880, by government officials engaged in extending colonial domains. Henry Morton Stanley, a land hunter, helped win for King Leopold II of Belgium the mineral-rich Congo Free State. The countrymen of adventurers like Rene Caillie dreamed of a French Africa from Algeria to Congo. Britons cherished a Cape to Cairo corridor to complement their holdings in the eastern and western parts of the continent. Germany wedged colonial territories between other colonial claims in Togo, Cameroon (Kamerun), southwest Africa, and East Africa.

Although only a small part of Africa was under foreign rule before 1880, all but two of the independent countries of sub-Saharan Africa were under European control by 1900. The two exceptions were Liberia, established by freed American slaves in the 1840s, and the ancient Empire of Ethiopia. In 1884 Otto von Bismarck convened the Berlin Conference of colonial powers in Africa to draw the boundaries separating their possessions. During the next half-century, Europeans settled in various areas of the continent, traded, extracted minerals, and established governments reflecting the different policies and institutions of the colonial powers.

Post-Independence Period (Since the 1960s)

Many factors helped to create a climate in which most of the European-ruled colonies in Africa eventually became independent. These included the participation of Africans in World Wars I and II; the growth of African nationalist movements; the Atlantic Charter of 1941, proclaiming the right of all peoples to choose the form of government under which they would live; and changing European economic and political concerns with respect to the efficacy and burdens of empire. The burdens of most African states as they exist today were created by the colonialists, and the states they enclose were given their independence when France, Britain, Belgium, and Portugal found it uneconomical to continue to rule them.

The wave of African independence began in 1957. Led by Nkrumah of the Gold Coast (Ghana), Houphouet-Boigny of the Ivory Coast, and Sekou Toure of French Guinea (Guinea), a host of sub-Saharan countries in rapid succession broke ties with their colonial rulers. Occasionally, the changeover was accompanied by violence, as in Zaire, Mozambique, Angola, and Zimbabwe. Since 1957, forty-three nations have joined the four previously independent countries of Ethiopia, Liberia, Sudan, and South Africa. South Africa became an independent union with dominion status within the British Commonwealth in 1910, and Sudan separated from Egypt and the United Kingdom in 1956. Namibia, under de facto South African control, became independent in 1990.

Africa's political evolution during the past three decades has been tumultuous, with nearly two thirds of the countries undergoing nonconstitutional changes in government. Although more than half of the nations are led by military leaders or committees, some have now returned to constitutional civilian rule. Relative tranquility and stable leadership exist only in a few countries. There is political trauma in most countries with authoritarian regimes. Most of the African states have not been able to overcome the liabilities that colonialists created with the artificial borders and structures they imposed on the Africans.

Secession attempts have threatened some nations. Eritrea sought independence in 1962, when Ethiopia assumed direct control and terminated Eritrea's federated status. Shaba (formerly Katanga) unsuccessfully attempted to secede from Congo when it became independent in 1960, and Biafra from Nigeria in 1967.

Cultural and religious differences have led to periodic civil wars in Sudan and Chad. Warfare also has erupted between states. Somalia and Ethiopia fought over the possession of the Ogaden region. Tanzania invaded Uganda in 1979 to oust the barbaric government of Idi Amin and to retaliate for Ugandan attacks on its territory. Libya forcibly annexed a portion of northern Chad in 1980–1981 and pushed farther south in 1983, halting only after regional and international pressures were applied. Nigeria and Cameroon also have had tense relations over poorly defined borders.

The various forms of government in sub-Saharan Africa also reflect the heritage of both colonial administrative and political institutions and indigenous historical and social backgrounds (Figure 7.2). Ethiopia's former constitutional monarchy, for example, was deeply rooted in the country's centuries-old royal history. Nigeria's attempt at American-style federalism, on the other hand, represented an effort to maintain unity in one of Africa's largest states by accommodating its ethnic, cultural, and historical differences in a decentralized system. Africa's ethnolinguistic groupings are characterized by strongly developed traditional structures, which often cross political boundaries imposed by colonial powers with little or no regard for linguistic and cultural similarities. Despite the impact of modernization in urban areas, traditional ethnic loyalties remain strong and have impeded the development of national consciousness. Opposition often has been based on ethnolinguistic and regional special interests.

African states continue to experience changes in governmental form and process as they experiment with ways to organize political power effectively and to devise a durable basis for citizen participation in the political system. The end of the Cold War and the collapse of the Soviet Union had major effects on some states. With the end of the Cold War many Western countries,

Figure 7-2. A Christian boy in Nasir, southern Sudan. A key feature of the cultural geography of Africa is the way most people identify with an ethnic or religious group within a nation. These groups are generally associated with a specific, if not precisely bounded, territory. In Sudan, the Islamic Arab group of the north has tried to increase their influence over the Christian African population of the south, resulting in serious conflict. (Photo: UNICEF by Betty Press.)

including the United States, stopped pouring money into the coffers of dubious governments they had supported in attempts to prevent the spread of communism; they instead started using the aid to promote reform. Angola and Mozambique abandoned Marxism and introduced a multiparty constitution. Despots were toppled in Benin, Congo, and Ethiopia. In Ghana, one-party rule crumbled. In villages across sub-Saharan Africa election boxes have sprouted, bringing hope that from them would grow more accountable governments, better-run economies, and greater respect for human rights.

Elsewhere, old leaders have been replaced by technocrats who are more in tune with the International Monetary Fund (IMF) and the World Bank than with the peasants who make up most of their populations. There is an upsurge in the demand for multiparty democracy. However, many of the leaders of this movement are opportunists and tribalists camouflaged in democratic uniforms. African leaders have responded with demands for change in three ways: resisting change, managing change, or accommodating change. During the 1990s, forty-two sub-Saharan African countries were one-party states or military dictatorships. Some have held elections of varying credibility. In only ten of these countries have the governments changed. South Africa ended constitutional one-race rule and has now drafted a new constitution. Several African states such as Sierra Leone, which are blessed with rich deposits of diamonds, gold, and other precious minerals and metals, have, since their independence, concentrated investments in the capital, and have provided few services, either in education or health care in the countryside.

In some countries such as Cote de Ivoire (Ivory Coast) elections have been flawed; elections are freer but are still unfair. A few old dictators found new ways of continuing their rule. The big failures, such as Congo, have come about not because democracy did not work, but because it was thwarted. In 1999 Nigeria elected its first civilian government, ending fifteen years of military rule.

The most dispiriting thing about Africa is not that it is the world's poorest continent, nor even that it is the only one where people were poorer at the end of the 1980s than they had been at the beginning of that decade. It is that even if Africa's economy were to grow at the rate projected by the World Bank for the rest of the 2000s, Africans would have to wait another twenty-five years to clamber back to the incomes they had in the mid-1970s. Africa has lurched backwards at a time when poor countries elsewhere in the non-Western world have sprung ahead. In 1965 Ghanaians were less poor than South Koreans or Thai; Nigerians were better off than Indonesians. Today the total wealth of Africa, with twice the population of the United States, is little more than that of Belgium. Disappointment crowds into the continent: unfilled bellies, untreated and untreatable disease, unschooled children, and unfinished wars. Can Africa reverse this dismal trend?

The 1960s were a time of optimism and hope for Africa, when Africans were snapping their shackles to take a rightful place among the world's independent states. Four decades later, there is no optimism about Africa's immediate future. Famine, corruption, terror and tyranny are widespread, and could well become worse. In the old days, most Africans would extol the virtues of socialism without meaning or understanding it. Now they extol the virtues of democracy without meaning or understanding it.

There are a host of reasons for Africa's failure and slide into chaos: a colonial system that, by its very nature, could not impart democracy; the prevalence of tribalism—the African feeling, often justified, that only the tribe guarantees security; an ugly elitism that encouraged the newly rich to turn their backs on the masses; the failure of European colonial powers to bequeath American-type federal systems that would have allowed regions and tribes to share power; the penchant by aid-givers for grandiose development schemes that overwhelmed small African ministries and usually withered in failure; the neglect that set in swiftly like rigor mortis after the failures; and the overload of humanitarian horror stories that has made much of the world shut its eyes almost in self-defense.

Africa had a warmth and innocence forty years ago that created a feeling that the continent had a chance to solve its problems and forge ahead. Four decades later, it is difficult to find that feeling. However, while the Africa of wretched refugee camps and bloody ethnic wars still grinds on in Angola, Sudan, Liberia, Somalia, Rwanda, and Burundi, in some parts of the continent radical changes such as political opposition, outspoken newspapers, and elections are emerging. In 1994 democracy came to South Africa, Malawi, and Mozambique. Some thirty African countries have abandoned their experiments with socialism in favor of the free-market creed. As part of the structural adjustment, African governments are trying to spend within their means, keep their exchange rates competitive, free up prices, strip out subsidies, stop meddling in business, and sell off state enterprises. Ghana, Tanzania, Gambia, Burkina Faso, Nigeria, and Zimbabwe have improved their industrial output, exports, savings, and income per person.

WHY IS AFRICA UNDERDEVELOPED?

Social scientists have tried to explain Africa's underdevelopment by several theories. Among these theories are

1. The absence of modernizing institutions
2. Center–periphery dependencies
3. The political economy

The Absence of Modernizing Institutions

According to this theory, the phenomenon of African underdevelopment is, for the most part, a consequence of the absence of modernizing institutions such as science and technology, labor stratification, role differentiation, capital accumulation, and achievement motivations. In the Asian Pacific section of the non-Western world, Chinese, Japanese, and Indian values (the cultural incentives that have encouraged virtues such as education, self-reliance, relentless struggle, and the quest for self-improvement) and capitalism (the economic incentive) with all the necessary requisites—capital, raw materials, and a laboring class—have worked in a complementary fashion and rendered development possible. In Africa such an effective unity of the culture and economy is lacking.

Center–Periphery Dependencies

According to this theory, the causes of African underdevelopment are for the most part externally generated. Extension of underdevelopment in Africa is a consequence of European and Arabian slave trades, European colonialism, and imperialism. Imperialism, by draining the indigenous wealth of Africa, made it impossible for Africa to develop. The past and present unequal economic relationship between the developed metropolis (Europe) and its underdeveloped satellite (Africa) played a major role in the region's underdeveloped status. (The metropolis and satellite relationship has also been called the center and periphery relationship.) Under this relationship, in Africa, peasants were compelled to produce "compulsory crops" and then sell their labor to European-owned mines, factories, or plantations. This mode of production distorted the African economy and led to the gradual destruction of the peripheral African farmers' attempts at self-sustenance.

The process of industrialization that Europeans introduced into Africa systematically made the African farmer a wage laborer for foreign-owned plantations and factories and, by paying the African laborer very low wages, the European owners of the means of production extracted high surplus profits from their capital investments. The results of this colonial mode of production were high savings and investments for the European owners, and a lack of savings, absence of investments, and a spirit of dependency for African farmers and wage earners alike. The European owners have now been replaced by multinational corporations based in Britain, the United States, Japan, and Germany, in which the center nurtures technology, innovative thinkers, and managers, while the periphery, as in Africa, produces extremely low wages.

The limited amount of technology sent to Africa is concentrated in cities, which results in the development of the urban areas and the underdevelopment of the rural regions, thus perpetuating center and periphery relationships. This phenomenon distorts the relationship between cities and countryside. Job-seeking farmers flock to the cities to secure the relatively few available employments. The results are that the lands from which they come become unproductive and the cities become overcrowded, thus leading to concentrations of urban poor on the one hand and under-cultivated lands on the other.

Political Economy

The political economy school suggests that the causes of underdevelopment are internal factors that are unique to the underdeveloped African countries. The internal factors such as underutilization of natural resources, low labor productivity, economic dependence on foreign capital, and urban-centered development, which are products of colonial history, have become integral aspects of the institutions of most countries.

Contrary to the dependency theory, which views the main explanations of underdevelopment as a whole in the center–periphery relations, political economy theory proposes that more adequate explanations are found in relationships that are internal to the countries. Presently the cities are the new perpetuators of the expropriation of the poor, and of rural peasants in particular. African cities are the product of colonial political economy. Traditional African cities such as Timbuktu were supplanted by new cities that catered to the colonial economies. Colonial domination has been replaced by urban domination of the rural sector. Africa as a whole is still a peasant society, and the urban-led development process is largely extractive. The urban bias has resulted in misallocation to the cities of material resources required by the rural periphery for its development, affluence for a selected few urbanites, and the perpetuation of rural backwardness and poverty.

These theories of underdevelopment also apply to the Asian part of the non-Western world. What, then, produced growth in Asia in recent decades and stagnation in Africa? In Asia a set of common policies imposed on a receptive culture and an amenable social structure by determined political elite has played the central role in development during the postcolonial period. Also, a favorable combination of external factors aided Asian development. Minority groups of Japanese, Chinese, Korean, and Indian entrepreneurs played a disproportionate role in development. Unlike Africa, the Asian nations generally did not have a tradition of tribal land ownership. In addition, in China, Japan, and India, land reforms swept away a feudal system of land ownership which had hampered individual incentives and agricultural innovation. Furthermore, Asian political systems have been stable. The reigning elite in all areas held on to office and allowed some degree of discussion, dissent, and protest. And they all stressed economic development as the primary goal of their regimes.

POPULATION GROWTH AND POOR AGRICULTURAL PERFORMANCE

Sub-Saharan Africa's population is estimated at over 600 million, and it is growing more quickly than any other region in the world. The high population growth rates are primarily due to Africa's position in the second stage of the demographic transition model. In this stage, crude death rates suddenly decline and birth rates remain at very high levels or even experience an increase. Because the difference between the crude birth rate and crude death rate is very high, the rate of annual increase is also very high. During the past half-century, countries of Sub-Saharan Africa have experienced a dramatic decline in death rates, including infant mortality rates (Figure 7.3). However, fertility rates have remained stubbornly high throughout the region.

If its present growth is not altered, its population would triple by the year 2028. But while Africa's population grows by 3.1 percent annually, the region's food supply increases by only 1.1 percent per year. This means that every year Africa's dependence on uncertain food imports grows more acute. And, in painfully practical terms, it means that each year more Africans will

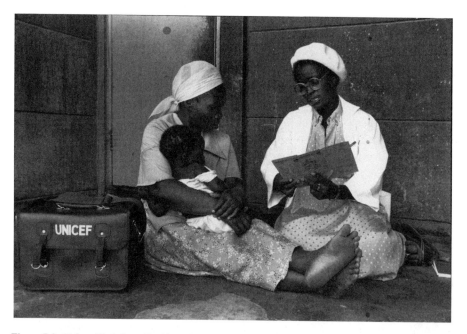

Figure 7-3. Tafara, Zimbabwe. Health workers visit homes to help women understand the significance of improved sanitation and hygiene in the prevention of many diseases that are endemic in sub-Saharan Africa. Improved sanitation and public health facilities, including vaccination of children, have led to declines in infant mortality in Zimbabwe and several other sub-Saharan countries. (Photo: UNICEF by Carolyn Watson.)

starve. The suffering that was triggered in the Horn of Africa by severe drought is being built in to the demographic structure of the entire continent.

The southern edge of the Sahara desert expands and removes another three- to six-mile-wide belt of arable land from between Mauritania and Ethiopia each year (Figure 7.4). Up to 28,000 square miles of farmland is lost to desert

Figure 7-4. Land degradation is advancing at an alarming rate in sub-Saharan Africa, particularly desertification in dry land areas such as the Central Plateau of Burkina Faso in Sahel. In the village of Ribou, near Yako, soil and water conservation measures, erosion-control systems including the construction of vegetative cover of bunds, and agro forestry are being undertaken to restore agricultural environment. A tree nursery contains eucalyptus, prosopis, papaya, acacia, and neem seedlings which are raised for planting to check the advancing desertification. (Photo: IFAD by J. Hartley.)

annually in the countries of the Sahel region. Encroachment of the Sahara threatens a third of Africa's fertile land. Although traditional farming systems worked well in sub-Saharan Africa when population densities were low, they became strained and ineffective when population growth accelerated in the 1950s. There is a link between rapid population growth, poor agricultural performance, and increasing environmental degradation. Farmers of the Sahel no longer can afford to let their fields restore fertility by letting them remain fallow for a while. Nomads no longer move their herds before they are able to overgraze and destroy pastures. As the population in sub-Saharan Africa expanded, mobility was curtailed and farmers had to remain in one place even though their farming methods were not suited to permanent farming. This led to agricultural failure and environmental degradation.

Africa's startling environmental losses and its steady declines in agricultural productivity do not bode well for a continent in which the economy is so heavily based on agriculture. Although little can be done to eliminate drought, which occurs periodically in Africa, much can be done to avoid famine. Drought has been transformed into famine by resource degradation, high population growth rates, and the absence of growth in farm output. Famine, in turn, has been aggravated by mistaken national policies and armed conflict. Nonetheless, Africa does have the potential to produce sufficient food for its increasing population and thereby reduce its vulnerability to future droughts. This potential depends greatly on the ability of African governments to implement effective national policies that support small farmers and encourage the development and use of relevant technology (Figure 7.5).

A problem in developing an agricultural strategy for Africa as a whole is the wide variations in the situation of subregions and countries. For example, in Sudan, Ethiopia, Mozambique, Somalia, Liberia, and Chad, the most important actions for agriculture are outside of agriculture—reducing civil strife, establishing sound principles of governance and pluralistic institutions—as well as generating rapid increases in food production. By comparison, macroeconomic policy changes are of greatest importance to stimulating agriculture in the countries of western and central Africa. Improved government management combined with investment in infrastructure is of highest priority for agriculture in Congo. Continuing to improve policy and technology transfer are most important in better-performing countries such as Kenya, Botswana, Tanzania, and Nigeria. Political and social stability are prerequisites in all areas.

Most of the increases in food supply in Africa have occurred due to expansion of cultivated area rather than yield increases. There are many reasons for this. For one, there has been little investment in irrigation, which was a major input into Asia's Green Revolution. In addition, unlike Asia, there has been little progress made by farmers in yield-increasing agricultural technologies. There is a technological revolution in agriculture occurring in

Figure 7-5. Siaya District, Nayanza Province, West Kenya. A Siaya farm operator stall-feeds the cows on Napier grass as part of the concept of zero grazing, whereby the animals are not roaming around for feed but are fed in stalls. About 60 percent of Siaya farm operators are women. African women's contributions to food production systems and national economies are very significant. Improvement of women's status will simultaneously strengthen African society as a whole, as well as enhance the continent's broader development prospects. (Photo: IFAD by Fiona McDougall.)

Asia. The fruits of this revolution are not being captured by Africa to a significant degree.

Neglect of roads connecting town to country, and the prevailing focus of government infrastructure investment in the megacities has, in many countries, cut the agricultural sector off from urban and export markets. It has also cut off farmers from the source of improved inputs and equipment, which is in the cities. It is from secondary towns that most services are provided to farming communities, and where the immediate collection markets for agricultural produce are usually found. Many African countries have focused so much of their resources on the megacities that these essential physical links with agriculture have been neglected. To improve agriculture, this situation must be corrected. Neglect of rural areas has resulted in the frequently appalling health and education status of rural populations (Figure 7.6). Expanded physical and social infrastructure investment in rural areas and in secondary towns is, therefore, one major strategy for agricultural development in sub-Saharan Africa.

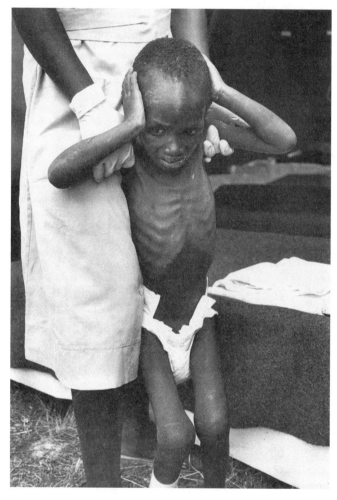

Figure 7-6. A child in Goma, Zaire. Poor economic conditions, malnutrition, and social problems continue to worsen in sub-Saharan Africa, where malnutrition affects one out of every three children. This disturbing, yet preventable, state of affairs causes untold suffering and, given its wide scale, presents a major obstacle to the development process. Most experts believe that the status of women is the key driving force contributing to malnutrition, poverty, rapid population growth, and inadequate progress in increasing crop yields. Women with low status tend to have weaker control over household resources, less access to information and health services, and lower self-esteem. In sub-Saharan Africa women's status and the long and short-term nutritional status of children are linked. (Photo: UNHCR by L. Taylor.)

Recognition of the essential role of women in all aspects of African agriculture is also important. Women are often the main decision makers on the farm, and are important in natural resource management as users of the soil and collectors of fuelwood and water. In Botswana, women contribute almost 70 percent of the value of crop production. In Kenya, 33 percent of all rural smallholder households are headed by women. In Congo, about 70 percent of the farm holdings are managed by women, as the result of significant male migration to jobs in the cities. Similar migration is reported on a large scale in Lesotho and Zambia. A greater focus on women is needed for agricultural development.

Family Planning in Africa

Traditionally, African peasants see children as an investment in the future: There will be more workers to help fetch water and firewood, till the land, and provide for their parents in old age. A woman's status in rural communities is greatly enhanced by the number of children she has—particularly sons. When a woman first marries, her surest means of gaining the acceptance and respect of her in-laws—among whom she must now live—is to start bearing children as quickly as possible. If she doesn't, her husband may take a second wife.

But many African women find their health declining as they have more children. With their grueling workloads and low level of nutrition, they are often physically exhausted by continued pregnancies and births. Many closely spaced births are seen as a major contributor to chronic anemia, a problem affecting a majority of women in the developing world. The unrelieved cycle of alternating pregnancy and nursing drains their energies, leaving both mothers and children more vulnerable to ill health.

Although effective family planning programs are important to reduce population, many specialists note that birthrates also go down when the over-all conditions of women improve—as a result of education and a widening sense of their ability to contribute to the family in ways other than by having many children. It has also been observed that a woman's earning power can be a positive factor in her practice of family planning. Women who earn money enjoy more respect from family members, hence have more autonomy. They have greater self-esteem and are more likely to want to plan and control the size of their families.

WHY CAN'T AFRICA FEED ITSELF?

Food airlifts are fairly common to Africa. In 1994 food was airlifted to Rwanda. In 1984 it was to Ethiopia. In 1992 United States Army cargo planes carried desparately needed food to starving Somalis as part of a new international effort to check the spreading starvation. From the arid, sun-baked mesas of Ethiopia to teeming refugee centers in Malawi and Mozambique, millions of people depend entirely on donated food. Why can't Africa feed itself?

When most of the African nations gained independence in the early 1960s, the continent was self-sufficient in food. Four decades later, war, drought, overpopulation, a collapsing environment, and disastrous policies have created a serious food crisis (Figure 7.7). The Ethiopian famine of the mid-1980s claimed a million lives. Today, over 20 million people are at risk of starvation in Ethiopia, Somalia, and Sudan in the Horn of Africa, the most famine-plagued part of the globe. Malnutrition, disease, and starvation are stalking more than 16 million people in southern Africa, according to U.N. reports in 2002.

Even the strongest agricultural nations live from crop to crop. When the rains did not come to southern Africa in 1992, eleven countries had to import grain—including South Africa and Zimbabwe, fertile lands that traditionally have had surpluses. Thirty million people are at risk of starvation in southern Africa, which is far more developed than the Horn of Africa and is expected to escape widespread famine; but hunger-related deaths have been reported in Zimbabwe and Mozambique.

Civil wars have caused the greatest privations (Figure 7.8), and no country has suffered more than Somalia. Many African conflicts have lasted a decade or more, destroying farms and roads. Peasants flee to cities for safety, where they depend on aid. Rapid population growth and farming methods that damage the land have created serious environmental problems. On the island of Madagascar, the Betsiboka River has turned crimson from erosion of the red soil.

Assaults on the food supply have become a key strategy in Africa's civil wars. Governments have sought to deprive rebel movements by destroying local economies and forcing the exodus of civilians. In northern Ethiopia, southern Sudan, and north-central Mozambique, raids on food crops by government forces and associated militia were supplemented by restrictions on commerce and relief shipments, forcing migration from rebel areas. During the Ethiopian famine in 1984–1985, the worst-hit province, Tigre, with a third of the affected population and rebel stronghold, received only 5 percent of the relief food. In Sudan's famine in 1986–1988, the region that suffered most, Bahr el Ghazal—again, a rebel stronghold—received less than 2 percent of the relief food. In Somalia, the fertile region between the Juba and Shebelle rivers was raided by former President Mohammed Said Barre's troops and by competing clans. Tempted by the prospect of land-grabs and political spoils, merchants financed raids and backed attacks on relief shipments, deeping famine and boosting their profits. Some leaders are all too willing to use food and famine for their own cynical ends.

In many cases, government policies work against the farmer. Kenneth Kaunda, who ruled Zambia from 1964 until 1991, sought to make his urban

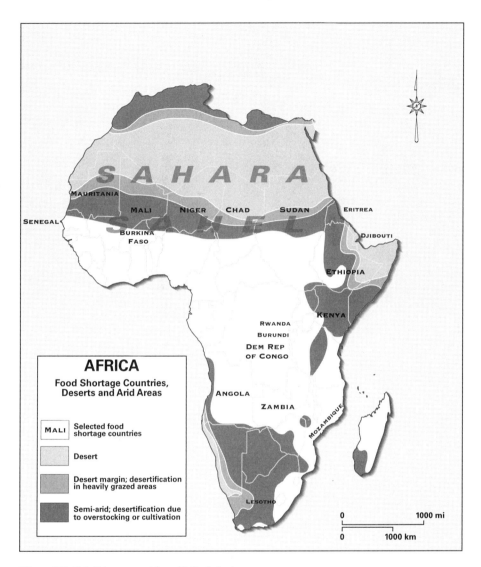

AFRICA

Food Shortage Countries, Deserts and Arid Areas

| MALI | Selected food shortage countries |

Desert

Desert margin; desertification in heavily grazed areas

Semi-arid; desertification due to overstocking or cultivation

Figure 7-7. Sub-Saharan countries with food shortages.

supporters happy by keeping food prices low through government subsidies. Many farmers left the land, discouraged by the low prices. The result: Zambia imports much of its food, only 10 percent of arable land is farmed, and crops often rot because truck drivers refuse to travel poor rural roads.

In neighboring Zimbabwe, President Robert Mugabe's government has confiscated half of the 4,500 commercial farms, almost all owned by whites, to win support from the black majority. The aim is to resettle black peasants, who account for most of the population and are desperate for land. As efficient commercial farms become small subsistence plots, food production has plummeted.

Figure 7-8. Refugees from Rwanda in Tanzania following ethnic conflict in Rwanda. Basic food rations of maize, beans, oil, and salt are provided by the World Food Program and distributed by the Tanzanian Red Cross. In parts of sub-Saharan Africa ethnic conflicts have raged out of control and weak governments have degenerated into "collapsed states." Tens of millions of people fled for their lives. Over 14 million people have yet to return home. (Photo: UNHCR by B. Press.)

Western Africa has escaped widespread shortages, but even that region cannot grow enough food for its people. Under pressure from the World Bank and other international institutions, African countries have been restructuring their economies and devoting more resources to agriculture. Sub-Saharan Africa could feed itself again, if the technology was made available, the wars were stopped, and the agricultural policies were changed (Figure 7.9). The question is, will any of that happen?

RECONCILING THE ENVIRONMENT AND DEVELOPMENT NEEDS

Sub-Saharan Africa's varied landscapes—tropical forests, savanna grasslands, and desert—are experiencing a wide range of environmental problems. Many of these problems arise from population pressures, the legacy of colonialism, and the political economy of apartheid in South Africa. During the colonial period fertile land was taken over for European-owned commercial farms and impoverished African peasant farmers were forced to cultivate marginal lands in remote areas for subsistence. The land was severely overgrazed in former black homelands in South Africa because pastoralists were not permitted to move their cattle to fresh grazing lands. The process of land degradation was

Figure 7-9. Farmers using cattle to thresh teff (a cereal grain) near Alamoto, Wollo district, Ethiopia. In the past 30 years, agriculture has made remarkable progress in expanding food supplies in the developing countries through a combination of better seeds, expanded irrigation, and higher fertilizer and pesticide use. However, Africa has not made significant progress. In sub-Saharan Africa, more than 260 million people—about a third of the population—lack adequate food. In 2003 twenty-five sub-Saharan African countries faced food emergencies. (Photo: IFAD by F. Mattioli.)

accelerated by forced relocation of people under apartheid and by restrictions on rural–urban migration. Drought, overgrazing, and erosion ravaged the environment of South Africa's former homelands.

In Zimbabwe the best fertile lands were set aside for the Europeans, and on the poor lands, which were designated as "Native Reserves," the pressures of population and over-cultivation led to severe environmental problems. Overuse and misuse of productive land have also led to environmental degradation throughout sub-Saharan Africa. Marginal lands on mountain slopes such as the Drakensberg Mountain in South Africa, and the arid and semi-arid savanna lands in Botswana and Namibia have been rendered unproductive through soil erosion and expanding desert fringes.

Despite growing international interest in African environmental issues, there is still no consensus on how to protect the environment. Most industrialized countries favor more ambitious goals and timetables for putting environmental safeguards in place than do the less-developed countries of the area. African leaders worry that their countries' economic needs will be ignored in international deliberations on the environment. They are concerned that policies adopted will be shaped according to the perspectives of the industrialized countries on environmental problems. These fears were reflected in the 1990 report of the South Commission, which was chaired by Julius Nyerere, the former president of Tanzania. Commenting on the calls for global efforts to limit chlorofluorocarbon emissions and protect tropical rainforests, the report observed that "the North is in effect demanding that the South should give priority to environmental protection over development objectives." Environmentalists in the industrialized nations perceive such statements as evidence that African leaders do not appreciate the need or urgency for global environmental protection measures.

The clash is not a simple conflict between development interests and environmental interests. It is a struggle between two different environmental agendas, one reflecting the experiences, interests, and politics of advanced industrial countries, the other reflecting the experiences, interests, and politics of African countries. Although African countries have become much more concerned about environmental issues over the past two decades, their ability to protect their interests in global negotiations on the environment is weaker now than it was in the 1970s. Given sub-Saharan Africa's poverty and growing political marginalization, African voices are often ignored in the global debate over the environment. Dependent on foreign aid, Africans are not in a position to resist pressures from environmentalists and governments in industrialized nations. But there can be no effective long-term solution of Africa's environmental problems and development needs unless African perspectives and realities are taken into account.

The environmental conservation movement in Africa was inspired and run by European colonizers who imposed their ideas on the continent. Paradoxically, it was the European colonizers' enthusiasm for hunting that first prompted concern for Africa's wildlife. In 1897 the British prime minister, Lord Salisbury, proposed limits on ivory exports from East Africa. This led to the first international convention on the preservation of African wildlife in 1900. In 1933, the colonial powers agreed to curb threats to African wildlife by creating national parks and reserves. These early initiatives excluded African participants and ignored African views.

One reason Africans were excluded from conservation planning was the colonizers' sense of cultural and moral superiority, which caused them to adopt a paternalistic attitude in most of their dealings with indigenous peoples. This sense of moral superiority was reinforced by technological superiority that enabled Europeans to exploit the continent's vast natural resources on a much larger scale than Africans had done. In imposing their Western-style conservationism on Africa, however, Europeans ignored the fact that Africans were already practicing their own indigenous form of conservation with considerable success. This impeded the growth of a modern African environmental movement.

After independence, an African environmental movement grew out of the efforts of poor, uneducated, and mostly rural people who sought to limit the environmental damage caused by inappropriate development policies that only served to worsen African living standards. Over the past four decades, a severe ecological crisis precipitated by chronic economic and political instability has taken its toll on the poor. To them, the destruction of the ecosystems has meant lengthening workdays, falling livelihoods, and deteriorating health. Thus, the African environmental movement was spurred by adverse effects of environmental degradation on life support systems and poverty. In contrast, in the United States and Europe environmentalism was spurred by adverse effects of rapid industrialization.

To regain some control over their lives and to improve their living conditions, in some parts of Africa villages have founded self-help organizations. These groups drew on communal traditions that place a high value on self-reliance. In Kenya this led to the birth of the *Harambee*, or self-help movement. In Tanzania the cooperative tradition in rural communities became embodied in the concept of *ujamaa*, which is synonymous with familyhood and interdependence. An important feature of almost all village self-help groups is the central role of women, who have focused on environmental problems that present obstacles to development. In Burkina Faso, for example, the Naam movement—a coalition of voluntary groups—was founded in 1967 by a teacher who wanted to mobilize villagers against poverty and environmental degradation by setting up rural development programs. Using local materials and low-cost technology, and building on the experience of its members, village associations built wells and dams, planted village woodlots, developed simple water filters, and helped spread the benefits of modern medicine. All this was accomplished by increasing local awareness of environmental dangers. By 1985, there were over 1,350 Naam groups in Burkina Faso and similar organizations in Senegal, Mauritania, Mali, Niger, and Togo.

The Green Belt Movement in Kenya, which has recently gained international prominence, was founded by women concerned about the effects of deforestation and desertification on poor rural communities. The organization draws upon local expertise to encourage self-reliance. The women of Kenya's Green Belt Movement have planted over 10 million trees in 1,000 greenbelts throughout the country. The movement has also succeeded in creating a groundswell of support for environmental issues on a national scale.

Throughout Africa, there has been an explosion of grassroots activity. The Sahel contains more than 15,000 village self-help groups. In Kenya alone, there are 20,000 women's groups. Many of these organizations are engaged in development-oriented work, of which environmental protection is a natural component. Prominent regional and subregional environmental organizations now exist in Senegal, the Ivory Coast, Zimbabwe, and Cameroon. Notwithstanding these successes, environmental movements in Africa do not enjoy wide governmental and public support. They are relatively isolated and weak because attention is generally focused on more pressing economic and political issues.

In countries such as Chad, Liberia, and Somalia, which have experienced repression and war on a scale that is hard for most people to imagine, it has been difficult for environmental groups to develop. The countries with particularly heavy concentrations of environmental groups such as Botswana, Burkina Faso, Kenya, Togo, and Zimbabwe are generally more stable. It is no coincidence that the least stable countries such as Ethiopia, Somalia, and Sudan also tend to have the worst environmental problems.

The central issue in sub-Saharan Africa, as in other parts of the world, is how to reconcile the need for environmental protection with the requirement for sustained economic growth. African countries lack the resources to acquire environmentally safer technology, and their economies are in serious trouble. Their dilemma is that they cannot ignore either the economy or the environment. However, as a result of economic crisis, many countries have been willing to sacrifice the environment for short-term economic benefits. Between 1950 and 1983, for example, 24 percent of Africa's forests disappeared, cut for fuel and timber exports. In the Ivory Coast, Africa's biggest timber exporter, the area of closed forests declined by two thirds in twenty years, from 12 million hectares in 1956 to four million in 1977. Liberia, which relies on wood exports for over 11 percent of its total export earnings, has also been depleting its forests rapidly. In Nigeria, once the world's largest tropical log exporters, timber shipments fell off dramatically after many years of over-cutting. Africa's forests are disappearing at a significantly higher rate than forests in South Asia.

Africa's economic problems also have enabled foreigners to exploit conditions on the continent in ecologically harmful ways. As landfill space became scarcer in European countries and the costs of treating the wastes skyrocketed, some European companies turned to Africa in search of dumping grounds. In 1988 over 8,000 drums of highly toxic waste were shipped from Italy to Koko in Nigeria. Angola, in dire need of foreign exchange, signed a contract with a Swiss company to store 5 million tons of waste. Congo signed an $84 million contract with a Dutch firm to accept 1 million tons of waste. Guinea Bissau was expected to earn $600 million in a deal with another Swiss company. Almost all African countries have now banned the importation of toxic wastes, but they lack monitoring facilities and are vulnerable to illegal dumping.

Reconciling environmental and developmental needs will not be an easy task. Africans could elect to shift their economic growth policies away from polluting industries such as waste disposal, offshore oil development, animal husbandry, agribusiness, and surface mining to concentrate more resources on nonpolluting industries such as organic farming, high-technology industries such as telecommunications and waste management, and the development of renewable energy sources based on solar power, biomass energy, and geothermal energy. Although this might be ideal for the environment, it is not economically practical for most African countries, which rely on agricultural products or minerals for the bulk of their exports. Furthermore, developing high-technology industries requires a huge, ongoing investment in research, which is more than most African countries can afford.

The impact of political systems on the environment has recently emerged as a major issue. A recent report on sub-Saharan Africa by the World Bank gives the same weight to "good governance" in ensuring sustainable development with environmental protection as it does to sound economic planning. It is held that the absence of democratic structures and institutions through which a state's actions can be monitored by its citizens and through which citizens can participate in their government's decisions is a major stumbling block to environmental protection. The link between a country's political system and its economic and ecological health is particularly relevant to Africa, but the relationship is not always clear. Ethiopia, a former Marxist state, has one of the most degraded environments in Africa. But Congo, which also has an authoritarian and undemocratic government, has preserved its forests and natural resources by remaining isolated from the rest of the world. These examples suggest that there is more at work here than the form of government alone. It is the interaction of political, social, and economic factors that determines a country's ability to manage its environmental problems and promote sustainable development.

Natural Resource Management and Sustainable Development

The natural resource base in many African countries is deteriorating sharply. There is now widespread evidence of soil erosion and degradation, water pollution, siltation of irrigated areas, pasture degradation, forest destruction, and disappearance of wild lands. Natural resource development has not been consistent with economically, socially, or environmentally desirable outcomes. Future strategy must include land and water use planing, land tenure reform, better wild lands and forest management to combine sustainable production of various products with conservation, better soil and water management on farms by farmers, and siting of infrastructure with environmental impact and agricultural development in mind.

Natural resource management requirements vary enormously by ecological zone, not only between countries but within countries. Requirements in humid forest areas are quite different from requirements in highly populated and fertile farming areas, pastureland, or semi-arid and arid lands. Taxes on natural resource use (forest taxes, mining royalties) and subsidies for conservation are needed to promote environmental and conservation objectives.

The effects of demographic pressure on sustainable land use and resource management can be seen in Rwanda. Increasing land scarcity has forced Rwandan farmers to expand the area under food crops at the expense of pasture, fallow, and forest. However, it has also encouraged them to grow

more perennials and to grow more crops in dense associations. Although the
expansion of cultivation contributes to erosion, especially on steep slopes,
perennials and dense associations are a form of intensification that makes land
use more sustainable.

Forests

About 30 percent of Africa's land area is under forests. Thirty-four percent of
Africa's forest lands are shrub lands and 38 percent are savanna woodlands
used for fuelwood harvesting, farming, or grazing. Only 28 percent of the
forest land is closed forest. By contrast, in Latin America and Asia two-thirds
of the forest area is closed forest. Timber production in 2002 amounted to
120.7 million meters of tropical log round wood logs. Africa's share of
production was about 11 percent; Asia-Pacific region produced 60 percent
and Latin America about 29 percent. Africa's wood exports are declining
(Southeast Asia and Latin America have greatly increased their wood
exports). Forest area in Africa is declining at about 3.7 million hectares per
annum, and the rate of decline is accelerating.

The most important causes for deforestation are agricultural encroachment,
infrastructure development in delicate areas, and timber and fuelwood
harvesting. Growing and migrating human populations and international
demand for timber drive this process. Sometimes agricultural projects have
facilitated the substitution of crop land for forests and pasture.

Government forestry and park services have not been able to manage
forests efficiently almost anywhere in Africa due to inadequately trained staff
and a policies that often encourage destructive practices. Open-access land
tenure in forest areas has permitted migrants easy entry into forests. This has
been caused in part by government land nationalization, which displaced
traditional forest people. Traditional forest people had some incentive to
maintain forests when customary land rights conferred to them exclusive user
rights in the forests. Governments have not been able to substitute traditional
people's forest management with effective government control of the forest.
As a result, the forests are often exploited by loggers, poachers, and farmers
who do not own or have exclusive rights to the forests, and hence have little
incentive to preserve them.

Open-access forests allow free harvesting of wood fuel. The resulting price
of wood fuel is lower than the environmental cost of its gathering. Wood fuel
prices are often so low that alternative sources of household energy cannot
compete unless they are subsidized. Wood fuel is not replanted in this
situation, until transport costs to consuming centers exceed replanting costs
around those centers. This has been a major problem in southern Sudan and
Sahel, but is common almost everywhere in Africa.

Another set of government policies that encourage excessive forest exploitation includes low stumpage fees on logging, low export taxes for logs, and
generous logging concession agreements setting few responsibilities for

loggers. This has stimulated more logging than is ecologically sustainable in West Africa, and in parts of central and eastern Africa. With weak supervision by government forestry services, the result is widespread abusive logging and felling.

To deal with these problems, some form of land use and natural resource planning will be necessary. Land use plans in forests should identify conservation areas, parks, areas allocated to sustainable logging, mining areas, farming areas, and areas for infrastructure development. Generally, the most important actions to deal with degradation of forest resources are to (1) reduce population growth and (2) to intensify agricultural production at a rate that exceeds population growth, encourage sedentary agriculture and livestock raising, and discourage migration into the forests.

Land Degradation, Soil Loss, and Desertification

All cultivated crops—or trees, bushes, and grasses—depend on a thin layer of topsoil. When the balance of components found in topsoil—moisture, bacteria, worms, chemical compounds, and a variety of carbons released by decaying matter—are upset, the soil becomes impoverished. When the balance of the soil is upset, each of the components begins to die out and the rich, fertile soil turns into wasteland. Desertification begins. Like a cancerous growth, one area of desertification spreads to other areas and soon the true desert begins to encroach on once healthy land.

Most of Africa's rangelands and rain-fed croplands are at least moderately affected by desertification, and 30 percent of Africa's irrigated lands are similarly affected. The most dramatic manifestation of land degradation and desertification is the ongoing drought in the Sahel, Ethiopia, and Sudan (Figure 7.10). Drought, in conjunction with other factors that degrade the environment, accelerates the process of desertification.

The main causes of land degradation in Africa are over cultivation, over grazing, deforestation, and the massive population explosion. Each of these factors occurring by itself would lead to severe environmental and economic problems; the combination of all four occurring simultaneously, with the added threat of cyclic droughts, points to a major catastrophe. In the old days, before national boundaries had solidified and when the population of Africa was much smaller, the traditional methods of shifting cultivation allowed land to remain fallow for extended periods of time. This allowed the land to regenerate. Given small, scattered communities, the collection of twigs for fuelwood did not adversely affect the forest. An adequate plant cover stabilized the water cycle, and therefore local rains were much more predictable. Plant cover also performed the vital task of knitting together the soil and preventing large-scale soil erosion. Herders and nomads had vast areas over which their cattle could roam.

Figure 7-10. The thirst for water is likely to become one of the most pressing issues of the twenty-first century. In the arid and semiarid regions of Africa there is potentially a desperate situation in which high water stress is combined with low per capita income. A muddy pond in a dried up river bed is the only source of water for the 3,000 residents who live in the three villages of Metogo, in the Tigray region of Ethiopia. The contaminated water causes diarrhea and other illnesses in children, and combined with poor personal hygiene, also causes them to suffer from scabies and other skin diseases. (Photo: UNICEF by Mark Thomas.)

In the past five decades, however, this scenario has changed. Since 1950, Africa's population has tripled. At the same time, national and local boundaries solidified, thus preventing traditional nomadic movements from area to area. In addition, large tracts of fertile land were put under cash crops, and the former farmers of these areas relocated to either marginal lands or squeezed into already overcrowded areas. The spread of large-scale plantation farms also pushed millions of peasants into smaller holdings, with little room to rotate crops. The introduction of land ownership and title deeds meant that shifting cultivation could no longer be practiced, and lands were parceled out permanently. Peasants on lands that are no longer sustainable tend to move into available virgin territory, burning down trees and vegetative cover to start new cultivation. All these factors combine to severely degrade the land. Huge tracts of range land in Africa, from Sahel to Lesotho, are churned into dust by the hoofs of animals as they travel vast distances in search of grazing lands. In many areas—such as northern Uganda, Somalia, northern Kenya, Senegal, Mauritania and northern Nigeria—nomadic communities looking for grazing land are coming into conflict with agricultural communities.

AIDS IN SUB-SAHARAN AFRICA

In the late 1980s AIDS emerged as one of the major epidemics coursing through Africa. In many cities the spread of the deadly virus among young adults—parents and family breadwinners—has reached astonishing levels. The highest concentrations of AIDS in Africans are in Botswana, Zambia, Zimbabwe, Tanzania, Cameroon, and Congo (Figure 7.11). A host of medical, cultural, and economic factors have made Africa vulnerable to the heterosexual spread of AIDS. The rampant extent of sexually transmitted diseases appears to boost the transmission of the AIDS virus. Promiscuity has helped drive the epidemic. Although data do not exist for comparing sexual behavior on different continents, surveys show that extramarital sex is commonplace in Africa.

Prostitution, always an engine of sexually transmitted diseases, has played a major role in the spread of AIDS in Africa. Typically, a small group of infected prostitutes pass the virus to large numbers of men, who take it to their wives and girlfriends. Prostitution is encouraged by migratory labor patterns rooted in the colonial past and in current poverty. Millions of couples are separated for months at a time as men work in mines or plantations or move to cities for any paying job. For many women, especially those with little education who have left the dreary cocoon of the village, selling sex may seem essential for economic survival.

In the mid-1980s, as the world first became aware of the new epidemic in Africa, experts in their more optimistic moments could hope that AIDS might be contained within certain social and geographic boundaries. It appeared largely confined to cities and to several adjacent countries of central and

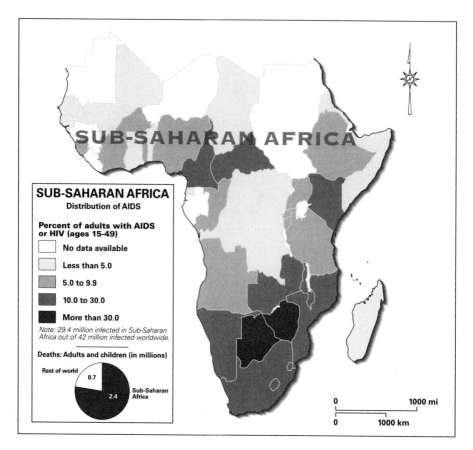

Figure 7-11. Distribution of AIDS in Africa.

eastern Africa. In these regions, for reasons that remain unidentified, AIDS began to explode sometime in the late 1970s—about the same time the virus began to race through the homosexual population in the United States. Although the cities are the hardest hit, AIDS is reaching everyone, taking the harshest toll among the working class and the poor (Figure 7.12). The disease has infiltrated rural areas, which are often linked to cities by back-and-forth migration and family ties.

In southern Zambia over 8 percent of pregnant women were infected in 2000, and in a rural area of Rwanda, 10 percent carried the virus. In southwestern Uganda, 12 percent of the villagers and 35 percent of people in market towns were infected. The neighboring districts of Tanzania are similarly blighted. To the south of the older AIDS belt, in Zimbabwe AIDS is spreading rapidly and may already infect at least 10 percent of urban adults. Farther south, AIDS has gained a solid foothold among the black population of South Africa. Nearly 40 percent of the adult population in Botswana has the AIDS virus, compared with about half of 1 percent in the United States. Botswana is the hardest hit country on the continent, but is considered among

Figure 7-12. At the macrolevel, the impact of AIDS in Africa is being felt gradually. But at the household level, the blow is sudden and catastrophic. Jane, one of nine children whose parents died of AIDS, a mango-filled bowl on her head, stands on a dirt road winding through maize fields in the Mzuzu district of northern Malawi. With a population of nearly 12 million, Malawi has one of the highest poverty rates in the world, exacerbated by drought, a dramatic rise in the prevalence of AIDS, and the influx of refugees from civil conflict in Mozambique. As devastating as war, AIDS is tearing into the heart of African societies. Taboos against discussing sex, lack of education about the transmission of HIV, women's second-class status, and the high cost of treatment fuel the epidemic. (Photo: UNICEF by Cindy Andrew.)

the most prosperous and stable. Its economy has grown at an average annual rate of 9 percent, thanks in large part to its resources, including the world's richest diamond mine. The healthy economy could be fanning the flames of AIDS in Botswana; the country is crisscrossed by good, safe roads, and the active economy means truckers on the move. Truckers in Africa have been shown to be major spreaders of the disease. They tend to have sex with both prostitutes and unmarried women at multiple stops.

Some have also blamed the AIDS explosion in Africa on the total lack of power among women (Figure 7.13). In many African countries, women can't insist that their husbands remain faithful or wear condoms. They cannot

Figure 7-13. A woman in Niger, where the female literacy is one of the lowest in sub-Saharan Africa. Studies have shown that improvements in women's education can dramatically improve child health, reduce child mortality and fertility rates, and increase household incomes. Women, as the "gatekeepers of their homes," have traditionally had frontline responsibility for protecting the health and well-being of their families. A commitment to improving education for Africa must be considered a development and investment priority. Africa is the only region that has experienced declines in education since the 1980s; without intervention, it is projected that by 2015, 55 percent of girls between the ages of 6 and 11 will not be in school. (Photo: Embassy of Niger.)

refuse to have sex or leave their husbands even when their health and their lives are at stake.

In West Africa AIDS has reached its highest concentration in the small former Portuguese colony of Guinea Bissau, where over 10 percent of the adult population carried the virus in 2000. In Abidjan, Ivory Coast, which is host to millions of immigrants from neighboring countries, 30 percent of adults were infected. AIDS-related illness is already the leading cause of adult deaths in Abidjan. With good roads and many large commercial farms worked by migrants, who are visited by busloads of prostitutes after payday, rural areas of Ivory Coast have become vulnerable to AIDS too.

Uganda, where a million people out of a total population of 24 million are infected with AIDS, was the first African country to start a major anti-AIDS education program in 1987. Using posters, radio, schools, and pamphlets in twenty-two languages, the campaign is pervasive and awareness seems universal; the program is making a difference.

REGIONS AND COUNTRIES OF AFRICA

The Sahel Region: Survival in a Fragile Ecosystem

The Sahel region of Africa lies to the south of the Sahara, stretching in a wide belt from Mauritania and Senegal across Gambia, Guinea Bissau, Mali, Burkina Faso, Niger, and Chad to Sudan. In 2000 the total population in Sahelian countries was estimated at 50 million. The population is growing at an annual rate of about 3 percent. At the same time, the amount of arable land declines on a regular basis because of the spreading desert. This decline of farm land proportionally affects the food production.

The decline in food production was also caused by the drive toward cash crop production generated by relations and mechanisms that linked this region to the world economy. No serious measures were taken at the central government or the village level to stabilize the sand dunes and arrest the expansion of desert. Nuclear and extended families in marginal lands, whether in settled villages or maintaining seasonal migration with their herds of animals, dealt with the natural resources of their areas as if they could not be exhaustetd. The degradation and stress on the carrying capacity in grazing areas and the destruction of the topsoil came gradually, almost unnoticed until it became serious, in the savanna belt of Sudan, which represents the eastern extension of the Sahel.

Over the last decade, the combined effects of drought, desertification, and economic underdevelopment have exerted severe pressure on the Sahelian population. Poverty has spread. It affects all social classes in the Sahel region, from the most remote places to state capitals and large cities. In urban centers, sharp increases in the price of basic goods, an extremely high unemployment rate, low salaries, pitiful living and health conditions, lack of health care, and a high population density have led to severe economic strain. In rural areas, the accelerated deterioration of the environment, the depletion of soils, the uncertainty of agricultural production, the loss of cattle due to drought, and the large number of people leaving rural areas have led to a noticeable breakdown of basic social order. Farmers migrate, shepherds settle, and women, children, and the elderly are abandoned. To survive has become the basic daily issue for many Sahelians.

The survival of populations in the Sahel region is directly associated with the scarcity of food and the acceleration of environmental degradation. At the beginning of this century, the Sahelian countries imported only 1 percent of the grains needed to feed their people. Sixty years later, when independence was declared, imported grains represented about 4 percent of the household consumption. It has now tripled to 12 percent. This volume is expected to continue to increase in the years to come.

At one time, emigration was one of the ways people escaped the pressure from natural scourges. This is still true, despite country borders. Also, people tend to move to the south where there is more rain or they move from rural areas to the cities. This migration resulted in a loss of people from the regions most hit by the drought, rapid population growth in the cities (6 to 10 percent annually in Sahelian cities), higher population density in the southern regions of the Sahelian countries, and an increase in migration toward countries located on the coast of the Gulf of Guinea, particularly Cote d'Ivoire. Migrations, malnutrition, and famine encourage the spread of diseases, the disastrous results of which are often overlooked. Refugee camps and ghettos are centers for devastating endemic diseases.

In most of Sahel the rains have been plentiful in recent years, ever since the drought of 1984. But when the rains finally came after the drought, they generated a number of problems such as floods and swarms of grasshoppers, for which the inhabitants of Sahel were unprepared. In Burkina Faso, 10,000 people were affected by floods and over half of them lost their homes. The rains have promoted a rapid reappearing of plant life, making the land ready for a grasshopper invasion. In Niger, grasshopper swarms have devastated about 47 million acres. The Sahel appears to be caught in a huge vicious cycle of natural disasters.

Is there any hope for the future of the Sahel region? Can the profoundly fatal trends caused by environmental factors and the inadequacy of development policies be stemmed? Is a recovery possible? More and more officials and international agencies are paying attention to the need to preserve the natural environment to carry out a balanced integration of the needs of a growing population within a sound framework in development planning: sustainable development.

Timbuktu: A Meeting Place of Black South and Nomadic North

Timbuktu is mythic both in its former wealth and its present desolation. But this city of crumbling mud-brick edifices and narrow, winding alleyways owes its existence to strategic location. Sweeping in from beyond the huge dunes that form the town's doorstep, Tuaregs have mounted hit-and-run attacks against Timbuktu and a score of other settlements on the desert's edge. In reprisal, the mostly black armies of Mali and Niger have razed Tuareg settlements and forced thousands of nomads into exile. The cultural landscape of the city is an eclectic mixture of West African and Arab influences.

At its height, during the mid-sixteenth century, the city had a population of about 60,000. A prime caravan stop and center of manufacturing, it dominated West Africa in trade and exports. The Niger River provided a crucial avenue of trade between central and West Africa, and it irrigated the flood plain upon which much of the city's food was grown.

Five hundred years ago, raids by Tuaregs brought down the wealthy kingdom of Mali, whose fabled capital and mosques were located in Timbuktu.

Twenty-first century hostilities are spreading ethnic hatred and economic destruction that threaten the stability of both Mali and Niger; two of the region's most vibrant but poorest democracies. The conflict has troubled nearly all of the outpost towns along the northern bend of the Niger.

With desert dunes surrounding it in all directions, and trapped in a severe climate, the fact that fabled Timbuktu rose and prospered for 800 years is remarkable. Now, as the desert creeps slowly southward all across sub-Saharan Africa, Timbuktu stands more isolated by sand and heat than ever.

The Horn of Africa

The Horn of Africa is strategically located with respect to the Persian Gulf–Southwest Asia region. This northeastern tip, or "Horn," is comprised of Somalia, Ethiopia, and Djibouti. Key neighboring states are Kenya on the south and Sudan in the west. The political–military situation in the Horn is complicated by internal and regional conflicts, instabilities, and tangled external alliances. Somali irredentist claims to neighboring territories inhabited by ethnic Somalis led to an undeclared Somali–Kenyan war in the late 1960s and then to a Somali invasion of Ethiopia's Ogaden region in 1977–1978. In 1982 Ethiopian troops attacked several points along the disputed Somali–Ethiopia border.

The Horn was partitioned at a relatively late date in the colonial history of Africa, the main beneficiaries being the French and the Italians. The French occupied the port of Obock in 1884. They constructed the port of Djibouti on the African coast, and later built a railway inland to Addis Ababa. The coastal region known as Somaliland eventually was divided among France, Britain, and Italy. Italian interest in the Horn dates from the establishment of Eritrea as a colony whose boundaries were defined in 1889–1891.

In recent years the Horn has been devastated by serious drought, famine, and tribal warfare. Stories of hunger and war continue to emanate from this part of the Middle East. In 1992 starvation in Somalia elicited an outpouring of compassion and generosity from around the world, as did the Ethiopian famine of 1984–1985 (Figure 7.14). The ouster of Somali dictator Mohamed Siad Barre in 1991 unleased open warfare among the clans. Fighting and drought plunged Somalia into chaos and mass starvation. Civil strife and famine left more than 350,000 Somalis dead.

The 1992 famine in Somalia was confined to the farmland in the southern part that was laid waste during the war to oust dictator Said Barre and the strife between the clans that followed. The fiercest fighting was in Mogadishu, which was split into two sections, supposedly under the control of warlords: Ali Mahdi Mohamed in the north and Gen. Mohamed Farah Aideed in the larger south.

Somalis share a common history, language, and religion—just the ingredients needed to form a nation. But Somali society evolved around clans that roamed the arid plains with their camels, sheep, and goats, making alliances or warring with other groups over the limited resources of water and grazing lands (Figure 7.15). Armed with knives and spears, Somali men constantly shifted loyalties to ensure the welfare of their group. Today's warlords and gangs are armed with hundreds of millions of dollars' worth of modern weaponry supplied by the United States and the former Soviet Union during the Cold War.

A north–south civil war in Sudan between Arab Muslims (in the north) and black Christians (in the south) has forced displacement of two million people in the country. Nearly 275,000 have fled to nearby countries. The civil war, along with drought, famine, and floods, has killed more than a million Sudanese.

Sudan's war began in 1955, but its roots are deep in the nation's past. Nowhere in North Africa is there a country whose people are more fundamentally dissimilar. Northerners, who form the majority, speak Arabic and are predominantly Muslim. Southerners speak a variety of languages and most

Figure 7-14. A woman teaches a group of boys in a school in the town of Baidoa, Somalia. Despite increased instability in Somalia, international agencies continue to provide assistance in health and education. (Photo: UNICEF by Betty Press.)

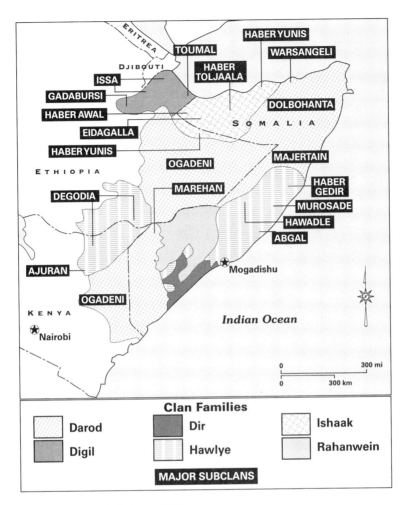

Figure 7-15. Major subclans in the horn of Africa.

follow indigenous religions or Christianity. The south was historically a reservoir of resources—mainly ivory and slaves—exploited by the north.

In Ethiopia famine was aggravated in the 1980s by collective-farming programs. Victory by rebel forces in 1991 brought about the return of private farms. The people whose images of suffering so shook the world during the 1984–1985 famine are now rebuilding their country. Ethiopia's dictator, Mengistu Haile Mariam, like Said Barre in Somalia, was overthrown shortly after the end of the Cold War. Poised strategically near the entrance to the Red Sea, both Ethiopia and Somalia had traded their loyalties to the rival superpowers in return for money and weapons.

An island of relative stability, Djibouti has had a defense agreement with France since gaining independence in 1977. With 3,000 French soldiers, plus ships and warplanes, Djibouti is an important staging area for supplies to the Horn of Africa.

In newly independent Eritrea, the impact of a 1980s drought was heightened by a secessionist war with Ethiopia. After thirty years of fighting to break free of Ethiopia, Eritrea faces its reconstruction. In their quest for stability, Eritreans have done what other Horn of Africa nations have yet to achieve—put aside their weapons and tempered both ethnic and religious differences to become one people, bound by a shared national identity.

The birth of Eritrea is causing concern to African neighbors who are themselves facing separatist movements. Eritrean independence will encourage secessionists in other African countries. Angola, Cameroon, Senegal, and South Africa all face potential splits. But any movement wanting independence will have to overcome two conditions that allowed the world community to accept Eritrea: the fact that Ethiopia agreed to it and that the Eritrean Liberation Front (EPLF) held a U.N.-monitored referendum. Not many other movements in the region are in a position to do this. Southern Sudan, which has little in common with its Islamic and Arabic north, is a prime candidate for separation, but independence would be forcibly resisted by the north, and tribal rivalries in the south would prevent a majority favoring independence.

What causes the perennial troubles in the Horn of Africa? People there, as in much of the African continent, have leapt from small traditional societies to twenty-first-century nationhood in only a few decades. Ancient tribal rivalries, illogical borders imposed by colonial powers, and the legacy of repressive and corrupt regimes supported by the Cold War superpowers are responsible for much of the tragedy in the Horn of Africa.

West Africa

West Africa comprises the former British colonies (such as Nigeria, Ghana, Togoland, Gambia, and Sierra Leone) and French colonies (such as Senegal, Mauritania, Guinea, the Ivory Coast, Dahomey, and Niger). Legacies of the colonial period are evident in the political and economic geography of West Africa. Politically, it is fragmented into a large number of states whose boundaries were derived from European power politics. Boundaries are not based on physical or human geography, and the countries they delimit—such as Gambia and Togo—often have awkward shapes.

In general, the British in their African colonies followed a policy of indirect rule that gave support and guidance to native policies and institutions, defended tribal life, and helped tribal leaders adjust their local administration to modern conditions. French policy was different. The French aimed at rapid cultural assimilation of their African possessions with France. The use of the French language in schools and administration was an important cultural feature of the French policy.

This region contains a significant diversity in environments, economies, and lifestyles. It includes forests, savannas, and deserts. A number of prosperous cities had evolved by the end of the fourteenth century. European activities in West Africa began during the fifteenth century. Trade in slaves, gold, ivory, and spices took firm hold in West Africa, in part because this area was closest to European colonies in the Americas. African middlemen from coastal areas raided the interior for slaves, which weakened the interior savanna states and strengthened the coastal forest areas.

In the eleventh century Islam first crossed the mountains and savannas that divide the forested tropics of West Africa from the parched Sahara. Islam gained a toehold as the religion of chieftains and traders. In the eighteenth century Muslim traders who had carried on commerce among the region's coastal and desert lands for centuries, settled in the area.

The Western Coastal States

From Senegal to Liberia there are a number of small states whose geography and development are related to differences in colonial experience. Senegal and Guinea were administered by France, Gambia and Sierra Leone by Britain, and Guinea Bissau by Portugal.

The heartland of Senegal and its neighboring countries is inhabited by the Wolof speakers. Their rulers became increasingly committed to the slave trade as their main source of wealth, and as a result the people suffered the devastation wrought by internecine warfare. Many were enslaved by their own overlords. Insecure and frequently threatened by their own masters, the Wolof welcomed the overthrow of their native oppressors and the substitution of French administration and Islamic culture in the late nineteenth century.

The people of Guinea differ widely. During nearly eighty years of conquest, collaboration, and domination, the French tried to impose a uniform system of administration. Their aim had been to promote the interests of a handful of French traders and settlers who were seeking to exploit the country's resources. But the French had shown little interest in, and had made no attempt to understand, the differing cultural traditions of the peoples they incorporated into their Guinea dependency.

The small state of Gambia became independent in 1965 (Figure 7.16). Guinea Bissau became independent in 1974, after a prolonged war of liberation which severely damaged the economy of the country.

The republic of Liberia is unique in origin and development among the countries of sub-Saharan Africa. Its origin dates from the efforts made in 1821 by the American Colonization Society to establish a home for freed slaves on the west coast of Africa. The first settlers landed in 1822 at a harbor later named Monrovia after President James Monroe. The country was declared a self-governing republic in 1847, with a constitution similar to that of the United States. About the size of Tennessee, it has an estimated population of between two and three million. Descendants of freed slaves make up

Figure 7-16. Pedal powered rice thresher in use on farmland along the lower Gambia River. The Gambia is about four fifths the size of Connecticut, and much of it is water, mangroves, and freshwater swamp. It is bordered on three sides by the Republic of Senegal, putting it in a vulnerable geopolitical situation. (Photo: IFAD by C. Rycroft.)

about 5 percent of the population. The indigenous people belong to four main ethnic groups comprising sixteen major tribes. The country's religions are Christianity (10 percent), Islam (20 percent), and animism (70 percent).

Liberia has been sunk into a civil war since 1989. Before the war tore the country into separate fiefs, Liberians, many of whom were descendants of freed American slaves, were relatively prosperous. Liberia's exports were iron ore, rubber, and timber, and to a lesser extent, uncut diamonds, coffee, and cocoa. The modern period of development started in 1925 with the coming of the Firestone Company, which at that time was given a large land grant for rubber plantations. Despite the abundance of rich lands, food is scarce, because years of heavy fighting and forced conscription of the young have halted farming.

Cote d'Ivoire, Ghana, Togo, and Benin

These countries are similar in resource endowment. Differences in their development are based on colonial history, postcolonial development strategies, and policies. As part of the French West Africa, Cote d'Ivoire, a New Mexico–sized nation, received less attention from France than the larger colonies of Senegal. Muslims make up at least 50 percent of the population.

Cote d'Ivoire became independent in 1960 and has had a stable government. The economy of the country is based on coffee, cocoa, and timber. Cote d'Ivoire remains relatively prosperous by regional standards, despite the fall in coffee and cocoa prices during the 1980s, which depressed the nation's two major export industries.

Ghana (formerly the Gold Coast) became independent in 1957. Under the British rule it relied heavily on the export of cocoa. Since independence, Ghana has tried to find an alternative to cocoa in the event of a price failure on the world market. Ghana, like other African states, consists of a great variety of peoples whom the colonial powers did nothing to unite and may even have strengthened in their differences. In recent years regional inequalities have increased in Ghana, with major concentrations of wealth in the Accra-Tema area and the areas that have benefited from the Volta River Project.

In 1960 the French-administered part of the former German colony became Togo. The French colonial territory of Dahomey became independent in 1960 and the area has been known as Benin since 1975. Both Togo and Benin are among the least-developed areas in West Africa.

Nigeria

Nigeria's attempt to accomodate diverse regional groups within a federation illustrates the difficulties faced by many heterogenous African states. In most instances, neither federalism nor strong central unitary government has been able to override the diverse ethnic groups with tribally rooted regional identities. In Nigeria the federal structure has caused continued friction and confrontation among the country's many ethnic communities and has nurtured traditional rivalries among the the three dominant ethnic groups: the Hausa-Fulani of the north, the Ibo of the east, and the Yoruba of the west (Figure 7.17). The Ibo and Yoruba in particular have feared political domination by the northerners. A consequence of these rivalries has been successive changes in the federal structure as different governments have tried to bring a devolu-tion of power among the three dominant tribal forces. Some of the larger minority groups have aspired for separate statehood.

During the Biafran civil war at least 1 million people died, most of them Ibos in the southeast, who were trying to secede from Nigeria. In recent years the Yorubas in the southwest have felt aggrieved. The northern-dominated military clique that has run Nigeria for a decade is not willing to release its grip on power. It annulled the 1993 presidential election, which was clearly won by a Yoruba.

Ethnic problems have been complicated by military misrule. Nigeria, the most populous country in sub-Saharan Africa, has been ruled by soldiers for twenty-five of its thirty-five years as an independent country. Its military regimes have tended to be corrupt and authoritarian; its civil regimes were merely corrupt. But never did it have a government as ruinous and oppressive

Figure 7-17. From a mobile health truck, a Yoruba woman health worker checks health cards while another speaks with the group of women with their children who are awaiting attention, in the village of Odolan, in the southwestern state of Oyu, Nigeria. One in five African children is Nigerian, in a country with 117 million people speaking a large number of languages. Rich in resources, Nigeria remains a low-income country whose children and women continue to suffer from malnutrition, inadequate health care, and limited education. (Photo: UNICEF by Giacomo Pirozzi.)

as the military dictator, who after seizing power in November 1993, systematically destroyed Nigeria's institutions and persecuted its most prominent citizens for the sole purpose of perpetuating himself in power. General Abacha dissolved elected state governments, disbanded the federal cabinet, gagged the press, and suppressed labor unions. His regime unleashed a campaign of terror against the Ogani people in Nigeria's oil country. Following his death in 1998, Nigeria has made some headway in stabilizing the economy. However, the years of military dictatorship hindered economic development, and change will be slow.

Nigeria is a major source of oil imports to the United States. Nigeria is expected to raise oil production to more than 3 million barrels a day by 2007 from 2.2 million in 2002. The oil installations in Nigeria sit next to some of the most destitute patches of the country, where villagers with no running water bathe, fish, and defecate in rivers polluted by oil spills, either from the wellheads or by the widespread illegal siphoning that enriches local gangsters. Such vast wealth being drained from so poor a region has long been a volatile source of resentment for local people, who have occupied platforms and forced negotiations for profit-sharing.

The Ogani people, a mostly poor, 300,000-member ethnic group, shares its land near the outlet of Niger River with the work crews and rigs of Shell Petroleum Development Company of Nigeria. Nigeria's military has attacked Ogani hamlets and unarmed villagers and burnt their homes. At the heart of the problem is a conflict of interests between the Ogani and the foreign oil company. For years the Ogani have demanded that the government protect their environment and share more revenue with the oil-producing lands. The Ogani have accused Shell of destroying their lands.

Petroleum production accounts for 80 percent of Nigeria's government revenue. Nigeria exports between 60 and 90 percent of its oil—a lightweight or "sweet" crude considered ideal for gasoline production—to the United States. Shell, which generates about half of this country's output, is by far Nigeria's largest producer. For years villagers have complained that Shell's operations have poisoned their once-rich crop land and devastated the wetlands of the Niger River delta, which form the world's largest mangrove swamp. At the same time, residents of these oil-producing zones have complained that Shell and the Nigerian government together have done little to develop the area.

The inhabitants of the oil-producing areas are becoming more and more impoverished because their farmlands, rivers, and vegetation are dying due to irreversible destruction of the environment. Devastation can be seen in the burned and badly tarred fields around damaged oil installations. While gas flares that from a distance resemble giant bonfires burn off millions of cubic feet of natural gas, most of the rural world in the Niger delta remains without electricity or other modern amenities.

The ethnic clashes and suspension of democracy by the military rulers had a negative impact on the economy. The history of Nigeria's experience is a case study on the frustration that ethnic diversity and corrupt military rule generate. Nigeria should be one of Africa's most prosperous and successful countries, but its repressive, divisive and corrupt military regimes have left Nigeria a shambles. Despite the formal change to civilian government, Nigeria is still largely run by its corrupt elite.

Equatorial Africa: The Congo Basin

Equatorial Africa comprises Zaire, Rwanda, Burundi, the Republic of Congo, Central African Republic, Cameroon, Equatorial Guinea, and Gabon. Zaire, the Republic of Congo, and the Central African Republic are located in the Congo River Basin. Cameroon, Equatorial Guinea, and Gabon are on the coast.

The Congo River cuts an enormous arc through the heart of the African continent. Lying mostly within the country of Congo, the river flows 2,700 miles from the headwaters of the Lualaba, crossing the equator twice, draining the vast rain forest nestled in the Congo Basin. Some consider the Chambeshi River the source, adding 200 miles to the Congo's length. Countless tributaries lace the forest, feeding the waters that make the Congo, at ten million gallons a second, the second-most powerful river (after the Amazon) in the world. This river system offers more than 8,500 miles of navigable waterways, an unparalleled network of virtually maintenance-free highways reaching into every corner of the country and beyond.

The river is divided into three parts. For the first 1,300 miles from the source it is called the Lualaba. It flows due north, draining the upland savannas of mineral-rich Shaba Province. Navigation reaches are interrupted by thunderous rapids and gorges. At Kisangani the river, now called the Congo, begins its long, easy curl through the central forest. As it bends toward the southwest, the river widens to nine miles, its waters dotted with myriad islands. Kinshasa lies at the head of Livingstone Falls, actually 220 miles of cataracts and rapids where the river crashes through the Crystal Mountains, the western rim of the Congo Basin. The ocean port, Matadi, lies at the foot of the falls. The river there is called the *bas fleuve* (lower river). There it spreads out, wide and deep enough for oceangoing ships to sail down the final hundred miles to the Atlantic.

The Congo nurtured glorious kingdoms where music and art flourished. But along the riverbanks the Arab and European slave traders were at their most brutal. In one of the darkest chapters of the European colonization of Africa, Leopold II, King of the Belgians, exploited the region—nearly eighty times larger than his own country—as his private domain.

The forests of the Congo Basin have been called one of the lungs of the world. Fed by as much as a hundred inches of annual rain and incubated by the fierce tropical sun, the teeming forest—which covers much of the basin's 1.5 million square miles—is a fecund world. Scientists estimate that a typical 4-square-mile patch of tropical forest might contain 750 species of trees (a comparable area of temperate forest might hold ten). The same area of forest may also hold 1,500 species of flowering plants, 125 species of mammals, 400 species of birds, 100 species of reptiles, and 60 species of amphibians. And these are merely the known species.

The Bantu peoples, the vast majority of the Basin's 200 or so ethnic groups, migrated into the forest a scant thousand years ago. They live in their villages, located in small clearings, between the river and rainforest.

Zaire (Congo)

Zaire (or the Congo) is the second-largest sub-Saharan African country by area (after Sudan) and the third-largest by population (after Nigeria and Ethiopia). Despite immense natural resources, its population is among the poorest in the region and in the world. Long beset with problems, the economy of Zaire has gone from bad to worse, despite perennial efforts at stabilization with the cooperation of international financial agencies. The most vulnerable victims of the economic crisis are the impoverished masses, whose ranks have continued to swell in recent years. Their plight is of all the more concern because their abject poverty contrasts so sharply with the wealth of the country's natural resources and ostentatious lifestyles of its elite.

Zaire could rank among the richest nations on earth. Its natural resources are immense. It is the world's largest exporter of industrial diamonds and cobalt. Mineral exports accounted, in 1988, for about two thirds of the foreign exchange earnings of the country and more than half of government revenues. Its huge lakes abound with fish and hydroelectric potential, and its forests could provide raw material to paper mills or furniture factories for decades.

Agriculture is the dominant sector for employment, providing jobs to more than 70 percent of the economically active population. But its growth rate per capita has been poor. Nature is not to blame for this. The agricultural sector in Zaire enjoys natural advantages that would be the envy of many other sub-Saharan countries. The population density is low, and about half of the land area is covered with forests. Rainfall is plentiful throughout the country. The northern and southern halves of the country, which is divided by the equator, enjoy complementary weather patterns with a warm/cool cycle in the north coinciding with a cool/warm cycle in the south. This complementarity has long been regarded as a major stabilizing factor in ensuring food supplies throughout the year. The agricultural production pattern is dualistic; millions of subsistence farmers coexist with a plantation sector that produces primarily industrial and export crops.

The modern manufacturing sector is relatively small and relies largely on foreign capital and marginal skills. It coexists with a pervasive informal sector, which is more often referred to as the *second economy* or *parallel economy*. This sector is notable for its enormity and for its extensive range of doubtful practices. It is a refuge sector that figures prominently in the survival strategies of most Congolese.

Since independence in June 1960, Zaire has been plagued by political instability, such as cholera epidemics, a lack of trained manpower, and a huge foreign debt (Figure 7.18). Travelers arriving in Kinshasa, the capital city, are struck by the tens of thousands of inhabitants wandering along the city's avenues. Many of them are unemployed. All day long they palaver and look for part-time jobs to help them get by. In the last forty years the population of Kinshasa has exploded from 500,000 to over 3 million inhabitants. Most of the city's new residents are former peasants who have been attracted to urban life.

Rwanda and Burundi

Rwanda, a country about the size of Maryland, is in east central Africa, bounded by Tanzania, Burundi, Zaire, and Uganda. The population at the

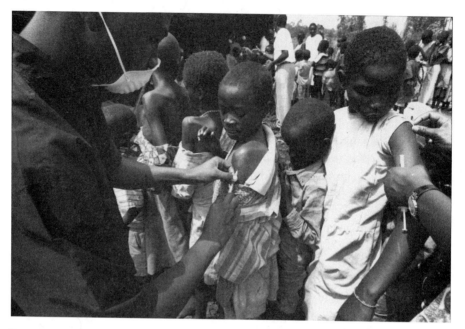

Figure 7-18. Two girls receive cholera vaccinations from health workers, while other children wait in line in the town of Goma, Congo. Cholera is transmitted by fecally contaminated food and water. This is most common in sub-Saharan Africa, often among displaced or refugee populations. Overall, some 79 million people in Africa are at risk from the disease according to World Health Organization. (Photo: UNICEF by Betty Press.)

beginning of 1994 was about 8.2 million. Months of war and ethnic bloodletting claimed an estimated half a million lives. The roots of Rwanda's conflict reach far into the past, and the problems that Rwandans face present a bleak future.

Rwanda was ruled from 1973 until April 6, 1994, by President Juvenal Habyarimana, a member of the Hutu tribe. Habyarimana was killed in a plane crash on April 6. The Hutus represent about 85 percent of Rwanda's population, but they were dominated for centuries by the minority Tutsi, who account for about 14 percent of the population. Even before Rwanda gained independence from Belgium in 1962, the country was plagued by tribal warfare, and Habyarimana's death touched off new conflicts. Government-trained Hutu militias began mass attacks on Tutsis and on moderate Hutus suspected of cooperating with them. Then, the Tutsi-led Rwandan Patriotic Front—which first invaded from Ugandan exile in 1990—began a new offensive. After two months of fighting, the rebel front captured Kigali, the capital, and on July 19, 1994, swore in a provisional government. It drove the remnants of the old Hutu-led government and its army out of their last refuge, in the far southeast of the country, and into Zaire. Perhaps one fifth of the inhabitants of Kigali, once a pleasant place of tree-lined avenues and colorful market, were butchered.

Ethnic hostility is nothing new here or elsewhere in Africa. In Rwanda it is rooted in a centuries-old domination by the cattle-owning Tutsi minority of the Hutu peasant majority. More recently, many Tutsis were deprived of power by the Hutu majority in 1960 and have since dreamed of revenge. Tutsis and Hutus may look different—Tutsis are a taller, Nilotic people, and Hutus are darker and stockier—but they have for centuries shared a common culture in Rwanda. They have lived in hamlets alongside each other on the steep hillsides. Yet they turned on each other. Why? No one seems able to say.

Burundi is desperately poor and mainly agricultural. Only an estimated 300,000 of its six million people work in business or industry. One third of the government is financed by aid from the international community. Seventy percent of the adults are illiterate, and the army eats up about 25 to 40 percent of the gross national product. Secondary schools are so crowded that they are forced to turn away students. Burundi shares with Rwanda the tribal division between Hutus and Tutsis: Burundi is about 85 percent Hutu and 15 percent Tutsi. In Bujumbura, the capital, neighborhoods are almost completely segregated by ethnic group.

In the summer of 1994, after a Tutsi-dominated government took power in Rwanda, about 140,000 Rwandan Tutsis who had been living in Burundi for more than thirty years went back home to Rwanda. With them they took the commercial backbone—40 percent of the business & civilian workers and 50 percent of the taxi drivers and journalists. But Burundi has avoided the chaos of its troubled neighbor largely because of a tenous, antagonistic relationship between its Hutu-dominated government and the Tutsi-dominated military—a relationship that has staved off greater violence even as it has paralyzed normal government function.

Republic of Congo and the Central African Republic

Thick rainforests cover nearly one half of the Congo Republic. The interior of the Republic of Congo drains into the Congo River, but the coastal area drains into the Atlantic. There is some commercial agriculture based on cocoa, coffee, oil palm, and groundnuts, but the bulk of the population is engaged in subsistence farming, with cassava and plantain as main crops. Most of the accessible forests have been cut. Petroleum was discovered in 1957 and has contributed significantly to the national economy. Lack of infrastructure has hampered the development of the country.

The Central African Republic was formerly French Equatorial Africa. The southern part of the country is rich in timber; northwards there are savanna lands and parklike forests that extend gradually into the Sahel. This area is a transition zone where traditions of black Africa, the culture of Islam, and Christianity coexist and struggle with each other. It is a landlocked country, and its development suffered greatly from lack of political leadership.

Cameroon, Equatorial Guinea, and Gabon

Cameroon, a former German colony, was a U.N. Trust territory under France. In 1960 it became independent. The plantations for coffee, cocoa, and oil palms produce significant amounts for export. There is a small but important mining industry based on the exploitation of bauxite, iron ore, uranium, and diamonds. Oil has been discovered close to the Nigerian border and revenues from oil form a significant part of the national economy. In October 2002 the World Court ruled that the disputed oil-rich Bakassi peninsula in the Gulf of Guinea belongs to Cameroon. Nigeria and Cameroon had fought over the territory for more than a decade. Future development of the country depends on improvement of the infrastructure and maintenance of political stability.

Equatorial Guinea, a former Spanish colony, became independent in 1963. It is small and, in general, undeveloped. There are important timber resources, and coffee and cocoa are grown for export.

Gabon has significant mineral deposits, large forests, and some oil resources. Timber was at one time the principal export, but now oil constitutes the major export of Gabon. The country has a higher per capita GDP than its neighboring countries. But most of the wealth is concentrated among the people in urban areas, and the rural countryside is still poor.

East Africa

East Africa, comprising Kenya, Tanzania, and Uganda, is an area of striking physical landscapes. They range from the tropical coastline through hot, dry savanna to alpine mountain ranges and from temperate, fertile highlands to desert. Before the first European traders, missionaries, and conquerors arrived in the mid-nineteenth century, the people of the area had already had a great deal of contact for many centuries with foreigners—Arabian traders in particular, but also with people from India. Under these influences a highly developed culture arose along the coast of East Africa, which reached its peak between 1200 and 1500.

Demands from American plantations caused an increase in the slave trade in East Africa after 1770, and it reached considerable dimensions between 1840 and 1870. As a result, the age, gender, and reproduction profiles of many African peoples were seriously distorted; in some regions, entire populations were wiped out. During their raids the slave traders penetrated deep into the hinterland of Kenya and Tanzania. West of the East African Rift Valley, in present-day Uganda, well-organized African kingdoms participated in the slave trade.

European conquests did not begin until 1880. The British were at first mainly interested in Uganda, with its strategically favorable position at the upper reaches of the Nile and its apparent wealth. From 1884 on, Germany claimed large areas of Tanganyika. During negotiations in Berlin between 1885 and 1890, Britain and Germany agreed to fix limits of the spheres of interest. Britain was granted Kenya and Uganda so that a railway could be built to the coast, whereas Tanganyika, which at that time included Rwanda and Burundi, came under German influence. Subsequently, Germany also ceded Zanzibar to Britain. From 1919 Britain administered Tanganyika under a League of Nations mandate. Thus, Kenya, Tanzania, and Uganda were, until their independence, under a common colonial power

Twice the size of Uganda but with far less agricultural potential, Kenya is, nevertheless, the one stable country in East Africa. The violence that preceded the independence of Kenya in 1963, and the relative tranquility that followed it, were the reverse of events in neighboring Uganda. The most important economic activity in this largely agricultural country is centered in the south, with production for export coming from the lands that were owned before independence by the Europeans. Among the chief plantation crops are coffee, sisal, and tea, but an important export is pyrethrum, which is used as an insecticide. The port of Mombasa is the terminus of the Kenya and Uganda Railway. Tribal differences constitute an important obstacle to continued development of the country. A detribalized urban black middle class is emerging in Kenya.

The number of people in Kenya's capital, Nairobi, has tripled in the last decade to 4.5 million. To some extent, Nairobi's growth and urban problems such as poor infrastructure, water supplies, roads, telephones, and electricity, are shared by most other African capitals. Increasingly in the past ten years, corruption and mismanagement have undermined the foundations for energy, telecommunications, and transportation—all sectors of patronage and power. The World Bank and Western donors plan to invest millions to privatize energy and telecommunications and to rebuild roads in Kenya, but progress is painstakingly slow.

Uganda, independent since 1962, is primarily an agricultural country. Large herds of cattle, sheep, and goats are the basis for an important trade in hides. Uganda has mineral resources, but their exploitation has been hampered by transport problems. Years of political instability and civil war caused much destruction of resources. Many forest and woodland areas were either shelled to destroy the enemy or scorched altogether by fire. Uganda, which was self-reliant in food, is facing food problems because of mismanagement of the environment during the period of political instability (Figure 7.19).

In 1961 Tanganyika became independent; in 1964 it joined in a political union with Zanzibar and adopted the name Tanzania. In addition to food crops, the principal products are sisal and cotton, but in two thirds of Tanzania agricultural production is hindered by the tsetse fly and insufficient water. Dar es Salaam, the leading port, is connected by rail with both Lake Tanganyika and Lake Victoria. Cultivation of cloves is concentrated in Zanzibar, which

Figure 7-19. A poor neighborhood of Kampala, Uganda. In recent years Kampala has grown rapidly and the town has spread over the surrounding hills. Africa has the highest urban growth rate of all world regions: 5 percent per year. The current pace and scale of change often strain the capacity of local and national governments to provide even the most basic services to urban residents. An estimated 25 to 50 percent of urban inhabitants in developing countries live in impoverished slums and squatter settlements, with little or no access to adequate water, sanitation, or refuse collection. In such situations, both environmental quality and human health and well-being are at risk. (Photo: UNICEF by Jorgen Schytte.)

produces about 60 percent of the world's supply. The development of Tanzania, after independence, was based on socialist ideology involving state control of the economy and regrouping of rural population and work on a communal basis. The collective system discouraged initiative and resulted in decline of agriculture. Since 1984 there has been some liberalization of economic policy.

Southern Africa: A Region in Transition

Southern Africa is a vast region of diverse peoples and cultures. The region has been inhabited for thousands of years, and many of its current problems have roots deep in the past. Ancestors of the Bantu-speaking peoples, who comprise the largest number of blacks in southern Africa, began migrating southward from central Africa at the beginning of the Christian era, crossing into present-day Zimbabwe some time before the fifth century A.D. By the year 1500, they had settled throughout the region and had occupied most of the east coast of present-day South Africa.

Portuguese explorers reached Angola in 1483 and Mozambique in 1498, marking the beginning of centuries of Portuguese influence. The Portuguese first reached the Cape of Good Hope in 1846, but permanent white settlement did not begin until the Dutch East India Company established a supply station in 1652. In subsequent decades, additional Dutch, French Huguenot refugees, and Germans settled in the Cape area to form the Afrikaner element of South Africa's white population. At the end of the eighteenth century, during the Napoleonic wars, Britain seized the Cape of Good Hope; subsequent British settlement and rule marked the beginning of a long conflict between the Afrikaners and the English-speaking settlers. The inhospitable Namib Desert constituted a formidable barrier to European exploration of South West Africa (Namibia) until the late 1700s; Germany annexed the coastal region in 1883.

Partly to escape British political rule and cultural hegemony, many Afrikaner farmers, known as Boers, began the "great trek" northward in 1836, coming into contact and conflict with various African groups and establishing two independent republics (Transvaal and the Orange Free State) in 1852 and 1854. Following the Anglo-Boer wars of 1880–1881 and 1899–1902, the defeated Boer republics were incorporated into the British Empire. In 1910 the two former Boer republics and the two British colonies of the Cape and Natal were joined to form the Union of South Africa, a dominion of the British Empire whose white population controlled most domestic matters. In 1934 the union achieved status as a sovereign state within the empire. Racial discrimination in South Africa became increasingly institutionalized after the ruling National Party came to power in 1948. A strong resurgence of Afrikaner nationalism in the 1940s and 1950s led to a decision, through a referendum in the white community, to establish a republic. This decision took effect in May 1961, and in October 1961 South Africa withdrew from the Commonwealth.

The issues that motivated most sub-Saharan countries in their quest for independence thirty years ago are still dominant in southern Africa. Colonial rule lasted longest there, and the white population was the largest and most firmly rooted in Africa. The wars to end Portuguese rule in Angola and Mozambique (which gained independence in 1975), the struggle to defeat the white minority in Rhodesia (now Zimbabwe, independent in 1980), the effort to terminate South Africa's control over Namibia, and the efforts to end apartheid in South Africa have been particularly bitter. For black Africans, such colonial and racial issues remain critical, while many whites in southern Africa associate these same concerns with a threat to their position and survival. These factors have created a general atmosphere of regional hostility and mistrust.

South Central Africa: Zimbabwe, Zambia, Malawi, Mozambique, and Madagascar

Zimbabwe Zimbabwe became independent in 1980. Since then, Zimbabwe has sought to improve its domestic and international credibility by balancing the need for change with that of building confidence in its government. The democratic institutions established by the constitution continue to operate, and parliamentary elections were held in 1985.

Zimbabwe inherited a strong and diversified economy with a significant private sector. The government has pushed population growth down below the African average, to 2.3 percent. This was achieved by setting up a family planning network well suited to the needs of the rural society. Along dusty roads in remote bits of the country, 800 women ride bicycles to deliver contraceptives and advice to peasant women. By meticulously visiting each village, these women, known as "community-based distributors," reach more than 70 percent of Zimbabwe's population. Families earning less than Z$400 ($50) a month—which is most of them—are given contraceptive pills free. These are the most popular form of birth control, partly because women can hide their use from their men folk. Others are charged Z$1.20 for a month's supply. Unlike many other African governments, which rely on foreign aid, Zimbabwe's pays the salaries of the 800 women and buys the contraceptives.

The government has supported efforts by the Zimbabwe National Family Planning Council, an agency backed by the United States (which says birth control is one of its four goals of foreign aid), to persuade Zimbabwean men to discard their traditional resistance to family planning. A few years ago there were regular reports of men beating their wives when they discovered that they were using contraceptives. The hefty cost of supporting a large family has helped persuade some men of the value of limiting its size. To encourage others, the council recently launched a "male motivation campaign," which sends advisers to talk to men at their place of work. It also stresses the need to control the spread of HIV by the use of condoms. Zimbabwean women now have a rate of contraceptive use of 43 percent, far higher than the average of 14 percent for sub-Saharan Africa. The country's total fertility rate, which measures the average number of children born to a woman during her life, is 5.3. This is well below the sub-Saharan average of 6.5.

Politically and economically, Zimbabwe has been on the edge since 2000, when the government ordered seizure of white-owned farms that were on property taken from blacks during the British colonial rule. White farmers agree that land reform is needed to undo colonialism's legacy in Zimbabwe, where whites make up 1 percent of the population but own 70 percent of the most fertile land. But the program's fast pace and hardball tactics have spawned violence and aggravated the food crisis. Many white farmers have been killed since the campaign began in 2000, and nearly 3,000 have been evicted without compensation. At least 300 white farmers have been arrested. The country's farm production has been devastated. Half of Zimbabwe's 12 million people need emergency food aid, according to U.N. estimates in 2002. An estimated 150,000 black farm workers on white-owned farms have lost their jobs. Although most of the black farm workers are skilled farmers, they have not received any of the seized land. The United States and European countries have condemned the Zimbabwe government's action and have imposed economic sanctions.

Zambia Formerly known as Northern Rhodesia, Zambia became independent in 1964. It is a plateau country, and the accessible areas along the railroads have attracted most of the development. A crucial factor in Zambia's development is its landlocked position. The country's economic heartland, the Copper belt, lies about 2,090 km from Beira in Mozambique and 2,740 km from Durban in South Africa. The Zambian economy relies greatly on the copper mining industry. During the colonial period, a selective migration policy encouraged the movement of able-bodied males from rural to urban areas to ensure a continuous flow of cheap and unskilled labor to industrialized areas of Zambia, colonial Zimbabwe, and South Africa. This policy led to concentration of development in a few modernized enclaves within a general territory characterized by underdevelopment. During the postcolonial period, Zambia has continued to ignore the problems of rural areas.

Malawi A small and poor country, Malawi lies astride the Great Rift Valley of eastern Africa in the narrow strip of land along Lake Malawi. It is primarily an agricultural country with maize, cassava, and millet as major crops. Commercial agriculture contributes to the exports of tobacco, tea, and sugar.

Rapid population growth has led to destruction of forests and woodlands on marginal areas such as hillsides and steep slopes in Malawi, and has had an adverse effect on natural resources. Overcultivation, overgrazing, and deforestation have produced declining agricultural fertility and negative ecological consequences, particularly in central and southern parts of the country where the population pressure is high.

Mozambique Mozambique attained its independence on June 25, 1975, after more than 470 years of Portuguese influence and colonial rule. The transition was the culmination of at least a decade of fighting, led principally by the Revolutionary Front for the Liberation of Mozambique (FRELIMO). It was marked by dramatic internal change and upheaval. A one-party socialist state was installed, and some 180,000 out of 200,000 Portuguese settlers, seeing their privileged position undermined, abandoned the country and fled to South Africa, Rhodesia (now Zimbabwe), or back to Portugal.

Post-independence Mozambique's new political, economic, and social policies, coupled with the impact of involvement in Rhodesian conflict, had a devastating effect on the economy. Perhaps the most significant upset came when 90 percent of the Portuguese settlers abandoned the country after independence, and Mozambique found itself bereft of private capital and both skilled and managerial services. With the backing of South Africa, Rhodesia, and ex-Portuguese settlers, the antigovernment Mozambique Resistance

Movement (MRM), later known as RENAMO, was created. During the past fifteen years, the rebels of the Mozambique National Resistance (RENAMO) and the members of the Mozambique Liberation Front (FRELIMO), the formerly Marxist party that ruled the country from 1975, have been engaged in a civil war, the victims of which include nearly a half million people who died of war-induced starvation and disease. In 1992 the two groups signed a peace accord. Since then RENAMO-controlled sections of the country have been opened up to relief agencies from the outside world. An estimated 5 million people—about a quarter of the country's population—have been displaced by the war, and massive efforts are being made to return them to their homes. But as people move, their first need is to eat, so they cluster around food distribution points, sometimes aggravating food-dispensing and health problems.

Madagascar The island of Madagascar lies 240 miles off the east coast of Africa. Larger than France, it became independent in 1960. Rice is the principal food crop, but the quality is poor and yield is low. The island has large forests rich in tropical products. Mineral resources are largely undeveloped, but it produces significant amounts of graphite and quartz crystals.

North of Madagascar lies a small group of islands comprising the Republic of Comoros. It became independent in 1975 and has a population of about 400,000.

Seychelles, Mauritius, and Reunion islands are to the east. The Republic of Seychelles, with a population of 73,000, enacted a law in 1995 guaranteeing to protect from extradition anyone willing to pay a $10 million citizenship fee.

Southwest Africa: Angola, Namibia, and Botswana

Angola Angola was one of the largest of the Portuguese territories. Portugal restricted the development of the country to the settlement projects for poor Portuguese farmers and limited manufacturing to the finishing of Portuguese semi-manufactures. Portuguese policy distorted the economic development of Angola. Though the country is potentially prosperous by African standards, the Portuguese made little effort to involve the indigenous people in the production of wealth other than as unskilled laborers. The departure of Portugal in 1975 left large gaps in the economy, which have not been filled during the last twenty years.

The Portuguese hasty withdrawal resulted in the immediate loss of almost the whole of Angola's trained personnel, and completely destabilized the country's economy. Years of hostilities between the South African-backed guerrillas and the Marxist government party since independence in 1975 disrupted economic activities. In 2002 Angola's warring parties signed a cease-fire accord after more than two decades of conflict. Rich in oil, diamonds, and other natural resources, Angola is rife with disease, malnutrition, and the violence of war. A country of about 13 million people, Angola is sub-Saharan Africa's biggest oil producer after Nigeria. Sixty percent of Angolan oil is now pumped by ChevronTexaco; the United States buys more than half of all the oil Angola produces. Recent discoveries of deep-water reserves off the coast will probably double production within five years. Why is a country so naturally rich mired in poverty? The oil companies have paid billions, but the civil war has consumed much of the money, while the rest has been deposited into the offshore accounts of powerful people. Little has found its way to ordinary people (Figure 7.20).

Namibia After World War I, South Africa was given a League of Nations mandate to administer the former German colony of South West Africa (Namibia) until it was ready for independence. In many ways South Africa treated South West Africa as an integral part of its national territory; after the Second World War it refused to place it under a U.N. trusteeship, and instead continued to administer the territory under South African law, including the introduction of apartheid. In 1966, the U.N. General Assembly revoked

Figure 7-20. Benguela Province, Angola. A man and a boy collect water from a pump provided by UNICEF. Angola's economy was ravaged by a 27-year civil war; millions of land mines make farming dangerous. Hunger haunts much of the country. If geology were destiny, Angola, with rich deposits of oil and diamonds and a relatively small population, would be one of Africa's most prosperous countries. Instead, civil strife and brazenly corrupt government have left it in ruin. (Photo: UNICEF by Adrian Pennink.)

South Africa's mandate, and in 1971 the International Court of Justice stated that South Africa was obligated to terminate immediately its administration of Namibia.

Faced with a growing insurgency mounted against it by the South West Africa People's Organization, and international pressure on South Africa, Namibia's independence came in 1990. Namibia's mineral resources are the driving force in the economy and are likely to remain so for years to come. The output of mines in 1991 was valued at 1.08 billion runs ($385 million), some 20 percent of the gross domestic product.

Botswana In 1966 Bechuanaland, a British protectorate since 1885, became independent as Botswana. It is one of the few strong and functioning parliamentary democracies in Southern Africa. Because nearly half of the country is desert, one of its greatest problems has always been poor water supply. One of the most important public works has been the construction of large dams and the boring of a system of wells. The exploitation of minerals such as copper and nickel deposits and diamonds make a major contribution to Botswana's economy.

With a little over 1.6 million people living in an area the size of France, Botswana's population and environmental problems are not as severe as some of the other countries of southern Africa. But as human and livestock population grow, and as mining expands, additional sources of water supply will be required. Escalating demands for water can have negative consequences on the environment.

South Africa: Transition to Democracy

South Africa is a country of more than 455,000 square miles, slightly larger than California and Texas combined. But most of its 40 million people are concentrated in the urban areas to the east, between Pretoria and Johannesburg and around Durban on the Indian Ocean, and to the southwest around Cape Town along the Atlantic Ocean. Much of the vast north-central area is desert and largely uninhabited. The Johannesburg and Cape Town metropolitan areas are growing at a steady pace. Central Johannesburg is the region's economic engine, generating 37 percent of the regional and 6 percent of the national gross domestic product. Near downtown, hundreds of black families have crowded into high-rise apartment buildings since the end of apartheid restrictions. Over 800 miles to the southwest of Johannesburg is Cape Town, the capital of the vast Cape Province and center of a metropolitan area of about 2.4 million residents, including the undercounted black population that has recently drifted into the western parts of the province. The western Cape area is known for the seaport, diversified industry, and a resurgent tourist trade.

The United States has maintained an official presence in South Africa since an American consulate was opened in Cape Town in 1799. After the South African government officially adopted its apartheid policy in 1948, relations between South Africa and the rest of the world community were troubled. This policy, which strictly segregated the races, denied the majority black population any vote in the national affairs. Some 85 percent of South Africa's population (45 million) is nonwhite, including 74 percent black. The five largest black tribes comprise 84 percent of the total black population: Zulu (6 million, or 34 percent); Xhosa (3 million, or 18 percent); Sepedi, North Sotho (2.5 million, or 14 percent); Seshoeshoe, South Sotho (1.8 million, or 10 percent); and Tswana (1.4 million, or 8 percent).

Under the apartheid, Afrikaans, a derivative language of the Dutch brought here by the white settlers, enjoyed a privileged position in the government and education, and was seen as the language of power and control. To many of the country's 30 million black Africans, Afrikaans came to represent the brutal apartheid system with its twin pillars of racial separation and white dominance. To them it stood as one of apartheid's most visible symbols, and they despised the way it was forced on them. It was the compulsory use of Afrikaans in black schools that touched off the simmering tensions in Soweto in 1976 and led to the uprisings that shook South Africa.

South Africa adopted a homeland policy in the 1950s which set aside 13 percent of South Africa's land for about 70 percent of the population. The homeland policy reflected South Africa's contention that there was no "black majority" in South Africa, but an assortment of separate tribal minorities. Under the homeland policy the blacks were stripped of citizenship and legal rights within South Africa once their homeland became "independent. The United States refused to recognize the independence of Transkei, Venda, Ciskei, and Bophuthatswana "homelands."

In 1990 South Africa freed black leader Nelson Mandela from prison and began to pursue a policy to bring democratic rule in the country with a new constitution. The quest for transition to black-majority rule was marked by violence. Most of the clashes were between supporters of the African National Congress, the nation's biggest black political group, and those of the Inkatha Freedom Party, the Zulu-based party that had its strongest support in Natal. In 1991, the South African government repealed most remaining racially discriminatory laws, including the Black Land Act of 1913, the Development Trust and Land Act of 1936, the Population Registration Act of 1950, the Group Areas Act of 1966, and the Black Communities Development Act of 1984. The results of the apartheid laws are still evident today; residential areas are strictly segregated by race, and Africans have long commutes to jobs in the larger cities.

In the new South Africa, Afrikaans is just one of the eleven official languages (Figure 7.21). Nine million people speak Zulu as their first language, and 7.4 million speak Xhosa. Afrikaans, with 6 million speakers, runs third, and in white business and academic enclaves it is rapidly losing ground to English, which is the first language of only 3.4 million South Africans but is

South Africans' First Language
(Percent of Total Population)

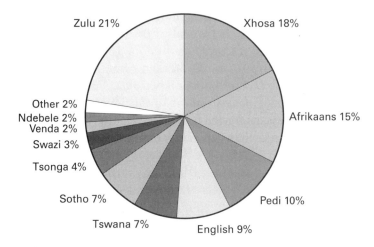

Figure 7-21. South African languages.

widely understood across ethnic lines. The nation's five Afrikaans universities have moved toward dual-language instruction in varying degrees.

In June 1993, after a year and a half of negotiations, the government and the main opposition group, the African National Congress, agreed for the black majority in South Africa to cast their first votes in April 1994. Voters elected a constituent assembly that wrote a new constitution and served as the first postapartheid parliament. The African National Congress won 62.7 percent of the national vote, the old ruling National Party won 20.4 percent, and the Inkatha won 10.5 percent.

The 1994 South African elections were to racism what the collapse of the Berlin Wall was to communism. They marked the end of the world's last racial oligarchy. Three and a half centuries of colonialism and apartheid had created one of the most unequal societies in the world. South Africa's 13 percent white population owned 86 percent of the country's land and more than 90 percent of its wealth. In 1998 half of South Africa's 30 million blacks remained unemployed, half were illiterate or semi-illiterate, half were under the age of 20, half lived below the poverty line, and fewer than half lived in homes with running water and electricity. Three million didn't live in homes at all—they squatted.

In June 1999 South Africa held its second multiracial general election, which resulted in an overwhelming win for the ruling African National Congress. As the euphoria of the election faded, the country was left with the reality of overseeing the transformation of a country burdened by the legacy of systematic deprivation of property ownership, decent education, fair wages, and basic services for the black majority.

The South African economy is still Africa's largest and most broadly developed. The base of the economy has evolved from agriculture to mining and, more recently, to manufacturing which now accounts for nearly 25 percent of the gross domestic product (GDP). The mining industry is an important sector of the country's economy, employing people from both within and outside of South Africa's borders. Although diamonds and gold have captured most foreigners' attention, other important minerals that are exported, such as coal, chrome, manganese, platinum, uranium, and vanadium, have been invaluable contributors to the country's foreign exchange. But the long-term prospects for the bedrock of South Africa's wealth in gold and other minerals remain poor. The shafts have gotten deeper, the ore poorer, the cost of extraction higher. In recent years employment in the mining industry has dropped from 525,000 in 1987 to 360,000 in 1994. In 1993, taxes on mining profits accounted for just 2.5 percent of the national budget, down from 12 percent in 1986.

Economic Challenges Facing South Africa Having finally achieved democracy, South Africa faces the more daunting challenge of repairing its social fabric, restoring its civil order, rebuilding its economy, and redistributing its land and wealth. South Africa's annual per capita income is $2,560, placing the country in the middle range of the world's economies, but at a level six times higher than the average of the rest of sub-Saharan Africa. But income disparities along racial lines are notorious in this country. Average income among whites is roughly eight times that of the black population. Whites still have a corner on the skills needed to sustain a technologically sophisticated, industrialized economy. Since 1975, the income gap within each of the two major racial groups has been widening, while the gap between the races has been narrowing. The real income of the emerging black middle class of unionized labor, white-collar workers, and small businessmen—the top fifth of all black wage earners—has risen by 40 percent since 1975. But the income of unemployed and rural blacks has dropped by 40 percent. Half of the black population now lacks "formal" employment—double the percentage of a generation ago. They eke out a meager existence as domestic workers, casual laborers, itinerant farm laborers, and pensioners. Nearly a fifth of blacks are squatters or backyard shack dwellers; two thirds live in homes without electricity; 70 percent lack running water.

Low-income whites—made up mainly of miners and factory workers—exposed to job pressure from blacks, and from declining fixed-capital investments, have lost 40 percent of their average real income. High-income whites have broken even since 1975. Meanwhile, Indians and mixed-raced Coloreds—the two other races in South Africa—have been more upwardly mobile. One of the biggest policy pressures the new government faces is whether to target the poorest of the poor or those who already have a foothold the formal economy.

Land reform is another major problem. The major issue is not so much the availability of land but its continued productivity. Large-scale white commercial farming accounts for roughly 90 percent of the value added in agriculture. Over the past three decades, farming profitability and subsidies have been declining. In 1960, agriculture accounted for 12 percent of the GNP; in 1994 it was only 4.7 percent. Millions of acres of idle state land, some of which is arable, arc available for distribution. White farmers may be willing to sell millions of acres more, if the price is right. But the history of large-scale land redistribution programs, in neighboring Zimbabwe and elsewhere, has been marked by sharp drops in farm productivity. The nation's black-run government has given land reform a back seat to other priorities. Land transfer programs remain under-funded by a government preoccupied with AIDs and crime, and doubtful that giving land to poor peasants will do much to better their lot. The government has set 2015 as the target for turning over 30 percent of the commercial farmland to non-whites.

In the meantime, South Africa's acute housing shortage is creating flare-ups all over the country between squatters and homeowners. In Durban and Cape Town, large housing projects under construction are being occupied by squatters, even though would-be homeowners have paid deposits on the units. South Africa needs to build 300,000 housing units a year to meet the needs of the unhoused; it is currently building 30,000.

In health care and education the biggest challenge is to equalize opportunities and make more resources available to blacks. The economic stakes are high. In the best of futures, South Africa not only lifts its own black majority off the floor, it also becomes a growth engine that can help rescue the economic hard cases to its north—Angola, Mozambique, Malawi, and Rwanda.

One of the problems South Africa is facing today is the exodus of white, wealthy, educated South Africans in growing numbers, draining the country of expertise it desperately needs to meet the development challenges. The exodus is in response to the increase in violent crime. Much of the new terror is confined to the white suburbs of Johannesburg. These areas were well protected under the old government and the residents worried about crime little more than suburban residents do in the United States. During the first half of 1995, 6,030 people emigrated—about twice the number of five years before. Most white South Africans go to Australia, England, the United States, Canada, or New Zealand. The loss of the educated elite is a serious blow to development efforts.

South Africa's Role in Revitalizing Sub-Saharan Economy The decades of apartheid separated not just white from black but also the region's richest and most advanced economy—South Africa—from its poor neighbors. South Africa is beginning to end that separation through a surge of investment in southern Africa. Investment is going into industries such as retailing, banking, brewing, mining, transportation, satellite television, and tourism. South African Breweries has invested in state-run brewing companies in Tanzania, Zambia, Botswana, Lesotho, Swaziland, and Mozambique. South African retailer Shoprite Checker has opened stores in Zambia and is building a shopping center in Maputo, Mozambique; Pick 'n Pay, another retailer, has opened stores in Namibia, Botswana, Zimbabwe, and Kenya. South Africa is building railroads in Zaire, hotels in Kenya, and prospecting for mineral deposits in Zaire, Burkina Faso, Guinea, Mali, and several other countries of West Africa. South African telephone companies are investing in the national networks of several countries with fiber optic lines or cellular systems. The South African electric company is investing in rehabilitating power grids of Mozambique, Angola, and Lesotho, and has plans to integrate them with South Africa's electrical network. South African Railways is working to upgrade the ports of Beira and Maputo to relieve congestion in South Africa's major seaport at Durban.

Nowhere has South Africa's penetration of new markets in sub-Saharan Africa been as spectacular as in French-speaking Zaire, formerly ruled by Belgium. As western companies have withdrawn from Zaire in exasperation over its corruption and chaos, South African concerns have moved in, seeing its mineral wealth and huge needs for new roads and railways as economic stepping stones to the rest of the continent. Restoring existing railroads and building new links would connect South Africa by modern rail with every country as far north as Tanzania, replacing costly truck routes and slow-moving lake barges. One of the problems in the development of sub-Saharan Africa is the lack of transportation connecting nearby countries.

South Africa's investment could help change the economic landscape of sub-Saharan Africa—a marginalized region where small markets, weak infrastructure, and harsh environment have not attracted much of the world's capital. But South Africa needs to do more. It needs to open its markets for exports from the poor sub-Saharan countries, so that they are able to pay for the imports they need from South Africa. South Africa has one of the most closed economies in the region. A host of trade barriers stop African goods from reaching its markets.

Would a dynamic South Africa, blazing an investment path across the continent, offering a market that is open to all, be enough to rejuvenate sub-Saharan Africa's economy? Maybe, over a long period. Over time the influence of pockets of economic productivity developed through investment should spread, and infrastructure should strengthen at local levels, facilitating the development of the entire region.

Southern African Development Community

Twelve southern African countries stretching from the Cape to Kilimanjaro (South Africa, Lesotho, Swaziland, Namibia, Botswana, Zimbabwe, Mozambique, Mauritius, Zambia, Angola, Malawi, and Tanzania) belong to the

Southern African Development Community. The purpose of the Community is to cooperate in a scheme to create a southern African economic community with free trade by 2000, and a free movement of people. By cooperating, the twelve countries hope both to earn some political clout and to integrate their way to prosperity. Other parts of the non-Western world, as well as the West, are forming regional trading blocks such as ASEAN (in Southeast Asia), SARC (in South Asia), NAFTA (in North America), and the EU (European Union). Southern Africans fear being left out.

The Southern African Development Community began in 1980 as a loose grouping of countries to share the scarce water that flows over their land, an important commitment in a region often parched by drought. They agreed that no country would be allowed to dam its rivers without first consulting others downstream. They promised to cooperate on electricity development, mining, and tourism. The group adopted protocol in 2000 that would eliminate internal trade barriers and export subsidies within the region.

There are difficulties in the way of creating a common market. Among other factors, almost all of the economic power of the region lies at its southern tip: South Africa's economy is nearly four times as big as that of all the other eleven members combined. South Africans are 35 times richer, measured by GNP per person, than people in Mozambique, the region's poorest country. If the twelve governments agree to allow people to move freely where they wish, many will head for South Africa. There are already an estimated 3 to 8 million illegal immigrants in South Africa. South Africa has begun to crack down and deport them. Partly to help stem this flow, South Africa wants its hinterland to prosper.

At present, only an estimated 10 percent of southern Africa's trade takes place within the region; in the European Union the figure is over 60 percent. Intraregional trade is growing; South Africa's exports to its own continent, 70 percent of which go to the Southern African Development Community, jumped by over a quarter from 1993 to 1994. Lifting trade barriers will help development. For the present, as was once true in Asia, many countries export the same things—mostly raw materials that go to Europe.

WESTERN ECONOMIC AID TO AFRICA

Every year the rich world pumps in billions of dollars of aid to try to breathe life into Africa's listless economies. The countries of the European Economic Community alone spend more than $9 billion helping Africans build roads, plant saplings, and fill bellies. Yet Africa stays poor. One reason—just one—is that as the rich world gives with one hand so it takes away with the other. The EU is one of the main offenders.

The EU sends cheap European beef to West Africa. Ostensibly designed to help poor African consumers, the beef program is really aimed at helping rich

European farmers. They produce beef that no one will buy at the price at which they want to sell, so they are subsidized by the European taxpayers to dump it in West Africa, where it destroys the livelihoods of poor farmers. Thanks to the tsetse fly, the countries in which this beef is dumped—Cote d'Ivoire and Ghana—rear few cattle of their own. But these countries have long enjoyed a thriving trade with cattle farmers in the Sahel—Mali, Burkina Faso, Niger, Chad—directly to the north. Traditionally, herdsmen used to walk their animals, often for days, to markets in the Sahel, where merchants bought them and then drove to markets in the south. Since the mid-1980s, however, when the EU started dumping beef, the merchants have increasingly given up. European beef can be bought in West Africa at half the price of that produced in the Sahel. The amount of frozen and chilled beef dumped by Europeans has leapt sevenfold in seven years. The Sahel cattle farmers cannot compete. Their climate can support few alternatives to cattle farming. They are among the vulnerable in a continent of paupers.

The EU's beef dumping policy undermines large EU projects expressly designed to support cattle farmers: building refrigerated abattoirs in Burkina Faso, improving cattle breeds in Mali, and fattening cattle in northern Cote d'Ivoire and Ghana. The EU does not want to concede that its beef dumping policy clashes with programs to support cattle farmers in Africa because it does not want to recognize that the EU agricultural policy rests on a bigger fraud: systematic overproduction of food in Europe paid for by Europe's taxpayers to please a powerful lobby, Europe's farmers.

Africa has also received aid from the World Bank. The Bank was originally a development fund, but has become the West's policeman for economic policy in Africa and elsewhere. The International Monetary Fund, a bank for governments to exchange currencies and draw credit, has since 1986 set aside funds to help African countries to change their economic policies. Since they were founded with other United Nations agencies after the Second World War, the Bank and, to lesser extent, the Fund have been driven by the breezes of economic fashion. Over the years, in Africa it has tried industrialization and economic pump priming. It backed large, prestigious projects, funded white elephants, and is responsible for several ecological disasters. It tried "poverty alleviation," and finally in 1980 the Bank was given the task of correcting economic policies on behalf of Western aid donors. The rule was simple. Western countries said: "No aid until you do a deal with the IMF and the Bank."

For most African countries who had borrowed heavily in the 1970s (on World Bank advice) and were facing low commodity prices, rising interest rates, and no new investment, there was no alternative. The belief in the West at that time was that if imports were slashed, currencies floated, subsidies removed, state companies sold off, and government spending cut, the economies would be back on track within four or five years. When the Bank and the Fund applied these policies—which they called "adjustment"—in

African countries, it brought severe economic problems. Thousands were turned out of jobs with no social security systems and no alternative sources of employment. Prices rocketed and wages fell. The unforeseen side-effects of adjustment were so severe that the Bank was forced to set up special programs to save the poorest countries from starvation (Figure 7.22). But the Bank still believed that this would last only a year or two. That time span for recovery has been revised until now no one dares predict when things will get better.

Other side-effects raised doubts about the Bank's policies. A cut in imports in the short term affected longer-term development plans, so that the very engines of recovery were starved of input and spares. Professionals in Africa, faced with choices such as earning $60 a month as a doctor in Tanzania or making $150 a day driving a taxi in Britain, France, or the United States, chose the latter. Africa's expensively trained, skilled workers headed to Europe and the United States. Worst of all, the Bank's investments were failing.

The Bank is not seen in Africa as a "listening bank." African countries see the Bank's priorities as driven by its own concerns rather than by their

Figure 7-22. School lunch program in Harare, Zimbabwe. Food security is among the major challenges facing African countries, where more than 16 million people are on the brink of starvation. Sub-Saharan Africa faces a particularly difficult challenge in the non-Western world. Here, agroclimatic constraints are more difficult than in much of Asia; the cost of accessing water is higher; and irrigation, transportation, and communications infrastructures are far more limited. Other factors such as widespread political instability, the HIV/AIDS crisis, rapid population growth, and relatively slow economic growth also make it hard for many African countries to muster the needed investments and policy reforms to increase food production. Africa's food bill could rise from $6.5 billion in 1997 to $11 billion by 2020. Paying that off could be politically and economically unsustainable. If African nations are unable to pay for needed imports, food shortages and malnutrition could rise to catastrophic proportions. (Photo: UNICEF by Jorgen Schytte.)

realities. Generally, the development plan for African countries such as Mozambique has been written by the Bank with little or no Mozambican input. The Bank and the Fund stand for antibureaucratic, free-market values, yet they are two of the largest bureaucracies in the world, employing 6,000 staff and 3,000 consultants, and churning out millions of tons of paper and memos. Their employees are so well paid that hardly anyone ever leaves. There is no reward for success, and no punishment for failure. They profess two tenets of faith: first, that there is no alternative to their policies; and second, that things are getting better.

In Africa, the Bank sees itself as a doctor. The patient is sick and needs drastic surgery, and the Bank resents being blamed for the pain. If the Bank workers are the doctors, the Fund workers are the hospital administrators. There is little self-questioning. It is no wonder that in Africa the aid policies of the World Bank and the Fund are seen as evil, as a conspiracy of the West against Africa and other developing nations.

In 2000 the United States Congress approved the African Growth and Opportunity Act (AGOA), which reduced or eliminated tariffs and quotas on more than 1,800 items. This has prompted the development of apparel industries in Kenya, Lesotho, Uganda, and other countries. Asian apparel manufacturers are the principal investors because the trade law allows them to sidestep quotas in their own countries. By shifting to Africa, Asian manufacturers can operate quota-free under the law. Kenya has 50,000 AGOA-related jobs; Lesotho created 10,000 new jobs in 2002. Although jobs have been created, most of the people getting rich from AGOA are not African but Asian investors.

HOW CAN AND HOW SHOULD SUB-SAHARAN AFRICA DEVELOP?

Both the models of economic development that Africa inherited from the colonial past and the socialist models that many countries uncritically accepted during the postcolonial era have failed to serve the region. The development policies of Western donors have also failed. A large part of the responsibility for the region's development crisis lies on the shoulders of African governments themselves. The biggest of Africa's constraints lies in its failure to develop people and institutions capable of running their own countries. African governments must end regional conflicts, reduce corruption, protect human rights, improve schools, and expand social services.

The challenge of the twenty-first century for sub-Saharan Africa as a whole is to seek solutions to the continent's three major issues. First, there is a need to develop less nationalistic but more region-oriented policy for development. Second, new institutions that are capable of creatively developing Africa's dormant material resources and existing traditional values must be created.

The new agenda should include agriculture as the engine of growth and place much more emphasis on people. Major efforts are needed to build African capacities—to produce a better-trained, healthier population and to greatly strengthen the institutional framework within which development can take place. Without this framework no amount of foreign aid will help, and even economic reforms will not succeed. Third, the merits of market economies and free trade should be acknowledged, as the Asian Pacific nations have done, to make social and economic development possible.

The problem is how to turn these challenges into reality for half a billion African people. How can African leaders be persuaded that profound changes are due and that rhetorical agreement is not enough, and how can the entrenched bureaucracy and business elite—which stand to lose in the short-term from long-term economic reforms—be overcome?

FURTHER READINGS

Adepoju, Aderanti and Christine Oppong, eds. 1994. *Gender, Work, & Population in Sub-Saharan Africa.* London: James Curry.

African Development Bank. 2002. *African Development Report 2002: Africa in the World Economy, Rural Development for Poverty Reduction in Africa, Economic and Social Statistics on Africa.* Oxford: Oxford University Press.

An-Na'im, Abdullahi, ed. 2002. *Cultural Transformation and Human Rights in Africa.* London: Zed Books.

Barrett, Christopher B., Frank Place, and Abdillahi Aboud, eds. 2002. *Natural Resources Management in African Agriculture: Understanding and Improving Current Practices.* New York: CABI Pub, in association with the International Centre for Research in Agroforestry.

Barnett, Tony and Piers Blaikie. 1992. *AIDS in Africa.* New York: Guilford.

Bassett, Thomas J. and Donald Crummey, eds. 2003. *African Savannas: Global Narratives and Local Knowledge of Environmental Change.* Portsmouth, NH: Heinemann.

Bryant, Coralie, ed. 1988. *Poverty, Policy and Food Security in Southern Africa.* Boulder, CO: Lynne Rienner Publishers.

Chazam, Naomi and Timothy M. Shaw. 1988. *Coping with Africa's Food Crisis.* Boulder, CO: Lynne Rienner Publishers.

Christopher, A.J. 1994. *The Atlas of Apartheid.* New York: Routledge.

Christiaensen, Luc J. 2002. *Growth, Distribution and Poverty in Africa.* Washington, D.C.: World Bank.

Cleaver, Kevin M. and Gotz A. Schreiber. 1994. *Reversing the Spiral: The Population, Agriculture, and Environment Nexus in Sub-Saharan Africa.* Washington, D.C.: World Bank.

Davidson, Basil. 1988. *Modern Africa: A Social and Political History.* London: Longman.

Edie, Carlene J. 2003. *Politics in Africa: A New Beginning?* Belmont, CA: Wadsworth Thomson.

Fukui, Katsuyoshi and John Markakis, eds. 1994. *Ethnicity and Conflict in the Horn of Africa.* Athens: Ohio State University Press.

Hope, Kempe R. 2002. *From Crisis to Renewal: Development Policy and Management in Africa.* Leiden, The Netherlands: Brill.

Jones, Stuart, ed. 2002. *The Decline of the South African Economy.* Northampton, MA.: Edward Elgar.

Kalipeni, Ezekiel, ed. 1994. *Population Growth and Environmental Degradation in Southern Africa.* Boulder, CO: Lynne Rienner Publishers.

Keeley, James, 2003. *Understanding Environmental Policy Processes: Cases from Africa.* Sterling, VA: Earthscan.

Lemon, Anthony and Christian M. Rogerson, eds. 2002. *Geography and Economy in South Africa and Its Neighbours.* Burlington, VT: Ashgate.

Leonard, David K. and Scott Straus. 2003. *Africa's Stalled Development: International Causes and Cures.* Boulder, CO: Lynne Rienner Publishers.

Mamdouh, Shahin. 2002. *Hydrology and Water Resources of Africa.* Boston: Kluwer Academic.

Rotberg, Robert I. 2003. *Africa's Discontent: Coping with Human and Natural Disasters.* Cambridge, MA.: World Peace Foundation.

Scherrer, Christian P. 2002. *Genocide and Crisis in Central Africa: Conflict Roots, Mass Violence, and Regional War.* Westport, CT.: Praeger.

Stock, Robert. 1995. *Africa South of the Sahara: A Geographical Interpretation.* New York: Routledge.

Tarver, James D. 1995. *The Demography of Africa.* Westport, CT.: Praeger Publishers.

Williams, Robert. 1987. *Political Corruption in Africa.* Hampshire, England: Gower.

Chapter 8

Future Prospects and Challenges

The preceding regional chapters have discussed the cultural patterns, nature–society relationships, development issues, and environmental issues in various parts of the non-Western world. In this chapter various threads of ideas discussed in the preceding chapters are pulled together to explore the future prospects of the non-Western world and the important challenges it faces. Before we discuss future prospects and challenges, and growth and change in the non-Western world since 1950s, let us look briefly at the non-Western world as it has changed from 1000 to 2000.

THE NON-WESTERN WORLD: 1000–2000

For Christians in the Western world the year 2000 marked a new millennium. To the non-Christian population of the non-Western world the year 2000 was not special. The year 2000 was 5760 in Israel; Heisei 12 in Japan; and 1420 in Islamic countries of the Middle East. But, like any anniversary, 2000 provides an opportunity to survey the last 1,000 years in the non-Western world.

Europe and the rest of the Western world was pretty much a backwater in 1000—a collection of petty kingdoms just emerging from the chaotic Dark Ages. The cultural heritage, sophistication, and technical knowledge of the Greco-Roman civilizations had largely been lost. Scholarship was confined to scattered monasteries and books remained scarce. Power over individuals was wielded by the two great institutions: the Holy Catholic Church in the realm of the spiritual and religious life, and the feudal system in the secular sphere. Except in the fields of theology and religious philosophy, Europe in 1000 was relatively backward.

In China, India, and the Islamic Middle East the intellectual life of 1000 was brighter. China was the best-organized and most technologically advanced society in the world. China's civil service fanned out from the palaces of the Soong Dynasty to govern about 100 million people. Survival was precarious for the Chinese peasants, but the bureaucracy provided an avenue of upward mobility. Most villages had elementary schools. Chinese medicine—acupuncture and herbal pharmacology—was the product of centuries of development. Chinese poets and painters created art that made Western art look crude. And Chinese workshops turned out marvels such as printed books, compasses, and bombs.

Regional kingdoms with distinctive Hindu cultures flourished in India in 1000. The Brahman priests and land-owning groups dominated sociopolitical organization and shared power with local ruling families. Bengal, Gujarat, and South India were leading in long-distance trade. Sanskrit was used in official records, formal education, and court literature. Patronage of arts, literature, and science by regional kingdoms encouraged creative efforts. Interest in astronomy and medicine continued during the period of maritime expansion in Southeast Asia. Mathematics made great progress and the use of ciphers and Indian numerals were later carried by Arabs to Europe. The West learned about Indian products, as they did about the number system, from Arab traders. Fabrics from the Indian port of Calicut became known as calico. Other familiar words that describe textiles, such as *chintz*, *cashmere*, and *bandanna*, also came out of India. As the year 1000 ended, the Turkish invasions of the Indian subcontinent started plundering the fertile plains of northern India and riches of the Indian temples.

In the Middle East Arab scholars, drawing on translations of ancient Greek texts and borrowing ideas from India and China, broke new ground in medicine, mathematics, and physics. Persia (Iran) was undergoing a true renaissance of arts and letters. The contributions of Islamic nations to the sciences put them far ahead of European culture in 1000 in an intellectual sense. In Africa, the Kingdom of Ghana was at its apex—its markets brimming with the wealth of Africa, its sculptors creating masterworks in gold. But the flow of information was slow, and contacts with other countries were limited.

How did the non-Western world change during the thousand years from 1000 to 2000? The discovery of the sea route by Europeans to India, China, and Africa was a major factor that ushered in an era of change. It led to the movement of ideas, goods, and colonizers to Asia and Africa. Most of the non-Western world to which the Europeans traveled in search of spices, silk, and gold became dominated, in due course, by the Western colonial empires. For nearly 200 years between 1750 and the end of World War II, the British, French, Dutch, and Belgians held vast colonial possessions in Asia and Africa. The British Empire, the world's largest and most powerful, began to unravel after World War II with India's independence in 1947. After India gained independence, there was little to stop Britain's dominoes from toppling: Palestine in 1948; Ghana, the first of its African colonies to go, in 1957; and in 1997, its last significant outpost, Hong Kong. Other European empires also crumpled.

During the last fifty years, since independence of most of the non-Western world, the principal focus of the nations in Asia and Africa has been on economic and social development. The process and patterns of development in various regions have been discussed in earlier chapters. Here, we briefly review the process of growth and change in the non-Western world as a whole.

GROWTH, CHANGE, AND DEVELOPMENT

Have the lives of ordinary people in the non-Western world become worse or better since the 1950s? The widely held answer seems to be that poverty is increasing. Yet, there has been a steady and dramatic improvement in indicators of the quality of life for ordinary people in non-Western countries in the last fifty years (Figure 8.1). The assertion that extreme poverty is on the rise is a standard feature of published commentary. For example, the July–August 1994 issue of *World Watch*, published by the Worldwatch Institute, announced on its cover: "After 50 years of big World Bank loans, the developing world—by most measures—has only grown poorer." Despite the commonplace character of such assertions, there has been little effort to look at this issue over sufficiently long periods of time to observe the broad sweep of trends.

How can we measure poverty? Economists typically give a shorthand answer to this question—they measure it by income. And by income, the economist typically means income in money. Money income can be used for each household in the country, and can be related to the amount required to purchase a minimum package of goods and services, such as food, clothing, and shelter. Those whose incomes are below this level are poor. Tracking such data over time answers the big questions. The alacrity with which economists produce such numbers, however, obscures basic problems—some conceptual, some practical—in relating money incomes to real quality of life across widely differing cultures, economic arrangements, and average income levels. Here we do not examine the income dimension. Instead, we look at basic social conditions such as decline in infant mortality, higher nutrition intake, and higher literacy that money and other resources make possible (Figure 8.2).

What does the overall trend show? For non-Western countries as a group, infant mortality has declined from 180 per thousand births in 1950–1955 to 69 per thousand in 1990–1995. Put another way, infant deaths have fallen from 1 out of every 5 babies to less than 1 in 14. Though the number of babies born annually has more than doubled during the period, the absolute number of infant deaths has declined steadily. This decline has been general—all countries

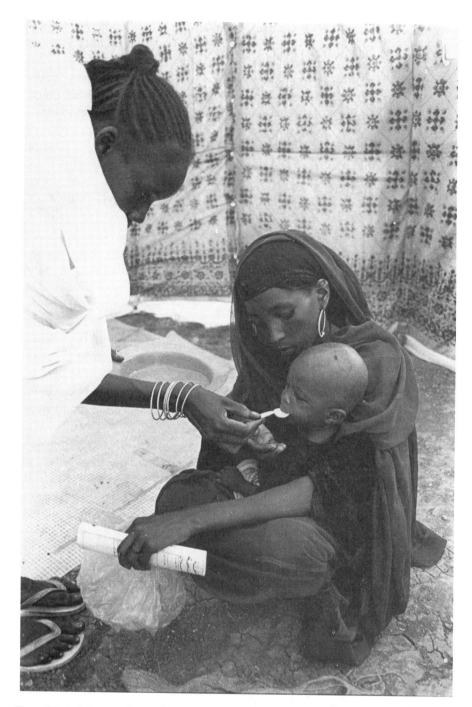

Figure 8-1. In Sudan, supplemental feeding of children has reduced the infant mortality (younger than 5 years) from 292 per thousand in 1960 to less than 172 per thousand in 2000. Better nourishment is partly responsible for the decline in mortality from 98 to 62 per thousand in Asia and from 135 to 95 in Africa between 1970–1975 and 1990–1995. Supplementary feeding is made available in many non-Western countries by governments and international agencies. (Photo: UNICEF by Jeremy Hartley.)

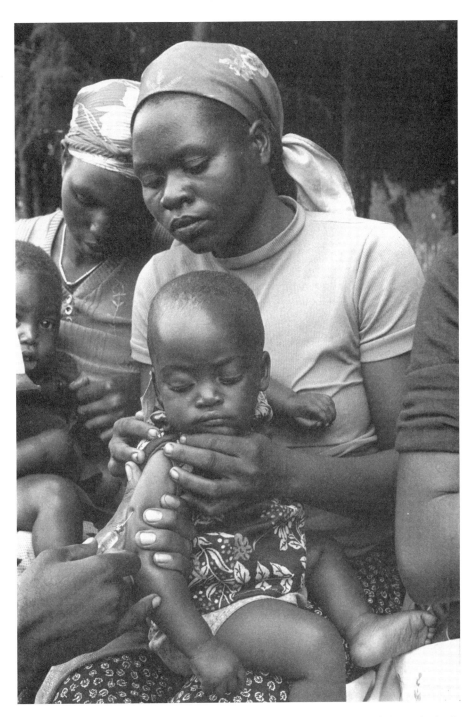

Figure 8-2. Immunization of children under one year old in the Kigali area of Rwanda. Immunization in many countries has also contributed to lowering of child mortality. In Rwanda mortality declined from 142 per thousand in 1970–1975 to 110 per thousand in 1990–1995. Health programs targeted at children and women are reducing mortality rates throughout the non-Western world. (Photo: UNICEF by Bert Demmers.)

have experienced it—although it has fallen much faster in some countries than in others. In a broad sense, the population explosion of the past several decades is the clearest indication that infant mortality fell substantially in non-Western countries. There is no broad evidence of increased fertility—the evidence is strongly in the direction of lower fertility rates—so the rapid population growth must have come from increased survival of children. Infant mortality is a useful proxy for broader health and well-being measures. If starvation is endemic among the larger population, more babies will die. When fewer infants die, it reflects a broader improvement in living conditions. The significant trend of declining infant mortality reflects a real improvement in the quality of life in many non-Western countries.

Life expectancy at birth in non-Western countries increased from 40.7 years in 1950–1955 to 62.4 years in 1990–1995. This means that each year, on average, life expectancy has increased by more than six months. At the same time, basic data on food production and availability produced by the Food and Agriculture Organization of the United Nations show that food production has outgrown population increases during the past four decades, which means that per capita food consumption has been rising. Altogether, it has risen by about 35 percent since 1950. During the past three decades it has risen 4 to 5 percent per decade. It is estimated that 33 percent of the population in 1975, or over 900 million people, suffered from serious malnutrition, defined as having an energy intake during the year of less than 154 percent of the basic metabolic requirement. (The basic metabolic requirement is the energy intake required for maintenance without physical activity.) By 1988–1990, the number of seriously malnourished in non-Western countries fell to 20 percent of the total, or nearly 720 million. This seems to be about the same proportion as was malnourished in England at the beginning of the nineteenth century. A trend of high and static or rising rates of malnutrition was confined to three African countries—Rwanda, Togo, and Zambia.

The improvement in nutrition over time probably reflects several factors, including higher productivity in agriculture, lower transportation costs, and better techniques for preserving food. The growth in agricultural productivity reduced by about half real prices of the three basic grains—wheat, rice, and corn—between the late 1950s and the early 1990s. Over the past century the fall in prices has been even steeper: since 1850, maize prices have fallen by about 80 percent in constant dollars.

Despite this favorable trend, some observers have warned that the past is no safe basis for predicting future trends. They contend that future trends are likely to be unfavorable. A major issue is whether the Green Revolution, for example in India and China, was an isolated case of serendipity that postponed a crisis, or one of a series of examples of humanity's capacity to increase agricultural productivity through scientific progress.

The fear of future agricultural calamity has a long history, impervious to actual trends. There has been substantial progress in food availability during the past several decades and a significant decline in the real price of basic agricultural commodities, particularly since 1980. Whether these trends will continue is uncertain. Economists generally would argue that higher prices would stimulate any needed increase in production. Such an increase, however, would be likely to adversely affect the nutritional intake of much of the non-Western world's poor—just as low prices of the 1980s were favorable to them. Overall, average people in non-Western world are eating a more adequate diet than at any previous time in modern history.

Literacy, which is almost universal in the Western countries, rose from 35 percent to 67 percent between 1950 and 1990 in the non-Western world, according to UNESCO data. The number of literate people in the non-Western world increased more than sevenfold during the period. The overall literacy rate increased faster in the 1980s than in precious decades, reflecting entry into the adult population of people in whom educational investments were made earlier, as well as the gradual dying off of older, illiterate people. The main reason for the decline in illiteracy appears to owe much more to extension of education to children than to the passing of older, illiterate people.

The explosion of formal education in non-Western countries is perhaps the most striking characteristic of the post–World War II world (Figure 8.3). Total enrolled students rose from about 100 million in 1950 to 738 million in 1990. The growth occurred first at the elementary level, where the student population in 1950 was 38 percent of the primary-aged population, to 78 percent in 1970, and around 97 percent in 1990, based on UNESCO data. Secondary education in 1950 was the province of a very small elite, with about 5 percent of the relevant age group enrolled in school. By 1990, enrollments were half of the relevant population. A large mass of the working age population in the non-Western world is now literate. Better education has been shown to be linked to a wide variety of other variables: health practices, willingness to innovate, educational aspirations for one's children, family planning, and productivity. That suggests that the potential for continued progress in the non-Western world resulting from the past investments in children is quite favorable.

Literacy and basic education have continued to spread rapidly in the non-Western world. Once the domain of an elite minority, literacy is now accessible to the great majority of children. More remains to be done on quality and quantity improvements, but the record of progress is substantial.

Overall, the non-Western world's poor countries have made as much progress in health and education in a generation as the rich West did in a century. On average, their infant mortality has more than halved, while the school enrollment has risen almost 50 percent. Though their GNP per person is still only 5 percent of that in rich Western nations, their citizens' life expectancy has risen by 17 years to 61 (life expectancy is 76 in the rich West).

These figures from the United Nations' annual Human Development report are good—but not good enough. Averages, as so often, hide striking differences. Some countries have made huge improvements: in Sri Lanka, for

Figure 8-3. Three girls do homework outside their house in Zhi Village, Shaanxi Province. Progress in women's education made major strides in China during the past three decades. Overall, women's status and opportunities have improved in China because of better education. But women in rural areas still face enormous disadvantages which take many forms, including sex-selective abortion and domestic violence and abuse. The bulk of the peasant women from poorer areas remain disadvantaged in their mobility because of the household registration system (*hukou*) or registration location, which prevents permanent migration to urban areas and affords fewer opportunities. The central government has announced its intention to conduct a gradual overhaul of the *hukou* system, which is a holdover from the 1950s when the Maoist command economy required tight controls over the flow of labor. (Photo: UNICEF by Roger Lemoyne.)

instance, the proportion of children dying in infancy has gone down by more than 70 percent since 1970. Others have barely progressed: only 4 out of 10 Pakistani children go to primary school, a rate unchanged in a generation. Variations among countries and regions are substantial in the non-Western world. Differential progress results from two separate strands. First, progress comes from broader education and access to a growing worldwide store of knowledge. Second, differences in economic growth among regions allow poor people in some countries greater opportunities. They benefit from higher incomes, more effective government promotion of development, and a greater social infrastructure, made possible by a larger overall amount of resources available to the society.

Most of the Asian and African countries began in the 1950s at approximately the same starting point for infant mortality, with a rate of about 180 per thousand. Since then, South Asia and Africa have had disappointing rates of economic growth. East Asia, however, has had extremely rapid economic growth, drawing on market-based economic policies and extensive investment in education. All three regions reduced infant mortality, cutting the rate by half or more. Nevertheless, East Asia's progress has been *spectacular,* while progress in the other regions has been *substantial.* East Asian rates of infant mortality in the early 1990s were similar to those in the developed Western countries in the late 1960s.

What can be done to prompt the laggard countries? Solid economic growth will help. But it is not enough. Nor, more surprisingly, is it a prerequisite. Better health and education, a better life overall for the poorest, do not have to wait until the whole nation gets richer. As the U.N. Human Development report points out, some very poor countries have done well in health and education. The characteristic they share is governments, national and local, that direct their modest spending to make sure that the poor—especially women—have access to public services. Political elites of the non-Western world more interested in big armies, big projects, and big subsidies for powerful interest groups are the worst enemies of the poor.

For most of modern history, the bulk of the non-Western world's peoples have lacked political and economic freedoms (free speech, free press, the power to choose political leaders, and the ability to pursue a desired occupation). Conditions facing women have been far more onerous than for men. In most societies, women have been constrained to remain in the patriarchal household until married (frequently without their consent) and then subjected to inferior status in the marriage relationship.

What about the contributions of rich Western countries and Japan to aid development efforts in the poor non-Western countries? For the past generation, many billions have been spent on development assistance—often in the name of the poor, but without reaching them. Multilateral agencies such as the World Bank and regional development banks are putting more emphasis on basic services such as clean water, primary schools, and baby clinics.

But these agencies are not the main suppliers of foreign public sector capital. The individual governments are the main suppliers, and they have not advanced in the same way as multilateral agencies.

Today, as in the past, country-to-country aid often ends up in the pockets of the "donor" country's businesses. Much aid money—more than a third of disbursements made by France and Germany, to take two notable examples—is tied: the money must be spent on goods or services from the donor country. Even untied aid may well go the same way, buying consultants, conferences, and general bureaucracy.

Even the aid money spent in the recipient country often does not assist those who most need it. UNICEF, the U.N. agency for children, reckons that in 1990 more than 80 percent of the bilateral aid to education went to secondary and higher education, though primary schooling matters most. Much the same is true of health. Relatively low-cost efforts at immunization, hygiene, and maternity care help vast numbers of people, yet primary health care gets about 1 percent of international aid flows. Donors are more tempted to see the concrete results of their money in the form of well-equipped hospitals in the capital city. Building large hospitals or universities is all too often an opportunity for graft for the recipient country.

Development aid that is properly directed and used in well-governed countries of the non-Western world can make a real difference. Western countries and Japan, who are trying to help, should remember the poorest of the poor who need help the most.

THREE MAJOR CHALLENGES

Within the framework of growth, change, and development outlined in the preceding section, the non-Western world faces three challenges as it prepares to enter the twenty-first century:

1. Adoption of an ecodevelopment paradigm for sustainable development and conservation
2. Integration of rural poverty alleviation programs, environmental priorities, and population and development strategies
3. Resolution of ethnic and religious conflicts

Ecodevelopment for Sustainable Growth

Since the 1950s, the philosophy and practice of environmental management in non-Western countries' development planning may be described as using a *frontier economic model* in which, if local resources exhaust, people move onto the next untapped frontier or create a new one with a new source of energy or new technology. Development under the frontier economics paradigm treated the environment as an infinite supply of physical resources (water, soil, air, energy, and raw materials) to be used and as an infinite sink for the by-products of development and consumption in the form of various types of pollution (waste) and ecological degradation.

Large irrigation projects in India, China, and Egypt involved a transformation of the environment to solve the increasing demand for more food and energy. Many of these projects were partly responsible for the loss of forest and environmental degradation during the past four decades. India's Narmada River Development Project and China's Three Gorges Project (Figure 8.4) illustrate two examples of megaprojects in the non-Western world, which can have negative overall impact on the ecology and environment. Ambitious programs for transforming river basins and reorganizing agriculture are attractive development goals. But the power of megaprojects to alter the conditions of human life for the better is matched by their power to destroy much that is valuable in the environment (Figure 8.5).

The opposite of the frontier economics paradigm in environmental management is the *deep ecology* philosophy, which espouses a value system based on environmental ethics rather than on the money and material orientation of economics. The deep ecology school of thought emphasizes a different relationship between nature and human socioeconomic activity, one that focuses on ethical, social, and spiritual aspects which have been largely ignored in the frontier economics view. Deep ecology has provided the conceptual basis for

Figure 8-4. The waters of the Yangtze have spilled over rich farmlands near Wuhan in central China. To control floods and generate hydroelectric power, China has built the Three Gorges Dam, which will transform a 350-mile stretch of the mighty Yangtze into a long, narrow lake. After decades of bitter debate, years of construction, and uprooting of 700,000 people, the Three Gorges Dam closed its gate in June 2003 and began filling the reservoir behind the dam. A visionary project long ago extolled by Mao Zedong himself, the dam has come to symbolize the Chinese Communist Party's drive to conquer nature, and it is still touted as the mark of a great nation's arrival. (Photo: P. P. Karan.)

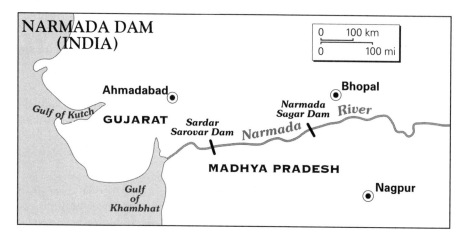

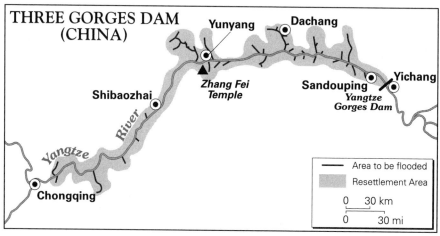

Figure 8-5. Dams and the environment: Narmada Dam (India) and the Three Gorges Dam (China).

India's Narmada River Development Project and China's Three Gorges Project

The Narmada Valley in India is the site of one of the world's largest multipurpose water projects: the Narmada River Development Project, which involves the construction of thirty large dams and many small ones on the river and its fifty-one main tributaries. The project will transform the basin which covers 94,500 square kilometers between the Vindhya and Satpura ranges in central India. It will increase food production and hydroelectric power generation. The construction of dams and reservoirs will also displace an estimated one million people and submerge 350,000 hectares of forest land and 200,000 hectares of agricultural land. The construction of one of the major dams of the Narmada Project—the Sardar Sarovar Dam—is facing major opposition from tribal groups that hunt and forage in the jungle canyons and from villagers who are being displaced by the inundation from the reservoir, which will submerge 250 villages and almost 40,000 hectares of lands.

A movement to save the river began in the 1980s as a struggle for just resettlement and rehabilitation of people being displaced by the Sardar Sarovar Dam, but the focus has shifted in recent years to preserving the environmental integrity and natural eco-systems of the entire valley. The movement has used the project as a symbol of Indian development planners' fascination with costly megaprojects at the expense of the environment and the poor. Partly in response to the movement, the World Bank decided to cease funding of the project in 1992 (Figure 8.6).

At about the same time in 1992, the National People's Congress of China approved construction of the Three River Gorges hydroelectric project on the Chang Jiang (Yangtze) River as part of the country's ten-year development program. The Three Gorges, a highly controversial project, has been widely discussed both in China and abroad. It will be the world's largest and most complex hydroelectric dam, and will take fifteen to eighteen years to build at a cost of over $11 billion. China des-perately needs the additional power generated by the project. It will also relieve the danger of flooding in the chronically flood-prone areas of the middle and lower Chang Jiang. By generating electricity equal to burning about 40 million tons of coal, the con-struction of the dam will reduce China's emissions of sulfur dioxide and carbon diox-ide. By lowering demand for coal, the Three Gorges project would ease pressure on an overburdened rail transport network in China.

The Three Gorges project will have negative social and environmental impacts. The reservoir will submerge 2 cities, 11 counties, 140 towns, 326 townships, 1,351 villages, and 23,800 hectares of cultivated land. More than 1.1 million people would have to be resettled, which accounts for one third of the cost of the project. Ecologists have expressed concern that the Yangtze dolphin, with a population of about 200, making it one of the world's most endangered species, along with the Chinese stur-geon and other fish species would be threatened by the construction of the Three Gorges project. The dam and the reservoir will destroy some of China's most scenic landscapes. In addition, as the dam reduces the flow of the river, the quality of Shanghai's municipal and industrial water supply could deteriorate. The wetland hab-itat of the numerous endangered species such as the Siberian crane along the down-stream lakes could also be destroyed by the dam. Finally, the silt trapped behind the dam would deprive downstream regions and the river estuary of vital nutrients. At the same time, the silt buildup behind the dam may impede power generation.

There is considerable opposition to the building of the Three Gorges project. About one-third of the 1992 National People's Congress either voted against or abstained from authorizing the project. The International Three Gorges Coalition headed by Green China has opposed the project, along with the Overseas Chinese Ecological Society, the Friends of the Earth, and Probe International.

several nonviolent environmental movements in the non-Western world such as the Chipko movement in the Himalaya, Naam movement in Africa, and the Sarawak Indigenous People's Allliance in Malaysia.

The application of deep ecology concepts would lead to radical changes in the traditional approach to development. The deep ecology approach tends to focus on the least possible human modification of the environment and strives to achieve a symbiosis with nature. With the current levels of population growth and land degradation in many non-Western countries, the deep ecol-ogy approach to development appears highly impractical. It is difficult enough to stabilize the population and land degradation, let alone decrease them to achieve symbiosis with nature.

Ecodevelopment, another paradigm of environmental management in devel-opment, attempts to integrate the social, ecological, and economic concerns in

Figure 8-6. The Narmada River, near Rajpipla, rises in central India and has deposited large quantities of alluvium in its lower course in Gujarat. To irrigate this productive agricultural land, the government proposed construction of a series of dams on Narmada and its tributaries, submerging 2.5 million hectares and displacing perhaps as many as 1 million people. Protests from the local people and environmentalists led to cancellation of the project. (Photo: P. P. Karan.)

development for the future. This approach tends to incorporate many of the social equity and cultural concerns raised in deep ecology. The basic promise of the paradigm is that solutions to environmental and economic problems must come from and fit into the local context. This fledgling ecodevelopment paradigm can provide a fully integrated sustainable development model for the non-Western countries. By addressing the problem of depleting resource levels, the degradation of the environment, the destruction of life-support systems in some areas, and the aesthetic impact of development processes, the concept forces the need to ecologize the economy.

The ecodevelopment model implies that ecological calculations need to be embodied much more substantially into the economic, political, and social decision-making processes. Cooperation between the natural and social sciences is needed to develop the understanding of how social institutions are to incorporate ecological concerns. The development of sustainable practices will demand methods of ecological calculation that draw on the scientific understanding of natural processes and the social and scientific understanding of the social processes.

These methods of ecological calculation will need to be translated into policy instruments for achieving sustainable development in non-Western countries. The making of development policy in most non-Western countries is split between many agencies. The current institutional mix is not well suited to the integration of social, ecological, and economic considerations into policy making. This is a complex issue and is unlikely to be resolved quickly. As a first step, it might be useful for countries to try to integrate ecological, economic, and social concerns at the local or regional level. The aim should be to integrate local and general forms of knowledge in the most appropriate way to allow the adoption of sustainable technologies and practices. The challenge ahead for the non-Western world is quite simply the development of detailed strategies for the application of the ecodevelopment concept across the range of current environmentally unsustainable uses of the resources and the inequity within each society.

In addition to the ecodevelopment paradigm for environmental management and development, three strategic approaches are required to solve the highest-priority environmental and natural resource problems. First, basic economic and environmental policy reform is needed to reverse the current mismanagement of the environment and the natural resources. Policies must be changed to reflect the real value of the natural resources and their products, including the environmental costs of production and use. Emphasis must be placed on strengthening the implementation and enforcement of environmental regulations and the development of incentives to improve the quality of the environment and the management of the resources. This includes incentives for greater empowerment and participation of the local populations and increased land and resource ownership and management rights.

Second, the human and institutional capacity in non-Western countries to analyze and manage natural resources and environmental problems needs strengthening in both the public and private sectors. A better balance is required between institutions responsible for resource use and those involved in protecting, rehabilitating, and planning for sustainable development. Solutions will involve better monitoring and the enforcment of regulations, the development of incentives for improved environmental stewardship in public and private institutions and communities, public participation in environmental impact assessments, improved technological capacity, and training for the private sector and government authorities. National and international policy development for many non-Western countries is severely hampered by the lack of information on trends in the conditions of the natural resources and environmental systems and on the economic and social costs of depletion and degradation.

Third, improved public access to information on development plans and decisions is essential to assure government accountability and open decision making. Responsible public policies on the environment and natural resource use can be enhanced by an informed public and a political system open to the concerns and participation of those affected by the development programs, which will require increased attention to environmental education for all levels of society in the non-Western world.

Integration of Rural Poverty Alleviation Programs, Environmental Priorities, and Population and Development Strategies

With the exception of Japan, people in most of the non-Western world are largely agrarian and pastoral folk. In 1988, rural people accounted for about 65 percent of the population of low-income non-Western world countries. The dependence of poor people on their natural resources, such as soil and its cover, water, forests, animals, and fisheries, is self evident; neglect of the environmental resource base results in a misleading picture of productive activity in rural communities. Nevertheless, neglect of the resource base has been a common thread running through various studies of poverty in the non-Western world. Until very recently, environmental resources made but perfunctory appearances in planning models, and they were cheerfully ignored in most development studies.

The situation now is different. The shift in attitude began slowly with the first U.N. Conference on Environment in 1972 and accelerated in the 1980s. Today no strategy of development would be regarded as adequate if the environmental resource base were absent from it. The focus now is to weave together development, environment, and population policies. A major factor contributing to poverty in many parts of the non-Western world has been the rapid growth of population. Unrelenting population growth, widespread poverty, and environmental degradation demand integration of development, environment, and population policies (Figure 8.7).

Most non-Western countries have treated population policy as essentially exogenous to the development process and environmental policy. However, experience has shown the importance of improving development-environment-population coordination. The challenge in the non-Western world is to articulate population and development policies and projects, and mesh them with priority environmental and social programs. Inadequate integration has led to the inefficient use of resources allocated to development programs and weak linkages with population policy and protection of environment.

The integration of poverty alleviation programs such as food, fertilizer, and credit subsidies, the indirect subsidies of irrigation operations, integrated rural development projects, employment creation projects, and small income generating projects with development goals will ensure that the programs as they operate will result in a sustained increase in the GDP through the increased productivity of resources, the conservation of the environment, and human development (Figure 8.8). The link between agricultural development and the alleviation of poverty is clearly visible in most of the non-Western world in land reform, irrigation development, and the increasing yield per hectare of cropped areas. Increasing cropping intensity should contribute to higher incomes and the absorption of labor.

The poverty alleviation programs in most of the non-Western world are essentially top-down ventures which are heavily dependent on the government

Figure 8-7. Fish catch brought ashore at Majanji land place, Lake Victoria, Uganda. Fishermen use boats powered by outboard engines supplied by grants from international agencies. The main objectives are to increase food production and the fish catch, and improve the health of the population. (Photo: International Food and Agricultural Development by C. Rycroft.)

bureaucracy. As a consequence, the perceived needs of the poor people do not get sufficient attention. The activities chosen are often ill-suited to the local resource endowments, which results in large leakages and inefficiencies in the implementation of programs. Usually the employment creation projects are

Figure 8-8. Dressmaking courses for Palestinian women in Lebanon. Greater participation of women in the labor force and profound changes in their status will be necessary for economic, social, and political development in the non-Western world. Women's employment is overwhelmingly in the agricultural sector. By contrast, women's employment in economically advanced countries such as South Korea, Singapore, and Japan is in clerical, sales, and service sectors, and in manufacturing. Women's employment in the most highly paid professional and managerial category is still small in the non-Western world. (Photo: UNRWA by M. Nasr.)

weakly integrated with area development, showing a lack of flexibility both in selecting activities that suit local resource endowments and environment, and in devising methods of implementation. Further, the upper-income households with larger landholdings in rural areas seem to have been the major beneficiaries from the assets created. Assets created exclusively for the benefit of the poor in the non-Western world, such as housing and programs to help the marginal and poor farmers, are relatively rare.

Integration of development, environment, and population policies faces a number of problems that affect both policy formulation and policy implementation. These problems include inadequate remuneration and operating funds, patronage in promotion and posting practices, excessive centralization, and attitudinal and communication problems which prevent effective contact between public servants and the poor, illiterate farmers. Considering past experience, improvement in this area is bound to be slow. Administrative decentralization can help the rural poor to the extent that resources are moved closer to the poor beneficiaries. However, the impediments to effective integrated policies typically appear to lie in the domain of political will and political economy of various non-Western countries.

Resolution of Ethnic and Religious Conflicts, Civil Wars, Border Clashes

The major dangers emerging in the twenty-first-century non-Western world are proliferation of nuclear and biological weapons, terrorism, the rising militarization of China, and the spreading violence related to drug trafficking from the Golden Triangle of Southeast Asia and the Golden Crescent of Southwest Asia. But a greater danger to the development of the area comes from high levels of organized violence between states or between contending groups within a state (Figure 8.9).

Ethnic rivalries, civil wars, border clashes, and other conflicts are on the rise in the non-Western world. From Algeria and Afghanistan to Tibet and the Philippines, there are a record number of conflicts. Strife infests lands as diverse as Cambodia, South Africa, Egypt, Sri Lanka, Israel, India, and Pakistan. In these countries turmoil has disrupted economies, politics, and security. The non-Western world is having a problem generating regionwide peace. There is no accurate count of the dead from the numerous civil wars, ethnic and religious rivalries, border clashes, terrorist strikes, lingering insurgencies, and other scattered conflicts.

Figure 8-9. Somali refugees arriving by boat in Mombasa, Kenya. Conflict between rival armed clans and warlords, mass murder, and famine in the 1990s led to the flight of thousands of refugees from Somalia to Kenya and other neighboring countries. Somalia is a chaotic, poor, battle-weary Muslim country with no central government. It is a dysfunctional state, with little infrastructure, a collapsed road system, and poor communication. Without stability in Africa's embattled regions, and staving off more of the kind of ethnic cleansing that already has taken place, it would be difficult to pursue economic and political progress. (Photo: UNHCR by P. Moumtzis.)

It has been thirty years since Cambodians first began killing each other. Thousands are still being killed each year, and tens of thousands made homeless. Political solutions to the conflict have repeatedly failed. Originally a war over ideology, it has now turned to the control of northwest Cambodia's hardwood forests. Khmer Rouge make more than $10 million a month from the cross-border sale of timber from the 10 percent of Cambodian territory under their control. The profits of the illegal timber trade finance rebel arms purchases. Thai logging firms, in cooperation with Thai soldiers, import timber felled in Khmer Rouge areas. Cambodia's civil war is destined to smolder on, just as its forests continue to disappear.

Ethnic hostilities have scorched the Middle East. In Muslim republics of Central Asia the fate of about 10 million ethnic Russians who now find themselves living outside the borders of Russia could become one of the most explosive problems. They have quickly devolved from privileged citizens of a superpower to unwanted and embittered minorities. In Tajikistan, for example, thousands of Russians, along with other ethnics, have fled a raging civil war. To the Muslims of Central Asia who suffered from the capricious Soviet nationalities policy, the Russian "colonists" are only getting their comeuppance. Stalin redrew the borders of the republics, liquidated ethnic elites, and ordered deportation of entire peoples.

In sub-Saharan Africa colonial rule was built on favoring certain ethnic groups, usually minorities, and using them to rule over the other tribes. That is what the Belgians did with the Tutsis, who make up about 15 percent of Rwanda's population and who were slaughtered by vengeful Hutu militia units in 1994 (Figure 8.10). The roots of ethnic strife run into the colonial past and further back. Some tribes benefited from the colonial rule and now, like the Tutsis, have paid a terrible and unfair price. The story is the same in country after country in sub-Saharan Africa.

Whenever an ethnic or religious majority within a country tramples on the rights and lives of minority people within its borders, the world outside rarely does more than cry foul. The sovereign rights of nations clash with the rights of victims. Support for the rights of victims is tepid in the non-Western world. The grim plight of southern Sudan underscores the pernicious strength of sovereignty. Since Sudan's independence in 1956 the southern region has been ravaged by intermittent civil war as the Christian and animist black Africans of the south chafe under the domination of the Muslim Arab–influenced Sudanese of the north. Arab militias, with the connivance of the Sudanese government, are guilty of massacres, kidnapping, rape, slavery, and forced Islamization in the south.

A partial list of the non-Western world's most flagrant conflicts and human rights violation underscores the extent of the problem and challenges us to explore solutions.

Figure 8-10. Refugees from Rwanda arriving in Tanzania to escape the ethnic bloodletting. Roughly 1.1 million people fled to Tanzania and eastern Zaire (Congo) after massacres in Rwanda in 1994, and nearly 800,000 people died in Rwanda during the conflict. In 2003 violence was raging in both Liberia and in ethnically riven Zaire in Africa's Great Lakes Region. The war in Zaire started in 1998, when rebel factions supported by Ugandan and Rwandan troops mounted a failed military push on the Congolese capital of Kinshasa. Since then, the Congolese war has claimed more than 3 million lives, not just in battle, but also as a consequence of sustained degradation in the region's quality of life and environment. Restoring a measure of normality to unending ethnic wars is among the toughest challenges facing African countries. (Photo: UNHCR by P. Moumtzis.)

- In East Timor the Muslim government of Indonesia seized the territory just as Portugal granted it independence in 1975, and tried to quash nationalist moves for autonomy or independence with serious human rights violations.

- Iran's Islamic government is trying to wipe out the Bahai minority by denying them education and jobs so long as they declare themselves to be Bahais. Mujahedeen-e-Khalq, opposed to the Islamic Republic of Iran, has often killed civilians and assassinated Iranian officials. Iran backs Islamist groups, including Lebanese Shi'ite militants of Hezbollah, Hamas, and the Palestinian Jihad.

- Iraq under Saddam Hussein's government inflicted severe abuses on the Kurds in the north and Shi'ite Muslims in the south. Iraqi militants trained in Taliban-run Afghanistan helped Ansar-al-Islam, an Islamist militia based in northeast Iraq, kill Iraqi kurds. Saddam's forces used nerve agents and mustard gas against Kurds.

- The Egyptian government has failed to prevent harsh Muslim discrimination against Coptic Christians. The Egyptian regime has often used mass arrests to crack down on dissident groups such as Egyptian Islamic Jihad and Jamaat-al-Islamiya that want to violently overthrow the government, which is viewed as corrupt, impious, and repressive, and replace it with an Islamic state.

- China's government, its tyranny exposed by the assault on pro-democracy marchers in 1989, still stifles democratic opponents with arbitrary arrests, sham trials, and torture. East Turkistan Islamic Movement is one of the more extreme terrorist group founded by Uighurs in Xinjiang. It seeks an independent state called East Turkistan. China has used war on terrorism as an excuse to suppress political dissent in Xinjiang.

- In Myanmar the government allows no criticism and holds more than 1,500 prisoners.

- In Israel, Hamas and Al Aqsa Martyrs Brigade, which combine the ideas of Palestinian nationalism and religious fundamentalism, have carried on countless suicide bombings to destroy Israel. Two marginal Israeli groups—Kach and Kahane Chai—have used terrorism to pursue their goals of expanding the Jewish state across the West Bank.

- Tibetan nationalism and culture have been relentlessly suppressed during fifty years of Chinese military occupation.

- Kashmir suffers under Islamic terrorist organizations such as Lashkar-e-Taiba and Jaish-e-Mohammad, which have conducted terrorism to claim Kashmir for Pakistan. At least 35,000 people have died in political violence since 1990.

- Ethnic and political armed conflicts continue in Liberia, Cote D'Ivoire, Zaire, and several other African countries.

There are also other internal battles in the countries which inhibit the development of stable democracies and free-market economies in many nations of the non-Western world.

North Korea presents a major international problem with the potential to create havoc. North Korea is the world's only unreconstructed Stalinist country. It occupies a prominent place in the war on terrorism because North Korea has sold advanced missile technology to other states such as Iran, Pakistan, Yemen, and Syria whose territories are used by terrorists as bases for operations. Pakistan provided technology to enrich uranium to Iran, North Korea, and Libya (Figure 8.11).

The brutal global competition for investment and trade is forcing companies and workers in several non-Western nations to tighten their budgets and constantly upgrade their skills to compete. Those who have succeeded are thriving; those who don't are left behind. The political resurgence of Islamic fundamentalist parties in Middle Eastern countries (the Welfare Party in Turkey), the unions in India and unemployment in China are all signs that left-behinds are starting to challenge the winners. These internal tensions will

Figure 8-11. Entrance to the old city of Medina, through the gate in the fortress built by the Turks in Tripoli, Libya. Tripoli was under Turkish control until 1911, when it was annexed by Italy. Libya was created in 1952 by the unification of three historic Ottoman provinces. In 1969 a revolution replaced the monarchy with a military dictatorship. Libya spent more than two decades supporting anti-Western terrorist groups. The United States and the United Nations imposed sanctions on Libya for its role in terrorist attacks, including the 1988 bombing of the Pan Am flight over Lockerbie, Scotland. It remains on the list of countries that sponsor terrorism because of its refusal to own up to its role in the Pan Am bombing. (Photo: P. P. Karan.)

increasingly shape the political geography and development of the non-Western world (Figure 8.12).

In many non-Western countries, the wealthy live behind high walls, secluded from the people on the other side, resulting in the absence of a sense of community, the lack of a sense that all are in this together. The absence of this feeling seriously inhibits many non-Western nations from developing into stable democracies—particularly as global economic forces widen the gap between winners and losers. In many countries a sense of hopelessness provides a fertile ground for ideologies of hatred, which provoke regional instability and hinder progress toward greater democracy, tolerance, prosperity, and freedom. Development in these countries is held back by what some scholars have called political and economic "freedom deficits." A nation's form of governance, ethnic tolerance, and how it treats minority groups are among the major challenges for most of the countries of the non-Western world. Clashes and conflicts are damaging to the hopes for the future.

Figure 8-12. An Islamic Center in Bahrain. Minarets of mosques dot the cultural landscape of the Muslim world. Muslim holy wars, or *jihad*, began in Arabia more than 1,300 years ago, and territorial conquest spread during the next 13 centuries to the Middle East, Europe, Africa, and Asia. During this period attempts were made to Islamize the conquered territory. When Muslim countries became colonies and protectorates of Britain, France, Spain, Italy, Holland, and Russia, the fear of *jihad* declined. Now, since decolonization in the 1950s and 1960s, *the jihad* movement is back again—stronger, more assured, more structured, and richer, with vast oil money financing it. To most people, the *jihad* now is simply one of the components of international terrorism. For some Muslims, Europe, the United States, and other non-Muslim countries are *Dar-al-Harb,* or Land of War. Muslim countries are *Dar-al-Islam,* the Land of Islam, God, and peace. The increasing Islamic extremist violence around the world present a major threat to peace and development, particularly in the non-Western world. Pressure by responsible Muslim leaders and clerics on *jihadis* to give up violence will demonstrate that there are true moderates who believe in pluralism and tolerance. (Photo: Bahrain National Museum.)

THE TWENTY-FIRST CENTURY

Despite political and economic hindrances, most countries in the non-Western world are, in general, experiencing progress in the first decade of the twenty-first century. There is movement toward democratization, greater electoral transparency, and popular participation in major national elections, all of which were lacking only a few years ago (Figure 8.13). Corruption, nepotism, and cronyism are all under the spotlight from China to Chad and Central Asia to South Africa as barriers to national interests, growth, and political stability. There is evidence that undemocratic practices, graft, and corruption are being rolled back, and markets and economies are being formalization and constructed along internationally recognized systems and regulatory norms. This bodes well for the future of the non-Western world, even though the reforms are far from over.

For Japan, the major economic power, which has been in an economic slump since 1990, anything more than a modest recovery is not expected in the first decade of the twenty-first century. However, on the upside, there is little likelihood of further deterioration in economic conditions, with the Japanese economy having weathered the worst in the last decade of the twentieth century. Aside from the impact of the aging population and declining fertility, the long-term resilience of the Japanese economy cannot be overlooked. In recent years, the Japanese government has invested enormous sums in infrastructure development, and this will stand the Japanese economy in good stead when the full recovery begins. A recovery driven by exports and increasing household spending boosted Japan's economy to 6.4 percent growth in 2003, the fasted expansion since 1990. With unemployment rate falling to a three-year low of 4.7 percent in March 2004, there is a growing feeling that Japan's recovery will continue.

China, the largest country in terms of population, remains committed to reform as the most effective means to ensure economic growth and political legitimacy. Dissent within the Communist Party will continue to reflect various concerns about the pace and depth of reform and its effect on social and political cohesion. Risks to business and government alike from financial and legal reform processes are tangible, but so are rewards. China has the potential to become an economic powerhouse, but the potential for backsliding is just as real. Human rights violations, including tightening the grip on the media, Internet chat rooms, and dissident essayists continue as vexing problems.

For India, the largest democracy, development prospects are positive in the first decade of the twenty-first century. There is real commitment to economic and social reforms within the framework of a vibrant democracy. India's software service industry has been carefully nurtured since the 1980s, and is highly regarded internationally. Other knowledge-intensive industries are likely to emerge from India's tertiary institutions in the medium term. Continued strong growth is expected in the call center industry and in software

Figure 8-13. Two girls participate in a literacy program in Noakhali District, Bangladesh. Investment in human resource development, particularly in education of girls, will be essential for social and economic development in the non-Western world. Until recently, in most non-Western countries few women attended secondary school or university, and few worked outside the home. Over the past 50 years, larger and larger proportions of women have completed secondary school. The proportion of women attending university, although much smaller, is also growing. More recently, women have started taking up paid employment in greater numbers, particularly in manufacturing, clerical, and service sectors. Women's life expectancy has improved across the non-Western world. Yet during early childhood, girls are still more likely to die than boys in some countries, while in others, unusual birth rates for boys and girls in recent years point to the prevalence of sex-selective abortion. (Photo: UNICEF by Jorgen Schytte.)

development, particularly as the U.S. economy revives. In May 2004, India's 660 million registered voters elected a government that will focus on economic development in the villages.

In the Middle East, the liberation of Iraq and Afghanistan provides a special opportunity to advance a positive agenda in the region that will strengthen security in Southwest Asia and North Africa. A transformed Iraq has the potential of becoming a key element of a very different Middle East in which ideologies of hate will not flourish. The Israelis, Palestinians, and neighboring Arab states united in June 2003 behind the vision of two states, Israel and Palestine, living side by side in peace and security. They agreed to a "road map" to achieve that goal. Israel realizes that it is in Israel's interest for Palestinians to govern themselves in a viable state that is peaceful, democratic, and committed to fighting terror. Palestinian leaders increasingly understand that terror is not a means to Palestinian statehood but is instead the greatest obstacle to statehood. Despite optimism, the area from Algeria to Afghanistan and Turkey to Sudan remains one of the most volatile regions of the non-Western World with tensions between Islam and modernity, fundamentalism and democratic aspiration, ethnic strife, suicide bombing and terror attacks.

The formation of the African Union in 2002, modeled after the European Union, offers optimism for the future of sub-Saharan Africa. With its own parliament, central bank, and court of justice, the African Union promises to impose standards of good governance on its member countries. Its Peace and Security Council has a mandate to intervene in regional conflicts involving war crimes, genocide, and crimes against humanity. Sustained political stability and sweeping economic reforms are the twin priorities of the newly formed African Union. The success of the African Union will depend on the individual states' commitment to reforms and political stability. With few exceptions, peace, security, and good governance elude much of Africa in 2004. It is a continent in chaos with numerous "failed" states, and rampant corruption. Is there hope for Africa? May be with education and development oriented leadership.

FURTHER READINGS

Amnesty International Report 2000. New York: Amnesty International USA.

Bloom, David E. and Jeffrey G. Williamson. 1998. Demographic transitions and economic miracles in emerging Asia. *World Bank Economic Review.* 12(3): 419–456.

Chetham, Deirdre. 2002. *Before the Deluge: The Vanishing World of the Yangtze's Three Gorges.* New York: Palgrave Macmillan.

Heymann, Philip B. 2003. *Terrorism, Freedom, and Security.* Cambridge: MIT Press.

Heaton, George, Robert Repetto, and Rodney Sobin. 1991. *Transforming Technology: An Agenda for Environmentally Sustainable Growth in the 21st Century.* Washington, D.C.: World Resources Institute.

Howard, M.C. ed. 1993. *Asia's Environmental Crisis.* Boulder: Westview

Karan, P. P. 1999. Environmental Management in Development Planning: Some Paradigms and Global Comparisons. In *Preserving the Legacy: Concepts in Support of Sustainability.* Edited by Allen G. Noble and Frank J. Costa. Lanham, MD: Lexington Books.

Kennedy, Paul. 1993. *Preparing for the 21st Century.* New York: Random House.

Mason, Andrew, ed. 2001. *Population Change and Economic Development in East Asia: Challenges Met, Opportunities Seized.* Stanford, CA: Stanford University Press.

Mason, Karen Oppenheim. 1995. *Is the Situation of Women in Asia Improving or Deteriorating?* Asia-Pacific Population Research Reports, No. 6. Honolulu:East-West Center.

Pinstrup-Andersen, Per and Rajul Pandya-Lorch. 1994. *Alleviating Poverty, Intensifying Agriculture and Effectively Managing Natural Resources.* Food, Agriculture, and the Environment Discussion Papers No. 1. Washington, D.C.: International Food Policy Research Institute.

Tolba, Mostafa L. 1992. *Saving Our Planet: Challenges and Hope.* London: Chapman and Hall.

United Nations. 1994. *Population, Environment and Development.* New York: United Nations.

Venkataramiah, E. S., ed. 1988. *Human Rights in the Changing World.* New Delhi: International Law Association, Regional Branch, India.

Index